# A Regional Geography of Western Europe

F. J. Monkhouse

Formerly Professor of Geography in the
University of Southampton

## Fourth edition

Longman

LONGMAN GROUP LIMITED
London

Associated companies, branches and representatives
throughout the world

First published 1959
Second edition 1964
Third edition 1968
Fourth edition 1974

ISBN 0 582 48424·3

Filmset by Keyspools Ltd, Golborne, Lancs.
Printed in Hong Kong by
Dai Nippon Printing Co., (H.K.) Ltd.

# Contents

*Contents*

# 10 The lowlands of northern France: II     219

*Contents*

viii

*Contents*

*Contents*

xii

# List of plates

## List of plates

# Acknowledgements

For permission to reproduce photographs we are grateful to the following:
Aerofilms: Plates 2, 11, 29, 30, 31, 36–46, 51, 53, 61, 63; Photo Alix: Plates 64, 65;
Phot'r Aeroport Lille-Lesquin: Plate 20; J. Allan Cash: Plate 58; Cliché Combier
a Macon: Plate 57; Compagnie Aérienne Française: Plate 33; Documentation
Française Photothèque: Plate 28 (photo Renault), Plate 56 (photo M.E.L.),
Plate 48 (photo B. Beaujard S.F.P.B.P.); Photothèque EDF: Plate 35 (photo
Brigaud), Plate 52 (photo Sodel); KLM: Plates 1, 3–8, 10, 12, 13, 16–18; Loic-
Jahan: Plates 47, 59; N.A.M.-foto: Plate 27; Alain Perceval: Plates 32, 34, 49, 50;
Jean Roubier: Plate 54; Sabena; Plates 9, 14, 21–27, 55; S.A. des Charbonnages
Winterslag: Plate 15; Swissaire – Photo A. G. Zürich: Plates 60, 62.

**Geographies for Advanced Study**

Edited by Professor Stanley H. Beaver, M.A., F.R.G.S.

# Preface to first edition

In his introduction to *Great Britain: Essays in regional geography*, edited by the late Professor A. G. Ogilvie, Sir John Russell wrote: 'The purpose of regional geography is to describe the regions of a country as they are and to discover the causes that have made them what they are.' It is in pursuing such an aim that the geographer feels that his subject has gone some way to attain a coherence of content which systematic studies, though of course essential and affording satisfying specialisation, sometimes seem to lack.

I must say at once that I do not seek to defend my apparent definition of western Europe as comprising France (less Corsica) and the Benelux countries. This is a matter of editorial apportionment, since other parts which one might reasonably expect to include in western Europe were for practical reasons allocated to colleagues. Nor does this work offer a regional study of each of these four sovereign states as individuals, but is based on major structural and physical units (outlined in Chapter 1) which inevitably disregard manmade frontiers. Thus 'Maritime Flanders' includes the contiguous portions of France, Belgium and the Netherlands, while 'the Ardennes' and 'the Scarplands and Vales of Lorraine' each comprise parts of Belgium, France and Luxembourg.

I fully realise the magnitude of my task and the shortcomings of the result. Much of the satisfaction which I derived some years ago from making a survey of the Kempenland, a small unit-area in northeastern Belgium, came from visiting this area and studying its features in the field. Ideally I should have treated each of the other regions and subregions in similar detail, but life, space and the editor's patience are all too short. I have indeed been fortunate in visiting most parts of western Europe, though in a necessarily more superficial way than the Kempenland; I have stood on top of Mont Blanc and at the bottom of one of the deepest Belgian collieries, I have walked over the heathlands of the eastern Netherlands and across the mistral-swept Rhône delta, and for several summers I have towed my caravan across Europe, halting where we pleased. But I am still conscious of the gaps, the defects, in my personal acquaintance with the west European landscape.

There have been other difficulties. Paradoxically one of these is the wealth of available material, for few parts of the world have been so thoroughly studied and described by geographers. The classic *Tableau de la Géographie de la France* of Paul Vidal de la Blache, published at the beginning of this century, has been succeeded by numerous monographs, many of them elegant, accurate and methodical pieces of work. Belgian and Dutch geographers have also been active, and my footnotes, frequent as they are, can refer to but a small proportion of the vast literature. Of statistical information too there is an embarrassing wealth; even the Grand Duchy of Luxembourg, of much the same size as Derbyshire, publishes an *Annuaire Statistique* exceeding five hundred pages. A major problem therefore has been to preserve some balance in the detailed descriptions, in the presentation of facts. Another difficulty results from the dynamic quality of western Europe, for the postwar years have experienced changes with which it is virtually impossible to keep pace; much of what is here written will inevitably have been modified before this book appears.

In this part of the world one or more alternative forms of place-names are frequently found. Briefly, the policy adopted in this text has been to adopt the official form sanctioned by the particular country, in French or Dutch as the case may be. A few exceptions involve names which have been anglicised or for which there is an accepted form for English readers. It would be sheer pedantry to use the official forms for Antwerp, Bruges, Brussels, Lyons, Marseilles, Picardy and the Scheldt; for these and a few other cases the official name is indexed with cross-reference to the form actually used.

I am happy to express my thanks to numerous friends. Professor S. H. Beaver, who is General Editor of these *Geographies for Advanced Study* and who first suggested that I should undertake this task, has given freely of his help at all stages, and I owe more than I can readily say to his exceptional critical ability. My colleagues in the Department of Geography at Southampton have throughout contributed suggestions and advice. During the course of the work much assistance and hospitality has been received in the four countries from Government departments (notably the statistical offices listed on p. 679), communal authorities, industrial firms and private individuals too numerous to list; to them I collectively convey my sincere thanks.

The heavy labour of typing the manuscript was carried out by Miss D. M. Cross, Miss H. Tranmer and Miss B. Wotton of the staff of the University of Southampton. The maps and diagrams were drawn with infinite care and patience by Mr A. Carson Clark, cartographer in the Department of Geography at Southampton. The aerial photographs used as half-tone illustrations were obtained through the courtesy of Miss M. D. Roberts, Assistant Librarian of the vast *Aerofilms* collection, and Mr R. H. Austin of *Sabena Belgian World Air Lines*.

*Southampton, December 1957*                                        F. J. M.

# Preface to fourth edition

The opportunity of a completely new and reset fourth edition has enabled all statistical and other factual material to be thoroughly revised. While the physical foundations on which this study is based remain fundamentally stable, the superimposition of the effects of man's activities create far-reaching changes in these critical days of dynamically evolving technology and fluctuating regional economic and social progress. Recent years have seen important even dramatic changes: the introduction of large-scale national and regional plans; modifications in agricultural policy, notably a move away from small producing units, a big decline in the labour force and an appreciable increase in output; the development of large industrial groups and consortia to meet the demands of new technologies in industry; the marked decline of coal as a prime energy resource, involving the closure of many 'old' basins and its partial replacement by oil, natural gas and nuclear power; the modernization of communications, as indicated by the electrification of railways, the spread of motorways, the growth of a web of pipelines for oil, gas and feedstock, the construction of container-ports and oil and bulk-cargo terminals; and the rapid but uneven growth of population, especially in the conurbations of Paris, Brussels and the Dutch Randstad. Most statistics have been updated to 1969–71, with the exception of French population figures for which the Census of 1968 has been used. Some of the maps have been redrawn and several plates replaced. In accordance with the official policy of metrication, all quantities are given in SI units, though imperial equivalents are appended for convenience.

*Ennerdale, March* 1972                                                    F. J. M.

# 1
# Introduction

Western Europe is rich in regional names which can be used by the geographer to facilitate his analysis and description of unit-areas with a marked individuality. Many of these were former administrative units. In Belgium names such as *Brabant, Hesbaye* and *Flandre (Vlaanderen* in Flemish) have been used for centuries; some, such as Brabant, survive as the names of presentday provinces, others, like Hesbaye, no longer have this administrative significance but are still used to refer to specific parts of the country. In the Netherlands the names *Friesland, Groningen* and *Limburg* have been in use for centuries, and still denote presentday provinces.

It is in France that these wider regional names survive in such numbers, shorn of any administrative significance. About forty feudal units retained their identity as *gouvernements* under the *ancien régime* until the outbreak of the French Revolution (Fig. 1.1), when they were swept away and replaced by eighty-three highly centralised *départements*, later increased in number to ninety, and in 1964 to ninety-five as a result of changes in the Paris region (p. 191). Many of these provincial names are still in common usage; two examples will illustrate this point. *Provence* is derived from the name *Provincia*, a Roman state with its capital at Aix. Even when the province was annexed to the French kingdom towards the end of the fifteenth century, it retained much administrative autonomy, together with its own language and legal system. But in 1791 the *gouvernement* was split up into the *départements* of Bouches-du-Rhône, Basses-Alpes and Var. Though Provence administratively vanished, the name now affords a convenient term of reference to the Mediterranean littoral between the Rhône and the High Alps. *Languedoc* affords a second example, a name derived from a thirteenth-century linguistic term, the *langue d'oc* of southern France, contrasting with the *langue d'oïl* of the centre and north of the country. The name was later applied in a more limited sense to one of the ancient provinces and is now used to refer to the western Mediterranean coastlands extending inland to the escarpment of the Cévennes, that is, the *départements* of Ardèche, Gard, Hérault and Pyrénées-Orientales.[1] It is interesting to note that the name has now been revived officially as an economic planning region (p. 4), with its headquarters at Montpellier, though Pyrénées-

Orientales has been added for administrative convenience.

Within these larger divisions may be demarcated a considerable number of more detailed units known as *pays*. These are of great diversity and their names are of varied origin. Some are derived from feudal administrative units or families (*Valois, Vexin*), others from prominent physical features (*Pays des Buttes, Gâtinais, Champagne humide*), from a nearby urban focus (*Bordelais, Soissonnais, Laonnais*), or from types of land use (*Landes, Boischaut, Ségalas, pays noir*). The origin of many is lost in antiquity, while others have been coined in quite recent times. Most are, however, based on distinctive and characteristic features of geology, relief and land use which distinguish them from their neighbours, and for that reason the regional geographer can make good use of them.

FIG. 1.1. The ancient provinces of France
**L** indicates the Grand Duchy of Luxembourg; and **N** the Netherlands.

Based on (*a*) W. R. Shepherd, *Historical Atlas* (1930), p. 146; and (*b*) R. L. Poole, *Historical Atlas of Modern Europe* (1902), plate 58.

It was as long ago as 1746 that the Abbé Guettard published a map of the *zones concentriques* of the Paris Basin, a revised edition of which, with accompanying *texte descriptif* contributed by Monnet, appeared in 1780. This stressed that the surface of the earth n'est point formée d'un mélange confus de matières, mais que ces matières y sont distinguées les unes des autres et y observent tel ordre, que pendant une certaine étendue de pays, on trouve que telle ou telle matière en forme le fond. . . . De là naît naturellement la division des terrains que nous distinguons sous les noms, par exemple, de pays à craie, et de pays à coquilles, etc.[2]

There were several other early attempts to discuss and to demarcate the regional units of various parts of France.[3] It was P. Vidal de la Blache, one of the greatest of French geographers, who developed the concept of regional studies to become one of the most fundamental aspects of geography. In 1888 he wrote an article entitled 'Des divisions fondamentales du sol français',[4] which in the words of Gallois was 'destiné aux maîtres chargés de l'enseignement de la géographie'. In 1903 appeared Vidal de la Blache's great work, *Tableau de la Géographie de la France*, forming the first volume of the monumental *Histoire de France illustrée*. After an introductory survey of the 'personnalité géographique de la France', he went on to a detailed description of each of the main regions. This work stimulated, on the one hand, detailed monographs which dealt with individual unit-areas; early examples include *La Picardie*, by A. Demangeon (1905), and *La Basse-Bretagne*, by C. Vallaux (1907). Gallois himself produced in 1908 a detailed *Étude sur la Région Parisienne* (*op. cit.*), in the form of a systematic description of Beauce, Hurepoix, Gâtinais, Puisaye and the rest. On the other hand, several general regional geographies of France appeared, more or less based on Vidal de la Blache. In 1909, for example, Joseph Fèvre and Henri Hauser published an attractive geography of France entitled *Régions et pays de France*, in which under twelve main divisions many hundred of *pays* were described. They say as introduction: 'Le point de départ d'une division naturelle de la France est dans la distinction des "pays", dont les noms, familiers aux habitants, ont victorieusement persisté à côté des dénominations administratives anciennes ou récentes' (pp. 6–7).

Rarely do the *pays* conform to any administrative unit, which does make it difficult to obtain relevant statistical information. In 1943 the Service National des Statistiques inaugurated an official enquiry, 'pour objet la détermination d'ensembles territoriaux homogènes, régions, contrées ou pays naturels, susceptibles, pour l'étude et la présentation statistique, de remplacer le cadre administratif traditionnel ou tout au moins de se juxtaposer à lui'. After the war the newly formed Institut National de la Statistique et des Etudes Economiques set up a Commission Centrale, including several distinguished French geographers, among them E. de Martonne. They produced in 1948 an impressive volume entitled *Régions Géographiques de la France*, with a detailed folding map classifying no less than 520 unit areas grouped into four orders of magnitude. Each was precisely defined in terms of its constituent *départements*, *cantons* or *communes*,

3

and its area and population were given. Thus although the basis of division was the *pays*, the exact boundaries provided a basis for statistical plotting.

As part of state planning in France, and specifically to even out the radical contrasts in economic development in various parts of the country, the government in 1955 set up machinery to produce regional plans to dovetail within and to amplify the details of the several postwar national plans.[5] Twenty-one regions were delimited, known as *circonscriptions d'action régionale*, and a plan for each has been formulated within which the state, local authorities and private interests can cooperate, and through which investment can be directed. These regions, though created by grouping existing *départements* with broad common interests and problems, were given many of the old provincial names, as shown in the following table.

| NAME | HEADQUARTERS | NAME | HEADQUARTERS |
|---|---|---|---|
| *Région parisienne* | Paris | *Bretagne* | Rennes |
| *Champagne* | Reims | *Limousin* | Limoges |
| *Picardie* | Lille | *Auvergne* | Clermont-Ferrand |
| *Haute-Normandie* | Rouen | *Poitou-Charente* | Poitiers |
| *Centre* | Orléans | *Aquitaine* | Bordeaux |
| *Nord* | Lille | *Midi-Pyrénées* | Toulouse |
| *Lorraine* | Nancy | *Bourgogne* | Dijon |
| *Alsace* | Strasbourg | *Rhône-Alpes* | Lyons |
| *Franche-Comté* | Dijon | *Languedoc* | Montpellier |
| *Basse-Normandie* | Rouen | *Provence: Côte* | Marseilles |
| *Pays de la Loire* | Nantes | *d'Azur: Corse* | |

While France is exceptional in the number of regional names, the result of her physical diversity, Belgian geographers have not been backward in their utilisation of such units. In 1913 M. Leriche[6] defined the natural regions of the country, and in 1927 P. L. Michotte discussed the basis of *régions géographiques*.[7] A. Demangeon, in *Belgique-Pays Bas-Luxembourg* (1927), the second volume of the *Géographie universelle*, delineated such regions as 'Le pays Lorrain', 'Le pays industriel', 'Les pays du Rhin et de la Meuse'. J. Halkin, in his attractive *Atlas classique* (1934), divided Belgium into a number of distinct unit regions, indicated on Fig. 1.2. Again, in 1940 Mlle M. A. Lefèvre produced a map, with accompanying text, defining the geographical regions.[8] Many studies have also been written of individual regions.[9] A notable contribution was by R. Blanchard, who produced in 1906 a masterly study of Flanders,[10] which cut across frontiers and dealt with the French, Belgian and Dutch portions as a homogeneous whole.

Belgium is administratively divided into nine provinces, forty-one *arrondissements*, 211 cantons and 2 379 communes, officially used as the basis of most statistical returns on various scales. It is significant, however, that the Institut National de Statistique distinguishes and utilises ten 'régions climatologiques' and fourteen 'régions agricoles'.[11] The latter is the basis of their triennial publication *La Statistique agricole* and is shown on a *Carte formée des régions agricoles* published in 1951; regions include, for example, 'Polders et Dunes', 'Région limoneuse' and 'Haute Ardenne'.

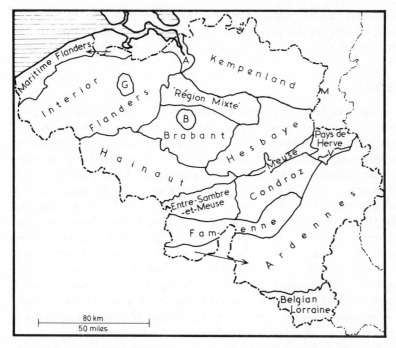

Fig. 1.2. The regions of Belgium
The abbreviations are as follows: **A,** Antwerp district; **B,** Brussels district;
**G,** Gent district; **V,** Verviers district. The area denoted as *'Région Mixte'*
comprises a number of small districts—in the west *'Petit Brabant'*, in the
centre the *'Campine brabançonne'*, and in the east the *'Hageland'*.

Based on J. Halkin, *Atlas classique* (1934), plate 18.

Statistics of agricultural distributions and production are tabulated for
each unit.

In the Netherlands, despite its less varied landscape, *pays* names are to
be found. The *Betuwe* or 'goodland' of the clay-floored floodplain between
the Maas and the Lek contrasts with the sandy heathland of the *Veluwe*
or 'badland'. The *Bon Pays* (*Gutland*) of the scarplands of southern Luxembourg differ markedly from the *Oesling* (the Ardennes plateau) of the
north.[12]

In the regional analyses which follow, reference is made to many hundreds of *pays* in western Europe.

The physical elements of western Europe must form the basis of any logical
pattern of regional division, and at first glance three main categories of
relief regions can be distinguished (Fig. 1.3). The ancient uplands include
Armorica, the Central Massif, the Vosges and the Ardennes. The younger
fold ranges of the Jura and the French Alps lie in the southeast along the
Swiss and Italian frontiers, and the Pyrenees border Spain. The residual

5

lowlands—coastal plains, basins and valleys—border the North Sea and the English Channel on the north, the Bay of Biscay on the west and the Mediterranean Sea on the south, and form re-entrants within the uplands.

## The uplands

The ancient uplands have experienced through long periods of geological time a complex series of geomorphological vicissitudes: alternations of folding, peneplanation, *en bloc* uplift and renewed denudation. Widespread earth movements of Carbo-Permian times were responsible for their basic structures. The Palaeozoic and still older rocks were folded to form a series of vast ranges across central Europe, sometimes given the general name of *Altaides*, which once extended from southwestern Ireland to southern Russia. The trends of folding in the west are referred to as *Armorican*, after the Breton name *Ar-Mor*, 'the country of the sea'; the structural lines run at first from west to east, gradually changing in central France until their direction is almost from northwest to southeast. Further east the trend is southwest to northeast (*Variscan*), as in the Ardennes and Vosges. A most complex structural 'apex' occurred in the south of the Central Massif of France where these fold systems met. The name *Hercynian* is sometimes applied collectively to all these Carbo-Permian fold systems.

They were slowly reduced to peneplains by a lengthy period of denudation in Permian and Triassic times, to be covered during the prolonged Mesozoic and Tertiary marine transgressions by limestones, sandstones and clays. Renewed denudation, followed by *en masse* movements, produced a series of upland blocks projecting from the surrounding sedimentary plains. During the Alpine orogeny of mid-Tertiary times, these uplands formed stable bastions against the fold movements from the south, and in fact helped as 'outer horsts' to determine the alignment of the newer mountain ranges. In addition, the blocks suffered at that time renewed *en masse* movement with tilting and considerable faulting; in some areas volcanic activity was associated with the disturbances. Since then denudation has modified the surface features still further. Thus they comprise massifs of Pre-Cambrian and Palaeozoic rocks—slate, schist, sandstone, quartzite, limestone, together with intrusive masses of granite and with some superficial products of volcanic activity. Smaller areas of newer rocks are preserved in basins and depressions within the uplands or on their margins.

In the northwest is *Armorica*, a triangular peninsula projecting into the Atlantic Ocean. Its geological definition appears clearly on Fig. 17.1, but, it must be admitted, in respect of its eastern boundary more clearly on this map than on the ground. Although geologically there is such a profound change from the ancient rocks of Armorica to the limestones of the lowlands of northern France, there is no corresponding change in landscape and land use; the characteristic *bocage* of small fields of pasture interspersed with hedgerows, copses and orchards extends well to the east. In this case it is necessary to be arbitrary, and to define a boundary which simply follows the geological division.

The *Central Massif of France* is enclosed by the 300 m (1 000 ft) contour

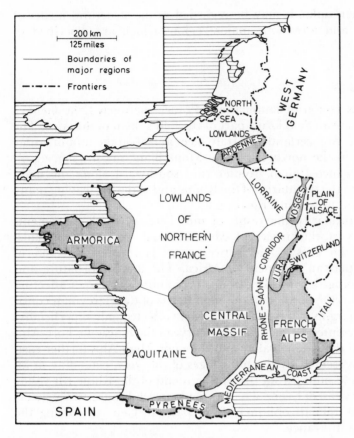

Fig. 1.3. The major regions of western Europe
The upland and mountain regions are distinguished by a stipple.

and occupies roughly a sixth of the area of the country. It stands prominently above the surrounding lowlands, with a markedly steep drop along its uptilted eastern and southeastern margins to the trough of the Saône-Rhône valley and the Mediterranean coastlands.

The *Vosges* rise along the western side of the rift valley of the Rhine. The western boundary is difficult to define, since the upland mass slopes gradually downward into the scarplands of Lorraine; one can choose the line of the low Muschelkalk hills which form the eastern boundary of the Keuper and Lias Clays of Lorraine.

Finally, the *Ardennes* form the western section of a group of uplands

7

lying across the basin of the Rhine, known collectively as 'the Middle Rhine Highlands'. The Ardennes are situated for the most part in southeastern Belgium, although a small portion extends into France as far west as Hirson, and they also comprise the northern third of the Grand Duchy of Luxembourg.

These Hercynian uplands may be regarded as the structural nuclei of western Europe, and form four major regions which are described in Chapters 17 to 20.

## The fold ranges

The mountainous region of southeastern France, between Lake Geneva and the Mediterranean Sea, forms part of the fold system of the Alps. The frontiers of France, Switzerland and Italy meet in fact on the summit-ridge of Mont Dolent, in the northeast of the Mont Blanc massif (Fig. 22.5). From here the Franco-Italian frontier runs southward along the main watershed between the tributaries of the Rhône and of the Po, leaving many lofty mountain groups within France.

The *Alps* are primarily the result of mid-Tertiary earth movements which upfolded vast thicknesses of Mesozoic and Tertiary sediments, accumulated in the geosyncline between the Hercynian foreland of Europe and the plateau continent of Africa. The direction, nature and degree of this folding depended both on the compressive forces affecting the geosyncline and the position of the rigid horsts of the Hercynian continent. The outer margins of this folded zone were affected only superficially, and are now represented by the sweeping curve of the limestone Fore-Alps which lie between the Rhône valley and the main High Alps further east. They are also represented by the hill ranges of the *Jura*, extending in an arc for 250 km (150 miles) from the southern end of the Rhine rift valley to the Rhône valley east of Lyons. The frontier between France and Switzerland crosses these uplands obliquely from Basel to Geneva, leaving the southwestern Jura in France.

A third system of fold mountains comprises the *Pyrenees*, the crestline of which for the most part demarcates the Franco-Spanish frontier. These complex mountains, rising abruptly above the Basin of Aquitaine, form a comparatively narrow series of ranges, and though not as lofty as the highest Alpine peaks, they are remarkably continuous and afford few well-defined passes. Structurally they owe their origin mainly to the Tertiary orogeny, but the particular fold movements occurred rather earlier than those of mid-Tertiary times which were mainly responsible for the Alpine ranges.

## The lowlands

The basins, coastal plains and valleys which comprise the lowland areas of western Europe are more easily defined after these seven upland and mountain regions have been demarcated. It is possible to describe them in terms of the major river basins (Fig. 1.4). The main continental water-parting runs northeastward from the eastern Pyrenees, along the southeastern edge of the Central Massif to the Plateau de Langres, and so to the 'Belfort Gate' and the Rhine at Basel. To the south and east of this line most of the drainage finds its way through the Saône-Rhône system to the Mediterranean. To the west and north are the basins of the Garonne, Loire, Seine, Scheldt (*Schelde, Escaut*), Meuse (*Maas*) and Rhine (*Rhin, Rhein, Rijn*).

It is not practicable to describe each of these river basins as individual units. This is partly because they come into such close juxtaposition and their watersheds interlock in a most complex manner, partly because their basins naturally include areas of the uplands already defined. It is more convenient to distinguish seven separate lowland areas; though differing in scale from the extensive lowlands of northern France to the restricted Plain of Alsace, each has an undoubted individuality.

FIG. 1.4. The major drainage basins of western Europe

*Introduction*

In the north, occupying the Netherlands, two-thirds of Belgium and part of the extreme north of France, are the *North Sea lowlands*, bounded on the south by the chalk ridge of Artois, and on the southeast by the line of the Sambre-Meuse valley. Then to the south lie the extensive *lowlands of northern France*, a structural depression enclosed by the Ardennes, the Central Massif and Armorica, and filled with varied sedimentary rocks. The heart, the focus of these lowlands, as indeed of France itself, is Paris, and the term Paris Basin is commonly applied. The major problem is where to draw the boundaries on the west with Armorica (where as has been shown it is necessary to be arbitrary) and on the east. Here the lowlands merge into the *scarplands and vales of Lorraine*, another region with an undoubted individuality, not limited to France but continued northward into the *Bon Pays* of Luxembourg and the *Côtes Lorraines* of southeastern Belgium. The compromise effected in drawing the boundary utilises the watershed between the Meuse, which has cut a long south–north furrow through the edge of the Corallian escarpment, and the almost parallel Aire, the most westerly of the Seine's family of rivers.

There is a broad gap, the 'sill' of Poitou, between Armorica and the Central Massif, through which the lowlands of northern France are continuous with those of *Aquitaine*. The last is an undulating triangular lowland, about one-seventh of the area of France, occupied by a fan of rivers flowing from both the Central Massif and the Pyrenees, and focusing on the Gironde estuary.

The coastal plain of southern France, between the uplands and the Mediterranean Sea, is sometimes known as the *Midi*. From the point of view of structure and relief it exhibits great diversity, but on to this the climate has imposed a unifying stamp reflected both in the landscape and the way of life. To the north the Midi is continued by the *Rhône-Saône Valley*, forming a lowland re-entrant far into central France. Indeed, another low 'gateway', the Porte de Bourgogne or Trouée de Belfort, leads from the upper Saône valley into the Rhineland. The valley of the Rhine from Basel to Mainz consists of a rift valley bordered by the Vosges and the Black Forest. The *Plain of Alsace*, varying in width from 15 to 40 km (10 to 25 miles), lies on the western side of the great river which for about 150 km (90 miles) forms the international frontier.

In this way, then, fourteen major physical regions, each with a marked individuality, have been defined (Fig. 1.3), and are used as a basis for presenting a systematic survey of the regional geography of France and the Benelux countries.

[1] This more limited district is strictly known as *Bas-Languedoc* (see pp. 424–38).
[2] Quoted by L. Gallois, *Régions naturelles et noms de pays: étude sur la Région Parisienne* (1908), pp. 8–9.
[3] These are conveniently summarised by Gallois, *op. cit.*, ch. 1 (pp. 8–34), 'La notion de région naturelle'.
[4] *Bulletin littéraire* (1888–9), ii, 1–7, and 49–57.

[5] I. B. Thompson, *Modern France: a social and economic geography* (1970), especially Chapter 5; P. Bauchet, *La Planification française* (1966); G. Caire, *La Planification, techniques et problémes* (1967).

[6] M. Leriche, 'Les Régions naturelles de la Belgique', *Revue Université de Bruxelles*, **19** (1913–14), pp. 185–218.

[7] P. L. Michotte, 'Cartes-types des régions géographiques de Belgique', *B.S.R. Belge G.*, **50** (1926), pp. 301–7.

[8] M. A. Lefèvre, 'Carte des régions géographiques belges', *Bull. Soc. belge Etud. géogr.*, **10** (1940), pp. 49–74.

[9] See M. E. Dumont and L. de Smet, *Bibliographie géographique de la Belgique* (1954), an impressive volume of 450 pages with a large number of entries.

[10] R. Blanchard, *La Flandre: étude géographique de la Plaine Flamande en France, Belgique et Hollande* (1906).

[11] Cf. S. W. E. Vince, 'The agricultural regions of Belgium', *London Essays in Geography* (1951), pp. 255–87. By using intersecting isopleths of crop densities, he produced twenty-seven subregions within ten main regions.

[12] G. Baeckeroot, *Oesling et Gutland* (1942)

# Part I
# The Lowlands

# 2
# The North Sea lowlands:
# general features

For long periods of geological time the North Sea and its margins have been an area of depression and of resultant sedimentation.[1] The structural boundary of this depression on the south is formed by the Palaeozoic rocks of the 'massif of Brabant', separating it from the syncline of the Paris Basin further south (Fig. 2.1). The 'floor' of the depression is essentially the surface of the peneplain of Hercynian Europe, including horstlike masses which contain coal-bearing rocks at various, though considerable, depths. The filling-in of this depression by sedimentation has proceeded since Permian times. The many deep borings put down by the Dutch and Belgian geological survey departments have reached Permian and Lower Carboniferous rocks in the southeast of the Netherlands and in northeast Belgium, although further north these lie at vast depths as yet unproven.[2] Triassic and Jurassic rocks have been found at depth beneath the surface of the Kempenland and parts of the southern Netherlands, but they do not occur on the surface, as they do on the outer margins of the Paris Basin.

In Upper Cretaceous times a widespread marine transgression spread far beyond the North Sea depression, during which an extensive cover of chalk rocks was laid down. The Chalk now appears on the surface in the Paris Basin, and it is seen also in the neighbourhood of Mons, further east in the Hesbaye and Herve regions near Liège, and in South Limburg. Elsewhere it has either been removed by subsequent denudation before any Tertiary rocks were deposited, as over much of the plateau of Brabant, or it is deeply masked by newer deposits. Thus the anticlinal chalk ridge of Artois dips beneath the Tertiary rocks of the Flanders Plain in Belgium, and in the Kempenland and South Limburg colliery shafts pass through Chalk and other Cretaceous rocks at considerable depths on their way down to workable Coal Measures.

In early Tertiary times a further widespread marine transgression covered the Netherlands, most of Belgium and the Paris Basin. The resultant deposits are to be found over much of the surface of central Belgium. Those of Eocene age include the Flanders Clay on the Flemish plain and the sands of Brabant and Hesbaye. Oligocene sands and clays form a narrow interrupted belt along the southern border of the Kempenland, and occur more

extensively to the east in Limburg. These older Tertiary rocks in the Netherlands are deeply buried beneath younger deposits.

In late Tertiary times (Miocene and Pliocene) occurred the last of the
major transgressions, and the sea again extended southwards over much of
what is now Belgium and even into northern France. Vast amounts of
coarse sandy sediment were laid down in the North Sea basin. The extent
and depth of this late Tertiary transgression seem to have fluctuated, for
occasional beds of brown coal among the sands and clays indicate temporary conditions of lowland swamp in which vegetation flourished.

Towards the end of Pliocene times began the steady shift northwards of

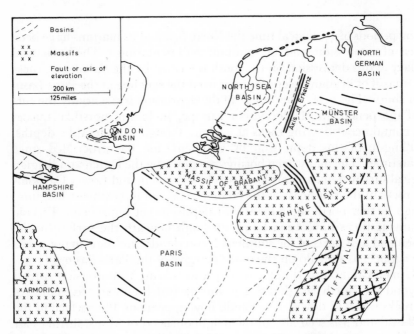

Fig. 2.1 Diagrammatic representation of the structural boundaries of the
North Sea basin

Based on J. H. F. Umbgrove, *Symphony of the Earth* (1950), p. 45.

the coastline, as the seas receded. This was mainly the result of a widespread
tilting movement; it seems that areas to the south of a line indicated approximately by the present Belgo-Dutch frontier were slowly uplifted, with the
result that surviving patches of Lower Pliocene rocks now lie in southern
Belgium and northern France at a height of approximately 150 m (500 ft).
To the north of this line, conversely, the tilting movement was downward,
so that the Lower Pliocene strata are found progressively deeper; at Utrecht
borings have located them at 370 m (1 200 ft) below sea level.[3]

There was a marked difference between the subsequent development of
the physical features of the North Sea lowlands to the south of this line of

tilting and those to the north. The former areas comprise the Plain of Flanders and the 'low plateaus' of central Belgium, the latter include the composite Scheldt-Meuse-Rhine 'delta'. Furthermore, the former lay well to the south of the maximum extension of the continental Quaternary ice sheets, while much of the northern area was either directly or marginally affected by these glaciations.

## The southern lowlands

This section of the North Sea lowlands for the most part consists of the basin of the Scheldt, together with the narrow valley of the Meuse from where it leaves the 'coal furrow' of southern Belgium to where it opens out into its composite floodplain with the Rhine.

The various rivers which comprise the Scheldt system flow more or less parallel across the Flanders Plain and central Belgium. The greater part of each of their courses trends from southwest to northeast, that is, approximately parallel to the North Sea coast. This river system developed, during the gradual emergence of the Pliocene sea floor, as a series of initially independent consequents. Many of the basic features of the Flanders Plain and the low plateaus of central Belgium were formed as the result of active erosion by these rivers in Quaternary times; the valleys of today are far too extensive to have been eroded by rivers of their present size. This enhanced downcutting was due partly to the increase in volume as a result of snowmelt on the uplands to the south, partly to various changes in base level. The denudation almost completely removed the newer Tertiary deposits over the whole of Belgium, except for the Kempenland in the northeast and the isolated cappings on the hills in Flanders, Brabant and even as far south as Artois in France. These hills rise from the gently swelling interfluves between the wide shallow valley troughs. This denudation therefore exposed the older Tertiary rocks such as the Flanders Clay and the sandstones of Brabant and Hesbaye. In central Belgium river erosion went even further and cut completely through the Tertiary deposits to expose ancient Cambrian and Silurian rocks in some of the valleys (Plate 22).

In immediate postglacial times extensive sedimentation was effected by the heavily laden rivers, so that the floors of their valleys are thickly covered with alluvium, in places to a depth of over 30 m (100 ft). Across these deposits the rivers meandered in floodplains as much as 6 to 8 km (4 to 5 miles) in width, towards the still fluctuating coastline. The rivers' courses, like the coastline, have now been artificially stabilised, but abandoned meanders can still be traced among the maze of drainage channels. These valleys, then, together with their gentle interfluves and occasional higher relics, comprise the main physical features of Flanders and the low plateaus of central Belgium.

Apart from some interesting changes due to river capture, particularly in French Flanders (see p. 144), there is a further important element in the

Scheldt drainage pattern. The middle Scheldt (that is, the section below the Lys confluence at Gent), the Durme and the Rupel together form a continuous west–east line, lying broadly at right angles to the northeasterly direction of the Lys and the upper Scheldt. This line is continued by the lower courses of the Dyle and the Demer, but while the middle Scheldt and Durme flow towards the east, the Demer, Dyle and Rupel flow to the west, with the result that both trends focus on the lower Scheldt and its estuary. The westwards-flowing Demer has eroded a distinct 'furrow' between the southern edge of the Kempen plateau and the general northward slope of the low plateaus of central Belgium. This furrow, therefore, taps the consequents flowing northwards from the plateaus of Brabant and Hesbaye—the Senne, Dyle, Geete and upper Demer—and so leads their waters to the Rupel and hence to the Scheldt estuary.

The only other major Scheldt tributary is the Nethe, which, by means of its two main headstreams, the Groote- and Kleine-Nethe, drains the gentle western slope of the Kempen plateau of northeastern Belgium. This plateau forms a broad and indeterminate watershed between these headstreams of the Nethe and a few right-bank confluents of the Demer, and those flowing north to the lower Meuse. The Nethe is wholly regularised in its lower course (it is actually siphoned under the Albert Canal), and finally joins the Rupel near the Senne-Dyle confluence.

Thus the drainage of virtually all Belgium to the north and west of the line of the Meuse makes its way to a single outlet. The only exceptions to this hydrographic unity are the Ijzer (*Yser*) and the Aa, each of which breaks through to the North Sea after following the usual southwest to northeast trend in its upper course.

The present Meuse below Liège flows northwards in a quite deeply incised valley. Though it now receives few tributaries from the west, its past changes of course have profoundly affected the physical landscape of northeastern Belgium and adjacent parts of the Netherlands. It is probable that the river once flowed eastwards beyond the position of Liège to the proto-Rhine; then it was diverted westwards over the Kempenland, and later still it developed its present northern course, succeeded lower down near Mook by a great bend westwards. These various changes of the Meuse have not been confined merely to the actual course of the river but have also involved alterations in base level. At times, notably when the melting of the ice sheets at the close of the Quaternary glaciation returned water to the seas and therefore produced a higher base level, the response of the river to its resultant gentler gradient was extensive deposition because of the reduction of its load-carrying capacity. At other times, the result both of lower glacial sea level and of the tilting which raised the land south of an axis more or less along the Belgo-Dutch frontier, the gradient of the river and therefore its erosive capacity were increased. The result has been the formation of a terraced valley, bordered by the Kempen plateau on the west and that of South Limburg on the east.

The results and interrelations of the erosional and depositional processes of the Meuse have been analysed in considerable detail by Mlle M. A. Lefèvre,[4] who has distinguished between the 'aggradational' or 'depositional' floodplains built up when the river was unable to carry its load because of a decrease of gradient, and the 'degradational' or 'erosional' floodplains where the surface has been progressively lowered by the river as its channel migrated. Mlle Lefèvre applies these principles to the lower Meuse basin and distinguishes four '*unités cycliques*' or 'fluvial complexes'. Cycle IV, the oldest, is represented only by a series of flats at a height of about 200 m (650 ft) above sea level, traceable in the Condroz and Herve regions to the south, in South Limburg, and along a west–east line to the north of Aachen. Mlle Lefèvre suggests that this level represents the valley of a former course of the Meuse when it flowed eastwards to join the Rhine, incised in a still older erosion surface at about 230 m (725 ft). The Meuse was later diverted northwards, then westwards, and finally again northwards to its present position, producing three further 'fluvial complexes', each of which is represented by a degradational floodplain (*e*) upstream and an aggradational floodplain (*r*) further downstream (Fig. 6.2). The aggradational floodplain of Cycle III is a *plateau du cône alluvial (IIIr)* laid down as the Meuse gradually changed its course in a series of slowly moving curves. It forms a horizontal 'fan' of coarse sand and gravel, with its apex just to the northwest of Maastricht at a height of about 100 m (340 ft). It is bounded quite steeply on the east by the later degradational terraces of the Meuse and on the southwest by the Demer valley, but it slopes very gently northward into the Netherlands and westward towards the Scheldt estuary. The deposits thin off from 9 to 12 m (30 to 50 ft) near the apex, to about 5 m (15 ft) near the Dutch frontier. Cycle II was responsible for a degradational floodplain which has been cut into the edge of the Kempen plateau, thus forming a distinct terrace between Maastricht and Maaseik at 40 to 45 m (130 to 150 ft) above sea level. Cycle I represents the modern floodplain of the Meuse and its tributaries; the degradational plain is the present valley floor in the neighbourhood of Maastricht, and the aggradational plain is represented by the present joint floodplain of the Meuse-Rhine and the alluvium-covered floors of the shallow valleys draining northwards across the frontier to the Meuse.

## The northern lowlands

During the span of the Pleistocene, the glacial epoch produced considerable effects both on those parts of the North Sea lowlands actually covered by the ice sheets and also on the periglacial fringes to the south.[5] These lowlands lay on the very margins of the maximum advance of the Scandinavian continental ice sheets. This maximum occurred in the third glacial period (known as the *Riss* or in northern Europe as the *Saale*),[6] when the ice sheet extended just to the south of the Zuider Zee. This limit is indicated by a discontinuous series of low sandhills, extending south-eastward as the Utrecht-Gelderland ridge, then interrupted by the Rhine valley, and continued to the southeast of Nijmegen and into Germany almost to Krefeld (Fig. 2.2). It would hardly be correct, however, to regard

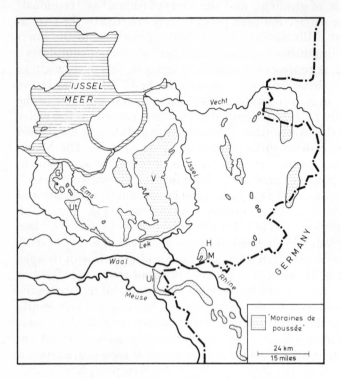

FIG. 2.2. The '*moraines de poussée*' of the southern Netherlands
Abbreviations: **G,** Gooiland hills; **H,** the Hettenheuvel;
**M,** the Montferland; **Ui,** the Uilenput; **Ut,** the Utrecht ridge;
**V,** Veluwe.

Based on K. Oestreich, 'La Genèse du paysage naturel', *Tijdsdr. IC. ned. aardrijksk. genoot.* **55** (1938), 562.

these hills as terminal moraines in the accepted sense, although some Dutch geologists[7] go so far as to call them 'moraines frontales'. They consist almost entirely of masses of sand and gravel, with little clay, and so these areas are included in the category of 'sand country' in the regional divisions described below. The ridges may represent a series of *kames*, deposited along the edge of the ice by subglacial streams. On the other hand, they may have been caused by ice pressure from the north, thus 'rucking-up' or 'bulldozing' the glacial drifts and possibly also the fluvial sands and gravels deposited in the preceding *Mindel-Riss* interglacial period. It can be clearly seen in several sand quarries that layers of sand and gravel have been folded and even overthrust in a remarkable way, if on a miniature scale. If this supposition is correct, the name 'push moraine' (*moraines de poussée*, or in Dutch, *stuwwallen*) is justified. These same sandy ridges occur in the Veluwe, in eastern Gelderland and in Overijssel (Fig. 2.3). All this sandy area, to the south of the Vecht valley, is described by Tesch (*op. cit.*) as the 'région des moraines frontales'.

To the north of the Vecht valley lies an extensive area in eastern Friesland and Groningen which Tesch calls the 'région de la moraine inférieure'; this represents, in fact, the ground moraine of the *Riss* glaciation. Sand, with irregular gravel patches, is still dominant, but there are considerable tracts of till. Sometimes two or three distinct layers of this occur, separated by sands and gravels which may well indicate slight fluctuations of this most advanced part of the continental ice sheet. Further west, in Noord-Holland, the glacial clays occur at greater depths under newer deposits. The surface areas of clay are shown on Fig. 2.3. Some isolated upstanding

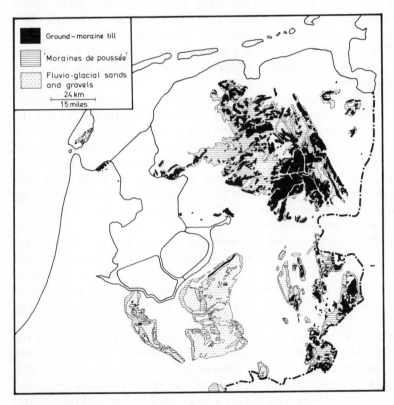

FIG. 2.3. Glacial and fluvioglacial deposits in the Netherlands
The areas of the *moraines de poussée* differ slightly from those shown on
Fig. 2.2, since they are drawn from different sources, and interpretations
of the various deposits likewise differ.

Based on *Kleine Overzichtskaart van Nederland*, 1:600000, produced by the Netherlands Geological
Survey (1947).

masses form the nuclei of Wieringerlant and the island of Texel. Till also underlies part of the Wadden Zee; it was convenient that it occurred so near the line of the main dyke across the mouth of the Zuider Zee, since this material, dredged from the sea floor and dumped into position, formed a compact basis for the dyke (see p. 49). In Friesland some mounds of sand and clay are of a drumlin-like character.

Occasional erratics are found, some of which are almost certainly of Scandinavian origin. In the province of Groningen and in the neighbouring parts of Drenthe some of these erratics have been assembled by man in the distant past to form dolmens, the famous '*Hunnebedden*' or burial places, claimed to represent the oldest traces of human occupation in the Netherlands.

The Quaternary glaciation was but a temporary interruption to the development of the drainage system of the Rhine. By the beginning of the Pleistocene these northern lowlands were dominated by a great proto-Rhine, to which the Scheldt, Meuse and Thames were confluents. This system formed the outflow for the drainage of much of central and western Europe. This proto-Rhine and its confluents have built up a vast joint deltaic area, really comprising a complex series of contiguous and over-lapping deltaic fans.

During the Pleistocene, sedimentation continued in the areas outside (i.e. south of) the immediate ice sheet.[8] As the ice fluctuated, so did the base level of the rivers, corresponding to the changing sea level which resulted from a withdrawal of water when the ice advanced or a return of water when it regressed. Some periods of extensive deposition of gravel and coarse sand took place at various times when the rivers were heavily charged with detritus. Other periods of renewed erosion occurred during stages of low sea level, when the rivers entrenched their beds deeply into their own deposits to form terraces.

The chronology of these river terraces has been worked out in considerable detail; a brief summary must suffice.[9] The highest Rhine terrace, found in West Germany below Bonn, but not represented in the Netherlands, indicates the position of the river in late Pliocene times. This is succeeded by the so-called High, Middle and Lower Terraces of Pleistocene age (Fig. 2.4). The High Terrace is found on the surface only in the south of the Netherlands, extending across the West German frontier between the valleys of the Meuse and its parallel northwards-flowing tributary the Niers, and further west along the present Belgian frontier. The Middle Terrace forms a much more extensive gravel sheet between the main distributaries of the Rhine, and covers a large area in Noord-Brabant and Limburg. The Lower Terrace occurs very extensively to the east of the IJssel Meer and along the Meuse valley, but it too is masked in the west and north of the Netherlands by recent superficial deposits. It is most hazardous to attempt to correlate these terraces with the whole glacial cycle, but some authorities tentatively ascribe the Middle Terrace to the

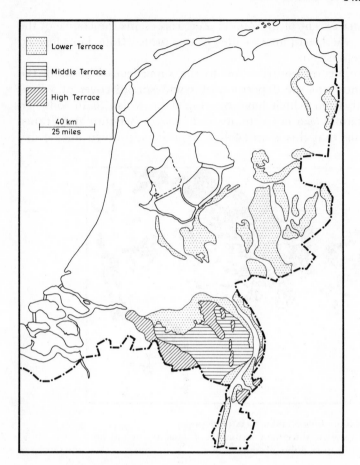

Fig. 2.4. The river terraces in the Netherlands

Based on *Kleine Overzichtskaart van Nederland*, 1:600000, produced by the Netherlands
Geological Survey (1947).

*Riss* glacial period and the Lower Terrace to the date of the *Würm* (*Weichsel*)
glaciation, the ice sheets of which did not advance further south than the
Elbe valley.

In addition to this river deposition, the higher sea level during some
interglacial phases resulted in the deposition of marine sediments. The most
notable interglacial transgression is ascribed to the period following the
*Riss* glaciation. The resultant marine deposits were first studied in the
embayment to the south of the IJssel Meer, known as the Geldersche
Vallei, drained by the small river Eem; as a result, the name *Eemian* has
been given to them. These deposits, mostly consisting of marine clays and
sands, are also found in Noord-Holland, along the coast of Friesland, in
the islands of Terschelling and Ameland, and in parts of Groningen. It is
suggested that the position of most of these Eemian deposits, lying more or

23

less over the former extent of the Zuider Zee, represents the course of the preglacial Rhine; the broad lower valley of this proto-Rhine later formed the Zuider Zee depression.

One further important contribution to the superficial deposits of the North Sea lowlands was the deposition of a widespread cover of a fine-textured material, from which have developed brownish loam soils. To this is given the names *loess* in Germany and *limon* in Belgium and France (Fig. 2.5). It seems that this is an aeolian deposit, laid down during dry

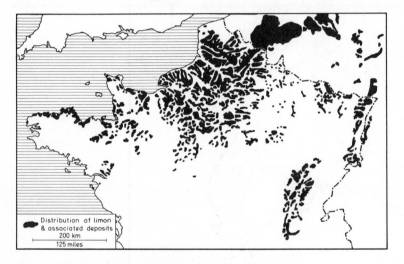

Distribution of limon
& associated deposits
200 km
125 miles

FIG. 2.5. The distribution of *limon* and associated deposits
The French frontier is shown, since the distribution of *limon* deposits within and without this is taken from different sources.

Based on (*a*) *Atlas de France*, sheet 10, 'Dépôts et formations récents'; and (*b*) *Internationale Bodenkarte von Europa*, 1 : 250 000, sheet VI.

steppelike interglacial or perhaps immediately postglacial periods. Wind, blowing outwards from high pressure centres established over the ice sheets to the north, exerted its sorting and transporting power on the finer elements among the vast supplies of unconsolidated materials deposited by fluvioglacial action beyond the margins of the continental ice sheets.

Limon occurs at all heights in central Belgium and the Paris Basin, both on the highest interfluves and plateaus and, though usually reworked and redeposited by subsequent river action, on the river terraces. Thicknesses of 21 m (70 ft) have been recorded. As a result, the underlying solid geology, whether it be Chalk as in Hesbaye, Artois and Picardy, or Tertiary sands and clays as in Brabant and Hainaut, or Tertiary limestones in the central Paris Basin, is in places wholly masked. The stamp of the limon on landscape and agricultural economy is so marked that a distinctive zone of limon-covered country can be traced right across Europe from the Paris

Basin, through central Belgium, and on across Germany (where the loess-covered region is known as the *Börde*) from the Rhine to Silesia.

## Postglacial developments

The greater part of the western half of the Netherlands, as well as the valley floors of the great rivers and the narrow strip immediately behind the Belgian coastline, is now covered with recent deposits, laid down since about 20 000 B.C., sometimes to considerable depths. The chronology of the

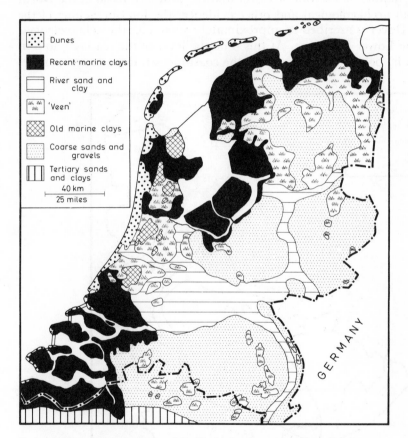

FIG. 2.6. The surface deposits of the Netherlands and northern Belgium
The areas of the various deposits are much simplified, especially of the river sands and clays, which form long 'ribbons' along all the streams. The term *veen* is as used by the Geological Survey, and includes both the *laagveen* and *hoogveen*, whether reclaimed or not (see also Fig. 3.6). The greater part of the *hoogveen* in the east has now been removed. The dunes include both the 'old' and the 'new' dunes.

Based on *Kleine Overzichtskaart van Nederland*, 1:600 000, produced by the Netherlands Geological Survey (1947).

postglacial period has been worked out in detail in Scandinavia, and it is possible to attempt a correlation with the sequence of events in the Low Countries.

At the end of the Pleistocene, sea level seems to have lain at about 60 m (200 ft) below its present position, the result of the considerable amount of water still contained in the *Würm* ice sheets. The floor of the present North Sea then formed continuous land between Britain and the continental low-lands of today. A gradual marine advance took place in the post-*Würm* period, the so-called 'Flandrian Transgression', which finally formed the English Channel, the Strait of Dover and the southern basin of the North Sea. From archaeological and other evidence, the final breaching of the Strait of Dover is ascribed to approximately 5000 B.C., the acknowledged end of the Lower Holocene. At this time the level of the sea lay 5 to 6 m (16 to 20 ft) below the present, and the coastline ran more or less parallel

FIG. 2.7. The regional divisions of the North Sea lowlands
The numbers are as follows: 1, the coastal lands of the Netherlands; 2, Maritime Flanders; 3, the Dutch river valleys; 4, the heathlands of Belgium and the Netherlands; 5, Interior Flanders; 6, the central low plateaus of Belgium and the Netherlands. These are described in Chapters 3 to 8 respectively. The letters refer to regional subdivisions described in the text.

to, but a few km seaward of, its present position. During the last few millennia the story in detail is complex. On the one hand there has been the accumulation of sand-dunes and marine muds, the deposition of river silt, and the growth of fen peat (Fig. 2.6). On the other hand, there has been a slight but continuous relative rise of sea level, which is still in progress at the rate of some 100 to 150 mm (4 to 6 in) per century, probably owing to the continued sinking of the floor of the North Sea Basin.

On to the results of these natural processes has been superimposed the contribution of reclamation and coastal defence, a fascinating story, though repeatedly interrupted by temporary setbacks due to storms and river floods; the last of these disasters flooded 16 000 ha (400 000 acres) in 1953. Today some two-fifths of Dutch territory and a considerable area of the maritime plain of Flanders would be inundated without the protecting coastal defences.

## Regional divisions

It is clear from this brief introduction that several regional subdivisions manifest themselves (Fig. 2.7). There is such a distinctive contrast between the embayed coastline of islands and estuaries from the Ems to the Wester Schelde (Chapter 3), and the long straight coast of Maritime Flanders from the Wester Schelde to the neighbourhood of Calais (Chapter 4), that these must be considered separately, with their hinterlands. The alluvium-floored tracts of the Rhine-Meuse floodplain form a broad belt across the centre of the lowlands (Chapter 5), and extensive areas of sand comprise the most westerly part of the heathlands of the North European Plain (Chapter 6). The plain of Interior Flanders (Chapter 7) is succeeded inland by the low plateaus of central Belgium and of the extreme southeast of the Netherlands (Chapter 8).

[1] For a full account, see A. J. Pannekoek, ed., *Geological History of the Netherlands* (1956).

[2] Much detailed information has also been obtained from borings put down by the *Nederlandse Aardolie Maatschappij*, an oil company in which the Royal Dutch Shell and Esso groups have equal participation.

[3] A map with contours showing the depth of the base of the Pleistocene (exceeding 600 m (*c.* 2 000 ft) in Noord-Holland) is given in Pannekoek, *op. cit.*, p. 8.

[4] M. A. Lefèvre: (*a*) 'Le Cône alluvial de la Meuse', *Annales de la Société scientifique de Bruxelles, Série B, Sciences physiques et naturelles*, **48** (1928), pp. 121–38; (*b*) 'La Basse-Meuse: étude de morphologie fluviale', *Bull. Soc. belge Etud. géogr., Mémoire I* (1935).

[5] A. Brouwer, 'De Glacigene Landschapstypen', *Tijdschr. K. ned. aardrijksk. Genoot.*, **57** (1950), pp. 20–32, affords a most useful summary with several maps.

[6] Some Dutch geologists have given to the *Riss (Saale)* glaciation the local name of *Drenthian*, the only glacial phase in which a Scandinavian ice-sheet actually covered part of the Netherlands.

[7] Notably P. Tesch, 'L'origine du sous-sol des Pays-Bas', *Tijdschr. K. ned. aardrijksk. Genoot.*, **55** (1938), p. 548.

27

⁸ G. C. Maarleveld, 'Fluvie-glaciale Afzettingen in Midden-Nederland', *Tijdschr. K. ned. aardrijksk. Genoot.*, **72** (1955), pp. 48–58.

⁹ The Maas terraces are discussed by J. I. S. Zonneveld, 'De Kwartaire Rivierterrassen in Midden-Nederland', *Tijdschr. K. ned. aardrijksk. Genoot.*, **72** (1955), pp. 329–43; he analyses, dates and names the various erosional terraces of the Maas, and provides a detailed map. See also Pannekoek, *op. cit.*, pp. 72–3, for a discussion of the Pleistocene, with a full bibliography and a chronological table showing the relationship of the terraces to the glacial phases.

# 3
# The coastal lands of the Netherlands

## The development of the coast

The past sequence of events affecting the coastline of the North Sea has been described above in outline. At the end of the Lower Holocene, the coastline of what is now the Netherlands lay more or less parallel to but a few kilometres offshore from its present position, and the Strait of Dover had been recently breached. A great offshore bar then developed as a result of sand accretion, sweeping in a curve from the coast of western Flanders to the Scheldt-Meuse-Rhine delta, where the distributaries interrupted its continuity, and continuing again along the coast of what is now Zuid- and Noord-Holland. The bar was probably initiated during the change from the 'Boreal' to the 'Atlantic' climatic phase. Its nucleus consisted of sand mixed with masses of shelly fragments, forming a basal layer (Fig. 3.2) on which windblown sand accumulated to form dunes, usually referred to as 'the old duneline'. These shelly sands now afford a valuable source of lime for agriculture.

As the dunelines developed into an appreciable barrier, the sea was finally excluded and mud steadily accumulated in the shallow freshwater lagoons. The surface level gradually rose as a result both of this accretion of mud and of the growth of fen peat. The resultant layer, known as the Lower Peatbed, is interrupted here and there by irregular patches of mud, sand and gravel indicating the courses of former streams which wandered vaguely over the marshland. A change to a slightly cooler climate seems to have interrupted this peat accumulation, but a return to moister, milder conditions just before the beginning of the historic period caused renewed plant growth and the formation of the Upper Peatbed.[1] These peat accumulations are known collectively as 'low fen peat' or *laagveen*, indicated on Figs. 2.6 and 3.6. They occur extensively in Zuid- and Noord-Holland, in Friesland and in Groningen, and in places the thickness is as much as 5 m (16 ft).

During the first millennium A.D. the position of this offshore bar gradually changed, the result of erosion in the south and of increased accretion in the north. The southern part of the old bar and duneline, extending from near The Hague (Fig. 3.1) to the French coast at Sangatte, was completely destroyed, so that the present coastline (described in the next chapter) now lies 5 to 8 km (3 to 5 miles) further inland. In the north accretion caused the position of the bar to move seawards until it reached a solid mass of till which now forms the 'core' of the island of Texel, and then curved eastward through the line of what is now the Frisian Islands. On this bar a second series of dunes was built up, which have been closely dated by means of archaeological evidence as originating from the beginning of the fourth century A.D.

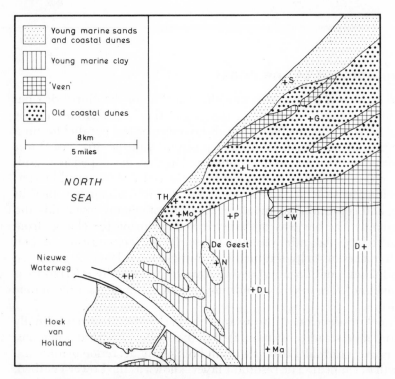

FIG. 3.1. The coastal lowlands in the neighbourhood of The Hague
The initials refer to the following towns: **D,** Delft; **DL,** De Lier;
**G,** The Hague ('s-Gravenhage); **H,** Hook of Holland (Hoek van Holland); **L,** Loosduinen; **Ma,** Maasland; **Mo,** Monster; **N,** Naaldwijk; **P,** Poeldijk; **S,** Scheveningen; **TH,** Ter Heide; **W,** Wateringen.

Based on the 1:50000 series, *Geologische Kaart van Nederlanden*, sheets 30, 37.

The two dunelines can still be traced along the coasts of Zuid- and Noord-Holland, the older ones lying 7 or 8 km (4 or 5 miles) inland of the newer dunes bordering the present beach. This zone forms such a valuable coastal defensive barrier, particularly when strengthened in various ways, that only a few short lengths of sea dyke are required between The Hague and Den Helder, although the land to the east is well below NAP[2]; this is almost the only section of the Dutch coast without sea dykes. The inner dunes now form gently undulating terrain known as *Geestgronden* between the new duneline and the polders (Fig. 3.2).

Behind this dune wall, then, lay in Roman times a broad desolate plain covered with peat fens and shallow meres, above mean sea level but liable to inundation by spring tides; these marshes were known as the *Wapelinge*, after an old Frisian word for water. An extensive shallow lake, the *Lacus*

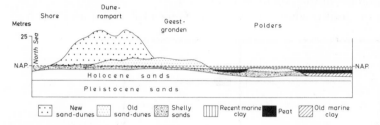

FIG. 3.2. Diagrammatic section across the dune and polder lands in Noord-Holland

Based on P. Tesch, 'The physiographic regions of the Netherlands', *Geogrl Rev.* **13** (1923), 511. Length of section is 16 km (10 miles).

*Flevo*, formed the progenitor of the Zuider Zee. Some of the Rhine waters flowed into this lake, which drained northwards through a broad channel known as the Vlie, to reach the North Sea through a gap in the dune wall. This gap is now represented by the Terschelling Zeegat between the islands of Vlieland and Terschelling, and the main shipping channel leading between these islands to the port of Harlingen is still known as the Vliestroom.

During historic times sea level has risen continuously, and it is evident that but for more than a thousand years of hard and sustained human effort the sea would today cover all Zeeland, the western part of Noord-Brabant and most of Zuid-Holland. The peninsula which projects northward between the North Sea and the Zuider Zee to form the province of Noord-Holland would consist merely of a narrow strip of dune islands (Fig. 3.3).

Until approximately the beginning of the fourteenth century the sea had a net gain on the land. There are, it is true, records as early as the seventh century of reclamation around the shores of the *Lacus Flevo*, and some large dykes were constructed in Friesland and Groningen. A shallow channel across what is now Friesland, the *Friesche Middelzee*,[3] which drained northwards between the dunes of what are now the islands of Terschelling and Ameland, was reclaimed by 1300. Men had even reclaimed most of the broad estuary of the Dollard, into which flows the Ems (*Eems*), but here enthusiasm outran technical ability, for in 1413 the sluices gave way and the waters flowed back, covering thirty villages. By 1300, therefore, notwithstanding some local and often temporary gains, the sea had advanced considerably. The new dune rampart north of Den Helder was breached in several places (so forming the Frisian Islands), and the mudflats within the dunes were inundated to form the Wadden Zee. This extended southward into the *Lacus Flevo*, flooding the low-lying peatlands around its margins and so forming the Zuider Zee, under which numerous towns and villages vanished. The dune wall south of Petten remained intact, but westerly projecting gulfs of the Zuider Zee (the Beemster and the Schermer in the north and the IJ in the south) covered all land below sea level to within 3 to 5 km (2 or 3 miles) of the North Sea (Fig. 3.3).

Further to the south, what is now the province of Zeeland and much of

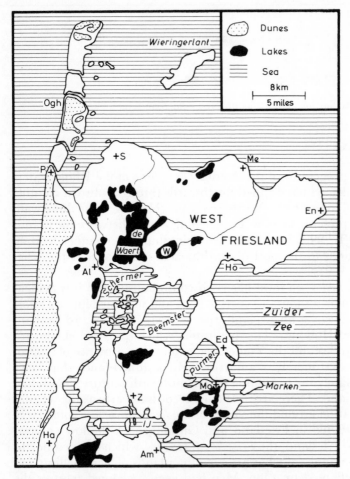

FIG. 3.3. Noord-Holland at the beginning of the fourteenth century
The abbreviations are as follows: **Al,** Alkmaar; **Am,** Amsterdam; **Ed,** Edam; **En,** Enkhuizen; **Ha,** Haarlem; **Ho,** Hoorn; **Me,** Medemblik; **Mo,** Monnikendam; **P,** Petten; **S,** Schagen; **W,** the Wogmeer; and **Z,** Zaandam.

Based on a folding map in *La Néerlande: études générales sur la géographie des Pays-Bas* (1938), facing p. 68, entitled 'Holland's Noorderkwartier in 1300', illustrating a contribution by J. B. L. Hol and H. van Velthoven, 'La lutte contre les eaux'.

southern Zuid-Holland became an archipelago of more than sixty islands separated by tidal channels, into which the Rhine-Meuse-Scheldt distributaries poured their waters. The main islands had more or less attained their present outlines by 1300, but many subsequent changes in detail have taken place, partly through the southward shift of the major distributaries (see p. 92), and partly by the gradual regularisation of shipping channels.

Other changes occurred in the coastline as a result of storms which at intervals breached the dykes and caused vast inundations. Many floods of great magnitude have been recorded, the result of storm surges set up when exceptionally high tides coincided with onshore gales; the fourteenth and fifteenth centuries seem to have been particularly prone. In 1413 the Dollard was flooded, as mentioned above. One of the most disastrous events was the 'St Elisabethsvloed' of 1421, which drowned 10 000 people and inundated a vast area between Dordrecht and Geertruidenberg, so forming a new arm of the sea, the Hollandsch Diep, and leaving the desolate reed-covered Biesbosch (which still exists). As the techniques of coastal defence improved, really disastrous floods became rarer, but they still occasionally happened; in 1825 much of Friesland was inundated, and other serious floods occurred in 1877, 1881, 1883, 1889, 1894, 1906, 1911 and 1916. Inundations were sometimes caused by deliberate breaching for strategic or malicious reasons, as in 1944 by the Germans in the island of Walcheren. But the floods of February 1953 were the worst for at least a century (pp. 36–7).

Defence against flooding whether by the sea or the rivers, with the complementary function of land reclamation and improvement, involves the building of sea dykes and river dykes behind which basic unit areas, known as *polders*,[5] can be reclaimed and maintained. The problems of the rivers, their regularisation and dyking, and their polder lands, are described in Chapter 5. It is necessary now to consider problems of coastal defence and the creation of the sea- and lake-polders, with special attention to the greatest polder scheme of all—the partial reclamation of the Zuider Zee.

## The sea dykes

Dykes are built to safeguard areas of land which would otherwise be either permanently inundated or temporarily flooded by exceptionally high tides. These, together with the lands liable to river floods, comprise 40 per cent of the total area of the Netherlands (Fig. 3.4), and include the very heart of the country, its chief cities and ports, and its most productive agricultural land.[6] The sea dykes extend continuously from the Dollard along the coasts of Groningen and Friesland to the Zuider Zee. In some places there is a double dyke, occasionally even a treble series (Fig. 3.7), consisting of a high outer rampart with a crest 4·5 m (15 ft) above NAP, made of clay faced with concrete or basalt blocks, and one or more overgrown older dykes a kilometre or so inland. The several lines indicate pro-

PLATE 1. The struggle against the sea: a dyke-burst in Zeeland in 1953

gressive stages of reclamation. The Frisian Islands are faced with sections of dyke to amplify the dunelines; the whole of the eastern shore of Texel, for example, is dyked. From the coast of Friesland the main Zuider Zee dam (Fig. 3.8) cuts for 29 km (18 miles) across what was once the open sea to the shores of Noord-Holland, so protecting the reclaimed polders and the low-lying lands around the former shores of the Zuider Zee.

From Den Helder to the Hook of Holland runs a sweeping curve of coast, nearly 100 km (60 miles) long, bordered by the new dune belt with a maximum width near Zandvoort of about 5 km (3 miles). Dykes are only necessary in this section round the northern tip of the peninsula of Noord-Holland, where they link up with the Zuider Zee dykes, and in minor dune breaks, as near Petten where there is a 5 km (3 mile) wall, the Honds-bossche Zeewering. This section of coast is nevertheless open to attack from the sea, and constant measures are necessary to check erosion of the dunes. Large numbers of groynes cross the beaches to well below low-water mark, fortified by sunken mattresses of willow boughs (known as *kraagstuk* or *zinkstuk*), or in recent years of polypropylene, to afford protection against tidal scour and to enhance protective accretion. On some of the sandflats fronting the dunes, osier fences are constructed to form 'drift dykes' which help to stabilise moving sand. Extensive planting of marram grass further restricts sand movement. Some of the narrower dune belts are faced with bitumen-covered stone, and sea walls and promenades front the many

34

holiday resorts. On the whole, this section of the Dutch coast, while needing constant care and maintenance, does not normally cause any major concern.

It is the delta region, with its islands, 3 000 polders and deep-water channels, which affords such critical problems. Approximately 1 100 km (700 miles) of dykes surround the Zeeland islands and border the mainland coast on either side of the estuaries. Some are merely low earthen banks; others are massive structures, such as the Westkapelle sea wall, which protects the southwestern corner of Walcheren island and is exposed to powerful attack by storm waves; its overall width, including fronting groynes and fascine work, is about 90 m (100 yd).

FIG. 3.4. Areas of the Netherlands liable to inundation
The areas liable to inundation by the sea are shown in black, those by the rivers with a stipple. The Zuider Zee polder yet to be reclaimed is outlined by a pecked line. The barrages under construction or completed as part of the Delta Plan are indicated; they will be completed by 1978.

Based on W. C. Leeuw, *The Netherlands as an Environment for Plant Life* (1935), Fig. 1.2, with revisions.

Difficulties arise from the fact that the land in the centre of these islands and behind the mainland dykes is frequently appreciably lower than the beach, the result of drainage and compaction of the terrain. Another problem in the delta region is tidal scour, which removes material from the foreshore and so undercuts the dykes, causing them to slump forward. This is particularly liable where the banks are built on clay resting upon sand, though groynes and fascine work help to combat this danger. While the upkeep of much of the defensive work is the responsibility of each commune, the problem became so acute that the administrators of certain polders in Zeeland were empowered in 1870 to receive assistance from the State and the province; these are officially known as *calamiteus* polders.

A further problem in the delta region is the progressive salinisation of water in the river estuaries and creeks. As the shipping channels are deepened, the influx of salt water increases, especially when the river discharges are low, so that salt water goes far inland, thus harming the pastures, and making water in the ditches undrinkable for cattle.

It has long been clear that there were two possible methods of coping with the ever-present threat in the delta region. One was to strengthen and raise every dyke by about 2 m (7 ft), a tremendous undertaking. The other was to build massive dykes across the estuary entrances, except for certain shipping channels, and so exclude the tidal seas. This would form freshwater basins, incidentally of great help to agriculture, both for the pastures and the market gardens. One contribution towards this end was completed in July 1950, when the Briellsche (Brielle) Maas was closed off from the sea. [7] One dam was built at the mouth near Oostvoorne, a second where the estuary divides from the Nieuwe Maas.

But three years later the floods of February 1953 made it clear that an overall 'Delta Plan' was a matter of urgent priority. The cause of the disaster of 1 February was a storm surge which raised the water level of the southern North Sea far above predicted heights; this increase was as much as 3 m (10 ft) at Hook of Holland. The storm surge was associated with gale force winds and storm waves of exceptional power during a period of spring tides. Many of the dykes were overtopped, and the inrushing water eroded the inner slopes and weakened them so that breaches were readily formed (Plate 1). Others were undermined by frontal wave attack and so slumped bodily forward. There were sixty-seven major breaches, some of 300 metres' width, and many kilometres of dyke were otherwise damaged. The area flooded was officially stated to total 150 000 ha (375 000 acres), while about 47 000 houses were destroyed or damaged and 1 800 people lost their lives. [8] The estimated cost of the Delta Plan, some £200 million, was seen in its true perspective against a loss of over £100 million as a result of this one event. Serious though the disaster was, it might have been much worse, for Dutch experts have calculated that even more adverse combinations of weather, tides and river floods are quite possible, which might result in flood levels exceeding the 1953 records by a metre.

The Dutch mobilised their resources and skill; within a month of the disaster only eight breaches remained, and by July only four were not yet closed, three on Schouwen-Duiveland and one on Zuid-Beveland. The last gap, at Ouwerkerk, was sealed before the end of the year, when concrete caissons were towed into the breaches and sunk in position.

The flooding and consequent salinisation of so much land was a grievous blow, and moreover 25 000 head of cattle in this prosperous dairying region were lost. The experience derived from the reclamation of Walcheren, which was under salt water for sixteen months after the war of 1940–45,[9] was of immense help and the recovery programme was carried out with remarkable rapidity. The work of desalinisation and the removal of the vast quantities of sand which covered so much of the farmland were executed by companies under government supervision; the cost was borne by the State, except for certain improvements to which the proprietors contributed. The government took the opportunity to carry out some redistribution of land, on a compulsory basis; a number of small submarginal farms were enlarged or amalgamated, the dispossessed farmers being settled on the new lands in the IJssel Meer polders. Considerable drainage improvements were also effected.

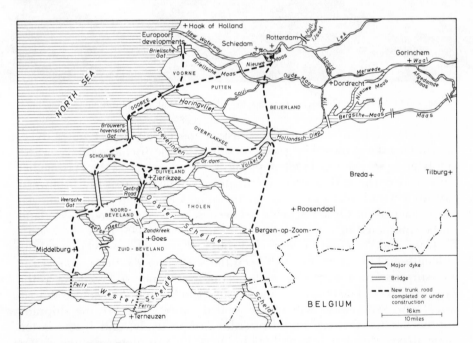

FIG. 3.5. The Delta Plan
All dykes are shown, completed, in progress or projected, though the whole scheme will not be finished until 1978. The bridge across the Oosterschelde is the longest in the world outside the Americas.

Based on various official Dutch maps.

PLATE 2. The Veersche Gat dyke, between the islands of Walcheren and Noord-Beveland

The 'Delta Plan' involves the construction of four major outer dykes interlinking the islands (Fig. 3.5), with sluices for the discharge of river water and floating ice, and locks for shipping.[10] These are across the Haringvliet between Voorne and Goeree (completed in 1968); across the Brouwershavensche Gat leading to the Grevelingen between Goeree and Schouwen (1970); across the Ooster Schelde between Schouwen and Noord-Beveland (to be completed in 1978); and across the Veersche Gat between Noord-Beveland and Walcheren (completed 1961) (Plate 2). These dykes, totalling in length 30 km (20 miles), will keep the sea out of the delta, converting the estuaries into a large non-tidal sheet of fresh water, to be known as the Zeeuwse Meer. The mouths of the Wester Schelde and the Nieuwe Waterweg (New Waterway) will not be sealed, since these are the shipping approaches to Antwerp and Rotterdam respectively, and traffic is too heavy to pass through locks without immense inconvenience. If tidal waters should build up in the Waterweg, they will be diverted through sluices on the Oude Maas into the Zeeuwse Meer, which will act as a vast temporary reservoir. A controlling dam was built (1955–58) across the Hollandsche IJssel to the east of Rotterdam, with large sluices and navigation locks, to protect the vital low-lying polders of Zuid-Holland and Utrecht from flooding.

Other subsidiary dykes are necessary partly to prevent dangerous currents from concentrating in the channels during the building of the major dykes. The small Zandkreek dyke between Zuid-Beveland and the eastern end of Noord-Beveland was completed in 1960. Inner dykes across the eastern end of the Grevelingen and between Overflakkee and Beijerland will be constructed; the latter will separate the Volkerak from the Haringvliet. In 1965 a fine prestressed concrete bridge, 5 022 m (about 3 miles), was opened across the Ooster Schelde (Plate 3); this forms part of a new trunk road ('de Centrale Weg'),[11] from Rotterdam southward over the islands. Another outer road will run from Rotterdam over the Veersche Gat dyke to Middelburg. Yet another highway further east ('the Benelux road') will run directly south from Rotterdam, utilising the Volkerak dyke, hence via Bergen-op-Zoom to Antwerp.

The whole scheme will be completed, it is hoped, by 1978. There have, it is true, been some doubts and objections,[12] mainly from the Zeeland fishermen.

Some Dutch engineers look still further ahead and envisage a similar series of excluding dykes to link the Frisian Islands, and so enable the

PLATE 3. The Oosterschelde bridge, between the islands of Duiveland and Noord-Beveland

Wadden Zee to be reclaimed.[13] This will provide the Netherlands with a smooth coastline, unbroken but for the carefully protected shipping channels. But this lies far in the future.[14]

These problems concerning the indeterminate margin of land and sea are emphasised by the very considerable area that lies between the mean high- and low-water marks, not including the reclaimed lands. The official land area of the Netherlands is 33 779 sq km (13 042 sq miles), but the total area to the mean low-tide mark is 40 893 sq km (15 789 sq miles).[15]

## The polders

The sea dykes and the river dykes provide for the exclusion of extraneous water from the areas they protect. The unit of organised reclamation behind these main dykes is the *polder*, which may vary in size from a tiny irregular-shaped patch of land reclaimed from a small tidal inlet or a piece of fen, to major units such as the Oost Polder of the Zuider Zee scheme, of about 54 000 ha (133 000 acres). Some polders lie well below sea level, occupying former areas of open sea or deep lakes. Pumping is constantly required to remove excess water through rainfall and seepage, and so to maintain the watertable at a predetermined level. Other polders lie just above NAP and are surrounded by lower dykes; from these water can usually be removed through sluices by gravity flow at low tide. Still others are well above sea level, but may be subject to temporary winter water-logging; a system of ditches and channels will usually provide adequate natural drainage.

The low-lying polders reclaimed from the sea or from lakes are known generally as *droogmakerijen*, literally 'dry-making'. Each unit is enclosed by a ring-dyke, for the centres of lake polders in particular are considerably lower than their margins, a tendency emphasised by compaction resulting upon drainage. Outside the ring dyke is a peripheral canal, known as a *ringvaart*, into which is pumped water from a close rectilinear pattern of drainage channels intersecting the polder floor. Formerly these lake polders were characterised by a ring of windmills which worked the pumps, standing on the dykes. In the nineteenth century these were largely superseded by steam pumps, and in this century by diesel engines or electric pumps. Most windmills are now inoperative, but many remain as a characteristic feature of the polder landscape.

Several interesting major polder schemes have been successfully accomplished. One of the earliest large-scale enterprises was the drainage of the Beemster, a lake to the southeast of Alkmaar, which was reclaimed between 1609 and 1612, using a ring canal and twenty-six windmills. Many other deep lakes were drained in Zuid-Holland, forming the Zuidplas Polder in Schieland to the northwest of Rotterdam, reclaimed between the years 1828 and 1839, and the Prins Alexander Polder, which was covered by a lake 6·4 m (21 ft) deep and became finally dry by 1874. The largest scheme, before the Zuider Zee plan was started, was the reclamation of the Haarlemmermeer[16] which lay in the triangle between Haarlem, Amsterdam and Leiden (Fig. 3.9); it covered 16 000 ha (40 000 acres) and was nearly 3·5 m (12 ft) deep. After the extensive floods of 1836 which inundated much of Leiden and Amsterdam, citizens of these towns were stimulated to action. A ring dyke was built and then steam pumps began to remove the water, a process completed by 1852.

Reclamation from the sea has also produced several major gains, apart from the recovery of the small tidal creeks and marshes around the Zeeland islands. In the north of Noord-Holland several polders were created from the Zuider Zee long before the present scheme. The Zijpe Polder was reclaimed in 1597, and in 1847 an extensive gain was made when the Anna Paulowna Polder (Fig. 3.8) was created out of a shallow gulf to the southeast of Den Helder. Another accomplishment was the reclamation of the Binnen IJ (Fig. 3.3), which as late as 1865 formed a wide arm of salt water extending westward from the southern Zuider Zee almost to the North Sea coast near Velsen. This had long been dyked, but it virtually cut Holland in two, and perpetually menaced with flooding Amsterdam on its southern shores. It was finally reclaimed by a major effort between 1865 and 1876. The North Sea (Noord-Zee) Canal was constructed from Amsterdam to IJmuiden (Fig. 3.11), and the IJ itself was converted into a series of polders ranging from 2·5 to 5 m (8 to 17 ft) below NAP. The peat cover was stripped off and today the underlying marine clays form fertile farmland.

Although each polder is reclaimed as a unit, its maintenance must be integrated with that of its neighbours, as well as with the navigable waterways. This requires detailed organisation and vigilant administration. The local administrative body is the *Waterschap*. These organisations consist of representatives elected by landowners within the polder or group of polders concerned. Formerly powerful autonomous bodies, their powers have necessarily been reduced as the growing complexity of drainage schemes, together with the often conflicting needs of navigation, have necessitated increasingly centralised administration, with financial assistance from the *Department van Waterstaat* and the provincial *Waterstaats*.

The method used in complex drainage areas, notably in Noord- and Zuid-Holland, is to create a group of polders within which a common water level is maintained and from which the disposal of excess water can be organised. Unless a polder borders the sea or a major river, it is necessary to utilise temporary storage areas until the water can be passed away. These storage areas are known as *boezem* and may be lakes, portions of canals, or rivers; the unit served by a single *boezem* or interconnected group of them is a *boezemgebied*. The water level in the *boezem* is maintained to avoid fluctuations which may on the one hand endanger the dykes and on the other affect navigation. Noord- and Zuid-Holland are covered by seventeen *boezemgebied*; several are very large, notably the Schermerboezem (Fig. 3.8) which serves most of Noord-Holland to the north of the North Sea Canal, the Rijnlandsboezem which occupies 100 000 ha (250 000 acres), including the former Haarlemmermeer, and the Delflandsboezem in the southwest.

The net result of a millennium of effort is that there are today about 2 500 polders, of which 400 000 ha (a million acres) are drained by gravity flow, and about a million ha (2·5 million acres) by pumping. A variety of soils overlies these reclaimed areas (Fig. 3.6). Along the coasts of Groningen

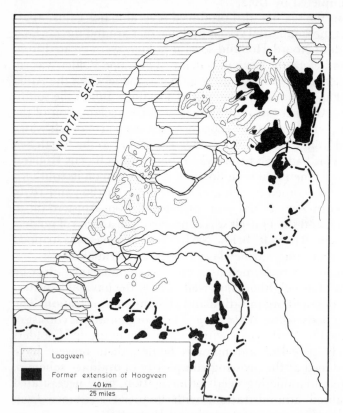

FIG. 3.6. Hoogveen and laagveen in the Netherlands
**G,** Groningen. Much of the *hoogveen* has now been removed, especially in the northeast. Areas in West Germany are not shown.

Based on W. C. Leeuw, *The Netherlands as an Environment for Plant Life* (1935), Fig. 2.4.

and Friesland, and again in the islands of Zuid-Holland and Zeeland, are the heavy soils derived from recent marine clays, forming the chief arable lands. In many parts of Noord- and Zuid-Holland are the peat soils of the *laagveen* (Fig. 3.6). These are mostly under permanent grassland, forming rich dairying lands, and the watertable is usually kept at a higher level than in the arable districts. The recent river clays, derived from alluvium deposited along the floodplains of the Rhine-Maas distributaries, are not as good as the marine clays for agriculture, and much is under permanent pasture.

Reclamation is still going on; the tidal mudflats are being reclaimed along the coast of Groningen and Friesland, there is one polder to complete in the Zuider Zee, and while the Delta Plan is not primarily intended as a scheme of actual reclamation, it will add between 10 000 and 16 000 ha (25 000 and 40 000 acres) of new land.

Some lakes in Noord- and Zuid-Holland (such as the Alkmaarder Meer and the Aalsmeer) still remain reserved as *boezem*. The numerous lakes of Friesland have hardly been touched, as most of them lie in uneven hollows on fluvioglacial sands and gravels, and the resulting poor soils would not be worth the cost of reclamation. But with these exceptions the polderlands, covering much of the Netherlands below roughly the one-metre contour (above NAP), form as a result of man's unending efforts the main agricultural districts of the country.

## Regional divisions

The main regional divisions may be described under five heads: (*a*) the coastal lands of Groningen and Friesland; (*b*) the Dutch Frisian Islands; (*c*) the IJssel Meer reclamation area; (*d*) Noord- and Zuid-Holland, with the western part of Utrecht province; and (*e*) the southwestern islands and estuaries (Fig. 2.7).

## The coastal lands of Groningen and Friesland

The coastal lands of the two northern provinces extend from the Dollard round to the Noord-Oost Polder of the Zuider Zee. This section of coast is remarkably smooth, the only prominent indentation being the rectangular Lauwers Zee. Considerable reclamation has been effected along the coast, in essence a natural process although artificially assisted and accelerated. The tidal mudflats are colonised by a succession of plants, in the initial stages with eel grass (*Zostera*), which assists the accretion of mud. When the level has been raised dense communities of marsh samphire (*Salicornia*) establish themselves, causing mud to accumulate still more rapidly. Then comes the familiar rice grass (*Spartina*), introduced along the Dutch coast only in 1924 but which has spread rapidly, and so the marsh gradually develops above the ordinary high-tide level. Finally the turf-forming grasses appear, thus producing the 'saltings' which are useful for grazing. This accretion of mud is assisted by the construction of wickerwork fences, nailed to rows of piles driven into the mud flats.[18] The mud which collects in them is colonised by marsh plants. In due course a low dyke is built on the seaward side of the salting to prevent inundation by exceptionally high tides, and as the salt is leached out by rainwater the pastures on the heavy clays become increasingly 'sweet'. In a number of places can be seen two or even three parallel dykes a kilometre or two apart and enclosing small polders, evidence of this progressive reclamation, with small villages strung out along the inner dyke. This process is illustrated most strikingly along the shores of the Dollard, where the main dyke is now nearly 180 m (200 yds) inland of the high-tide mark, in Groningen near Uithuizen (Fig. 3.7) where in the last century three new polders were formed, and in Friesland between Holwerd and Nieuwebildtzijl.

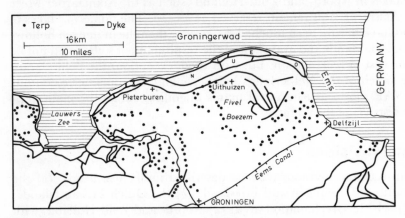

FIG. 3.7. Dykes and '*Terpen*' on the coast of Groningen
The letters indicate polders reclaimed since 1853 through the fixation of tidal mudflats by natural accretion of mud, the growth of plants, and artificial assistance by means of osier fences, as follows: **E,** Ems polder; **L,** Lauwer polder; **N,** Noord polder; **O,** Oost polder; **U,** Uithuizer polder; and **X,** Xegenboeren polder.

Based on a folding map in *La Néerlande: études générales sur la géographie des Pays-Bas* (1938), facing p. 76, illustrating a contribution by J. B. L. Hol and H. van Velthoven, 'La lutte contre les eaux'.

The marine clay lands extend inland for 15 to 30 km (10 to 20 miles), most of the land being in polders, although the surface is a few metres above NAP and normally drains by gravity flow.[19] The peat lands further inland, however, are largely below NAP, and extensive lakes lie in the peat hollows and in depressions in the sand country further south (see p. 140). The peat to the southeast of Groningen has been mostly removed (see p. 138), and little outward sign can be detected in the agricultural landscape of the transition from the coastal clay lands to the improved sands.

No month near the coast has mean temperatures below freezing (Groningen, 1°C (34°F), January mean), although prolonged spells of frost may occur, especially further inland where the lakes may freeze at any time in winter. The mean annual rainfall at Groningen for the period 1921–50 was about 740 mm (29·3 in), although the figure for 1953 was 680 mm (26·9 in) and that for 1954 was 900 mm (35·4 in).

The coastal lands form rich farming country,[20] and nearly four-fifths of the area is under rotation grass, clover, potatoes (for which Friesland is the chief growing area in the country), cereals (particularly wheat and barley

44

in Groningen), chicory and mustard. Although the emphasis is on arable crops on the claylands, large numbers of Friesian cattle are grazed on the coastal pastures and on temporary leys. There are few large towns, and the emphasis is therefore less on liquid milk than on the production of factory-made butter and cheese, frequently on a cooperative basis.

These northern provinces are fascinating, with the spacious landscape interrupted only by the prosperous-looking farmhouses with their glazed-tile, sometimes part-thatched, roofs, straight treelined roads, and quiet villages. Many of these settlements are situated on or near artificial refuge mounds. More than 500 of these can be traced (Fig. 3.7), although many others have vanished; frequently the soil of which they were built has been spread on the nearby fields. In Friesland these mounds are known as *terpen*; they are usually small, with only a few houses and sometimes a church. In Groningen, where they are called *wierden*, they are much larger. The mounds stand usually 2·5 to 3 m (8 to 10 ft) above the surrounding lands, an adequate margin for most floods, but the largest known, at Hoogebeintum, is 12 m (39 ft) high and covers an area of about 9 ha (22 acres). Most mounds were built in late Roman times when sea level was lower than at present, and when they were required as refuges only at rare intervals. After the thirteenth century it became necessary to build complete dykes along the coast, since sea level had risen and major inundations had become more frequent; the refuge mounds therefore became unnecessary. Those with churches survived as centres for their respective villages; others were abandoned, for as reclamation developed the people left the refuge nucleations, and in these coastal lands the population is now widely dispersed either in large farmhouses or in small scattered hamlets.

There is little urban development except for the provincial capitals, Groningen and Leeuwarden. This is partly because the two provinces have depended almost wholly on an agricultural economy for many centuries, partly because this was always a remote corner of the Netherlands and an oddly isolated part of western Europe. No great routes crossed here, either from the sea with the difficult approaches through the tidal flats and the lack of natural harbours, or from the land with the interrupting gulf of the Zuider Zee to the west and the desolate moorlands to the east. Only the provinces of Zeeland and Drenthe have a lower proportion of urban population than have Groningen and Friesland.

The city of Groningen is situated where the areas of clays, sands and peat bogs meet; it is described on p. 139 in connection with the reclamation of the bogs and heaths. It is linked by the recently enlarged Eems Canal to the Dollard at Delfzijl. This little port has developed in some measure as an outport for Groningen (which can itself be reached by coasters), and it forms a servicing port for the prosperous agricultural region of the northeast. It imports coal, fertilisers, timber and animal feeding-stuffs, and exports large quantities of strawboard, paper, potato-flour and dextrine from the factories of Groningen. Delfzijl handled 900 000 tons of freight in

1968. It now has a large aluminium refinery, using bauxite from Surinam and gas from the nearby field at Slochteren (p. 139), and a new chemical plant. In Friesland, Leeuwarden (88 000) has the same dominating position as Groningen. It was once a port on the Friesche Middelzee, but by the end of the thirteenth century this long arm of the sea had been reclaimed. The old town is still surrounded by a moat, and several minor canals, used by small barges carrying agricultural produce, fertilisers, oil, bricks and timber, focus on it from the port of Harlingen, from Groningen by the Hoendiep, and most circuitously from Zwolle and Meppel in the south. Today Leeuwarden is the administrative centre for a rich agricultural district and it has famed markets for cattle, butter and cereals; only the market at Rotterdam handles more cattle annually in the Netherlands. Once the city was renowned for gold and silver work; the Friesch Museum in the town contains a silversmith's forge, an attractive collection of Frisian silverware, glass, pottery and numerous other products of former thriving local handicrafts. These have been replaced by a variety of modern industries, carried on in small efficient factories: the manufacture of shoes, vinegar, paint, soap, electroplate, and (as an agricultural centre) of butter, cheese and, oddly enough, margarine.

Harlingen is a small artificial port, built during the years 1870–77 to serve Friesland. The approach through the Wadden Zee by the Vliestroom channel is so narrow and winding that it is used only by small coasters, although there are regular services to London and Hull. It handled only about 250 000 tons of freight in 1968, mostly exports of dairy produce and strawboard, and imports of oil, timber and miscellaneous raw materials for the industries of Leeuwarden. The town stands in an area which has been devastated by floods several times in history; the village of Almenum, which disappeared in the flood of 1134, was on the same site, and in 1566 another serious flood devastated the whole district, since when enlarged dykes have prevented any further incursions. Several small industries have developed, notably the building of coasting vessels and barges, the canning and salting of fish, and leather-tanning.

A number of people in Friesland still speak Frisian, or more strictly West Frisian. The pure language, which has quite a considerable literature, is spoken in the countryside, the so-called *Landfries*, but a Frisian-Dutch dialect (*Stadsfries*) has gained ground in the towns.

## The Dutch Frisian Islands

Between the dyked coast of Groningen and Friesland and the line of the Frisian Islands lies the Wadden Zee, a considerable extent of tidal waters. The *Wadden* consist of sheets of mud and sand, mostly exposed at low tide, and crossed by a dendritic maze of creeks. The shoals have been notorious since the earliest times for the wrecking of ships; in 1799 the bullion-transporting *Lutine* (whose bell still summons the members of Lloyd's when some serious event has occurred) foundered off the island of Vlieland.

The Frisian Islands are strung out in a smooth curve, with Texel following the trend of the Noord-Holland coast just east of north, while the others are aligned progressively further and further in an easterly direction. Each island, with the exception of Texel which has a 'core' of glacial drift, consists of sandflats with a line of dunes fronting the open sea, and all except Vlieland, which is wholly sandy, have small areas of marine clay on their inner sides. They represent fragments of the northern parts of the offshore bar already described, breached in many places between the eighth and twelfth centuries.

The larger islands are separated by straits (known as *zeegaten* or *gaten*), mostly with deepwater channels, although the gap between Texel and Vlieland is much shallower than the others. Navigation is made difficult by 'submarine deltas', which fan out as sandbanks on the seaward side of the *gaten*; the powerful ebb tides sweep sand from the Wadden Zee through the *gaten* out into the deeper waters of the North Sea, where the strength of the tidal currents is checked.

The largest island is *Texel*, about 22 by 11 km (13·5 by 6·5 miles) at its maximum extent, separated from the mainland to the south by a deep channel, which is kept clear of sand by a powerful tidal race. The southeast of the island consists of a mass of glacial clay, rising to a height of 15 m (49 ft) in a low hump known as Het Bergje. The west coast is fronted by a continuous dune rampart and by a broad beach of fine sand, while the east coast is dyked along almost its whole length. In the northeast extensive mud- and sandflats form the breeding grounds of gulls, terns and avocet; this part is locally known as *Eierland* and formerly there was a considerable export of eggs to Amsterdam. The small population mainly lives in the little town and ferryport of Oudeschild, several inland villages, and the seaside resort of De Koog. A once valuable fishing industry is now of negligible importance. Considerable flocks of sheep provide milk from which the famous 'Texel green cheese' is made, and a few thousand cattle and some pigs are kept.

Most of southwestern *Vlieland* is an expanse of bare sand, a large part of which is covered by the highest tides. Further north there are lines of groyne-protected dunes, with a sea wall on the southeast. Some small flocks of sheep and goats and a few cattle are kept. The small village of Oostvlieland is a popular summer resort, linked by ferry services to Harlingen.

*Terschelling*, 25 km (16 miles) long but only 3 km (2 miles) in breadth, has a wide area of dunes in the centre, with extensive sandflats both to east and west, and a broad sandy beach on the north. Along the south coast a low stone dyke encloses some small polders, with a string of tiny settlements. Most of the land is under permanent grassland or is used for fodder crops; some cattle are kept, their milk being processed at a dairy factory near Hoorn. An interesting if minor local occupation is the collection of whortleberries from the scrubby heathland for export to the mainland.

*Ameland*, about 20 by 3 km (12 by 2 miles) in size, lies only 8 km (5 miles) from the coast of Friesland, separated from it by the tidal banks of the Friesche Wadden. In 1875 a causeway was built across, exposed at high water, but it is not now used and has been deliberately breached in places to allow the passage of fishing boats. The island has the usual pattern of beach, dunes, small polders, and a stone dyke along the south coast. A ferry is run at high water across to Holwerd on the mainland.[21]

The only other island of any size is *Schiermonnikoog*, consisting mostly of dunes and sandflats, but with one large dyke-protected polder. A ferry from Oostmahorn on the shores of the Lauwers Zee brings visitors across to Oosterburen, which possesses several hotels. There are other Frisian islands, merely rather higher sandflats, uninhabited save for the lighthouse keepers on Rottumeroog.

## The IJssel Meer reclamation area

The gulf of the Zuider Zee has long offered an obvious challenge to the enterprising Dutch, for it penetrates far south into the heart of the country, and some 300 km (200 miles) of dykes were required to safeguard the low-lying lands around its margins. The expense of maintenance of these dykes was one of the arguments put forward when the legislation for the reclamation scheme was being discussed in the Dutch parliament in 1918. To a densely populated country, the additional agricultural land offered an immense opportunity, for the area of the Zuider Zee was about 3 700 sq km (1 430 sq miles). It was estimated that 2 300 sq km (860 sq miles), or about 60 per cent of the whole, could be reclaimed, thus adding approximately 10 per cent to the cultivated area of the country.

The Zuider Zee proper, with a maximum width of about 65 km (40 miles), lies to the south of a narrower section between Noord-Holland and Friesland (Fig. 3.8). The floor of the southern part lay 2 to 5 m (8 to 16 ft) below mean low water, and before enclosure there was a small tidal range of about 0·3 m (1 ft). Discharge channels from neighbouring polders, several small rivers, and one major Rhine distributary, the IJssel, flowed into the Zee. The IJssel not only has a mean discharge of about 2 500 cu m (8 000 cu ft) per second, but it carries vast loads of sediment.

Many schemes were discussed over the years before a final plan was adopted in 1918. This involved the construction of a major dam or *Afsluit-dijk* across the narrow mouth where the Zuider Zee opened into the Wadden Zee. Within this enclosed area a series of polders was to be reclaimed, leaving a much reduced body of water, the IJssel Meer, into which the rivers could discharge. This would in effect serve as a large-scale *boezem*, the level of which could be controlled by sluices in the main dyke. In times of obstructed discharge, as when exceptionally high storm tides are experienced in the Wadden Zee outside, the sluices could be kept closed and the level of the IJssel Meer would then rise, acting as a reservoir.

48

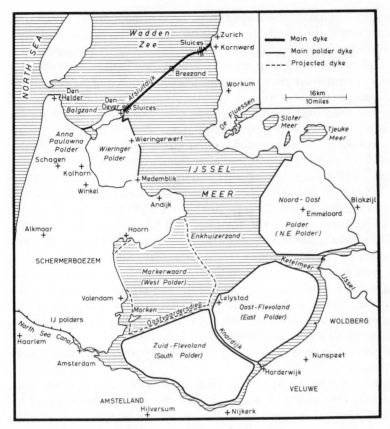

FIG. 3.8. The reclamation of the Zuider Zee
The state of the project is shown as at early 1973. Only the dykes and
canals concerning the Zuider Zee polders are shown.

Based on (*a*) various official sources; (*b*) P. Pinchemel, 'Le Polder du Nord-Est (Pays-Bays)',
*Annls Géogr.* **62** (1953, 348, 350; and (*c*) J. W. Thierry, 'The Enclosure and Partial Reclamation
of the Zuider Zee', *Geogrl J.* **77** (1931), p. 226.

Work started in 1920 with the construction of a short dyke connecting
Noord-Holland at Van Ewijcksluis with Wieringen island, which was
completed in five years. The clay for this section was dredged from the
Balgzand, a shallow bay to the southeast of Den Helder. Work on the main
dyke began in 1927. Vast quantities of sand were dumped on to some
shallow banks to form the artificial island of Breezand; here were constructed two harbours for dredgers and hoppers. The dyke was then extended in each direction from this island.[22]

The *Afsluitdijk* had to be of immense strength since it is exposed to storms
from the open sea. It not only crossed open water with a mean depth of
3 m (10 ft), but it had to negotiate deeper channels of up to 12 m (40 ft).
The core of the dam was made of till, which is tough and tenacious when
wet, conveniently dredged from the nearby floor of the sea between

49

Wieringen and Friesland, and tipped directly from hoppers on to the site. This clay core was backed on the inner side by a massive sandbank deposited in the early stages from hoppers, then by suction dredgers through pipes. This sandbank was covered with more clay, and then flanked on both sides by enormous brushwood mattresses, sunk as a protection against tidal scour. Both sides of the dam were faced with stonework laid on rubble. By 1932 there remained only the sealing of the final gaps; this operation presented serious problems, since as the gaps narrowed so the force of the tidal flow was increasingly concentrated within them. The two gaps, in the Middelgronden and Vlieter channels, were finally closed on 28 May 1932.

The result was a dyke 30 km (18 miles) in length between Den Oever, on what was Wieringen island, and the coast of Friesland near Zurich. Its overall width exceeds 120 m (400 ft), including a platform 34 m (112 ft) wide along the inner side for the roadway and for a future double-track railway. The height of the crest is about 7 m (24 ft) above NAP, which gave a margin of about 3 m (10 ft) above the highest storm tides recorded to that time. Two groups of sluices were built through which excess water from the IJssel Meer is discharged at low tide, one at the western end of the dyke near Den Oever, the other near the opposite end. Each sluice is 12 m (40 ft) wide, and the gates close automatically when the rising tide reaches a certain level. Each set of sluices is accompanied by a navigation lock; the one at Den Oever can accommodate vessels up to 2 000 tons, the other takes vessels up to 600 tons.

By 1937 the water in the Meer was quite fresh. This now provides, incidentally, a valuable source of water; its summer level is maintained at 25 mm (10 in) above that of winter, so that water can be obtained for agricultural purposes—for market gardens, water-meadows and the dairy industry. The saltwater fish have been replaced by pike, perch and eels; the last come from the Sargasso Sea and pass through the sluices in millions, to return there years later (if not smoked and eaten!) to spawn and die. In actual fact, about 10 000 tons of fish, of which a fifth consisted of eels, were caught in 1968 by the IJssel Meer fishermen.

**The Wieringer Polder**

In 1927, when the work on the *Afsluitdijk* was well advanced, the construction began of the first of the polders, which was to occupy the site of the Wieringermeer, a right-angled re-entrant of the sea in the northeast of Noord-Holland. Great preliminary care was taken, even to making a small trial polder at Andijk on the margin of the Drechterland peninsula near the southeastern corner of the new polder. This was intended for experiments with methods of desalinisation and then with possible crop successions on similar soils to those which would be found in the new polder.

The first task was the construction of the outer bounding dyke, 16 km (11 miles) in length, from Medemblik to Den Oever, completed early in

1930. While this was being built, the main internal drainage canals were dredged out and two pumping stations were constructed. The problem of the disposal of water from the Anna Paulowna and other adjoining polders to the west, which had previously drained to the Wieringermeer, was overcome by the construction of a canal along the western shore of the Wieringermeer, connected both with the old polder drainage system to the west and with the canals in the new polder. This runs into a small lake, the Amstel, left as a storage reservoir to the south of the dyke between the mainland and the former Wieringen island, and discharging into the open sea. Another main canal runs along the south of the new polder.

The enclosing dyke was completed in February 1930, and pumping at once began; by the end of August the polder (which had been 3 m (10 ft) deep) was dry. This was the largest area in the Netherlands ever to have been reclaimed from the sea, and amounted to nearly 20 000 ha (50 000 acres), or 9 per cent of the land to be won by the whole IJssel Meer scheme. Internal canals divide this polder into four self-contained sections, each with its own watertable. Within these sections, the main drainage channels, navigable by small barges, further separate the land into rectangular strips, and these are subdivided by feeder drains into units of approximately 20 ha (50 acres), each bounded at one end by a metalled road.

A major problem was to get rid of the salt in the clays, which can only be removed by long-continued leaching. Throughout the winter of 1930–31 all rain water was pumped away, so gradually removing the dissolved salt. This was accelerated by spreading gypsum (calcium sulphate) over the land, to form a highly soluble compound with the sodium chloride in the soil. By the end of the winter of 1930–31 the higher parts of the polder were free from salt, but in the lower lands the process was to take three further years. The whole area was deep-ploughed several times in order to mix the light superficial sands with the underlying clay, and to expose as much material as possible to the beneficial effects of weathering.

So far all the work had been done by state-employed contractors, but in September 1931 the first farmers arrived as state tenants. They were leased holdings of one or more of the 20 ha (50 acres) units; intended dairy farms were usually of one or two units, arable farms of two or three. The considerable demand for holdings was typical of Dutch initiative, and it was possible to select rigorously applicants with the necessary enthusiasm, aptitude and technical knowledge. By the end of 1934 forty-five holdings totalling 1 000 ha (2 500 acres), or about 5 per cent of the total, were being farmed, and by 1940 the entire polder was under cultivation. The early crops of rye were gradually replaced by more profitable wheat, potatoes and other roots. Three villages were created, complete with schools, churches and amenities generally, including electricity supplies from the Grid: Wieringerwerf (the administrative centre), Middenmeer and Slootdorp.

The years of occupation, 1940–44, were difficult for the polder farmers, especially with shortages of fertilisers. But worse was to follow, for in 1944, when the end of the war was imminent, the German forces carried out an extensive programme of flooding, presumably for defensive purposes. Two breaches were blown in the outer dykes in the northeast by the retreating enemy, and the polder was inundated, fortunately only by fresh water from the IJssel Meer. Nevertheless, the floor of the polder inside the breaches was deeply scoured by inrushing water, and buildings and roads were swept away. The inhabitants immediately started work to seal the gaps. Fortunately the pumping houses were undamaged, and after the liberation auxiliary pumps were brought in. By December 1945 the land was dry and in the following summer it was again under cultivation. But almost all the farms and villages had to be rebuilt, and this work was not concluded until 1953. Today it is once again a prosperous agricultural area.

## The Noord-Oost Polder [23]

The second polder to be tackled was the Northeast, with an area of 48 000 ha (119 000 acres), lying in the angle between the lowland of southern Friesland and northern Overijssel. Work on the enclosing dyke did not begin until 1936, and progress was slow. This dyke extends south to the former island of Urk, and then curves southeastward to the south of the island of Schokland; the dyke was completed in 1940 during the German occupation. The deep-water channel of the Zwarte Water and the IJssel outfall was left to the south of the polder. Three pumping stations were built at the apices of the polder, and the ground had dried out by 1942. The land immediately inside the western dyke lies at about 4 m (13 ft) below NAP, rising gradually eastward. In the eastern half the watertable is maintained at 5·7 m (18·7 ft) below NAP, i.e. nearly 2 m (6 ft) below the surface.

Three main canals were dredged out before the polder was dry, with another along the western perimeter on the inner side of the dyke, to which drains a close network of minor canals and ditches. Some 96 per cent of the surface consists of young marine clays, sometimes with an admixture of sand. Considerable areas of fine sand are found, especially on and around the former islands of Urk and Schokland, and in the northeast occur peat deposits. The land was divided into 2 160 units, mostly of the usual 20 ha (50 acres) size, though some smaller lots of about 10 ha (25 acres) are used for intensive horticulture. About 2 000 ha (5 000 acres), mainly in the northeast and on the sandy patches of Urk and Schokland, were planted with conifers. Eleven villages have been built (Fig. 3.8), and 470 km (295 miles) of roads were constructed. Emmeloord, with about 20 000 people, supplies the administrative, social and shopping services for the population (Plate 4). Houses are built in terraces, with broad treelined grass verges and service roads. Schools, churches and public buildings have been carefully designed and sited, and the main shopping street has covered arcades. The town stands to the north of a small harbour where the three main canals meet, and light industries (at present mainly the servicing of agricultural

PLATE 4. The town of Emmeloord, Northeast Polder of the IJssel Meer

machinery) are expected to develop around the port area.

Progress was, however, much slower than in the case of the Wieringer Polder, at first because of the difficulties of the war years, then because so much of the national effort after 1945 had to be devoted to reconstruction; notably the flooded areas of Zeeland and of the Wieringer Polder had first to be recovered. By 1949 the population had reached 3 000, then there was a rapid increase to 13 000, and by the end of 1969 it had reached 35 000. The whole polder was handed over from initial state development to its permanent cultivators, to form about 1 200 individual farms, by the beginning of 1958. About 40 000 ha (100 000 acres), or four-fifths of the total area of the Noord-Oost Polder, was under cultivation in 1968, nearly half under industrial crops, 28 per cent under arable, 8 per cent under permanent pasture, and 4 per cent under horticulture.

## The remaining polders

In the original plan there remained the large southeast and southwest polders. It was decided that the former was too big to handle as a unit, and accordingly it was divided into two, the Oost Polder[24] (known as Oost-Flevoland) and the Zuid Polder (Zuid-Flevoland). The former comprises 54 000 ha (133 000 acres), the latter 40 000 ha (99 000 acres). The West

53

Polder (to be called the Markerwaard) will total 60 000 ha (149 000 acres), and will be completed, it is hoped, by 1975, thus realising a scheme spread over sixty years which will have cost the equivalent of £200 million.

Work on the Oost Polder was delayed by the destruction wrought by the storm of February 1953, which necessitated the employment of much Dutch drainage equipment, dredgers and hoppers. However, work slowly progressed and a dyke was built out northwestward from the coast near Harderwijk. On a dump of material in the very centre of the southern part of the Zuider Zee, Lelystad was created, to serve first as a base for workmen and equipment, later to be developed as a town. Dr Lely, incidentally, produced before the end of the nineteenth century the plan which is the basis of the whole scheme, and was Minister in charge of its early development; it is fitting that his name should be thus commemorated as the future 'capital' of the new polder. A ship canal, 400 m (1 300 ft) in width, runs southwestward to the IJ Meer and to Amsterdam; this was dredged out during the winter of 1956–57 before the polder had been pumped dry.

At the rate of about 90 m (100 yd) a day the dyke was pushed forward during 1955–56, until on 13 September 1956 the last gap to the northeast of Lelystad was filled, and Oost-Flevoland was thus enclosed by a dyke 90 km (56 miles) in length. Three pumping stations were built, and locks were constructed to take shipping of up to 600 tons near Lelystad, and up to 300 tons near the IJssel estuary, to enable vessels to pass into the IJssel Meer from the neighbouring canals. An additional dam was built around the southeastern perimeter of the polder, completed also in 1956, leaving a narrow ring-channel between it and the mainland. In addition, a road bridge, 1 100 m (1 200 yd) in length, crosses the channel between Oost-Flevoland and the Noord-Oost Polder near Urk, and 70 km (45 miles) of main roads have been built. The sites and layout of other towns were carefully chosen.

The Oost Polder, which slopes gently northward from 2 m (7 ft) below NAP in the south to 4 m (13 ft) below in the centre, is divided into two sections, with watertables of 5 m (16 ft) and of 6 m (17 ft) below NAP respectively. It represents a major contribution to the agricultural land of the country, since 96 per cent of its surface is estimated to be of the category of 'very good soils', compared with 70 and 80 per cent for the Wieringer Polder and the Noord-Oost Polder respectively. Pumping proceeded by the spring of 1957. By 1968 24 000 ha (60 000 acres) were scheduled as agricultural land, almost all under arable crops. Work has followed rapidly on the Zuid Polder, and by the end of 1970 about 17 000 people were living in the southern polders.

## Noord- and Zuid-Holland

From the northern tip of the Den Helder peninsula to the Haringvliet and the Hollandsch Diep lies the largest continuous area of Dutch territory below N.A.P., yet it is one of the most densely populated parts of the world. At the end of 1970, Zuid- and Noord-Holland had densities of population of 1 058 and 849 per sq km (2 740 and 2 199 per sq mile) respectively, compared with the average of 389 per sq km (1 008 per sq mile) for the Netherlands as a whole. The density in western Utrecht is also very high, but as this province includes the sandhills of Gooiland (see p. 135), the average is reduced to 614 per sq km (1 590 per sq mile), which is nevertheless the third highest in the country. This density is due on the one hand to a remarkable urban development with its attendant flourishing commercial and industrial activities, on the other to an intensity of agriculture which is rarely equalled.

The western part of the region consists of lines of sand-dunes. In the south are the lowest portions of the Rhine interfluves, separated by distributaries flowing between massive dykes. Here are the low-lying polders to the north of Rotterdam. Further north several large groups of polders are the floors of reclaimed lakes, notably the Beemster and the Haarlemmermeer (Fig. 3.9). A number of lakes still remains, many lying in hollows left by peat-cutting and some retained as *boezem*. There is everywhere a maze of drainage and navigation canals, minor channels and ditches.

Soils are remarkably varied (Fig. 2.6), for they have developed from sands in the west, tracts of new marine clays in the southwest, some old marine clays on the floors of the drained lakes or where the peat has been removed, fen peats, and river clays and sands in the south.[25] The following table summarises the areas of each of the main soil types of Noord-Holland and Zuid-Holland:

*Soil types (percentages)*

| | OLD SEA CLAY | YOUNG SEA CLAY | RIVER CLAY | PEAT | DUNE SANDS | INLAND SANDS |
|---|---|---|---|---|---|---|
| Noord-Holland | 21 | 44 | — | 18 | 10 | 6 |
| Zuid-Holland | 14 | 59 | 5 | 14 | 6 | — |

Source: *Jaarcijfers voor Nederland*, 1957–58 (1960).

## Agriculture

A large part of the region is devoted to dairy-farming. The peatland polders and many of the older lake polders are for the most part under permanent pasture, where a high watertable is maintained. The proportion of permanent pasture amounts to 34 per cent of the total farm land of both Noord- and Zuid-Holland. The climate on the whole is mild and moist, and grass grows for much of the year. The mean temperatures at Den Helder range from 3°C (37°F) in January (appreciably warmer than in the east of the country) to about 17°C (62°F) in August. The 1921–50 mean of rainfall was about 680 mm (26·8 in), spread out through the year, for even the driest months (April and May) still had nearly 40 mm (1·4 in) each. As a result, dairying is based on grazing on permanent pastures, and cattle are kept out of doors for most of the year; little short ley pasture and few fodder crops are grown, although meadow hay is cut for winter feed.

In 1968 there were about 555 000 cattle (of which 294 000 were dairy animals) in the two provinces, or about 14 per cent of the total in the country. In Zuid-Holland a vast urban market exists for liquid milk. In Noord-Holland, by contrast, much milk is sent to large factories for processing into butter and cheese. The farms still produce a considerable output

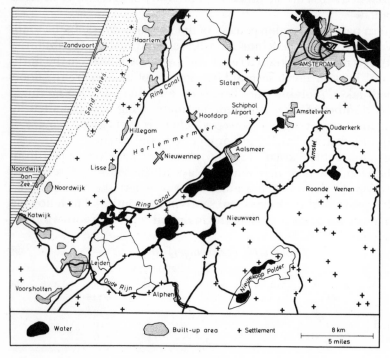

FIG. 3.9. The polders southwest of Amsterdam
The reclaimed Haarlemmermeer lies within the ring canal to the south of Haarlem.

Based on *Chromo-Topographische Kaart van het Koninkrijk der Nederlanden*, 1 : 50 000, sheets 24 (E), 25 (W), and 25 (E).

of cheese, notably the Gouda variety made in western Utrecht and eastern Zuid-Holland, and the red-crusted Edam cheese produced further north on the polder farms bordering the IJssel Meer. Much of the cheese business is now centralised and highly organised; for example, a large proportion of Edam cheese is sold in the famous market at Alkmaar in Noord-Holland. Bullocks are reared in some areas; in the neighbourhood of Schiedam they are fattened on the residues from the distilleries.

PLATE 5. The bulb-fields near Hillegom

Some arable farming is practised, but this does not compare in extent or importance with the Zeeland islands or with the Friesland-Groningen coastal claylands. The main districts under crops are the newer polders to the northwest of Rotterdam, in the fertile IJ district, and on the old marine clay floors of the reclaimed lakes. Here cereals, potatoes, sugar beet and vegetables are grown.

Horticulture and fruit cultivation are carried on to supply both the towns and also a well-organised export market, especially in Great Britain. Market gardens are important to the east of The Hague on the sandy soils (the *Geestgronden*), which being light and warm are extremely productive when heavily fertilised. Other significant areas are to the north of Alkmaar and in the triangle enclosed by Medemblik, Enkhuizen and Hoorn. The district to the south of The Hague, known as the Westland, and the neighbouring Delfland and Schieland, have an immense area under glasshouses. Zuid-Holland had 4 674 ha (11 550 acres) under glass in 1968, out of a total of 6 955 ha (17 186 acres) in the whole country. More than half of this was devoted to tomatoes, and about a fifth each to grapes and cucumbers, the rest under melons, peaches and strawberries, all mostly for export.

One of the most profitable sides of horticulture is bulb-growing, for which the Netherlands is justly renowned; the output is almost entirely for export. There is a string of centres along the sandy strip to the east of the dunes extending between Leiden and Haarlem, concentrated at Sassenheim, Lisse and Hillegom. The heavily fertilised sandy soils are admirable

57

for bulb-raising (Plate 5), and some 12 000 ha (30 000 acres) were devoted to it in 1970. In spite of the competitive development of Lincolnshire, millions of bulbs are exported annually from the Haarlem district to Great Britain and elsewhere. There is an elaborate cut flower trade, both for home and export, centred near Leiden, around Utrecht and at Aalsmeer near Schiphol. Nursery gardens are widespread, the most extensive being at Boskoop, 16 km (10 miles) north of Gouda; its azaleas, rhododendrons, clematis and roses are world-renowned; 767 ha (1 895 acres) were devoted to the cultivation of flowers (other than bulbs) in the two provinces in 1969, out of a total area in the whole country of about 2 500 ha (6 200 acres).

All this diverse agricultural activity, carried on with an intensity and an enthusiasm rivalled perhaps only in Denmark, produces a valuable contribution to the Dutch economy. The horticultural districts have the densest rural population in the world, although the large dairy farms of the permanent grass polders and the arable farms of the lake polders do not require as much labour. There are numbers of prosperous villages, some (as in the inter-riverine areas of Zuid-Holland) grouped around former refuge mounds, others (as in the polders further north) strung out along roads following the dykes. In the sand areas behind the dunes there is a chaos of villages interspersed with glasshouses, domestic houses and market gardens. This then is one contribution to the high overall density of population in these provinces.

## Towns and industries

Commercial and industrial development, which though long-established has nevertheless kept pace with modern progress, accounts for a complementary development of urban life. Most of the towns grew up in the Middle Ages as commercial centres on the banks of navigable waterways. In Noord-Holland several such towns bordering the Zuider Zee, once important as centres of commerce, have suffered because of their position on the coast of a shallow near-inland sea. Today these towns—Enkhuizen, Edam, Hoorn and Medemblik—are little if any bigger than they were in the seventeenth century, some indeed much smaller, and they now function as quiet, pleasant market centres.

The only Zuider Zee town to flourish in modern times is Amsterdam itself, by reason of its development of administrative functions, an enormous commercial life and a great range of industrial activities. Its main asset as a port is the magnificent North Sea (Noord-Zee) Canal, a waterway 24 km (15 miles) in length (Fig. 3.11), completed in the year 1876, by which the city firmly turned its back on the Zuider Zee and looked, as it necessarily was obliged to do in order to maintain its position, towards the North Sea. The city grew up in what must have been in many ways an unpromising position among tidal flats and sandbanks. Near the point where the little river Amstel entered the southern shore of the IJ, a dam was built early in

PLATE 6. Amsterdam

the thirteenth century to provide a sheltered harbour. Here seagoing craft could transfer their cargoes to smaller vessels which penetrated the inland waterways, hence the growth of the city's entrepôt trade. The 'Dam' today is a broad open place, the heart of the city's life. The urban area gradually extended southward in a semicircle, with the houses built on piles driven into the marsh. Its outward growth can be traced from the concentric semicircular canals crossed by radial channels (Fig. 3.10); it is said that the city in effect stands on three hundred islands. Each stage of growth had to be carefully planned, involving extensive drainage as the built-up area expanded southward. Occasionally drastic flooding forced its citizens to undertake ambitious large-scale reclamation schemes, and the city then spread a stage further on to the newly available land.

Since the war of 1914–18 the city has developed rapidly. In 1921 the area of the municipality was quadrupled, and considerable building programmes were put into operation. To the north of the IJ, for example, garden cities were built, Oostzaan in 1920–21 and Nieuwendam in 1925–26. In 1926 a plan was published for the overall development of 'Greater

Amsterdam', but this was superseded by the famous 'Master Plan', published in 1934 after several years of intensive research, and which finally received Royal Assent in 1939.[26] This bold plan envisaged a population of almost a million in the year 2000, but this figure has already been surpassed (1·04 millions in 1970). It involves the building of a number of garden-cities to the west of the present city, industrial development in the port area, and carefully integrated systems of communications, including a 'belt railway' raised on a 6 m (20 ft) embankment and a series of major radial highways. Although of course seriously delayed by the war of 1939–45, the plan is now making considerable progress; several garden cities are being developed.

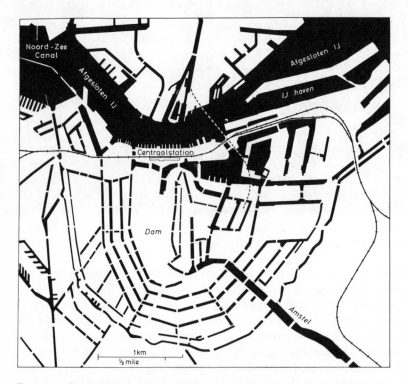

Fig. 3.10. Central Amsterdam
Water areas are in black. This brings out (*a*) the ramifications of dock-basins along the North Sea Canal and the Afgesloten IJ, and (*b*) the pattern of concentric semicircular *grachten*, indicating the outward expansion of the city to the south as drainage and reclamation progressed. The word 'Dam' indicates the position of the main square, on the site of the original dam separating the river Amstel from the IJ. A group of six new *tuinsteden* (garden suburbs) is being developed to the west of the area shown on this map, with a planned total of 45 000 houses. Compare Plate 6.
  The site of the projected road tunnel is shown by a pecked line.

Based on *Falk-Plan Amsterdam* (n.d.).

Amsterdam is itself a magnificent city of 831 000 people (Plate 6), with wide functions. Although the political seat of the Netherlands government is at The Hague, Amsterdam is in fact the capital. It is an important commercial, financial and cultural centre; for long it has had close relations with the now reduced Dutch overseas possessions; and it is still a great entrepôt centre. Its port lies mainly along the eastern waterfront, the Afgesloten IJ, which is separated by the Oranje locks from the IJssel Meer, and there are some new basins for special purposes (such as the Petroleum-Haven) to the west. While it falls considerably behind Rotterdam in tonnage of shipping and freight accommodated, in 1970 it handled 20·7 million tons of seaborne freight (though only 9 per cent of the Dutch total[27]). It is well connected with inland waterways, and in 1952 these connections were immensely improved with the opening of the Amsterdam-Rhine Canal (see p. 96 and Fig. 5.3). A new international airport at Schiphol was opened in 1967.

Amsterdam, with its suburbs, is second in the Netherlands only to the Rotterdam conurbation as an industrial district. This extends along the North Sea Canal to IJmuiden (Fig. 3.11), and along the north bank of the IJ. Varied branches of the metallurgical and engineering industries are carried on, many of a precise nature and requiring a high degree of fabrication. Dutch engineering firms have a reputation for specialised machinery, including plants designed to process colonial products (machinery for sugar refineries, margarine factories, oilfields and tin mines), refrigeration machinery and electrical equipment. Although not as important as at Rotterdam, there is considerable shipbuilding activity; the *Oranje* (20 166 tons gross), for example, was built there for the Netherlands Royal Mail Line. Marine engineering is also highly developed; one firm, Nederlandsche Werkspoor, accounts for a fifth of the total Dutch output of marine engines, and several foreign firms build Werkspoor engines under licence. Plants which assemble cars, lorries and aircraft from parts made elsewhere include the Citroën and Ford plants at Hembrug (a few km west of the city on the shores of the North Sea Canal) and the Fokker works on the northern side of the port. A wide range of consumer goods, as one would expect in a capital city, includes clothing, pharmaceutical chemicals, footwear, paper, printing and bookbinding. Food-processing industries, as again one would expect in a port, comprise chocolate- and cocoa-making, sugar-refining, tobacco-processing, flour-milling, brewing (notably the delightful Amstel lager) and distilling. Others are specifically associated with the 'colonial trade'—oil seed crushing, rubber and timber manufactures. An oil refinery was completed in 1965 on the banks of the North Sea Canal at Zaandam, and another (with associated petrochemical plants) was opened in 1968; the latter is supplied by pipeline from the Europoort terminal (p. 68). Large areas of reclaimed land on either side of the Canal are scheduled for industrial expansion. The long-established diamond-cutting industry still exists but on a much reduced scale.

Few other large towns are found in Noord-Holland, partly because of its predominantly agricultural character, partly because it lies between the Zuider Zee (hence the decay of its former ports already mentioned) and the long sand-dune coast, with an almost complete lack of harbours.

The one North Sea port of any importance is IJmuiden, which only came into existence with the cutting of the North Sea Canal. New moles have been built at the North Sea entrance, and enlarged locks were completed in 1967; these, the largest in the world, can take vessels of 100 000 tons. The port handled 7·01 million tons of freight in 1968, and is also important as the main Dutch fishing port; about 89 000 tons, nearly half of the total tonnage of fish landed in the Netherlands, were handled there.[28] In the Middle Ages the Dutch took considerable part in the herring fisheries of Europe; this was referred to as the *principale goudmijne* and was one cause which led to the growth of the Netherlands as a mercantile country. Fishing then was carried on from the Zuider Zee ports; indeed, the IJmuiden harbour was only built in the 1890s.

Adjacent to the northern side of the IJmuiden port basins are the blast furnaces and steel works of the *Koninklijke Nederlandsche Hoogovens en Staalfabrieken N.V.*, the only fully integrated steel plant in the country (Fig. 3.11). This was originally constructed as a result of the serious shortage of steel during the war of 1914–18, in order to mitigate this vulnerable position. It was decided that the industry could be more advantageously supplied with high grade ores imported by sea than with poorer ores from adjacent countries such as France. A site of some 2 900 ha (7 000 acres) was

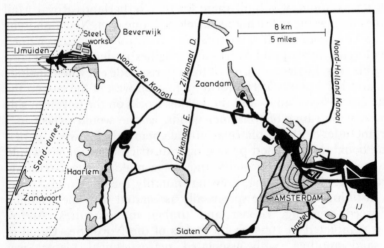

FIG. 3.11. The IJmuiden iron and steel works, the North Sea (Noord-Zee) canal and Amsterdam
The built-up areas are shown in generalised form by means of a stipple.

Based on *Chromo-Topographische Kaart van het Koninkrijk der Nederlanden*, 1:50000, sheets 24 (E) and 25 (W).

chosen to the north of the seaward end of the North Sea Canal. It was intended to develop from the first a fully integrated steel plant, but heavy postwar rises in costs made this impossible with the limited capital available. Three blast furnaces were erected between 1923 and 1929, and by 1939 the output of pig iron had reached about 280 000 tons. In point of fact this was then considerably more than the Netherlands itself could consume, so rather curiously the country became one of the world's largest pig iron exporters. K. N. Hoogovens did later decide to develop the making of steel, and in 1938 a small oil-fired open-hearth furnace was put into operation, using about 40 per cent locally produced pig and the rest scrap. A rolling-mill was also erected in 1939 close to the steel works, but even before production started it was dismantled by the Germans and transported to the Hermann Goering works at Watenstedt. This plant was recovered after the war and began operations again in 1947, producing principally steel plates for the shipbuilding industry.

After the war the Netherlands was faced with a vastly increased consumption of steel for the reconstruction of her damaged cities, communications and industries, for her new specialised manufactures, and for her contribution to European defence. In 1950 Dutch industry was using 1·5 million tons of steel, but by 1955 this had risen to 2·4 million tons, a figure rather surprisingly only half a million tons less than the Belgian consumption, even with their long-established tradition of heavy industry. The Netherlands thus has become a very considerable importer of crude steel. The Government, in conjunction with the industrialists, planned to expand the IJmuiden plant as part of the country's postwar economic development. The open-hearth steel furnaces were increased to five and their capacity has been considerably stepped up. Several rolling mills and a tinplate plant were built at IJmuiden. As a result of these various developments, Dutch production of steel rose rapidly, as the following table shows:

*Output and consumption of steel (thousand tons)*

|  | 1938 | 1952 | 1954 | 1958 | 1970 |
|---|---|---|---|---|---|
| Crude steel | 52 | 685 | 929 | 1 437 | 5 041 |
| Finished steel | — | 444 | 707 | 1 197 | — |
| Total finished steel consumption | — | 1 760 | 1 988 | 2 324 | — |

Source: *Mémento de statistiques*, published by the ECSC, Luxembourg, annually.

During recent years further developments have occurred, including the installation of new deepwater ore docks, and of basic-oxygen steel converters which reached an annual output of 6 million tons by 1972. In 1971 K. N. Hoogovens merged with the West German firm of Hoesch, Europe's first trans-frontier steel merger, so forming the second largest unit in the ECSC.[29]

With customary Dutch thoroughness, various byproduct plants were erected on adjacent sites. Coke oven gas is utilised in a nitrogen fixation plant to produce ammonium sulphate, benzol, toluol and tar, while the remaining gas is piped through a grid to Amsterdam, Zaandam and Haarlem. Another company was formed, in conjunction with a Maastricht concern, to manufacture Portland cement from furnace slag, with an annual output of 200 000 tons, and another slag-processing plant produces roadmaking materials. A large power station was built to the east of the steel works, utilising part of the blast-furnace gas for electricity production, and supplying much of the province of Noord-Holland. There are also a jam factory, a tobacco factory and a paper factory.

Some of these concerns are situated in the municipality of Beverwijk on the north side of the canal, where lives much of the labour used at the port of IJmuiden. Beverwijk has grown rapidly, and is designed to expand still further as one of the 'new towns'; the plans being developed anticipate a population of 150 000 by 1980. The built-up area will expand to the northeast, absorbing some small existing villages, and a completely new town centre will replace the present one. Considerable areas to the west and southeast of the town have been reserved and are being developed as industrial sites.[30]

Haarlem, with a population of 172 000, is the fifth largest urban centre in the Netherlands, lying 6 km (4 miles) to the east of the North Sea. The little river Spaarne winds through the town. Haarlem grew up as the home of the Counts of Holland, and developed prosperous industries at an early date, although like so many others it suffered vicissitudes during the wars of the sixteenth century. Today, besides being the centre of the bulb industry, it has a variety of industries—engineering, railway rolling-stock and chemicals. Alkmaar is the market centre for much of Noord-Holland. It was once a small fishing village, surrounded by water (hence its name 'all sea') until the surrounding polders were reclaimed, when it became the centre of a rich pastoral district; its cheese market is well known.

While Amsterdam clearly dominates the urban life of Noord-Holland, in Zuid-Holland and western Utrecht by contrast there is a cluster of conurbations, known as the '*Randstad Holland*'. These include notably The Hague and Rotterdam (whose outskirts are only 13 km (8 miles) apart), which together contained in 1970 over 14 per cent of the total population of the Netherlands, and also Utrecht.

The city of Rotterdam is second to Amsterdam in size; in 1970 its official communal population (including within the city boundaries Delfshaven and Kralingen on the north side of the river, Charlois, Katendrecht and Feijenoord on the south, and even Hook of Holland 30 km (18 miles) away) was 687 000. The total for the 'agglomeration', including Schiedam and Vlaardingen to the west, is 1 061 000.

Much of central Rotterdam was rebuilt following extensive war damage (Plate 7).[31] One of the most interesting new features is the *Lijnbaan*, a

PLATES 7, 8. Rotterdam: (*above*) the port, with Waalhaven and Botlek on the left; the New Waterway diagonally across the view; and Schiedam, Vlaardingen and Maassluis in the centre background; (*bottom*) the petroleum port of Botlek on the right, Rozenburg to bottom left and Vlaardingen on the top left.

shopping centre built to the west of the town hall. While most of the streets were planned on usual lines—broad avenues, shops and flats above—the *Lijnbaan* consists of an attractive shopping district from which vehicular traffic is excluded. This project was started in July 1952 and completed in October 1953. A metro system is under construction, the first stage being opened in 1968.

Rotterdam (Fig. 3.12) is very much greater than Amsterdam as a port. It stands about 30 km (18 miles) from the sea, mainly on the northern bank of the Nieuwe Maas formed by the junction of the Lek and the Noord (see p. 94 and Fig. 5.3). It was near the confluence of the small river Rotte, which wanders in from the north, that the old town grew up in the four-teenth century. At first its trade was subordinate to that of Dordrecht, for long the leading Dutch port, but in the seventeenth century it began to forge ahead. The size of shipping grew in the late eighteenth and nineteenth centuries, while the problem of silting in the estuaries became increasingly acute, the result of the tendency of the Rhine distributaries to move south (see p. 92). Until the mid-eighteenth century shipping used the direct Briellsche Maas (Fig. 3.12), for long the main outlet of Lek water, but silting formed in this channel a large bank (which is now the island of Rozenburg), and this route was finally abandoned for another more than twice as long. This went southward through what is now the Noord and the

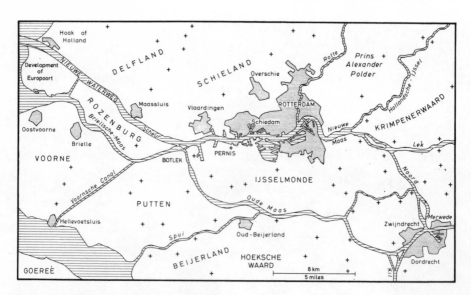

Fig. 3.12. Rotterdam and the neighbouring waterways
The main built-up areas (generalised) are shown by stipple, individual village centres by a cross. Outside the conurbations are extensive areas of low-lying polders, with villages usually strung out along the dyked roads.

Based on *Chromo-Topographische Kaart van het Koninkrijk der Nederlanden*, 1 : 50 000, sheets 37 (W and E).

Dordsche Kil, and so out to the sea through the Haringvliet between Voorne and Goeree-Overflakkee. In 1830 a channel (the Voornsche Canal) was cut across Voorne and used for thirty or forty years, but difficulties of navigation steadily increased as silting encumbered the Goeree channel with sand- and mudbanks. Many ships preferred to enter either through the Grevelingen channel between Goeree and Schouwen, then proceed round the eastern end of Overflakkee and down the Haringvliet to the Voornsche Canal, or even (particularly if they were coming from the south) through the Ooster Schelde and the Mastgat. All these routes were regrettably circuitous.

The final solution was a direct cut westward to the North Sea, the New Waterway (*Nieuwe Waterweg*), following mainly the line of the Scheur, the northern channel formed when the island of Rozenburg split the Maas into two. This involved cutting through the sandspit of the Hoek van Holland, and it took six years to construct, from 1866 to 1872. At first, however, this New Waterway (still known above Maassluis as the Scheur) was only 3 m (10 ft) deep, and until 1885 larger vessels were still obliged to approach by the longer alternative circuits. It has been subsequently enlarged several times, and can now be negotiated by vessels drawing up to 10 m (33 ft). Ships enter between moles, nearly 800 m (half-mile) apart, at Hook of Holland (*Hoek van Holland*), which handles the considerable ferry traffic with England. Dredging is constantly necessary in the New Waterway, but with a mean tidal rise of about 1·7 m (5·5 ft) there is a useful natural scour, carefully directed and utilised by training walls.[32]

The port of Rotterdam consists of quays along both banks of the Nieuwe Maas (Plate 8), together with numerous basins, all with unlocked connection with the river. It is used regularly by Holland-Amerika and Rotterdam-Lloyd liners, and by many cargo vessels. In 1970 Rotterdam itself handled 219 million tons of seaborne freight (80 per cent of the Dutch total), while if all the subsidiary ports along the New Waterway are included, the total was 228 million tons (84 per cent). Approximately 65 000 ships use the port and its subsidiaries each year. Rotterdam is the leading world port in terms of tonnage of freight handled. It is well ahead of London, and also of Antwerp and Hamburg combined, and, a still more impressive fact, it handles appreciably more freight than the port of New York. Much of this freight consists of bulk imports of crude oil, mineral ores, cereals, timber, and such foods and raw materials as groundnuts, soya-beans, sugar and bananas. One feature has been the enormous growth of container traffic; the port handled over 200 000 of these containers in 1970, a quarter to or from North America.

One major contribution to its importance is its situation relative to the Rhine distributaries (Fig. 5.3). The Noord and Waal form a highway leading southeastward into West Germany. The line of the Waal, the Maas-Waal Canal, the Maas and the Juliana Canal provides a route to Limburg and beyond to southern Belgium. A through route can be followed to Antwerp via the Noord, the Hollandsch Diep, the Zuid-Beveland Canal and the Scheldt estuary, and several alternative minor waterways lead northward to Amsterdam. As a result, the port handles about a third of the freight carried on the Dutch inland waterways (which totalled 242 million tons in 1970).

Since 1950 great developments, still in progress, have taken place in the port of Rotterdam. At the eastern end of the island of Rozenburg has been constructed the port of Botlek,[33] to handle bulk imports of mineral and vegetable oil, and of chemicals. Several industrial undertakings have been built, including a huge Esso refinery, a shipyard for supertankers, and a chemical factory. On a still bigger scale is the development of *Europoort*, at the North Sea end of the island of Rozenburg opposite Hook of Holland.[34] On the site Shell, Caltex and Esso have built huge terminals, the Gulf refinery was opened in 1965, a B.P. refinery in 1967, and the 290 km (180 miles) Rotterdam–Rhine pipeline was laid to Kelsterbach in West Germany. The port also handles bulk cargoes of ore for western Europe generally. A ship canal has been cut parallel to the New Waterway. Excavation of the dock basins is well advanced, and *Europoort* will function as a major gateway for western Europe, mainly coping with bulk cargoes. At present it can take 250 000-ton tankers, with a 20 m (60 ft) draught, through a new entrance direct from the North Sea.

The Rotterdam conurbation forms the largest single industrial region in the Netherlands. From Vlaardingen through Schiedam and up-river to Dordrecht are some fifty shipyards and other establishments are engaged in ancillary industries. The output of ships is varied, for the industry both supplies the Dutch mercantile marine and executes many foreign orders. These include tankers, container ships, motor coasting steamers (a speciality of the Dutch yards), tugs, dredgers, hoppers and floating cranes. Warships are built both for the Royal Netherlands Navy and for foreign customers; the famous Polish submarine *Orzel* was a product of a Dutch yard. Vessels built include the *Rotterdam* (1959, 38 650 gross tons, flagship of the Holland-America Line), the *Nieuw Amsterdam* (1938, 36 667 tons gross), the *Statendam* (1956–57, 24 300 tons), the *Ryndam* (1951, 15 015 tons) and the *Maasdam* (1952, 15 024 tons). There has been a considerable postwar expansion in Dutch shipbuilding activity; several 200 000 ton tankers and 100 000 ton bulk-carriers have been constructed. Marine engineering is also well developed, while the manufacture of lock gates, caissons, pontoons, pumps and bridges is an obvious reflection of the country's own requirements. Dutch firms carry out contracts for port works, drainage and regularisation schemes in many parts of the world. There is a vast range of other metallurgical industries and the usual port industries: five oil refineries and petrochemical complexes, distilling, vegetable-oil refining, the manufacture of paper, timber products, car assembly (Chrysler, Simca) and many more; it would require an industrial directory to list the multifarious activities. Special mention may be made of Unilever's two huge factories, one making soap at Vlaardingen, the other margarine at Feijenoord, and of the distilleries at Schiedam, world famous for gin.

Vlaardingen, on the Nieuwe Maas between Rotterdam and Hook of Holland, has grown enormously in recent years, partly because of the development of its port and partly because of the introduction of new industries, while it also has some importance as the third fishing-port in the Netherlands. It is being developed as a 'new town';[35] the first stage, to house 25 000 more people, was completed by 1961, and further developments envisage a total population of 140 000. The method used is to build large rectangular blocks of flats of varying height, with community buildings and small parks. The first phase is being carried on in the western suburbs, and the new district is called Westwijk.

The Hague (known in Dutch both as 's-Gravenhage and Den Haag) is an attractively laid out town, with broad treelined avenues and imposing squares, substantial houses and Government buildings, new well designed residential suburbs, pleasant gardens and wooded parks, in all 'an animated and cheerful city'. Originally situated 3 to 5 km (2 to 3 miles) from the coast, it has expanded into the dunelands, and Scheveningen (one of the most popular seaside resorts on the North Sea) and Loosduinen are now officially within the commune. Its population has grown rapidly from 56 000 in 1830 to 206 000 in 1899 and to 719 000 in 1970. The functions are primarily political and administrative, for it is the seat of government where the States-General meets (although Amsterdam is the actual capital), and it has been the seat of the Permanent Court of International Justice since 1922. Formerly the city had little commercial or industrial importance, but in the last few decades the number of banks and offices has increased, and some industries have been established. These include printing (notably the government stationery office), paper-making, clothing, minor metal manufactures, furniture and food-processing. Scheveningen is the second Dutch fishing port; in 1968, 37 000 tons of fish were landed there, about 30 per cent of the Dutch sea-fisheries' catch, mostly consisting of herring, which are salted at several large plants beside the harbour.

Eight km (5 miles) to the southeast of The Hague is the quiet attractive town of Delft, with a population in 1970 of 84 000. It stands on the Schie, and the old town is enclosed by a rectangular moat, the Singel-Gracht. It was long famous for its pottery, although the industry nearly died out in the eighteenth century; a certain revival has taken place since the end of the nineteenth century. Delft has a variety of light industries—the making of cigars, dyes, alcohol, gelatine, margarine, yeast and electric cables—and it is a pleasant residential town with a certain attraction for tourists. Other important features include the Topografische Dienst, which produces the official Dutch topographical maps, and the large Hydraulic Laboratory which carries out research investigations.

Leiden, a town of 101 000 inhabitants, lies about 35 km (22 miles) northeast of The Hague, 8 km (5 miles) from the coast of the North Sea. It stands among the branches of the Oude Rijn, which flow sluggishly through and around the town. A former flourishing cloth trade now survives only in the manufacture of blankets and special livery-cloth, and at the height of its prosperity in the early seventeenth century it had a population considerably greater than it has today. Leiden is in effect a cultural centre, and with its traditions of the past it also has some importance for the tourist trade. The few industries include printing and publishing, distilling and cigar-making, but these are of no great value.

Dordrecht (89 000) stands mainly on the south bank of the Oude Maas, near the meeting of the Noord, the Wantij and the Dordsche Kil. Until the seventeenth century Dordrecht was the leading port of the Netherlands, but silting and the increasing size of ships caused Rotterdam, 25 km (15 miles) nearer the sea, to forge ahead in the nineteenth century. Nevertheless the deepening of the Oude Maas has helped Dordrecht, and it has extensive inland waterway connections. With Zwijndrecht on the opposite bank of the river it handles over a million tons of freight, although this in point of fact amounts to less than one per cent of the total freight handled by Dutch ports. Its industrial activities are of much the same character as those of Rotterdam although on a smaller scale: shipbuilding, marine engineering, various metallurgical industries, chemicals, a Unilever oil-seed crushing-plant, and high quality glassware.

Utrecht (279 000), the fourth city of the Netherlands, is situated on the Kromme Rijn where it splits into the Vecht (which wanders off northwards to the IJssel Meer) and the Oude Rijn. The rivers are here markedly entrenched, and the city grew up on the high firm banks; the canals that intersect the town lie far below the level of the bordering houses. It has long been an important centre of communications, for it stands in the centre of the 'isthmus' between the IJssel Meer and the Lek, at the junction of the peat polderlands to the west and northwest, the river clay lands to the south, and the morainic hill country to the east. The Merwede and the Utrecht-Rhine Canals, several times enlarged, link Utrecht with Amsterdam and with the Lek. The completion of the Amsterdam-Rhine Canal (see p. 96) has further improved the position of the town, as will the new state highways.

As a result of this central position Utrecht has many metropolitan functions; it is the seat of the Roman Catholic archbishopric, the head-quarters of the *Nederlandsche Spoorwegen* (the State Railways), and it has a celebrated university. It is an important industrial town, with numerous engineering activities, the manufacture of railway rolling-stock and chemicals, tobacco processing, and an immense output of factory-made dairy produce. To the northwest, along the Merwede Canal, have developed new industrial suburbs.

In this section on the Dutch coastal lands, considerable space has been devoted to these towns, the inevitable result of a remarkable development of city life within a small area of western Europe. The southern part of Zuid-Holland, with the great cities of Rotterdam, The Hague and Utrecht, is commonly referred to as 'Randstad Holland' (p. 64).[36] Nevertheless, it must not be forgotten that a mere 8 km (5 miles) from Amsterdam lie the fertile arable lands of the IJ Polders, that only a kilometre or two north of Rotterdam is the deep Prins Alexander Polder, and that many of the workers of Utrecht live on the wooded Gooiland Hills not far to the east. In this part of the Netherlands intensely developed urban and rural ways of life are in close juxtaposition.

## The southwestern islands and estuaries

This subregion comprises the whole of the province of Zeeland (except for Zeeuwsch-Vlaanderen which is part of Maritime Flanders) (see pp. 86–7), together with the extreme south of Zuid-Holland. This is the delta region, including the four major estuaries—the Wester Schelde, the Ooster Schelde, the Grevelingen Maas and Volkerak, and the Haringvliet. Between the first two are the islands of Walcheren, Zuid-Beveland and Noord-Beveland,[37] although the first and second of these were actually converted into a peninsula when causeways were built to carry the Flushing to Bergen-op-Zoom railway. The island of Schouwen-Duiveland and the peninsula of Tholen separate the Ooster Schelde from the Grevelingen Maas, and Goeree-Overflakkee divides the latter from the Haringvliet. This, as has been shown (p. 35), is the main area of exposure to flooding, comprising some 1 800 sq km (700 sq miles) of dyked islands and peninsulas consisting mainly of reclaimed heavy marine clays; the floors of the polders are well below the perimeter dykes and the mean level of the sea. It is the area that will be transformed by the 'Delta Plan' already described (see p. 38). In May 1960, a phase of the Plan was finished when the dyke linking Noord- and Zuid-Beveland was completed, in April 1961 the Veersche Gat dyke between Walcheren and Noord-Beveland was finished (Plate 2) and in 1970 the Brouwershavensche Gat leading to the Grevelingen was sealed.

This is one of the main arable districts of the Netherlands. No less than 59 per cent of the total area of Zeeland is officially classified as arable land, only 14 per cent under permanent pasture. About a quarter of this farmland grows wheat, and barley is also important. Approximately a quarter of the Dutch sugar beet and flax output is grown, together with a considerable area of potatoes, onions, leguminous crops and other vegetables. Cultivation is intensive and yields are generally high; the wheat yield in Zeeland reaches 39 quintals per ha (31 cwt per acre), compared with the quite high figure of 35 q (28 cwt) for the Netherlands as a whole. In Zuid-Beveland there is a large area of orchards and bush fruit, especially red currants. Although this region as a whole is predominantly arable, in

1968 of the 80 000 cattle in Zeeland about a quarter were dairy animals. This figure is, however, by far the lowest for any Dutch province, the next being Limburg with 195 000.

A certain amount of inshore fishing is practised among the islands; for many years the oyster and mussel beds of the Ooster Schelde have been carefully managed. The loss of these is one disadvantage of the Delta scheme which has in fact caused some opposition. [38]

In spite of the intensive and prosperous agriculture, only the provinces of Friesland and Drenthe have a density of population lower than that of Zeeland; its density of 177 people per sq km (458 per sq mile) in 1970 was rather less than half that of the country as a whole and only about a sixth that of Zuid-Holland. This is due to the absence of large towns; a mere 18 per cent of the population lived in towns of 20 000 or over, compared with 64 per cent for the Netherlands as a whole, and only Drenthe had a smaller urban population. The only town of any size is Flushing (*Vlissingen, Flessingue*), on the southern tip of Walcheren. It is the third port of the Netherlands, and has regular container handling services with Harwich. It has extensive oil- and coal-bunkering facilities, and also a shipbuilding yard. The capital of the province is Middelburg, once a seaport, now linked by canal to Flushing and to the Veergat on the north of the island. It is a pleasant, quiet administrative and market centre, with the old town still surrounded by a moat. Veere, at the northern end of this canal, is another former port, which with several other tiny places have ceased to be of any importance as a result of the silting-up of their harbours and the increased size of shipping.

The population then is dispersed among the arable lands of the islands. Some villages are grouped around refuge mounds, others are strung out along the lines of ancient dykes or on sandy ridges that indicate the positions of former silted channels.

---

[1] For a table of the subdivisions of the Upper Holocene, with the sequence of the vegetation, its dating, and its archaeological associations, see A. J. Pannekoek, *Geological History of the Netherlands* (1956), p. 108.

[2] The datum used by the Netherlands *Topografische Dienst* is the mean tidal level at Amsterdam. This was first calculated in 1875, and was known as AP (Amsterdamsch Peil). When the new precise levelling of the Netherlands was carried out in the years 1922–36, a revised datum, NAP (Nieuw Amsterdamsch Peil), was used.

[3] The origin and silting-up of the Middelzee is described by H. Halbertsma, 'Enkele oudheidkundige aantekeningen over het Middelzee', *Tijdschr. K. ned. aardrijksk. Genoot.*, **72** (1955), pp. 93–105.

[4] J. van Veen, 'Overstromingen Tijdens de negen Stormvloeden sinds 1877', *Tijdschr. K. ned. aardrijksk. Genoot.*, **73** (1956), pp. 1–6; this describes, with detailed maps, each of the last nine floods since 1877.

[5] P. Wagret, *Les Polders* (Paris, 1959), gives an authoritative and beautifully illustrated account; English edition, *Polderlands* (London, 1968).

[6] A delightfully written and authoritative account of all the varied aspects of Dutch reclamation is provided by Joh. van Veen (chief engineer of the *Rijkswaterstaat*), *Dredge, Drain, Reclaim: the art of a nation* (2nd edition, 1949). This includes a large number of

photographs, diagrams and maps. A concise summary of the endless Dutch struggles against the sea is afforded by A. G. Maris, *De Dijken: een nationale Uitgave* (1954), a well-illustrated volume of 188 pp. A very detailed account is given by A. M. Lambert, *The Making of the Dutch Landscape* (1971), well illustrated and with a very full bibliography.

⁷ K. F. Valken, 'De Afdamming van de Briellsche Maas en haar Consequenties', *Tijdschr. econ. soc. Geog.*, **42** (1951), pp. 113–18.

⁸ Details of the disaster are given by *The Battle of the Floods* (1953), published for the benefit of the Netherlands Flood Relief Fund in Amsterdam. See also W. E. Boerman, 'The storm floods in the Netherlands', *Geography*, **38** (1953), pp. 178–82, and K. C. Edwards, *ibid.*, pp. 182–7, 'The Netherlands floods: some further aspects and consequences', G. W. Hoffman, 'The 1953 flood in the Netherlands', *Geogr. Rev.*, **44** (1954), pp. 423–5, gives considerable bibliographical detail of the causes and consequences of the floods. J. H. G. Schepers, 'Een Stormvloed teisterde Zuidwest-Nederland', *Tijdschr. K. ned. aardrijksk. Genoot.*, **70** (1953), pp. 126–55, describes the effects of the floods, with tables, maps and aerial photographs. The problems of reconstruction are discussed by M. W. Heslings, 'Het Herstel en de Sanering van het Rampgebied in Zuidwest Nederland', *ibid.*, **70** (1953), pp. 273–308, and by S. Herweijer, 'Het agrarisch Herstel en de Herverkavelingen in het Rampgebied', *ibid.*, **72** (1955), pp. 297–306.

⁹ An account of the recovery of Walcheren is provided by Joh. van Veen, *Dredge, Drain, Reclaim: the art of a nation* (2nd edition, 1949), pp. 122–7.

¹⁰ J. Koopman, 'Het Deltaplan en zijn Waterstaatskundige, Economische en Sociale Aspecten', *Tijdschr. K. ned. aardrijksk. Genoot.*, **73** (1956), pp. 113–33; this contains numerous plans and photographs. The Delta Plan is also discussed by M. C. Verburg, *Het Deltaplan. Verleden, Heden en Toekomst van het Deltaplan* (1955); S. E. Steigenga-Kouwe, 'The Delta Plan', *Tijdschr. econ. soc. Geogr.*, **51** (1960), pp. 167–75; and J. Lingsma, *Holland and the Delta Plan* (1964).

¹¹ J. M. Roof, 'De Centrale Weg als Zeeuwse Verkeersspil', *Tijdschr. econ. soc. Geogr.*, **47** (1956), pp. 48–53.

¹² A summary of the many socio-economic changes involved in the implementation of the Delta Plan is given by M. C. Verburg, 'De Functie en de Resultaten van het economisch-geografische Onderzoek met Betrekking tot de structurele Wijzigingen als Gevolg van het Deltaplan', *Tijdschr. econ. soc. Geogr.*, **47** (1956), pp. 311–22; this has a bibliography of eighty-three references.

¹³ A map of the Netherlands of the future, after both the Delta Plan and the closing of the Frisian *zeegaten* are completed, according to J. Th. Thijsse, is given by Schepers, *op. cit.*, p. 150.

¹⁴ In December 1960 an official Dutch commission published a 1 200 pp. report on coastal defences, urging a strengthening and enlarging of the entire dyke system.

¹⁵ As computed by the Stichting voor Bodemonderzoek (Soil Survey Institute) at Wageningen in 1950.

¹⁶ A detailed study of the Haarlemmermeer is given in a monograph by Chr. van Paassen, P. J. Kouwe and G. A. Wissink, *De Haarlemmermeer* (1955), Publicatie No. 11A uit het Geografisch Instituut der Rijks Universiteit te Utrecht; this deals fully with the problems of a polder community in highly urbanised surroundings. An account of the century of progress since the Haarlemmermeer was drained is provided by G. A. Wissink, 'Bij het Eeuwfeest van de Haarlemmermeer', *Tijdschr. K. ned. aardrijksk. Genoot.*, **72** (1955), pp. 200–18.

¹⁷ N. Oostinga, 'Water- en Afvalwaterproblemen in de Provincie Groningen', *Tijdschr. econ. soc. Geogr.*, **55** (1964), pp. 2–7.

¹⁸ F. Verger, 'Les conquêtes sur la mer de la Zélande au Jutland', *Annls Géogr.*, **65** (1956), pp. 270–87. This article includes some excellent photographs of reclamation sequences.

¹⁹ An account of the marine clay lands, their improvement and utilisation, and the associated problems of coastal defence in western Friesland, is given by P. du Burck, P. J. Ente and L. J. Pons, 'Het Zeekleigebied van Westfriesland', *Tijdschr. K. ned. aardrijksk. Genoot.*, **73** (1956), pp. 140–51; this includes a number of detailed maps and soil profiles.

²⁰ Chr. van Welsenes, 'The development of the agricultural area of northern Groningen', *Tijdschr. econ. soc. Geogr.*, **51** (1960), pp. 175–80.

²¹ L. H. Bouwman, 'Agrarische Hervorming op Ameland', *Tijdschr. econ. soc. Geogr.*, **46** (1955), pp. 282–6.

²² J. W. Thierry, 'The enclosure and partial reclamation of the Zuider Zee', *Geogrl. J.*, **77** (1931), pp. 223–37, provides much information, with illustrations, about the early stages of the project. See also Ch. A. P. Takes and A. J. Venstra, 'Zuyder Zee reclamation scheme', *Tijdschr. econ. soc. Geogr.*, **51** (1960), pp. 162–7; and Ch. A. P. Takes, 'The settlement pattern in the Dutch Zuiderzee reclamation scheme', *Tijdschr. K. ned. aardrijksk. Genoot.*, **77** (1960), pp. 347–53. M. H. M. van Hulten, 'Plan and Reality in the IJsselmeerpolders', *Tijdschr. econ. soc. Geogr.*, **60** (1969), pp. 65–76, gives a detailed survey of the scheme from the official point of view. A series of maps shows the planned settlements in East Flevoland between 1954 and 1965, when they were reduced in number from twelve to four.

²³ W. M. Otten, 'De Noordoostpolder 1942–52', *Tijdschr. K. ned. aardrijksk. Genoot.*, **69** (1952), 300–14, contains numerous maps and photographs; and Ph. Pinchemel, 'Le polder du Nord-Est (Pays-Bas)', *Annls Géogr.*, **62** (1953), pp. 347–63; this contains numerous large-scale maps and photographs.

²⁴ J. F. R. van de Wall, 'De Groei van het Ontwerp voor de Oosterpolder', *Tijdschr. K. ned. aardrijksk. Genoot.*, **70** (1953), pp. 315–28, discusses the early stages of the reclamation of the Oost Polder.

²⁵ C. H. Edelman, *Soils of the Netherlands* (1950), affords a most detailed account, illustrated by a folding map on the scale of 1 : 400 000.

²⁶ Aspects of the planning of Amsterdam are discussed by W. Dougill, 'Amsterdam: its town planning development', *Tn Plann. Rev.*, **14** (1931), pp. 194–200; and 'Amsterdam: The General Extension Plan', *ibid.*, **17** (1934), pp. 1–10. See also G. L. Burke, *The Making of Dutch Towns* (1956), pp. 141–53.

²⁷ In 1970, the Dutch ports handled 264 million tons of seaborne freight, of which 103 were imports, 36 exports, the balance in transit or bonded store.

²⁸ This figure refers only to sea fisheries; in addition there were further landings from inshore fisheries (unspecified, but about 40 000 tons).

²⁹ Summaries of the Dutch steel industry are provided by (a) L. A. Pennock, 'De Koninklijke Nederlandsche Hoogovens en Staalfabrieken N.V.', *Tijdschr. K. ned. aardrijksk. Genoot.*, **65** (1948), pp. 544–7; (b) 'The Dutch iron and steel industry', reprinted from the *Monthly Statistical Bulletin*, **26** (1951), no. 11, of the British Iron and Steel Federation; and (c) A. M. Lambert, 'Dutch steel making: past, present and future', *Geography*, **56** (1971), pp. 241–3. A detailed account of the merger is given by D. K. Fielding and G. Krumme, 'The "Royal Hoesch Union"', *Tijdschr. econ. soc. Geogr.*, **59** (1968), pp. 177–99, with maps, lists of plants and their functions, subsidiaries and associates; the central company is now known as Estel N.V.

³⁰ J. M. Richards, 'New towns in the Netherlands', *Progress*, **45** (1956), pp. 147–57.

³¹ A detailed summary (of 287 pp.) of the first ten years in the postwar reconstruction of Rotterdam is provided by C. van Traa, *Rotterdam: de Geschiedenis van tien Jaren Wederopbouw* (1955).

³² J. W. de Vries, 'Uit de Geschiedenis van de Rotterdamse Waterweg', *Tijdschr. K. ned. aardrijksk. Genoot.*, **70** (1953), pp. 4–19, with the aid of detailed maps, describes the construction, maintenance, problems, etc., of the waterway, including the influence of radar on navigation.

³³ E. Wever, 'Pernis–Botlek–Europoort; un complex à base de pétrole?', *Tijdschr. econ. soc. Geogr.*, **57** (1966), pp. 131–41.

³⁴ K. P. van der Mandel, 'Europort: the gateway to Europe', in *Progress* (1958), vol. 46, pp. 199–208. See also W. Evers, 'Europoort', *Geographische Rundschau*, **11** (1959), pp. 298–304; H. Kuipers, 'The changing landscape of the island of Rozenburg (Rotterdam Port Area)', *Geogrl. Rev.*, **52** (1962), pp. 362–78; and F. Posthuma, 'Port modernisation: the lessons of Rotterdam–Europoort', *Progress*, **57** (1968), pp. 143–51.

35 J. M. Richards, 'New towns in the Netherlands', *Progress*, **45** (1956), pp. 147–57.

36 J. Winsemius, 'Urbanisation in the western part of the Netherlands (*'Randstad Holland'*)', *Tijdschr. econ. soc. Geogr.*, **51** (1960), pp. 188–99; and W. Steigenga, 'The urbanization of the Netherlands', *Tijdschr. econ. soc. Geogr.*, **54** (1963), pp. 46–52. Various aspects of planning in the Netherlands are discussed by A. K. Dutt, 'Levels of Planning in the Netherlands, with particular reference to regional Planning', *Ann. Ass. Am. Geogr.*, **58** (1968), pp. 670–85; and R. H. Buchanan, 'Toward Netherlands 2000: The Dutch National Plan', *Econ. Geogr.*, **45** (1969), pp. 258–74. See also an official Government publication, *Second Report on Physical Planning in the Netherlands* (The Hague, 1966).

37 C. Hage, 'Noord-Beveland', *Tijdschr. econ. soc. Geogr.*, **42** (1951), pp. 86–98.

38 The results of the closing of the estuaries under the Delta Plan on the cultivation of oysters and mussels, together with the lobster and shrimp fisheries (especially in the Ooster Schelde, centred on Yerseke), is described by A. G. U. Hildebrandt, 'De Gevolgen van de Afsluiting van de Zeegaten voor de Visserij', *Tijdschr. econ. soc. Geogr.*, **47** (1956), pp. 189–98.

# 4
# Maritime Flanders

The coastal plain from the estuary of the Wester Schelde in the northeast to where the chalk hills of Artois reach the Channel coast at Sangatte, a few kilometres west of Calais, forms a distinct regional unit, referred to as 'Maritime Flanders'. About 56 km (35 miles) of this North Sea coast are in France, 68 km (42 miles) in Belgium, and 13 km (8 miles) in the Netherlands, while a further 64 km (40 miles) form the southern shore of the Wester Schelde. The whole length provides a remarkably straight and unembayed coastline, characterised by a broad extent of sandy beach uncovered at low tide, and backed by a continuous barrier of sand-dunes strengthened in places by artificial defences. Behind this again lies a flat plain, seamed with drainage channels and extending landwards for some 10 to 15 km (6 to 10 miles) to approximately the 5-metre (16 ft) contour.

## The evolution of the coast

The evolution of this coastal plain has already been described down to the end of the Lower Holocene, at about 5 000 B.C. On the offshore bar, which extended far to the northeast beyond the Scheldt, Meuse and Rhine breaches (see p. 29), accumulated a line of sand-dunes behind which lay a marshy lowland. Here sedimentation was considerable, and with the onset of the mild damp conditions of the Atlantic phase, the growth and decay of vegetation led to the formation of peat beds. This continued into the Sub-Boreal phase, although under those cooler and drier conditions much less peat accumulated, but with the return of a milder damper climate peat accumulation was again accelerated. Neolithic finds in Flanders testify to the presence of man in the region at this time.

The development of the coastlands of Flanders in historic times has been studied in detail by Belgian geologists and botanists.[1] There have been several phases of marine transgression. The *Dunkirk I* phase, from the second century B.C. to the first A.D., was responsible for considerable sedimentation near Veurne and Ostend. The second phase, *Dunkirk II*, occupied the period from the fourth to the eighth centuries; at its maximum in the fifth century this transgression covered the coastal plain as far inland

76

as the 5-metre contour, and much silt and fine sand was deposited. Only a few sandy islands, the remnants of the former duneline, remained above the water level. Conversely, tidal channels were cut down into the peat beds; their courses can still be traced by deposits of coarse sand, for when the level of the surrounding peatlands was later lowered through drainage and resultant shrinkage and compaction, the winding sand-filled channels were left outstanding.

From the eighth century onwards the sea slowly receded, and the progressive drying-out of the shallow lagoons was assisted both by natural sedimentation and by some reclamation by man; documents as early as the tenth century relate to the building of dykes. Considerable protection was afforded by the accumulation of another line of dunes (see p. 30), which like its predecessor originated as an offshore bar built up by the waves.

There was a further but less extensive transgression in the tenth century, referred to as *Dunkirk III A*. It caused several breaks through the new duneline, but the artificially strengthened defences helped to limit the extent of this inundation. The estuary of the Ijzer (in French *Yser*) became a broad sheet of water, and the enlarging of a breach near Knokke was responsible for the Zwin. An extensive marshy depression (probably caused by peat-cutting), known as the Groot-Moeren, which extended across the position of the present French frontier, was also flooded.

Towards the end of the eleventh century a renewed transgression (*Dunkirk III B*) particularly affected the Zwin estuary, resulting in a rapid growth in the importance of the port of Bruges. The deposits associated with the *III A* and *III B* transgressions cover the now reclaimed areas referred to as the *Middelland*, found along and to the east of the Ijzer estuary and between Blankenberge and Bruges.

Reclamation went steadily on, furthered especially by grants of land to the Cistercian religious houses. But as in Groningen and Friesland many setbacks were experienced, for sometimes too extensive an area was reclaimed with inadequate protection, so that some storms did grievous damage. In the succeeding centuries catastrophes occurred at intervals; in 1377, when the Wester Schelde was enlarged into its present estuary form, twenty-two villages were inundated with great loss of life. A very disastrous flood occurred in 1404, and as a result the *Graaf Jansdijk* was built by the Counts of Flanders to buttress the dune wall; this can still be traced in places, well inland of the present coastal defences. Other inundations were sometimes a result of neglect during the wars to which Flanders was grievously and frequently subject, sometimes deliberately caused as part of military strategy; the so-called *Polders historiques d'Ostende* to the south of that town were flooded by the beleaguered Dutch between 1601 and 1604. These polders incidentally were maintained as water areas until 1800 to serve an unusual purpose; at low tide the sluices were opened and water from the polders flowed strongly seawards, helping to scour the shipping channel and maintain an adequate depth of water in Ostend harbour.

Unlike the Netherlands, since the seventeenth century little serious flooding has taken place in Belgium. No major rivers bring massive contributions of flood water to the coastal lowlands, the strengthened duneline is straight and continuous, and no area actually lies below the Ostend datum, although some land is below high-tide level. The only area flooded since the seventeenth century in Belgium has been the Ijzer estuary, twice deliberately for defensive purposes in 1783 and in 1914–18, once in 1928 by the collapse of a temporary dyke during a storm. A very small area to the east of De Zoute was inundated by the floods of 1953. There have been inundations, however, both in Dutch and French Flanders, along the estuaries of the Scheldt and the Aa.

Marine erosion has pushed the coastline a little landwards in historic times. Between Dunkirk and Nieuwpoort and again near Ostend the present coastline lies a few hundred metres inland of its position in the tenth century. Testereph and Scarphout were formerly ports which had silted up by the twelfth century, but today their sites lie some distance offshore. There are other such records, but for the most part the coastal defences which protect against inundation have also served against erosion.

The features of the Flanders coastal plain are described under first the beach and dune rampart, and second the polderlands (Fig. 4.1).

## The beach and dunes

The broad beach, uncovered in places for a width of nearly 400 m at low tide, consists of sand, strikingly free from pebbles, which is fortunate for the Belgian resorts. The set of the currents and a longshore drift move some sand and mud, although this is largely checked by groynes (Plate 9).

Behind the beach rises a long rampart of dunes, cut through only at Dunkirk and by the Aa estuary at Gravelines in France, and at four places in Belgium—at the mouth of the Ijzer below Nieuwpoort, at Ostend, near Zeebrugge where the ship canal from Bruges reaches the sea between the moles, and at the shallow mud-covered inlet which marks the former mouth of the Zwin estuary. Between the Ijzer mouth and Dunkirk the dune belt is over a kilometre wide, and between Ostend and Wenduine and again near Knokke it is nearly as wide. On the other hand, to the west of Ostend it becomes a narrow single duneline. The highest dune is the 'Blekker', which rises to 51 m (167 ft) near Oostduinkerke, and many more exceed 30 m (100 ft). The duneline is chaotic in appearance, a tossing sea of sand, with clusters of crests separating broad depressions (known as *pannes*), but with a steep uniform slope falling to the beach. An irregular cover of vegetation consists of marram grass planted to help stabilise the sand, patches of scrubby bushes—osiers, willows, gorse and aromatic shrubs, and here and there plantations of conifers.

This coastline within Belgium is an almost continuous holiday resort, for apart from the major centres, Ostend and Blankenberge, there are many

Plate 9. The Belgian coast near Heist

-*baden* and -*plages* fronted by promenades and concrete sea walls.[2] Among
the dunes are individual villas, hotels, holiday camps and huge caravan
parks. The remains of Hitler's 'Atlantic wall' are still visible—massive gun-
turrets that have slumped down the dunes, and pill-boxes that have been
converted into public conveniences or refreshment kiosks.

Apart from the tourist industry and the presence of packet ports, manufacturing industry has recently expanded. The old town and citadel of
Calais stand on what was a dune island, surrounded by several basins and
canals, and approached from the sea between long converging jetties. The
port works stand on piles which go down through the sands into the
Flanders Clay. The new town, with the industrial suburbs of St Pierre, has
developed to the south; factories make lace, rayon, clothing and embroidery, and there are several food-processing establishments and timber yards.
A large factory, owned by British Titan, makes titanium dioxide for
paint, plastics and paper. Calais is important as a ferryport at the terminal
of the shortest sea route between Britain and the Continent, and imports
of timber, ores, chemicals, cellulose and other bulky raw materials are
unloaded for the northern industrial area of France. About 4 700 ships used
the port in 1969, with a total net tonnage of 4·4 million, and over a million
passengers entered. There has been considerable British industrial development in the Calais area. Ten British firms employ a fifth of the local labour
force.

Dunkirk (*Dunkerque*), its tremendous scars from the summer of 1940 now

79

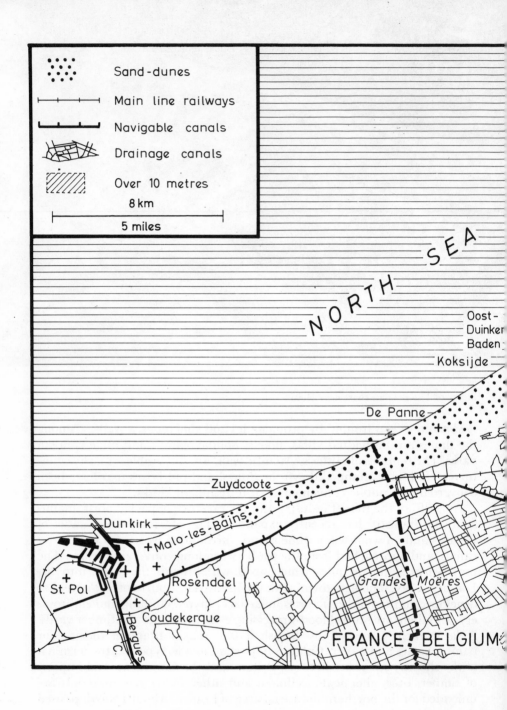

Fig. 4.1. The Flanders coast southwest of Ostend
The complicated pattern of the drainage canals is much simplified.

Based on *Cart de Belgique au 1 000 000^e*, sheets I, II, VII, VIII.

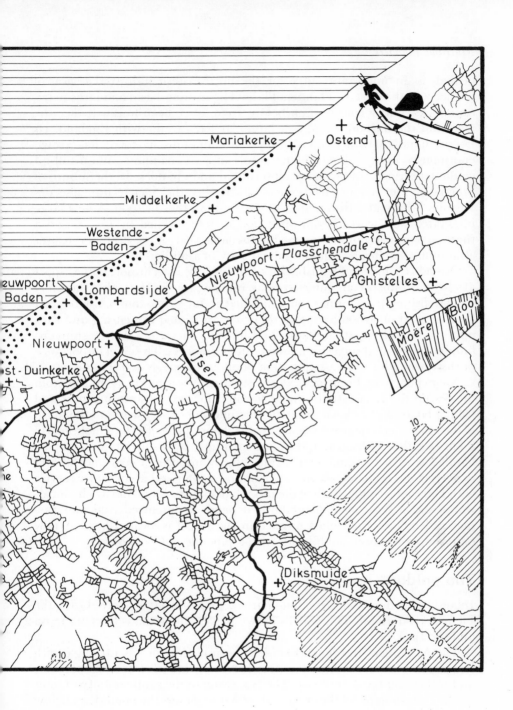

Mariakerke

Ostend

Middelkerke

Westende-
Baden

Nieuwpoort-Plasschendale C.

Ghistelles

euwpoort
Baden

Lombardsijde

Bloot

Moëre

Nieuwpoort

IJser

st-Duinkerke

10

Diksmuide

10

10

10

healed, is an important entry for the northeastern industrial region of France and the western Flanders Plain. The turning-basin and large maritime locks, under construction before 1939, have been finished since the war, and the harbour handles a large car ferry traffic with England. Its freight handled, which totalled 17·1 million tons in 1969, has grown enormously in recent years, the result of its expanding roll-on/roll-off container services and its large oil terminal and ore dock. In the suburb of St Pol-sur-Mer a large oil refinery, owned by the Société française des Pétroles B.P., had a throughput of 5·41 million tons in 1969. A new large integrated steel works began operation in 1962, owned by *Usinor*, and a thermal power station was opened in the same year. A big Péchiney-Kaiser aluminium smelter has an annual capacity of a million tons.

Ostend (*Oostende* in Flemish, *Ostende* in French) is an important ferryport at the terminus of an international railway route. It is also the chief Belgian fishing port, for in 1969 it handled about 34 000 tons of fish out of a Belgian total of 50 000 tons, and there are associated fish-curing and canning plants, refrigeration plants, and fertiliser factories. A large shipyard builds trawlers and such specialised craft as dredgers. The chief importance of the town, which has a population of about 60 000, is as a seaside resort.

Nieuwpoort (in French *Nieuport*), situated about 3 km (2 miles) from the sea up the Ijzer estuary, has a harbour for small tramp steamers and fishing boats, and its local industries include a chemical works to the south of the town. Zeebrugge is a wholly artificial port, protected by a mole nearly 8 km (5 miles) in length, and linked to Bruges by a ship canal. The port handles a varied commercial traffic, mostly imports of coal and oil and exports of coke, chemicals and cement and has a regular container service with Harwich. To the south of the inner harbour the large Solvay chemical-works and a coke oven plant both depend on imported coal and raw materials. The largest glass furnace in the world is located here. A new oil terminal has been completed, with a pipeline to Gent (p. 157).

## The polders

Inland of the dune belt lies a long narrow strip of what is referred to as the Flemish polderland. This widens in two places, along the valleys of the Aa and the Ijzer.

The Aa polders, in French Flanders, occupy more or less a triangle with its apex at St Omer (where the river leaves the low clay-covered plateau) and its base on the dune coast. The Aa, rising to the southwest of St Omer on the eastern slopes of the chalk hills of Artois, enters the polderland below that town, and flows to the sea beyond Gravelines between high dykes built well above the surrounding countryside.

The Ijzer follows in its upper course the general southwest to northeast direction of the Flanders rivers (see p. 17), but then makes an abrupt right-angled bend northwards and breaks through to the North Sea coast near

Nieuwpoort. It probably owes this change of course to the *Dunkirk II* marine transgression, which produced several shallow embayments into one of which the upper Ijzer was diverted. The estuary seems to have extended as a broad sheet of water as far inland as Loo until the tenth century, but gradual reclamation has since reduced it to the narrow tidal creek of today. Several sluices at Nieuwpoort are used to regulate the levels of the coastal canals and to dispose of floodwater brought down by the river. These sluices were operated to flood the Ijzer valley as part of the defence of Nieuwpoort in the war of 1914–18.

The surface of the polderland is interrupted only by depressions, usually the result of peat cutting or of digging clay loam for brick-making, and by sandy hillocks rising 6 m (20 ft) or so above the general level. Some of these hillocks near the coast are the remnants of older dunes, those further inland are 'islands' of Pleistocene sand; they sometimes form village sites. The soils are variable; patches of yellow sand, black silt and grey or blue marine

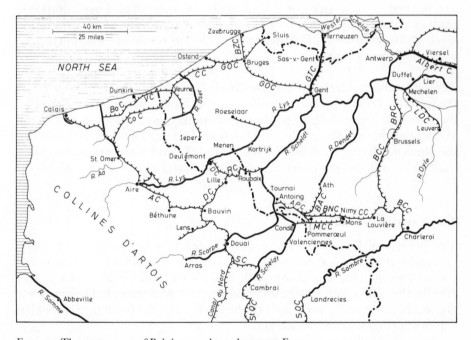

FIG. 4.2. The waterways of Belgium and northeastern France
The abbreviations are as follows: **AC,** Aire Canal; **APC,** Antoing-Pommeroeul Canal; **BAC,** Blaton-Ath Canal; **BNC,** Blaton-Nimy Canal; **BCC,** Brussels-Charleroi Canal; **Bo C,** Bourbourg Canal; **BRC,** Brussels-Rupel Canal; **BZC,** Bruges-Zeebrugge Canal; **CC,** Centre Canal; **Co C,** Colme Canal; **DC,** Deûle Canal; **GOC,** Gent-Ostend Canal; **GTC,** Gent-Terneuzen Canal; **RC,** Roubaix Canal (continued to the Scheldt as the Espierres Canal); **SC,** Sensée Canal; **SOC,** Sambre-Oise Canal; **St QC,** St Quentin Canal; **VC,** Veurne Canal.

Based on W. Seghers, *Kaart der Binnenscheepvaartwegen van N.-W. Europa* (n.d.).

clays can be seen within a few metres of each other, although the clays usually predominate.

The polders are covered with a maze of drainage ditches (Fig. 4.1), many in orderly geometrical patterns, others in irregular chaos; some of the latter were formerly tidal creeks. They lead into larger channels and then into a few major outfalls. The rivers Ijzer and Aa also help. The small navigable waterways (Fig. 4.2), along which it is possible for a barge to move from Calais to Bruges more or less parallel to the sea, play little or no part in the drainage since they are usually enclosed within dykes some metres above the surrounding countryside; frequently a drainage canal at a lower level runs parallel to a waterway, and may even pass under it in a concrete siphon.

The polders are divided for drainage purposes into units, under the control of elected syndicates, many dating from developments in the twelfth century. In each polder the watertable is maintained at a specific level; excess water is removed by gravity when the sluices into the main outfalls are opened at low tide, or occasionally by pumping. One additional problem, the result of much of the polders lying below normal high-tide level, is the infiltration of salt water into the subsoil should too much fresh water be pumped away.

These Flemish polderlands may be divided into several units (Fig. 2.7). In the west the French polders lie within the Aa basin, succeeded eastward by the more extensive Belgian polders, and along the southern shores of the Wester Schelde are the polders of Dutch or Zealand Flanders. In addition, the lands bordering the Scheldt estuary and the Antwerp region itself must each be considered separately. These are lettered 2a to 2d respectively on Fig. 2.7.

## The French polders

The polders of French Flanders, though nowhere below mean sea level, remained as marshland much later than did those of Belgium. Little in the way of reclamation was accomplished until the eighteenth century, and even in the nineteenth winter flooding was still widespread. These polders are wet because of the proximity of the chalk-edge to the west, from which copious spring-water is discharged.

The reclaimed polders are now the scene of a prosperous arable farming. Some cattle are reared, both for dairying and for meat, to supply the industrial towns in the Lille area and on the northern French coalfield, but livestock are not so important as in Belgian Flanders. As the marshes were reclaimed, they were put under cereals, beans and clover, and some districts concentrated upon flax-growing. These crops are still grown, although the area under flax has notably declined, and the largest area is now devoted to sugar beet, for which the northeast is the most important producing region in France; several large refineries have been built since the 1914–18 war. There are many prosperous market gardens, and chicory is a local speciality in sandy areas.

Several factories processing agricultural commodities are situated at points along the banks of the canals, equipped with wharves to handle imported coal and raw materials. These include distilleries, breweries, chicory mills, vegetable canneries and saw-mills, and they help to provide full employment in this agricultural countryside.

The population lives either in villages straggling in linear pattern along the embanked roads and on slight eminences, or in large prosperous-looking though isolated farmsteads, for there are few towns. St Omer stands at the junction of the polder land with Interior Flanders, where the Neuffossé Canal is linked with the canalised river Aa. It is a small market town, with a few factories manufacturing clothing and underwear. Other towns are Bourbourg, also with some small factories, and Bergues at the junction of three waterways surrounding the town, which give it a Bruges-like appearance.

## The Belgian polders

In Belgium about 50 per cent of the polders are under permanent grass-land, while much of the remainder is under rotation grassland, with oats and green crops for fodder. Large dairy herds produce milk for the towns of central Belgium. Sheep, the basis of the medieval Flemish woollen industry, were grazed on the salt-marshes and grass-covered mudflats. Some sheep are still to be seen, mostly in Oost-Vlaanderen near the Dutch frontier, but are few in number in comparison with past centuries. Pig-rearing is usually associated with dairy farming. Further south, on the slightly higher lands towards Interior Flanders, sugar beet, flax and malting barley are grown. The demands of neighbouring urban markets have resulted in market-gardening on the sandy soils where the dune belt meets the polders; these produce early vegetables, notably potatoes and carrots.

Farms usually stand on sandy ridges or hillocks away from the damp pastures, and with an occasional line of pollarded willows or poplars they form the only interruptions to the sweeping open countryside. The many dispersed villages consist of little more than a nucleus of a church, an inn and a few shops, situated at a road confluence or where a road crosses a canal. A few small market towns include Veurne (in French *Furnes*), the focus of four waterways, six roads and a railway, the market centre of the frontier district; it has a few small processing industries.

Bruges (its official Flemish form is *Brugge*) is the largest town, with a population of about 51 000, though an agglomeration total of 114 000, situated on the edge of the polderland 13 km (8 miles) from the sea, to which it is linked directly at Zeebrugge by a ship canal and also by a much longer waterway (the Gent-Ostend Canal) which wanders leisurely across the plain to Ostend. The old town, encircled and intersected by canals, exists as an attractive tourist centre and as a market town for the northern districts of the province of West-Vlaanderen. On the north side of the town considerable industrial developments have taken place alongside the canal basins, including small shipbuilding yards, engineering works which construct bridges and rolling-stock, breweries, flour mills, a yeast factory and several timber yards. A number of craft industries still cater profitably both for tourists and for export—lace-making (largely a domestic industry), embroidery, wood-carving, fine printing and glass-painting.

## Dutch Flanders

In the north the strip of polderland widens and trends almost at right angles along the southern shore of the Wester Schelde. Most of these polders are in Dutch territory, forming what is called *Zeeuwsch-* (or *Zeeuws-*) *Vlaanderen* (Zealand Flanders).[3] They are bordered by tidal marshes and mudflats seamed with creeks. As late as the fourteenth century, the northern corner of Zealand Flanders consisted of an archipelago of islands intersected by branches of the Zwin estuary. Silting took place, stimulated by dyking along the Wester Schelde, to the great detriment of Bruges at the head of the Zwin. The coastline is now protected by a thick earth dyke, reinforced with stone-facing along virtually its whole length. Substantial flooding has nevertheless occurred at times, the last in February 1953 (see p. 36), when the dykes were breached near Terneuzen and on either side of the northward-projecting Hoek van Ossenisse. One piece of reclamation has been completed since the war of 1939–45; the broad creek known as the Savojaards Plaat, which dried out at low tide leaving only the Braakman channel, has been dyked off from the open sea. The Braakman was the outlet of a canal from Gent to the Wester Schelde as early as the tenth century, and also the outlet of the Sasvaart in the sixteenth century from Gent via Sas-van-Gent. This canal had silted up by the end of the eighteenth century, and finally the Gent-Terneuzen ship canal was cut across the polder lands in 1827.

This canal, two-thirds of which is in Belgium, has been enlarged several times, so that it can now take 60 000 ton ore-carriers, as determined by the dimensions of the triple sea locks at Terneuzen where the canal enters the Wester Schelde. One internal lock at Sas-van-Gent in the Netherlands near the frontier, larger than the sea locks, was constructed to cope both with floodwater, since extensive flooding on the upper Scheldt and the Lys is relieved by way of this canal, and also with exceptionally high tides in the Wester Schelde; the sea locks are opened for several hours before and after high tide. It is 30 km (20 miles) long, with a width of 50 m (160 ft) at the surface, and has a minimum depth of 5 m (17 ft). In 1969 the canal transported over 12 million tons of freight.

These Zealand Flanders polders are low-lying, some well below mean sea level, notably the Pauluspolder to the south of the Ossenisse peninsula. The reclaimed heavy marine clays are almost entirely under arable cultivation, although dairying, pig-rearing and (on the salt marsh pastures) sheep-grazing are practised. The main crops are cereals and roots grown in rotation, together with market-gardening and fruit cultivation. Large prosperous-looking farms are dispersed over the open countryside, and villages are few and scattered, occasionally curiously forlorn in appearance, sometimes rather attractive. Some, such as Sluis, are decayed ports; this formerly stood on the shores of the now silted Zwin, although it is still connected to Bruges by a small canal constructed during the régime of the United Netherlands. Biervliet was a fishing village, where it is said the method of curing herrings was invented; a herring-vane surmounts the spire of the town hall.

Terneuzen (sometimes known simply as Neuzen) stands at the seaward end of the ship canal to Gent, now the centre of a huge American-controlled chemical complex.[4] The port tranships raw materials into barges, some transit traffic passes through to Gent, and it has a small fishing industry. The canal does not handle cargo originating locally (this, mainly fruit and agricultural produce, is despatched by rail).

## The Scheldt estuary

The estuary of the lower Scheldt is dyked on both sides, for most of the bordering polderlands lie well below high-tide level.[5] The lowest official point in Belgium is actually at Austruweel (800 m downstream from Antwerp on the river bank), just one metre below the Ostend datum. In the east the alluvial soils change gradually to the sands of the western Kempenland, while to the west is the fertile *Waasland* or *pays de Waes*.

The distance between Antwerp, where the Scheldt is nearly 550 m (600 yds) wide, and the mouth of the estuary (indicated by a line between Flushing and Breskens), is 93 km (58 miles) of which 55 km (34 miles) lie in Dutch territory. This outlet is known as the Wester Schelde, between the islands of Walcheren and Zuid-Beveland to the north and the low-lying dyked coast of Zealand Flanders to the south. This estuary, a vitally important outlet for Antwerp, seems to have become established only in historic times, and it was not until the fifteenth century that it became the major outlet of the Scheldt system with a continuous navigable channel. The altitudes involved are so slight that without regularisation a mere accident of tidal scouring can convert a minor creek into a main outlet, and artificial alteration is easy. Until 1866, for example, some of the water of the river Scheldt escaped through the Ooster Schelde, the estuary to the north of the Walcheren-Zuid Beveland islands, but in that year a dam was built to carry the Flushing railway between Zuid-Beveland and the mainland, and the gap was sealed.

The long story of 'the Scheldt question' is a direct result of the fact that the greater part of the estuary is under Dutch sovereignty, which for many years sought to cripple the trade of Antwerp by denying maritime access to it, hence the closure of the Scheldt from 1648 to 1792. It was not until 1863 that the Dutch right to levy tolls on Scheldt navigation was finally bought out by Belgium and other interested maritime countries. Today the Wester Schelde (the western part of which is known as the Honte) has a dredged and buoyed fairway, at its narrowest over 140 m (150 yds), and with a least depth of 7·3 m (24 ft) right up to Antwerp. In effect vessels drawing up to 10 m (33 ft) can reach the port at high water.

## The Antwerp region

The influence of Antwerp (in Flemish *Antwerpen* and in French *Anvers*) is sufficiently marked to justify the appellation of the *région Anversoise* to an area on either side of the lower Scheldt from the Rupel confluence to the frontier, where the waterway bends almost at right angles. The city lies almost entirely on the right bank of the river, beyond its easterly 'elbow', with an extensive dock system downstream of the built-up area (Fig. 4.3). Apart from two small basins constructed during the Napoleonic period, most of these docks were built in the latter part of the nineteenth century; they are connected with the river by means of three locks. The large Hansa Dock, completed in 1932, is linked directly to the river further downstream as well as to the other docks. The total water area of these docks is about half as much again as those at London or Liverpool, and there are about 50 km (30 miles) of quays, of which 8 km (3 miles) stretch along the river frontage of the city. The barge docks are the focus of inland waterway traffic down the Scheldt system from Flanders, along the Albert Canal from Liège (see pp. 128–31), and up the estuary from the Netherlands and the Rhine via the Zuid-Beveland Canal. Considerable extensions of the dock-system are in progress; a series of new docks, with modern handling and storage equipment, has been constructed downstream of the city. The huge Zandvliet lock, which can accommodate ships of 70 000 tons, was opened in 1967.

Antwerp is one of the world's great ports, and through its docks passes about four-fifths of the foreign trade of the Belgo-Luxembourg Union. In 1969 unloadings at the docks totalled 62·4 million tons (48·9 by sea, 10·2 by inland waterways), and loadings amounted to 33·6 million tons (24·1 and 6·8 respectively);[6] these figures include transit and entrepôt traffic. A wide range of commodities is included—imports of mineral oil, ores, timber, foodstuffs, raw materials generally, and exports of manufactured goods, especially steel, chemicals, glass and textiles.[7]

Mainly as a result of these port functions and of its long commercial and industrial traditions, Antwerp was a city of 227 000 people in 1970; with its half-circle of densely inhabited contiguous communes to the east and south, the total population of the conurbation was about 670 000. A

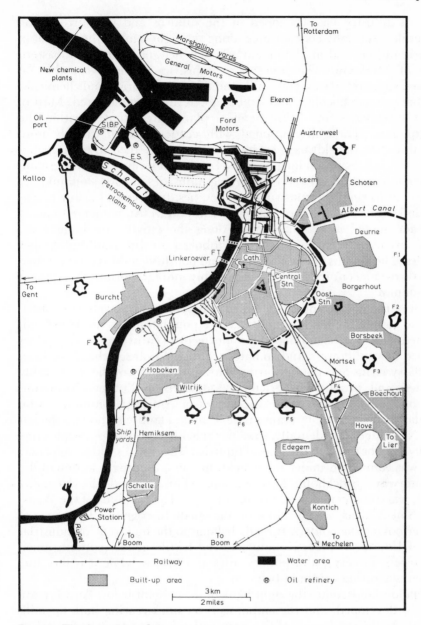

Fig. 4.3. The Antwerp region
Water areas are in black. The two oil refineries marked in the new dock area
are Esso-Standard and SIBP. The world's widest tunnel was completed in
1968 under the Scheldt to take a section of the *E3* (Stockholm–Paris–Lisbon)
motorway. **F,** indicates each of the perimeter forts. **VT,** vehicular tunnel under
the Scheldt; **FT,** foot tunnel. **Cath,** Cathedral.

Based on (*a*) *Kleine Falk von Antwerpen (Falkplan)* (n.d.); (*b*) W. Seghers, *Kaart der bevaarbare Water-
wegen van Belgie en Noord-Frankrijk*, inset plan, 'Antwerpen'; and (*c*) official information.

variety of industry has developed in the suburbs and the surrounding countryside, especially concentrated along the right bank of the Scheldt in Hoboken and beyond in Hemiksem and Schelle, and in the northeastern suburb of Merksem. The usual port industries include vegetable oil refineries, sugar refineries, flour mills and tobacco factories, and chemicals, soap, margarine, chocolate and rubber goods are manufactured. Most of Belgium's refineries and petrochemical plants are situated within the Antwerp area. These are supplied with crude oil both directly from terminals on the Scheldt used by small tankers, and since 1971 through a pipeline 105 km (65 miles) long from the Europoort terminal at Rotterdam. The varied metallurgical and engineering industries include shipbuilding, marine engineering, the construction of cranes, bridges and heavy machinery, and car assembly (Ford, Chrysler and GMC). An immense range of 'consumer goods' is manufactured. Along the estuary are large glass, pottery, brick and cement works. At Hoboken are tin, lead and copper refineries. The famous diamond-cutting and polishing industry, established for a little over a century, is now considerably more important than that of Amsterdam.

Much of the polderland of the *région Anversoise* is intensively cultivated, largely to supply the demands of the city's population. In the Waasland, reclaimed since the beginning of the fourteenth century, market gardens specialise in cauliflowers and tomatoes, and there are orchards of bush fruits, dairy farms and poultry farms. This must be one of the most highly cultivated and productive agricultural districts in Europe. Numerous prosperous looking villages are the homes of Antwerp commuters who travel daily into the city by train to the Tête de Flandre station on the left bank. (No bridges, incidentally, span the Scheldt at Antwerp; people cross either by ferry or through the several tunnels.) The world's widest vehicular tunnel was completed under the Scheldt in 1969, forming a section of the E3 motorway (Stockholm–Paris–Lisbon). This, named the Kennedy Tunnel, was also opened to rail traffic in 1970. The 'capital' of the Waasland is Sint-Niklaas, which stands on the northern edge of a low range of hills overlooking the polders. It really belongs to the hierarchy of industrial towns of Interior Flanders, manufacturing textile goods (cottons, linen, lace, carpets, hosiery), and pottery, tiles and bricks, while it is the chief clog-manufacturing centre in Belgium.

The polderlands along the right bank of the Scheldt below Antwerp are much less developed, and the emphasis is on stock-rearing both for milk and veal. As the sandy soils of the Kempenland are approached, market-gardening becomes more important; a speciality is the cultivation of asparagus. A few small villages are situated mainly on sandy 'islands' above the polders. Only one settlement of any size, Lillo, near one of the old defensive forts around the perimeter of Antwerp, stands near the lonely and rather desolate banks of the Scheldt.

[1] R. Tavernier, 'L'Evolution de la plaine maritime belge', *Bull. Soc. belge Géol.*, **56** (1947), p. 332.

[2] O. Vanneste and G. Declercq, *Le Littoral et son hinterland: essai d'une étude d'économie touristique* (1955).

[3] S. E. Steigenga-Kouwe, *Zeeuws-Vlaanderen* (1950), Publicatie no. 2 uit het Geografisch Instituut der Rijks Universiteit te Utrecht; this is a very full account, with detailed maps.

[4] M. C. Verburg, 'The Gent-Terneuzen development axis in the perspective of the European Economic Community', *Tijdschr. econ. soc. Geogr.*, **55** (1964), pp. 143–50.

[5] R. Havermans, 'Het Waterstaatkundig Landschap in de Antwerpse Noorderpolders', *Bull. Soc. belge Etud. géogr.*, **23** (1954), pp. 59–84.

[6] The balance in each case was handled by rail within the docks area, and is included in the returns 'enregistré par l'administration des douanes'.

[7] M. de Roeck, 'Le Port d'Anvers: situation et problèmes', *Report of the International Geographical Week, Brussels* (1958), pp. 54–9.

# 5
# The Dutch river valleys

The broad alluvium-floored valley of the Rhine distributaries and the closely parallel Maas forms a distinctive region across the southern part of the Netherlands, extending westward from the West German frontier near Nijmegen. Deposition of alluvium in this delta region has been facilitated because the rivers enter the sea in the neighbourhood of a tidal node, an area of limited tidal range.

## The Rhine and its distributaries

The proto-Rhine in immediately preglacial times entered the sea further to the north than at present, by way of the valley of what is now the Eem and through the proto-Zuider Zee (see p. 31). Since then the main Rhine outlets have been gradually displaced further to the south. This tendency was probably initiated by the blocking of the northern outlets by the ice sheets of the third glacial advance (see p. 19), but in postglacial times this has been largely a result of the fact that the tidal range increases southward towards the Strait of Dover. This amounts to only 1·5 m (5 ft) at Texel Gat, increasing to more than 4 m (13 ft) in the Scheldt estuary. The southerly distributaries therefore experience a more rapid fall of water level at low tide than those to the north, which causes an increased scouring action by the ebb tide in collaboration with the river current. Thus the southern outlets have been progressively deepened and widened, and the northern ones (except for the IJssel) have become correspondingly silted up, and reduced to little more than backwaters. In Roman times the main stream flowed westwards along the line of the Kromme Rijn and the Oude Rijn, so reaching the sea to the west of Leiden (Fig. 5.1); this was for long the northern frontier of the Roman Empire, for the main Rhine outflow formed a prominent defensible obstacle. Today the main discharge is by the Waal, the most southerly distributary, which carries three times the volume of the Neder Rijn and six times that of the IJssel.

The Rhine enters the Netherlands from West Germany near Lobith, approximately 160 km (100 miles) from the sea. Its régime is variable as a result of the different contributions of its numerous tributaries; the flow can vary at Lobith from 1 400 cu m (50 000 cu ft) per second to nearly 11 000 cu m (400 000 cu ft). Two periods of high water are experienced, during late autumn and winter, and again in early summer following snow-melt in the Alpine head-streams. Between these maxima, low water occurs in January and February during the winter freeze (which may be very pronounced in central Europe, as in 1947 and 1956), and again in late August–October before the effects of the autumn rains are felt so far down-stream. In the spring of 1972 the Rhine was at its lowest level for many years, the result of an unusually snow-free winter in its headstream area.

The Rhine divides initially a few kilometres within the Netherlands; the main stream continues westwards as the Waal, while a right-bank distributary forms the Neder Rijn. The latter utilises for 16 km (10 miles) an artificial channel cut in 1710 to stabilise the river for navigation, for the Waal at that time was drawing off so much of the flow that the Neder Rijn and IJssel were rapidly silting up. This Pannerdensch Canal was therefore cut to make a more direct connection between the Waal and the Neder Rijn (Fig. 5.2), so avoiding serious flooding.

The Neder Rijn itself sends off from just above Arnhem the circuitous distributary of the IJssel (Plate 10), which wanders casually northeastwards then northwards in a series of meanders, finally entering the IJssel Meer.

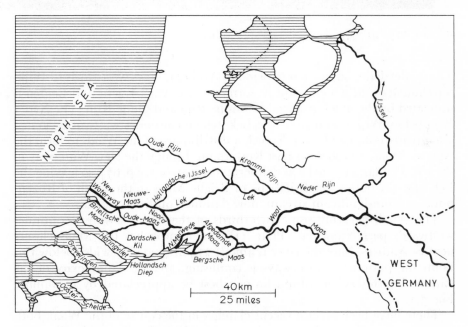

FIG. 5.1. The Rhine-Maas distributaries
The major outer dams, projected or completed, for the Delta Plan are marked (see p. 38).

Based on P. R. Bos and J. F. Niermeyer, *Schoolatlas der Gehele Aaarde* (1936), plates 13–16.

PLATE 10. The Rhine-IJssel divergence near Arnhem

The Neder Rijn, 90 m (300 ft) wide at Arnhem, flows westwards to Wijk-bij-Duurstede, at which point its former course via Utrecht and Leiden is indicated by the much reduced Kromme Rijn and Oude Rijn. The Neder Rijn below Wijk is known as the Lek, which continues westwards, joined and greatly enlarged by the Noord, a distributary of the Waal, to form the Nieuwe Maas, and so flows past Rotterdam through the New Waterway to the sea. This last channel was deliberately created (see p. 67), so leaving the Lek's former outlet, the Briellsche or Brielle Maas to the south of Rozenburg, as an insignificant stream, now dammed off from the sea.

The Waal, carrying some two-thirds of the Rhine's water, continues westwards past Nijmegen (Plate 11) and approaches the Maas closely near St Andries; here the river is almost 275 m (300 yds) wide. Below this point the pattern of waterways is confusing, and the complexity of the various interlinked distributaries can best be appreciated by examining Fig. 5.1.

There have been several recent changes in the course of the Waal, both natural and artificial, the latter designed to check flooding and to improve navigation. The bulk of Waal water now passes through the Nieuwe Merwede, cut in the latter part of the nineteenth century, and so via the Hollandsch Diep and the Haringvliet to the North Sea. Part of the Waal water, however, flows as the Noord to join the Lek and so to form the Nieuwe Maas already mentioned.

## Navigation on the Rhine distributaries

The main artery of navigation through this maze of waterways is the line of the Waal–Merwede–Noord–Nieuwe Maas (Fig. 5.3), focusing on Rotterdam and its outlet to the sea through the New Waterway. No locks are required on this through route, 130 km (80 miles) in length, other than where branch canals enter, and large Rhine barges, drawing 3 m (10 ft) or more and with a freight capacity of up to 4 000 tons, can navigate with ease, while small seagoing steamers can pass up the waterway into West Germany.

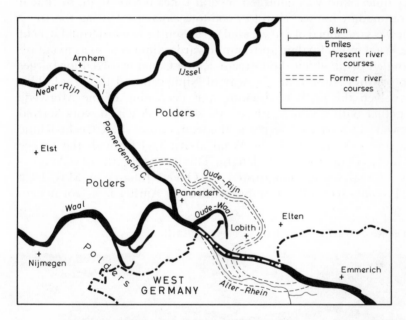

FIG. 5.2. The regularisation of the Rhine near the West German-Dutch frontier

Based on R. Schuiling, *Nederland* (1934), i, facing p. 243.

The Waal is linked at several points with the Maas, since it flows in close proximity to it soon after entering the Netherlands, and the inter-riverine area was for centuries the scene of extensive flooding. The rivers are now separated by massive dykes, and connections have been established where they approach, as at St Andries, where the locks can take 2 000-ton barges. In 1928 the Maas-Waal Canal, just 13 km (8 miles) long, was built to link the Maas at Mook with the Waal below Nijmegen, involving locks at either end which can accommodate 2 000-ton barges. This now forms the most important and direct link between the Maas navigation and Rotterdam.

The Neder Rijn–Lek waterway is far less important than the Waal, although 2 000 ton barges can use it under normal conditions. It joins the Noord a few kilometres above Rotterdam, and so affords direct contact between that port and Arnhem.

A number of minor canals provide links, although somewhat inadequate, between Rotterdam and Amsterdam. For many years the latter has been concerned about a direct connection with the Rhine. For long the only route was by way of the Zuider Zee and the river IJssel, but later connections were developed via Utrecht to the Lek at Vreeswijk, and also via Gouda. The Merwede Canal to Utrecht was enlarged in 1893 and was continued south to the Lek at Vreeswijk as the Utrecht-Rhine Canal, and thence to Gorinchem on the Waal. This waterway had an overall length of 70 km (44 miles) and was enlarged several times before 1939, so that it could accommodate barges of up to 2 000 tons capacity. During the 1930s the project was sanctioned of a new canal to run southeastward from Utrecht to join the Waal much further upstream towards Nijmegen, so as to cut off the rightangled bend which the Utrecht-Rhine Canal involved for barges moving to or from Amsterdam by way of Nijmegen and the Waal. This scheme involved the further widening and deepening of the Merwede Canal, together with a new southeasterly section on which work started before the war. This passes Utrecht to the west, crosses the Utrecht-Rhine Canal and the Lek, and joins the Waal above Tiel through the Prince Bernhard lock, 335 m (1 100 ft) in length. This waterway, the new Amsterdam-Rhine Canal,[1] was inaugurated by Queen Juliana in May 1952 (Fig. 5.3). It is almost exactly the same length as the Amsterdam-Gorinchem

PLATE 11. The River Waal at Nijmegen

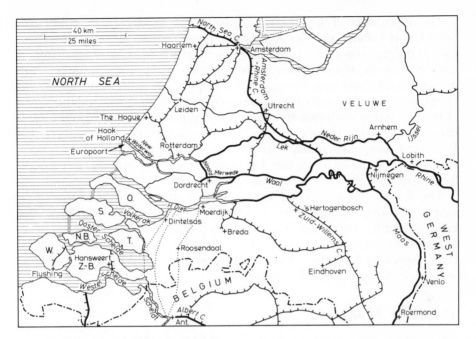

Fig. 5.3. The waterways of the Rhine-Maas estuaries
The links between the Hollandsch Diep and Antwerp which have been contemplated at various times are indicated by dotted lines.[2]
   The abbreviations are as follows: **HDiep,** Hollandsch Diep; **N-B,** Noord-Beveland; **O,** Overflakkee; **S,** Schouwen; **T,** Tholen; **W,** Walcheren; **Z-B,** Zuid-Beveland.

Based on (*a*) R. Schuiling, *Nederland* (1936), ii, 420; and (*b*) W. Seghers, *Kaart der Binnenscheepvaartwegen van Noord-West Europa* (n.d.).

connection, but it shortens the distance between Lobith and Amsterdam by 40 km (25 miles), or by about twenty hours for a barge journey.

   The Rhine and its connections occupy such an important place in Dutch inland navigation that it is useful at this point to summarise the overall picture for the country as a whole. In 1970 the Netherlands' waterways transported 242 million tons of freight. Of this, 90 million tons represent internal movement within the country, or a third of all freight carried by road, rail and water. The Dutch inland fleet consists of over 20 000 barges, of which 1 300 are of over a thousand tons capacity, together with more than 2 000 tugs.

   The situation of the Netherlands relative to the Rhine valley implies that the waterways must play an important part in international traffic. In 1970 about 149 million tons of foreign freight negotiated the Dutch waterways, both imports for Dutch consumption and exports of Dutch produce, together with transit freight which passed along the waterways from one foreign country to another, while the balance involved transhipment at Dutch ports.

The importance of the Rhine navigation is shown by the freight figures recorded at Lobith, the German-Dutch customs post. About 112 million tons of freight passed this point in 1970, of which 64 moved upstream. A large proportion of this upstream traffic consisted of grain, oil, timber, iron ore and other bulk raw materials transhipped at Rotterdam and other Dutch ports for despatch to West Germany, France and Switzerland. Most of the remaining upstream freight originated in Belgian ports, and moved direct to the same three countries. Downstream traffic was mainly from West Germany, particularly coal (some in transit to Belgium and France), steel and manufactured goods for export from Rotterdam, and potash from Alsace for the Dutch chemical industry.

The Rhine makes a second vital contribution to the Netherlands: as a source of water for agricultural, industrial and domestic purposes, and large quantities are abstracted at various points. But increasing pollution has caused growing concern, the result of the accumulation of waste in the river, especially from the potash industry of Alsace and from the chemical and other effluent-producing industries of the Ruhr.

## The river Maas

The river Meuse, having pursued a lengthy course through the scarplands of Lorraine and across the Ardennes, follows the 'coalfield furrow' (pp. 500–3) between Namur and Liège. It flows northwards for about 160 km (100 miles), forming the frontier between Belgium and the Netherlands

PLATE 12. The regularised Maas near Bergharen

from Lanaye to Maasbracht (except in the Maastricht district), and then becomes a wholly Dutch river, the Maas. To the east of the international section lies the plateau of South Limburg, while in the west is the continuous line of the Hesbaye-Kempenland-Peel plateaus. Past changes in the course of the Maas, discussed on pp. 18–19, have resulted in the formation between Liège and Maasbracht of a quite steepsided valley, some 3 km (2 miles) broad and with three distinct terraces on each side (Fig. 6.2). Particularly in the west, this valley edge is pronounced; near Daalgrimbie, for example, the plateau descends prominently from about 90 m (300 ft) to the river terrace at 45 m (150 ft). Further north the plateau-edge becomes progressively less marked and recedes further from the river, although the floodplain is still bordered by low bluffs rising 15 m (50 ft) or so, until the river begins to swing westwards and approach the Rhine. The last feature of any prominence to separate the two valleys is the sandy ridge of the Uilenput (see p. 135), to the south of Nijmegen. At Heumen, near the West German frontier, the Maas, now nearly 200 m (660 ft) in width, is at only 9 m (30 ft) above sea level, and as a result, it meanders across its floodplain towards the sea. The seasonal variation in volume in its lower course is very marked. The river finally reaches the Hollandsch Diep through the Bergsche Maas, cut in the latter part of the nineteenth century to form a direct outlet distinct from that of the Waal just to the north.

## Navigation on the Maas

While the Rhine is of course the premier waterway artery of the Netherlands, the Maas is of importance, particularly for the south of the country.[3] The improvement of navigation downstream from Maastricht obviously assists the economic development of South Limburg, which is rather remote from the rest of the country, and was formerly valuable for the exploitation of the coalfield there (Fig. 8.3).

The regularisation of the Maas, both to improve navigation and to assist in flood control, is a long story. The river is now contained between massive embankments, several large meanders have been cut through, and five locked barrages have been built to stabilise depths for navigation. The Rhine and the Maas below Mook were separated by dykes, with links via the Maas-Waal Canal and the St Andries lock already mentioned. The outcome of these schemes, completed just before the war of 1939–45, was to make the Maas navigable for vessels of at least 1 500 tons, and as a result of postwar dredging and further improvement the river can now be negotiated by 2 000-ton barges.

It will be appreciated, however, that these measures were concerned with the Maas below Maasbracht, where it becomes wholly a Dutch river. From Lanaye to Maasbracht, with the exception of the short stretch through the city of Maastricht (Fig. 8.3), the frontier runs along the centre of the river, which meanders through its valley, its course impeded by

gravelbanks and sandbanks, islets and backwaters. With Belgian un-
willingness to undertake any joint scheme of regularisation, unilateral
action by the Netherlands to improve the river was impossible. The solution from the Dutch point of view was the construction of the lateral Juliana
Canal along the right bank, wholly in Dutch territory, between Maastricht

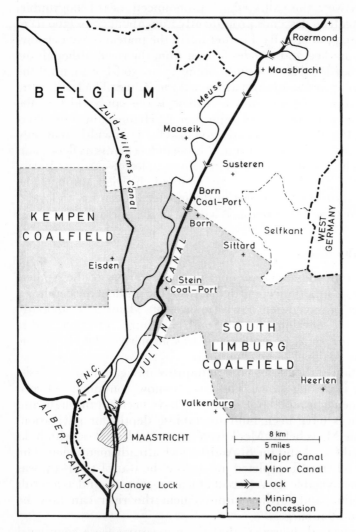

FIG. 5.4. The Juliana Canal
**BNC,** Briegden-Neerharen Branch Canal.
   *Note.* The Selfkant was returned to West Germany in 1963 by
the treaty of 8 April 1960.

Based on W. Seghers, *Kaart der Binnenscheepvaartwegen van Noord-West Europa* (n.d.).

and Maasbracht (Fig. 5.4), while the Belgian solution was the construction of the Albert Canal (see pp. 128–31). The portion of international river between Maastricht and Maasbracht has therefore remained virtually unnavigable.

The Juliana Canal leaves the Maas in the northern suburbs of Maastricht (Fig. 6.9). The river is canalised within the city and lined with quays, but it ceases to be navigable below the barrage at the point where the canal takes off, a barrage designed to keep the depth uniform within Maastricht. The Juliana Canal is 34 km (21 miles) in length, and the fall in level of 14 m (45 ft) is accommodated by four locks. The canal has an overall width at water level of 46 m (152 ft) with a bottom width of just over 15 m (50 ft) and a depth of 5 m (16·5 ft); it can accommodate 2 000 ton barges. Apart from the river-port of Maastricht and two basins opening off the canal at Maasbracht, two canal ports were constructed specifically to serve the South Limburg coalfield (see pp. 174–8). The canal was completed and opened in 1936.[4] It carries annually about 15 million tons of freight, of which a fifth formerly consisted of coal, and nearly half of building materials (cement, bricks, stone).

## The river polders

Most of the Rhine-Maas distributary pattern is now constrained within regularised channels, since this rectification is intimately bound up with the interrelated problems of navigation, already discussed, and of flood control. The gradients of the rivers are slight, and they therefore tend if uncontrolled to wander across the plain, depositing vast quantities of alluvium and fine sand. Gradually their beds have been raised above the surrounding country, a dangerous state of affairs made worse by the slight sinking of this adjacent land as a result of drainage and compaction. It has long been necessary therefore to create defences along the river banks against flooding, and there seem to have been small dykes as early as the eighth century, which were progressively enlarged and strengthened. Slowly other improvements were effected; meanders were cut off, groynes and training walls were built, and major rectifications of the actual course. But floods continued to be a menace because technical skill was inadequate to build unbreachable dykes against the tremendous volume of floodwaters which both rivers can bring down. Selected sections of dyke were therefore kept deliberately weaker or lower than the rest, through which floodwaters could escape into reserved areas which acted as temporary reservoirs, and so relieve the pressure on the dykes protecting lands further downstream.

Sometimes an exceptional river flood would far exceed the bounds of these storage areas, causing widespread destruction and loss of life. The most serious floods resulted from the proximity of the Waal and the Maas, especially in the neighbourhood of Heerewaarden, where the two rivers are only 300 m apart. As the Waal with its larger volume and greater powers of sedimentation has a higher bed, in times of flood its water flowed into the inter-riverine area and then into the Maas. But usually that river was also in flood, and thus not only were the inter-riverine lands inundated but the flow of the Maas was obstructed, and so floods backed far up the valley. This happened so frequently that large areas of formerly fertile river clays degenerated into sour swampland, useful only as temporary pasture.

From 1880 a long programme of river works was put into effect. The Maas and the Waal were separated by an enormous dyke. When the Bergsche Maas was cut as a direct outlet for the Maas, the former course of the river lower down was sealed off except for locks at either end. After the floods of 1926–27, when the Maas dykes burst in several places and the inter-riverine area was widely flooded, a further programme of works was undertaken, already described. The scheme was completed by 1939, and the menace of Maas floods has been virtually removed.

The Rhine distributaries are dyked along almost their whole length westward from the Dutch frontier, except near Arnhem where the sandy uplands of the southern Veluwe come close to the north bank of the Neder Rijn (see pp. 135–7). The Maas is also dyked along both banks below Grave, and along the right bank upstream for a further 15 km (10 miles) to Mook.

Much of the land between or adjacent to these rivers would be liable to inundation without this protection. Indeed, west of a line from Utrecht to Gorinchem the rivers flow through country below NAP, which would be inundated anyway without the sea dykes. East of this line to about the Amsterdam-Rhine Canal, the surrounding land is well below even the mean summer level of the rivers, and further east again the land, though higher, is still below the level of winter floods. Between the main river dykes themselves lies a considerable extent of land, for they are necessarily built well back from the summer channels; these lateral strips are usually inundated in winter, but afford summer pastures. Outside the main dykes are the river polders, enclosed units wherein pumping may be either occasionally or continuously necessary to remove excess water.

## Land use

These polders are covered with river clays and occasional patches of gravel and coarse sands. The soils derived from these riverine materials are not generally as good as from the marine clays, since the alluvium tends to be damp and often rather sour, the result of constant infiltration of water. Between 50 and 80 per cent of these valley lands are therefore under permanent pasture, and an even higher proportion is found to the south of Utrecht. This is therefore a predominantly dairying area, though further east, where the land is rather higher and a low watertable can be maintained, mixed farming becomes more important (Plate 13).

Since the war of 1939–45 increasing attention has been paid to these low-lying areas of damp river clays; they are known generally as *Komgrondenge-bieden* (basin soil districts). Because of the damp, rather sour soils and also because of isolation due to the absence of roads and railways and the stretches of unbridged rivers, they have long constituted areas of agricultural underdevelopment. Since 1945 the state has carried out schemes of drainage, installed pumping stations, provided financial help and advice for colonists, and fostered programmes of research. The work was furthered in 1953 by the creation of the *Stichting tot Ontwikkeling van Komgrondengebieden* (Foundation for basin soil districts) as a coordinating and stimulating organisation. It supervises the work of local committees, encourages cultural and social activities, assists in the building of farms, and maintains a 'groundwater level research establishment'. Between 1945 and 1968 about 33 000 ha (80 000 acres) were opened up and divided into holdings, and work is in progress on a further 10 000 ha (24 000 acres). [5]

The most prosperous of the inter-riverine alluvial areas lies between Arnhem and Nijmegen, the *Over-Betuwe*, usually known simply as the *Betuwe* or 'the good land'. This is the chief orchard district in the Netherlands, with many trees growing in grassy meadows, and extensive market gardens.

The alluvial valleys include the long narrow floodplain of the IJssel, enclosed by the sandy heathlands of Overijssel on the east and by the prominent edge of the sand country of the Veluwe on the west. The IJssel wanders through its floodplain between dykes along much of its course. The Vecht, flowing from West Germany, approaches within 14 km (9 miles) of the lower IJssel, then swings away northwards to make a separate entry into the IJssel Meer by way of a narrow stretch of water deliberately left between the Northeast and East polders (Fig. 3.8). Several small river polders in the lower IJssel valley are below NAP. The IJssel valley is mainly under pasture, with dairying and pig-rearing, and some orchards.

## Settlement and towns

The interfluvial lands are not densely populated in comparison with many parts of the Netherlands, for the liability to flooding has precluded much settlement except for a few towns on locally favoured sites. Such places as Heusden and 's Hertogenbosch are placed several kilometres away from the river, on the edge of the floodplain. Even in the Betuwe there are few settlements of any size; Elst is a pleasant little town right in the centre, with a market and various fruit-preserving industries, and a few more villages are set among the orchards. Tiel, an old town on the north bank of the Waal, had some commercial importance in the Middle Ages, and today has several jam-making and fruit-preserving factories. [6] Lower downstream is Gorinchem, another old town with a varied history; it was one of the first places to be captured by the 'Water Beggars' in 1572. Its old patterned brick and stone houses and fortified gateways, and its long-established cattle market, contrast strikingly with modern factories which make glucose and mustard, refine sugar, and preserve fruit.

The two main towns of this central alluvial valley are Arnhem on the northern banks of the Neder Rijn, and Nijmegen on the southern side of the Waal. They stand opposite to each other, 16 km (10 miles) apart, on the outer edges of the floodplain, where the Veluwe hills and the Uilenput ridge respectively (Fig. 2.2) afford firm sites. Both towns have grown outwards and upwards on to the slopes of these hills. Arnhem, the capital of Gelderland, and an important route centre, had a population of 133 000 in 1969. Its position has always made it of strategic importance, right down to the closing stages of the war of 1939–45, when desperate attempts were made by Allied airborne troops to secure the river-crossing, in conjunction with similar attempts at Nijmegen. Arnhem has become a prosperous commercial town with large markets, and is an important industrial centre with a variety of manufactures—rayon, rubber, pharmaceutical chemicals, clothing, light metallurgical work, barges and rivercraft. It has a tin-smelting plant, which smelts about a fifth of the world's output.

Nijmegen (149 000 people) is also an important route centre, and its river port on the Waal (Plate 11), served also by the Maas-Waal Canal from the south, handles over a million tons of freight each year. It too has a varied industrial life, including the manufacture of electrical apparatus, light engineering products, tungsten wire, rayon, river craft, chemicals and food products. The town is also the centre of a considerable brick-making activity. The bricks are made from the alluvial clays; many of the claypits are worked only in summer, for they are inundated in winter. Coal for the kilns is brought by water from the Ruhr. An atomic power station, of 50 mW capacity, was completed in 1968.

The IJssel valley stands out as a strip of denser population by comparison with the heathlands on either side. Some towns are actually on the river banks, and have been trading ports for centuries, such as Zutphen, Deventer and Kampen. The port of Deventer was once easily accessible to seagoing ships, and the *Handelshaven* is still there, although but little used. Today it is a prosperous town with cotton and flour mills, a chemical works, and some light engineering factories. Lower down the valley is Zwolle,[7] the capital of Overijssel, which stands on slightly higher ground between the IJssel and the Vecht, here only 14 km (9 miles) apart. Zwolle is an important railway centre and market town, and retains much of its old world charm, with the old town surrounded by a broad tree-lined moat. The lowest town along the valley is Kampen, on the left bank of the IJssel some 6 km (4 miles) above its entry into the short arm of the IJssel Meer between the two big polders. It was once a member of the Hanseatic League, and in the fifteenth century it was a thriving port before the harbour silted up. It too retains much of its old interest, with a moat and several fine gateways, and is now a quiet market town.

A second important line of towns in the IJssel valley is strung out where the western edge of the floodplain meets the eastern slope of the Veluwe; the largest is Apeldoorn (124 000 people). These towns have manufactured paper for centuries, and today Apeldoorn and Renkum have large modern paper mills. Apeldoorn itself is a prosperous residential town; near by is the royal summer palace of Het Loo.

## The Geldersche Vallei

The Geldersche Vallei forms a low trough between the Utrecht-Gelderland ridge on the west and the hills of the Neder-Veluwe on the east. It is not, however, strictly an alluvial valley, although it contains numerous streams, and was probably occupied by a small tongue of ice when the continental ice sheet was at its maximum (see p. 19). Except in the north, where there are clays, most of its soils are either sandy or peaty. The depression forms a link between the floodplain of the Rhine and the southern shores of the IJssel Meer. It approaches the Rhine floodplain near Wageningen on the Neder Rijn, although the river is carefully shut off from the Vallei by a large dyke. The northern part is drained by a series of streams coming from the Veluwe, and coalescing near Amersfoort to form the river Eem. The whole area is low-lying; although oddly enough the plain north of Amersfoort is known as the Hoogland, this is only in comparison with the lands bordering the IJssel Meer, which are well below NAP and were formerly subject to flooding. A dyke now borders the IJssel Meer coast; with the completion of the South Polder, a ring canal between the dykes now separates it from the Vallei.

About 60 per cent of the area of the Vallei is under permanent pasture, and it is a prosperous dairying and pig-rearing district. It is not very densely populated; there are scattered farms and a number of villages. Baarn, in the west of the Vallei, is the centre of a large-scale poultry-farming activity. The only town of any size is Amersfoort, the market centre for the district, a focus of railway routes rounding the southern end of the IJssel Meer, and an industrial town with small metallurgical manufactures and textile mills. An assembly plant for the British Leyland company has been opened there.

---

[1] W. H. Brinkhorst, 'Het Amsterdam-Rijnkanaal', *Tijdschr. K. ned. aardrijksk. Genoot.*, **69** (1952), pp. 285–99.

[2] R. Tausma, 'The projected Antwerpen-Rhine canal', *Tijdschr. econ. soc. Geogr.*, **55** (1964), pp. 150–64.

[3] C. F. Egelie, 'De Problemen van de Scheepvaartwegen in het Gebied de Maas', *Tijdschr. K. ned. aardrijksk. Genoot.*, **71** (1954), pp. 321–38; this deals with the navigation of the Maas and the Rhine connections, and provides a detailed map.

[4] F. J. Monkhouse, 'Albert and Juliana: two great waterways', *Scottish Geographical Magazine*, **72** (1956), pp. 163–76.

[5] J. A. C. van Burg, 'Komgrondengebied in Ontwikkeling', *Tijdschr. K. ned. aardrijksk. Genoot.*, **73** (1956), pp. 49–65; this provides numerous detailed maps and a number of plates.

See also A. M. Lambert, 'Farm consolidation and improvement in the Netherlands: an example from the Land van Maas en Waal', *Econ. Geogr.*, **37** (1961), pp. 115–23.

⁶ J. Visscher, 'Tiel als Streekcentrum', *Tijdschr. econ. soc. Geogr.*, **42** (1951), pp. 136–42.

⁷ K. Dekker, 'Zwolle: ritme en functie van een middelgrote Stad', *Tijdschr. econ. soc. Geogr.*, **53** (1962), pp. 57–61.

# 6
# The heathlands of Belgium and the Netherlands

## General features

Heathlands occupy much of the North European Plain, extending in a broad belt from the basin of the middle Oder to northeastern Belgium. Though differing in detail, these heathlands have many features in common: poor leached soils developed on superficial sheets of sand and gravel; a considerable extent of bare sand, often blown into dunes; a vegetation cover of the characteristic heath associations, notably the dominant ling (*Calluna vulgaris*); and in the higher bleaker parts extensive tracts of moorland which have developed where waterlogging has been caused by an underlying impervious layer. Reclamation and improvement have progressed slowly; some parts now carry conifer plantations, while other areas provide either reasonably useful and carefully fostered pastures or rather poor arable land on which is grown rye, potatoes and sugar beet. But the extent of unreclaimed heath is still considerable.

The sheets of sand and gravel on which the heathlands have developed are of two different types. Those which occur to the north and east of the Rhine-Maas valley across the south-central Netherlands are of glacial or fluvioglacial origin. Sheets of sands and gravel, occasional erratics, patches of till and much-dissected morainic ridges occur in eastern Friesland, southern Groningen, Drenthe, Overijssel and eastern Gelderland (Fig. 6.1). The West German–Dutch frontier runs southward through their eastern parts, and on either side the name Bourtanger Moor (Moer) is applied. Between the IJssel valley and the IJssel Meer lies the sandy region of the Veluwe, with the narrow Gooiland ridge further to the southwest. The Hettenheuvel-Montferland hills form two small detached heathlands between the Rhine and the valley of the Lijmers, and a small patch, called the Uilenput after its highest point, straddles the frontier in the acute angle between the Waal and the Maas.

Lying across the Belgo-Dutch frontier and extending southward for 110 km (70 miles) between the valleys of the lower Maas and the Demer, is another continuous area of heathland—Noord-Brabant and northern Limburg in the Netherlands, and the Kempen (in French *la Campine*) in Belgium.[1] The sands and gravels upon which these have developed are,

FIG. 6.1. The heathlands of western Europe
The areas of heathland are derived from various geological and land use
maps, and from plotting in the field.
**H,** Hettenheuvel; **M,** Montferland. The southern limit of the Quaternary
glaciation is marked only in the Netherlands.

however, of fluvial origin, laid down by the immediately postglacial
Meuse, vastly swollen in volume and bearing an immense load of coarse
sand and gravel (see pp. 18–19 and Fig. 6.2).

## The character of the heathlands

The surface features of the heathlands are dominated by sheets of sand,
diversified by intercalated layers and occasional superficial patches of
gravel, a thin veneer of alluvium in the valley floors, and some peat in the

higher depressions. Because of the extremely permeable nature of these sands, surface streams are usually absent, and the watertable occurs at some depth except where an impervious pan causes waterlogging. The podsol-type soils developed on the sands are dry, partly because of their low waterholding capacity and partly because they are subject to rapid

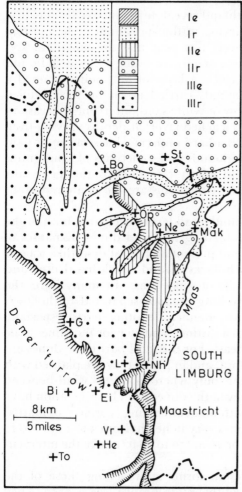

FIG. 6.2. The terraces of the Lower Meuse Valley
The abbreviations *Ie* to *IIIr* are explained on pp. 18–19. Commune centres are indicated as follows: **Bi,** Bilzen; **Bo,** Bocholt; **Ei,** Eigenbilzen; **G,** Genk; **He,** Herderen; **L,** Lanaken; **Mak,** Maaseik; **Ne,** Neeroeteren; **Nh,** Neerhaven; **Op,** Opitter; **St,** Stamproy; **To,** Tongeren; **Vr,** Vronhoven.
 The international frontier is indicated by a heavy pecked line, except where it follows the river Meuse (Maas). Only the left-bank terraces are shown.

Based on M. A. Lefèvre, 'La Basse-Meuse: étude de morphologie fluviale', *Soc. belge Etud. géogr., Mémoire I* (1935).

evaporation from their friable surface. They suffer constant leaching from the swiftly percolating rainwater, and this results in the removal of the soluble bases, particularly calcium; the soils are thus deficient in nutrients and lack fertility. Only a small amount of humus forms, derived from the matted fibrous remains of mosses, lichens and woody heath plants, and as this is not neutralised it remains highly acid in character.

The typical soil profile of the heathland reveals first a surface layer of dry, compact and rather acid peat,[2] varying in thickness from 25 to 200 mm (1 to 8 in); in depressions, however, this peat may be much thicker, forming a dark layer of a metre or so (2 or 3 ft) consisting of raw acid humus mixed with some silt. Below the peat is a layer of sand, often stained a chocolate colour by humus compounds carried down by the acidified rainwater, and this passes into yellow or white sand, interrupted occasionally by layers of pebbles. Below this leached layer, at depths varying from 700 mm to a metre (18 in to 1 yd), is a hard impermeable stratum or pan, sometimes consisting of humus compounds and sometimes of sand grains or gravel stained reddish-brown and solidly cemented by the ferric salts deposited from percolating solutions. Under this are the unaltered sands and gravels.

The surface sand layer is to be found at all levels, occurring both in the form of extensive sheets and as undulating hills and dunes. Expanses of yellow, dazzling white or greyish sand present an almost desertlike aspect, level but for wind-ripples and tiny hillocks of sand which has drifted and accumulated around occasional tufts of spiky grass. In many parts the sand has accumulated into low swelling mounds separated by hollows, arranged in a confused and chaotic manner. In other parts, especially on the exposed higher areas, there is a distinct tendency for the dunes to be orientated from southwest to northeast. For the most part these dunes are fixed with coarse grass and heath flora, and in places they are planted with conifers, so that surface sand appears only where footpaths wind between the dunes. Occasionally, however, even the dunes fixed by vegetation have one side of bare sand, sometimes with an overhanging 'cornice' of matted ling and grass roots. These fixed dunes vary in height from 3 to 12 m (10 to 40 ft) and exceptionally even to 15 or 20 m (50 to 70 ft) above the intervening hollows.

In places the sand accumulates in forms approaching those of the migratory dunes of the Landes in southwestern France (see p. 355). They display a grouping in long interconnected trails, with the axis of each dune more or less at right angles to the prevailing winds, and with curving, almost crescentic, 'wings'. The horizontal movement is not great, because the unvegetated and therefore 'unfixed' areas are small in extent. The movement of the sand is within the dune area itself: the wind piles up, destroys, levels and hollows out, producing a chaotic and ever-changing relief. On the open windswept plateaus the sand is in constant motion where there is no fixation by vegetation. Many of these dune areas owe their existence to the direct or indirect influence of man in the past: to the clearance of woodland, to the overgrazing of heath, to the lowering of the water-table as a result of the draining of intervening hollows and valleys, and to the excavation of sand and gravel.

On these sands occur heathlands, given the name of *heide* in both Belgium and the Netherlands, although in the former the terms *heyde*, *bruyères* and *landes* are also used. The rainfall totals in these areas range from about 600 to 750 mm (24 to 30 in). It is true that the sandy permeable soils and the frequent strong winds on the exposed plateaus considerably reduce the 'effective total' of the rainfall, with the result that the heathlands are colonised in the unreclaimed and unimproved parts mainly by plants with xerophytic characters, capable of withstanding these conditions.

These rainfall totals are, however, sufficient to support tree growth, and it seems that the present heathland has resulted from the destruction or degeneration of former woodland; the dominant trees probably comprised oak, birch and hornbeam. Medieval texts, old maps and place names containing woodland elements[3] bear evidence to the former extensive woodlands in the present heath areas of both Belgium and the Netherlands, and botanists by pollen analysis of peats and by the examination of surviving patches of woodland plants support this evidence. But large clearance schemes by religious houses, the slow but gradual widening of the perimeter of arable land and of pasture around the villages in the valleys, and the wholesale cutting for fuel by the armies which repeatedly fought over the Low Countries, all took their toll. Once the woodland had been cleared, natural regeneration became increasingly difficult, for clearance allowed the rapid destruction of the mild humus which forms under deciduous woodland and its replacement by a thin acid layer in which heathland associations flourish. Further, regeneration was often prevented by the grazing of sheep, goats and rodents which destroyed the young seedlings. Another adverse factor was the development of the 'hard-pan' layer, which forms readily when the soil has been deprived of its protective deciduous cover and cannot easily be penetrated by the roots of young trees. Perhaps the highest and bleakest parts, over 75 or 90 m (250 or 300 ft), where the soils are exceptionally poor and the surface is much exposed to strong winds, have never been wooded; it is possible therefore that the high heathland is primitive and is the natural type of plant community developed on these soils under the particular climatic conditions. But in most areas the heathlands are the result of the destruction of a former woodland cover.

It is not easy to describe the heathlands in general terms, since their aspect varies considerably from place to place as the plant associations change. The most characteristic feature is the dominance of ling. The growth is usually close, but even with old woody and 'leggy' plants the height of the layer is rarely over 450 or 600 mm (18 or 24 in). In spring there are tints of pale green with the new growth, in autumn tones of deep purple or sepia, but after a widespread fire (a common occurrence, both deliberate and accidental) whole tracts are of unrelieved black or grey. One can walk for kilometres across these heathlands, their dreariness and monotony relieved only by pine plantations, occasional meres, and the apparently rather aimless paths and tracks. While ling is overwhelmingly dominant, several other layers can be distinguished—bilberry, dwarf gorse, mosses and lichens.

A more varied type of vegetation, known as 'mixed heath', is found locally among the ling. *Erica cinerea*, or purple bell-heather, sometimes occurs, and on sunny slopes it forms considerable stretches of colourful landscape which contrasts with the sombre ling. In the damper areas, as in shallow depressions, the cross-leaved heath (*Erica tetralix*) is common. A group of species characterised by their tolerance of high soil acidity, by some degree of adaptation to summer drought, and by a very low demand on plant nutrients in the soil, includes broom, dwarf whin, juniper and gorse. The bracken fern is not a true heath plant but it does occur in some places, and there are extensive thickets of brambles.

Over many parts a more open heath is found, especially where constant burning or grazing has kept the ling from full development. These grass heaths occur beyond the arable lands and improved pastures around the villages, where the ling, frequently fired, sometimes grazed, sometimes cut for litter, has retreated. True heath plants are much less numerous, and are replaced by heath-grasses, notably *Agrostis* sp., *Festuca* sp. and wavy hair grass (*Deschampsia flexuosa*), growing in low clumps or tufts separated by bare sand, or sometimes forming a more or less continuous turf carpet.

Scattered silver birch grow sporadically among the grass-heaths and even occasionally in the *Calluna* heath; sometimes they are so numerous and continuous as to be called birch woods. In the lower heathlands, particularly on the valley margins, the birch grows in association with dwarf oak and other deciduous trees, and sometimes such tracts justify the name 'oak-birch heath'. Scrubby woodlands of dwarf oak, willow, hazel, alder and ash may form a dense layer 2 m (6 ft) or so in height, often interlaced with brambles, while the slender trunks of the silver birch rise 4 to 6 metres (15 to 20 ft) above the thicket. Here and there are isolated conifers, sub-spontaneously spreading from neighbouring plantations. Occasionally, too, dwarf oaks form continuous thickets, with an associated shrub layer which includes broom, buckthorn, bilberry and bracken.

A characteristic feature of the heathlands is the large number of small lakes and meres, some on the alluvial floors of shallow valleys, others in depressions on the higher parts of the plateaus. They consist of irregular sheets of shallow water which vary in extent with the rainfall, except where they have been artificially restrained by embankments. In the damp depressions around these lakes, aquatic and heath communities come into close juxtaposition. In addition, the broad, gently sloping valleys contain swampy areas; the lines of the streams and the ditches leading into them are indicated by reeds, alders and willows.

In many parts appear extensive areas of what can be called generally 'wet heath': these are known as *Moeren* or *Gooren* in Belgium, and as *Hoogveen* or *Moeren* in the Netherlands.[4] The vegetation associated with them suggests a transition between heathland and aquatic communities. In the waterlogged hollows are found *Carex* sp., *Phragmites* sp. and sometimes alders, then comes the wet heath dominated by the blue moor grass (*Molinia coerulea*), with the crossleaved heath (*Erica tetralix*), and higher still the drier grass-heath with patches of ling.

On the higher parts, at altitudes exceeding 75 m (250 ft), are to be found small areas of true peat-bog, akin to the *Hochmooren* of Germany and the Pennine 'Mosses'. They occur in the higher parts of the northeast Kempenland, in the Peel district of Dutch Limburg, in the Bourtanger Moer, and in other parts of the eastern Dutch heathlands. Even though the soil is sandy and highly permeable, the upland hollows become waterlogged because the hardpan is well developed and the drainage on the indeterminate watersheds is so poor that much surface water remains stagnant. The bog is closely related to the heath which surrounds it, for it has the same poverty of mineral nutrients and the same high acidity; the difference is that its surface is permanently damp while the true heath is mostly dry. The characteristic plant association comprises blue moor grass, which often occurs in great tussocks, *Sphagnum* and other bog-mosses, cotton grass and heath rushes. Considerable thicknesses of highly acid and nutrient-poor peats develop in these hollows. These form the bleaker parts of the upland heaths, and can properly be termed 'moors'.

It is probable, however, that the bog peat covering in the higher sandy areas of both Belgium and the Netherlands was formed under conditions of higher rainfall after the end of the last phase of the Quaternary glaciation. There is now, it seems, enough rainfall for them to maintain themselves if undisturbed, but the present summers are too dry for the *sphagnum* mosses to develop to any extent. The more accessible areas have been drained, the peat cut and used for fuel, and the underlying sands reclaimed for agriculture, and so the bogs have been reduced to mere fragments of their former extent.

## Reclamation of the heathlands

The reclamation of the heathlands in both Belgium and the Netherlands has proceeded for many centuries; records date back to the twelfth century describing attempts mainly by the religious houses. Throughout the centuries the perimeter of cultivated land around each isolated heathland village was pushed outwards. Occasionally official stimulus was applied, notably in Belgium in the sixteenth century, when grants of land were made to individuals on condition that these areas were cleared of heath and made productive, and again in the eighteenth century during the reign of the Empress Maria-Theresa.

In both countries the farmers in the small scattered communities pursued a way of life which enabled them to win a meagre subsistence from their limited environment. They owned strips of improved arable land on which were grown crops of rye, potatoes and buckwheat, and patches of enclosed valley pasture. In addition they exploited in various ways the neighbouring common heathlands. These heathland common rights included the grazing of sheep and the cutting of turves and ling. The last was of considerable value, for when dried it provided litter for the stock; the young shoots were browsed by large flocks of sheep; the woody stems and roots served as fuel, valuable in a largely treeless region for they were burnt with dried peaty clods dug from the wet heaths or bogs; and the stalks were chopped and mixed with mud for the lath-and-daub method of cottage construction.

Efforts were made to improve the sandy soils for cultivation by the use of compost and dung provided by the animals, the development of various crop rotations, and occasionally the development of simple irrigation systems to improve the meadows where the village lay near a river. But these schemes of improvement were of a small-scale nature, compared with the area of heathland which remained virtually untouched except in the immediate neighbourhood of the villages. In fact, in both countries the opposition to government edicts which aimed at furthering any large-scale schemes by external interests was considerable, for the communes jealously guarded the common rights on the heathlands.

In the latter half of the nineteenth century, however, both Belgium and the Netherlands included in their programmes of economic development a great increase in the extent of agriculturally productive land in order to help meet the demands of their growing populations. A law was passed in Belgium in 1847, for example, by which the state was authorised to order the compulsory sale of unimproved communal heathlands. The new occupant was granted a reduction or even complete remission of taxes and tithes, in return for which he was obliged to convert the waste into arable land or pasture. As a result, many communes themselves embarked on policies of improvement in order to avoid losing their lands, and there was considerable state encouragement and financial help by way of technical assistance and interest-free loans. In the Netherlands particularly, co-operative organisations developed. In 1888 the *Nederlandsche Heidemaatschappij* (the Dutch Heath Society) was founded. Helped by the government, it serves as a distributor of financial assistance, carries out reclamation schemes and leases the land to approved tenants, furthers research projects and disseminates information about their results. The Belgian Ministry of Agriculture, at its *Station de l'Etat pour l'Amélioration des Plantes* at Melle, sponsors research into mixtures of grass seed suitable for dry sandy soils—quick-growing, drought-resistant and with tenacious binding roots.[5]

In the Netherlands much reclamation has taken place in the high peat moors, the stimulus coming sometimes from cities such as Groningen, from individual communes and from private companies. Groningen started reclamation as long ago as the sixteenth century, when its citizens began to remove peat from the surrounding moorlands for fuel, using canals to transport it to the city. When the peat had been stripped off, agricultural settlements, known as *veenkoloniën*, were established. Manure from the flocks and herds and garbage from the cities were dug in, and in the nineteenth century cheap chemical fertilisers, mainly from Germany, were used. In the northeastern moorlands these reclaimed lands are now growing potatoes, rye and oats, mainly for industrial purposes; factories making starch, glucose and strawboard have been established.

Irrigation schemes have been tried in both countries to improve the dry soils for both horticulture and pasture, and at the present time irrigation is still used in a limited way. In some of the market-gardening areas along the southern margins of the Kempenland water is taken from navigation canals; near Herentals, for example, smallholdings and market gardens are supplied with water from a short cul-de-sac off the Herentals-Bocholt Canal. Many of the meadowlands in the shallow valleys within the heathlands are intersected with ditches which serve as drains in winter and as irrigation channels in summer. In dry summers the efficacy of these systems is particularly noticeable by the contrast between the brown heathland beyond the irrigated area and the green meadows. These areas are supplied with water by gravity from streams and canals. But the higher heathlands, where improvement is most needed, cannot be irrigated because of the absence of streams on the plateau surfaces, and the area improved is only a small proportion of the total extent.

Some of the sandy heath, then, has been improved for arable farming, particularly in the Netherlands. In Belgium, however, during the last century there has been little overall increase in the arable area; most communes in fact show a decrease. This is not because heathland has not been improved, but because the nature of the farming system in the Kempenland as a whole has changed. Under the influence of the nearby markets offered by Antwerp, Mechelen, Brussels and other towns in central Belgium, the emphasis is now on cattle-keeping for milk and veal, and the area of permanent pasture has been greatly increased at the expense of cereals. What arable land remains either consists of intensively cultivated market gardens along the heathland margins or is under fodder crops.

The establishment of plantations of soft woods often affords the most profitable, sometimes the only possible, utilisation of tracts of sandy soil, and also helps to meet the increasing demand for constructional timber, pit props and pulpwood. Extensive planting has been carried out in the higher eastern parts of the Kempenland and in the Veluwe by the respective states, the communes, various public bodies and private individuals. In the Belgian province of Limburg, for example, the proportion of communally owned woodland forms about one-third of the total. This is the most profitable way in which the communes have been able to make the heathlands contribute to their revenues, especially as the state assists them in the costs of clearing and of planting. As a result, one of the most characteristic, if alien, features of the heathland landscape is the frequent occurrence in plantations of stands of Scots pine and occasionally of Corsican pine. These trees have the advantage of attaining maturity within thirty or forty years. They are usually planted in long straight lines forming square or rectangular blocks intersected by rides. Only occasionally do these conifers occur less formally; a few scattered pines have colonised adjacent oak-birch heath, and here and there clumps of trees have been planted in the dune areas to assist their stability, or for shelter and decorative purposes in the vicinity of collieries, factories and housing estates. About one-sixth of the Belgian heathlands have been planted with conifers, about twice as much as the proportion in the Netherlands.

Finally, it must not be forgotten that other changes have taken place in the heathland landscape. Villages and towns have grown up, factories have been built, and roads and railways now link formerly isolated settlements. Most significant of all, the Kempenland is underlain by exploitable deposits of coal, and it has become a considerable industrial area. Industrial developments have not been as prominent in the Dutch heathlands. Coal has been located under the Peel at depths exceeding 900 m (3 000 ft), and also further north in Gelderland, but it is unlikely that there will ever be any exploitation. Some factories have been built in the Dutch heathlands, mainly for processing agricultural produce; occasional interesting introductions include the cotton textile industry of a group of towns in the Twente area of central Overijssel.

The individual heathlands are numbered on Fig. 2.7 from 4a to 4f.

## The Kempenland

This area of heathland extends westward for about 100 km (60 miles) from the steep slope overlooking the Meuse valley to the reclaimed polders around the Scheldt estuary. The southern boundary is indicated by the line of the rivers Rupel, lower Dyle and Demer, while the heathlands continue northward to the Dutch frontier. The main features of the Kempenland relief may be described under three headings: the plateau, the plateau edge and the plain.

The Kempen plateau is demarcated more or less by the 50-m (160-ft) contour, although much of the eastern part exceeds 75 m (250 ft), and in the extreme south, where the Kempen is linked to the plateau of Hesbaye, the height just exceeds 100 m (330 ft). Some Belgian geologists consider that the Kempen plateau is partly of tectonic origin, and that it is the result of a gentle anticline trending approximately from west to east along a line to the north of Liège. But the consensus of opinion is that the plateau represents a depositional surface surviving between the Meuse on the east and the Demer on the southwest, both of which have been entrenched not only into the Quaternary sands and gravels but also into the underlying Tertiary rocks. The surface consists of gentle swelling eminences, alternating with shallow marshy depressions. The plateau forms a broad somewhat indeterminate watershed between rather vague streams which drain northwards to the Meuse and southwards to the Demer. There are areas of marsh and much artificial drainage.

To the west and north the plateau descends inconspicuously towards the plain. To the southwest and east, however, it is more sharply defined by the valleys of the Demer and Meuse respectively, forming a marked change of slope where the rivers have cut their terraces into the deposits during a degradational phase in their cycles. This is quite a steep slope (Fig. 6.3),

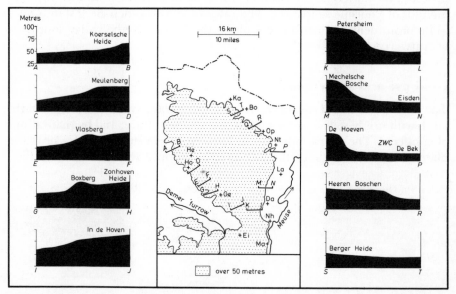

FIG. 6.3. Profiles of the edge of the Kempen plateau
Various sheets of the *Carte topographique et militaire de Belgique* were used to determine precise heights along the lines of profile. The vertical exaggeration is ten times.

The commune centres are indicated as follows: **Bo,** Bocholt; **Da,** Daalgrimbie; **Ei,** Eigenbilzen; **Ge,** Genk; **He,** Helchteren; **Ho,** Houthalen; **Ka,** Kaulille; **La,** Lanklaar; **Ma,** Maastricht; **Nh,** Neerharen; **Nt,** Neeroeteren; **Op,** Opitter; **ZWC,** Zuid-Willems Canal.

embayed by the valleys of numerous streams between low spurs and isolated knolls. In the neighbourhood of Diest, the Demer's right-bank tributaries have cut back deeply into the plateau, leaving interfluves orientated from northeast to southwest, frequently separated by transverse valleys now left streamless because of the lowering of the watertable in the more deeply eroded Demer valley. The superficial deposits have been removed, and these interfluves now form rounded hillocks of heavily iron-stained compacted sandstone; these are in fact exposed Lower Pliocene (*Diestian*) sandstones. The hillocks are known as the Diestian Hills; their summits rise from 9 to 40 m (30 to 130 ft) above the Demer valley floor.

The Kempen plain slopes away gently northward into the Netherlands and westward to the Scheldt. It is almost impossible to say where the plateau ends or the plain begins, although the 50-m (160-ft) contour might be taken as a somewhat arbitrary line of demarcation. The plain is rarely absolutely level, for it is interrupted on the one hand by sand-dunes, on the other by the gentle slopes of the river valleys and by marshy depressions containing meres and small lakes. Drainage is so vague and indeterminate that considerable areas are patterned with drainage ditches and channels leading into such northwards-flowing streams as the Mark and the Dommel, and ultimately to the Meuse. A few small hills rise as faintly swelling mounds of Pliocene sandstone. The town of Heist-op-den-Berg stands on a quite prominent eminence overlooking the Groote-Nethe valley southeast of Antwerp.

## Land use and settlement

The higher eastern *Limburgsche Kempen* is characterised by much heathland, with sandy soils supporting but scanty agriculture, and by plantations of conifers.[6] The sparse population lives mostly in small villages near the plateau edge on or about the fifty-metre contour. Several in the north—

PLATE 13. Dinxperlo, near the edge of the heathlands and the Rhine plain

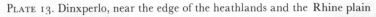

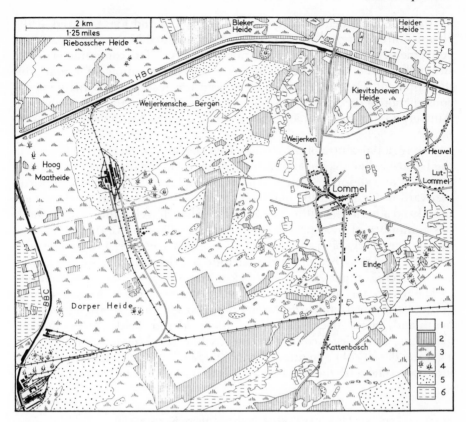

FIG. 6.4. Land use in the Kempen heathlands near Lommel
The numbers in the key are as follows: **1,** arable land; **2,** coniferous plantations;
**3,** heathland; **4,** marsh; **5,** bare sand and dunes; **6,** permanent pasture. Waterways are
shown by a thick black line, roads by a double line, and railways by a single barbed
line. Houses and industrial buildings are shown in solid black. The two factories in the
west are metallurgical refineries.

The abbreviations are as follows: **BBC,** Beverloo Branch Canal; **HBC,** Herentals-
Bocholt Canal.

Lommel (Fig. 6.4 and Plate 14), Neerpelt, Overpelt, Bocholt, Reppel—are
located along the line of the Herentals-Bocholt and the Zuid-Willems
Canals which closely follow the 50 m (160 ft) contour. Another line of small
villages stands on the terraces along the western banks of the Meuse. In the
central Kempenland the number of hamlets is small, and most of them lie
on the lower slopes of valleys which form slight re-entrants into the plateau,
notably Genk in the Stiemerbeek valley. Others stand on spurs of the
plateau projecting into the Demer valley. Very few villages are to be found
on the high plateau itself. One such is Asch, at a height of 80 m (260 ft); it is
a focus of roads across the plateau, a minor railway junction, and a small
servicing centre. During the last sixty years housing estates have been built

for the labour needed in the collieries (see p. 126 and Fig. 6.7) and at the chemico-metallurgical works described below, sited in the open heathland conveniently near the industrial units they serve. The commune of Genk, situated on the high heathlands, is a specific example of remarkable development. Communications have been much improved, including the construction of the Albert Canal (see p. 128–31), and of the motorway from Antwerp via Hasselt to Liège, hence linking with the Aachen-Köln auto-bahn.

The regional centre of the eastern Kempenland is the town of Hasselt in the Demer valley. As the administrative centre of the province of Limburg, a market and shopping centre, with main line connections running north-eastward to Genk and the higher plateau, with a busy port on the Albert Canal and a variety of industrial activities, Hasselt well fulfils its function. It has a number of food-processing industries—flour mills, distilleries pro-ducing a remarkable range of spirits, tobacco factories, breweries and a gelatine works. Other industries include a brick and tile works, timber yards, several tanneries, a glue works, a soap works and fertiliser factories.

The character and aspect of the lower *Antwerpsche Kempen* change gradually westward towards the city of Antwerp. There is progressively less heathland, more deciduous trees, more fenced fields, more market-gardening and dairy-farming, and more villages and small towns indicating a greater density of population. Several large villages are situated near road junctions. The settlements avoid valleys that are liable to flood; thus Heist-

PLATE 14. Lommel, a heathland village in the northern Kempenland

op-den-Berg clusters around the slopes of a hillock rising to nearly 45 m (150 ft), while only a kilometre away the floor of the Groote-Nethe valley is less than 7·5 m (25 ft) above sea level. In the northern part of the western Kempenland, villages avoid the marshes and meres along the valleys of the rivers which flow northwards into the Netherlands.

The regional centre of this part of the Kempen is Turnhout, a prosperous market, industrial and administrative town, on the railway line between Antwerp and Tilburg, and with a busy port on the Desschel-Turnhout-Schoten Canal. One group of factories, many of them owned by old-established companies, is situated within the city itself, in blocks among the houses and shops, with frontages along the streets. Several of these factories carry on various aspects of Turnhout's leading industry— the manufacture of drawing-paper, stationery and fine papers; it has important printing and bookbinding trades, and is the world's largest centre for the manufacture of playing-cards. Other old established industries include the manufacture of coarse linen, twill, sacking and canvas, and lace is still made as a piecework domestic industry, mainly for export. Then there is the manufacture of cigars, pottery, leather and various foodstuffs, and a small diamond-cutting industry carried on by a branch of a big Antwerp firm. A second and newer group of factories, producing bulky commodities, is built to the northwest of the town near a basin on the Turnhout-Desschel-Schoten Canal—timber yards and saw mills, a cement works, a flour mill, and a small steel works making agricultural implements. Turnhout is the centre of one of the main Belgian brick-making districts and numerous brick yards, making about a quarter of the Belgian output, are sited along the banks of the Desschel-Turnhout-Schoten Canal on either side of the town. The kilns stand on the canal banks, behind which lie large claypits, some abandoned and water-filled, others still in operation, from which is excavated the fine clay (*terre glaise*). Cement is also made near Turnhout and Beerse. The *Ravels* works to the east of Turnhout has its own fleet of barges, to bring lime from the kilns near Visé in the Meuse valley. Barges return with clay from the Ravels pits to another cement works owned by the same company at Visé-Loën, a nice example of industrial development at each source of the two main raw materials linked by cheap water transport.

Mol is another small industrial and market town on the main line railway between Antwerp and Neerpelt. Within the town several old-established factories make cigars, leather goods, pottery, small articles of metal and wood, textiles and clothing. Three mills specialise in the production of patterned blankets; the frontages of the buildings lie along the main street. Belgium's main atomic energy plant is situated near Mol. Herentals has similar small-scale industries, including also the manufacture of copper and bronze articles and of glassware. Many establishments are little more than artisan workshops, and such units as tanneries, brickyards, distilleries and flour mills are dispersed at each market town.

## Modern industrial development

Apart from these small industries, localised in the towns and villages, the Kempenland contains a number of major industrial units deliberately sited in the heathlands. These, with the large collieries, make the Kempenland one of Belgium's important industrial regions.

The material losses to Belgium through the German occupation of 1914–18 were enormous but, as in the case of northeast France, certain positive advantages and opportunities resulted from enforced reconstruction. Not only could factories be built on efficient lines and installed with modern plant, but industry need no longer be tied to old-established districts on the southern coalfield by reason of the capital values of site and plant. The Kempenland offered considerable advantages; the cheapness of land for spacious factory sites, the unpopulated areas available for the layout and segregation of noxious or dangerous industries, the gradual development of the new coalfield, and the proximity of the port of Antwerp were all encouraging factors. The region was reasonably well served by railways and waterways, and the building of the Albert Canal in the 1930s was a major contribution. Of the nineteen industrial establishments shown in Fig. 6.5, all but two lie on the banks of a waterway, and most are at a rail and water intersection.

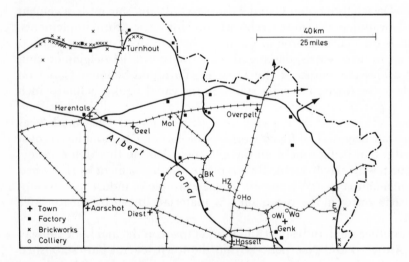

Fig. 6.5. The location of the major industrial establishments in the Kempen heathlands
The factories were located from large-scale maps and from information supplied by the various companies, and plotted on a small-scale map. They are named on a map in F. J. Monkhouse, *The Belgian Kempenland* (1949) (p. 146).

The six collieries are indicated by initial letters (for their names, see Fig. 6.6). The canals are shown by heavy lines (for their names see Fig. 6.8), the main line railways by barbed lines.

In the period of reconstruction, then, a number of new factories was built, and the firms which already had small establishments before 1914 took advantage of the capital available through reparations and government loans to rebuild or enlarge their works. These include four large zinc refineries, mostly owned by Liège groups, where refining had developed in the nineteenth century. Several establishments produce a variety of other nonferrous refined metals—lead, silver, copper and cadmium—and a factory at Oolen refines uranium and radium. These concerns also manufacture a variety of chemical derivatives such as sulphuric acid. A chemical works near Beerse refines copper and makes copper nitrate and copper sulphate, the latter mainly for export to France and Italy to spray in solution on the vines. The Reppel works specialise in arsenic derivatives (including an insecticide for use against the cotton boll-weevil), exported in large quantities to America. At Tessenderloo a chemical factory, destroyed during the war of 1939–45, was rebuilt in 1947 and produces chemicals such as caustic potash, bleaching powder, potassium sulphate, muriatic acid and liquid chlorine. There are four large explosives works, segregated in uninhabited open land behind lines of protective sand-dunes. Belgium is one of the leading producers of glass, manufactured before the war of 1914–18 almost entirely in the Liège area. A large establishment, employing over fifteen hundred workers, was built in 1921–23 at Mol-Gompel; this is now one of the world's largest producers of sheet glass. A smaller factory, making laboratory ware, bottles and glass insulators, is situated north of Mol. The glass sands are worked in the communes of Mol and Gompel, some of a quality approaching the famous deposits near Fontainebleau; other supplies are imported from Heerlerheide in South Limburg in the Netherlands. An atomic energy plant is situated near Mol. A Ford motor assembly plant was opened in 1963 at Genk on the banks of the Albert Canal, and in April 1963 the Allegheny–Longdoz steel plant, the result of an American–Belgian merger, began production of stainless steel in the same district.

## The Kempen coalfield [8]

Before the war of 1914–18 the whole of the Belgian coal output was obtained from the Sambre-Meuse field (*Bassin Sud*), and production rose steadily during the nineteenth century as Belgium developed as one of the most highly industrialised countries in the world (see pp. 500–5). The output of coal increased from 2·6 million tons in 1835 to 23·5 million tons in 1900, at which total it remained more or less stationary until 1914. But the actual consumption of coal increased much more rapidly than did this production, and it became progressively more obvious that the southern field alone would soon be unable to supply Belgium's needs. This was indicated by the increase in imports of coal and coke, which in 1835 had amounted to less than 10 000 tons but by 1900 had attained 3 million tons. Increasing attention was therefore paid to the possibility of the existence of exploitable coal deposits in other parts of Belgium.

During the latter part of the nineteenth century considerable developments had taken place in the South Limburg coalfield on the eastern side of the Meuse valley (see pp. 174–8). Belgian geologists and mining experts were increasingly interested in the possibility that these coal deposits might well extend into the Kempenland. The coal-bearing strata are effectively hidden under a considerable depth of newer deposits, and much geological speculation therefore took place. The first mention of the possibility of a coal basin in northern Belgium was in fact as early as 1806, and as time went on many distinguished geologists contributed to the body of published material. It was evident that only trial borings could verify the various suppositions; the first was put down in 1877 to the north of Liège. Success was finally attained when a company sank a boring at Zuiden near Asch, and on 2 August 1901 this reached a coal seam at a depth of 541 m (1 775 ft), from which a sample was triumphantly brought to the surface. Fifty years later a *fête commémorative* was held at Genk to celebrate this momentous event.[9] Geological prospecting has gone on steadily, and more than a hundred borings have now been put down, the deepest of which, at Wijvenheid, attained a depth of 1 912 m (6 273 ft).

The existence was proved of a coal basin extending westward for 80 km (50 miles) from the Dutch frontier towards Antwerp, and 1 300 sq km (500 sq miles) in area. The coal does, however, lie at a considerable distance below the surface, and half of the exploitable reserves are estimated to occur at depths exceeding 900 m (3 000 ft). The borehole evidence was sufficiently conclusive to encourage the granting of concessions. At first the Belgian government, stimulated by the example of the Netherlands (see p. 176), considered the question of exclusive state ownership and operation of the coalfield. Possibly because of the enormous cost obviously involved in initial exploitation and the necessity of attracting both Belgian and foreign capital, the government contented itself with demarcating three state reserves, occupying about a sixth of the proven area, strategically placed in the west, centre and east of the field. At the present time ten concessions are held by individual companies, together with the three still unexploited state reserves; their positions and extent are shown on Fig. 6.6, with the six active collieries. Two of these are in the commune of Genk, on the heath-covered plateau which forms the watershed between the Demer and the Meuse systems at a height of about 75 m (250 ft) above sea level. Another is in the east of the coalfield overlooking the Meuse valley, and the others lie to the northwest of Genk, the most westerly being the Beringen-Koersel colliery.

In 1906, when the first concessions were granted, the companies started the immense task of developing the field. The overlying deposits of sands and gravels, unconsolidated and often waterlogged, meant that technical problems of shaft-sinking were considerable, and in fact the shaft-freezing

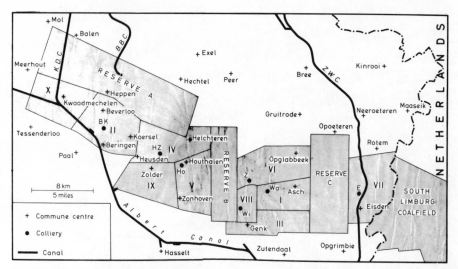

FIG. 6.6. The Kempen coalfield
The collieries are indicated by their initial letters, as follows: **BK,** Beringen-Koersel;
**E,** Eisden; **Ho,** Houthalen; **HZ,** Helchteren-Zolder; **Wa,** Waterschei; **Wi,** Winterslag;
**Z,** Zwartberg. Helchteren-Zolder and Houthalen were amalgamated in 1965, and the
Zwartberg colliery was closed in 1966, the result of an ECSC decision.
    The individual concessions are numbered from I to X.
    Waterways are indicated by abbreviations as follows: **BBC,** Beverloo Branch Canal;
**KDC,** Kwaadmechelen-Desschel Canal; **ZWC,** Zuid-Willems Canal.

Based on maps in various volumes of the *Annales des Mines* (Bruxelles).

process had to be used. This process was slow and immensely expensive.
The deepest shaft is at Zwartberg, which reaches a depth of 1 019 m (3 314
ft) and took four years and three months to complete. The development of
the underground workings was also long and costly, and was further
retarded by the war of 1914–18. As a result, the first coal was not raised until
1917 from Winterslag (Plate 15), followed by two more collieries in 1922
and by the others at later intervals. The first colliery to produce a million
tons in a year was Waterschei (1·08 million tons in 1930). Helchteren-
Zolder and Houthalen amalgamated in 1965, and Zwartberg was closed in
1966.

    The Kempenland was not at first sight a promising area for industrial
development. The surface consisted of heathland, with few settlements and
with almost no local sources of labour. In the decade following 1920 there
was a marked shortage of labour in most branches of Belgian industry,
especially in the less attractive of these. This shortage was met, particularly
in the collieries, by the importation of labour from other countries, and
from 1922 onwards trainloads of foreign workers arrived in Belgium. The
result is shown by the fact that while the seven Kempen collieries employed
only 2 951 men in 1920 during the stage of initial exploitation, this figure
had risen to 18 657 in 1935 and to 30 000 in 1964. Today, though the mining

PLATE 15. The Winterslag colliery, Genk, Kempenland

force is declining, foreign workers comprise three-tenths of this total mining force, and a higher proportion, three-sevenths, of the underground workers. The effects can be appreciated in the commune of Genk[10] in the heart of the heathlands, the fourth largest commune in Belgium, and containing the two collieries of Winterslag and Waterschei which produce one-seventh of all Belgian coal. The population of Genk was 1 776 in 1846 and still only 3 422 in 1910. But by 1970 it was no less than 58 000, of whom about 17 000 were foreign, half of them Italians. The result of this population increase, not only in Genk but in other communes on the coalfield, was that provision had to be made within the former virtually empty heathlands of settlements where the workers and their families could live. This is the reason for the housing estates, built near the collieries on the lines of 'garden-cities', known in the Kempenland as *tuinwijks* or *zwijnwijks* (Fig. 6.7).[11]

Thus a great building programme was necessary, both for the colliery installations and for housing the labour. In one respect the situation of the collieries in the open heathlands was a positive advantage, for the installations and the housing estates could be laid out on spacious and often attractive lines. Each colliery purchased its land on leasehold terms from the commune; in Genk the original three collieries bought about one-ninth of the total area.

Over parts of the Kempenland, therefore, the dark sombre stretches of heathland are now replaced by large modern collieries and new towns. As

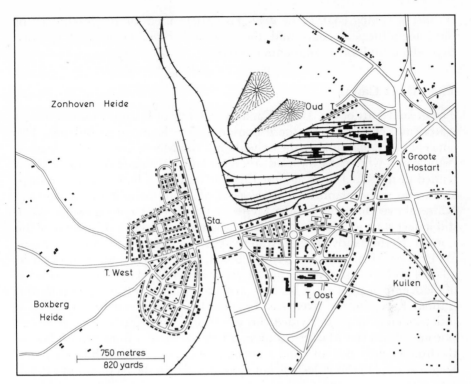

Fig. 6.7. Housing estates in Genk commune in the Kempenland
**T,** *Tuinwijk*. The colliery spoil heaps are indicated by hachuring.

Based on a manuscript map made available by the SA des Charbonnages Winterslag.

one travels across the open country, in the distance can be seen the tall chimneys, cooling towers, concrete pit-head installations and vast pyramidal spoil dumps. But much is still heathland; more than a quarter of Genk commune is of untouched heath and another quarter has been planted with conifers. The ceaseless activity at the collieries and the dense agglomerations of population in the housing estates actually emphasise the emptiness and loneliness of the heathlands within which they stand as relatively isolated 'industrial oases'.

Until recently progress has been steady during the seventy years of development, and the Kempen field has increased its proportion of the Belgian total. Output in 1965 reached 9·7 million tons, 45 per cent of the total. But despite the success of the Kempen collieries, the Belgian government, in response to the Coal and Steel Community's programme of reduction of output, was obliged to close the Zwartberg colliery in 1966. This caused considerable unrest, culminating in riots. Output is now about 8 million tons, contributing three-quarters of Belgium's much reduced output. The type of Kempen coal varies considerably, from semi-anthracite to highly volatile long-flame coals. Especially valuable to Belgium, which is short of coking coal, is the *demi-gras* variety used for the production of hard metallurgical coke, and the *gras* and *Flému* coals used for gas, byproducts and soft-coke manufacture.[12]

## The Albert Canal

The greater part of the Albert Canal, today one of Europe's busiest inland waterways, crosses the southern margins of the Kempen heathlands. The concept of a canal linking the Scheldt and the Meuse goes back at least to Napoleon I, who realised the advantages of the position of Antwerp ('It is a loaded pistol that I hold against England's throat', he is reputed to have said), and so he planned a '*Canal du Nord*' from Grimlinghausen on the Rhine above Düsseldorf to the Meuse at Venlo, thence to Antwerp. Work did in fact start in 1808, but was soon abandoned. Under the régime of the United Netherlands several waterways were built, notably the Zuid-Willems or Maastricht-'s Hertogenbosch Canal (Fig. 6.8), completed in 1826. This leaves the Meuse just below Maastricht, skirts the eastern edge of the Kempen plateau to Bocholt, and then runs to 's Hertogenbosch and ultimately rejoins the river near Engeln. The final recognition of Belgian independence in 1839 divided this canal into three parts: a short Dutch portion within the Maastricht area, a Belgian section from Smeermaas to the frontier near Bocholt, and a northerly Dutch portion. Thus of its total length of 130 km (80 miles), 75 km (47 miles) are in the Netherlands. It will take barges up to 450 tons, and although there are twenty-two locks to negotiate, in 1969 the Belgian portion transported 4·4 million tons of freight. The canal performs a very useful function in serving the towns and the agricultural areas of both the eastern Kempenland and the Dutch province of Noord-Brabant.

In 1844 the newly independent Belgium took advantage of the existing eastern section of the Zuid-Willems Canal, and began to construct from this waterway at Bocholt a new canal, known as the Meuse-Scheldt Junction or Kempen Canal. Until the ultimate completion of the Albert Canal, this was the only water route from Liège to Antwerp. But the most rapid voyages between the two cities by this canal took forty-three hours for a motor-barge and seventy-seven hours for a tow of four dumb-barges. Several other serious disabilities included ten locks and numerous swing and lift bridges which had to be negotiated; the depth was only about two m (7 ft) and the barge capacity was limited to six hundred tons; and barges were obliged to pass through Dutch territory in the Maastricht area on their way to Liège. When the Albert Canal was built it incorporated the western section of this Junction Canal, and the remaining portion was renamed the Herentals-Bocholt Canal (Fig. 6.8).

Even before the war of 1914–18 a growing sense of the inadequacy of these canals had developed a preoccupation with the problem of creating a new major waterway across northeast Belgium. This would not only form a direct all-Belgian route between Antwerp and Liège, but would provide necessary cheap transport for the output of the newly developed Kempen field. Various companies interested in the coalfield considered that the construction of a canal would prove to be a most important factor in its development. It was also argued that it would have a strategic value as a defence across the northeast of the country, duplicating the obstacle of the Meuse.

Various projects were put forward in the years following the war of 1914–18. One canal was actually started in 1923, following a direct line between Hasselt and Visé, and involving fifteen locks and a tunnel, but this was soon abandoned owing to the immense engineering difficulties and obvious great cost. After lengthy deliberations a route from Hasselt via Eigenbilzen to the Meuse valley at Visé was adopted.[13]

The Albert Canal, 130 km (80 miles) in length (Fig. 6.8), proved to be an immense undertaking which took ten years to complete; ironically and bitterly it was officially opened during the German occupation on Christmas Day 1940, for the intended opening at Liège in July 1939 was post-

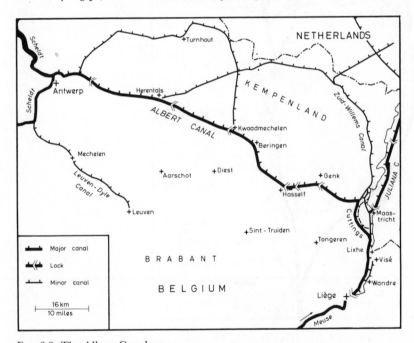

FIG. 6.8. The Albert Canal
The abbreviations are as follows: **DTC,** Desschel-Turnhout Canal; **HBC,** Herentals-Bocholt Canal; **TSC,** Turnhout-Schoten Canal; **ZWC,** Zuid-Willems Canal. A connection between the Juliana and Albert Canals, by way of the huge Lanaye locks, now enables 2 000-ton barges to pass through (see Fig. 6.9).

Based on A. Delmer, *Le Canal Albert* (1939), of which vol. ii consists of maps, including four sheets covering the canal on a scale of 1 : 100 000.

poned owing to a disastrous breach in the embankments near Hasselt. The
canal takes off from the Meuse below Monsin Island (Fig. 18.10), utilising
the old Liège–Maastricht Canal, which runs parallel to and on the west side
of the Meuse, as far as the Ternayen lock near Lanaye. This canal, built in
1850, was enlarged to the overall dimensions of the new waterway between

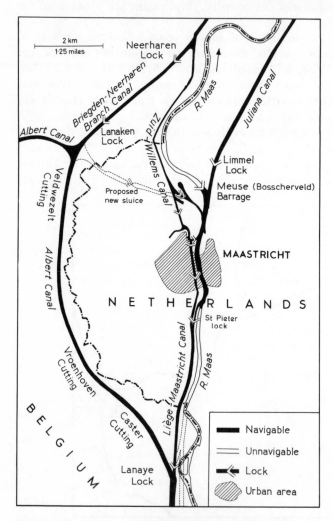

Fig. 6.9. The Albert and Juliana Canals in the Maastricht district
The proposed new connection between the port of Maastricht
and the Albert Canal, and possible developments in the
neighbourhood of the Lanaye lock, are shown by pecked
lines. The proposed new channel of the Meuse in the south
will rejoin the river a few km upstream, so avoiding the
bends and islets of the section bypassed.

Based on various large-scale Belgian and Dutch maps and plans.

new embankments. The major physical obstacle was the upland 'neck' linking the Kempen and Hesbaye plateaus, which the canal had to pierce in order to circumvent the western boundary of the Maastricht area. A series of vast cuttings was made (Fig. 6.9); the 'Tranchée de Caster' was excavated through the St Pietersberg ridge, and then followed the immense Vroenhoven-Veldwezelt cuttings, nearly 10 km (6 miles) long, some 180 m (200 yds) wide and in places over 60 m (200 ft) below the surface of the plateau. The huge quantities of excavated earth were removed to other sections further west to build the embankments. From Briegden to Genk the Eigenbilzen cutting was made through a series of low hills, and then the canal was continued westward along the Demer valley into the Scheldt lowlands. For some 50 km (30 miles) it incorporated enlarged sections of the old Meuse-Scheldt Junction Canal and its Hasselt Branch. Along most of this 'lowland course' it is contained within embankments 180 m (200 yds) in width at their base. The canal enters the port of Antwerp by way of the Strasbourg and Lefebvre Docks.[14]

The fall of 56 m (184 ft) between Liège and Antwerp is negotiated by six groups of triple locks, the locations of which are shown on Fig. 6.8. A seventh lock at Monsin is intended to ensure that the level of the Meuse at Liège remains stable at about 60 m (200 ft) above sea level, and is normally kept open. Sixty-five bridges were constructed, which (with one exception) were destroyed during the war of 1939–45, but have been subsequently rebuilt. Canal ports were developed, apart from the important terminals at Liège and Antwerp, notably three coal-ports specifically constructed to handle Kempen coal. The port of Genk, managed by the Société du Port Charbonnier de Genck S.A., was constructed jointly by the Winterslag, Zwartberg and Waterschei companies with whose collieries it is linked by rail, and is used also by Houthalen. This basin has unlocked connection with the canal, and is extremely well equipped for handling coal, with extensive sidings and mobile overhead loading bridges. Kempen coal can be shipped from the Genk coal-port to Liège in about seven hours, and to Antwerp in nine or ten hours. The Zolder and Beringen ports are situated further west along the canal to serve the Helchteren-Zolder and Beringen-Koersel collieries respectively. Two large ports on the Meuse valley section of the canal, at Lixhe and Haccourt, handle large quantities of cement from neighbouring works. About 38 million tons of freight were transported in 1969.

The construction of the Albert Canal made possible another valuable contribution to the pattern of Belgian waterways. A link canal, the Briegden-Neerharen Branch, 5 km (3 miles) in length and involving two locks, was constructed in 1935 around the northwestern perimeter of the Maastricht district (Fig. 6.9). It connects the Zuid-Willems Canal, before it enters the Netherlands from the north, with the Briegden Basin on the Albert Canal, so providing a continuous all-Belgian water route along the eastern edge of the country.

## The heathlands of the southern Netherlands

These southern heathlands are merely the continuation of the Maas 'fan' across the frontier, described on pp. 18–19. The heathland dips gently northward to the alluvium-covered floodplain of the Maas, though in the

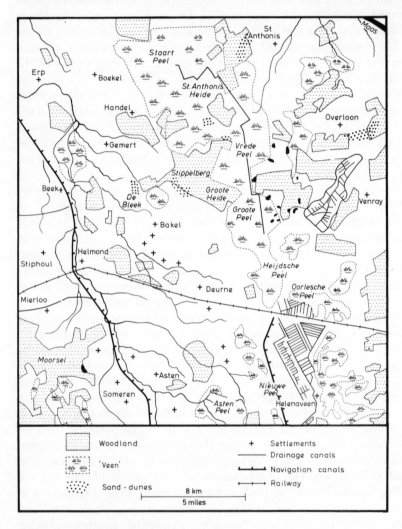

FIG. 6.10. An area in the Peel
This area lies to the north-east of the Belgian frontier, between the Zuid-Willems Canal (the waterway in the west of the map) and the Maas valley. The highest point (the sand-dunes of the Stippelberg) is about 30 m above NAP, but the general altitude of this rather desolate area is about 20–23 m. The areas of *veen* and woodland are necessarily generalised. Near Helenaveen, deep borings have reached coal at a depth of 987 m.
Based on *Topografische Kaart van het Koninkrijk der Nederlanden*, 1:200000 sheet 18.

west bluffs rising to 15 to 20 m (50 to 75 ft) overlook the drained polders bordering the Ooster Schelde. Several small streams flow vaguely north-wards to the Maas from a watershed which lies mainly in Belgium; their shallow valleys form narrow 'tongues' of alluvium across the heathlands, and the streams are regularised in their lower courses.

In the east the plateau projects prominently northwestward, forming a flattish ridge 50 m (170 ft) in height known as the Peel, lying across the provincial boundary between Noord-Brabant and Limburg. It forms a low secondary divide between streams flowing northeast to the middle Maas and those going northwest to the Aa and the lower Maas. Under the surface of the Peel lies a considerable thickness of Chalk, and below that again the Netherlands Geological Survey has proved the existence of a deep coal-field, for coal was reached near Helenaveen at a depth of 987 m (3 238 ft) in August 1906. These coal deposits are separated from the South Limburg field by a downfaulted trough where the Upper Carboniferous strata have been carried down to 2 400 m (8 000 ft) below the surface. This Peel field has seams accessible by modern techniques, although the immense develop-ment costs which will be entailed have precluded any initial exploitation and none is likely. Other hidden fields have been proved further north in Overijssel and Gelderland.

The heathland is similar in character to that of the Kempen to the south, although it is generally lower. Numerous depressions in western Noord-Brabant indicate former channels of the Scheldt, others in eastern Noord-Brabant those of the Maas, now filled with peat mosses. The Peel (Fig. 6.10) still contains one of the largest areas of peat bog in the Netherlands.

This is one of the most scantily populated areas in the Netherlands, served by few roads and with only a few scattered villages. It is, however, crossed by the main line railway between Eindhoven and Venlo, near which occasional *veenkoloniën* have been created, such as Helenaveen (Fig. 6.10),[15] where in 1853 the brothers Jan and Nicolaas van de Griendt, pioneers of reclamation in the Peel, founded a company to develop a colony. The first stage was the cutting and removal of peat for sale (which is still in progress in some districts); then the company gradually introduced agricultural enterprises (horticulture, cattle- and poultry-rearing), and individual tenants rented plots of land. In 1940 631 people lived there, but unfortu-nately the district was badly damaged during the final stages of the war of 1939–45; this has been made good. Further north the Peel is even more sparsely populated, with only a few scattered villages. To the southeast of the Peel proper the bleak moors continue towards the edge of the Maas valley. A few villages are located near the Belgian frontier at a height of about 45 m (150 ft). Further north settlements increase in frequency on the sides of the long re-entrant valleys, and farms are scattered among sur-viving patches of heath.

A string of towns lies along the northern edge of the sand country bordering the clay lands, from Bergen-op-Zoom in the west in an arc

PLATE 16. The Philips electrical works at Eindhoven

through Roosendaal, Breda and 's Hertogenbosch to Grave on the Maas. A second line of larger towns lies further south—Tilburg in the Leij valley, Eindhoven in a shallow embayment where a fan of tributaries converges to form the Dommel, and Helmond on the Zuid-Willems Canal. All these are long-established market towns which have recently developed such industries as electrical, metallurgical and light engineering, the manufacture of textiles, chemicals, cigars, rubber and leather goods.[16] Eindhoven is the home of the vast Philips electrical company,[17] with a population in 1859 of under 5 000, but in 1970 this had risen to 190 000, and it is now the fifth city of the Netherlands. Also at Eindhoven is the main factory of the Van Doorne Automobielfabriek NV, which since 1928 has manufactured motor trucks, road-tankers and other commercial vehicles. In 1958 the company started production of DAF cars, now supplying 40 per cent of the Dutch market and even rivalling Fiat and Volkswagen in the production of 800 and 1 100 cc vehicles.

## The minor heathlands of the central Netherlands

Several small patches of sand country lie between the southern shores of the IJssel Meer and the Rhine-Maas distributaries. Little remains of true heath, although considerable areas are carefully maintained as parks. The Utrecht-Gelderland ridges run discontinuously southeastward from the IJssel Meer to the Neder Rijn. These ridges are only 6 to 10 km (4 to 6 miles) wide but stand quite boldly above the polderlands of the Vecht valley to the west and of the Geldersche Vallei to the east.

The ridges are either planted with coniferous woodland or are built upon. The Gooiland Hills are only 15 km (10 miles) from Amsterdam and less than that from Utrecht, and so small villages have developed during the last few decades into residential towns from which 'commuters' travel in daily to work—notably Hilversum (which in 1969 had a population of 100 000). With numerous specialised light industries and the main Dutch radio station, this has been described as 'the Chislehurst of Holland—a discreet and wealthy suburb', attractively laid out. Further south, a line of small towns, including Doorn (the home for so long of the exiled ex-Kaiser Wilhelm II), is situated along the southern edge of the hills among market gardens (which flourish on the heavily fertilised light warm sands), orchards and woodlands.

Another distinct line of these sandy hills trends southeastward from the Waal at Nijmegen across into West Germany near Kleve, continuing southeastward towards Krefeld; this forms a somewhat indeterminate watershed between the Maas and the Rhine. The highest point in the Dutch section of these hills is the Uilenput 96 m (315 ft). Nijmegen rises steeply from the southern bank of the Waal on to the north-facing abutment of this ridge (Plate 11), where its new suburbs have grown (see p. 104). On the wooded hills to the south of the town are pleasant residential villages.

A third outlying patch of sandy hills lies between the Rhine where it enters the Netherlands and the drained marshlands of the Lijmers valley. The hills culminate in the Hettenheuvel 106 m (345 ft) and the Montferland 83 m (272 ft), and are wooded with conifers.

## The Veluwe

This extensive area of sandy country, the name of which means literally 'barren land', occupies a broad triangle between the IJssel Meer, the IJssel and the Lek. The land is highest in the east, the *Over-Veluwe*, and a string of hummocky *bergen* can be traced from the Woldberg southward in a gentle arc (Fig. 6.11) attaining about 107 m (350 ft). The *Neder-Veluwe* slopes gently westward from about 45 to 15 m (150 to 50 ft). The margins of the Veluwe are much dissected by streams flowing east to the IJssel, south to the Neder Rijn and west to the Geldersche Vallei; their valleys are characterised by a curious asymmetry. [18]

The sands are remarkably continuous and as a result the Veluwe is the largest area of sparse population in the Netherlands, bearing extensive tracts of coniferous plantations (Plate 17). Wide expanses of ling still exist, some now in nature reserves, and the several large estates include the royal

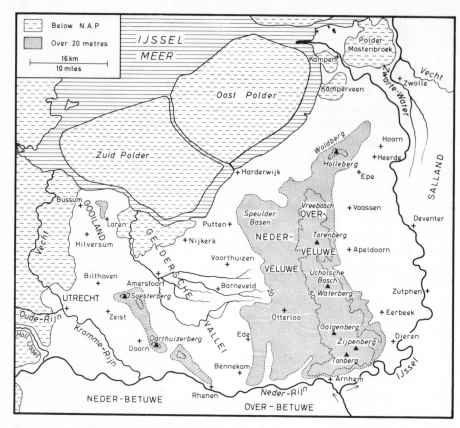

FIG. 6.11. The Veluwe and its neighbourhood

PLATE 17. The Veluwe

summer residence. About 3 km (2 miles) north of Arnhem is the well-known open-air 'Folk Museum', which displays houses, bridges, windmills, etc., typical of each of the Dutch provinces. A few hamlets and resorts are located in the Neder-Veluwe and further west still some larger towns lie in the valleys of the streams draining to the Geldersche Vallei, notably Ede; industrial developments have made this a commune of 72 000 people.

## The East Gelderland-Overijssel heathlands

These heathlands extend between the valleys of the Lijmers and the Vecht, a stream which flows westwards from West Germany to the IJssel Meer. In the centre of the district is a line of distinct morainic hills; these sandy humps, each with a distinctive -*berg* name, rise to a highest point of 80 m (262 ft). In the east much of the heathland is above 60 m (200 ft), the highest point, the Gelgenberg 70 m (229 ft), actually lying just over the frontier in West Germany. These higher areas are almost entirely of sand, interrupted by the broad Twente depression, where the convergence of numerous streams has produced an extensive though thin veneer of alluvium. Some areas of heath still survive, interrupted by strips of alluvium; there are large blocks of coniferous plantations; and reclamation has provided considerable although scattered areas of pasture (especially on the shallow valley-floors) and some arable land. The peat bogs along the frontier region have been almost entirely removed. In the northeast of Overijssel, for example, to the east of the river Vecht, the bogs have been worked for peat since the twelfth century.[19] So much peat has been removed that extensive irregular lakes have been formed, and the medieval arable landscape has been replaced by meadows, swamps and shallow meres. The work of reclamation continues, and the wasteland in Overijssel has been reduced from 15 to 5 per cent of the total area during the last decade.

The high heathland in the east is thinly populated; there are, however, a few *veenkoloniën* in the northeast of Overijssel. Further west a much closer pattern of settlement has developed, particularly in the Twente,[20] where several large towns are engaged in the cotton industry, notably Enschede, Hengelo and Almelo. Other industries (clothing, engineering, electro-technical activities and the production of chemicals) are related to the dominant textiles. It is perhaps surprising that Overijssel has a larger proportion of its gainfully employed population engaged in industry than any other Dutch province.

## The northeastern heathlands

North of the Vecht valley the sandy areas continue through Drenthe into Groningen and eastern Friesland, and eastward across the West German frontier. The most striking relief feature is the low undulating sand ridge of

PLATE 18. The reclamation of the moorland in Drenthe

the Hondsrug,[21] which extends southeastward from near Groningen to the corner of Drenthe.

It was on the sands in the centre and east of Groningen and Drenthe that the high peat bogs were formerly so widespread. Here are the *moeren*, such as the Oostermoer to the east of the Hondsrug and the desolate Bourtanger Moer extending into West Germany. Some high bog remains, especially along the frontier, but much has been cleared, especially in the province of Groningen where the *veenkoloniën* are most numerous. Many were systematically established in the seventeenth century on the moors adjacent to the city. In the early nineteenth century the *Stadskanaal* was cut south-eastward to the German frontier, and a series of straggling villages with surrounding rectangular drainage patterns was established. Fields of potatoes, rye, oats and occasionally sugar beet have replaced the desolate peat moors.[22] Root crops are grown for fodder and cattle are kept, both stall fed and grazed on permanent pastures, providing manure for the sandy soils. Pigs are fed on skimmed milk, and poultry and bees are other items in a remarkably prosperous economy. Reclamation still goes on in Drenthe (Plate 18), and by 1968 only 17 000 ha (42 000 acres) was still classified as 'waste', out of the total area of 268 000 ha (650 000 acres).

The sandy heathlands as well as the moors have been greatly reduced in extent, particularly in the lower western parts, and in places they carry market gardens and orchards, notably of bush fruits. Much land in Friesland and Groningen has been converted into permanent pasture. These reclaimed lands have now a remarkably dense population for a rural area, and are virtually indistinguishable from the coastal districts on the fertile clays. A close pattern of villages amid a prosperous agricultural landscape is the reward of nearly four centuries' effort.

Groningen,[23] the 'regional capital' of the north and, with a population of 169 000 in 1970, the seventh city of the Netherlands, is situated at the northern extremity of the Hondsrug where this sandy ridge meets the coastal claylands and the former peat bogs to the southeast. Its new harbour was opened in 1967, following the enlargement of the Eems Canal. The city is a market centre for the densely populated agricultural neighbourhood, and has a variety of industries connected with the processing of agricultural commodities—flour-milling, brewing and distilling, and the making of industrial alcohol and strawboard, as well as such newly introduced industries as the manufacture of chemicals, rayon, and electrical apparatus.

An interesting development in the last thirty years has been the discovery and working of mineral oil near Schoonebeek in southeastern Drenthe. The first oil was produced in 1944, the first gas in 1947. In 1970 the output of oil totalled 1·9 million tons, a not inconsiderable contribution to the Dutch requirements,[24] but it is believed that the wells have passed their peak.

Vast deposits of natural gas, said to be some of the largest in the world, have recently been discovered at Slochteren;[25] the gas consists of 90 per cent

PLATE 19. The natural gasfield at Slochteren

methane. A consortium (the Dutch Gas Union) has been created, including the State, the State Mining Company and the Shell and Esso companies, to develop this source of energy. When in full production it will supply a quarter of Dutch energy requirements. A web of pipelines has been constructed to other parts of the Netherlands and to neighbouring countries. Gas production has grown from 1·1 million m³ in 1961 to 43·4 million in 1971, of which about 17·2 million was exported to her EEC partners. Reserves are expected to last about twenty years. Another large gas field was discovered in 1970 under the municipality of Emmen, in the extreme east of Drenthe. Development is in progress, and it is planned that the entire production will be sold to West Germany (Plate 19).

The municipality of Emmen is the scene of some interesting developments, for it is one of the Netherlands' scheduled 'new towns'.[26] Emmen is a municipality about 15 by 20 km (10 by 12 miles) in extent, comprising a number of individual hamlets and fen-colonies. The population, as returned in the censuses, therefore, is deceptively high; it totalled 19 425 in 1899 and had reached 80 000 by 1969. Only about 18 000 actually live in the town of Emmen itself, for it is a servicing focus for the agricultural area around. It has been the centre of peat-digging for centuries and the peat has now almost disappeared. New industries are being introduced into a scheduled industrial zone in the southeast of the municipality, where chemical factories, strawboard mills and a nylon-spinning factory have been built, and others will follow. The aim is to check the drift of population from these eastern heathlands to the overcrowded districts of the western Netherlands. A new town is growing to the east of the old urban centre, separated from it by woodland to be retained as a park. Further schemes may result in a total population of fifty to sixty thousand in the centre and about a hundred thousand in the municipality.

## The Laagveen of Friesland

Further west in Friesland extensive areas of 'low fen' still lie in waterlogged hollows among the sand country, and peat-cutting has added to this extent of stagnant water. Eight per cent of the area of the province of Friesland is still classified as waste. To the southeast and south of Leeuwarden, the provincial capital situated on the clay lands, there is an extensive area of irregularly shaped lakes with interconnecting channels. Few of the meres have been drained, unlike the clay-floored lakes of Noord- and Zuid-Holland, because their sandy floors would provide such poor soil that it would not be worth the cost of reclamation. (In years of hard frosts, incidentally, the famous 'Eleven Towns' skating race is held, over a distance of 200 km (125 miles) linking the chief towns of the province.) But such is the reputation of Frisian dairy-farming that even on these sandy areas stock-rearing has developed, using fertilisers to grow fodder crops and importing cattle food for stall-feeding.

Few large settlements exist in the *veen*-area of Friesland, although many small, often quite isolated, hamlets, most of them fen colonies, do occur. Heerenveen, for example, has a tiny nucleated centre and a population spread out in individual farms and hamlets over much of the considerable area of the commune. Some colonies, curiously, were founded by a charitable society during the famine of 1816–17; each family settled was supplied with some land and a few animals. The settlement at Veenhuizen, just over the Groningen border, was originally established for 'orphans, paupers and beggars', and that at Ommerschans near Meppel for 'the idle and the disorderly'. These are today thriving little settlements. Many fen villages stand solitarily among the meres and their interconnecting creeks; Giethoorn, for example, to the northwest of Meppel, consists of houses scattered among devious channels, accessible only on foot by way of narrow bridges or more usually by punt. Sneek is a busy little town on the transition zone between the fen and the coastal claylands, with an important butter and cheese market. It has also a holiday function similar to that of some of the centres in the Norfolk Broads. Shallow reedy meres provide interconnected waterways to the IJssel Meer, and so Sneek is a renowned sailing centre with several regattas each year.

[1] N. P. J. de Vries, 'The Benelux central region: some results of a survey of two frontier regions', *Tijdschr. econ. soc. Geogr.*, **55** (1964), pp. 164–71.

[2] For details of these peat soils, see C. H. Edelman, *Soils of the Netherlands* (1950), pp. 78–86.

[3] See F. J. Monkhouse, *The Belgian Kempenland* (1949), p. 38, for a map of Kempen place names containing woodland elements.

[4] There is apt to be some confusion in the various terms applied in different countries because of the temptation to translate in terms of cognates. The word *Hoogveen* is applied in the Netherlands to the acid wet heaths and sometimes to the true bogs, while *Laagveen* indicates the basic fen peats of the lowlands (see p. 29 and Fig. 3.6). The Belgian terms *Moeren* and *Gooren* are used for the wet heaths. On the higher areas, where true peat bogs have developed, similar to the upland mosses of Britain, the Belgians use *Moeren* or *Hochmoeren*, the Dutch *Hoogveen* or *Moor*. In Germany, *Flachmoor* indicates the lowland fen-peat, *Moorgeest* the wet heath and *Hochmoor* the high peat bog.

[5] A detailed bibliography of works relating to the improvement of the Kempen heathlands is given by F. J. Monkhouse, *The Belgian Kempenland* (1949), pp. 234–5.

[6] A. Bodeaux, 'Les Landes à callune de Campine et les conditions de leur reforestation', *Revue de l'Agriculture* (1957), pp. 1509–37.

[7] *De Turnhoutse Kempen: Haar economische en sociale betekenis* (1953), published by the *Vlaams Economisch Verbond* (Antwerpen).

[8] General monographs concerning the Kempen coalfield include the following: H. Basselman, *Das Kempenbekken und seine Bedeutung im belgischen Kohlenbergbau* (1935); C. Demeure, *L'Industrie belge du charbon et du coke* (1930); P. Gruselin, *Le Bassin minier de la Campine* (1925); G. de Leener, *Le Charbon dans le Nord de la Belgique* (1904); and K. Pinxten, *Het Kempisch Steenkolenbekken* (1937).

⁹ A detailed account of the long preliminaries and the final success of these explorations is given by André Grosjean, *Prologue aux fêtes commémoratives de la découverte du charbon en Campine (août 1901–août 1951) (Extrait du Bulletin de l'UILv)* (Bruxelles, 1952): 'Dans un document de 1903, ceux-ci avaient dépeint leurs propres sentiments en disant: "Nous nous étions lancés comme dans une mer inconnue à la recherche d'un nouveau monde", et l'on a pu, à juste titre, comparer leur aventure à celle de Christophe Colomb' (p. 13).

¹⁰ The industrial development of Genk is fully discussed by J. Thomas, *Genk, Centrum voor Nijverheid* (1954), with numerous detailed maps and photographs.

¹¹ F. J. Monkhouse, 'Housing estates in the Belgian heathlands', *Tn Plann. Rev.*, **25** (1954), pp. 195–206.

¹² This distribution and use of Kempen coal is described by F. J. Monkhouse, 'The movement of coal in Belgium, with special reference to the Kempen Field', *Trans. Inst. Br. Geogr.* (1951), publication no. 17, pp. 97–110.

¹³ F. J. Monkhouse, 'Albert and Juliana: two great waterways', *Scottish Geographical Magazine*, **72** (1956), pp. 163–76; V. Neesen, 'The Albert Canal as shipping artery and site for the location of industry', *Tijdschr. econ. soc. Geogr.*, **55** (1964), pp. 172–8; and R. Lievens, 'Le Canal Albert, axe des transports du Limburg belge', *Rev. Navig. intér. rhén.*, **30** (1958), pp. 8–14.

¹⁴ A full account of the construction of the Albert Canal, including a volume of maps, is given by A. Delmer, *Le Canal Albert* (1939).

¹⁵ R. Kok, 'Een Eeuw Helenaveen', *Tijdschr. econ. soc. Geogr.*, **46** (1955), pp. 243–52; this affords a detailed account of the founding of the colony and the development of a settlement based on horticulture.

¹⁶ P. C. A. t'Hoen, 'Postwar industrial development in the south of the Netherlands', *Tijdschr. econ. soc. Geogr.*, **51** (1960), pp. 180–8.

¹⁷ N. de Vries, 'De N. V. Philips' Gloeilampenfabrieken en Eindhoven', *Tijdschr. K. ned. aardrijksk. Genoot.*, **65** (1948), pp. 534–43.

¹⁸ The problem of these valleys is examined in detail by (*a*) C. H. Edelman and G. C. Maarleveld, 'De Asymmetrische Dalen van de Veluwe', *Tijdschr. K. ned. aardrijksk. Genoot.*, **66** (1949), pp. 143–6; and (*b*) G. C. Maarleveld, 'Over de Erosiedalen van de Veluwe', *ibid.*, pp. 133–42, which deals with various types of valley formed during the periglacial climate of the Würm glacial period. See also H. Lehmann, 'Periglaziale Züge im Formenschatz der Veluwe', *Erdkunde*, **2** (1948), pp. 69–79.

¹⁹ M. K. E. Gottschalk, 'De Ontginning der Stichtse Venen ten Oosten van de Vecht', *Tijdschr. K. ned. aardrijksk. Genoot.*, **73** (1956), pp. 207–22.

²⁰ J. Buursink, 'De Twentse Industrieformatie', *Tijdschr. econ. soc. Geogr.*, **55** (1964), pp. 233–41.

²¹ G. H. Ligterink, 'De Hondsrug en het Dal van de Oer-Eems', *Tijdschr. K. ned. aardrijksk. Genoot.*, **71** (1954), pp. 105–21.

²² C. van Welsenes, 'The development of the agricultural area of northern Groningen', *Tijdschr. econ. soc. Geogr.*, **51** (1960), pp. 175–80.

²³ C. van Welsenes, 'De stad Groningen', *Tijdschr. econ. soc. Geogr.*, **54** (1963), pp. 145–53.

²⁴ Details are given in an article under the auspices of the *Nederlandse Aardolie Maatschappij*, 'Olie en Welvaart in Z.O. Drenthe', *Tijdschr. econ. soc. Geogr.*, **46** (1955), pp. 217–21, including a map of concessions.

²⁵ T. M. Thomas, 'The North Sea Gas Bonanza', *Tijd. econ. soc. Geogr.*, **59** (1968), pp. 57–70, contains a detailed map of the Dutch oil and gas wells.

²⁶ J. M. Richards, 'New towns in the Netherlands', *Progress,* **45** (1956), pp. 147–57.

# 7
# Interior Flanders

Between the polderlands of the maritime plain and the low plateaus of central Belgium lies an area known as Interior Flanders (in Flemish *Binnen-Vlaanderen*). It forms a triangle with its base along the southeastern edge of the chalk hills of Artois and Cambrésis and its apex at the junction of the rivers Scheldt and Rupel above Antwerp. The region may be broadly defined as lying between the 5 and 50 m (16 and 160 ft) contours; the latter generally coincides with a steeper and quite prominent slope on the eastern side of the Dendre valley, rising to the low plateaus of central Belgium. Interior Flanders consists of three geological elements: the recent alluvium deposited over the valley floors, the Eocene rocks (Flanders Clay in the southwest and sands to the north) on the interfluves between these valleys, and a few higher relict patches of newer Tertiary rocks (mostly Pliocene sands) in the south.[1]

## The physical features

As described above (p. 17 ), the upper Scheldt and its tributaries the Lys (*Leie*) and Dendre (*Dender*) developed courses almost parallel to the North Sea coastline. Their valleys are 3 to 5 km (2 to 3 miles) wide, filled in with alluvium often to depths of 30 m (100 ft) or more, across which the rivers meander in great loops, many of which have been cut off either naturally or as a result of the regularisation they have undergone. Gradients are gentle; the Lys, for example, falls only 8·5 m (28 ft) from the French frontier to its confluence with the Scheldt at Gent in a distance of 108 km (67 miles).

The tributaries of the three main streams within the Belgian portion of the plain are numerous but short, rising on the indeterminate watersheds between each. The only tributary of any size is the Mandel, which flows parallel to the Lys in its upper course before it turns almost at right angles to join the main river near Grammene. The upper courses of the Lys and Scheldt, however, display a considerable complexity, and it is clear that river capture has modified their pattern. The Lys rises on the Artois hills and flows in a northerly curve in a trench through the chalk country, leaving it for the claylands near Aire on the edge of the plain. These claylands are naturally wet and swampy, since copious springs emerge from the Chalk, and in spite of an extensive grid of drainage channels similar to that of the polderlands, flooding is still liable following periods of heavy rain. This part of the upper Lys valley, sometimes given the name of the *Pays de Weppe*, is almost a basin, as is shown by Fig. 7.1, since to the north the low

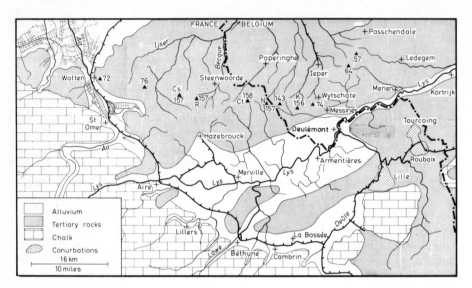

FIG. 7.1. The plain of western Flanders
The simplified geological outcrops illustrate the main pattern of relief: the edge of the chalk hills of Artois to the southwest, the Eocene sands and clays forming a low plateau mostly over 50 m (150 ft), and the alluvium, seamed with drainage channels, of the Aa valley, Maritime Flanders in the extreme northwest, and the almost enclosed upper Lys Basin. Small patches of Pliocene sands form higher points on the west–east ridge which forms a divide between the rivers of Maritime Flanders and the Lys.

The individual hills are indicated by abbreviations as follows: **Cs,** Mont Cassel; **Ct,** Mont des Cats; **K,** Kemmelberg; **N,** Mont Noir; and **R,** Mont des Récollets. The canals are named on Fig. 4.2. Heights are given in metres.

Based on various French topographical and geological maps.

plateau of Ieper (*Ypres*) and to the south the Gohelle chalk platform project eastward, rising to over 30 m (100 ft). The basin then distinctly narrows below Armentières, since the Flanders Clay plateau of Ploegsteert and Messines and the hills of Ferrain approach the banks of the river from north and south respectively. Twenty-five km (16 miles) below Aire the Lys is joined by the Lawe, also flowing from the hills of Artois, and at Deulémont on the Belgian side of the frontier it receives the Deûle. It seems that the Deûle once continued northeastwards beyond Lille as the then upper part of the proto-Scheldt. It was captured by a tributary of the Lys, and so the river now makes, below Lille, a sharp right-angled bend to the north. Its deserted lower valley is followed by the Roubaix Canal and its Belgian continuation, the Espierres Canal (Fig. 4.2), which joins the Scheldt at Espierres and thus resurrects the former river course.

Further to the southeast river capture has been even more active. The upper Scarpe once flowed northeastwards to join the Dendre, but this section was captured by a northwards-flowing subsequent stream, leaving only the small truncated West Dendre. This subsequent developed still more actively and captured the upper waters of yet another consequent, the lower part of which is now the eastern Dendre, and then successively two more, the former headwaters of the Senne and the Sennette. This subsequent is known as the Haine, which joins the Scheldt at Condé; its valley is followed by the Mons-Condé Canal and by the western part of the Centre Canal, so forming a useful west–east link across the Franco-Belgian coalfield. The Haine rises only 3 km (2 miles) from a left-bank Sambre tributary.

The most striking diversification of Flanders is the result of isolated patches of Pliocene sands resting on the Flanders Clay, forming the higher interfluves in the south and southwest. In Belgium, between the Dendre and the Scheldt, appears the gently undulating ridge of the Ronse hills; they form several rounded summits, notably the Pottelberg (157 m (515 ft)) to the east of Ronse. Other outlying hillocks extend for 50 km (30 miles) across southwestern Belgium into France. The prominence of these summits was to elevate them to a strategic eminence in the war of 1914–18 far beyond their actual altitude, and their names have achieved a notorious place in military history (Fig. 7.1). The ridge first becomes evident near Passchendale and trends southwestward to the south of Ieper, culminating in Belgium in the Kemmelberg 156 m (512 ft). It then extends westward into France, capping the Ieper clay plateau (which forms a watershed between the polders of the upper Ijzer to the north and the Lys basin to the south), and culminating in a string of summits. After a distinct break in this ridge, caused by the cutting back of the upper valley of the Becque, it rises again to Mont des Récollets and Mont Cassel, and ends quite markedly in the west, overlooking the Aa valley near Watten; it drops in a short distance from 72 m (236 ft) to less than 2 m (6 ft) above sea level. The line of hills is dissected by the numerous north-flowing tributaries of the Ijzer.

Another element contributes to the diversification of the relief of French Flanders. Several areas of the Chalk form projecting spurs and isolated masses, separated by faulting or by river erosion from the Artois hills to the west; such is Vimy Ridge, another name famous in the annals of war.

The southern part of French Flanders, between the Lys valley and the Chalk of Cambrésis to the southeast of Valenciennes, is one of considerable diversity, resulting in a number of *pays* (Fig. 7.2). The low hills in the angle of the Deûle and the Lys are known as the *Ferrain*, and the chalk uplands which project as a low promontory east of Lille towards Tournai form the *Mélantois*. The Eocene plateau between Lille and La Bassée is the *Carembault*. The *Pévèle* extends southward from the edge of the chalk hills of

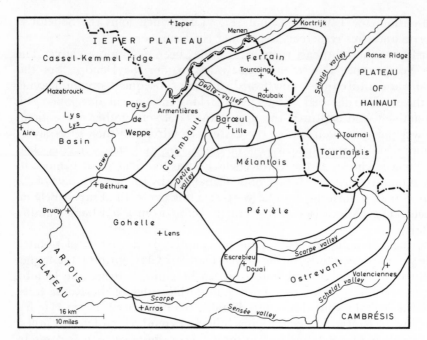

Fig. 7.2. Regional units of western Flanders
This map is intended to provide a key to the general position of the regional
units referred to in the text. The boundaries are frequently necessarily arbitrary,
although various criteria (geological outcrops, significant contours, etc.) are
used where possible.

Mélantois to the valley of the Scarpe, forming a basin of Eocene clays overlying the sands which outcrop on the margins, particularly in the southwest,
to form low hills. The clay plain itself lies at about 40 to 50 m (130 to 160 ft),
and is covered with streams and drainage ditches. The *Ostrevant* is a *pays*
situated between the Scarpe and Sensée-Scheldt valleys, an area of sands
and clays overlying the Chalk, and consequently rather dry. It is low in the
east, but rises towards Douai as undulating wooded hills. Underlying the
Ostrevant is the concealed basin of the Nord coalfield. The *Gohelle* lies
between the Pévèle and the Artois chalk hills, and forms a gently undulating
plain crossed by the upper Deûle; like the Ostrevant, it is underlain by a
concealed coalfield, the Pas-de-Calais basin. Other *pays* can be distinguished; the *Tournaisis* lies between the Pévèle and the Scheldt valley
near Tournai, the name *Escrebieu* is often applied to the Douai district, and
the *Baroeul* is the area between Lille and Tourcoing.

## Agriculture

Interior Flanders has been for centuries one of the most closely settled and
densely populated areas in Europe. It has long possessed a flourishing

146

agricultural, industrial and commercial economy, and many of the towns have been prosperous centres of urban life since medieval times, as their architectural glories testify.

Agriculture is carried on intensively, much of it virtually on a horticultural scale, for holdings are small, particularly in the northern parts of the province of Oost-Vlaanderen. Long before the Agrarian Revolution in England, the hard-working Flemings had discovered the value of heavy manuring of the sandy soils, and had thereby obviated the necessity of a period of fallow. The proximity of the large towns has encouraged market-gardening, and hops, potatoes, sugar beet, chicory, flax and even wheat are grown in small patches, often by spade cultivation. On many holdings more than one main crop is produced each season; turnips, for example, sometimes follow a cereal. High yields are general, the result of heavy manuring both with artificials and dung. Clover and fodder crops are included in the rotations to feed dairy cattle; each holding usually has a small herd of two or three animals, sometimes stall-fed, to produce milk, butter, cheese and veal. The number of cooperative dairies has grown in recent years, but these are still inadequate to stimulate a really flourishing dairying industry; it is merely one contributory item in a mixed farming economy.

Towards the south in West-Vlaanderen, Hainaut and French Flanders, the size of the farms increases, mechanisation replaces the patient laborious spade cultivation of northern Flanders, and larger fields of wheat and sugar beet become dominant. Some specialisation has developed in industrial crops—flax in the valley of the Lys near Kortrijk and Tielt and in the Scarpe valley, tobacco in the Ieperle valley, and chicory between Kortrijk and Roeselare and near Aire, while potatoes are extensively grown in the sandy soils. Dairy farming also increases in scale southward; many farms in French Flanders have herds of twenty to a hundred animals to supply the densely populated industrial districts. Some permanent pastures occur in the water-meadows in the upper Lys basin and on the flat floors of other river valleys, and much clover and fodder beet are grown as supplementary feeding.

## Industry

Industry is carried on in close association with agriculture throughout Flanders. Many factory workers live in the country, often owning a small-holding which they cultivate on a family basis, and travelling daily some distance to their work. Domestic industry has declined, it is true, but it is still practised quite widely. The three main groups of activities are still the mining, metallurgical and textile industries, though there have been considerable recent attempts at diversification (tyres, electronics, car assembly, clothing) to provide work for those redundant because of a decline in these staple activities, especially in textiles and mining (see note, p. 291).

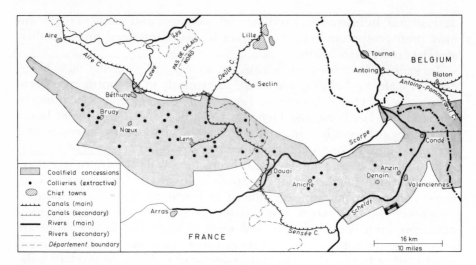

FIG. 7.3. The coalfield of northern France
There is a slight discrepancy between the areas of the concessions shown on this map and on Fig. 18.8, the result of different interpretations as shown on the two source maps. A number of these collieries has been closed during the last few years,

Based on the *Atlas de France*, plate 44, with revisions from various sources.

## The coalfield of northern France

Underlying the sands and clays of French Flanders is a synclinal depression where the rim of the Artois ridge dips steeply to the northeast. Below the Chalk lies the concealed coalfield of the Nord and the Pas-de-Calais; the Coal Measures, exposed on the surface further to the east in Belgium, are found progressively deeper to the west, and cease to be exploitable just southwest of Aire.[2]

As in southern Belgium, the field is situated rather unfortunately from a structural point of view, since it was subject not only to the Hercynian orogeny, but also to the complex fracturing associated with the stages of uplift of the Ardennes during early and mid-Tertiary times (see pp. 483–7). In places overthrusting has forced older sedimentary rocks above the Coal Measures, especially in the southwest of the field, and moreover the workable coal is separated by faults which divide the field into several individual productive areas. The two main basins are those of Douai-Valenciennes in the east and Béthune-Lens in the west, separated by barren ground (Fig. 7.3). The coal is worked at considerable depths, the mines averaging well over 400 m (1 300 ft) and at times attaining 900 m (3 000 ft) below the surface. Moreover, the earth movements have affected the Coal Measures in detail; many individual seams are interrupted and displaced by faults and sometimes they dip at high angles. The large number of thin seams makes for difficult and expensive exploitation; the average thickness

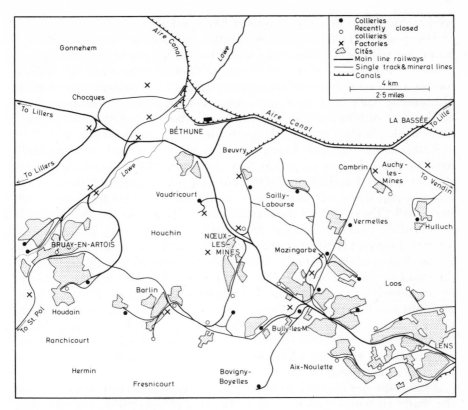

FIG. 7.4. The Béthune-Lens industrial region
Names of towns and villages are lettered in their correct positions, without symbols (other than the *cités-ouvrières*). Several more collieries have been closed in recent years.

Based on *Carte de France au 50 000ᵉ*, sheet XXIV/5.

worked is only about a metre and some seams are as little as 0·3 m.

Despite these many physical disadvantages, the field is still of some importance to France, since in 1971 its active collieries produced 15 million tons, rather less than half of the total national output of 34·5 million. About two-thirds came from the Pas-de-Calais section, the most important producing areas being around Lens, Noeux, Béthune and Bruay (Fig. 7.4). In the *département* of Nord, the main districts are near Douai (Plate 19) in the west, Aniches, and as far east as Anzin and Condé, the regional centre being Valenciennes. Largely because the coalfield was entirely restored and re-equipped in the decade following the war of 1914–18, a high proportion of mechanical operation takes place. In the post-1945 period too, much modernisation has been effected; this has been systematised in two stages, the first 1947–56, the second still in progress. The number of collieries has been reduced to a quarter since 1947 as a result of the policy of concentration. But it has recently been announced that the field will be wholly shut-down by 1983, as part of EEC policy.

The quality of coal is extremely variable, not only in various parts of the basin, but with depth; the upper seams consist mainly of high volatile gas coals, the lower ones of semi-anthracite. Thus in 1969 about 7·6 million tons of anthracite and semi-anthracite (*maigre*), 2·2 million tons of semi-bituminous coals used for metallurgical coke production (*demi-gras*), 7·6 million tons of bituminous coals (*gras*), and about 1·5 million tons of long-flame coals (*flambant gras*) made up the output of this northern field.

Rather more than half of the coal produced is consumed on the coalfield itself at the coke ovens, patent fuel plant and thermal-electric power-stations. More than half the French coke output (which totalled 9 million tons in 1969) was made at pithead cokeries, most of them large units built since 1948. Two-thirds of these cokeries are situated in the Pas-de-Calais section of the field near Fléchinelle (the most westerly unit), Ferfay, Bruay, Grenay, Lens and Hénin-Liétard. The three Nord cokeries are mainly in the Douai district to the west of Valenciennes. Considerably more than half of the coal gas manufactured in France is produced at these cokeries, mainly for use in industry; it is distributed over the northern industrial area by a gas grid, but this byproduct coal gas is being rapidly replaced by natural gas piped from Slochteren in the Netherlands (p. 139) and by refinery gas from the Seine valley. A dozen large power stations, fuelled either by coal or coal gas, are owned either by *Electricité de France* or the *Houillères nationales*; the largest is at Hornaing in Nord.

A large amount of coal dust and small coal is unavoidably obtained from the shattered seams, and modern methods of recovery from the screening and washing plant enable much former waste material to be utilised. As a result, over 5 million tons of *briquettes* (large blocks used as steam-raising fuel) and *boulets* (small 'ovoids' burnt in domestic stoves) and manufactured each year by mixing the dust with pitch obtained from the tar distillation plants, mainly at Aniche, by far the most important centre, and also at Anzin, Bruay, Courrières, Noeux and Oignies.

About two-thirds of the coal produced in the northern field is consumed elsewhere, and Lens and Douai are the main handling centres. It is significant that both are on inland waterways; coal moves by canal towards Paris and to many parts of northern and central France. Some is used in other industrial areas of northeastern France, notably in the textile factories of the Lille-Roubaix area.

A very considerable chemical industry has developed on the coalfield, associated with the byproducts of the cokeries. Thus in 1969 about 170 000 tons of coal tar, 57 000 tons of sulphate of ammonia and 44 000 tons of benzine were obtained, the raw materials for a wide range of chemical and pharmaceutical products, fertilisers, aniline dyes, detergents, plastics, acids, motor fuels and industrial alcohol. The main plants are in the neighbourhood of Béthune, Liévin and Courrières. A large tyre factory was recently opened at Béthune. A small oil refinery at Valenciennes had a throughput of 870 000 tons in 1969; it is linked by pipeline to the terminal at Dunkirk.

## The metallurgical industry

Many of the towns in Belgian Flanders, particularly Gent (see p.155), Tournai, Kortrijk and Ronse have a variety of metallurgical manufactures, including sheet steel at Zelzate, textile machinery, electric motors and diesel engines.

The two French *départements* of Nord and Pas-de-Calais form the most important part of the *Région Nord* of the Chambre Syndicale de la Sidérurgie Française (Fig. 11.7). No iron ore is mined in this region, and ore and pig iron come both by rail from Lorraine and by sea through the port of Dunkirk from Mauretania, Brazil and Liberia. In 1969 about 5·1 million tons of pig iron were produced, and about 5 million tons of steel. About a third of the latter consisted of 'Martin steel' made in basic open-hearth plant, though an increasing amount is made in new Basic Oxygen converters. As might be expected, a considerable variety of steel-using industries, both light and heavy, provide quantities of scrap for the steel hearths.

The metallurgical industry has developed both on the coalfield and away from it. The major concentration on the coalfield is around Valenciennes, both along the canalised Scheldt and to the west of it. The largest company in the northern industrial region is Usinor (Union Sidérurgique du Nord de la France), incorporated in 1950. It owns large integrated plants to the south of Valenciennes at Trith and further west at Denain; extensive developments have taken place at these establishments under the postwar modernisation plans. Usinor has recently amalgamated with the Lorraine-Escaut company, with a combined capacity of 8 million tons of steel.

While much semifinished steel is sent away to the Paris industrial district, to Lille and to southern Belgium, a varied range of metal-using industries is active within the coalfield area—rails, locomotives, boilers, chains (a speciality at Anzin), steel wire at Trith, textile machinery and agricultural implements. Douai is the centre of various engineering industries.

Although Lille's chief industrial importance depends on textiles, numerous metallurgical and engineering establishments make, as might be expected, a range of textile machinery and also agricultural implements for the Flanders Plain and the Paris Basin. In the industrial suburbs which have grown up to the east of the city, particularly in the post-1918 period of construction, heavy engineering is carried on. This includes the construction of locomotives and rolling-stock for the Région Nord of the SNCF, electric motors and boilers. Roubaix-Tourcoing, 8 km (5 miles) away to the northeast, also has textile machinery works. Further west, at Isbergues in Pas-de-Calais, is a large modern integrated steel-plant, largely rebuilt in the post 1945 years and again modernised since 1960.

## The textile industry

The Flanders Plain has been one of the world's leading textile-manufacturing areas since the Middle Ages, though during recent years there has been a considerable decline, with the closure of many mills and the reduction of the labour force by over a third during the last decade.

In early times there was a concentration on woollens, first using local wool from sheep on the neighbouring hills and then importing Cotswold wool. This branch of the industry, now consuming wool from South Africa and Australia, is still important in French Flanders, especially in the Roubaix-Tourcoing conurbation and near Cambrai, but the main centre in Belgium moved as early as the fifteenth century from Flanders into the Verviers district to the east of Liège. Some interesting specialisations in woollen manufacture survive at such towns as Gent, Kortrijk and Eekloo.

Linen has also flourished for centuries along the Lys valley at Armentières, Wevelgem, Kortrijk, Gent and a multiplicity of smaller places, and also at Roeselare, Lokeren, Aalst, Ronse, Roubaix, Lille and Valenciennes. The industry had such advantages as locally grown flax, the pure water of the Lys for retting, and a dense, hard-working population. As late as the nineteenth century most flax used was still grown locally in the Belgian province of West-Vlaanderen and in French Flanders, cultivated mainly on small-holdings and harvested on contract by large firms who retted the flax and sold the fibre to the mills. Today, however, home-produced flax supplies only a fifth of the requirements and the rest is imported. Fine linens still constitute a major product and are a valuable export item.

Cotton is now the pre-eminent textile in Belgian Flanders, despite competition from Japan and India in recent decades. More than half of the spindles are located in and around Gent; factories are situated within the city itself and at such growing suburbs as Gentbrugge, Wetteren and Ledeberg. The industry has also spread along the valleys of the Scheldt (at Oudenaarde and Ronse) and of the Dendre (at Aalst, Ninove, Geeraardsbergen and Ath). A number of individual small firms specialise in different branches of the industry, though a few large combines have been created through mergers. Even the small independent companies have for the most part grouped themselves into marketing organisations. An immense variety of both thread and fabrics is made. A special line at Gent, Aalst and Dendermonde is the manufacture of cotton blankets for use in the tropics.

The mills of Belgian Flanders dominate the cotton industry in that country, but those of French Flanders have important rivals in the lower Seine valley near Rouen, in Alsace and in the Central Massif. Nevertheless Lille, Roubaix-Tourcoing, Armentières and La Bassée have many large factories, and specialisations include the manufacture of muslins and voiles at Lille itself.

These long-established branches of the textile industry have helped to create both a tradition and a labour force. As a result, other textiles (jute, rayon and nylon) are now produced, in more or less the same centres, Gent and Kortrijk being dominant in Belgium, and Lille and Roubaix-Tourcoing in France. A vast range of associated industries in both countries uses yarns and cloths; in fact almost every town in Flanders, and in central Belgium too, possesses some branch of the textile industry. Some of these towns, such as Brussels, Vilvoorde and Lier, lie further east on the central plateaus and will be mentioned later. Others are in Flanders itself; Tournai, for example, has long been famous for carpets, Lille has an immense output of readymade clothing, and the Roubaix-Tourcoing agglomeration makes clothing, hosiery, knitting wool, carpets, tapestries and furnishing fabrics.

## The waterways

The waterway system of Flanders comprises the regularised Scheldt and its almost parallel tributaries Lys and Dendre, interlinked by several transverse canals (Fig. 4.2), and also connected with the waterways of the Paris Basin across the Artois watershed and with the Sambre-Meuse system to the southeast. The river Lys, the most northerly of the Scheldt family, has been embanked for most of its length, and cuts have been made across several loops. Six locks are required to maintain a minimum navigational depth of about 2 m (7 ft). Although the river is usually very sluggish, there is a considerable difference in regime between the low-water flow of late summer and the high-water of winter. The river is navigable for barges as far upstream as Aire.

The Scarpe, which is wholly a French river, joins the Scheldt a kilometre from the Belgian frontier. It is canalised from Arras for a distance of nearly 65 km (40 miles), and as it crosses the northern coalfield by way of Douai it forms a very useful waterway, particularly as it is linked northward to Lille by the Deûle Canal and southward to the Scheldt by the Sensée Canal. Douai, at the junction of these several canals, has extensive basins and wharves, for it is an important coal depot.

The Scheldt is an important waterway both to France and to Belgium. Above Cambrai in France the river is unnavigable, but navigation is continued southward across the watershed to the Seine system by the St Quentin Canal. Below Cambrai the river has been canalised, and a navigational depth of 2 to 2·5 m (7 to 8 ft) is maintained by sixteen locks in France and a further six in Belgium. Thus the Scheldt affords 63 km (39 miles) of waterway in France and a further 200 km (125 miles) in Belgium. It crosses the eastern part of the Nord coalfield, flowing through such important towns as Cambrai and Valenciennes, and its banks are lined almost continuously with wharves and warehouses. It serves too the rich agricultural area in the neighbourhood of Cambrésis, with the considerable production of sugar beet and cereals; several sugar refineries are located on its banks. Then in Belgium the river flows across the densely populated plain of Flanders through such textile towns as Tournai and Oudenaarde before its junction with the Lys at Gent.

The Scheldt and its tributaries are interlinked in France by a continuous chain of transverse canals, so that it is possible for barges to move south-eastwards from Calais and Dunkirk as far as the Scheldt, following a line broadly parallel to the Belgian frontier at a distance of about 30 km (20 miles). This traffic first utilises the Calais Canal and the canalised river Aa to St Omer, and continues along the short Neuffossé Canal to Aire. The Aire Canal then runs southeastward through Béthune, and at Bauvin joins the Deûle Canal. The last is a very important waterway, 64 km (40 miles) in length, since it links the Lys and the Scarpe across the western part of the coalfield, it serves the industrial centre of Lille, and a branch canal bordered by almost continuous coal wharves serves the Lens section of the Pas-de-Calais field. The Roubaix (or Espierres) Canal continues the line of the Deûle to the northeast of Lille, crosses the frontier, and joins the Scheldt at Espierres. Finally, the Sensée Canal leaves the Scarpe near Douai and completes the chain by linking it to the Scheldt near Etrun. The Sensée is specially useful, since it forms the main connection between the various coalfield waterways and Paris by way of the St Quentin Canal. The chief items carried on these waterways are, as might be expected, coal and coke; oil, pyrites, salt and soda (the last two from Lorraine) are other important items.

It is a reflection both of the economic orientation of the Flanders Plain towards the lower Scheldt and Antwerp and also of the pattern of natural drainage that few waterways connect the Lys-Scheldt system with the North Sea coast. The river Ijzer has been canalised, but is of very fluctuating depth and is sometimes unnavigable for several months in summer. It is linked by the Ieper-Ijzer Canal with the town of Ieper; formerly this continued south over the watershed to the Lys as the Ieper-Lys Canal, which was destroyed during the war of 1914–18, and it was decided that its rebuilding was not worth while. Further east is the Gent-Ostend Canal, begun as long ago as 1614, and completed to the coast at Ostend by 1753; it is a useful waterway, 68 km (42 miles) in length, serving the agricultural plain of Flanders.

The chalk ridge of Artois extends southeastward from the Boulonnais, forming a range of low hills which presents an appreciable barrier between the waterways of the Flanders Plain and those of the Seine system. It is crossed by the St Quentin Canal, a waterway 92 km (57 miles) long, which leaves the canalised Scheldt at Cambrai and negotiates the watershed by means of forty-two double locks and two tunnels near the divide, descending to the Oise Lateral Canal at Chauny, and so to Paris. The importance of this link is such that it has been enlarged several times; in 1928, for example, the summit divide tunnels were widened and deepened. Electric tractors are used for haulage to increase the working capacity of the canal. A second waterway crossing was achieved in 1965 by the completion of the

Canal du Nord (Fig. 9.5).

The Scheldt system is connected with the Sambre-Meuse by two link-canals. The Mons-Condé Canal is a straight west–east waterway 25 km (16 miles) long, running from the French Scheldt at Condé across the frontier to Mons, and so serving both the French and Belgian portions of the coalfield. A second link, wholly within Belgium, joins the Scheldt near Antoing with the Mons-Condé Canal at Pommeroeul. Several other interconnections have been developed in this area. The Blaton-Ath Canal crosses southward from Ath in the Dendre valley to the Antoing-Pommeroeul Canal. The Centre Canal continues the Mons-Condé Canal eastward through the coalfield area to join the Brussels-Charleroi Canal at Houdeng-Goegnies. The Centre has the steepest gradient of any Belgian waterway, with an average rise of about one in 230, although it needs only six locks. Modern electrically-operated barge-lifts are used.

The waterways within the western part of the Scheldt system and their links with neighbouring rivers therefore serve much of the coalfield of northern France, the important French industrial complex of Lille-Roubaix-Tourcoing, and the Belgian textile area of the Lys-Scheldt valleys, as well as the cities and ports of Gent and Antwerp and a dense agricultural population in the Flanders Plain. During the last decade, the waterway links between Dunkirk, Lille and Valenciennes have been enlarged to take 3 000-ton barges (Fig. 4.2).

## Population and settlement[3]

It is not surprising that Interior Flanders has such a dense population. Most of the rural population is dispersed widely over the countryside, with individual houses situated within smallholdings, and perhaps only a church to indicate the commune centre; Flanders is in fact a type area for 'dispersed' rural settlement.

The industrial towns, comprising as a rule an old centre, often walled and water-ringed, with a girdle of new suburbs, are strung out along the main and subsidiary valleys; these have been mentioned already in connection with their long-established textile industries. In the *département* of Pas-de-Calais, Lens, Béthune, Bruay, Noeux and many more towns form a densely populated industrial district; the old towns, the new housing estates (*cités-ouvrières*) and industrial estates, the collieries, coke ovens, byproduct plants and spoil-dumps are spread over the countryside (Fig. 7.4). In the east is the Valenciennes basin, where Douai,[4] Denain and Anzin have developed similarly (Plate 20).

Gent[5] (*Gand* in French, *Ghent* in English), surpassed in size in Belgium only by Brussels and Antwerp, has long been an important city in the Flanders Plain. The Lys and the upper Scheldt meet in the southeast of the city, and the lower Scheldt, tidal up to the Gentbrugge weir, then flows gently eastwards towards Antwerp and its estuary. Several minor rivers and

PLATE 20. Colliery number 10 at Oignies, Pas-de-Calais. The waterway in the foreground is the Canal de la Haute-Deule

PLATE 21. Industrial suburbs in Gent along the Gent-Terneuzen Canal

drainage canals intersect the city, the ship canal from Terneuzen on the Wester Schelde enters the docks in the northeast (see p. 86), and a smaller canal comes eastward across the plain from Bruges and Ostend. Wherever one goes in Gent, in fact, one has to cross water; there are said to be over two hundred bridges within the city, and the built-up area actually lies on twenty-three islands (Plate 21).

Gent has had a long and prosperous history; as early as 1500 it had a population of over 100 000, the result of its rich industrial and commercial activity. In 1970 the population of the commune was 149 000 but several adjacent suburbs bring the population of the agglomeration to over 230 000. It is a useful port, second to Antwerp in Belgium; in 1969, 3 254 seagoing ships were accommodated, and it handled about 8·5 million tons of freight. Vessels of up to 10 000 tons can dock there.

As has already been made evident, Gent is the dominating centre of all branches of the Belgian textile industry except woollens, and it has an immense variety of related manufactures, such as carpets and clothing. Textiles today, however, account for less than half of its industrial importance. Chemicals (especially dyestuffs), fertilisers, metallurgical products and glassware are made, and around the docks (Plate 21) and in the eastern and northern suburbs are flour mills, saw mills, tanneries, paper mills (one of these produces half of Belgium's consumption of newsprint), a low temperature carbonisation plant, and a huge electrochemical works. The Belgian-Shell company owns a bitumen refining plant, and a Texaco refinery was opened in 1968, using crude oil brought by pipeline from the Zeebrugge oil terminal (p. 82). Other factories are situated along the banks of the ship canal to the north. A modern integrated steel plant (*Sidmar*) at Zelzate, between Gent and Terneuzen, has a capacity of 2 million tons. These modern industrial developments and the new suburban housing estates contrast remarkably with the old inner town, where stand some of the architectural glories of Belgium—the *Hôtel de Ville*, the *Halle aux Draps* (Cloth Hall), the cathedral and other attractive buildings.

Lille lies on the right bank of the canalised Deûle; the old town was contained within massive triangular fortifications, which with the imposing pentagonal citadel were largely the work of Vauban. During its long history the town has generally prospered, but it has suffered periodically from the wars which so often beset Flanders, for as a great strongpoint it was frequently involved, often besieged and sometimes taken; even in the war of 1914–18 it was heavily shelled although it was declared an open town at the outbreak of hostilities. Lille's outstanding growth has been during the last century and a half, when it has become the leading commercial and industrial city of northeastern France, although so near the Belgian frontier from which attack has come three times in the last century. Outside the city a close ring of industrial suburbs spreads into the countryside and has absorbed the former individual villages. Lille had a population in 1968 of 191 000, though with Roubaix, Tourcoing and the other communes which comprise the official agglomeration the total was 881 000. It is a vital communications centre, for here a main line railway from Calais and Dunkirk to Strasbourg crosses the main Paris–Brussels and Paris–Gent lines, the motorway to Paris is complete, and that to Antwerp is under construction. There is a useful river port, since the Deûle Canal links the Scarpe with the Lys. Lille's manufactures are many and varied; it is the largest single textile-making town in France, it has a range of metallurgical and chemical industries, and there are sugar refineries, flour mills, tobacco factories, distilleries, breweries, tanneries and chocolate factories. With Roubaix and Tourcoing, Lille[6] has now become one of the eight official *métropoles d'équilibres* (p. 199), and is the headquarters of the Picardie planning region.

The towns of Roubaix and Tourcoing, with their neighbouring communes, now form part of the Lille agglomeration. They lie only a kilometre or so from the Belgian frontier and 11 km (7 miles) from Lille, to which they are virtually connected by continuously built-up areas. Each has a long industrial history; as early as the eleventh century Tourcoing was famed for its velveteens and serges. As at Lille, industrial expansion was rapid in the nineteenth century and the textile industry, particularly wool, flourished. The two towns produce four-fifths of all French woollen yarn, and other items such as carpets, tapestries, furnishing fabrics and clothing. Textiles are predominant, but other manufactures include leather, rubber, miscellaneous metallurgical products and chemicals. Many Belgian workers cross the frontier daily to factories in the two towns.

The Flanders landscape is thus a remarkable palimpsest on which a millennium of vicissitudes has left its impressions. Before its final nineteenth-century division between France and Belgium, it had belonged to the Counts of Flanders, then it was successively under Burgundian, Austrian, Spanish and French rule. During the war of 1914–18, French Flanders suffered the devastating results of the most concentrated and prolonged static warfare that the world has ever experienced; two rich *départements* were ruined, the most important industrial regions of France were devastated. Southern French Flanders was a shattered wilderness in 1918: towns such as Lens, Arras and Cambrai (the centre of which was mined when the Germans evacuated in 1918) suffered immense damage, and many collieries and mining villages were wiped off the landscape. Some compensation did result in the long run, for the coalfield was rebuilt on modern lines. But the vast war cemeteries, the occasional plaque stating that a village once stood here, and the memorials (as at Vimy) are tragic monuments to the sufferings of Flanders nearly sixty years ago.

[1] R. Nistri and C. Prêcheur, *La Région du Nord et du Nord-Est* (1959); and the *Atlas du Nord de la France* (1961).

[2] R. Gendarme, *La Région du Nord: essai d'analyse économique* (1954). For detailed reviews of recent developments, see I. B. Thompson, 'A geographical appraisal of recent trends in the coal basin of northern France', *Geography*, **50** (1965), pp. 252–60; and 'A review of problems of economic and urban development in the northern Coalfield of France', *Southampton Research Series in Geography* (1965), no. 1, pp. 31–60.

[3] J. Beaujeu-Garnier, 'Géographie de la population de la région du Nord de la France et problèmes d'aménagement régional', *Bull. Soc. belge Etud. géogr.*, **30** (1961), pp. 67–92.

[4] J. R. Leborgne, 'Le site et l'évolution urbaine de Douai', *Annls. Géogr.*, **59** (1950), pp. 109–21.

[5] M. E. Dumont, *Gent: Een Stedenaardrijkskundrige Studie* (1951), provides much detail, including an atlas volume.

[6] P. Bruyelle, 'Les grandes villes françaises, Lille-Tourbaix-Tourcoing', *Notes et Etudes Documentaires* (1965), no. 3206, p. 111.

# 8
# The central low plateaus of Belgium and the Netherlands

## General features

The land rises gently towards the east and the southeast from the edge of the Flanders Plain, forming what can be called 'the central low plateaus'. This rise is of the order of 1 m per 1·5 km (3·5 ft per mile), from about 45 m (150 ft) above sea level to a height of 200 m (650 ft) near the southern margin of the region, where the land then falls quite steeply to the long curve of the Sambre-Meuse valley; the highest point is actually 220 m (722 ft) above sea level, to the northeast of Namur. This profile is well illustrated by the main line from Brussels to Liège via Tienen. From Brussels there is an up-gradient of the order of from 1 in 200 to 250 as far as Ans on the plateau above Liège, where the line reaches its maximum altitude of 180 m (590 ft). It then descends to the valley floor at about 68 m (225 ft) in a distance of less than 6 km (4 miles), with an average gradient of 1 in 32. This difficult section of line, although opened as early as 1842, had to be operated by cable haulage for goods traffic until 1871, and, until the recent electrification of the line, trains were assisted by banking locomotives.

It might reasonably be argued that this area ought not to be included in the broad regional unit of the North Sea lowlands on grounds of relative altitude. But the countryside has the general character of a lowland, certainly in comparison with the much higher Ardennes to the south, and indeed the area is commonly known as 'the low plateau of Middle Belgium'.

Palaeozoic rocks such as slates and quartzites, together with some associated igneous intrusions, underlie the plateaus at no great depth in the centre and south. The Senne and Dyle have cut down their valleys through the newer overlying strata, thus exposing the basement rocks; these are quarried for road-metal and setts in a number of places. Porphyritic diorites are worked at Quenast (Plate 22) and Lessines. Small outcrops of Devonian and Carboniferous rocks are also revealed in the valleys to the east of Mons. At Ecaussines in the Sennette valley and again at Soignies in the Senne valley are extensive limestone quarries; the bluish limestone, known in the district as *petit granit*, has long been worked for building stone, and when cut and polished it has an attractive marbled surface. Upper

PLATE 22. Quarry at Quenast in the valley of the upper Senne

Carboniferous rocks appear on the surface in the south of the Hainaut plateau. This is part of the 'coal furrow' of southern Belgium (see pp. 485–6), which is exposed further east within the narrow trench of the Sambre-Meuse beyond Charleroi, though in the Mons-Centre districts the coal is concealed beneath newer deposits.

The Chalk adds another contribution to the solid geology of these plateaus. It outcrops near Mons, again between Tienen and Liège, and beyond the valley of the Meuse over the greater part of South Limburg and the Pays de Herve. Frequently, however, a superficial cover of recent deposits occurs.

These Palaeozoic and Mesozoic rocks furnish abundant evidence of the complexity of the structural history of the plateaus. Some Belgian geologists consider that the Palaeozoic rocks represent an anciently established 'horst' or massive block, the southern bounding edge of the North Sea basin (Fig. 2.1). This was involved in the Hercynian folding at the end of Carboniferous times (see p. 483), and may even have formed part of the 'foreland' against which the folding took place. There is, however, evidence that the ancient rocks were themselves folded to form a very complex 'Brabant anticline' (Fig. 18.2), though much less intensely affected than the Ardennes further south. The northward limb of this fold dips gently under an increasingly thick cover of newer rocks, forming the Kempen syncline which contains Coal Measures.

Then followed the prolonged sequence of alternate denudation, marine transgression and deposition in Tertiary times already described (pp. 15–16). The net result was the formation of the present widespread cover of Older Tertiary rocks, consisting mostly of Eocene sands (although clays predominate in the southwest), together with occasional surviving patches of Oligocene and Pliocene sands.

Uplift and late Tertiary denudation combined to produce a broad surface dipping gently northward from the High Ardennes away to the North Sea basin. Belgian geomorphologists distinguish a '*surface plane*' at 180 to 200 m (590 to 650 ft) along the southern edge of the Brabant and Hesbaye plateaus, which has been correlated with similar surfaces to the south of the Meuse valley on the margins of the Ardennes. But the 'furrow' eroded by the Sambre and the Meuse, a relatively recent feature (see p. 489), lies transversely across this once continuous erosion plane, and thus separates the plateaus of 'High Belgium' from these central low plateaus.

This northward tilt of the low plateaus is naturally reflected in the courses of the main rivers in the eastern Scheldt basin (the Senne, Dyle, Gette and upper Demer), until each in turn is picked up by the east–west line of the Demer, Dyle and Rupel in yet another transverse 'furrow', south of the Kempenland plateau (see p. 18). Only in the extreme south, where, as has been described (see p. 145), the Haine flows to the west, and in the east, where the Méhaigne and Geer make their way eastwards to the Meuse, have streams developed athwart this northward tilt.

In the broad valleys of the rivers much alluvium has been deposited. In addition, forming a most important contribution to the agricultural economy, a widespread cover of limon (Fig. 2.5 and see p. 24) lies on the interfluves of the plateau surface. On this have developed brownish loams of excellent quality. Brabant and Hesbaye in fact have much in common with Beauce and with the *Börde* of Hanover and Magdeburg.

Large hedgeless fields grow wheat and sugar beet (Plate 23), producing high yields from the heavily fertilised loam-soils, with numerous prosperous-looking nucleated villages and occasional large isolated farms (Plate 24). The low plateaus have an average density of population of the general order of 150 to 200 per sq km (400 to 500 per sq mile). These figures, however, are swollen by the considerable urban population, for some of the towns have had a flourishing existence for a thousand years or more. If rural population alone is considered, the average is considerably less than in Interior Flanders, mainly because farms are much larger and there is less of the intensive smallholding system.

Differences are nevertheless evident between various parts of these low plateaus. Brabant and Hainaut may be considered as one region, for these names refer mainly to adjoining administrative provinces and they have geographically much in common. Further to the east, within the obtuse angle of the Meuse, is the plateau of Hesbaye. Across the north, from the Rupel to the Gette-Demer confluence, lies the 'furrow' between the Kempenland and the low plateaus; the transitional character of this

PLATE 23. The arable lands of the Dyle valley between Leuven and Mechelen

PLATE 24. A farm on the plateau of Brabant

district is indicated by the fact that some Belgian geographers name it the *Région Mixte*,[1] but nevertheless it does belong mainly to the 'northward slope' of central Belgium. Finally, beyond the Meuse valley are the eastern low plateaus, comprising the Pays de Herve of eastern Belgium and its continuation northward across the frontier into South Limburg. These six units are numbered from 6a to 6e respectively on Fig. 2.7.

## Brabant and Hainaut

The western low plateaus include the greater part of the province of Brabant and the eastern part of the province of Hainaut, corresponding more or less to the valleys and interfluves of the Dendre, Senne and Dyle. Both plateaus have an extensive *limon* cover, in Hainaut resting largely on clay, in Brabant mainly on sands. The floors of the valleys are broad and alluvium-covered. To the north the limon-derived soils gradually become sandier as the edge of the Meuse 'fan' is approached in the Demer-Dyle valley. The Palaeozoic rocks are never far below the surface, and are even exposed in places; as a result surface drainage is abundant even in the sandy country and very plentiful on the Hainaut clays. The plateau is much dissected, particularly in the south, by steepsided valleys.

Both Brabant and Hainaut are agriculturally of great importance, and wheat and sugar beet dominate in both in terms of area. The sandier soils of Brabant, however, carry a much higher proportion of arable, while in Hainaut there is more pasture, partly the result of the widespread damp claylands, partly due to the requirements of the mining towns for dairy produce. Hainaut is the chief horse-breeding region of Belgium; in spite of mechanisation many farms in central Belgium still use these heavy draught-horses.

In the neighbourhood of Brussels there is a concentration on market-gardening, dairying, pig and poultry farming, the production of flowers and nursery cultivation, in obvious response to the adjacent urban market. To the northwest of the city are immense areas of glasshouses, mainly producing early vegetables and flowers, while in the southeast beyond the Forêt de Soignes are more glasshouses devoted to grapes (Plate 25).[2]

The industrial importance of the Brabant-Hainaut region is considerable. The two outstanding areas are the Brussels conurbation, and the Mons (Borinage) and Centre basins of the southern coalfield of Belgium; it is, however, more convenient to describe the whole coalfield as a unit within the Sambre-Meuse valley (see pp. 500–5). Apart from these special cases, many towns have a great variety of industries. The Flanders textile industry extends eastward into Brabant—particularly at Brussels itself, Braine-l'Alleud and Anderlecht. In the Senne valley the towns of Halle, Braine-le-Comte and Soignies have miscellaneous metallurgical, textile and food-processing industries. At Clabecq[3] a large integrated iron and steel works is situated in the Sennette valley 25 km (15 miles) south of Brussels on

PLATE 25. Glass-houses at Hoeilaart, southeast of Brussels

the banks of the Brussels-Charleroi Canal; this affords an example of the location of a heavy industry away from both fuel and raw material, but with excellent communications with areas which can supply these needs and with a large accessible consuming market. A large oil refinery, also near the banks of this waterway, was opened at Felvy in 1971. Further east Leuven, Nivelles and a host of smaller towns, many within the Brussels orbit, all share the well-developed industrial life of Belgium. Leuven (in French *Louvain*) stands in a well-marked gap through the northern edge of the Brabant plateau. Its nucleus was a ninth-century castle on a wooded hill above the marshes of the river Dyle (hence the derivation of its name from *loo*, a wooded height, and *veen*, a marshland). Until the late fourteenth century it was a prosperous textile town, but then the city fell on hard times, remedied only slowly after the fifteenth century. Today it is a market centre for the surrounding agricultural countryside, and it has extensive food-processing industries, particularly brewing, flour-milling, the manufacture of potato starch and vegetable-canning. In addition, it has a number of metallurgical industries, including the manufacture of agricultural machinery, and chemical works, tanneries and saw mills. The Leuven-Dyle Canal links the town with the Rupel and the lower Scheldt, since the river Dyle itself is little used; the canal carries a considerable tonnage of fertilisers, flour, bricks and timber.

Vilvoorde is situated somewhat similarly to Leuven, where the Senne

165

cuts through the northern edge of the plateau of Brabant in a well defined gap, also followed by the Willebroek Canal. It too has had a long and prosperous history, and until it became involved in the fifteenth-century wars its cloth industry was thriving. Following a long period of decline, the town shared in the nineteenth-century expansion of Belgian industry and particularly in the prosperous period of 1896–1914. As a result, the manufacture of fertilisers, chemicals, electrical appliances, vegetable oils, glue, starch and leather is established on the banks of the Willebroek Canal in the suburbs, and many specialised factories (textiles and gloves) still operate within the town itself. There is also a coking plant and a car assembly plant.

## Brussels

The city of Brussels (in French *Bruxelles*, in Flemish *Brussel*), capital of Belgium, has for long been one of the main cities of Europe.[4] In 1970, while the population of the commune of Brussels itself was only about 170,000, the agglomeration (including eighteen contiguous communes) had a total of 1·1 million people. The city originated in the sixth century on one of the many islands among the marshland of the braided river Senne, hence the probable derivation of its name from *broek* (a marsh) and *sele* (a dwelling). The river now flows through the western part of the city, vaulted over for much of its course and incorporated within the city's drainage system, although it emerges into the daylight in the northwestern suburbs. The town developed rapidly from the eleventh century as its varied industrial and commercial activities increased. The built-up area grew on the drier terraces along the east bank, and it has now spread on to the sandstone plateau at 35 to 40 m (120 to 135 ft) above sea level, as compared with the valley floor at about 15 m (50 ft). There is a clear distinction between the 'lower town', with the commercial quarter, the spacious Grand' Place flanked by the magnificent fifteenth-century Gothic Hôtel de Ville, the docks and the canal port, and the residential 'upper town', the centre of which is the attractive Quartier Léopold, with its parks, boulevards and *places*. As the capital, Brussels has a wide range of administrative functions, it is a great commercial centre and is the main industrial district of Belgium. Its industries are extremely varied, including a wide range of metallurgical products, textiles (carpets, blankets, clothing), chemicals, paper, furniture and consumer goods generally. Heavy industry has developed notably along the canals in the northern and southern suburbs.

Brussels is a port in its own right, with a series of four large basins in the northwest of the city. The Brussels-Rupel Canal (Fig. 4.2), sometimes known as the Willebroek, enables vessels to reach the capital from the Scheldt estuary via the Rupel. The original waterway was built in the sixteenth century, but it was enlarged during the 1830s and again at the end of the century, and now has a depth of 6·5 m (21 ft) right into the port of

Brussels. Barges and seagoing vessels of up to about 3 000 tons can reach the port, but three locks and numerous bridges somewhat delay progress. Nevertheless, 4·4 million tons of freight were conveyed in 1969, an indication of the importance of this link between the chief port and the capital. From the southern end of the port the Brussels-Charleroi Canal (Fig. 4.2) leaves to cross the plateau of Brabant to the Sambre industrial region. The canal was originally constructed in 1827–32 to take vessels of some seventy tons, but successive works of enlargement have been carried through, and by 1922 barges of 300 tons could be accommodated. The main difficulty is a rise of about 100 m (350 ft), negotiated by utilising the valleys of the Senne and Sennette and with the aid of twenty-six locks and two short summit canals, followed by a further eleven locks down to Charleroi. In 1969, 4·7 million tons were conveyed along the canal including coal from the southern field, building materials and oil. This route is obviously so important that a project was put forward in the late 1930s for the creation of a 2 000 ton capacity canal; a modified scheme to enable 1 350 ton barges to use the canal was completed in 1965. It now provides a valuable waterway circuit around eastern Belgium, linking the southern and northern coalfields, the chief port and the capital.

Considerable developments have taken place in Brussels since the war of 1939–45, including a great extension of suburban housing estates and the building of vast blocks of flats and offices within the central area. Brussels is a most important railway focus, for seven main lines carrying international express traffic converge upon it, and the country's largest marshalling yard is at Schaerbeek in the northeastern suburbs. The two main stations are *Nord* and *Midi*, formerly linked only by circuitous beltlines both to west and east of the city, although only 3 km (2 miles) apart in a straight line. Their junction by an underground link was begun as long ago as 1903, but the interruptions of two wars and more urgent reconstruction delayed the completion until 1955. Since 1945 the *Nord* and *Midi* stations have been rebuilt and there is a new underground *Gare Centrale*.[5] Road communications too have developed since 1965, and the construction of several urban motorways is still in progress. The three ring roads (at distances of 1·5, 5 and 8 km approximately from the city centre) have been reconstructed, providing separate lanes for through and local traffic. Eight road tunnels have been built to carry ring traffic under the radial arteries and so prevent obstruction of flow at these busy intersections. The *autostrade* from Brussels to Ostend runs straight across country, bypassing to the south towns such as Aalst, Gent and Bruges. This highway was begun in 1936, and by the outbreak of war the Aalter-Jabbeke section was finished; the road was completed in 1956. Other motorways lead to Antwerp, Liège and Namur. The construction of the Brussels *métro* began in 1965. In all, Brussels is one of the most attractive and progressive capital cities in Europe, deriving much importance from its rôle as the administrative headquarters of the European Economic Community and of the North Atlantic Treaty Organisation.

## The plateau of Hesbaye

The northern part of Hesbaye has the prevailing northerly tilt of the central low plateaus, and several streams flow northwards to the Demer. In the south, however, two river systems have developed athwart the slope. The Méhaigne flows eastwards, having captured successively several north-flowing tributaries, former headstreams of the Gette, before it breaks southwards through the plateau edge to join the Meuse just above Huy. The Geer also flows eastwards through Tongeren, to join the Meuse above Maastricht.

Like the plateaus of Hainaut and Brabant, Hesbaye is largely limon-covered, but while in the north this superficial deposit rests on sand, in the south and east it is underlain by the Upper Chalk. The combination of the friable porous limon, sometimes over 15 m (50 ft) thick, and the permeable Chalk has resulted in a notable absence of surface drainage, except in the few shallow valleys of the Gette, upper Demer, Geer and Méhaigne. Compared with the dissected plateaus of southern Brabant and Hesbaye, therefore, the surface is much more uniform. Some broad shallow depressions are the product of subsidence following solution of the underlying Chalk. Particularly in the east shafts or 'pipes' occur in the Chalk due to localised solution down fissures. Now filled with sands or clays, they vary in diameter from 0·3 to 2 m (1 to 7 ft), and penetrate for a distance of from 1 to 20 m (3 to 65 ft) or more. These features are particularly well developed in the extreme northeast, where the Hesbaye plateau projects into the Maastricht territory. Belgian geomorphologists have given the name of 'plateau subkarstique de sous-sol crayeux' to this part.

The countryside consists of open fields; arable farming is predominant, and in southern Hesbaye the emphasis is almost exclusively on the cultivation of wheat and sugar beet on large holdings. Further north agriculture becomes more mixed in character, and includes market-gardening and fruit-growing on the sandy loams.

Southern Hesbaye has many small towns and villages nucleated into compact groups of houses and farms, and separated by stretches of open farmland. This nucleation was due originally to the clustering of houses within communal lands farmed on the openfield system. Most of these settlements have fewer than 5 000 inhabitants, with local agricultural industries and occasional specialisations, such as cutlery manufacture at Gembloux. Further north a line of larger towns is strung out along the medieval trade route from Antwerp and Bruges via Leuven to the Rhineland; these include Tienen in the valley of the Grande-Gette, Saint-Truiden and Tongeren, a line continued eastward through Maastricht and Aachen. As a result, these towns have a long commercial and industrial tradition. Tienen (*Tirlemont*) lies on the northern margins of an extensive sugar beet area, and in fact possesses the largest sugar refinery in Belgium, as well as other agricultural processing industries—flour mills, tanneries, starch factories—and it is the world's largest producer of citric acid.

The plateau of Hesbaye to the northeast of Tongeren just enters the Netherlands where the frontier makes its westerly loop away from the centre of the river Meuse to form the district of Maastricht (see pp. 172–3). The river Geer (known as the Jeker in the Netherlands) flows parallel to the Meuse and about 3 km (2 miles) to the west of it, thus demarcating the promontory of St Pietersberg to the southwest of the town. The surface of this hill, which attains 122 m (403 ft) in elevation, is partly covered with Oligocene sands which have given a heath-like appearance to the landscape, and much is planted with conifers or reserved as military training grounds.

The Chalk in the Maastricht area is the youngest of the system; the name *Maastrichtian* is in fact sometimes applied to these formations. It consists of a soft but compact sandy limestone, yellowish in colour, described as chalky tufaceous marl (the Dutch term is *tufkrijt*), which is highly fossiliferous. It has been quarried for many centuries, possibly since Roman times, since the stone is easily cut into blocks yet the surface hardens on exposure to the air. A vast labyrinth of galleries supported by residual pillars has developed during the centuries in these quarries, which can be entered near Slavante about 3 km (2 miles) south of Maastricht. The Chalk is still extensively quarried, mostly to provide raw material for the neighbouring cement works, both in the Netherlands and at Lanaye and Visé in Belgium.

## The 'Région Mixte'

This intermediate strip between the low plateaus of central Belgium and the Kempenland consists of districts known in the west as *Petit Brabant*, in the centre as the *Campine brabançonne* and in the east as the *Hageland*.[6] It follows more or less the line of the broad Demer valley, and represents a transition (interrupted by the alluvial floor of the Demer valley) from the sandy loams of Brabant to the coarser Pliocene sands of the Kempenland. The Demer has been regularised and straightened (Fig. 8.1), and its floor is a maze of cutoffs, minor drainage channels and ditches.

The light warm sandy soils on either side of the river, when heavily fertilised, are suitable for the intensive cultivation of vegetables, particularly of early varieties. Such crops as peas, sown at the end of January and picked in early June, asparagus, early potatoes, carrots and chicory are grown along the valley between Mechelen and Diest, a 'golden belt' of horticulture. Glasshouse produce, bush and orchard fruits, and flowers are also important. Numerous villages and towns, of 10 000 to 30 000 inhabitants, form market centres both for the southern Kempenland and the Demer valley, and have varied flourishing industries. Diest is a centre of flour-milling and various other forms of food-processing, brewing and distilling. Aarschot also carries on food-processing, Lier manufactures textiles and chemicals, and Duffel has textile and metallurgical works.

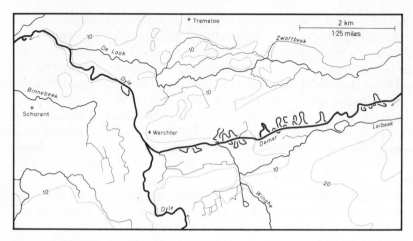

Fɪɢ. 8.ɪ. The Demer valley
The maze of minor drainage channels and ditches is not shown. The contour-
lines are in metres.

Based on *Carte de Belgique au 100 000ᵉ*, sheets X, XI.

The most important industrial town is Mechelen (*Malines*), with a
population of 66 000 in 1970. It is situated at only 8 m (25 ft) above sea
level on the banks of the tidal Dyle, which flows through the town in
several branches. Like Leuven, it is an agricultural and market-gardening
centre and has a wide range of industries. Its lace, famous for centuries, is

Pʟᴀᴛᴇ 26. Brick-works at Boom on the Rupel estuary

still a valuable export item. There are numerous furniture factories, varied textile and clothing factories, paper mills and printing works, a *Mercedes* car assembly plant, tanneries, and food-processing factories. Boom, situated on the north bank of the Rupel, is one of the main centres of brick-making (Plate 26); in fact about half of Belgium's output of bricks is made at yards which line the river banks between Boom and Rumst.

## The Pays de Herve

Lying between the Meuse valley and the West German frontier, and bounded on the south by the valley of the Vesdre, is the plateau of the Pays de Herve. Although this rather remote region is often grouped with the Condroz and the other southern plateaus because it lies 'beyond the Meuse', its surface rocks mostly consist not of Palaeozoic sandstones and shales but of Upper Chalk with a superficial cover of limon and Clay-with-flints (Fig. 8.2). It has in fact more of the character of Hesbaye than of the ridge and valley structure of Condroz (see p. 499). In the east, however, the valleys are cut down through the Chalk into the underlying Palaeozoic rocks. Zinc ores are associated with these rocks, and mines have been worked for centuries in the valleys near the West German frontier. The

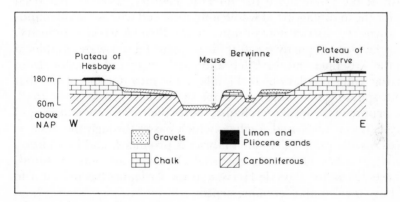

FIG. 8.2. The Meuse terraces below Liège
The length of the section is about 16 km (10 miles).

Based on a diagram in *Handboek der Geografie van Nederland* (1949), i, 251, illustrating chapter 3, 'Geomorfologie', by J. B. L. Hol.

zinc industry of Liège formerly depended on these and other small deposits in the Meuse valley, but the Belgian output of ore has now ceased, and the zinc concentrates used (for Belgium produced 262 000 tons of zinc metal in 1969) are imported from Australia, Mexico, Canada and Jugoslavia.

Almost all the plateau is over 180 m (600 ft) in altitude: the highest point is 354 m (1 161 ft) near Henri-Chapelle. Belgian geomorphologists have distinguished two clearly-defined erosion surfaces, the lower at 180 to 200 m

(590 to 650 ft), the higher at 270 to 300 m (900 to 1 000 ft); these correspond to similar surfaces in the Ardennes to the southwest. A few rivers have cut prominent valleys into the plateau surface, notably the Geule (in Dutch, the *Geul*) which flows across the northeast of the region into South Limburg, and the Berwinne flowing westwards to the Meuse. A few short streams drain the southern plateau and join the Vesdre, otherwise there is a marked shortage of surface drainage.

Mixed farming is carried on in the Pays de Herve on the clay soils; oats and fodder crops predominate on the higher plateau, wheat in the lower areas, with widespread pasture. The main emphasis is, however, on stock-breeding; it is a prosperous dairying district and numbers of animals are sold off to farmers further west.

Settlement is curiously dispersed, particularly in the west, a remarkable contrast to the plateau of Hesbaye where it is nucleated, although the same combination of limon on Chalk forms a broadly similar physical environment. This dispersion is largely the result of the widespread dairy-farming. A considerable number of people in the southern part of the Pays de Herve travel daily to work in Verviers.

Verviers is situated in the steepsided valley of the Vesdre, which joins the Ourthe to the southeast of Liège. The town has expanded on to the hill slopes south of the river. Since the fifteenth century, Verviers has been important for the manufacture of woollen textiles, and with some surrounding small towns the district now dominates the Belgian woollen industry. The reasons for this are partly geographical (plentiful soft water and local wool from the Ardennes and the Eifel) and partly historical (freedom from the restricting guild regulations of Flanders, the introduction of the first carding and spinning machines in Europe by William Cockerill in 1798, and the enterprise of the local merchants). After the construction in 1844 of the railway between Liège and Aachen, which passes through the town, it grew apace. A wide range of woollen fabrics is produced, and in addition leather goods, brushes, chemicals, glue and chocolate are manufactured. Its situation between the Pays de Herve and the Ardennes has helped it to become a busy market and servicing centre.

## South Limburg

The southern part of the Dutch province of Limburg consists of an 'appendix' that projects southward between West Germany and Belgium for more then 40 km (25 miles), and widens from a narrow corridor merely 5 km (3 miles) across to more than 30 km (20 miles) further south. All South Limburg lies on the east side of the Maas except for the district of Maastricht, where the town of that name stands mainly on the left bank of the river, while the frontier makes a loop some 4 km (2·5 miles) further to the west on to the plateau of Hesbaye.

The historical reasons for this apparent geographical anomaly are complex. The long-drawn-out negotiations which followed the break-up of the united Kingdom of Holland and Belgium after the revolution of 1830 culminated in the treaties of London in 1839. The King of Holland, in return for the cession to Belgium of what is now the province of Luxembourg, received in a personal capacity part of the province of Limburg. Included in this territory was the former enclave surrounding the city of Maastricht, which had been, with intermissions, a detached portion of Dutch territory since its capture from the Spaniards during the Thirty Years War (1618–48). The 1839 settlement made Maastricht contiguous with other Dutch territory, although both the city and the rest of Limburg remained in the category of personal possessions of the King of Holland until 1867, and in fact were individual members of the German Confederation. In that year, at the Conference of London, Limburg was fully incorporated into the kingdom of the Netherlands, and became a Dutch province.

At the end of the 1939–45 war, the Netherlands made strong claims for a number of frontier revisions at the expense of Germany.[7] One of these concerned the 'Selfkant', immediately to the east of the narrow corridor near Sittard. On 23 April 1949 the Selfkant was transferred to the Netherlands and placed under a special commissioner, while on 1 January 1952 it was incorporated into the province of Limburg (Fig. 8.3). In 1963, however, this territory was returned to West Germany by treaty.

South Limburg consists for the most part of a plateau of Cretaceous rocks, with some surviving patches in the northeast and west of Younger Tertiary sands and marls. The Cretaceous rocks consist mainly of Upper Chalk; in the west they are soft tufaceous limestones, in the east they comprise chalk.

Rarely, however, do the Chalk or the Tertiary rocks appear at the surface, except in the valley of the Geul. As far north as Sittard the surface is covered with loams, believed to be *loess* (*limon*) deposits of windborne origin. This may be so in part, but some Dutch geologists regard them as residual loams formed by the decomposition *in situ* of the Upper Chalk, reworked and redeposited by stream action, and with possibly a mixture of true loess material, as the name given to them (*loessoïde*) would indicate; the resultant soils are referred to as *loessleem* and cover almost exactly a quarter of Limburg. Whatever their origin, these loam soils are among the most fertile in the country.[8]

One further important element enters into the geological make-up of South Limburg. Across the centre of the region lies the westward continuation of the Upper Carboniferous rocks found along the northern edge of the uplands of central Europe; the Aachen and Eschweiler fields of West Germany can be traced over the frontier into Limburg, and then across the Meuse into the Kempenland. The Coal Measures of Limburg are concealed by younger rocks, except for minor outcrops in the extreme east in the valley of the Wurm, a left-bank tributary of the Roer. There are estimated to be 3 000 m (10 000 ft) of Upper Carboniferous rocks, mostly shales and sandstones. Several faults, running approximately from south-east to northwest, divide the field into blocks in which the depth of exploitable coal varies considerably. The overall dip is towards the northwest, and so workable coals near the upper part of the series are found at about 60 m (200 ft) depth in the east but at over 600 m (2 000 ft) in the west. Major faults bound the field, beyond which coal lies at great depths.

The present surface features of South Limburg are mainly the result of river action. As in the Kempenland and Noord-Brabant, the Maas and its tributaries have exercised profound effects in late interglacial and post-glacial times, and they are now markedly entrenched. The erosional and depositional terraces discussed on pp. 18–19 are well represented. The plateau is bounded on the west by the clearly defined alluvium-floored trench of the Maas, and is cut into three individual blocks by the Geul and the Geleen, its two right-bank tributaries. In the northeast, extending across the frontier into Germany as far as the Roer valley, is the *IIIr* level (described on p. 19 ), the highest gravel-covered terrace. Between the Geleen and the Geul this *IIIr* level again appears, mostly at over 90 m (300 ft), rising to a well-marked erosion level at 180 m (590 ft), from which project residual summits such as the Ubachsberg and the Vrouwenheide (each 217 m (712 ft) ). South of the Geul valley, the erosion terraces of both Cycles *II* and *III* are well developed, and the 180 m (590 ft) level is also quite extensive. Along the Belgian frontier to the south, parts of the 270 to 300 m (900 to 1 000 ft) erosion surface of the Pays de Herve extend into South Limburg, rising to the rounded summit of the Vaalserberg 322 m (1 056 ft), the highest point in the Netherlands, almost at the junction of the triple frontier. The rivers are here swift-flowing, and in places their valleys are steepsided with occasional rocky slopes.

South Limburg is a pleasant, prosperous-looking agricultural region, and farming is predominantly mixed. The loam soils are excellent for sugar beet and potatoes, there are extensive market gardens, and it is one of the chief fruit-growing districts in the country. Large orchards have been established under grass, with tree crops of apples, plums and pears, and also others intercropped with bush-fruit. It is an important dairy-farming and pig-rearing area. Many of the valleys are wooded, and clumps of fine beech trees add to the attractive verdant character of the countryside.

Nevertheless, Limburg has a high proportion of its occupied population engaged in industry—54 per cent, compared with 42 per cent in the Netherlands as a whole. This industrial importance was until recently mainly due to the presence of the coalfield and associated industries,[9] but with the progressive rundown and scheduled closure of the field in 1973, other industries are being introduced.

## The coalfield

For many years the importance of the Limburg field to the Netherlands was that it was the only productive one.[10] It was possibly the first to be worked in Europe, for it is recorded that the monks of Kloosterrade Abbey mined coal by opencast methods in the valley of the Wurm near the German frontier. Further sporadic operations were carried out during succeeding centuries but only on a small scale; in 1845, for example, some mining took place to supply fuel for the newly opened Maastricht-Aachen railway. It was not until 1895 that the first large-scale concession was granted to the Domaniale Company at Kerkrade, and during the next five years further leases were obtained by various companies with French, German and Belgian interests. The extent of these private concessions and the location of the eight collieries they developed are shown on Fig. 8.3.

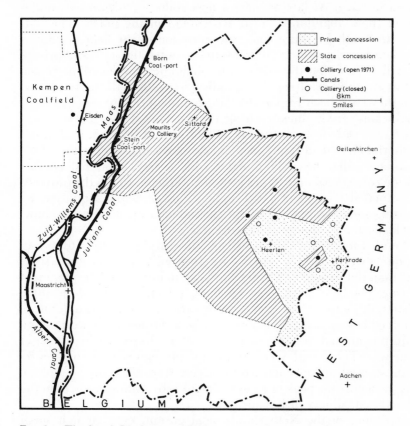

FIG. 8.3. The South Limburg coalfield
The boundary of concessions in the neighbouring Kempen coalfield is shown by pecked lines. In 1963 the Selfkant was returned to West Germany.
 Letters are used to indicate names of individual collieries as follows:
**D,** Domaniale; **E,** Emma; **H,** Hendrik; **J,** Julia; **L,** Laura; **M,** Maurits; **ON,** Oranje-Nassau; **W,** Wilhelmina; **WS,** Willem-Sophia.

Based on P. R. Bos and J. P. Niermeyer, *Schoolatlas der Geheele Aarde* (1936), Plate 11 B.

Alarm, however, was increasingly felt in Dutch political and industrial circles towards the end of the nineteenth century that the country's mining enterprise had passed under the control of foreign interests, and it was considered desirable for the state to assume a considerable measure of future responsibility. It was not intended that existing foreign concessions should be expropriated, but that private and state mines should exist side by side. The state therefore reserved to itself most of the non-conceded proven area by an Act of 1901, and in 1912 it formally extended its domain over the whole province, except for areas already conceded. A state company, the Staatsmijnen in Limburg, was established, and the first coal was produced in 1906. The palatial headquarters of the Staatsmijnen were established in Heerlen. Three other state collieries were built including the great *Maurits* undertaking in 1923. As late as 1964 a new colliery (*Bertrix*) was under construction (now abandoned) near Roermond in the north. The output of coal in South Limburg since the initiation of the field in 1895 is summarised in Fig. 8.4, which differentiates between the state and private mines. It will be seen that the former, although later developed, increased their output steadily; by 1924 they produced exactly half the total, and since 1926 they have been responsible for about 60 per cent.

The coal seams vary in thickness from about 0·5 to 2·5 m (2 to 8 ft). They are, however, considerably disturbed by folding and faulting, and moreover are interlaminated with dirt, so that careful washing is necessary. One great advantage is that the coal is found in wide variety; about half consists of high grade coking coal and 10 per cent of anthracite. In all, the province contains estimated reserves of 4 000 million tons, of which a quarter lies within existing concessions. Only about 500 million tons of the latter, however, are classified as 'economically workable'.

When South Limburg was liberated by allied troops in the autumn of 1944, the mines were standing idle as a result of military operations. Apart from some material damage the chief handicap to immediate development was a shortage of labour, partly because many miners had joined the allied armies, partly because of the aversion felt towards mining as a result of German forced labour decrees. There was also a shortage of materials and mining equipment, and maintenance had been neglected during the later years of the war. The overall recovery from the trough year of 1945 represented a substantial achievement; output rose from little over 5 million tons in 1945 to a postwar peak of 12·6 million in 1961. Maurits was then the biggest individual colliery in Europe.

The importance of the Netherlands' coal output, even though small compared with that of its neighbours, was that it was able to supply a considerable portion of the country's fuel needs, since 1945 some 80 per cent; actually, for several years before the war a slight surplus was available for export. Increasing postwar industrialisation in the Netherlands, coupled with the export drive and the rearmament contribution which the country must sustain, at first reduced the proportion of home consumption

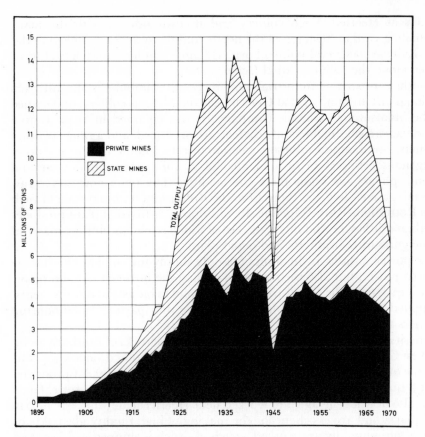

Fig. 8.4. Output of coal in South Limburg

Based on statistics obtained from successive volumes of the *Jaarcijfers voor Nederland*.

which the Limburg field could contribute. In each of the years 1955 and 1956, home consumption exceeded 17 million tons. After 1960 output was stabilised for a few years at 10 to 11 million tons annually, but the industry suffered increasingly from overproduction of some types of coal, and from the competition of cheaper imported coal, oil and natural gas (pp. 139–40). Accordingly, it was decided by the ECSC to run down the coalfield and close it in 1973. The Hendrik colliery was closed in 1967, and its buildings are now used as the headquarters of the NATO *Alfcent* Command, transferred to Limburg from France; Maurits also closed in 1967, and only four collieries remained open by 1971, in which year output was only 3·8 million tons.

The Limburg field is situated in a remote corner of the Netherlands, and the transport of such bulky items as coal and coke demands special organisation, both by rail and water. The Limburg mines were served by a standard-gauge line operated by the Mines Railway Department, with its headquarters at Heerlen. Each colliery had its own sidings, with the main marshalling yard at Susteren in the north, and the system was linked to the State Railway at several points. Formerly some 3 million tons of coal were carried along the Juliana Canal (see p. 101).

Another important industrial unit in South Limburg is the nitrogen fixation plant, built in 1930 at Geleen near the Maurits colliery, and owned by the Staatsmijnen-Chemie company; it was enlarged in 1949. Liquid ammonia, carbon dioxide and ethylene are produced, and a range of other products—ammonium sulphate, calcium nitrate, sodium nitrate and other nitrogenous fertilisers, nitric acid, alcohol, cleaning agents, detergents and solvents, phenol and many more commodities. This plant now uses as raw materials gaseous hydrocarbons from the Rotterdam terminal via a branch of the Rotterdam-Rhine pipeline. In addition, a distillation plant produces tar-oils, naphthalene and pitch, the last of which is used as binding material in a neighbouring briquette and ovoid plant.

The power stations at the mines not only supply the collieries with their required power, but also the coking plant and the nitrogen fixation plant. About a quarter of the generated energy, surplus to industrial requirements, is supplied to private consumers in Limburg and parts of neighbouring provinces through a grid.

Deposits of brown coal are found in the Miocene rocks of Limburg along the West German frontier. The deposits have been worked since 1917, but only one quarry, near Kerkrade, has remained active; in 1958 it produced about a quarter of a million tons, but it ceased production in 1961. Glass sands, also of Miocene age, are worked near Heerlerheide; they are nearly pure quartz and are excellent for the making of high quality glass. About 100 000 tons annually are worked, much of which is shipped to Liège and Mol-Gompel in Belgium.

## Settlements

Several mining towns have grown from agricultural villages during this century. The centre is Heerlen, which had a population of only about 6 000 in 1890; soon after this date exploitation of the coalfield began, and communications were improved by the construction both of state railway lines and the mines railway. The state mining company has its headquarters in Heerlen, and eight collieries lay within or near the commune. As a result its population in 1970 was 75 000. Other towns are Kerkrade near the West German frontier, Brunssum and Hoensbroek. Many of the workers formerly employed in the big Maurits State colliery live in or near Lutterade in the northwest, where several chemical byproducts plants are situated. New industries have been introduced to find employment for miners as the Limburg collieries are closed.[11] An example is the DAF autoplant at Born, established by the parent company of Eindhoven (p. 134). State subsidised industrial estates have been developed to the northeast of Maastricht at

Bertrix (served by a port on the Juliana Canal), near Brunssum, and to the southwest of Kerkrade (with factories making electronic and electrical apparatus, household goods, foodstuffs, and chemicals).

The regional centre of South Limburg is Maastricht (112 000 people in 1971), situated on the left bank of the Maas, with the suburb of Wijk on the opposite side. It has owed much to its being a crossing-point of the river since Roman times; the name is derived from the Latin *ad Mosam Trajectum*, where a ford was used on the important route to the Rhineland. The bridges have always been vital strategic points right down to 1939–45, when a Victoria Cross was won for an aerial attack on the *nieuwe Maasbrug*, constructed in 1932. A fine new bridge has been built since the war. During the latter part of the nineteenth century the town expanded, first as a result of improved waterways; the Maas is unnavigable below the town, but the Liège-Maastricht and Zuid-Willems Canals were useful. In the 1930s the lateral Juliana Canal was completed, thus linking Maastricht to the Maas below its international section (see p. 101). The development of railways also helped Maastricht, which is rather remote from the rest of the Netherlands, and the exploitation of the coalfield to the east afforded a great stimulus to industrial development. There are now various steel-using industries, brick, tile and cement works, a tannery, a soap works, a tobacco factory, a woollen mill, several rubber factories, a glass factory which has made the attractive *Crystal Maastricht* ware since 1834, and one of the largest paper mills in the country. It is still an important market town and shopping and servicing centre for this part of the Netherlands, spaciously and attractively laid out. With its remarkable collection of churches, ramparts and the oldest surviving town gate in the country, the city still retains much of its ancient interest and charm, and has an appreciable tourist traffic.

[1] As, for example, J. Halkin, *Atlas classique* (1934), plate 18, and see Fig. 1.2.

[2] S. W. E. Vince, 'Viticulture in Belgium', *Geogrl. J.*, **107** (1946), pp. 135–40, deals with the production of table grapes under glass.

[3] An immensely detailed account is by R. Mangelinckx, 'Clabecq et sa sidérurgie', *Rev. belge Géog.*, **87** (1963), pp. 260–344.

[4] P. Gourou, 'L'agglomération bruxelloise', *Bull. Soc. roy. belge. Géogr.* (1958), *fasc.* I–IV, pp. 1–83.

[5] M. Pardé, 'Sur la jonction ferroviaire entre Bruxelles-Nord et Bruxelles-Midi', *Annls. Géogr.*, **62** (1953), pp. 296–8.

[6] G. Scheys, 'Hageland, Boden en Landschap', *Bull. Soc. belge. Etud. géogr.*, **23** (1954), pp. 85–121.

[7] L. M. Alexander, 'Recent changes in the Benelux–German boundary', *Geogrl. Rev.*, **43** (1953), pp. 69–76.

[8] See A. J. Pannekoek, ed., *Geological History of the Netherlands* (1956), pp. 102–3, for a full discussion, with bibliography, of the problem of these deposits.

[9] L. Haas, 'Sociaal-economisch structuurbeeld van de Nederlandse provincie Limburg', *Tijdschr. econ. soc. Geogr.*, **56** (1965), pp. 32–7.

[10] F. J. Monkhouse, 'The South Limburg coalfield', *Econ. Geogr.*, **31** (1955), pp. 126–37.

[11] G. R. P. Lawrence, 'The changing face of South Limburg', *Geography*, **56** (1971), pp. 35–9.

# 9
# The lowlands of northern France: I

## General features

The greater part of northern France consists of a structural depression lying between the Ardennes, the Central Massif and Armorica. This has been filled in with sedimentary rocks ranging in age from the Jurassic to the Miocene, while in places a thin cover of superficial Recent deposits is present (Fig. 9.1).

A series of Jurassic limestones and clays appears on the eastern margins, and is continued in the south along the flanks of the Central Massif. Again in the west they can be traced in a narrowing outcrop from the coast of Calvados along the eastern margins of the Armorican Peninsula. In succession outwards from the centre of the basin can be seen the Portland, Corallian and Oolitic Limestones, best represented in the cuestas of Lorraine (Chapter 11). Between the limestone outcrops, river erosion has developed valleys along the various Jurassic clays (a narrow outcrop of Kimmeridge and the much more widespread Oxford and Lias Clays).

The Cretaceous rocks comprise the most extensive element in the surface geology, for they completely encircle the region, attenuated only in the south. The Lower Cretaceous (*Albien*) Gault Clay appears as a crescentic exposure in the east. A soft clayey sandstone known as *gaize* (equivalent in age to the Upper Greensand in England) forms the ridge of the Argonne, and other greensands outcrop in Puisaye in the south. The most widespread surface rock in the Cretaceous is the Chalk, except in the south where it is buried under Tertiary deposits.

The central part of the region is occupied by Tertiary rocks, including limestones, sandstones, marls and clays, and varying in age from the Lower Eocene, exposed only in the deeper valleys, to the Miocene in the south-west. The limestones are the dominating surface rocks in the centre of the region, forming a series of low plateaus.

These Mesozoic and Tertiary rocks are in many parts masked with superficial deposits. Residual clays, such as the Clay-with-flints, are common over the limestones and the Chalk, distinctive gravels occur on terraces in the valleys at different heights, and much alluvium has been deposited on the floodplains of the rivers. The most important of the superficial deposits

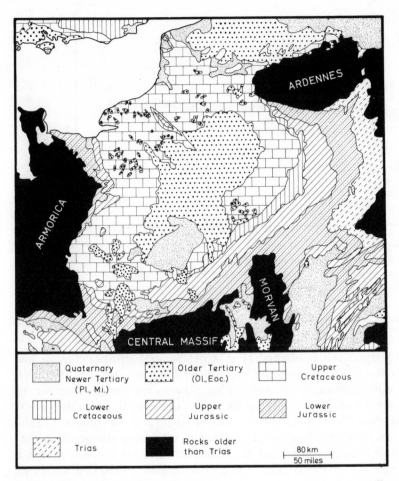

FIG. 9.1. Geological map of the Paris Basin

Based on the *Carte géologique de la France*, 1 : 1 000 000, published by the *Service de la Carte géologique détaillée de la France*.

is limon (see pp. 24–5); its widespread distribution in northeastern France is shown on Fig. 2.5.

These rocks were laid down during long periods of geological time in the structural depression (Fig. 2.1). In mid-Tertiary times the strata were affected by movements associated with the Alpine folding to the south, though of a gentler character on these outskirts of the orogenic zone. The resultant shallow basin form causes the strata to dip gently inward from the outer rim, and denudation therefore affected the higher marginal areas more markedly. The more resistant limestones and chalk alternate with the clays and marls, so that a succession of outward-facing cuestas and intervening clay vales has been produced.[1]

The folding movements also caused flexures which have produced signifi-

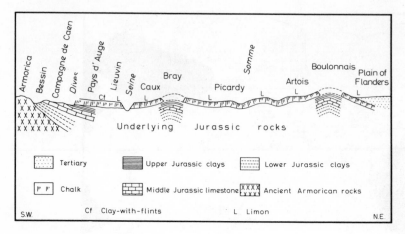

FIG. 9.2. Simplified section across northern France
The length of the section is about 450 km.
The superficial covering of Clay-with-flints in the west and limon in the
centre and east is indicated by letters; this covering is of course not
continuous.

Based on A. Cholley, *La France* (n.d.), pp. 77, 161.

cant results upon the landscape (Fig. 9.2). Several distinct though low
anticlines can be traced, trending in a more or less northwest to southeast
direction, and these cause marked undulations in the surface features. In
the northeast the anticline of Artois forms a prominent line of hills bordering the Flanders Plain. The Boulonnais, the structural continuation of the
Weald, is another anticline which has been extensively denuded, so that
infacing chalk cuestas now form a 'horseshoe' around a depression in which
Jurassic rocks are revealed (Fig. 9.11). Bray is also a denuded anticline,
with Upper Jurassic clays and limestone exposed in the centre (Fig. 9.12).

## The river systems

A whole pattern of rivers has developed, flowing transversely across this
tilted basin structure, and focused on the lower Seine. Most of the tributaries
drain from the south and east, and only a few short confluents, such as the
Essonne and the Eure, are received from the west. In addition, the right-
angled bend of the middle Loire trenches across the sequence of sedimentary
rocks in the southwest, while the northwards-flowing Meuse and Moselle
are involved in the eastern scarpland margins. A few short streams—the
Canche, Authie and Somme—cut across the chalklands of Picardy directly
to the English Channel.

The development of this drainage pattern has not only resulted in the
formation of a series of cuestas and vales on the margins of the basin, but
has caused the dissection of the inner part into a series of distinct unit-areas.

The centripetal effect of the Seine has caused repeated river capture, while successive rejuvenations have enabled the rivers to form strikingly incised valleys. The numerous individual *pays* so characteristic of France generally are to a large extent demarcated by river valleys, while others comprise portions of the valleys themselves (Fig. 9.3).

## The upper confluents of the Seine

The main watershed of central France between the Seine and Saône systems is formed by the Plateau de Langres, a Jurassic upland which links the ancient masses of the Vosges and the Morvan. From it flow northwards the Marne, the Aube, the upper Seine and the Armançon, together with the Meuse further to the east (Fig. 9.4), while numerous short streams descend the steep faulted southern side to the Saône trough.

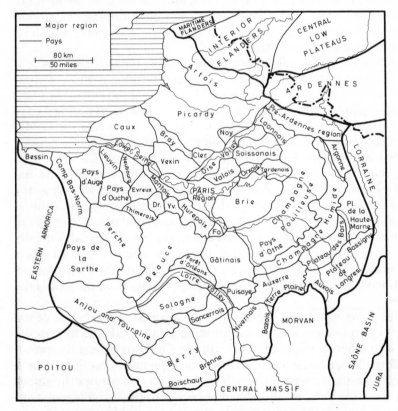

FIG. 9.3. The pattern of the *pays* in the lowlands of northern France
The abbreviations are as follows: **Cler,** Clermontois; **Dr,** Drouais; **Fo,** Fontainebleau; **Noy,** Noyonnais; **Yv,** Yvelines.

Based on a map, 'Régions géographiques de la France', 1 : 1 400 000, published by the *Institut National de la Statistique et des Etudes Economiques* for the *Ministère de l'Economie Nationale.*

The upper Seine, the Ource, the Aube and the Aujon rise at a height of about 450 m (1 500 ft) on the limestone plateau, known to the inhabitants as *La Montagne*. Their sources break out as springs in the deeply cut valley floors, and the rivers may disappear and reappear a number of times during the first few kilometres of their courses. It has been known during exceptionally dry periods for the bed of the Seine to be dry as far downstream as Châtillon. The neighbouring Marne and Meuse, however, have cut their sources further back through the Oolite into the Upper Lias clays that lie on the southwestern margins of the Vosges. These impermeable rocks afford a better water supply than does the limestone, and as a result the upper Marne has a larger and more regular volume than the Seine. Again, further to the west the Yonne rises on the crystalline rocks of the Morvan, while its tributary the Armançon flows from the Lias marls which flank that upland on the east. Thus the Yonne makes a considerably larger contribution to the volume of the middle and lower Seine than do the other headstreams; indeed, rapid runoff following sustained rainfall or a period of snowmelt in central France may in fact cause serious flooding, which on several occasions has affected Paris.

This batch of head rivers flows northwards across the succession of progressively younger Jurassic and Cretaceous rocks, forming a series of alternate vales and cuestas—the narrow Oxford Clay vale at the foot of the Oolitic Limestone plateau, then the Corallian cuesta, the Kimmeridge Clay vale and the Portland Limestone plateau (Fig. 9.4). The rivers meander across each of these clay vales, then by contrast cut through the next cuesta in steepsided winding trenches. They next enter the Gault Clay lands, to which is given the *pays* name of *Champagne humide*. Some river capture has developed here between the Portland cuesta and the Chalk; thus the Armançon turns abruptly west along the strike at St Florentin as a subsequent stream to join the Yonne above Joigny, and similarly further to the east the Ornain turns west near Bar-le-Duc to join the Marne at Vitry-le-François. The main rivers then cross the chalk country of *Champagne pouilleuse*, wandering sluggishly over the flat floors of their entrenched alluvium-lined valleys, fed by numerous springs issuing from the foot of the chalk slopes.

The Seine flows westwards for 65 km (40 miles) along the edge of the central Tertiary plateau, a direction initiated by the Aube further to the east. This is another example of river capture. One can regard the proto-Yonne and the lower Seine as an original consequent stream, joined by a powerful right-bank subsequent which in due course captured the upper Seine and the Aube; the small beheaded trunks of these rivers now continue their original northward trends to join the lower Marne.

Below Montereau the Seine is joined by the Loing, one of its few left-bank tributaries, the probable evolution of which is discussed below in connection with the middle Loire. The Seine here flows at 50 m (160 ft) above sea level and is 240 km (150 miles) in a direct line from the English Channel, although its official distance for navigation is no less than 493 km (306 miles), an indication of its meandering course. It crosses the limestone plateau through a broad trench cut into the Tertiary rocks, receiving its major right-bank tributaries, the Marne and the Oise, above and below

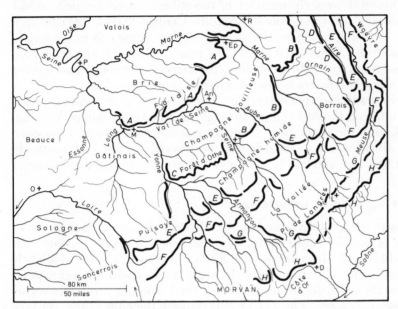

FIG. 9.4. The cuestas of the southeastern Paris Basin
The cuestas are shown in generalised form by heavy lines, and are lettered as follows: **A,** Tertiary (Falaise de l'Ile de France); **B,** Upper Chalk; **C,** Middle Chalk; **D,** Upper Greensand (*Gaize*) of the Argonne; **E,** Portland Limestone; **F,** Corallian Limestone; **G,** Oolitic Limestone; **H,** Lias.
   Some towns mentioned in the text are indicated by their initials as follows: **An,** Anglure; **D,** Dijon; **Ep,** Epernay; **L,** Langres; **M,** Montereau; **O,** Orléans; **P,** Paris; **R,** Reims; **T,** Troyes.

Based on (*a*) *Atlas de France,* sheet 9 (*Morphologie*); and (*b*) F. Machatschek, *Das Relief der Erde* (1938), p. 54.

Paris respectively. A number of terraces can be seen at different levels, the result of continued downcutting in ancient alluvium while the meanders were swinging freely. E. Chaput[2] has distinguished at least four terraces at specific levels: at 12 to 15 m (40 to 50 ft), at 30 to 35 m (100 to 160 ft), at 55 m (180 ft), and a few fragments of ancient surfaces at higher levels still. The flint gravels on the upper terraces contain remains of animal life, including bones of mammoth and reindeer.

## The middle Loire

It is necessary at this point to mention the incursion of the Loire into the lowlands of northern France; indeed, some of the northward-flowing headstreams of the Loing rise only 8 km (5 miles) from the Loire itself. It seems probable that the upper Loire once continued northwards to the proto-Seine system, cutting through the Portland Limestone cuesta, and so forming the most westerly member of the tributaries converging on the lower Seine. But this river, coming from the Central Massif, was captured by the back-cutting of a powerful stream flowing westwards to the Bay of Biscay, hence the rightangled bend. The much reduced Loing remained, now far too small for its broad valley (the *Plaine du Gâtinais*), and joining the Seine a few kilometres below Montereau (Fig. 9.10).

The Loire itself, greatly enlarged in volume by the accession of its near-parallel confluent, the Allier, flows through the Lias Clay plain of *Nivernais*, and breaks into the main basin through its southern Portland Limestone rim. The river swings westwards and northwards to its most northerly point near Orléans, and finally southwestwards towards the Bay of Biscay.[3]

### The right bank Seine tributaries

The course of the upper Marne has already been discussed, for it is one of the family of parallel upper tributaries which flow from the Jurassic rim on to the chalklands. It continues still further northwards as the chalk belt itself swings in this direction, until the river comes under the centripetal influence of the inwardly-dipping strata of the basin and bends westwards to the Seine confluence. The Marne cuts through the edge of the Tertiary escarpment just below Epernay, forming a striking steepsided valley in the limestone, and receiving numerous affluents from the clay-covered plateaus both to the north (*Tardenois*) and the south (*Brie humide*).

The Oise forms a complex drainage system, since not only do its head-streams rise in the Ardennes, but the Aisne and its tributary the Aire have their sources in the eastern scarplands not far from both the Marne and the Meuse (Figs. 10.1, 10.2). The Oise itself actually rises just within Belgium near Bourlers on the southwestern slopes of the Ardennes, flows westwards over the Gault Clay and Chalk, then through the rim of the Tertiary escarpment, and finally in a broad flat-floored valley with uniform plateau surfaces on either side to its junction with the Seine.

The upper Aisne is a longitudinal stream draining northwards through the Gault Clay vale to the west of the sandstone ridge of the Argonne, from which it receives numerous affluents. The river wanders peacefully through its broad marshy valley across the claylands, to be joined near Challerange by the Aire, the most easterly of the Seine system (Fig. 10.2). The Aisne then escapes from the north–south trend of the scarplands, and flows in a clearly defined trench across the chalklands and the limestone plateau. It receives another large tributary, the left-bank Vesle, which crosses the chalk country and penetrates the escarpment in a gap, near the entrance of which stands Reims. The Aisne itself continues westwards, its deeply cut

valley separating the distinctive *pays* of *Soissonnais* and *Valois*, to join the
Oise at Compiègne.

## The lower Seine and its estuary

The Seine below Paris forms a series of swinging meanders, incised 90 m
(300 ft) or more below the surface of the flanking chalk plateaus. Narrow at
first, the valley widens below Rouen, though still within its prominent
bounding walls. The river is bordered by reclaimed alluvial flats through
which the channel is regularised and confined between massive dykes. A
bore (the *mascaret*) is experienced for some distance upstream.

The broad estuary opens out towards the west; between Le Havre and
Trouville it is nearly 14 km (9 miles) across. A shipping-channel is dredged
from the deepwater Carosse roadstead off Le Havre upstream to Rouen
through ever-changing sandbanks. By way of this estuary the waters of the
Seine, the runoff from the surface of some two-fifths of France, find their
ultimate way to the ocean.

## The Somme and its neighbours

Part of the extreme north of these lowlands is drained by a few rivers which
flow independently to the English Channel—the Canche, Authie, Somme,
Béthune, Arques and other smaller streams. The only river of any size is the
Somme, which rises on the backslope of the chalk hills of Cambrésis near St
Quentin at a height of about 70 m (230 ft). Only 11 km (7 miles) to the
north is the source of the Scheldt, with an intervening dry gap at about
140 m (460 ft) above sea level; this is one of the natural routeways between
Flanders and the Seine basin. The Somme wanders westwards in a broad
flat-bottomed valley, alluvium-lined and in places marshy, followed by a
lateral canal. Below Amiens the river is trenched in the limon-covered chalk
plateau; it enters the sea through the broad Baie de Somme.

## The waterways

These natural waterways afford a valuable system of communications,
linking Paris[4] with the northern and eastern industrial districts of France
and with southern Belgium (Fig. 9.5). Much regularisation has, however,
been necessary; the depth of water is controlled by weirs with locks. Each is
paralleled along its upper course by a lateral canal; this was easier and
much cheaper than extensive regularisation of the rivers.

The Seine too has been improved for navigation. The river is not
navigable above Marcilly, although a lateral canal prolongs navigation as
far as Troyes for small barges. Between Marcilly and Paris numerous locks
and barrages are required, and cuts have been made through tortuous
braided sections. Below Paris the Seine provides a waterway in which a

depth of 3 m (10 ft) is maintained by weirs with large sluices, built during the interwar period both to check flooding and to assist navigation.

The Seine carries the greatest volume of traffic of any French waterway, since not only is it joined by several tributaries, but the lower river forms an

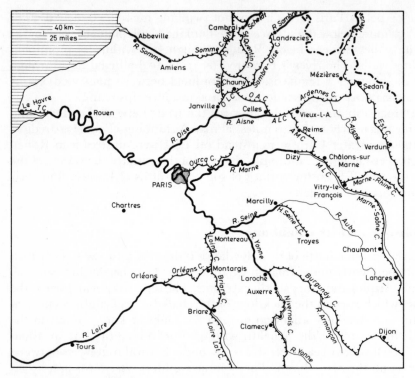

FIG. 9.5. The waterways of the Paris basin
Abbreviations are as follows: **ALC,** Aisne Lateral Canal; **AMC,** Aisne-Marne Canal; **C du N,** Canal du Nord; **MLC,** Marne Laternal Canal; **OLC,** Oise Lateral Canal; **TC,** Tancarville Canal. The Canal du Nord was completed in 1965.

Based on W. Seghers, *Kaart der Binnenscheepvaartwegen van N-W Europa* (n.d.).

important line of communication between Paris and its ports of Rouen and Le Havre. The various sections of the Seine are responsible for nearly 6 000 million ton-km of freight, about a third consisting of oil. Then, too, link canals connect the main rivers across the intervening plateaus between the Oise and the Aisne and between the Aisne and the Marne. Others link the Seine system with the Flanders waterways to the north (the St Quentin and Nord Canals), with the Sambre-Meuse system in the east (the Sambre-Oise and Ardennes Canals), with the Rhine to the southeast (the Marne-Rhine Canal), with the Saône to the south (the Marne-Saône and Bur-gundy or *Bourgogne* Canals), and with the Loire to the southwest (the

Nivernais, Loing and Orléans Canals) (Fig. 9.5). The links have not been easy to construct because of the complex relief features of the concentric cuestas.

## Regional divisions

Although the term 'lowlands' may be applied in a general sense, as a result of these diverse rocks, structures and drainage systems the relief is distinctly varied, including flat or gently undulating plateaus, deeply cut alluvium-floored valleys, steep cuestas and open vales. Land use is equally diverse. There are rolling expanses of arable lands with fertile loamy soils growing wheat and sugar beet; extensive tracts of poor grazing on bare chalk and limestone; heavy well-watered claylands with prosperous dairy farms; dense plantations of conifers on sandstone ridges; market gardens along the valley floors; and serried rows of vines on south-facing slopes. Moreover,

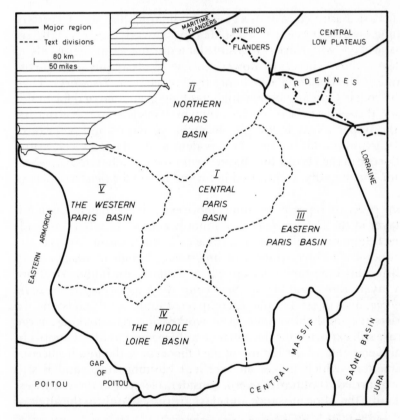

FIG. 9.6. Key map to the major divisions of the lowlands of northern France
The numbers **I** to **V** refer to the major areas described in each section of
the text. A more detailed pattern, including a large number of *pays*, is given
on Fig. 9.3.

this part of France has been important for millennia, and has a well-developed urban life with a considerable number of towns, large and small. The greatest of these is Paris, the heart, the focus, of these lowlands, as indeed of France itself. It is for this last reason that the name Paris Basin is commonly applied to the region as a whole. Sometimes, however, the term is used in a wider sense to include the eastern scarplands, but as pointed out above (p. 10) it is more convenient to include those areas east of the Meuse in Lorraine. For purposes of detailed regional description, five main divisions have been distinguished (Fig. 9.6).

## 1. The central Paris Basin

The central Paris Basin[5] consists of a gently undulating plateau of Tertiary strata dipping towards the centre. The oldest rocks, overlying the Chalk, are beds of plastic clays, which are responsible for a distinctive springline along many valleys. Above these are Lower Eocene sands (equivalent to the Thanet Sands in the London Basin, hence the French term *Thanétien*). Then succeeds the coarse *Calcaire grossier* which has long been quarried for building purposes; this seems to be of marine origin in its lower strata, of estuarine origin in the upper. Next follow the Beauchamp Sands and a series of marls, clays, gypsum and limestones equivalent to the Barton Clays at the top of the Eocene in the Hampshire Basin (hence the French term *Bartonien*). The gypsum, incidentally, is quarried in several places for plaster ('plaster of Paris').

Oligocene rocks are represented much more extensively than in England. The thin layer of the *Calcaire de Brie* commonly consists of a band of millstones, large fragments of siliceous limestone embedded within layers of the clayey·residue of a former stratum of limestone, though in places, as in southern Brie, this limestone does appear as a more continuous stratum, with marly layers above and below. Next come the famous *Sables supérieures de Fontainebleau*, beds of sand in places compacted into a solid sandstone. In some districts the sands have long been worked for glass-making; large quantities are still exported for this purpose to Liège and to Mol-Gompel in the Belgian Kempenland. At the top of the Oligocene is the tough siliceous Beauce Limestone which makes an excellent building stone and is still extensively quarried; it outcrops over a considerable area to the southwest of Paris. Finally, the Miocene sands and clays are present only in the angle of the middle Loire near Orléans.

These then are the Tertiary rocks of the central part of the lowlands. Denudation has removed some here and there, so exposing others, and thus has given considerable variety to the landscape. One can pass in a few kilometres from the level monotonous surface of the limestone plateau of Beauce to the fantastic sandstone rocks among the glades of the Forêt de Fontainebleau. The whole range can be seen in some of the deeper valleys and along the edge of the outward-facing escarpment which bounds its eastern and southeastern margins. The term *Ile de France* having been bestowed on the central plateau (it is thought first by Froissart in the fifteenth century), the escarpment is known as the *Falaise de l'Ile de France*.

The chief contrast in relief generally is between the higher surfaces of the intervening plateaus and the valley floors. The latter are cut down into the clays and lined with alluvium over which rivers meander, formerly with considerable areas of marsh, now for the most part dyked and regularised. Their valleys have long afforded routeways, notably along the Oise from Flanders and the Ardennes and along the Marne from Lorraine, now followed by main roads and railway lines, and lined with prosperous industrial towns—Chauny, Noyon, Compiègne, Creil and Pontoise in the Oise valley, Soissons and Attichy in the Aisne valley, and Epernay, Château-Thierry, La Ferté, Meaux and Lagny in the Marne valley. Indeed, in effect Greater Paris extends 'fingers of linear industrialisation', with metallurgical, engineering, chemical and food-processing industries, and of close settlement far along these valleys. Elsewhere the alluvial valley floors contain meadowlands (utilised by a rich dairying industry producing milk for the metropolitan market), woodlands, and market gardens[6] cultivated with typical French assiduity.

## The plateau-lands of the Ile de France

Although tongues of denser settlement project along the valleys, the limestone plateaus support an agricultural population of merely a rural order of density.[7] An indication of the land use figures of the seven *départements*, which mainly comprise the Ile de France, will be useful. These include the three new *départements* created in 1964 out of the former Seine (Seine-St Denis, Haute-de-Seine and Val de Marne), the three created out of Seine-et-Oise (Val-d'Oise, Yvelines and Essonne), and the existing Seine-et-Marne which comprises more than half of the official *région parisienne*. In this region, in 1968, arable occupied almost half of the total area (mainly wheat and sugar beet), permanent pasture only 5 per cent, and woodland about 22 per cent.

The paucity of permanent pasture is a result of the generally rather dry and well drained surfaces. What there is occurs as meadowland along the alluvium- and clay-covered floors of the valleys, and in a poor almost heath-like form on the patches of Clay-with-flints or on the limestone where the limon covering is absent.

Woodland covers parts of the valley floors and some of the outcrops of sand. Some forested areas have been deliberately maintained, notably the Forêt de Fontainebleau[8] on the sands between the limestones of Beauce and

Brie, and the Forêts de Rambouillet, Chantilly, Sénart and St Germain. Fontainebleau, with its varied trees, stretches of heath and fantastic groups of rocks, is a favourite outlet for Paris; it was, incidentally, the home of the famous Barbizon school of landscape painters—Millet, Corot, Diaz and others.

## Beauce

A journey from Paris in a southwesterly direction to Orléans crosses a wide expanse of Oligocene limestone of unusually level surface. This Beauce Limestone is about a hundred metres in thickness, much fissured and extremely permeable, and surface drainage is markedly deficient. But except in the south where some areas of heathland occur on the bare limestone, Beauce is blessed with a limon mantle sufficiently thick to hold moisture, providing an excellent loamy soil for arable farming. Here are the extensive wheatlands, with some sugar beet and barley; from the air one sees a chequerboard of cultivation, from the ground a monotonous vista of vast unfenced fields. Settlements are rare, and consist either of large prosperous farms or of nucleated villages built around a broad marketplace. Wells have to be sunk so deeply through the limestone that they are necessarily expensive and therefore infrequent. A few towns—Etampes, Malesherbes, Pithiviers and Chartres with its cathedral—are market and route centres, with such old-established industries as the manufacture of agricultural implements, and new decentralised activities such as the manufacture of radio, TV and other electronic items.

## Brie

The Plaine de Brie occupies the area between the middle Seine and the Marne. This has undergone considerably more denudation than has Beauce; the Beauce Limestone and the Fontainebleau Sands have been completely removed, exposing the *Calcaire de Brie* over considerable areas. This in its turn has been cut into by the numerous streams which flow northwestwards across the plateau, so revealing the underlying marls. Much of this Brie Limestone has been weathered, producing a surface mantle of residual clay, particularly extensive in the northeast where it causes considerable waterlogging with numerous tiny lakes and areas of marsh (Fig. 9.9); their extent has been reduced by reclamation, although some of the surviving lakes are used for pisciculture. This part is known as *Brie humide* in contrast to *Brie pouilleuse* of the limestone, over much of which, however, limon is fortunately present.

The agriculture of Brie is therefore more varied than that of Beauce because of the greater range of soils. Wheat and sugar beet are the chief crops grown on the limon-covered limestone. In addition, since 1940 such crops as colza, white mustard, cameline and flax (developed as a result of the need for vegetable oils during the German occupation) have been cultivated for industrial purposes. Some interesting specialisations include the production of rose-bushes on the heavy clay soils near Crisy-Suisnes. Fruit cultivation has been developed, with long rows of cordon trees.

The wetter clay soils in the north and in the valleys carry pasture, which, supplemented by fodder crops (particularly lucerne), enables a considerable dairying industry to thrive. About 95 000 cattle were found in Seine-et-Marne in 1968, of which half were dairy animals, providing milk both for the Paris market and also for a lucrative cheese-making industry. Brie cheese is famed and large quantities are exported, particularly to Great Britain. Though sheep are no longer so numerous as in the past, the limestone pastures, used in conjunction with the practice of folding the animals on stubble and roots, enabled 107 000 animals to be kept in Seine-et-Marne in 1968.

The plentiful supply of surface water and the accessibility of well water at no great depth have occasioned a pattern of agricultural settlement quite different from that of Beauce. Many dispersed farms and small villages are situated in valleys or depressions surrounded by orchards, and provide a pleasantly varied and prosperous looking landscape as compared with the rather open austerity of Beauce. The regional name is a common element, as in Valence-en-Brie, Le Chatelet-en-Brie and Rozoy-en-Brie.

## Tardenois, Valois and Soissonnais

Between the Marne and the Oise-Aisne valleys, the Tertiary limestones form the low plateaus of *Tardenois, Soissonnais* and *Valois*.[9] Their surfaces vary in detail, for they have been much dissected by the tributaries of the Marne, Aisne and Oise; the Marne, for example, cuts right down into the Chalk. Denudation has in fact removed more and more of the overlying Tertiary rocks as one goes northeastwards from Beauce. Tardenois has an interrupted covering of Brie Limestone, Soissonnais of Upper Eocene limestone, Valois of the Lower Eocene *Calcaire grossier*. Most of the limestones are limon-covered. Other rocks introduce variety into the landscape; surviving outliers of the *Sables de Fontainebleau*, for example, form a distinct east–west ridge across the plateau rising to over 240 m (800 ft), deeply dissected by the headstreams of the Ourcq and heavily wooded. Some of the streams have cut down through the limestones, forming broad flat-floored valleys; these were formerly marshy and although now drained they still have damp heavy soils. In Valois the tributaries of the Ourcq and the Oise have eroded less markedly to form somewhat narrower valleys, rarely penetrating the limestone to the underlying clays and sands.

These *pays* form areas of prosperous and varied agricultural activity. Wheat with sugar beet in rotation predominates on the limon soils, the cultivation of fodder crops in conjunction with pasture on the clays allows dairy-farming, and there is much fruit-growing and market-gardening in the valleys.

The northern part of Valois on the plateau above the left bank of the Oise carries a succession of fine deciduous forests of oak, beech and lime—the Forêts de Compiègne (140 sq km (55 sq miles) in area), d'Halatte, de Chantilly and several others. Further south between the Aisne and the Ourcq valleys is the Forêt de Villers-Cotterêts. Most of these woodlands grow on the *sables moyens de Beauchamp*, except for that of Compiègne on the Lower Eocene sands and clays. Some of the sandy areas have been planted with pines, notably to the east of Chantilly, the so-called *mer de sable* with its white sand-dunes. Soissonnais too has its woodlands—the Forêt de l'Aigle in the angle of the converging Aisne and the Oise, and the Forêt de St Gobain further to the northeast.

Population is concentrated in pleasant villages along the springlines in the valleys. Several larger towns, such as Laon and Soissons, have grown up as market centres and as points on the routeways radiating from Paris. Laon stands on a prominent outlier of limestone 180 m (600 ft) above sea level, isolated between two headstreams of the Ailette and overlooking the chalk plain to the east known as *Laonnais*. Many of the towns contain industries of a varied nature, sometimes long-established, frequently newly established, the result of 'industrial overspill' from Paris, to areas outside the metropolis but with rapid access to it: metallurgical, light engineering, electronic and chemical industries. Several large sugar refineries are at such towns as Nogent-sous-Coucy and at Eppeville. Glass is made at Thourotte (to the north of Compiègne) and at Chauny, using glass sands from the St Gobain and Coucy districts. Along the valley of the Oise, notably at Creil, Montataire (with its new *cité-ouvrière*) and Nogent-sur-Oise, are various metallurgical industries; a rolling-mill was opened by Usinor in 1950 at Montataire to provide sheet metal for the Paris industrial area. Creil has large repair shops for locomotives and Nogent has wagon-building and repairing works. Chemicals and pottery are also made at these last two towns. At Creil and Porcheville are two thermal power stations, each with an annual output of over 2 million kWh.

## The Seine and Paris

Paris has grown from a small Gaulish settlement to its position as the leading city of continental Europe.[10] Its gradual concentric expansion from a nucleus on the Ile de la Cité[11] (Plate 27) has resulted in its present official area (the *agglomération urbaine*) of 368 sq km (142 sq miles), while its dormitory satellites spread out into neighbouring *départements* (Fig. 9.7).[12]

For a distance of some 30 km (20 miles) from the Charenton sluice at the Marne confluence to the river-port of Gennevilliers, the Seine flows through Greater Paris (Fig. 9.8); 13 km (8 miles) of the river lie within the municipality. The banks are concreted and lined with wharves and quays, and a

PLATE 27. Paris. The Ile de la Cité

navigational depth of 3 m (10 ft) is maintained. The channel is intersected by several islands, and the chief impediment to navigation (particularly at high water) is the numerous bridges; twenty-seven cross the main stream within the city itself and another nineteen are downstream to Gennevilliers. Factories and wharves line the river through a continuous succession of industrial suburbs.

Traffic on the river is heavy, as can be expected from the large population and varied industrial activity of Paris. In 1969 the wharves within the city handled 6 million tons of freight, and the port ranked third in France to Strasbourg and Rouen, though if the whole of the *agglomération parisienne* is considered it was easily outstanding with no less than 27·2 million tons. Another four million tons passed along the river in transit. More than two-thirds of this traffic was incoming, consisting of coal (from the northern coalfield), wheat and sugar (from the eastern farmlands of the Paris Basin), oil, crude steel (from Lorraine), building stone (from the Morvan and the Central Massif), sands and gravels by way of the Seine tributaries, and a variety of raw materials (ores, chemicals, wool, cotton, petroleum, timber and wood pulp) imported via Le Havre or Rouen. The tonnage of outgoing waterborne freight was less than a third that of imports, since so much of the exports consist of small-bulk high-value goods which can stand rail or road charges. Cement, bricks, plaster of Paris, and refuse to be dumped in disused quarries outside the city were the main bulk items.

Three canals are within Paris itself. The St Martin Canal, 5 km (3 miles) in length, leaves the Seine just below the Pont d'Austerlitz, continues in a tunnel under the Place de la Bastille and emerges near the Faubourg du Temple to end in the Bassin de la Villette to the northeast of the Gare de l'Est. From this basin the St Denis Canal continues to the Seine at La Briche. This is quite a busy little canal for it serves important industrial suburbs. The two canals therefore form a direct water route across eastern Paris, short-circuiting the lengthy westward loop of the main river around the Bois de Boulogne. The Ourcq Canal joins the Bassin de la Villette from the east; it serves the eastern industrial suburbs of Pantin.

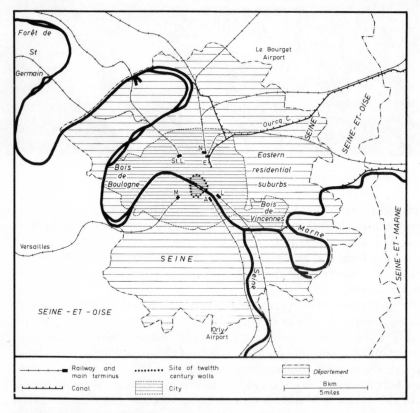

Fig. 9.7. Paris and its suburbs

The abbreviations of the railway stations are as follows: **A,** Austerlitz; **E,** Est; **L,** Lyon; **M,** Montparnasse; **N,** Nord; **St L,** St Lazare.

The medium shading indicates the area of the municipality, the more open shading the area of the former *département* of Seine. Seine and Seine-et-Oise were reorganised into six *départements* in 1964 (p. 189).

Based on (*a*) *Environs de Paris, Carte au 100 000ᵉ (Michelin,* sheet 96); (*b*) *Nouveau Plan de Paris (Carte Taride)*; and (*c*) G. R. Crone, 'The site and growth of Paris', *Geogrl. J.* **98** (1941), 37.

The functions of Paris are immensely varied. It is the seat of government of a highly centralised administration, a remarkable focus of communications (Fig. 9.7), a centre of trade, commerce and tourism, the largest industrial city in continental Europe, a vast residential and servicing centre, and in fact a world focus of life and thought. The chief industrial concentrations are in the northeastern suburbs in St Denis, St Ouen and Aubervilliers; in the eastern parts along the Ourcq Canal and in the suburbs of Pantin, Montreuil and Vincennes; in the Seine valley between Ivry and Choisy-le-Roi; and most important of all at a string of towns extending downstream from Billancourt on either side of the bend of the river as far as Gennevilliers and Argenteuil. Several works make steel castings for specific purposes at Ivry, Courbevoie, St Ouen and St Denis, and in the last-named district are produced wagons and rolling-stock, boilers, barges and other river craft, armaments, turbines and diesel engines. Although some factories were deliberately removed before 1939 to ostensibly safer areas, aircraft are manufactured at Levallois-Perret, Evry, Puteaux, Nanterre and Gennevilliers. Machine tools are made at Asnières and St Ouen. The two main French automobile producers, *Renault* and *Citroën*, are situated in the Paris district at Boulogne-Billancourt and Grenelle respectively. The former company was nationalised in 1945 when the *Régie Nationale des Usines Renault* was created, retaining the structure of a private concern but with ownership vested in the State. Its main factories extend along both banks of the Seine and on the intervening island of Seguin (Plate 28), and since nationalisation a huge new plant has

PLATE 28. Paris. The *Régie Nationale des Usines Renault*, Billancourt

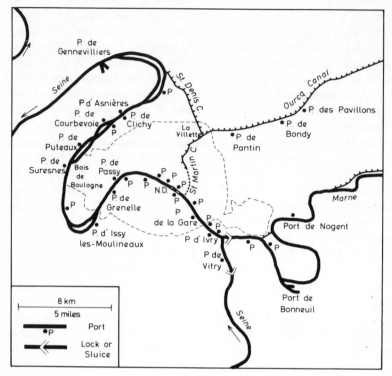

Fig. 9.8. The Port of Paris
The light pecked line indicates the boundary of the municipality of Paris.
The heavy pecked line indicates the underground section of the St Martin
Canal. **ND,** the Cathedral of Notre-Dame on the Ile de la Cité. Each
individually named 'port' is indicated by **P,** the more important being
named in full.

Based on W. Seghers, *Kaart der Binnenscheepvaartwegen van N-W Europa* (n.d.).

been built at Flins-sur-Seine, some 30 km (20 miles) downstream. The
Simca company has a large plant at Poissy. The necessarily vast public
utilities include thermal power stations (some of the largest in France),
gas works, sewage works and abattoirs.

In the industrial suburbs an extensive range of consumer goods is manufactured, not merely the world-renowned *haute couture* and *articles de luxe,*
but chemical products, electrical apparatus, food products, tobacco and
cigarettes, paper, books, soap, furniture, footwear, glassware, pottery,
radio and television, rubber products, linoleum, etc.

It is as difficult to give a figure for the population of Paris as it is for
London or New York. The *ville* in 1968 had a population of 2 591 000; the
official *agglomération urbaine,* which includes Paris *ville* and twenty-three
adjacent communes, had 8 197 000. Finally, if one takes the *agglomération*

198

*parisienne*, an overall total of nearly 12 million people is attained. The *zone suburbaine* includes a number of towns with a dual rôle; they have their own industrial activities and also house the commuters who travel daily to their work in Paris,[13] resulting in tremendous strains on the transport system. Eight 'new towns' are under construction or designated, four along each major axis to the northeast and southwest of the agglomeration. Paris is, in fact, undergoing almost complete rebuilding, with new high-rise blocks and 'complexes', subways and urban motorways. The growth of Paris (which has absorbed 45 per cent of the total French population expansion during the last twenty years, and includes a fifth of the labour force) has caused much national concern. Efforts have been made under the various national and regional plans to curb this tendency, to check unnecessary building and limit new industrial development. To reduce the disparity between Paris and the rest of France, eight existing urban complexes in various parts of the country are to be developed as *métropoles d'équilibres* ('balancing' or 'regional metropolises').[14] A new master plan for the whole Paris region has been published.[15]

## The Falaise de l'Ile de France

The eastern rim of the Ile de France forms a distinct outfacing escarpment, sweeping in a curve around its eastern and southern margins. It rises to about 210 m (700 ft), reaching its maximum point (287 m (942 ft)) in the Montagne de Reims (Fig. 9.9) near the town of that name. It then sinks gradually to the south until near Montereau it only attains about 150 m (490 ft) (Fig. 9.10). A sequence of rocks, from Oligocene limestones to the underlying Chalk at the base, is exposed on the face of the escarpment. Weathering and downwash have produced a thick cover of soil on the lower slopes.

The northern part of the escarpment, as a result of river erosion, is by no means continuous; in turn the Aisne, Vesle, Marne and Petit-Morin cut deeply through its edge. The last of these rises just beyond the escarpment in an area of marshland, the Marais de St Gond, still quite extensive in spite of reclamation, but its valley through the escarpment is far too well developed for such a small stream. Probably its former headwaters lay further to the east, but were captured by the Somme, a left-bank tributary of the Marne; the elbow of capture is near Ecury-les-Repos. The Marne to the west of Epernay forms a striking almost gorgelike valley.

The edge of the escarpment projects boldly eastward between each of the valleys, forming peninsula-like extensions of the plateau; a notable example is the Montagne de Reims between the Vesle and the Marne valleys (Fig. 9.9). Many minor valleys also interrupt the continuity of the Falaise, leaving spurs and isolated knolls rising above the plain to the east, such as Mont Aimé, a knoll separated from the Côte des Blancs to the south of Epernay. A little further to the west a similar hill, crowned by the village of Toulon-la-

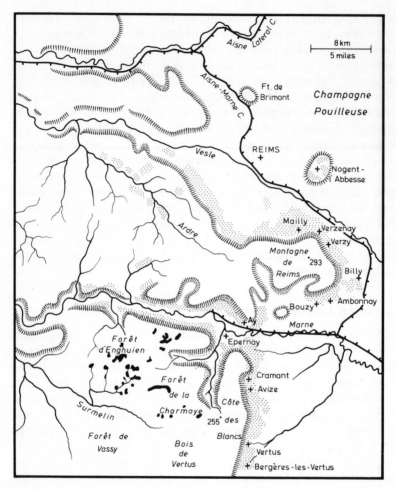

FIG. 9.9. The Champagne area
The area of vineyards (stippled) is very generalised. The edge of the *Falaise*
is shown by hachuring; spot heights are in metres. Some of the main
vine-growing centres are named. The small *étangs* in the southwest are
shown in black.

Based on: (*a*) *Carte de France et des frontières au 200000ᵉ*, sheet 17; (*b*) *Carte de la France vinicole*
(1949).

Montagne, is but a few metres lower. Some of these knolls were fortified to
protect the towns in the valley routeways.

To the south of the valley of the Petit-Morin the escarpment (known as
the *Côte Champenoise* or as the *Falaise de Champagne*) swings more continuously
westward, with the Seine flowing along its foot, until below Montereau
the river cuts abruptly northward towards Paris (Fig. 9.10).

Several towns stand in the gaps through the cuesta or near its foot—

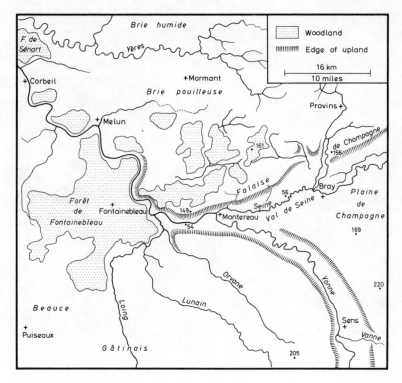

FIG. 9.10. The southern part of l'Ile de France
Spot heights are in metres.

Based on *Carte de France au 200 000ᵉ*, sheet 25.

Neufchâtel on the Aisne, Reims on the Vesle, Epernay on the Marne, and then the line of Romilly, Nogent and Bray along the middle Seine. Reims is grouped around its magnificent fourteenth-century cathedral (Plate 29), heavily damaged in the war of 1914–18, since the town was taken by the German army before the battle of the Marne and then occupied a vital defensive salient; the cathedral was not completely restored until 1938. The town has long been a market centre for the plains of Champagne to the east, as it lies on one of the main roads leading west to Paris, and today it is an important road and rail junction. Since the twelfth century Reims has had a flourishing textile industry based on the sheep of Champagne, and its fairs were renowned. Today it has grown into an important industrial town, with not only these old-established textiles, but also food-processing industries, flour-milling, sugar-refining, confectionery, the manufacture of vehicle components, general engineering, aircraft assembly and glass-making. It is of course one of the two centres of the champagne wine industry, Epernay being the other. Reims has not grown appreciably since the nineteenth century, in fact its population dropped from about

PLATE 29. Reims

100 000 in 1900 to a few thousands during the war of 1914–18. By 1938, however, it had risen to 117 000 and by 1968 this growth had been maintained to 153 000.

### The vineyards

Perhaps the best known feature of the limestone escarpment is the famous vineyards, or at any rate the famous product of those vineyards, called after the old provincial name.[16] The slopes of the Montagne de Reims, the northern edge of the Marne valley (Plate 30), and the Côte des Blancs (the main escarpment to the south of the Marne) are covered with long rows of vines. The vineyards, usually known after each neighbouring village, cover about 130 sq km (50 sq miles) (Fig. 9.9).

Except for the eastern aspect of the slopes, this district possesses no real physical advantages for the cultivation of the vine; the soils are rather poor, and the area is so near the northern limit of effective cultivation that bad or indifferent years are regrettably common as a result of too much rain, too little sunshine or late frosts. Both total yield and quality (as

202

PLATE 30. Champagne vineyards near Epernay along the Marne Lateral Canal

between a vintage and a non-vintage year) therefore vary considerably. It is to traditional skill and care in processing that champagne owes its reputation, although the uniform temperatures within the labyrinths of caves in the Chalk help in the maturing processes.

Until two centuries ago the Champagne grapes (almost all the *Pinot* variety) were used to make still wines, sold under the name of each particular vineyard. Then it was discovered by the renowned Dom Pérignon, of the Benedictine abbey of Hautvillers, that a delicate sparkling wine could be produced by means of carefully controlled fermentation. No longer is champagne sold under the name of the vineyard, since the final product is a blend, but under that of the firm which has processed it. The *cuvée* or blending of the juice from several vineyards after its first fermentation, followed by a lengthy maturing, clarifying and fortifying, are all most expert procedures.

The output of champagne wine is small, a mere 805 000 hectolitres out of the French total of 66·5 million in 1968. But in a good vintage year its value is considerable, since it constitutes one of the best known export wines.

## 2. The northern Paris basin

This comprises an area of low chalk-land which emerges from beneath the northern margins of the Tertiary strata of the Ile de France and continues northward to the Channel coast.[17] The gently undulating plateaus are largely limon-covered, and form one of the most important arable-farming areas in France, growing mainly wheat and sugar beet. A number of distinct units can be distinguished: the coastal margins, Artois, Picardy, the Pays de Bray, the Pays de Caux, the Vexin, the valley of the lower Seine and its estuary.

### The coastal margins

The coastline trends in a sweeping curve from the Strait of Dover to Cap de la Hève, the northern containing headland of the Seine estuary. Chalk forms the main element along this edge of the plateau (hence the name commonly applied to it of the *Falaises de Craie*), except in the Boulonnais where various Jurassic rocks are exposed. Since the formation of the Strait of Dover and the Flandrian transgression (see p. 26), marine erosion has severely attacked this cliffed coast, particularly in the south between the mouth of the Somme and Cap de la Hève; it is estimated that the latter has retreated 1 400 m (1 500 yd) during the last eight centuries. The action of the waves is emphasised by the fact that the Chalk overlies Gault marls and sands and Upper Jurassic clays, which are exposed at the base of the cliffs, so that masses of chalk constantly slump forward over these unstable 'lubricated' strata to the beach below.

One striking result of marine erosion is the formation of a type of 'hanging valley' known as a *valleuse*. Wave action has cut back in places more rapidly than the small chalk streams can erode their valleys, so that the mouth of each ends abruptly in a steep drop to the beach below (similar to the 'Seven Sisters' between Newhaven and Eastbourne). Many of the *valleuses* are now dry, the result of a lowered watertable. In places, however, the valleys open out to the coast at sea level and the cliffs are completely inter-rupted, as at Dieppe where the Arques reaches the sea and at Fécamp near the mouth of the Valmont.

The cliffs thus vary in height; to the west of Fécamp they rise for 75 to 90 m (250 to 300 ft) but between Veules and Quiberville they are only 35 to 50 m (125 to 175 ft). The highest sections are formed by the headlands; Cap de St Jouin rises to 390 m (400 ft), Cap d'Antifer to 116 m (381 ft) and Cap de la Hève to 107 m (351 ft). The cliffs have been heavily undercut to form caves, and there are many magnificent isolated stacks and arches.

On the other hand, a considerable amount of material has accumulated through longshore drifting. To the east of Cap d'Antifer this drift is from west to east, although now somewhat reduced by the construction of

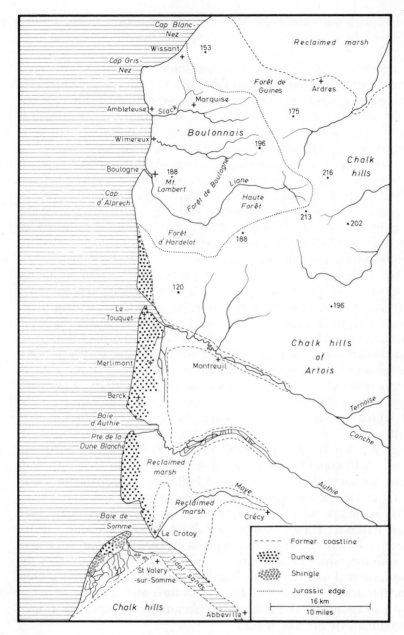

FIG. 9.11 The coastline of northern France
The approximate edge of the Jurassic rocks, exposed by denudation of the
Boulonnais anticline, is indicated by a dotted line. The margin of the coast
at the time of the Flandrian transgression, before sedimentation and
reclamation had taken place, is shown by a pecked line. Heights are in metres.

Based on various maps in A. Briquet, *Le Littoral du Nord de la France* (1930).

groynes. The material consists of flints derived from beds in the eroded chalk cliffs, and these have been built up as shingle beaches across the bays, as at Dieppe.

In the angle where the direction of the coast changes abruptly from west–east to south–north, the chalk plateau falls back to form the wide funnel of the Somme estuary, where sand and mud have accumulated. Flint shingle moves as far as the mouth of the Somme and contributes to the growth of the hooked spit of Le Hourdel across the estuary. Beyond that point only lighter materials, such as coarse sands, are moved, and sand spits backed by dunes have developed across the mouths of the Authie and the Canche. Between these spits and the edge of the chalk plateau are enclosed lagoons and marshland, much of which has been reclaimed and drained.[18] On the sand spit projecting northward across the Canche estuary has grown the modern luxury resort of Le Touquet. From Ault, therefore, to near Cap d'Alprech, the old chalk cliffs now lie well inland, fronted by reclaimed marsh, sand-dunes and sands (Fig. 9.11).

From Cap d'Alprech to Sangatte is a most interesting section, where the dissected anticline of the Boulonnais (see p. 207) reaches the sea; as a result, a striking variety of formations is revealed. The Chalk of Cap Blanc Nez contrasts with the Jurassic limestone of Cap Gris Nez, which rises 55 m (180 ft) from the sea. Pointe de la Crèche, about 3 km north of Boulogne, exhibits in section the complexities of the structure; the Upper Jurassic strata, including clays, sandstones and limestones, reveal striking folds. The beach is covered with massive blocks of sandstone derived from the weathering of the cliffs. Several small streams, notably the Liane (at the mouth of which stands Boulogne), reach the sea through broad clay-floored valleys.

This coast is not naturally favourable for the development of ports, but the proximity of England has encouraged the growth of the ferry terminals of Boulogne (connected with Dover and Folkestone) and Dieppe (with Newhaven); in 1969 about 510 000 passengers disembarked at Boulogne and 240 000 at Dieppe, and both ports have car ferry facilities and a small commercial harbour; Dieppe has a specialised import of tropical fruits. Coal was once by far the main import, but in these postwar years it is relatively unimportant. Oil, other hydrocarbons and timber are now the main items imported into Boulogne. The neighbourhood is one of the chief manufacturing areas of cement in France, as lime and clay are found in convenient juxtaposition, and a considerable amount is exported. Bricks, tiles and earthenware are also made.

Boulogne is the largest fishing port in France; of a total catch of about 428 000 tons in 1969, the port handled 129 000 tons. Dieppe was the sixth French fishing port with 11 000 tons. Most of the Boulogne fishing trade is in the hands of large trawler firms, and certain ancillary industries (curing, salting, packing, ice-making and the manufacture of fertilisers) are carried on. Fast night trains of refrigerator cars serve the Paris markets. Dieppe handles rather the smaller vessels which return daily, and it has a large covered fish market. The town has had a considerable recent expansion of industry: marine and electrical engineering, and the manufacture of man-made textiles. Fécamp is still one of the centres for fitting out the big *terreneuviers*, the trawlers which visit the Grand Banks of Newfoundland, based on St Pierre and Miquelon; cod and herring are processed.

Finally, this section of coast has a considerable tourist importance and its resorts are thronged during the summer months, both sophisticated places such as Le Touquet and the innumerable quiet *plages* among the dunes.

## Artois

The *Collines de l'Artois* consist of a long anticlinal ridge of chalk trending from northwest to southeast, where it is usually known as the *Cambrésis*. The general level rises towards the northwest, reaching a maximum of 217 m (709 ft) on the rim of the Boulonnais; the term *Haut-Boulonnais* is applied to this high chalk rim,[19] *Bas-Boulonnais* to the depression thus enclosed which opens on to the Channel. The surface of this breached anticline has a varied appearance, a result of the differential erosion of the diverse Jurassic and Cretaceous limestones, sandstones, marls and clays by the three small rivers Liane, Wimereuse and Slack. Residual hills stand up prominently from the clay lands of the valleys. The sands have an almost heathlike character, the clays carry pasture and copses, and the limestones have a cover of permanent grass. A small outcrop of coal at Hardinghen has been worked since the end of the seventeenth century, but only about 11 000 tons were produced each year in the decade before 1937, when mining ceased. However, this supply of fuel, together with some Jurassic iron ores, initiated an iron industry which survives as the presentday steel works at Outreau, with a plant opened in 1951, including an electric furnace for making special alloy steels.

The Artois anticline itself is asymmetrical; the rocks dip gently south-westward towards Picardy but more steeply to the plain of Flanders. Many small streams flow down the southern slope to join the Canche and the Authie, and others cut deeply into the northern slope to water the Flanders Plain. A few have begun to develop valleys along the crest of the anticline parallel to the strike, notably the Ternoise (on which stands St Pol), a tributary of the Canche. A right-bank tributary of the Ternoise flows from the northwest; it rises only 3 km (2 miles) from the Lys, which flows to the northwest for about 10 km (6 miles) also along the crest before swinging east down the slope to the Plain of Flanders.

Dry valleys are common, but there is also a surprising amount of surface water, largely because of the considerable limon covering. An undulating hill-and-dale relief is the result—open, with few trees, and with small nucleated villages and large farms growing wheat and sugar beet on the loamy soils. About two-thirds of the *département* of Pas-de-Calais was under arable in 1968 (although this administrative unit of course includes part of the Flanders Plain); rather less than one-third of the total arable was under wheat. Formerly the chalk lands were the grazing grounds of large flocks of sheep, but now cattle are eight times as numerous, although some sheep are still folded on fodder crops and grazed on stubble. A considerable area of fodder crops is grown for the feeding of cattle kept mainly for milk production.

## Picardy

The name of the ancient dukedom of Picardy (*Picardie*) has survived as a regional term, and most of it lies in the *département* of Somme, which the river more or less bisects. The undulating chalk lands rise to about 150 m (500 ft) to the north of the Somme valley, but to 240 m (791 ft) in the south on the rim of the Pays de Bray. The landscape is rather monotonous, consisting of sweeping expanses of chalk plateau interrupted only by dry valleys and by the larger marsh-floored valleys of the Somme, Authie and Canche.

The Chalk indeed appears on the surface comparatively rarely, although newly ploughed land reveals its characteristic pale bloom, for over much of the area lies the mantle of limon. Elsewhere, less usefully, are deposits of Clay-with-flints; these often carry woodlands or even uncultivated scrubland. The loam soils are intensively cultivated, for almost exactly two-thirds was under arable in 1968, and a third of that grew wheat. The rest was devoted to sugar beet and to fodder crops such as clover, colza and beet. A reflection of this arable activity is that over 19 000 tractors were in operation in 1968 in Somme; only two other *départements* (Seine-Maritime and Pas-de-Calais) possessed more. More than a quarter of a million cattle were kept, mostly stall-fed in large byres. The milk is sent to Paris and the industrial northeast, and there is some cheese-making, such as the attractive *Rollots* produced near Montdidier.

Another form of specialised agriculture is found along the alluvium-floored valleys, particularly that of the Somme, and on the reclaimed marshes behind the estuaries of the Canche and the Authie. Formerly they were used for peat-cutting, fishing and wild-fowling, but today they are occupied by intensively cultivated market gardens, utilising the heavily fertilised black peat soils. The floor of the Somme valley is so intersected by the braided channels of the river and irregular ponds formed by peat-cutting that cultivators are obliged to use flatbottomed boats to visit their holdings and to take crops to the Amiens markets.

When one crosses Picardy, either by train from Boulogne via Abbeville and Amiens on the way to Paris or by the new 'Nord' motorway, there is a remarkable impression of scanty population. One sees an occasional isolated farm,[20] a large sugar refinery standing among the fields, and here and there a steeple projecting from a clump of trees in a hollow or a valley. But numerous prosperous villages, many of them completely rebuilt since the wholesale devastation of 1914–18, are strung out along the valleys. In the marshy Somme valley they stand on the lower terraces away from the braided channels and ponds. Elsewhere they form small nucleated settlements in dry valleys, where the watertable is near the surface and well sinking is therefore less laborious and expensive than on the plateau. The average density of population in 1968 was about 80 per sq km (200 per sq mile).

This average is as high as it is partly because of the presence of Amiens, with its population of 118 000. The town stands mainly on the left bank of the Somme, with its old citadel on a chalk hill across the river near the junction of several tributary valleys. A settlement has stood on this site since Roman times, and in the medieval period it became an important focus of communications (notably on the route between Paris and Flanders), a commercial town and a centre for varied textile and metallurgical industries. Its superb Gothic cathedral, probably the finest in France, which remained almost unscathed in the 1914–18 war, is a testimony to its medieval splendour and importance. Today Amiens has textile, clothing, tyre, chemical and footwear manufactures and a wide range of food-processing industries.

Several other towns are located along the Somme valley; St Quentin (almost wholly rebuilt since the war of 1914–18, and with modern textile factories and engineering and electronics works), Péronne and Abbeville are the only ones of any size.

## The other chalkland *pays*

### The Pays de Bray

Although this small unit is on a different scale from Picardy, it is worthy of special mention. By road from Amiens to Rouen one traverses this *pays* transversely to the structure, from Dieppe to Beauvais the direction is longitudinal. In either case the contrast between the surrounding chalklands and this elongated ellipse of Upper Jurassic rocks is pronounced.

The Pays de Bray consists of an anticline from which the overlying Chalk has been removed, leaving infacing escarpments (Fig. 9.12). Within the anticline the Béthune flows northwest to the sea at Dieppe, the Epte first in a diametrically opposite direction then turning south to the Seine. The rim is also broken to the south by the Andelle, which has a short longitudinal upper course in the depression before bending south towards the Seine. As a result, a variety of rocks is exposed within the anticline. The infacing chalk slopes are underlain by Cretaceous Chalk Marl and Gault Clay, forming a clearly marked springline. Then follow Upper Jurassic clays and sands and in the centre some upstanding hillocks of Portland Limestone which rise to about 230 m (750 ft). Bray presents a varied landscape of woodlands, damp meadows, patches of sandy heathland and arable fields.[21]

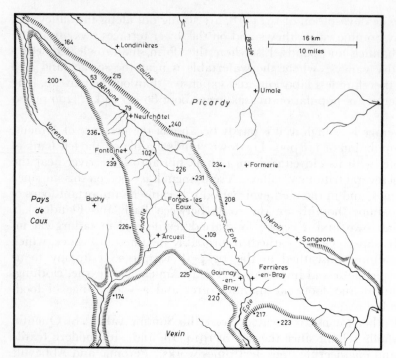

FIG. 9.12. The Pays de Bray
The edges of the denuded anticline, within which are exposed Cretaceous marls, Gault Clay and Jurassic clays, sands and limestones, are indicated diagrammatically by hachuring. Some small hillocks of Portland Limestone rise to the northeast of Forges-les-Eaux. Heights are given in metres.

Based on *Carte de France au 200000<sup>e</sup>*, sheets 8, 9, 15, 16.

Several small hamlets lie along the floor of the depression, followed by the road and railway from Dieppe to Beauvais. Neufchâtel-en-Bray, Forges-les-Eaux (the name is a legacy of an ancient iron industry using local ores and charcoal), and Gournay-en-Bray are the largest.

## The Pays de Caux

This block of chalk forms a plateau extending westward towards Cap de la Hève as a blunted triangular upland between the chalk cliffs and the incised meanders of the Seine.[22] At first sight it appears to have a fairly uniform surface level at about 150 m (500 ft), swelling almost indistinguishably to a maximum of 205 m (673 ft). It has been shown,[23] however, that although there is an overall general slope towards the coast of about 4 m per km (20 ft per mile), this is not a single surface but a series of broad shallow step-platforms, probably of marine origin. Many patches of impermeable Clay-with-flints occur, sometimes extensive enough to bear small lakes. Water draining from these patches finds its way down fissures or joints in the surrounding chalk, which it sometimes enlarges to form considerable sinkholes. Deeply incised valleys are rare, except along the southern margins where short streams flow rapidly down the edge to join the Seine. The steep slopes of the Seine's incised meanders are heavily wooded.

The limon-covered surface of the plateau forms excellent farmland, and the land is divided into open hedgeless blocks of cultivation or permanent pasture. But for the treelined roads, so typical of northern France, the orchards around the compact nucleated villages, and an occasional large walled farm, the landscape seems rather bare (Plate 31). Villages and hamlets appear at much more frequent intervals than in Picardy, however.

The Pays de Caux corresponds closely to the *département* of Seine-Maritime (although this also includes the lower Seine valley and the Pays de Bray), and its land use figures (for 1968) are indicative. Thirty-four per cent of the total area was under arable, 40 per cent (a surprisingly high figure) was under permanent grassland, and 15 per cent under forest. Large strips growing wheat occupy rather more than half of the arable area, and the yield of wheat per hectare is second only to that of Nord in France. Flax, sugar beet, potatoes and fodder crops make up the remaining area; the area under flax amounted to about 19 000 ha (47 000 acres) in 1968, nearly half of the French total.

PLATE 31. Part of the Pays de Caux

This district is important for cattle-rearing, more so than any other area of the Paris Basin, for in 1968 there were 650 000 head. Nearly half of these were dairy cows, producing milk for the Paris, Rouen and other urban markets, and for cheese-making; *Suisse Bondon* cheeses are a well-known product.

No large towns stand on the plateau; significantly Rouen, the *chef-lieu* of the *département*, lies below on the banks of the Seine. Numerous villages and hamlets are dotted around, some of them along the main railway line from Le Havre to Amiens, others near the heads of short valleys dropping down to the Seine.

## Vexin

The chalk plateau between Caux and the Tertiary rocks of the Ile de France to the south is known as Vexin. A division is sometimes made between *le Vexin normand* in the northwest and *le Vexin français* stretching southeast towards the Oise valley, although this has more historical than geographical significance.

Vexin differs from the other limon-covered chalk plateaus in the degree to which it is dissected by river valleys; the tributaries of the Thérain and other Oise confluents in the east and south, and the Epte and the Andelle in the west, have cut quite steep valleys, leaving small tracts of plateau surface as interfluves. The cultivation of wheat and fodder crops on the limon soils and dairying in the clay-floored valleys are the main agriculture activities. Vexin is crossed by the straight N14, the main road between Rouen and Pontoise, and so to Paris.

## The lower Seine valley

The physical characteristics of the lower Seine valley[24] have been described above (p. 187). The steep chalk slopes are thickly wooded, and the reclaimed alluvial flats bordering the dyked course of the river are utilised either as meadowland or for market-gardening. As the river meanders so these meadows occupy alternate sides of the river, becoming more extensive and seamed with drainage channels as the estuary is approached. The largest area is the *Marais Vernier*, which includes much land still of a marshy character and a large shallow lake. The marsh occupies a semicircle 16 km (10 miles) across between two northward-projecting spurs of chalk; the more westerly, the Pointe de la Rocque, is surmounted by a lighthouse, for it rises abruptly to over 45 m (50 ft) a few hundred metres from the tidal flats. This semicircle, bounded on the south by a steep chalk face rising to over 90 m (300 ft), represents the site of a former meander of the Seine, the cliff being the river-bluffs. On the opposite side of the estuary, a little lower down to the west of the Pointe de Tancarville, is another curve of chalk, the former complementary northward meander. The river current is now confined to a dredged channel leading directly through the *Embouchure de la Seine*, the 'estuary funnel', and these former meander-sites lie well to the south and north respectively. The only bridge across the Seine below Rouen is at Tancarville. The Normandy motorway between Caen and Paris follows the south (left) bank of the Seine, and another is planned for the north bank. The role of the lower Seine as a 'corridor of movement' is emphasised by the considerable river traffic, by the electrified railways linking Le Havre, Rouen and Paris, by the several high-capacity oil pipelines and by electricity grid lines.

Andresy, Poissy, Meulan, Mantes, Bonnières, Les Andelys, Elbeuf and many other towns are situated along the river.[25] They have wharves and quays, and a range of industries, using imported fuel and raw materials, has developed; these include the manufacture of textiles, tobacco and cigarettes, paper, cellophane, cement, bricks and chemicals. An oil refinery was completed in 1969 at Vernon, halfway between Paris and Rouen; its throughput in that year was 287 000 tons, and this is rapidly increasing.

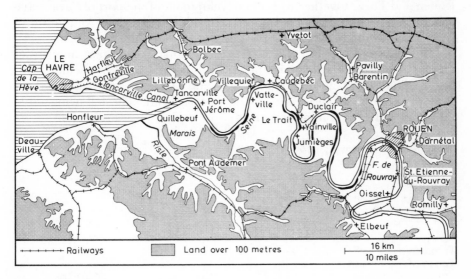

FIG. 9.13 The lower Seine and its estuary
The heavy black lines along the river indicate embankments.

Based on *Carte de France et des frontières au 200 000ᵉ*, sheets 8, 15.

The two largest urban centres along the lower Seine are Rouen and Le Havre; between them they contain over half of the entire population of Seine-Maritime.

Below Elbeuf the Seine makes a huge meander, leaving as a core the wooded spur of the Forêt de Rouvray (Fig. 9.13). Along the right bank of this meander on a terrace above the river (a position which has kept the city immune from all but exceptional flooding) grew Rouen,[26] 130 km (80 miles) from the sea and 240 river-km (150 miles) from Paris. It has been a town since pre-Roman times, and became successively the seat of a bishopric, the capital of a powerful feudal Normandy, an important centre of early industrial development, and a base for French maritime expansion. In the mid-nineteenth century the threat to its mercantile interests by the growth of the size of shipping, the progressive silting of the river below the port, and the rivalry of Le Havre developing as an outport led to a programme of engineering works after 1848. A dyked channel was constructed through the estuary to the roadstead beyond Le Havre. There is an appreciable tidal range, and vessels drawing 7·5 m (25 ft) can enter the port at mean high water springs, although the bulk of the shipping using the port consists of medium-sized vessels drawing 3·5 to 6 m (12 to 20 ft). The maritime port extends along both banks of the Seine for about 20 km (12 miles) to the Boïeldieu bridge in the heart of the city, to which point the river is tidal. Above the bridge the inland waterway port extends for a further 13 km (8 miles) to Oissel, for the navigational improvements of the Seine between Rouen and Paris, together with the development of the port of Paris, have benefited river transport enormously. In addition to some kilometres of river quays, numerous basins have free connection with the river.

If mineral oil is excluded, Rouen is the leading French port in terms of tonnage handled. If crude oil is included, however, both Marseilles (with 49·8 million tons of oil imported in 1969) and Le Havre (37·0 million tons) with their large refineries are of course far ahead. The following table summarises the main items imported:

*Seaborne trade of Rouen, 1969*
*(thousand tons)*

|             | IMPORTS | EXPORTS |
|-------------|---------|---------|
| Oil         | 1 959   | 3 091   |
| Coal        | 970     | 63      |
| Fertilisers | 1 089   | 60      |
| Foodstuffs  | 1 007   | 2 038   |
| Others      | 585     | 899     |
|             | 5 610   | 6 151   |

Source: *Annuaire statistique de la France*, 1970–71.

In the interwar period the volume of these imports into Rouen was much greater, but two of the largest bulk commodities (coal and oil) have been considerably reduced; in 1930, for example, Rouen imported 5 million tons of coal and in 1938 about 3·1 million tons, of which two-thirds came from Britain. Similarly with oil; prewar tankers delivered direct to the Shell refinery near Rouen, but today with their greatly increased size the oil is unloaded at Le Havre and piped to the refineries along the river.

Rouen is an inland waterway port second only in France to Strasbourg. In 1969 about 5·2 million tons of freight were loaded into barges, while 2·9 million tons were unloaded; in each case mineral oil was the dominant item.

The imported raw materials are used in the Rouen area, at factories along the lower Seine, and in the Paris region. Rouen itself is the centre of an important industrial district. Cotton manufacturing has been established since the eighteenth century when it was introduced into what had long been a textile district, first for wool then linen. Cotton factories extend along both sides of the Seine and along tributary valleys (though there has been a big recent decline in the industry), and a variety of other textile industries (rayon, nylon and clothing) has developed. A great variety of metal-using industries is found at Rouen and downstream along the Seine at Duclair, Mailleraye, Caudebec and elsewhere to Le Havre itself—ship-building, ship-repairing, wire and cables, diesel engines, refrigerating equipment, electrical and electronic engineering. Other industries include petrochemicals, and the production of paper at mills along the left bank at Grand-Quévilly and Oissel. Finally, the Shell refinery at Petit-Couronne above Rouen was the third largest in France in 1969 in terms of output (7·8 million tons).

Rouen has developed therefore as a port and industrial centre of considerable importance. From its original terrace-site on the north bank, the built-up area has spread up tributary valleys and (as a result of flood protection and regularisation measures) on to the south bank within the meander. Its population in 1968 was 120 000, though if the fourteen adjacent communes in the official *agglomération* are included the total is almost 370 000, the ninth largest in France. This is an indication of how the town's activities have expanded to draw neighbouring districts into its orbit. It is now linked with Paris by the Normandy motorway.

Between Rouen and the sea are several small ports (Fig. 9.13), including Duclair, Jumièges, Le Trait and Villequier. Some have industries, but others are merely mooring points for vessels negotiating the channel to Rouen. At Port-Jérôme, Esso-Standard have developed a refinery which (with a 1969 output of 4·6 million tons) is the sixth biggest in France (Plate 32). Crude oil is brought by pipeline from the tanker terminal at Le Havre. Near by is a large petrochemical factory, owned by Shell-St Gobain, which makes detergents. A few kilometres upstream of Port-Jérôme is the recently expanded Gravenchon refinery of the Mobil-Oil company; it had an output of 2·7 million tons of hydrocarbons in 1969. A new refinery has been opened at Vernon, 40 km (25 miles) upstream.

Le Havre, the second port of France in tonnage of vessels entered and cleared, is situated on the northern shore of the Seine estuary to the southeast of Cap de la Hève. Until the sixteenth century its site was an area of

PLATE 32. The Port-Jérôme oil-refinery on the Seine between Le Havre and Rouen

tidal marshes, from which its docks were excavated. Improvements have culminated in a deep-water channel leading into the port from the Carosse roadstead off Cap de la Hève; this enabled the ill-fated *Normandie* to enter at any state of the tide. Today the port accommodates Atlantic liners (handling 28 000 passengers in 1969), ferry steamers from Southampton and a large number of cargo vessels. In bulk of freight handled, Le Havre is again second to Marseilles; the outstanding imports in 1969 were crude mineral oil (37·0 million tons), refined mineral oil (1·3 million), coal (1·25 million), and agricultural products (1·3 million). Apart from oil, which dominates the scene, the imports are neither so bulky nor so diverse as those of Rouen. A few kilometres upstream of Le Havre, on the banks of the Tancarville Canal, is the Gonfreville-Seine oil refinery, built in 1933 and subsequently enlarged, with an output of 12·51 million tons of hydrocarbons in 1969, the largest in France; it is owned by the nationally sponsored Compagnie Française de Raffinage. A vast petrochemical complex has been developed. A pipeline has been constructed along the Seine valley from Gonfreville via the other refineries to Paris, and another pipeline has recently been completed to the Grandpuits refinery 40 km (25 miles) southeast of Paris in the *département* of Seine-et-Marne. A large offshore island is under construction at Le Havre, with oil discharge berths for 500 000 ton tankers.

216

Le Havre,[27] as a result of its multifarious commercial and industrial activities, has expanded inland from its site on the alluvial plain on to the surrounding chalk plateau. In 1968 its population had reached 200 000, or with its three neighbouring communes of Harfleur, St Adresse and Sanvic, forming the official agglomeration, about 247 000. Considerable destruction occurred during the war of 1939–45, but much rebuilding has taken place, and numerous lofty ferroconcrete buildings, including a fine railway station, have arisen behind the port area, together with several new residential districts. Its industrial activities have been greatly expanded, notably at an estate developed on reclaimed land to the east of the port alongside the Tancarville Canal. Industries include ship-repairing, general engineering, flour-milling, oilseed-crushing, sugar-refining, the production of petrochemicals, and aeronautical and automobile (Rénault) assembly.

[1] The standard work on the morphology of the Paris Basin is A. Cholley *et al.*, 'Carte morphologique du Bassin de Paris', *Mémoires et Documents* (1956), v, pp. 7–103. This detailed text accompanies a volume of four morphological maps on the scale of 1:400 000, published by the *Centre de Documentation cartographique et géographique* (Paris).

[2] E. Chaput, *Recherches sur les terrasses alluviales de la Seine entre la Manche et Montereau (Bulletin Service de la Carte Géologique de France, 1924)*.

[3] The monumental work on the valley of the Loire is R. Dion, *Le Val de Loire* (1934), a volume of 752 pp., copiously illustrated and documented.

[4] M. Chartier, 'Problèmes de la navigation fluviale dans la région parisienne', *Bull. Assoc. Géog. franç.*, (1965), 338/9, pp. 41–51.

[5] P. George and P. Randet, *La Région parisienne* (1959), in the series *France de Demain*.

[6] M. Phlipponneau, *La Vie rurale de la banlieue parisienne* (1956), provides a detailed study of horticultural activity.

[7] P. Brunet, *Structure agraire et économie rurale des plateaux tertiares entre la Seine et l'Oise* (1960), a detailed text of 552 pp.

[8] An account of the ancient forest, its changes and developments, is given by A. Kh. Iablokoff, *Un Carrefour biogéographique: le massif de Fontainebleau* (1953).

[9] M. Chamard, 'La Plaine du Valois', *Annls Géogr.*, **44** (1935), pp. 496–508.

[10] See, for example, A. Demangeon, *Paris; la ville et sa banlieue* (1934); G. R. Crone, 'The site and growth of Paris', *Geogrl J.*, **98** (1941), pp. 35–47; P. George *et al.*, *Etudes sur la banlieue de Paris* (1950); P. H. Chombart de Lauwe *et al.*, *Paris et l'agglomération parisienne* (1952). R. E. Dickinson, *The West European City* (1951), devotes a chapter (pp. 223–35) to the site and function of Paris.

[11] M. Foncin, 'La Cité', *Annls Géogr.*, **40** (1931), pp. 479–503, affords a detailed exposition of the historical geography of the Ile de la Cité.

[12] See J. Bastié, 'La Population de l'agglomération parisienne', *Annls Géogr.*, **67** (1958), pp. 12–38. He defines the *agglomération* as comprising 55 communes in addition to the *ville*. The *zone suburbaine* occupies another 161 communes. See also J. Bastié, *La Croissance de la banlieu parisienne* (1964); and G. Pourcher, *Le Peuplement de Paris* (1964), published by the *Institut National d'Etudes Démographiques*.

[13] A. Lucchi, 'Les migrations alternantes dans la région parisienne', *Annls Géogr.*, **75** (1966), pp. 39–56.

[14] These are Lille–Roubaix–Tourcoing; Nancy–Metz–Thionville; Strasbourg; Lyons–St Etienne; Marseilles–Aix; Toulouse; Bordeaux; and Nantes–St Nazaire.

[15] *Schéma Directeur d'Aménagement et d'Urbanisme de la Région de Paris* (1966).

[16] P. Marres, 'La Champagne', *La Vigne et le vin en France* (1950), pp. 76–81. See also

G. Colin, 'Le Dynamisme du vignoble champenois', *Rev. Géog. de l'Est*, **8** (1968), pp. 337–53.

[17] For a detailed, well illustrated and fully documented study of the Chalk in northern France, see Ph. Pinchemel, *Les Plaines de Craie du nord-ouest du Bassin Parisien et du sud-est du Bassin de Londres et leurs bordures: étude de géomorphologie* (1954). This contains a bibliography of 606 items.

[18] See A. Briquet, *Le Littoral du Nord de la France* (1930), for details and a number of maps; a more recent study is C. Prêcheur, *Le Littoral de la Manche de Sainte-Adresse à Ault. Etude morphologique* (1960).

[19] A detailed summary of the northern chalk cuesta of the Boulonnais, together with maps and a bibliography, is given by A. Coleman and A. M. Ferrar, 'Morphology of the North Boulonnais Chalk', *Geogrl J.*, **120** (1954), pp. 62–80. There is a most interesting analysis of the mapped erosion surfaces.

[20] R. Coque, 'L'évolution de la maison rurale en Amiénois', *Annls Géogr.*, **65** (1956), pp. 401–17, traces the evolution of the 'courtyard farm' and its relation to the rural economy.

[21] H. D. Clout, 'The Retreat of the Wasteland of the Pays de Bray', *Trans. Inst. Brit. Geog.*, **47** (1969), pp. 170–89; this analyses the development of a *bocage*-like landscape, largely as a result of changes in ownership, illustrated with some striking maps.

[22] A. Frémont, 'La partie occidentale du Pays de Caux (La Région du Havre)', *Annls Géogr.*, **65** (1956), pp. 98–122, deals in detail with the '*évolution économique*' of this area.

[23] B. W. Sparks, 'Erosion Surfaces around Dieppe', *Proceedings of the Geologists' Association*, **64** (1953), pp. 105–17, has a detailed map showing eight distinct erosion surfaces.

[24] A. Vigarié, 'Observations sur les caractères structuraux et morphologiques de la Région de Rouen', *Annls Géogr.*, **63** (1954), pp. 22–32.

[25] E. Vigarié, 'L'Ensemble portuaire de la Basse-Seine', *Tidschr. econ. soc. Geogr.*, **50** (1959), pp. 136–51.

[26] F. Gay, 'La croissance de la région de Rouen et ses problèmes', *Etudes Normandes* (1964), no. 171, pp. 1–16.

[27] F. Gay and J.-P. Damais, 'Le Havre, aspects géographiques et sociologiques de la croissance urbaine', *Urbanisme* (1966), no. 93, pp. 35–49; and J.-P. Damais, *La Nouvelle Ville du Havre. Reconstruction et Repopulation, fascicule 2, tome ix, of Mémoires et Documents du Centre de Documentation cartographique et géographique* (1961).

# 10
# The lowlands of northern France: II

## 3. The eastern Paris Basin

Beyond the edge of the Tertiary escarpment the eastern Paris Basin is occupied first by an outcrop of Chalk, then by a narrower tract of Gault Clay, and finally on the margins by the topmost Jurassic rocks. The last are at their narrowest in the extreme north, where they come up against the Palaeozoic rocks of the Ardennes massif and disappear completely near Hirson, but the exposures broaden as they swing southward in a great curve; the greater part are in Lorraine (Fig. 9.1). The same sequence appears in the south, although the belts of Chalk and Gault become increasingly attenuated, and it again culminates in the Jurassic limestone plateaus which in the east form a divide between the Seine and Saône basins and further west border the flanks of the Central Massif.

## The Chalk country of Champagne

The *pays*-name of *Champagne pouilleuse*, indicating a dry, dusty and 'beggarly' type of country, has for long been applied to the outcrop of Chalk, at its widest 50 km (30 miles) across, which sweeps in a curve for 150 km (90 miles) from the Oise valley, where the Chalk actually comes up against the Devonian rocks of the Ardennes, to beyond the Yonne. In the north between the Oise and the Aisne the chalk lands are known as *Laonnais*, after the town of Laon which lies on the edge of the Tertiary limestone to the west (see p. 194). Then follows the *Champagne pouilleuse* proper, succeeded southward by the *Pays d'Othe* between the upper Seine and the Yonne, and finally *Gâtinais* to the west of the Yonne. The last two are sufficiently distinctive to be considered separately.

The Chalk country rises very gradually in altitude, from about 75 m (250 ft) at the foot of the Falaise to 210 m (690 ft) on its eastern rim, where a not very prominent escarpment descends to the Gault Clay plain. These Chalk lands are wide and open, and for centuries sheep-grazing has been their main use; in 1968 there were still nearly a quarter of a million sheep in the two *départements* of Aube and Marne. Unlike the chalk country of the northeast, limon is almost completely absent, and the thin residues of *in situ* weathering are not of much value for arable farming. However, especially in the post-1945 years, heavy fertilisation has improved the meagre yields, and wheat and fodder crops are cultivated in increasing quantities. In many ways this is one of the most monotonous and thinly populated parts of the French countryside.

The chalk country is crossed by river valleys—those of the Oise, the Aisne, the Marne, the Aube and the upper Seine (Fig. 9.4). These rivers are obvious misfits in their present valleys; broad trenches were eroded during Pleistocene times when their volume was much greater. The present streams wander over the flat valley floors which they have rendered almost impermeable by a lining of alluvium. The rivers, which formed numerous backwaters and braided sections, have been regularised to check flooding, but for navigation purposes it usually proved easier to build lateral canals, such as that of the Marne which follows the main stream for 68 km (42 miles) upstream to Vitry-le-François.

Nevertheless, the essential shortage of water within the chalklands has nucleated most settlement within these valleys, and villages usually lie along the foot of the chalk bluffs at the springline. Some are little more than groups of farms, which possess both meadowlands and damp pastures on which cattle are pastured and also sheep-grazings on the chalklands beyond the valley bluffs. These valleys are also routeways, as they have been for many centuries, and the Marne is followed upstream by road, railway and canal from Châlons to Langres, the Seine similarly from Romilly through Troyes to Châtillon and thence to Dijon. At Châlons the northward trend of the road along the Marne is continued by N44 through Reims and Laon to the Channel coast; the chalkland offers a line of easy movement from north to south which bypasses Paris on the east. Some of the great medieval fairs were held at towns on these routes, notably at Troyes on the Seine and at Reims on the western edge of Champagne.

Troyes, the *chef-lieu* of the *département* of Aube, had a population of nearly 75 000 in 1968, and after Reims is the biggest town in this part of France. It has a nodal position at the junction of several railway lines and *routes nationales*, and has a port on the Seine Lateral Canal. The town has developed a diversified industrial life, many of its activities (such as the manufacture of textiles and paper) being established for centuries; the earliest Saxton county maps of England were printed on Troyes paper. Hosiery and knitwear are still important, now using imported wool and manmade fibres, and there has been recent diversification into electrical and electronic engineering. Châlons-sur-Marne is almost as well placed in respect of communications, for it lies at the crossroads between the route from Lorraine and Metz which continues due west to Paris, and the north-south route already mentioned. This town too has light industries, including food-processing, light and electrical engineering, and the manufacture of manmade fibres and textiles. Many other smaller towns stand along the valleys. Rethel, for example, on the banks of the Aisne, has been a manufacturing town and market centre for many centuries. Indeed, its population has changed little from 7 500 in 1851 to 8 000, but it has breweries, saw mills and small textile factories. The town is the centre of a small valley *pays*, known as *Rethelois*.

## The Pays d'Othe

This southern section of the *Champagne pouilleuse* between the upper Seine and the Yonne is diversified with irregular residual patches of the Lower Eocene *argiles plastiques*. The south-facing chalk escarpment, overlooking the clay vale containing the Armançon, is covered with these sandy-clay deposits, and forms a prominent ridge rising at its highest to 280 m (912 ft). This is one source of the water supply of Paris, for the Aqueduc de la Vanne, beginning in the Vanne valley, taps numerous springs and streams on the backslope. The ridge is much dissected by streams flowing both northwards down the backslope to the Vanne (a rightbank longitudinal tributary of the Yonne) and southwards down the shorter slope to the Armançon. Wooded spurs project in both directions between the deeply cut valleys, long and tapering to the north, short and abrupt to the south. More patches of Eocene sandy-clays occur to the north of the Vanne, but much bare chalk is apparent.

This interesting *pays* has a pleasantly varied land use and agriculture, the result of the differing geology and soils. The ridge is swathed with forest, while by contrast the open chalk country to the north provides sheep pasture. Cattle are grazed on water-meadows along the streams, sugar beet and cereals are cultivated on the plateau where the clay covering is present, vines are grown on south-facing slopes of the chalk escarpment, and orchards (particularly of cherries and cider apples) cluster around the villages. Several attractive small towns are found, many of them with suffixes *-en-Othe*. One indication of a past activity is a series of names such as La Forge-à-l'Eau, Les Minières and La Charbonnière; beds of ferruginous sands were worked and smelted with charcoal in the sixteenth and seventeenth centuries. The larger settlements are mostly along the Vanne and its tributaries; Sens, at the junction of that river with the Yonne, is the market town for the district.

## Gâtinais

This *pays* lies mainly between the rivers Yonne and the Loing, but also extends west of the latter towards the plateau of Beauce. It represents a further section of the Chalk belt, but is still more masked than the Pays d'Othe with residual Eocene deposits of heavy clays. The surface is much wetter as a result of this impermeable cover, and large numbers of shallow lakes or *gâtines* (hence the name of the *pays*) lie in undulating hollows in the clay. The only Chalk appears at the sides of the numerous open valleys where streams have removed the clay cover.

Considerable drainage and reclamation of the *gâtines* have been effected and the clay soils now carry pasture for cattle. Arable farming is concentrated on the gently sloping valley sides, especially where the underlying fertile marls of the Lower Chalk are exposed in the Loing valley. Much of the district is under woodland, especially where the Bois des Haies covers a considerable area. There is no shortage of water, and small villages are widespread. Montargis, in the Loing valley where several tributary valleys converge to form an open fertile plain, is the regional centre. It is served by the Briare Canal, with which it is also connected to the Orléans and Loing Canals (Fig. 9.5); although these are only secondary waterways, they form a helpful link system in the heart of France. Montargis has several small rubber, chemical, leather and food-processing factories.

## The Argonne

To the northeast of *Champagne pouilleuse* lies the much dissected massif of the Argonne, consisting of a clay-sandstone of greenish-white colour known as

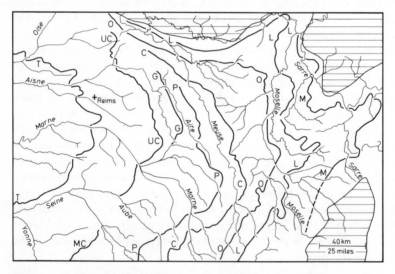

FIG. 10.1 The scarplands of the eastern Paris Basin and Lorraine
The escarpments are shown in generalised form by heavy lines, and are lettered as follows: **T,** Tertiary (Falaise de l'Ile de France); **UC,** Upper Chalk; **MC,** Middle Chalk; **G,** Upper Greensand (*gaize*) of the Argonne; **P,** Portland Limestone; **C,** Corallian Limestone; **O,** Oolitic Limestone; **L,** Lias; **M,** Muschelkalk (Trias). The Palaeozoic rocks are indicated by horizontal ruling.

Based on (*a*) *Carte géologique de la France*, 1 : 1 000 000, published by the *Service de la Carte géologique détaillée de la France*; and (*b*) F. Machatschek, *Das Relief der Erde* (1938), p. 54.

*gaize* (Fig. 10.1). The massif has been defined by the erosion of two parallel longitudinal streams, the Aisne to the west and its tributary the Aire to the east. The latter rises in the Kimmeridge Clay belt not far from the Meuse and flows northwards, entrenched down through the clay; in fact it may disappear into the underlying porous Corallian Limestone for several kilometres, particularly during a dry summer. It reappears further north and crosses the Portland Limestone plateau in a trench which again is occasionally waterless in summer. It then turns sharply west near Grand-pré through the northern part of the Argonne to join the Aisne, for here is an example of river capture (Fig. 10.2).[1] The Aire once continued its longi-tudinal direction northwards to join the Meuse, but an active west-flowing subsequent of the Aisne cut back into and finally through the Argonne, leaving the beheaded trunk of the proto-Aire to continue to the Meuse as the much reduced Bar.

Streams dissect each side of the Argonne, since there is much water in the valleys on these clay sands although the ridges are dry. The southern

FIG. 10.2. River capture in the Argonne
The upper Aire once flowed north-northwestwards to join the Meuse. It was captured by an active subsequent of the Aisne, which cut back through the Argonne. The beheaded trunk is now the Bar, which joins the Meuse below Sedan. Heights are given in metres.

Based on *Carte de France au 200 000ᵉ*, sheets 10, 17.

Argonne is divided longitudinally into two by the deeply-cut valley of the Biesme, which flows northwards for about 20 km (12 miles) until, like the Aire, it turns sharply west to join the Aisne. The steepsided transverse valleys are separated by sharp crests which rise to 230 m (750 ft) in places.

The Argonne is still a well-wooded district, despite the age-old activities of wood-cutters and charcoal-burners and the vast devastation of the two last wars. The ridges and valley sides are clothed with both deciduous trees and recently established plantations of conifers; the total area of woodland today is about 470 sq km (180 sq miles). The valleys and depressions, where not cleared and drained, are either marshy or covered with thick scrub, while some of the higher drier ridges present a heathlike appearance, with silver birch, brambles, bracken and ling.

The Argonne is a zone of scanty settlement. Some towns and villages are situated on the flanks of the uplands, with smaller settlements within the upland in the more open valleys, such as the pleasant town of Florent-en-Argonne in the longitudinal valley of the Biesme. Some villages were once centres of iron industries, using local ferruginous sands, charcoal and water power; small lakes were formed by damming streams (which resemble the 'hammer ponds' of the Weald), but are now used only for fishing. Many men are employed in forestry and at the saw mills and timber yards. Today some mixed farming is practised in the more open valleys, with an emphasis on dairying, and even cereals are grown.

The Argonne is still a zone of separation, as it has been for centuries, between Champagne and Lorraine, and it long formed one of the outer defensive barriers of the Paris Basin. The upland is not a single cuesta like the Jurassic hills further east but a much dissected upland, and the north–south trend of the ridges and valleys makes it difficult to cross transversely. One main road and railway run west from Verdun but they have to pursue a circuitous route from one valley to the next, and the railway is obliged to tunnel. Another railway and road utilise the Aire gap by way of Grandpré. But between these two transverse routes 30 km (20 miles) of forested ridges and valleys are crossed only by a single minor road.

## The pre-Ardennes region

A rather indeterminate region of Jurassic rocks, sometimes referred to as *Plaines et Plateaux pré-Ardennais*, lies in the extreme northeast between the chalklands and the Ardennes. The Meuse, after flowing through its long 'furrow' in the Corallian Limestone, continues in a series of large loops through a narrow Lias Clay vale before cutting north in a narrow gorge through the Ardennes. It receives two tributaries along the narrow outcrop of the Lias, the Chiers from the east which joins the main river below Sedan, and the short Sormonne which flows in a diametrically opposite direction to join the Meuse at Charleville. The Lias outcrop becomes progressively narrower to the northwest, finally vanishing against the Silurian rocks of the Rocroi massif in the Ardennes. To the south a parallel band of Oolitic Limestone forms a prominent cuesta overlooking the Lias vale, and then to the south again are narrow exposures of Oxford and Gault Clays, the Corallian being scarcely represented. Here the Jurassic rocks, sweeping to the northwest from Lorraine in an attenuating curve, end near Hirson.

The valleys of the Meuse and its tributaries form a prosperous farming area. The soils developed on the Lias Clay, enriched with calcareous down-wash from the cuestas and with river alluvium, are used for the cultivation of oats, trefoil and fodder beans, or are under short ley meadow grasses. The

FIG. 10.3 The Meuse valley industrial area in northern France
Each town shown has metal-using industries.

Based on *Carte de France et des frontières au 200 000*[e], sheet 10.

emphasis is on livestock, including dairy cattle, beef cattle, sheep and horses, and many large farms possess quadrangles of stables.

The *département* of Ardennes is included within the *Région Est I* of the *Chambre Syndicale de la Sidérurgie Française* (see Fig. 11.7). The Meuse valley from Sedan downstream to the Belgian frontier at Givet has metallurgical industries; such names as Neuve-Forge and Vieille-Forge are indicative of its old establishment. The initial advantages included charcoal from the well-wooded Ardennes and water power from the Meuse tributaries. In the fifteenth century refugees from Liège introduced nail-making, which has survived to the present day. The war of 1914–18 caused widespread destruction and the industrial life had to be completely rebuilt. Today the district has no blast furnaces, but a large steel works, built under the post-1945 modernisation plans, is situated at Blagny-Carignan on the banks of the Chiers 16 km (10 miles) upstream from its junction with the Meuse. Another steel works at Vireux, utilising pig iron from Lorraine, supplies steel for the factories at Charleville, Monthermé, Vrigne-aux-Bois, Ville-sur-Lumes, Nouzon, Fumay and many other places (Fig. 10.3). These manufacture tubes, nails, hardware, boilers, wire and other metallurgical products in great variety. The northern branch of the Est Canal and the canalised Belgian Meuse afford relatively easy access to Lorraine and to the southern Belgian coalfield, while the Douai-Cambrai-Charleville line enables Nord coal to come by rail.

The chief town of the *département* of Ardennes is Mézières, on the south side of a meander of the Meuse, while its twin, Charleville, stands some kilometres downstream on the north side of the loop below the confluence of the Sormonne. Each is an old fortress town, with modern suburbs and factories engaged in various branches of metallurgical industry. Sedan, situated just below the junction of the Chiers, likewise consists of an old fortress town on the right bank of the river and new industrial suburbs on the left bank. It is the centre of a long-established woollen industry, originally based on wool from sheep both on the Ardennes and on the limestone plateaus to the south, and on the plentiful supplies of water from the flanks of the uplands. A number of factories, both in the suburbs of the town and in neighbouring villages, still make fine woollens, velours and velvets.

This part of France has suffered grievously as a result of its strategic situation. Sedan was a fortified town as early as 1424. It was here that Napoleon III saw his army defeated in 1870, the whole area was devastated in the war of 1914–18, and much destruction occurred again in 1940–44. Ten years afterwards some of the towns still had a much smaller population than in 1938, but most of them have now recovered.

## The claylands of Champagne

A crescentic outcrop of Gault Clay flanks the chalk cuesta on the east, though it is much less extensive than the Chalk; from the Aisne valley southward it forms a strip only a kilometre or two across, widening to 30 km (20 miles) where it is crossed by the Marne flowing from Joinville almost to Vitry-le-François. The Gault then extends still further to the south as a narrow outcrop between the Chalk and the Jurassic limestones, occupied by a section of the Armançon which flows through the clay vale to join the Yonne.

Further west, between the Yonne and the Loing, the Gault Clay is diversified by outcrops of Upper Greensand. These form low sandstone ridges, known as the *Collines de Puisaye*, which trend east–west and rise to 375 m (1 227 ft). This higher land causes a series of streams to flow north with a reasonable gradient both to the Loing and the Yonne, thus avoiding the marshlands found in other Gault districts. The clay outcrop crosses the Loire near Cosne, and can then be traced as a narrow band along the northern edge of Berry, where it finally disappears.

Except where each river in turn has cut an alluvium-floored valley across the outcrop and for residual patches of sand or outcrops of Greensand, the Gault forms a continuous sheet of heavy impermeable soils, hence the name *humide*. Originally it must have been an area of extensive swamps, lakes and thick forests, and many shallow interconnected lakes and marshy depressions remain, particularly in the source region of the Aisne and in the angle of the Marne to the southwest of St Dizier, where the Etang de Lahorre covers about 250 ha (620 acres). Much reclamation, originally begun by religious houses in the Middle Ages, has been effected, and it has now a prosperous dairying (particularly for cheese-making) and mixed farming activity. The countryside is undulating rather than flat, and so while meadows are concentrated in damp depressions, arable land growing cereals and roots (particularly fodder beet) is found on the better-drained lower slopes, and orchards occur on south-facing aspects or clustered around hamlets. The most prosperous arable part of *Champagne humide* is *Perthois*, where the Marne, the Saulx and the Blaize have deposited alluvium over the clays. The small patches of sand form scattered higher areas of heathland among the claylands, where widespread afforestation has taken place.

Hamlets are small but widely distributed, since there is no problem of water supply. As in the Argonne, some of these settlements nurtured bygone iron industries based on patches of ferruginous sands within the clays. A few of the little towns still have metallurgical industries, now using Lorraine steel, as at St Dizier (which makes nails and wire), Bar-le-Duc, Wassy and Vitry-le-François. Other activities include the manufacture of bricks and tiles, cement (at Frignicourt), textiles (the legacy of the wool sales at Troyes and elsewhere from the *Champagne pouilleuse* flocks), pottery (at Pargny-sur-Saulx) and crockery (at Couvrot). At Sermaize-les-Bains is one of the largest sugar refineries in France. Both the Marne-Saône and Marne-Rhine Canals cross the central part of the region and so facilitate the movement of the bulky raw materials for these industries, as well as of agricultural products, and of fertilisers and lime for the heavy clay soils.

# The eastern Jurassic margins

The Jurassic outcrop swings south and southwest, forming an area which has been given by French geographers the collective name of *Plateaux de la haute Marne et de la haute Seine*. The succession of Jurassic rocks has been described in connection with the upper Seine and its several tributaries, which cross these outcrops more or less transversely (see p. 183 and Fig. 9.4). Several *pays* in this marginal area merit more detailed attention.

## Barrois

The *Plateau des Bars* consists of the western part of the Corallian plateau, a narrow belt of Kimmeridge Clay, and a low cuesta backed by the undulating plateau of Portland Limestone which dips gently westward towards *Champagne humide*. These various zones naturally display marked differences in land use. The higher parts of the limestone plateaus are either wooded or afford poor grazing, although their lower slopes are ploughed. Cattle, kept both for dairying and for meat, graze on the clay-floored valleys.

The limestone slopes of Barrois have quite a reputation for wine, and its yield is included under the general classification of 'Burgundy'. A large amount of *vin ordinaire* is produced, but the vineyards along the river Serein, a tributary of the Yonne, in the neighbourhood of Chablis, yield a superb dry wine of a unique pale gold colour. Another wine district extends northeast from Les Riceys across the Seine and Aube valleys; the best-known product is the *Vin Rosé des Riceys*. The vineyards of both Chablis and Les Riceys climb up the lower south-facing slopes of the limestone knolls and plateau edges.

Settlement is concentrated along both the main and side valleys. The three Bars, -sur-Seine, -sur-Aube and -le-Duc, stand in broad valleys cut by the Seine, the Aube and the Ornain respectively. They form prosperous market towns and centres of communication, and have numerous light manufactures such as tanning, the preparation of leather-goods and food-processing. Further to the south Auxerre stands in the valley of the Yonne (the *pays* name of *Auxerrois* is sometimes given to the surrounding district), and Tonnerre (similarly *Tonnerrois*) is on the left bank of the Armançon. These form a crescent of towns round the Jurassic rim of the eastern and southeastern Paris Basin.

## The Plateau de Langres

This limestone upland forms the watershed of central France between the Seine and Saône systems. In the neighbourhood of Langres itself the plateau attains about 470 m (1 550 ft), but this increases southwest to heights of over 600 m (2 000 ft). The plateau is an asymmetrical anticline, with a steep and much faulted southern slope to the Saône valley and a more gentle gradient to the north, across which are trenched the upper Seine and its family of tributaries. The steep edge overlooking the Saône valley has a maximum altitude of 636 m (2 087 ft). The general name of *Côte d'Or* is applied where the cuesta form becomes more pronounced further south, between Dijon and Beaune; this district really belongs to the Saône trough (see pp. 377–80).

The Langres plateau consists largely of Oolitic Limestone, though in some parts denudation has exposed the underlying Lias clays and marls. The Marne and the Armançon, as already emphasised, have cut back through the limestone on to these clays, where they take their rise. To the northeast of Langres the clay lands are known as *Bassigny*, further to the southwest as *Auxois*, and on the northern flanks of the Morvan as *Terre Plaine* (Fig. 9.3). An outcrop of Lias Limestone forms a prominent escarpment to the southeast of Langres.

The plateau has a varied agricultural pattern, as evidenced by the land use statistics for the *département* of Haute-Marne, in which much of the upland lies. Forty per cent in 1968 was wooded, including most of the higher plateau where the rainfall is quite heavy (Langres has an annual mean of 914 mm (36 in), at an altitude of just over 450 m (1 500 ft). There are woodlands of beech, chestnut and oak, and some extensive coniferous plantations. Twenty-five per cent was devoted to arable cultivation, almost exactly half of this under cereals (oats and wheat), the rest under fodder crops and potatoes. Some vines are grown, but not on any scale; the great Burgundy vineyards of the adjoining *département* of Côte d'Or lie on the eastern slopes of the plateau (see p. 377). About 25 per cent was under pasture, both the rather scrubby limestone grassland and the damp meadows on the Lias clays of the Marne valley; in 1968 there were 235 000 cattle (about half dairy animals) and some 50 000 sheep. In spite of the altitude and the appreciable rainfall, there is therefore quite a prosperous agricultural life.

Most of the small towns and villages are situated in the valleys, though Langres is an attractive walled town standing boldly on a north-projecting limestone spur between the Marne and a small parallel headstream to the west, and serving as a market centre for a considerable district.

The Langres plateau lies transversely athwart central France, so forming a distinct barrier to communications between Paris and the Mediterranean coast, but this is nevertheless crossed by several main railway lines. The most important line of the *Région Sud*, from Paris to Marseilles, follows the Yonne and Armançon valleys through the southern scarplands. It then climbs up the Oze valley through the Lias claylands to the summit at Blaisy-Bas at a height of about 400 m (1 350 ft), and penetrates the watershed through a 3-km (2-mile) tunnel before beginning the steep descent of the Oolitic slope to the railway junction of Dijon, thence down the Saône valley. A second main line, that of the *Région Est* from Paris to Basel, follows in turn the valleys of the Seine to Troyes, then of the Aube beyond

Bar-sur-Aube, and of the Marne from Chaumont to Langres; the watershed between Langres and Chalindrey is again negotiated by a tunnel. A markedly steep descent eastward down the Lias limestone edge, utilising the Amance valley, takes the line to Vesoul and so through the Belfort gap to Basel. Several main roads, none with any really severe gradients, focus on Langres from the north via the Marne valley, hence down to Vesoul and Besançon, and on Dijon from Paris and the west. Even two canals cross the divide. The Burgundy Canal links the Yonne with the Saône via Dijon, although it requires 189 locks, and the Marne-Saône Canal, with 114 locks, passes to the east of Langres in a tunnel through a limestone spur.

## Nivernais

Although almost separated from the rest of the Jurassic rim by the projecting 'peninsula' of the Morvan, an area of Jurassic rocks with a distinct individuality is contained between the Loire and the edge of the Morvan. This is given the *pays* name of Nivernais, after the regional centre of Nevers, and corresponds very closely to the *département* of Nièvre. The Loire flows across the western part, known as *Le Val du Nivernais* or as *Bas-Nivernais*. The central part is much higher, rising to 452 m (1483 ft) and is known as the *Plateaux* or *Côtes du Nivernais*. The eastern part, crossed by the Yonne, is *Bazois*.

Nivernais is structurally a complicated area, since it forms part of the northern end of one of the Tertiary rift valleys which characterise the eastern flanks of the Central Massif (see pp. 526–7), and it is crossed by a number of roughly north–south faults. While Oolitic Limestone predominates, an ancient 'wedge' of granite appears in the neighbourhood of St Saulge, while in the south a small down-faulted pocket has preserved Permian and Carboniferous rocks, including the Upper Coal Measures of the tiny Decize coalfield. Considerable overlying deposits of Pleistocene sands and gravels were deposited by the postglacial Loire on leaving the Central Massif with its swollen volume and immense load.

Nivernais is therefore a district with varied landscapes, soils and land use patterns. This is reflected by the figures for the land use categories; 118 000 ha (292 000 acres) of arable, 225 000 ha (556 000 acres) of pasture and 216 000 ha (534 000 acres) of woodland were returned in the *département* of Nièvre in 1968. Agriculture is of a mixed character; cereals (wheat predominant) and fodder crops occupy approximately the same area, and much permanent grass on the Lias clays and along the Loire valley supports 115 000 dairy cattle and considerably more of the white Nivernais stock bred for beef and for draught use. Vineyards on the terraces of the Loire below Nevers produce a light dry white wine which is mostly consumed locally, though a Nièvre wine with a very wide reputation is *Pouilly-Fumé*, produced in Pouilly-sur-Loire 40 km (25 miles) downstream from Nevers.

Some of the areas of gravel and sand carry a heathland vegetation of bracken and gorse. Considerable tracts are under oak-birch woodland, and parts of the heaths have been planted with conifers.

Population is not dense, averaging about 35 per sq km (90 per sq mile) over the region as a whole. There is no shortage of water and numerous villages occur along the tributary valleys of the Yonne and the Loire. Decize is a small town connected by a branch to the Loire Lateral Canal, by which coal was shipped to Nevers, the *chef-lieu* of the *département*. It has several light engineering industries, including the manufacture of aircraft parts. An ancient iron industry used the ferruginous ores of Berry and local charcoal, and today pig and raw steel are imported from Lorraine for light metal manufactures. Another old-established industry, the manufacture of crockery and earthenware, is still quite prosperous.

# 4. The middle Loire Basin

The river Loire, after leaving its downfaulted basin in the north of the Central Massif, crosses the Oolitic Limestone and then swings in a curve through the southwestern corner of the Paris Basin. The symmetrical arrangement of the strata, seen so clearly in the eastern part of the basin, is here lacking, partly because the land is more low-lying (hence differential denudation has had less scope), partly because much is masked with unconformable sheets of Tertiary sands, clays and gravels.

This region may be described under the several subregions of the valleys of the Loire and its major tributaries; the *Sologne*, within the angle of the Loire; *Champagne berrichonne*, or Berry; the *Collines du Sancerrois*; and the districts of *Brenne* and *Boischaut*.

## The middle Loire valley

From Nevers to the junction of the Maine near Angers, a distance of about 350 km (220 miles), the Loire flows in a broad trench usually varying in width from 5 to 10 km (3 to 6 miles) which rises by well-defined terrace steps to the rolling plateau country beyond. In places this trench narrows to a kilometre or so, and to the east of Tours above the southern bank rise steep cliffs. The river meanders over the floor of this flood plain, and the vast loads of material brought down by the winter floodwaters from the Central Massif are spread out in ever-changing banks of sand and gravel, between which the river braids its course in a tangle of feeble watercourses and islets covered with osiers and willows. In summer it seems a placid river, with expanses of white gravel and sand, and quiet backwaters.

In winter the many branches merge to form one swirling stream, covering the islets and filling the channel between the protective dykes built along almost its whole length through Touraine and Anjou, set far back from the summer course of the river. At times during these winter floods the waters spread out to form shallow lakes. Thus at Orléans the road and rail bridges are each more than 300 m (1 000 ft) long to cope with the floodwaters. At Tours the overall width of the river at flood is about 380 m (1 250 ft), and the road bridge crossing from the town to the bluffs on the south side is more than 430 m (1 400 ft) in length.

The proto-Loire cut a much broader valley than the present river would seem to justify. In Pleistocene times it deposited vast quantities of sediment brought down from the Central Massif, but since then it has eroded its bed in stages within the old floodplain, so forming a series of broad terraces. The present floodplain is for the most part floored with sands and gravels, but the terraces are covered with alluvium on which fertile soils have developed. Below Blois, where chalk outcrops overlook the valley, downwash has produced a rich calcareous soil. Much drainage and reclamation of the valley-flats has been carried out.

The several sections of the Loire valley have sufficient identity to have received a whole series of *pays* names. In the west of Nivernais it is known as the *Vallée Noire* or simply *Le Val*. Then succeed downstream the *Val d'Orléans*, the *Val de Blois*, the *Val de Touraine* and the *Val d'Anjou*.

Centuries of effort have made the terraces of the Loire valley one of the most attractive farming areas of France. It affords a pleasant agricultural

PLATE 33. The River Loire at Saumur

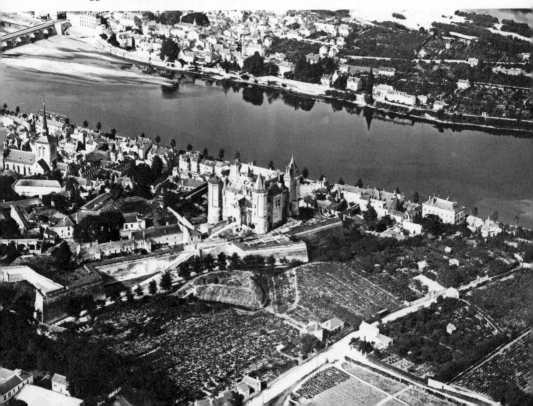

landscape of rich meadows on the floor of the floodplain, market gardens and nursery gardens on the lower terraces (especially near the towns), larger fields of wheat on the broad upper terraces, and extensive orchards and vineyards. There are numerous local specialisations; thus Anjou is famous for its artichokes,[2] potatoes are grown along the south side of the Val d'Orléans, asparagus in the angle between the Cher and the Loire to the south of Blois, mushrooms along the lower Indre valley,[3] and haricot beans in Touraine. In fact, the term 'Garden of France' has been justly bestowed on this valley, particularly on the Val de Touraine.[4]

The Loire valley has extensive vineyards on its slopes.[5] Touraine has long been famous for both white and red wines; the white wines of Vouvray, produced from grapes grown on the north bank between Blois and Tours, the red wines of Bourgueil also grown on the right bank but below Tours, and the Chinon vineyards on the north bank of the Vienne just above its confluence with the Loire, are all well known. The Val d'Anjou, in the neighbourhood of Saumur, produces a range of both sparkling and still wines, including the superb *Saumur pétillant* wines: crisp, dry and sparkling.

The Loire valley has several large towns, each the centre of a valley *pays*, each with an eventful history, with a lively industrial and commercial life superimposed upon the glories of the past. Orléans,[6] the *chef-lieu* of Loiret, had a population of 96 000 in 1968; situated on the northern banks of the Loire, it has long been a bridge town, helped by a string of islands. It is a gracious town, with broad streets and attractive squares. It has naturally developed as a market town, lying as it does between Beauce and Berry, and several industries have achieved considerable importance; these include food-processing (flour-milling, the making of biscuits and confectionery), numerous light engineering and metallurgical industries, vehicle components for Rénault, tyres (Michelin) and pharmaceutical chemicals. Further downstream is Blois, the *chef-lieu* of Loir-et-Cher; its crowded houses rise steeply up the limestone slopes of the valley-side to the castle which has dominated the town for many centuries. It too is a bridge town; five main roads converge from the north on the bridge, although only a single road from the south, and it is a prosperous tourist centre.

Tours is the largest town of the middle Loire valley. It has grown up on the south side of the valley within the long narrow triangle of level land between the Loire and the converging Cher. The town itself had a population of 128 000 in 1968; in recent years the built-up area has expanded over the interfluve and along the north bank of the Loire, and now the official *agglomération* has a population of about 201 000. The Loire is crossed by rail and road bridges, the latter carrying N10, the main road from Paris to Bordeaux, and the city is bypassed on the east by a new bridge carrying a section of autoroute. The city is an important railway junction, with large marshalling yards. As centre of the 'Garden of France', its importance rests largely on agricultural produce; a famous agricultural fair is held annually in May. Numerous industries[7] have been established, mainly the manufacture of agricultural machinery, fertilisers, pharmaceutical chemicals, rubber, rolling-stock and ball-bearings. Saumur, below the Vienne confluence, is important as a centre of the wine industry (Plate 33). Two nuclear power stations are in operation in the Loire valley at Avoine near Chinon, a third at St Laurent-des-Eaux on the loop of the Loire between Orléans and Blois.

These are the main towns, but a succession of small prosperous villages on either side of the river is situated on the terraces above flood danger. Some, such as Beaugency and Amboise, stand at minor Loire bridgepoints. Several have developed new light industries, including electrical engineering at Gien, and the making of vehicle components (Simca) at Sully.

One of the main features of the middle Loire valley is the remarkable number of *châteaux*, hence the popular term of 'château country'. This is partly due to historical and personal reasons, in that since the time of Charles VII the Bourbons had been particularly attracted by Touraine, and to the geographical features of this pleasant river valley, with numerous prominent sites within easy distance of Paris. Some of the châteaux originated as medieval fortresses, but after the Renaissance they developed highly ornate, even flamboyant, architectural features. They succeed each other at intervals along the river banks, each sited on some prominent bluff or spur—Amboise and the fortresslike Chaumont to the east of Tours, Chenonceaux (built on a bridge across the Cher), Valençay in the open country south of the Cher, Chambord (the largest of the Loire châteaux) and Cheverny away from the river to the east of Blois, and the château de Blois. Another group is found below Tours—the fortress of Luynes, Langeais, Villandry (with its superb formal gardens), the great ruin of Chinon, and many more.

## The Sologne

To the south of the angle of the middle Loire lies the Sologne,[8] a gently undulating plain 120 to 150 m (400 to 500 ft) above sea level and about 4 400 sq km (1 700 sq miles) in area, draining vaguely westwards to the Loire by way of the Loiret, Cosson and Beuvron, and to the Cher (hence again the Loire) by the Sauldre. The underlying rock is Chalk, but this is not visible except on sides of the valleys, for the region is covered with a thick mantle of Miocene clays and sands and in the south also with Clay-with-flints and gravels, the immense *cônes de déjections* of the proto-Cher and -Loire. The heavy clays and gentle gradients have resulted in impeded drainage, so that this region has long been characterised by marshes and a vast number of lakes. The Sologne once carried an ancient forest, gradually destroyed during the Middle Ages, to be replaced by the *étangs* and by heathland. As a result, in the early part of the nineteenth century it formed one of the poorest parts of France; the few inhabitants were poverty-stricken, undernourished and unhealthy, obtaining a bare existence by cultivating rye and buckwheat and by keeping flocks of sheep. The density of population was probably less than 100 per sq km (250 per sq mile).

Many reclamation projects have been started, though not all were successfully carried out. In 1859 at La Motte-Beuvron, in the heart of the Sologne, *Le Comité central de la Sologne* was organised to systematise and co-ordinate the various efforts at improvement, which had considerable success. Some of the reclaimed land is now under cultivation, and cereals are grown, not much wheat but rye and malting barley for the breweries of Orléans, and increasingly hybrid maize, while asparagus, potatoes and haricot beans are cultivated on the sandy soils in the north. The reclaimed claylands afford grazing for both dairy cattle and beef cattle. The breeding of rabbits, geese and turkeys has developed; the last are sent to Paris and even to England.

The most valuable improvements in the Sologne, particularly of the sands which in places overlie the clays, have been by afforestation. Considerable progress had been made by 1914, in spite of a disastrously cold winter in 1879–80 which destroyed vast numbers of trees, notably the not too hardy maritime pine. Much of the woodland was of necessity felled during the 1914–18 war, so that despite renewed activity in the interwar period, by 1939 the area planted was still less than in 1914. Since 1920 planting has been mainly by Austrian pine and Douglas fir, with some deciduous trees such as birch and oak. More felling was necessary in the 1939–45 period but more planting has since taken place. In all abo it 200000 ha (500000 acres) are under timber, but areas of heath still survive.

Population is scanty, concentrated in a number of small towns along the river valleys. They are mostly market towns, and possess industries connected with the exploitation of the forests; saw mills prepare pit props and sawn timber, and an important cooperage activity serves the wine trade. Selles and St Aignan each has a small pottery, while Romorantin possesses several small textile factories, the legacy of an activity based on the flocks of sheep that once grazed in the Sologne, and it also produces lingerie, footwear and ironmongery.

To the north of the Loire lies the Forêt d'Orléans[9] with an area of about 500 sq km (200 sq miles). It has developed on the same Miocene deposits as the Sologne, and is similar in many respects, although with only a few lakes.

## The southwestern *pays*

### Champagne Berrichonne

The low undulating plateau of Berry[10] slopes gently northward towards the Sologne from the edge of the Central Massif. It consists mainly of Oolitic Limestone in the south and Corallian Limestone in the north, with a narrow intervening strip of clay, and the plateau, 230 m (750 ft) in altitude in the south, falls to 90 m (300 ft) in the north. It is crossed by a number of rivers—the Cher and its tributaries in the east, the Indre and its head-streams in the centre, and the Creuse in the west. The whole region is sometimes divided into two—*la champagne d'Issoudun* to the west of the Cher in the *département* of Indre, and *la champagne de Bourges* to the east in the *département* of Cher, after the two main towns.

Much of the plateau carries a reddish-brown loamy soil, the product of limestone disintegration, and although somewhat dry this yields well when heavily fertilised. The *département* of Cher had actually 47 per cent of its area under arable in 1968, compared with only 20 per cent under pasture and 20 per cent under woodland; the figures for Indre were 57, 13 and 16 respectively. In this area modernisation and rationalisation of agriculture has made recent progress; rural depopulation has stimulated the creation of large mechanised farms, growing a rotation of cereals, sugar beet and legumes. Rather more than half of the arable grew cereals (wheat, oats, barley for malting, and some maize), the rest fodder crops. There were also in the two *départements* about 427 000 cattle, 350 000 sheep, 90 000 goats and 184 000 pigs, evidence of a mixed agriculture; some famous goat-milk cheeses from Berry can be bought in the Paris markets. Vineyards are common on the limestone slopes, but these rarely produce wine other than *vin ordinaire*.

Some quite extensive woodlands consist mostly of oak with an admixture of beech, hornbeam and birch. These woods once supplied charcoal to small local iron works, but they now provide timber for furniture-making at Châteauroux and St Amand.

The agricultural population of these open limestone plains is not dense; Cher averages 40 people per sq km, Indre about 36. Population is distri-buted in large villages along the river valleys. The regional capital is Bourges, with a population in 1968 of about 71 000. Situated at the con-vergence of two Cher tributaries (the Auron and the Yèvre), it has long been a major route centre; nine main roads and a number of railways con-verge on it, but the Berry Canal which passes through its western outskirts is now disused. Bourges is one of the old-established centres of metallurgical industry, and its present activities include foundries, ordnance works, the huge missile and aircraft factory of Nord-Aviation, textile and clothing factories,[11] Michelin tyres and several concerns making agricultural implements and hardware. Other industries include tanning and leather working based on hides from local herds at Levroux and Issoudun, milling, brewing at Châteauroux and Issoudun, and the manufacture of linoleum. Such towns as Vierzon, Mehun and Foëcy have brick, tile, porcelain and chemical industries; a modern development is the manufacture of elec-trical insulators using Jurassic fireclays. Châteauroux has textile industries, now making cloth for uniforms, and in the neighbourhood of Argenton the manufacture and embroidery of lingerie is still carried on. Near this town was developed a large US air-base; its closure in 1951, thus ending a major source of civilian employment, was a serious economic blow, only partially alleviated by the creation (with government stimulus) of an industrial estate with various light industries.

## Sancerrois

The Collines du Sancerrois, of Portland Limestone, rise to 434 m (1 424 ft) in the Massif d'Henrichemont, and drain north by rivers flowing to the Sauldre, which have cut deeply into the underlying rocks. Where surface deposits of Clay-with-flints and residual Eocene clays occur, there are extensive woodlands of oak and birch, and the higher parts are covered with a scrub of brushwood and brambles. The most favoured areas for agriculture and settlement occur in the valleys, where the Chalk has been exposed and the slopes are covered with a veneer of warm limy downwash soil. Here grow pleasant orchards of pear, plum and cherry, and a profitable specialisation on the higher slopes is provided by the cultivation of walnuts, producing about 700 tons of nuts per annum. Sancerrois has been a vine-growing region since Roman times, producing some light white wines, although it was badly hit by phylloxera. Sancerre itself stands well to the west of the Loire on a limestone knoll.

## Brenne and Boischaut

These districts lie to the south and west of Berry, between it and the Limousin crystalline plateau. They rise to about 150 to 250 m (850 ft), and are mostly covered with Middle and Lower Jurassic sandstones and clays. Some masses of reddish sandstone form low conical hills, covered with pines and broom scrub, but the greater part is a gently undulating erosion surface heavily plastered with impermeable clays. Brenne, like the Sologne, has numerous small lakes, marshes and peat bogs, of which only a little has been drained. About 350 of these reedy sheets of water survive, totalling 4 300 ha (10 600 acres), of which the largest covers nearly 180 ha (450 acres). Boischaut is higher, better drained and more wooded, though with considerable areas of rather bleak moorland and scrubby heath. Some mixed farming is practised on the better-drained clay soils, but population is inevitably scanty.

# 5. The western Paris Basin

The difficulty of demarcating a boundary between the Paris Basin and Armorica has already been stressed (see p. 6). Much of the western part of the Paris Basin forms part of the old province of Normandy,[12] which today broadly comprises Seine-Maritime on the east bank of the lower Seine, and Eure, Calvados, Orne and Manche to the west (Fig. 1.1). These *départements* form in fact a transition zone between the central Paris Basin and Armorica. Only Eure, Orne and Calvados are under consideration here, since Seine-Maritime has been described as the Pays de Caux, and Manche is included in Armorica.

The coast between the Seine estuary and the Baie des Veys (the joint estuary of the Vire and the Taute) represents a section across the northern margins of the Cretaceous and Jurassic rocks in France. From Honfleur to Trouville at the mouth of the river Touques, the Chalk and Upper Jurassic limestones reach the sea; the cliffs are generally steep, though wooded in places, and are fronted by an offshore wavecut platform, the Rochers des Creuniers. From Trouville to the mouth of the Dives the cliffs are still prominent, consisting of Cretaceous clays rising inland to over 90 m (300 ft). Then follows a break where the Dives has worn a broad valley, forming an estuary encumbered with sandbanks and a broad sandy beach backed by dunes, which continues to the marshy estuary of the Orne near Ouistreham. From here to the Pointe de Maisy, the eastern 'corner' of the Baie des Veys, the Oolitic Limestone of the Campagne de Caen reaches the sea, forming a low rocky coast with cliffed sections culminating in the 40-m (130-ft) Cap Manvieux to the west of Arromanches, alternating with valleys opening on to the shore. Offshore lies a wavecut platform with numerous boulders, rocky islets and shingle banks in places appearing above high-tide level.

No section of coast has ever been studied in such detail, nor has one seen such vital military events, as this part of Normandy. It was here that the liberation of Europe began, when the operation 'Overlord' was launched on 6 June 1944. Indeed, a little plaque on a wall at Ranville, to the east of the lower Orne, records it to be 'le premier village de France libéré'. Devastation from these military operations was inevitably immense; some villages were shattered and Caen itself was terribly damaged. Today the rebuilding is complete, but the 'Mulberry harbour' off Arromanches still survives, and a plaque on a monument near its seaward end records the name of 'Port Winston' bestowed on it.

# The relief regions

## The Chalk plateaus

The chalk outcrop extends across the valley of the lower Seine to form an area of open and gently undulating plateauland at an altitude of 135 to 180 m (450 to 600 ft). It is, however, dissected by the steepsided valleys of various Seine tributaries, forming a number of broadly similar *pays*— Lieuvin, Neubourg, Evreux, Ouche, Thimerais and other smaller ones (Fig. 9.3). The surface of the plateaus is patchily covered with residual tracts of Lower Eocene sands and clays, and limon in some parts lies over both the Chalk and these newer deposits. The valley floors are broad and inclined to be marshy, although for the most part they have been reclaimed to form excellent pasture. Between Evreux and Louviers are the beech-woods of the Forêt de Bord.

## Perche

The land rises westward to Perche, where a short west–east anticline has produced the swelling ridge of the Collines du Perche, attaining a height of 309 m (1 014 ft) in the north. The surface of this anticline has been planed off, exposing the underlying Jurassic rocks, notably the Oxford Clay, although the highest part of the ridge actually consists of Cretaceous sand-stones. The Collines du Perche form a watershed rising above the otherwise uniform unbroken level. The Blaise, Avre and Iton flow northwards across the chalklands to the Seine; the Rille, Touques, Dives and Orne also drain northwards direct to the English Channel; and the headstreams of the Sarthe and the Loir flow away southwest ultimately to the Loire. This watershed is very indeterminate and many streams rise within a few hundred metres of each other and flow away in opposite directions. The various Mesozoic rocks—chalk, limestone, sandstone—are largely covered with residual clays.

### The Pays de la Sarthe

To the southwest of Perche the varied Mesozoic rocks extend to the edge of the Palaeozoic massif. The river Sarthe flows in a southwesterly direction to its confluence with the Mayenne near Angers, hence the general name *Pays de la Sarthe*. Here once again is apparent the absence of a distinctive boundary between the Paris Basin and Armorica. The *Institut National de la Statistique* in its official map of the geographical regions of France dis-tinguishes a single area, the *Pays de la Mayenne et de la Sarthe*, for although the Pays de la Mayenne is of Palaeozoic rocks and the Pays de la Sarthe of Mesozoic rocks, the considerable overlying areas of residual clay result in a remarkably similar landscape and land use, a *bocage* country (see p. 458) of small fields of pasture, wooded hedges and copses, and orchards. The same transitional character is indicated by the regional name of *Maine*, one of the old provinces (Fig. 1.1); *Haut-Maine* is the basin of Le Mans in the Sarthe valley, *Bas-Maine* the basin of Laval in the Mayenne valley within the slate-country of eastern Armorica (see p. 469).

The original unity of the Pays de la Sarthe then is due to the fact that it occupies the basin of the Sarthe and its main headstream the Huisne, though three distinct types of landscape can be distinguished. The *pays argileux* is the *bocage* country referred to above. Areas of limestone, the *pays calcaire*, form the higher interfluves between the valleys and resemble the *campagnes* further to the north described below. Thirdly, a considerable cover of Cretaceous sands extends between the Sarthe and the Loir, forming the '*région des sables du Mans*'; names such as Sable-sur-Sarthe are indicative of its character. Much consists of heathland, though tracts of conifers have been planted, mostly maritime pines, exploited for resin since the beginning of the nineteenth century. Near Le Mans these light soils, when heavily fertilised, are used for market-gardening. Occasionally the sands are more compact and form a reddish stone, which has been used for churches and other buildings in Le Mans. Among these Cretaceous sands a small isolated patch of Jurassic clays appears to the southeast of Le Mans. This covers the floor of a former dome from which the overlying Cretaceous rocks have been denuded. Its damp rich soils form such a contrast to the dry hungry sands of the surrounding country that it is actually known as the *Oasis du Belinois*;[13] 'des ruisseaux jaseurs coulent en minces filets ou se brisent en cascatelles'.[14]

## The Pays d'Auge

A narrow strip of Oxford Clay between the Chalk and the Jurassic limestones has been eroded by the river Dives flowing north to the Baie de la Seine, so forming the broad valley, with gently sloping sides, of the Pays d'Auge. The river wanders across this plain, which is thickly covered with alluvium.

## The Campagnes Bas-Normandes

To the west of the Oxford Clay of the Pays d'Auge is a long north–south outcrop of Oolitic Limestone. It forms in the north the low plateau of Caen, which reaches the coast to the west of the mouth of the Dives at Ouistreham. This gives rise to the rocky coastline already described, which contrasts with the earthy cliffs of Cretaceous clays to the east of the Dives. The limestone extends southward, interrupted in the neighbourhood of Falaise by an easterly projection of Cambrian slates; the limestone here forms a quite prominent escarpment. Further south the Oolite follows the eastern edge of the Palaeozoic rocks, rising as the *Campagne d'Argentan* to the north of the town of that name, and forming a watershed between the north-flowing Orne and Dives and the south-flowing headstreams of the Sarthe. Further south the limestone plateau is known after the chief town of the upper Sarthe basin as the *Campagne d'Alençon*. The Oolite exposure trends away southward along the edge of the Palaeozoic rocks, becoming more attenuated until it disappears in the Sarthe valley near Saldé-sur-Sarthe.

The term *campagne* which has been applied to these limestone plateaus is akin to the word *champagne*, indicating an open gently undulating surface mainly given over to large fields and arable cultivation.

## The Plaine du Bessin

The river Aure and its long headstream the Dromme rise in the limestone country of the Campagne de Caen, and flow northwards in well-defined valleys to within 3 km (2 miles) of the coast near Port-en-Bessin. The Aure then makes a remarkable rightangled bend and flows westwards for nearly 30 km (20 miles) parallel to the coast, though separated from it by a limestone spur. This lowland, where the Lower Jurassic clays outcrop, is known as the Plaine du Bessin. Further west these clays are covered by the sediments deposited by the rivers Vire and Taute, which enter the Baie des Veys. Both sediments and clays have been largely drained and reclaimed by a close network of channels.

## Land use

It is clear from this description of the physical features of central Normandy that a great variation appears in the agriculture practised on the damp valleys and claylands, the limon-covered Chalk, and the limestone plateaus both with and without an appreciable clay cover. Climatically this part of Normandy has distinct maritime tendencies. Ste Honorine-du-Fay (to the southeast of Caen) experiences a range of only 13°C (24°F) between the mean January (4°C (39°F)) and July (17°C (63°F)) temperatures, while on the coast this range is still less marked and the January temperature is about 7°C (44°F). Rainfall averages 710 to 760 mm (28 to 30 in), 50 to 80 mm (2 to 3 in) less than that received by the more exposed Breton peninsula to the west, and it is evenly distributed throughout the year.

Central Normandy forms an agricultural transition area between Armorica and the Paris Basin proper. The limon-covered Chalk and the clay-covered limestone grow cereals and roots, as in the eastern Paris Basin, but with an emphasis on oats as the main cereal and on potatoes as the chief root crop. The clays and the reclaimed marshlands of the river valleys provide excellent pasture for dairy cattle, and in places they are intensively cultivated under market gardens, growing early vegetables. Large orchards of cider apples are found, especially in the Pays d'Auge; cider is the *vin du pays* of Normandy, although less so, it is said, than in the past, for both beer and wine are gaining ground at its expense. A potent liqueur, *Calvados*, is distilled locally from apple-juice.

The two *départements* of Calvados and Eure are included in the region under discussion, and the following figures are revealing:

*Land use, 1968 (Percentage of total area)*

|  | ARABLE | OF WHICH CEREALS | PERMANENT PASTURE | WOODLAND |
|---|---|---|---|---|
| Eure | 39 | 63 | 29 | 23 |
| Calvados | 20 | 58 | 64 | 9 |

Source: Ministère de l'Agriculture, *Annuaire statistique de la France,* 1970–71.

The significant facts are that Eure, the more easterly *département*, has twice as much arable as Calvados but less than half the proportion of pasture. This progressive transition westward towards the pastoral economy of Brittany is further demonstrated by the fact that the next *département* to the west, Manche, had 70 per cent of its area under permanent pasture and only 10 per cent under arable.

Mixed farming is therefore characteristic of central Normandy, but with an emphasis on arable in Eure and on livestock in Calvados, though in the latter the limestone Campagne de Caen forms an exception, for it is almost wholly under the plough. In 1968 there were 535 000 cattle in Calvados and 331 000 in Eure, producing milk for the Paris market and for cheese-making. This is the area of origin of the three well-known Normandy cheese—Camembert, Livarot and Pont-l'Evêque, each called after the original village of production. Camembert was first made in the village of that name in 1761 by Madame Marie Harel, to whose memory a monument fittingly stands in the main square. Various fresh cream cheese are also processed here—Gournay, Petit-Suisse, Bonde, Neufchâtel and others. Poultry and pig-rearing (223 000 pigs in the two *départements*) are obvious concomitants of the dairying industry, and horses are still bred in considerable numbers in his area; Perche is the home of the famous Percheron.

## Population and settlement

Population is dispersed widely in small villages along the river valleys in the chalklands to the east, and near the coast where breaks occur in the cliffs. The only place of any size in the eastern chalklands is Evreux in the valley of the Iton, a pleasant town of about 42 000 people, a market centre and the *chef-lieu* of Eure. A few small ports carry on inshore fishing and the collection of lobsters and shell-fish. The numerous seaside resorts include the fashionable Deauville and Trouville on the Côte Fleurie to the east of the Orne estuary; the suffixes *-sur-Mer, -les-Bains* and *-plage* are freely bestowed along this coast. A more recent expansion of tourism has taken place along the Côte de Nacre, west of the Orne; camp sites, caravan parks and marinas have been developed. Bayeux stands some distance from the sea on the river Aure, serving as the market town for the Pays de Bessin, with some old-established industries such as pottery and lace-making. Lisieux in the valley of the Touques has been a little market town for centuries, but the canonisation of Ste Thérèse in 1923 made it a famous place of pilgrimage.

Further west several towns lie along a natural routeway running from the Loire valley to the coast of Normandy east of the Cotentin peninsula, utilising the Sarthe valley in the south and the Orne valley in the north. The most important town in the south is Le Mans, the regional centre of the middle Sarthe basin, once capital of the duchy of Maine, now *chef-lieu* of the *département* of Sarthe. The old town stands upstream of the confluence of the

Sarthe and the Huisne, dominated by the cathedral on a prominent hill; the new town has expanded southward along the right bank of the main stream. Le Mans is now a regional centre of some importance for the Sarthe basin and for much of western Normandy; its population in 1968 was 143 000. It has a variety of industries, including the manufacture of Rénault automobiles and aircraft, agricultural machinery (notably tractors) and light metallurgical articles. A large chemical factory produces pharmaceutical drugs and fertilisers, and there are also a tobacco factory, clothing factories and an old-established works which makes stained glass. Le Mans is a major route centre, for here cross the north–south Caen–Angers and east–west Paris–Rennes routes, and the town is famous for its motor-racing circuit. Further north are the towns of Alençon, which is a market centre and also has nearby granite and kaolin quarries, and Argentan in the upper Orne valley.

The chief town of Calvados is Caen (with 110 000 people in 1968), a place of lengthy historical antecedents; it was indeed the residence of William the Conqueror. The town was grievously damaged during the initial heavy fighting following the Allied landings in the summer of 1944. It has been triumphantly rebuilt in modern style and has expanded rapidly; symbolically, its new university buildings were opened in the summer of 1957. It is linked to the sea at Ouistreham by the lateral *Canal Maritime*, 14 km (9 miles) in length. Caen combines the functions of a prosperous market centre for the varied agriculture of the *campagne* with modern large-scale manufacturing, notably the production of steel, and the recent introduction of rapidly growing light industry (car components, electrical and electronic parts). Caen, in fact, is the most rapidly growing town in northwestern France.

## The Normandy iron and steel industry

The iron ore fields of northwestern France (Fig. 11.7) occur for the most part near the western margins of the Armorican massif. Much of the ore is smelted near Caen, so it is convenient to describe the orefields here. The ferruginous rocks, mainly Ordovician oolites, are preserved for the most part in synclines within the Pre-Cambrian sandstones and quartzites. Where the iron-bearing beds were exposed on the surface by denudation, the carbonates were oxidised into hematites; most have been worked out as a result of their accessibility, tolerable richness (over 60 per cent metal in places) and non-phosphoric quality. Elsewhere the ore is a granular calcareous *minette*, with some 30 to 40 per cent iron, though less phosphoric than the Lorraine ores. Four individual synclines containing these ferruginous rocks can be traced; their trends stand out even on the small-scale map (Fig. 11.7).

The ironstones were worked as early as pre-Roman times, and on a small scale almost continuously until the mid-nineteenth century, by which time the readily accessible ores had been exhausted. In 1875 geological research revealed the presence of further deposits, with the result that several mining concessions were granted before the end of the century. Little development took place in this predominantly rural and agricultural area, where both capital and labour were unwilling, until foreign interests, notably German, were attracted by the proximity of the deposits to the coast. By 1914 twenty concessions had been granted, of which eleven were controlled by German groups.

By 1913 production had reached an annual output of 800 000 tons, the whole of which was sent out of the district. In that year 490 000 tons were exported by sea from Granville, St Malo and Caen, of which Rotterdam took 262 000 tons (then sent up the Rhine by barge to Duisburg and the Ruhr), Emden received 66 500 tons (which also went to the Ruhr via the Dortmund-Ems Canal), and the rest, mostly hematite, went to Great Britain—to South Wales, Middlesbrough and Workington.

The outbreak of war in 1914 had a notable effect on the French iron industry, when the northeastern industrial area, including the Briey and Longwy *minette* regions, were enemy occupied. France had to turn to other supplies of ore, and Normandy became of considerable importance. Output of ore reached a million tons in 1917, and although in the period of postwar reconstruction the recovery of *Lorraine Annexée* dwarfed the Normandy ore-fields, production has continued steadily.

During the occupation of 1940–44 the orefields were at first prosecuted vigorously, but of course production ceased following the invasion of Normandy and the ore-handling installations were seriously damaged. Production was at first small after the liberation, but this rapidly increased until by 1952 seven mines were yielding 2·5 million tons, a figure which after a slight drop in 1953 was until recently maintained (2·64 million tons in 1963). Output has now declined (1·9 million tons in 1969). About half this ore was once exported to Great Britain, the Belgo–Luxembourg Union and West Germany, but now little is exported.

Before the war of 1914–18 all the ore produced in the Normandy fields was sent to other consuming areas. In 1910 the industrialist Thyssen established the German-controlled Société des Hauts Fourneaux de Caen to erect coke ovens, byproduct plant and blast furnaces at Mondeville, to the northeast of Caen. The outbreak of the 1914–18 war intervened, but with the desperate need for munitions it was decided to go ahead, and the company, taken over by the French Government at the outbreak of war, was reincorporated as the Société Métallurgique de Normandie. In 1916 the coke ovens and a first blast furnace were put into operation. In 1920 about 54 000 tons of pig iron were produced for export. Between the wars the SMN extended the works into an integrated steel-making plant, and by 1940 there were six batteries of forty-two coke ovens, two blast furnaces, with Bessemer and open-hearth steel furnaces, and a large rolling-mill producing about a quarter of a million tons of steel. Half of this output was used locally at the shipbuilding yards at Blainville on the banks of the Canal Maritime between Caen and the sea, and at other engineering works in the neighbourhood. During the invasion of the continent in 1944, the Mondeville works were very heavily damaged, but most of the rebuilding was completed by 1951, and production now exceeds that of prewar years (about 600 000 tons of steel annually). A wide range of specialised steel-using industries has recently been introduced into the district, including general and electrical engineering, and the manufacture of car components. Chemicals and cement are made as byproducts at the steel works.

[1] J. L.-F. Tricart, 'La capture de l'Aire-Bar', *La Partie orientale du bassin de Paris. Etude morphologique* (1949), pp. 397–407.

[2] An account of the specialised horticulture of Anjou is given by I. Deguil, 'L'horticulture en Anjou', *Annls Géogr.*, **42** (1933), pp. 601–9.

[3] J. Lartaut, 'La culture des champignons dans l'Ouest de la France', *Norois,* **12** (1965), p. 409.

[4] G. Lecointre, *La Touraine* (1947).

[5] P. Marres, 'Les vignobles de la Loire et du Centre', *La Vigne et le vin en France* (1950), pp. 59–75.

[6] See P. Bachelard, 'Orléans et sa banlieue', *Norois*, **14** (1967), pp. 439–57; and S. Vassal, 'La Croissance de l'agglomération orléanaise', *Norois*, **18** (1971), pp. 647–69, which contains a number of maps.

[7] Y. Babonaux, 'L'industrialisation de Tours', *Annls Géogr.*, **57** (1948), pp. 243–9.

[8] A detailed study of the Sologne and its development is given by P. Guillaume, *La Sologne au cours des siècles* (1954). See also K. Sutton, 'La Triste Sologne', *Norois*, **16** (1969), pp. 7–30, a discussion of the historical geography of the Sologne, based on old surveys and maps; and (by the same writer), 'The Reduction of the waste in the Sologne: nineteenth century French regional improvements', *Trans. Inst. Br. Geogr.*, **52** (1971), pp. 129–44.

[9] C. Milleret, 'La Forêt d'Orléans', *Annls Géogr.*, **72** (1963), pp. 426–58, with several maps and plates.

[10] F. P. Gay, *La Champagne du Berry*, (1967), a monumental work of 549 pp.

[11] A. Douguédroit, 'L'Industrie du vêtement dans le Berry', *Annls Géogr.*, **69** (1960), pp. 584–93, with a detailed map.

[12] R. Musset, *La Normandie* (1960), a detailed survey of 220 pp. See also *Atlas de Normandie* (1966).

[13] J. Bienfait, 'Le Belinois', *Norois*, **3** (1954), pp. 219–30.

[14] E. Bruley, *Géographie des Pays de la Loire* (1937), p. 146.

# 11
# The scarplands and vales of Lorraine

It is not easy to define Lorraine as a geographical region, largely because it forms a transition zone between the outer cuestas of the Paris Basin and the massif of the Vosges. [1] The name has for long had a political connotation; for centuries it was a dukedom on France's eastern frontiers, not formally incorporated into that country until as late as 1766. In 1871 the eastern part (now the French *département* of Moselle) was absorbed with Alsace (Haut- and Bas-Rhin) into Germany, the annexed area being known as the *Reichsland* and to the French as *Lorraine Annexée*. This did not include all Lorraine; the part left in French hands consisted of the *départements* of Meuse, Meurthe-et-Moselle and Vosges. The annexed territory was returned to France in 1918, but it was again occupied by Germany in 1940 and it was clear that the conqueror's intention was to integrate the area within the Reich. Although in the period 1871–1918 the two provinces had been administered as a unit, in 1940 Alsace was added to Baden and Lorraine to the *Saar-Pfalz* (the Saar-Palatinate). The latter territory became after 1941 the *Gau Westmark*. Strong measures were put into effect to assimilate Alsace and Lorraine within the Reich, but the spirit of resistance burned strongly among those remaining in the provinces and among the many exiles; the cross of Lorraine symbolised the resistance of Free France. In 1944 the provinces returned to France.

On an administrative basis, therefore, contemporary Lorraine comprises the four *départements* of Moselle, Meuse, Meurthe-et-Moselle and most of Vosges. Geographically, however, it is more convenient to adopt the compromise suggested on p. 10, which takes the watershed between the Aire and the Meuse as the western boundary, the narrow but prominent outcrop of the *Muschelkalk* as the eastern. Lorraine, using this definition, consists of an area of Triassic and Jurassic rocks, with alternating outcrops of limestone and clay. The more resistant limestones form a series of cuestas (the *Côtes*), each with an eastward-facing slope dissected by deep valleys into spurs and outlying fragments, and a plateau-surface sinking gently to the west. Between them occur strata of clays and marls; where their dip is gentle the outcrop is extensive, forming broad undulating vales with abundant surface drainage and heavy clay soils. The valley of the Meuse is

246

entrenched in the Corallian Limestone of the *Côtes de Meuse*, with its main escarpment beyond the right bank of the river. It is succeeded eastward by the Oxford Clay plain of the *Woëvre*, and then the extensive Oolitic Limestone upland, the *Plateau de la Moselle*, terminating in the dissected edge of the *Côtes de Moselle* overlooking the Moselle valley. To the east again is the *Plateau Lorraine propre*, continued in the south by the *Hautes plaines de la Lorraine méridionale*; the terms *plateau* and *plaine* are here rather misleading

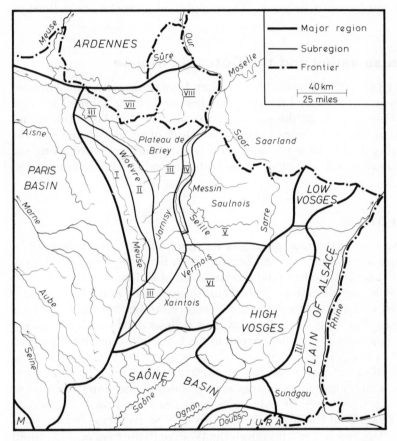

FIG. 11.1 The regional divisions of part of eastern France
The neighbouring regions of the Paris Basin and the Saône Basin are not sub-divided (see Figs. 9.3 and 14.3 respectively). The numerals **I** to **VIII** refer to the subregions of Lorraine as follows: **I,** The Meuse valley and the Côtes de Meuse; **II,** The Oxford Clay vale; **III,** The Plateau and Côtes de Moselle; **IV,** The Moselle valley; **V,** The Plateau of Lorraine; **VI,** The High Plain of Lorraine; **VII,** Belgian Lorraine; **VIII,** The *Bon Pays* of Luxembourg.

Based on a variety of sources, including (*a*) *Carte géologique de la France*, 1 : 1 000 000, published by the *Service de la Carte géologique détaillée de la France*; and (*b*) map of *Régions géographiques de la France*, 1 : 1 400 000, published by the *Institut National de la Statistique et des Études Économiques*.

since the surface of the latter is generally at a higher altitude than that of the former. Both are covered with Lias Clays in the west and with Keuper Marls in the east as far as the *Muschelkalk* cuesta.

This distinctive Lorraine region is not limited to France. The northern margin is indicated by the edge of the Ardennes, demarcated by the sudden outcrop of Lower Palaeozoic rocks. Between this clear geological demarcation and the French frontier are two areas of similar Triassic and Jurassic rocks—the *Bon Pays* of Luxembourg and the *Côtes Lorraines* of the Arlon district of southeastern Belgium. These eight subdivisions are defined in Fig. 11.1.

## The Meuse valley and the Côtes de Meuse

The Upper Jurassic rocks, notably Corallian Limestone, with some Kimmeridge Clay and Portland Limestone further west, form a broad curving outcrop. This appears on the surface to the southwest of Mézières, swings southward to where it attains a maximum width of 55 km (35 miles) in the neighbourhood of Commercy, and then trends southwestward along the flanks of the Central Massif to the neighbourhood of Châteauroux (Fig. 11.2).

### The river Meuse

The Meuse rises in the Lias district of Bassigny, and receives a number of headstreams across the plain of Lorraine, both from the Triassic ridges of the Monts Faucilles and from the claylands, in spite of some encroachments by the Moselle (see pp. 260–1). It then cuts through the Oolitic Limestone in a steepsided valley, to enter for a short distance the Oxford Clay vale near Neufchâteau. But from just below this town it flows northwards for 150 km (95 miles) in a trenchlike valley incised in the Corallian Limestone, parallel to but 8 to 14 km (5 to 10 miles) west of the escarpment (Fig. 11.3). During this long section the Meuse receives no surface tributaries other than a few streamlets which emerge as springs on the sides of the limestone valley. Formerly the river received tributaries both from the Lower Cretaceous ridges and valleys to the west, now captured by active Seine headstreams such as the Aire (see p. 223), and from the Woëvre to the east, now captured by the Moselle. The Meuse was obviously once much larger, as its deeply cut valley, with a floodplain over a kilometre wide, can testify. No longer is it an actively eroding but rather a depositing river; it wanders across its floodplain, with braided sections, stagnant backwaters and abandoned loops.

In its natural state the Meuse would be of little use for navigation, but it has been regularised and improved from Troussey, where it is linked to the Marne-Rhine Canal, to the Belgian frontier (Fig. 12.5). Part of the river has been incorporated into the northern section of the Est Canal; loops have

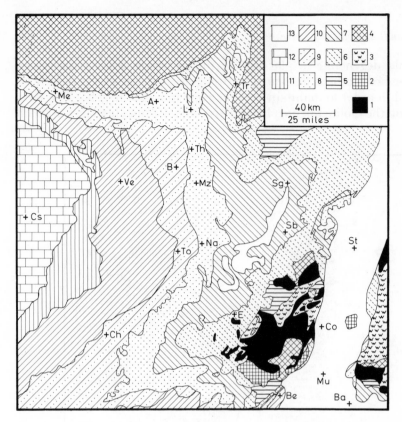

FIG. 11.2 Simplified geological map of part of eastern France
The numbers in the key are as follows: **13,** Quaternary, Tertiary; **12,**
Upper Cretaceous (including Chalk and Upper Greensand); **11,** Lower
Cretaceous (Gault Clay); **10,** Upper Jurassic (including Portland Lime-
stone, Kimmeridge Clay, Corallian Limestone and Oxford Clay); **9,**
Middle Jurassic (including Oolitic Limestone); **8,** Lower Jurassic
(including Lias clays and limestone); **7,** Upper and Middle Trias (Keuper
and Muschelkalk); **6,** Lower Trias (sandstones); **5,** Permian, Upper and
Middle Carboniferous; **4,** Lower Carboniferous, Devonian, Silurian,
Ordovician, Cambrian; **3,** Pre-Cambrian; **2,** eruptive rocks; **1,** granitic
and gneissic rocks.

A few towns, inserted to help location, are indicated by initials, as
follows: **A,** Arlon; **B,** Briey; **Ba,** Basel; **Be,** Belfort; **Ch,** Chaumont;
**Co,** Colmar; **Cs,** Châlons-sur-Marne; **E,** Epinal; **L,** Luxembourg; **Me,**
Mézières; **Mu,** Mulhouse; **Mz,** Metz; **Na,** Nancy; **Sb,** Sarrebourg; **Sg,**
Sarreguemines; **St,** Strasbourg; **Th,** Thionville; **To,** Toul; **Tr,** Trier;
**Ve,** Verdun.

Based on *Carte géologique de la France*, 1 : 1 000 000, published by the Service de la Carte géologique
détaillée de la France.

been cut through to straighten the course and four tunnels have been constructed through meander cores. Its natural régime is very variable; heavy
rains on the impermeable clays of the Lorraine plateau formerly caused
rapid runoff and serious flooding downstream, both in winter and in late
summer, while conversely after a long spell of drought in early summer the

river would degenerate in places to shrunken trickles among the gravel banks. The bed has been deepened by dredging, and many locks have been contructed in order to maintain an effective depth of 2 m (7 ft). The river flows not on the Oolite but on a layer of its own alluvium, in places as much

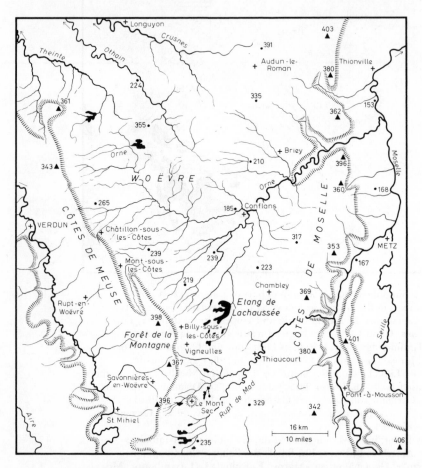

FIG. 11.3. The Côtes de Meuse and Moselle, and the Woëvre
The steep edges of the east-facing *Côtes* and of the western edge of the Meuse valley are indicated in a generalised way by hachures. Heights are given in metres. The map stresses (*a*) the limited narrow trench of the Meuse, with only a few short tributaries from either side; (*b*) the damp surface of the clay-covered Woëvre, with numerous small lakes and a dense pattern of streams, draining either east to the Moselle or north to the Chiers and so to the Meuse; (*c*) the dissected edges of the *Côtes*.
  A few of the many villages along the foot of the Côte de Meuse are shown (*-sous-les-Côtes*). Note, however, the misleading Rupt-en-Woëvre and Savonnières-en-Woëvre, which are not in the Woëvre as here defined.

Based on *Carte de France et des frontières au 200 000ᵉ*, sheets 17, 18.

250

as 9 m (30 ft), deposited in its more active days. This has produced an impermeable bed, and there is little loss by infiltration.

Despite difficulties, the French section of the Meuse and the Est Canal carries annually about 2 million tons of freight, including coal, oil, building stone and bricks. It passes through such important towns as Verdun (where it is contained in a tunnel under the fortifications), Sedan and Mézières-Charleville (see p. 226). Moreover, there is a useful transfrontier traffic; about three-quarters of a million tons of freight moves in each direction.

## The Côtes de Meuse

To the east of the Meuse valley is the line of the Côtes de Meuse. While the floor of the valley near Verdun lies at 200 m (660 ft), on the ridge-line only a kilometre or two to the east heights of 380 m (1 270 ft) are attained; the highest point of the Côtes de Meuse is actually 412 m (1 352 ft). The summit level of this ridge is remarkably uniform, but several deep dry valleys eroded by former Meuse tributaries from the east dissect it into a number of steep-sided flat-topped hills, particularly in the south. A clearly defined gap, utilised by the Marne-Rhine Canal, lies west of Toul (Fig. 11.6).

Much of the ridge is thickly forested, mostly planted by the Government department of *Eaux et Forêts*. The concentrated devastation of the war of 1914–18 destroyed about 14 000 ha (35 000 acres) of forest in the neighbourhood of Verdun, most of which had been replanted by 1938.

## Settlement

Several towns situated along the Meuse valley have functioned as fortresses for much of their existence—Neufchâteau, Void, St Mihiel and Verdun itself. The Corallian cuesta, with its outward escarpment backed by the Meuse trough, formed a definite transverse obstacle, a major defensive line against any thrust into the Paris Basin. The greatest of these fortresses—Verdun—stands at the crossing-point of the Meuse valley route through eastern France (Mézières, Sedan, Verdun, Toul, Dijon) and the vital east–west line from Metz via Reims or Châlons-sur-Marne to Paris. Limestone bluffs project westward to north and south of the town, and the old citadel was built on a massive hillock. Verdun has been a fortress since before Roman times; it was greatly developed by Vauban in the reign of Louis XIV, and was immeasurably strengthened between 1871 and 1914. As a result, Marshal Pétain's successful defence in 1916–17 ('*Ils ne passeront pas*') cost the lives of over half a million men. The fortified hills surrounding the town were the scene of constant assaults and repulses.

Settlements to the east of the Meuse are confined to the deeper valleys which have been cut down through the Corallian into the underlying clay, where water is obtainable and where meadows and small patches of arable

251

land occur. Economically the Côtes have little value, other than as a source of timber (notably pit-props), of building stone which is quarried at Euville, Commercy and elsewhere, and of agricultural lime and cement. The proximity of the Est Canal is useful for the export of these bulky commodities.

## The Oxford Clay vale

Between the underlying Oolites and the overlying Corallian Limestone occurs a considerable thickness of Oxford Clay, dipping gently westward. Its outcrop can be traced from near Mézières, trending southeastward to the Meuse at Stenay, then swinging southward to Neufchâteau. It is of no great width, varying between 20 and 25 km (12 to 15 miles), while to the south of Toul it forms only a narrow strip of 4 or 5 km (2 or 3 miles), where it is known as *Soulossois* (Fig. 11.6). Nevertheless, it makes a distinctive contribution to the Lorraine landscape, forming a gently undulating vale about 200 m (650 ft) above sea level.

The *pays* name *Woëvre* is applied to this clay vale, derived from the Latin word *wabra*, meaning a thicket. This element appears commonly in the local place names. Unfortunately, the generic 'Woëvre' is used outside the present accepted limits of the *pays*; thus Rupt-en-Woëvre and Savonnières-en-Woëvre each lie in the valley of a short Meuse tributary, well to the west of the Corallian crestline (Fig. 11.3). But the Woëvre in its present *pays* sense is restricted to the Oxford Clay vale.

The Oxford Clay consists of a heavy blue clay well over 200 m (650 ft) in thickness, overlain by some calcareous marls. Much of this superficial cover is derived from both the Oolitic and the Corallian Limestones, providing a soil which is inherently fertile, although heavy, rather cold and often waterlogged as a result of the impermeable substratum. The vale is characterised by abundant surface drainage, a multiplicity of wandering streams and shallow lakes; the latter increase considerably in size during the winter (Fig. 11.3).

It is probable that the waters of the Woëvre once drained westwards to the Meuse, as evidenced by the several high-level dry valleys through the Côtes de Meuse. The more active Moselle to the east, flowing in a much lower valley, has gradually captured the greater part of the Woëvre drainage. The streams rise near the eastern edge of the Côtes de Meuse at the junction of the Corallian and the clay, wander vaguely eastwards against the dip of the strata (and indeed against the general slope) until they converge to form a few larger rivers—Ache, Rupt de Mad, Orne (the master-stream of the district), and Fentsch, which then cross the Oolitic plateau in several striking gorges (see p. 254). The northern part of this clay vale drains by way of the Crusnes and the Othain to the Chiers below Montmédy, and so to the Meuse.

## Land use and agriculture

The Woëvre has some importance for agriculture, particularly in the slightly higher areas flanking the Côtes de Meuse, where calcareous down-wash has enriched the soil. Considerable artificial drainage has extended the area of arable land, notably for the cultivation of wheat, oats and potatoes, and permanent grassland supports dairying activity. Vineyards are found on the lower slopes of the Côtes de Meuse and their eastern outliers, and there are orchards, particularly of stone-fruits such as plums and cherries. But much of the Woëvre is too wet for farmland, and considerable tracts of woodland survive among the small lakes and marshes.

## Settlement

On a population map much of the Woëvre stands out with an average density of less than 20 per sq km (50 per sq mile). Villages are small and somewhat scattered, usually on the higher eminences of the Corallian outliers. Other settlements occur along the foot of the Corallian slope, including a long string of villages with the suffix *sous-les-Côtes*, especially along the steep continuous section between Verdun and St Mihiel. Sometimes a village lies well up the escarpment in a south-facing hollow, such as Moulainville, while at the foot of the escarpment near the springline is Moulainville-la-Basse. An example of a hamlet named from its location is Le Mont Sec, 24 km (15 miles) east of St Mihiel; the village perches on the northeastern side of a prominent little hillock.

# The Plateau and Côtes de Moselle

Rocks of Middle Jurassic age, mainly Oolitic limestones, clays and marls, appear on the surface near Hirson in northern France as a narrow belt between the chalklands of the Paris Basin and the Palaeozoic rocks of the Ardennes. This outcrop trends in a direction south of east, and is crossed by the alluvium-floored Meuse valley just above the Chiers confluence. To the east of Montmédy, however, the outcrop widens and swings away southward, forming a triangular plateau, the base of which lies along the Belgian and Luxembourg frontiers for a distance of about 40 km (25 miles), while its apex is situated 80 km (60 miles) to the south near Nancy. The northern part is known as the Plateau de Briey, then comes the Plateau de Jarnisy, and in the south the Plateau de Haye. A small portion of the upland, isolated by the right angle of the Moselle to the east of Toul, is known as the Forêt de Haye, and other outlying portions survive to the east of the Moselle between Nancy and Metz (Fig. 11.6). From where the valley of the Moselle cuts across the Jurassic plateau, the outcrop trends southwestward, first as a narrow belt, then widening to form the Plateau de Langres, the southern boundary of the Seine basin.

This Oolitic plateau, with an undulating surface of flat-topped ridges some 300 m (1 000 ft) above sea level, rises slowly eastward to a prominent escarpment (the *Côtes de Moselle*), overlooking in the north the Lias plateau of the southern Bon Pays of Luxembourg, and in the east first the Moselle valley as far south as the Meurthe confluence and then the clay plain of Lorraine. The escarpment in the north rises to a height of 423 m (1 388 ft), falling within a distance of only 5 or 6 km (3 or 4 miles) to the Moselle valley at about 150 m (500 ft). To the south of Toul the highest point on the main ridge rises to 506 m (1 660 ft), although in point of fact the maximum elevation attained in the *Côtes* is provided by an Oolitic outlier in the plain of Lorraine to the east, the prominent Butte de Vaudémont or de Sion (585 m (1 919 ft) ).

Both the plateau and the escarpment are deeply trenched by rivers. In the south a number of Meuse headstreams, which rise in the Keuper or Lias plain of Lorraine, cut right across the Oolitic plateau. The Meuse itself traverses the outcrop just above Neufchâteau, and the Moselle not only crosses it between Pont-St Vincent and Toul but also recrosses between Toul and Frouard. A remarkable river-capture is responsible for this seeming anomaly (Fig. 11.6, and see pp. 260–1). The Plateau de Haye is seamed with dry valleys which once drained northwestwards to the Meuse from the clay plains of *Xaintois* (see p. 275). The lowered watertable, the result of the much lower level of the Madon (a left-bank tributary which joins the Moselle at Pont-St Vincent), has left these valleys dry, except where they have been cut right down into the Lias clays. Here as a result springs have been formed, the waters of which mostly find their way northeastwards to the Madon.

Further north the plateau and escarpment are cut across by several left-bank Moselle tributaries, which rise in the claylands of the Woëvre, as already described, and flow eastwards. The Ache and the Rupt de Mad are both contained in steepsided valleys which become increasingly prominent as the escarpment edge is approached, their floors lying at 15 to 75 m (50 to 250 ft) below the plateau surface, and further north still the Orne (Fig. 11.9) and the Fentsch flow in deep almost gorgelike valleys. In the extreme north, near the frontier, the escarpment is incised by the northward-flowing Alzette and its tributaries the Kayl and the Dudelange (Fig. 11.15). The Chiers pursues an unusual course, for it rises in Luxembourg and flows westwards before cutting southwestwards through the Oolitic escarpment, then picking up its tributaries the Othain and the Crusnes, and finally joining the Meuse.

## Land use and agriculture

The soils vary considerably. Over the southern Plateau de Haye a kind of reddish sandy-clay is found, which tends to be dry and 'hungry'. On the lower valley sides calcareous downwash provides a much better soil, and the valley bottoms are covered with alluvium. In the north the more extensive occurrence of marls and clays allows the development of quite reasonable soils, used for arable farming. Some areas of coarse gravel and sand, often containing quite large sandstone fragments, are the remains of diluvial deposits of the former consequent rivers flowing northwestwards from the Vosges before the present cuesta and vale drainage system evolved.

Extensive forests occur, particularly in the south where a large part of the Plateau de Haye is wooded, and also the Forêt de Haye lies in the angle of the Moselle-Meurthe confluence. Less continuous patches of woodland are found in the north, particularly on the gravels.

Much of the Briey plateau is under arable, growing wheat and potatoes. Vineyards appear both along the southeast facing slopes of the Côtes de Moselle and on the sides of the valleys which cut across the plateau. Hops and stone-fruits such as plums and cherries grow in these calcareous soils.

## The iron ore deposits

The major significance of the Middle Jurassic plateau results from the fact that between the overlying Oolites and the underlying Lias occurs a considerable thickness of iron ore, known as *minette*, the largest deposits in Europe. The ore consists of either a chamosite (a silicate of iron) or a siderite (a carbonate of iron), of oolitic structure with minute spherical concretions within a calcareous matrix, except in the Nancy basin in the south where the matrix is markedly siliceous. The iron content varies considerably in the different beds from 24 to as much as 40 per cent, although the richer ores have been largely exhausted; the average content of ores now worked is of the order of 33 per cent. They contain from about 1·7 to 1·9 per cent of phosphorus, and so before the introduction of the Gilchrist-Thomas process neither wrought iron nor steel could be successfully made. The term '*minette*' was therefore contemptuously applied to these ores.

The overall thickness of the ore-bearing strata varies from 24 to 40 m (80 to 130 ft), within which as many as seven distinct beds may be distinguished. Near the top of the deposit is a bed of ore which has a relatively high iron content of 40 per cent or more, but is sandy or gravelly and exceedingly friable. Below this is to be found the 'calcareous red' bed (a ferruginous limestone), the best *minette* ore, with an iron content of 40 per cent; unfortunately these deposits are approaching exhaustion and indeed have been worked out in many areas. Beneath this again lies the 'calcareous yellow' bed, not quite so rich, but actively worked in the Orne valley. The most widespread bed is the 'grey', which is usually calcareous in France. It has a lowish iron content varying from 24 to 32 per cent, but today it is the most extensively worked for it occurs in layers of up to 6 m (20 ft) thick. Beneath this are the 'brown bed', the 'black bed' which is markedly siliceous, and the underlying 'green bed' 1 to 3 m (3 to 9 ft) in thickness but highly pyritous; these are but little worked.

The Jurassic and underlying strata dip gently southwestward; as a result, while the ore beds appear at the surface on the scarp faces and valley sides in the north and east, they occur at progressively greater depths to the west. Ore has in fact been proved as far west as Verdun at about 580 m (1 900 ft) below the surface. The low iron content obviously makes deep mining uneconomic, and the area shown on Fig. 11.4 represents the limit of the worked areas and concessions at the present time. Apart from the low iron content and phosphoric character of Lorraine ore, further geographical drawbacks are the difficult terrain with steepsided valleys and escarpments, the distance from adequate supplies of coking coal, and its vulnerable European position near the meeting-place of four countries.

On the other hand, the orefield has some positive advantages, apart from its estimated reserves of 8 000 million tons in France and a further 200 million in Luxembourg.[2] The dip of the strata is gentle, there is usually little structural disturbance so that the beds are continuous, and mining is highly mechanised and cheap. The deeply trenched valleys enable much ore to be won by horizontal galleries driven into the hillsides and even in some districts by open quarries, although in places shaft-mining is used. A large proportion of the ore is calcareous and therefore self-fluxing in the blast furnaces, while the juxtaposition of various qualities enables the siliceous and calcareous ores to be mixed to form self-fluxing charges. Finally, the geographical position which has brought travail to Lorraine three times in seventy years has paradoxically meant that at the heart of the industrial complex of western Europe it has shared in its development. France exported 19 million tons of ore in 1969, though nearly 7 million were imported. The contribution of Lorraine to the French iron and steel industry is shown by the following table:

*Output of iron ore in France (million tons)*

|  | 1929 | 1937 | 1952 | 1963 | 1969 | 1970 |
|---|---|---|---|---|---|---|
| Lorraine | 48·00 | 35·42 | 37·75 | 54·38 | 52·87 | |
| Normandy | 1·88 | 1·94 | 2·47 | 2·64 | 1·89 | |
| Anjou-Brittany | 0·53 | 0·38 | 0·58 | 0·77 | 0·65 | |
| Others | 0·32 | 0·08 | 0·38 | 0·10 | 0·02 | |
| France | 50·73 | 37·82 | 41·18 | 57·89 | 55·43 | 56·81 |

Source: Successive volumes of *Annuaire statistique de la France* (Paris) and publications of the *Chambre Syndicale de la Sidérurgie française*.

## THE ORE BASINS

The *minette* field is divided by faults and intervening barren ground into four individual districts: those of Nancy, Briey, Longwy and Moselle. Administratively the whole field comes under two regions of the *Chambre Syndicale de*

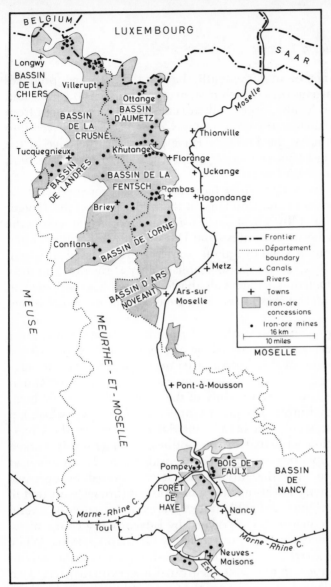

FIG. 11.4. The iron ore basins of Lorraine
The map indicates the *département* boundary between Moselle
and Meurthe-et-Moselle, i.e. the Franco-German boundary in
1871–1919 and 1940–44, when *Lorraine Annexée* (the *département*
of Moselle) was included in Germany. Iron ore mines in
Luxembourg are not shown.

Based on: (*a*) *Carte industrielle de la Lorraine* (1930); (*b*) *Atlas de France*, 'Richesse
minérales concessibles' (sheet 44) (1933); (*c*) *Cartes de France et des frontières au
200 000ᵉ*, sheets 11, 18, 27; (*d*) post-1945 information from various official sources.

*la Sidérurgie* (Fig. 11.7), namely *Est I*, which comprises the Longwy, the
greater part of the Briey, and the Nancy basins in the *département* of Meurthe-
et-Moselle, and *Est II*, which includes the Moselle field in the *département* of
Moselle.

257

The detached Nancy basin in the south, the first to be worked, produces rather low-grade siliceous ores, which moreover are sandy and friable and so are mostly smelted locally, using as fluxes calcareous ores brought from further north. Nevertheless, the ore is cheaply mined by adits driven into the steep eastern slope of the Forêt de Haye and along the edge of the outlier of the Bois de Faulx (Fig. 11.4); about a million tons have been produced annually in recent years.

The main mining areas in the Briey basin occur in the upper parts of the Orne valley between Joeuf and Conflans, in the upper parts of the Woigot valley to the northwest of Briey near Tucquegnieux, and further west in the upper Othain valley between Landres and Domremy. Most of the mining here is by shafts as much as 90 m (300 ft) in depth. Its isolated situation, together paradoxically with the transportable quality of the ores and their calcareous nature which makes them valuable for mixing, has resulted in an absence of iron and steel works in this plateau area, and much ore is sent away by rail.

The plateau of Briey ends abruptly in the north more or less along the international frontier, and is bounded on the northwest by the Chiers valley. The headstreams of this river and its neighbour the Alzette have dissected the cuesta-edge, where the ferruginous sandstones of the Chiers basin outcrop. These ores consist mainly of the sandy 'Upper Red' beds, which are particularly friable. The important centre of Longwy, which has given its name to the whole northern industrial basin, lies in the Chiers valley near its junction with that of the Godbrange. The ore is worked mainly by galleries opening out into the steepsided valleys, although at Hussigny it occurs so near the surface that it is obtained by opencast methods. Mining activity in this northern basin is continuous with that of Luxembourg; mineral lines and cable railways cross the frontier in several places, and several French mines are owned by Luxembourg companies.

The Moselle basin occurs in what was formerly German Lorraine. While ore beds have been proved from north of Pont-à-Mousson continuously to the Luxembourg frontier, mining is concentrated in certain districts. Two of these follow the narrow lower valleys of the Orne and the Fentsch, where galleries can be driven into the steep hillsides. South of Joeuf, in the Orne valley, deep mines are sunk into the plateau surface itself (Fig. 11.9). Much of the ore is siliceous, hence the need for supplies of calcareous ore from mines further west in the Briey basin.

Two groups of mines near Redange and Russange belong geographically and geologically to the Longwy region, but are in the *département* of Moselle (*Région Est II*). The reasons for this date back to 1871, when Germany defined the new frontier.

## Settlement

A major iron- and steel-producing region based on these orefields has

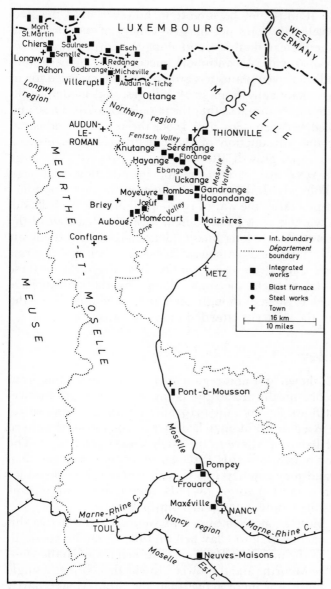

Fig. 11.5. The Lorraine iron and steel industry
Minor steel works and steel-using industries are not shown.

Based on (*a*) *Carte industrielle de la Lorraine* (1930); (*b*) *Cartes de France et des frontières au 200 000*, sheets 11, 18, 27; (*c*) post-1945 information derived from *Statistical Bulletin*, **28**, no. 2 (1953), and *ibid.*, **30**, no. 8 (1955), published by the British Iron and Steel Federation, with revisions.

developed in Lorraine, for the most part along the foot of the eastern escarpment between Maizières and Thionville; it is therefore convenient to describe this industrial development as a whole in the next regional section

259

(the Moselle valley). It must not be forgotten, however, that the steel industry has also developed along the narrow valleys of the Orne and Fentsch and within the Plateau de Briey, and along the northern valleys of the Chiers and its headstreams. A continuous succession of modern integrated steel works and coke oven plants has grown up, with crowded towns which have expanded chaotically from small villages, and modern well-planned housing estates. It is estimated that the population of the Orne and Fentsch valleys trebled between 1891 and 1906, the results of industrial expansion following the introduction of the Gilchrist-Thomas process, and there was further rapid growth after the war of 1914–18. The large labour requirements were met in part by the introduction of foreign workers, notably of Poles and Italians, as elsewhere in the mines and factories of western Europe.[3] After the war of 1939–45 another great influx of foreign and stateless workers took place to help meet the demands of the expanding steel industry. Today long lines of dense industrial settlements are separated by thinly populated plateau surfaces, with their arable farms and woodlands. While some drain of population has gone on from these intervening agricultural districts, the small villages on the plateau have continued their placid existence, though obviously benefiting from the expanding markets in the adjacent crowded industrial areas.

## The Moselle valley

The Moselle valley is shown as a unit region on Fig. 11.1, extending from the Meurthe confluence northward to the point where it leaves France. The Moselle, which flows for 500 km (319 miles) through west-central Europe, takes its rise in a number of small headstreams on the northwestern flanks of the granitic Ballon d'Alsace in the High Vosges (Fig. 19.1). The river flows more or less northwestwards, first over the crystalline rocks, then across the Triassic sandstone country (see p. 512) where it is enclosed for some distance within a forested gorge, over the undulating plain of Lorraine, and so reaches the Oolite outcrop at Pont-St Vincent.

It seems that the Moselle once continued its westerly trend across this Oolitic plateau, the narrow Oxford Clay belt and the Corallian cuesta in turn, so forming one of the main headstreams of its neighbour to the west, the present Meuse. The Meurthe and the lower Moselle then formed a single consequent stream, which was more active than the proto-Meuse, partly because its volume was greater, partly because its gradient was steeper, for the Meuse rises at a much lower altitude. Eighty km (50 miles) from their sources the Meuse and the Moselle are descending at a rate of about 1 and 4 m per km (3 and 12 ft per mile) respectively, and where the rivers approach most closely the floor of the Meuse is more than 45 m (150 ft) above that of the Moselle. The original Meurthe-Moselle consequent developed an active subsequent tributary which cut back through the Oolitic Limestone into the Oxford Clay vale and captured what is now the upper Moselle at Toul, forming a magnificent 'elbow of capture' (Fig. 11.6). The result is that the Moselle now flows across the Oolite to Toul on the edge of the Oxford Clay, but then turns abruptly north then northeast across the Oolite again to the Meurthe junction at Custines. A small obsequent, the Ane or Asne, occupies the 'Toul Gap' or the Val de l'Ane, the former course of the river, which is now utilised by the Marne-Rhine Canal (Fig. 11.6), and by the main railway line between Paris, Nancy and Strasbourg. Toul, at the eastern end of the gap, and dominated to the north by twin Corallian buttes, was for long a fortress town, making use of these steepsided hills for fortifications.

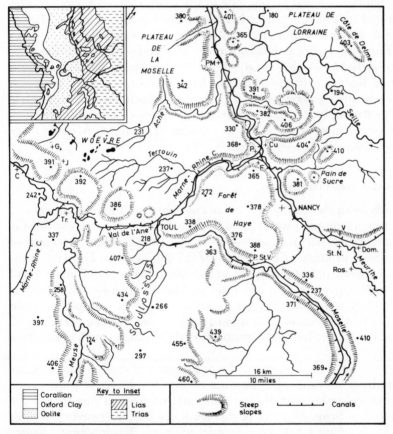

FIG. 11.6. The Toul gap
The abbreviations of towns are as follows: **C,** Commercy; **Cu,** Custines; **Dom,** Dombasle; **Fr,** Frouard; **G,** Gironville; **J,** Jouy-sous-les-Côtes; **P,** Pompey; **PM,** Pont-à-Mousson; **PStV,** Pont-St Vincent; **Ros,** Rosières-aux-Salines; **StN,** St Nicolas-du-Port; **Tr,** Troussey; **V,** Varangéville.

Based on *Carte de France et des frontières au 200 000ᵉ*, sheets 18, 27.

From the Meurthe confluence the Moselle winds northwards along the edge of the Lias plain in a broad alluvium-floored valley closely bounded on the west by the steep dissected edge of the Côtes de Moselle. In the angle of the Moselle-Seille confluence stands the old fortress town of Metz. Fifty km (30 miles) downstream near Thionville the river again changes direction towards the northeast, cutting through the well-marked north–south Virine cuesta of Liassic limestone in a distinct gap, and so it reaches the point of convergence of the French, West German and Luxembourg frontiers near Schengen.

The river is unnavigable above the Meurthe confluence, although from near Epinal to Toul its valley is utilised by the southern branch of the lateral Est Canal, which runs first on one side of the river, then on the other, and from Toul to Frouard it is paralleled by 24 km (15 miles) of the Marne-Rhine Canal. Between Frouard and Metz the river is canalised, and from Metz to Thionville sections of its course are utilised by the lateral *Canal des Mines de Fer de la Moselle* (Fig. 11.9). Below Thionville, to its junction with the Rhine at Koblenz, the Moselle has been canalised to take 1 500-ton barges, by means of barrages.[4] The scheme, including hydroelectric stations, was completed in 1964 (see p. 492). A project is now in progress, scheduled for completion in 1975, to canalise the French Moselle from Thionville to Pont-St Vincent, above Nancy.

## The Lorraine steel industry[5]

It has already been shown that Lorraine contributes almost 93 per cent of the total French iron-ore output; in addition the district is responsible for four-fifths of French pig iron, and just over half of the crude steel and of the finished steel products. *Est I* and *Est II* (as delimited on Fig. 11.7) contained at the end of 1969 54 of the 75 active blast-furnaces in France, 66 of the 77 Thomas converters and 27 of the 75 Martin open-hearth furnaces, together with six new Basic Oxygen converters. The total output of crude steel from the two regions in 1969 was 12 million tons out of a French total of 22·51 million,[6] a decline in the proportion due to the growth of the *Nord* region (p. 151).

Even before the war of 1939–45 the production of steel in Lorraine, as indeed elsewhere in France, was dominated by a few large integrated concerns,[7] which contrasts with the considerable number of dispersed individual steel-using firms. Since 1945 this tendency has increased; grouping and consolidation have taken place in order to enable development schemes envisaged under the Monnet Plan to be implemented. The huge Sidelor (the Union Sidérurgique Lorraine) was incorporated in 1950; it operates works at Micheville near the Luxembourg frontier, at Rombas, Homécourt and Auboué in the Orne valley, and at Pont-à-Mousson in the Moselle valley. Sollac (the Société Lorraine de Laminage Continu), also formed in 1950, controls steel works and rolling-mills at Hayange, Sérémange and

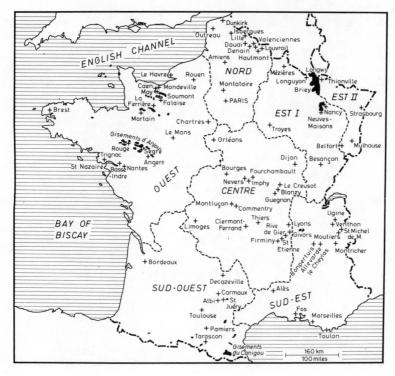

FIG. 11.7. The French iron ore fields and the centres of the iron and steel industry
The towns are shown in which major steel-making and steel-using industries are located, with the exception of those in Lorraine, which are shown in detail on Figs. 11.4, 11.5. The boundaries of the seven regions into which the industry is grouped under the *Chambre Syndicale de la Sidérurgie* are shown. Orefields are in black.

Based on: (*a*) *Atlas de France*, sheet 44, 'Richesses minérales concessibles' (1933); (*b*) post-1945 information derived from *Statistical Bulletin*, **28**, (1953, no. 2 and *ibid.*, **30**, (1955) no. 8, published by the British Iron and Steel Federation.

Ebange in the Fentsch valley. The long-established De Wendel firm owns integrated works at Hayange in the Fentsch valley and at Moyeuvre in the Orne valley; this firm was founded as long ago as 1805 by the Marquis François de Wendel, and it was one of his descendants who in conjunction with Schneider of Le Creusot bought the rights of the basic process of steel-making from Gilchrist and Thomas. In 1967 the three main Lorraine companies (de Wendel, Sidelor and Mosellane) were merged to form France's largest steel complex (*SACILOR*). This, with Usinor (p. 151) dominates French steel production. In 1971 Sacilor announced drastic rationalisation plans, including the closing of five blast-furnaces and fourteen rolling-mills, and the redundancy of 12 000 workers.

Three steel-making areas can be distinguished: the Longwy and Nancy

PLATE 34. The *Sidelor* steel-works at Rombas, Lorraine

districts within *Est I*, and the Moselle-Briey districts mainly included in *Est II* (Fig. 11.5).

### THE LONGWY DISTRICT

In the Longwy district the industry is situated in several narrow steepsided valleys. Sidelor have an integrated plant at Micheville in the upper Alzette valley near the Luxembourg frontier, but the greatest concentration of industry is around Longwy, in the Chiers valley near the junction of several tributaries. Not far from the Belgian frontier is the Mont-St Martin works, and further down valley are the Chiers, Senelle and Réhon works (Fig. 11.8). Several blast furnace plants are located in this frontier region, for, as was noted above, the friable ores cannot stand transport and are mostly smelted locally. The pig iron is sent out of the district, much of it to the *Nord* and Ardennes industrial areas. Thus the Arbed-controlled Société Minière des Terres-Rouges (see p. 287) has blast furnaces at Audun-le-Tiche, and others are at Godbrange, Redange, Villerupt and Ottange (Fig. 11.8). Several of these have been rebuilt under postwar modernisation plans. A number of steel-using industries has developed in the Longwy district.

264

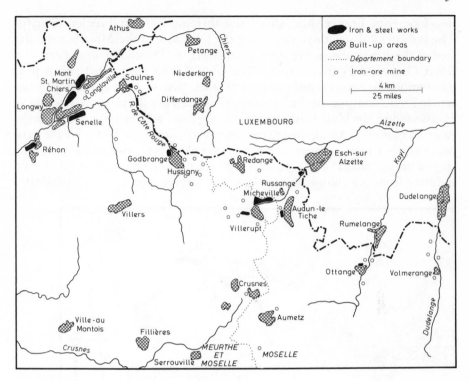

FIG. 11.8. The iron and steel industry in northern Lorraine
Details of the Luxembourg iron and steel works, not shown on this map, appear on
Fig. 11.15. The built-up areas are generalised.

Based on: (*a*) *Carte de France au 50 000ᵉ*, sheets XXXII/10, 11; XXXIII/10, 11; (*b*) post-1945 information derived
from various official sources.

## THE NANCY DISTRICT

The chief integrated plants in the Nancy region are at Pompey, Frouard,
Maxéville and Neuves-Maisons (Fig. 11.5). These are served by rail and
inland waterway transport, the first three by the Marne-Rhine Canal and
the canalised Moselle, the last by the southern branch of the Est Canal.
Further north Sidelor operates blast furnaces at Pont-à-Mousson, which is
incidentally one of the main centres in France for the production of cast-iron
pipes. It is interesting to note that the girders for the Eiffel Tower were
made at Pompey. Numerous steel-using and -finishing industries have
developed in the Nancy region, notably light engineering, electrical equipment and electric locomotives.

## THE MOSELLE DISTRICT

The metallurgical industry of the *département* of Moselle expanded tremendously between 1871 and 1914; the Treaty of Frankfurt brought
*Lorraine Annexée* into the German empire, and it shared vast industrial

developments. France thus inherited a thriving industrial region in 1919. The industrial district extends along the left bank of the Moselle near the foot of the limestone escarpment from Metz to Thionville, and along the lower Orne and Fentsch valleys. The several large integrated plants produce annually about 6 million tons of steel, that is, over a quarter of the whole French output. In the Moselle valley itself are the integrated works at Hagondange, the blast-furnaces of Uckange, and rolling-mills to the northeast of Thionville. Along the narrow floor and sides of the Fentsch valley are concentrated blast furnaces, steel works, coke ovens, old towns and new *cités-ouvrières*, roads and railways—a continuous alignment of heavy industry from Knutange downstream to Florange and Ebange. Similarly,

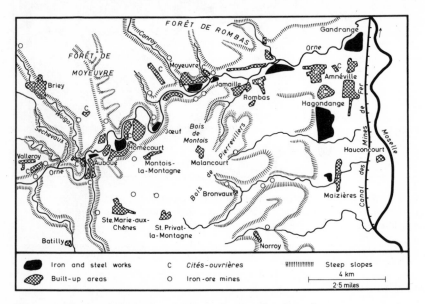

FIG. 11.9. The iron and steel works in the Orne valley, Lorraine
Note the deep shaft mines on the plateau as well as the adit mines on the steep sides of the valleys.

Based on *Carte de France au 50 000ᵉ*, sheet XXXIII/12, with later information.

further south in the Orne valley (Fig. 11.9) there is continuous industrialisation from Auboué to Sidelor's huge plant at Rombas (Plate 34) and the newly built plant at Gandrange. At Joeuf, incidentally, the Gilchrist-Thomas basic process was first used in France.

## Other industries

The main preoccupation of the towns of the lower Moselle valley from Nancy to Thionville is therefore the production of steel and a variety of steel-using industries. But in order to reduce the dependence on iron and

266

steel, in which a big run-down is taking place, efforts are being made to attract more diversified activities: electrical and general engineering, car assembly, chemicals, and new light industry. Nancy has a wide range of other industries, many of long establishment; these include glass-making, textile manufactures brought by Alsatian refugees after the Franco-Prussian War of 1870, electrical and general engineering, tanning and the manufacture of leather goods, chemical industries, brewing, the making of furniture and musical instruments, and food-processing industries; in short, a most intensively developed and varied industrial life. In addition, it is the chief financial and commercial city of Lorraine. As a result, the population of the Nancy commune in 1968 was 123 000, but with the nine other communes which make up the official *agglomération urbaine* the total is about 260 000. Nancy has considerable administrative importance as the *chef-lieu* of Meurthe-et-Moselle, and was for long the capital of the duchy of Lorraine; logically, it is the headquarters of the Lorraine planning region.

Metz,[9] the *chef-lieu* of the *département* of Moselle, is the only large town in this part of Lorraine not concerned directly with the iron and steel industry. Its position has resulted in its function as a fortress town since Gallo-Roman times. Under the direction of Vauban, it formed one of the strongest defence points on France's eastern frontier, and after it became German in 1871 it was made still more powerful, so that it remained in German hands until occupied by Marshal Pétain's forces in November 1918. Today the town has spread far beyond the narrow picturesque streets around the cathedral. While its communal population was 108 000 in 1968, with the contiguous residential and industrial suburbs the agglomeration total was about 166 000. A variety of light industries is carried on in and around Metz. It is an agricultural centre for the Moselle valley, for the neighbouring *côtes*, and for the district of Messin to the east. As a result, the food-preserving industries supply Parisian food shops (tinned and bottled fruit and vegetables, preserves and tinned meats). On the fertile soils of the floodplain extensive market gardens and orchards grow asparagus, strawberries, peas and beans, yellow plums, pears and cherries, and hop gardens to the south serve several large breweries in Metz. Although this part of the valley does not yield the famous Moselle vintages, vineyards have been cultivated on the limestone slopes since Roman times, and quantities of *vin ordinaire* are bottled in Metz. Other enterprises in the neighbourhood include limekilns, cement works and plaster works (using the raw materials from adjacent quarries), tanneries, flour mills, tobacco factories, timber-using industries and a Citroën plant. An oil refinery has been constructed at Hauconcourt near Metz, linked by pipeline to Strasbourg (p. 309).

## The plateau of Lorraine

This sub region, known to French geographers as the *plateau Lorrain propre*, extends eastward from the outliers of Oolitic Limestone along the right bank of the Moselle to the Muschelkalk outcrop (see p. 512) on the flanks of the Vosges. The central part of this plateau, the upper Nied and Seille basins, is given the *pays* name of *Saulnois*. The surface rocks consist mainly of clays—Keuper in the east, Lias in the west; a slight cuesta of Rhaetic Limestone affords a surface manifestation of the margin between these Triassic and Jurassic rocks. The Lias outcrops are rather more varied, consisting of clays, marls, shales and some gritty limestones (the Mid-Lias Grits), while the Keuper comprises more uniform impermeable heavy clay marls, but these differences do not really detract from the geographical unity. The surface of the plateau is diversified by deposits of diluvial gravels washed down from the Vosges by the swollen Pleistocene streams, and now forming a north–south zone of irregular hillocks mostly covered with woodland.

In the extreme north a small upfold of Triassic rocks (the Saarlouis Anticline) projects southwestward across the frontier from the Saarland into France. The newer rocks have been denuded from its upper surface, so revealing the Bunter Sandstone. This forms the forested Plateau de St Avold, consisting of a series of ridges which rise to 426 m (1 398 ft). This sandstone upland is bounded on its perimeter by a cuesta of Muschelkalk.

## Drainage

The Lorraine plateau is crossed by a number of rivers, the floors of which lie between about 180 and 240 m (600 and 800 ft), while in places the higher intervening levels attain 330 m (1 100 ft). The Sarre rises on the northern slopes of Mont Donon in the Vosges and flows northwards over the forested Bunter Sandstone. It then follows the Muschelkalk outcrop northwards from Sarrebourg to Sarre-Union. Here it crosses the strip of Pleistocene gravels, flowing in a narrow valley among undulating hills, and then wanders on to the clay plain, diversified by patches of the gravels and coarse sands. Finally it re-enters the Bunter Sandstone country, marking the frontier for about 11 km (7 miles) before it becomes wholly a West German river in the Saarland. The Nied, formed by the union of its two headstreams, the Nied Française and Nied Allemande, curves right round the southern and western rim of the Triassic upland of St Avold, draining the central part of the plateau. It is a slow-flowing river with a flatbottomed valley, and is marshy and liable to flood in places. The Seille, which joins the Moselle at Metz, also pursues a sluggish course over the claylands. Much of its former swampy floodplain has been reclaimed and the river is regularised, but the valley is still liable to inundation in wet winters.

One result of the cover of impermeable Keuper Marl and the gently undulating surface of the plateau is the presence of many irregular-shaped lakes (Fig. 11.10). Some to the west of Sarrebourg lie on the Keuper Marl among the forested hillocks of gravels; the largest of these acts as a reservoir for the Marne-Rhine Canal and the Canal des Houillères de la Sarre (Fig. 12.5). Other lakes in Saulnois are contained in hollows formed by

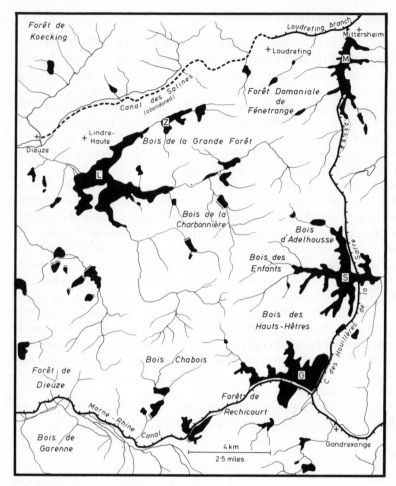

FIG. 11.10. The 'lake district' of northern Lorraine
This map gives some impression of the confused relief of the north-central
part of the Lorraine plateau. The lakes lie in the hollows among the
irregular hillocks of gravels resting on the Keuper clays. Many have been
dammed and are used for fish-rearing, some (notably the Etang de Lindre)
are *étangs périodiques*, and are drained at intervals for cultivation. The
Etang de Gondrexange lies near the watershed and acts as a feeder to the
Marne-Rhine and Sarre Colliery Canals.
   Some of the *étangs* are shown by abbreviations as follows: **G,** E. de
Gondrexange; **L,** E. de Lindre; **M,** Grand E. de Mittersheim; **S,** E. du
Stock; **Z,** E. de Zommange.

Based on *Carte de France au 50 000ᵉ*, sheets XXXV/14, 15; XXXVI/14,15.

subsidence due to the removal of underlying beds of common salt and
gypsum from the Keuper. Many have been artificially enlarged and are used
for pisciculture. The Etang de Lindre, for example (shown on Fig. 11.10),
is an *étang périodique* formed by damming the river Seille above Dieuze.

## Land use and agriculture

The climate of the Lorraine plateau, mainly because of its altitude, is rather cool and damp, with rainfall totals of 700 to 800 mm (28 to 32 in). Nancy, for example, just outside the southwestern corner of this subregion, has mean temperatures of −0·5°C (31°F) and 17°C (62°F) in January and July respectively, and a mean annual rainfall of 790 mm (31 in); an appreciable early summer maximum is indicative of the approach in eastern France to continental conditions. The soils vary considerably, the result of the diverse nature of the parent rocks. Considerable tracts of woodland cover the gravel ridges and notably the Bunter Sandstone uplands.

Mixed farming is widespread, with a dominance of permanent pasture on the Lias Clays and of arable land on the Keuper Marls. The best arable soils are developed on the Muschelkalk, where Sarrebourg is the market centre of a prosperous area. As in many rural areas adjacent to industrial populations, the pasture has strikingly increased since the war of 1914–18 at the expense of arable. Not only do the industrial districts require milk, which the farmers find profitable to produce, but the better wages obtained in industry have drawn labour from the land. As a result, the area under permanent pasture forms rather more than half of the total farm-land. But cereals are still grown, oats for fodder and wheat for human consumption each occupying about two-fifths of the cereal area, and barley for brewing the remainder. Vineyards grow on some south-facing slopes in the Seille valley, but conditions are not really favourable and the wines produced are rather rough *vins ordinaires*.

The *département* of Moselle corresponds roughly with the Lorraine plateau, and the official statistics for 1968 give some indication of the land use.

*Département of Moselle,*
*1968 (1 000 ha)*

| | |
|---|---|
| Total area | 623·2 |
| Woodland | 174·0 |
| Permanent pasture | 195·0 |
| Arable land | 150·5 |
|   Cereals | 95·2 |
|   Fodder crops | 30·2 |

Source: Ministère de
l'Agriculture, *Annuaire
statistique de la France*, 1970–71.

The importance of animal rearing is shown by the fact that in the *département* there were 126 000 head of dairy cattle and about 130 000 pigs, the usual concomitant of the dairying industry. Poultry are widely kept, notably immense numbers of geese, whose livers are destined to be the raw material of the unforgettable delicacy of the *pâté de foie gras Strasbourgeois*.

## The salt deposits

The plateau of Lorraine has two sources of mineral wealth. The Triassic and older Jurassic rocks are notable for their deposits of salts, as in Cheshire and Worcestershire in England and on an enormous scale in the North German Plain, as a result of evaporation in gulfs of the sea or in enclosed lagoons. The Lorraine salt deposits have been exploited for many centuries,

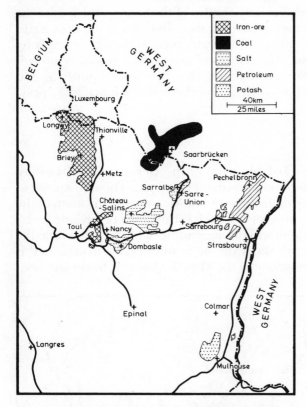

FIG. 11.11. The mineral resources of Alsace and Lorraine
The navigable waterways are shown as solid lines (for their names see Fig. 12.5). The iron ore fields are shown in more detail on Fig. 11.4, and the Saar-Moselle coalfields on Fig. 11.12.
The oilfield near Pechelbronn ceased production in 1969.

Based on (*a*) *La France: géographie-tourisme* (1952), edited by D. Faucher, ii, 345; and (*b*) *Carte industrielle de la Lorraine* (1930).

certainly since Roman times. Numerous place names contain salt-elements, including Château-Salins, Rosières-aux-Salines, Salonnes, Salival, Marsal, and possibly Saulnois itself. More than 2·0 million tons of sodium chloride were produced in 1968 from three main districts (Fig. 11.11).

In the north the saltfield of Sarralbe occurs in the Muschelkalk, and is exploited by brine-pumping at Sarralbe itself, Salzbronn and Haras. The salt provides the raw material for the Solvay chemical works at Sarralbe.

The output of the Seille basin comes from saltbeds in the overlying Keuper; until about 1866 rock salt was mined and brine was obtained from surface springs. Since then it has been necessary to pump the brine from deep borings; at Dieuze is a large chemical works.

The third producing area lies in the valley of the Sanon, which joins the Meurthe at St Nicolas-du-Port. These salt deposits occur in the Lias marls, and while a few rock salt mines still operate, most of the extraction is by pumping of brine solutions. The centres of production include Varangé-ville, Dombasle and Rosières-aux-Salines. There are several purifying and packing plants, and the Solvay works at Dombasle uses salt as its major raw material.

## The Moselle coalfield[10]

In the extreme north the Coal Measures of the German Saar Basin are continued across the frontier into Lorraine (Fig. 11.12). Though exposed in the Saarland, the relatively undisturbed Coal Measures to the south of the river Saar are overlain by progressively thicker deposits of Triassic rocks. After an interruption due to downfaulting southwest of Falquemont in the Nied valley, where as a result the seams lie at unworkable depths, coal is again found fairly near the surface in the Moselle valley. It has in fact been

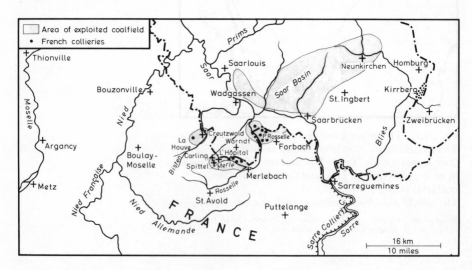

FIG. 11.12. The Moselle and Saar coalfields
The former boundary between the Saarland and West Germany is shown. German collieries in the Saarland are not marked.

Based on (*a*) *Saaratlas* (1934), sheets 4, 23; (*b*) C. C. Held, 'The new Saarland', in *Geogr. Rev.* **41,** (1951), 599.

proved at a depth of 790 m (2 587 ft) near Pont-à-Mousson, but no development has taken place and any future exploitation is unlikely.

The Saar coalfield was first worked by France during the Napoleonic era,
but almost the whole district passed to Rhenish Prussia in 1815 and exploitation steadily progressed in the nineteenth century. A certain amount of
prospecting took place and concessions were granted on the French side of
the frontier, but little development took place there. After the disastrous
Franco-Prussian War, when the whole basin became German, the field was
vigorously prosecuted as German industrialisation proceeded apace. By
1913 the Saar had an annual output of seventeen million tons, of which
*Lorraine Annexée* contributed almost a fifth.

Between 1920 and 1935 the Saar Territory was placed under a council
appointed by the League of Nations, and the coalfield was granted to
France for fifteen years. The collieries and coke ovens were operated by an
administration controlled by the French government, known as the *Mines
Domaniales de la Sarre*, with its headquarters at Saarbrücken.

The long, weary Franco-German negotiations concerning the future of
the Saar ended in June 1956. A number of major issues were settled, notably
the French agreeing to the incorporation of the Saar into West Germany
on 1 January 1957. In this agreement the French made concessions about
the future development of the *Grand Canal d'Alsace* (see p. 299), the Germans
about the canalisation of the Moselle. The problem of the frontier coalfield
was settled by allowing France to continue to work the Warndt colliery
from French territory until 1980.

The portion of the field which lies in the *département* of Moselle, returned to
France in 1944, is being actively prosecuted. There are three separate
districts. The chief mining area is in the valley of the Rosselle (a left-bank
tributary of the river Saar), particularly in the angle to the northwest of
Forbach. This district is known as *Petite-Rosselle*, and six large collieries (one
of which, situated just over the frontier at Warndt, is operated on lease from
West Germany) are in production. Further west is the Merlebach-Spittel
district with four deep collieries near L'Hôpital, Merlebach and Heiligen-
bronn, whose workings extend into the Saarland itself. These subfrontier
workings were one of the main stumbling-blocks to Franco-German
agreement. The third district lies further to the northwest in the valley of
the Bisten, another left-bank tributary of the Saar, where the colliery of
La Houve produces low-grade coal used in pithead thermal generators.

Although the coal occurs at depths much greater than in the Saarland,
the seams are relatively undisturbed and one in the Petite-Rosselle area
exceeds 3·5 m (12 ft) in thickness. Output rose steadily from 3·8 million
tons in 1913 to 6·7 million in 1938, and continued to increase to a peak of
15·7 million in 1964. There has since been a decline to 11·5 million in 1971
(though a third of France's total), and several collieries are soon to close.
The yield per underground worker averages 2·68 tons per shift, compared
with 1·75 for France as a whole, an indication of the thick uninterrupted

seams and the degree of modern mechanisation. This is in fact the highest output per worker in Europe, and compares favourably with that in the Ruhr (1·68) and in Belgium (1·15). Unfortunately for the metallurgical industry, the Moselle field produces none of the *demi-gras* (semi-bituminous coal) so well suited for metallurgical coking; about 65 per cent of its output consists of *flambant gras* (free-burning gas coals), and 17 per cent each of *flambant sec* (dry steam-coal) and *gras* (bituminous coal). About 2·8 million tons of metallurgical coke were made from locally produced coal in 1969, the bulk of the coal being used to produce thermal electricity, the rest for domestic use and steam-raising. France's very real need of metallurgical coke had led to continuous postwar research. Two modern cokeries were completed in 1952, one owned by the Houillères Nationales at Carling, the other by a group of steel firms at Marienau. These cokeries are now producing metallurgical coke from mixtures of various Saar and Moselle coals without using a proportion of Ruhr coal. Two large thermal power stations are owned by the Houillères Nationales, at Carling and at Grossbliederstroff. The Grand Blenod station, opened in 1969, produced in that year 5 074 gWh, the largest output by far of any French power station. At Carling too a large chemical plant, part of a carbopetroleum complex, straddles the border, including integrated plants at Fürstenhausen and Perl in the Saarland.

## Settlement

The distribution of population on the Lorraine plateau manifests the variety of relief, soils and economic development. The rural population lives in small villages, often on south-facing slopes above the clay vales. Market-towns usually stand at bridge points on the rivers, such as the trio of Sarrebourg, Sarralbe and Sarreguemines on the river Sarre. The salt industry and the northern coalfield have resulted in the growth of a number of small industrial centres. There is no dominating regional centre; the two main towns of this part of France are Nancy and Metz on the western margins.

# The high plain of Lorraine

The plain of Lorraine shares the same geological characteristics as the plateau to the north, a similar broad pattern of a western Liassic and an eastern Keuper section, with the outcrops curving southwestward in conformity with the concentric pattern of the Paris Basin. Its southern boundary, the watershed between the Meuse-Moselle drainage to the north and the Saône headstreams to the south, consists of a southwesterly prolongation of the Triassic rocks surrounding the High Vosges, known as the Monts Faucilles, with a double cuesta of Muschelkalk.

The plain of Lorraine lies at an average elevation well above 300 m (1 000 ft), diversified by a series of valleys occupied by the Moselle and its tributaries as they converge on the Nancy–Toul area. The rivers—Meurthe, Mortagne, Moselle—and their numerous headstreams rise on the western slopes of the Vosges (Fig. 19.1), and then cross the flanking Bunter Sandstone in gorgelike valleys. They trend northwestwards across the Muschelkalk, Keuper and Lias in turn, now flowing in broad rather marshy valleys, but with steep bounding slopes lying well back from the river. None of these rivers is much used for navigation, but the flat-floored Moselle valley provides room for the lateral Est Canal (Southern Branch). The Moselle receives only one left-bank tributary, the Madon, which drains the claylands to the southwest. These river valleys dissect the Lorraine plain and introduce a certain variety into the landscape.

Several individual districts have received *pays* names; thus *Xaintois* lies around Mirecourt in the Madon valley, and *Vermois* is in the converging angle between the Meurthe and the Moselle. The Rhaetic outcrop of calcareous sandstone, which separates the Lias from the Keuper in the Lorraine plateau, is present also in the plain, and can be traced south-southwestward as the escarpment of *Virine*, cut through in prominent valley-gaps by the Moselle tributaries. Irregular patches of gravels occur here and there, and strips of recent alluvium cover the floors of the valleys.

## Land use and agriculture

The character of the agricultural landscape is very similar to that of the Lorraine plateau. The patches of gravel and sand are wooded, the limestone-derived loams and some of the clays are under arable, the rest of the clays and the damp valley floors carry permanent pasture, some of which is irrigated as water meadows. Wheat, oats and potatoes are widely grown, and dairy cattle are numerous. Vineyards cover some south-facing slopes, particularly near Lunéville, although the rather high altitude, exposure and rainfall makes this an unfavoured area for viticulture.

## Settlement

Small towns and large villages are strung out along the lower slopes of the valleys. Many have small factories, often long-established from the days of water power, engaged in textile-spinning, embroidery, leather work, timber-using industries, the manufacture of glassware, pottery and chemical products. The chief town is Lunéville at the confluence of the Meurthe and the Vesouze; its activities include engineering (notably rolling-stock, made by a branch of the firm at Graffenstaden near Strasbourg), and the manufacture of textiles, embroidery and straw hats.

# Belgian Lorraine

This area of about 1 000 sq km (400 sq miles) lies in the extreme southeast of Belgium, known as the *Côtes Lorraines*. In the east a narrow tongue of a rather clayey red Bunter Sandstone extends for 25 km (15 miles) along the southern margin of the Ardennes. Then follows a succession of Jurassic calcareous sandstones, limestones, shales and marls, trending in roughly parallel outcrops from west to east. The Muschelkalk and Keuper, though well represented in the Grand Duchy of Luxembourg further to the east, are not present on the surface in Belgian Lorraine except in an insignificant area in the northeast adjoining the frontier.

As elsewhere in the scarplands, these rocks offer a varied resistance to denudation. The most northerly cuesta consists of yellowish Lower Lias Sandstone, known further east as the Luxembourg Sandstone. This cuesta to which is given the name of the Sinemurian Cuesta by geologists, trends eastward across the country to the north of Arlon (Fig. 11.13).[11] It is much dissected, rising to a number of minor wooded summits, the highest being the Hirtzenberg 465 m (1 526 ft) near Arlon. A few kilometres further south is the Charmouthian Cuesta, trending eastward from near Virton into the Grand Duchy, and consisting of Mid-Lias calcareous sandstones, known as the Habergy Sandstones from their extensive development near the small town of that name. Although a less prominent feature than the Luxembourg Sandstone cuesta, it rises towards the east to form several quite noticeable hills, one near the frontier reaching 411 m (1 348 ft). The third cuesta, in the south, comprises a short section of Oolitic Limestone, here known as the Bajocian Cuesta. This is one of the best defined of the Jurassic escarpments, for it can be traced for about 150 km (90 miles) from the Chiers valley almost to the Moselle. The Franco-Belgian frontier in the west runs to the south of the cuesta-edge, but elsewhere lies to the north of it. This anomaly in fact gave Belgium a tiny portion of the *minette* orefield, which small though it was did originally help to establish an iron and steel industry. The summit point of this cuesta within Belgium attains 403 m (1 322 ft) south of Halanzy, but it is appreciably higher in Luxembourg and France.

Between these sandstone and limestone ridges occur the various clays, marls and shales of the Middle and Upper Lias, within whose less resistant outcrops river systems have developed their east–west vales. The valley of the Semois lies between the edge of the Ardennes and the Luxembourg cuesta; this river rises near Arlon, and flows westwards over the clays and marls until it crosses on to the Palaeozoic rocks of the Ardennes. Most of the remainder of Belgian Lorraine drains to the Chiers and so to the Meuse. The Ton drains the vale between the Luxembourg and Habergy cuestas, the Vire occupies the vale between the Habergy and Longwy cuestas; the two streams meet just below Virton and flow southwest into France and so to the Chiers. One interesting river is the Messancy, which rises on the

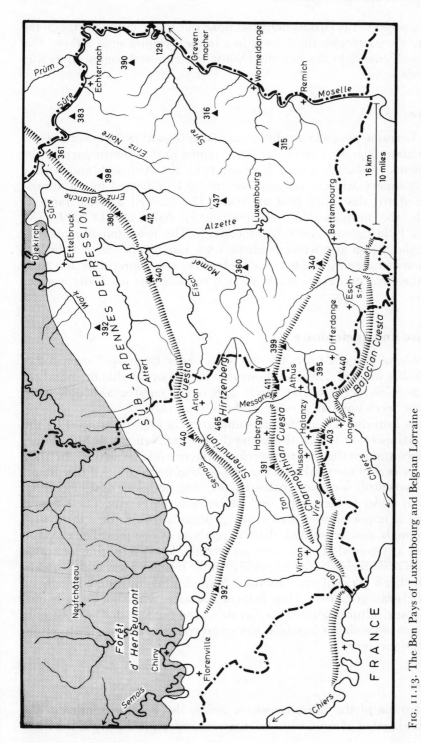

Fig. 11.13. The Bon Pays of Luxembourg and Belgian Lorraine
The Palaeozoic rocks of the Ardennes are stippled, and the trends of the main *Côtes* are indicated by hachures. Heights are given in metres, prominent summits by black triangles.

Based on *Carte de France et des frontières au 200 000*[e], sheets 10, 11.

southern slopes of the Hirtzenberg and flows due south, cutting through the Habergy cuesta to join the Chiers just inside Belgium near Athus. The Chiers itself cuts right through the Oolitic cuesta near Longwy on its way westwards.

## Climate

Belgian Lorraine ranges in altitude from 260 m (850 ft) in the lower western vales to about 450 m (1 500 ft) at a few points in the eastern parts of the escarpments. Although generally lower than the Ardennes and with a southerly aspect, winters are quite severe, as is indicated by an annual average of 103 days with frost at Arlon. The marked seasonal range is shown by the mean monthly temperatures for Arlon of 1°C (34°F) and 17°C (62°F) in January and July respectively. The mean annual precipitation for the region as a whole is about 1 500 mm (39 in), with a distinct maximum between November and February, not appreciably less than that of the Ardennes to the north, though summers are markedly warmer and drier.

## Land use and agriculture

The whole of Belgian Lorraine was once under forest, and even today almost half is wooded. Fig. 18.6 shows that the major woodlands, mainly of birch and pine, occur on the sandy soils of the cuestas, although small patches of beech and oak survive on the heavier clays.

Belgian Lorraine is regarded as a unit area (*la Région jurassique*) by the Belgian Ministère de l'Agriculture and the Institut National de Statistique, and agricultural statistics are therefore conveniently available. In 1961 just 35 per cent of the total area was classified as farm-land. Of this almost exactly two-thirds was under pasture (including both long and short leys), 3 per cent under fodder crops, and 10 per cent under oats. These figures indicate the importance of stock-rearing; of the 48 000 cattle a third were dairy animals, and in addition there were about 11 000 pigs. The clay and marl soils are somewhat intractable and require heavy fertilising for arable crops, but nevertheless about 22 per cent of the farmland was under cereals, and a further 6 per cent grew potatoes. Some fruit is cultivated, usually by means of 'grass orchards'. Thus Belgian Lorraine, while not being of outstanding agricultural significance (as shown by the fact that in 1961 only 2·2 per cent of Belgium's farmland was returned in this region), has a certain limited importance.[12]

## Iron ore

The extension of the Lorraine *minette* across the Belgian frontier in the neighbourhood of Musson and Halanzy was appreciated early in the nineteenth century. But the Belgian portion of the field covers only a little over 2·5 sq km (1 sq mile) and the yield is small; still, it stimulated developments in this southern district, and blast furnaces were built at Musson and Halanzy and a steel works at Athus near the Luxembourg frontier, which are still active. The *minette* has been mined in small quantities—a peak of 248 000 tons in 1900, but only 96 000 tons were obtained from the single mine in operation in 1963, and it has now been closed down.

## Settlements

The total population of the two *arrondissements* of Arlon and Virton, which coincide with the official *région agricole*, is about 92 000, with a population per sq km of about 87 (225 per sq mile), compared with 310 (803) for all Belgium. This population is mostly grouped in small nucleated villages in the clay vales, and the only place of any size is Arlon. It is a pleasant town, situated at a height of 410 m (1 350 ft), the administrative centre of the *arrondissement* and a prosperous market centre. It is an important route focus, for no less than eleven main roads converge upon it, and it is the frontier station for the Brussels-Namur-Luxembourg railway line. The little town of Athus is chiefly important for the integrated steel works of SA d'Angleur-Athus.

## The Bon Pays of Luxembourg

The regional name of the *Bon Pays* is given to the outcrop of Triassic and Lower Jurassic rocks which covers the southern two-thirds of the Grand Duchy of Luxembourg. The geological map (Fig. 11.2) shows that the Lower Palaeozoic rocks here recede to the northeast, forming a triangular embayment extending into West Germany beyond Trier. This re-entrant indicates the line of the broad Luxembourg Syncline, a downfold parallel to and contemporaneous with the Hercynian folding of the Ardennes, Eifel and Hunsrück (see pp. 483–6 and Fig. 18.2). Its surface reveals a much greater variety of Mesozoic rocks than in Belgian Lorraine to the west, where the Trias is scarcely represented. The Triassic and Jurassic rocks were subjected to a long period of differential erosion, and the several out-crops present the pattern of an acute angle pointing northeast, with successively younger rocks occurring towards the southwest. The oldest, the Bunter Sandstone, follows the edge of the Devonian rocks, but only the northwestern 'limb' of the outcrop appears in Luxembourg, the south-eastern in West Germany to the east of the river Sarre. The next formation, the Muschelkalk, is represented both in the north, where it succeeds the Bunter along the edge of the Ardennes, and in the east along the Moselle valley. The Muschelkalk here differs from its usual shelly limestone character, for it consists rather of sandstones and marls in the lower beds and of dolomitic limestones and sandstones in the upper beds. Within the angle of

279

the Muschelkalk, and broadly parallel to its two outcrops, occur the Keuper rocks, consisting mainly of clays and marls, but including also layers of sandstone, dolomitic limestones, and some gypsum which is quarried for plaster and cement. At the top of the Keuper are occasional outcrops of yellow Rhaetic Sandstone.

The central part of the Bon Pays, enclosed to the north and east by these older Triassic outcrops, consists of an extensive area of yellow calcareous Lower Lias Sandstone. This forms a triangular plateau, interrupted in the north by the valley of the Alzette, deeply eroded into the underlying Keuper rocks. To the southwest succeed the Middle and Upper Lias clays, shales and marls, and occasional beds of calcareous sandstones. Finally, in the extreme southwest, part of the northern edge of the Oolitic cuesta just appears in Luxembourg; limited though it is, it does provide the Grand Duchy with appreciable deposits of *minette*.

Mention must be made of the quite extensive Quaternary deposits, both Pleistocene gravels and coarse sands and the narrow strips of newer alluvium. The Pleistocene deposits are found on the high lands along the Ardennes margins, where they cover both the Bunter Sandstone and the lower parts of the Devonian rocks. They occur too on the higher areas in the west of the Bon Pays and along the foot of the Oolitic cuesta in the southwest. These gravels formerly contained workable quantities of alluvial iron ore (hydrated oxide of iron) in nodules or grains, redeposited from the *minette* ore beds to the south. The early Luxembourg iron industry in fact developed because of the accessibility of these non-phosphoric alluvial ores, which could be smelted with charcoal.

## Relief features

A pattern of drainage has developed in the Bon Pays which (except for the headstreams of the Chiers in the extreme southwest) focuses on the Moselle in the eastern angle of the country. In the north, flowing eastwards within a broad trough cut in the Bunter Sandstone, are the Attert and its parallel tributary the Wark, which join the Sûre flowing in the same direction. In the east such streams as the Syre flow direct to the Moselle, and the broadly parallel Ernz Blanche and Ernz Noire join the Sûre.

The central and western parts of the Bon Pays are drained by the Alzette and its numerous left-bank tributaries. This river rises in France, deriving headstreams from the Oolitic plateau, and then flows north across the central Bon Pays to its junction with the Sûre near Ettelbruck. As a result the river crosses each of the varied outcrops in turn. First it cuts through the Oolitic cuesta above Esch, next it flows over the Mid-Lias Clay in the broad Vallée de Roeser, and continues for 16 km (10 miles) deeply entrenched in the Luxembourg Sandstone (Fig. 11.14). As the river approaches the city of Luxembourg, its valley becomes virtually a gorge with sinuous winding loops; the surface of the sandstone plateau lies almost

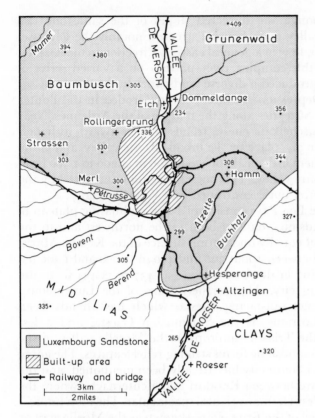

Fig. 11.14. The middle Alzette valley and the city of Luxembourg

The northward-flowing Alzette leaves the broad Vallée de Roeser, eroded in the Mid-Lias Clays, for a winding gorge cut across the Luxembourg (Lower Lias) Sandstone. A few km downstream from the capital city, the valley widens out as the steep sandstone slopes recede from the river, leaving the wide Vallée de Mersch eroded from the Keuper Marls and floored with recent alluvium. Heights are given in metres.

Based on (*a*) *Carte de France au 50 000ᵉ*, sheets XXXIII/10, XXXIV/10; and (*b*) *Geologische Übersichtskarte des Luxemburger Landes*, edited by J. J. Robert.

60 m (200 ft) above river level. It was on the rocky peninsula between the Alzette and its western tributary the Pétrusse that the tenth-century fortress was built which formed the nucleus of the city. One result of the deep meanders is that the railway from Liège to Metz and Strasbourg has to cross the Alzette three times, requiring a viaduct 260 m (850 ft) in length, and to pierce a meander-core by means of a tunnel. To the north of the city the Alzette passes on to the Keuper Marls, and its valley broadens out as the

Vallée de Mersch, although the dissected slopes of the sandstone rise steeply away from the valley floor. Several streams, notably the Pétrusse, the Mamer and the Eisch, flow in a general easterly direction to the Alzette.

The development of this complex river pattern on a varied series of geological outcrops has produced a diverse landscape. In the north the so-called 'Sub-Ardennes Depression', a broad trough eroded in the Bunter by the Attert, Wark and Sûre, lies along the margin of the Ardennes. Near its southern edge the Muschelkalk cuesta trends northeastward, although cut through completely in one place by the broad Alzette valley, and in the east it forms some prominent little peaks of 370 to 400 m (1 200 to 1 300 ft) in height overlooking the Sûre valley. This cuesta is again interrupted by the Ernz Blanche and the Sûre, but is continued into West Germany.

The central part of the Bon Pays consists of a low undulating plateau of Luxembourg (Lias) Sandstone, flanked both to the northwest and to the southeast by the lower but equally undulating surface of the Keuper Marls. Most of this plateau lies between about 300 and 400 m (1 000 and 1 300 ft), the highest point occurring in the Grunenwald at 437 m (1 434 ft) to the northeast of Luxembourg city. The northern edge of the Luxembourg Sandstone forms a distinct out-facing cuesta, which has already been traced across Belgian Lorraine as the Sinemurian Cuesta, and a less marked cuesta borders the Triassic outcrops in the Moselle valley in the east. In several places this sandstone forms striking relief features. The gorge of the Alzette near Luxembourg city has already been mentioned, and the winding valley of the Sûre between Reisdorf and Echternach (where the outcrop continues into West Germany) is also spectacular. The most impressive scenery is in the valley of the Ernz Noire (known as the Moellerdall or Müllerthal), a right-bank tributary of the Sûre in the extreme northeast. Not only has stream erosion cut deep gorges, but rainwater percolates into the fissures of this calcareous sandstone, enlarging them by solution and forming chasms, grottoes and caverns alternating with steep buttresses and fantastic rock pinnacles. The rocks vary in resistance to denudation, and in places strata of siliceous sandstones are much less easily attacked than the calcareous sandstones, so stand out boldly. Where harder strata outcrop across streams, rapids and falls occur, notably the famous Schiessentümpel on the Ernz Noire itself. These sandstones are densely wooded with beech, and the whole district, known as the *Petite Suisse*, is a much visited tourist area.

Towards the southwest the surface rocks consist of Middle and Upper Lias clays and shales, forming undulating country between 240 and 300 m (800 and 1 000 ft) high. The valleys occupied by the Alzette's headstreams have open cross-profiles, with gentle interfluves, though occasional bands of limestone and sandstone form steep escarpments. The Habergy Sandstone, mentioned above as forming the Charmouthian Cuesta in Belgian Lorraine, can be traced as a low cuesta, with a maximum altitude of 399 m (1 309 ft), from the Belgian frontier to the Alzette valley.

In the extreme south is the prominent north-facing Oolitic cuesta, forming heights which overlook the Chiers and Alzette valleys; the Gintzenberg near Dudelange, on which stands Luxembourg's radio station, attains 425 m (1 394 ft), and the Hatschenberg, also near Dudelange, is about 10 m (30 ft) less. A small detached mass of Upper Lias limestone, standing prominently on the watershed between the sources of the Chiers and an Alzette headstream, a kilometre to the north of the Oolitic cuesta, is known as the Zolver Knapp or the Butte de Soleuvre 422 m (1 385 ft).

The Moselle valley is sufficiently distinct to be mentioned specifically, since it forms a depression along the southeastern frontier; the official lowest point in the Grand Duchy is found in its valley at the Sûre confluence at 129 m (423 ft). The floodplain is covered with alluvium and gravels, and the valley slopes cut in the Keuper rise gently to the west. Where the Muschelkalk approaches the river the slopes are steeper, but faults have resulted in steplike southeast-facing terraces, each backed by a prominent escarpment.

## Climate

Considerable climatic variations are experienced over the Bon Pays, in spite of its limited size. The Moselle valley in the southeast lies to some degree in a rainshadow and has a southeasterly aspect; as a result it usually experiences a pleasant climate, with a mean annual rainfall of 660 to 890 mm (26 to 28 in), monthly temperatures varying from about 18°C to 3°C (65°F to 35°F), and long sunshine hours. The rest of the Bon Pays has a higher rainfall varying from about 800 to 950 mm (32 to 38 in), and is cooler and cloudier than the Moselle valley. Indeed, the highest mean rainfall figures for Luxembourg are found not in the much higher Ardennes, but in the southwest on the exposed Oolitic cuesta where the total is over 1 000 mm (40 in). Great local variations occur; sheltered south-facing valleys experience more pleasant conditions than do the open plateau surfaces.

## Land use and agriculture

The Bon Pays is, in proportion to its area, almost as much under woodland as the Ardennes (Fig. 18.6), even though there was extensive felling in the eighteenth and early nineteenth centuries by the charcoal-burners to provide fuel for the iron furnaces. The Luxembourg Sandstone carries considerable woodland, notably in the neighbourhood of the capital—the extensive Grunenwald to the northeast and the Baumbusch to the northwest. As Fig. 18.6 shows, woodland is widespread on the uplands but it has been cleared from the valleys for cultivation. Beech is the most common tree, though oak and oak-beech woods are still found. Conifers are planted extensively, especially on the sandstones, by the Administration des Eaux et Forêts.

The Bon Pays is a region of mixed farming, mainly practised on a subsistence basis, although the local variations in relief, soils and climate are reflected in differences in emphasis. The damp alluvial valley floors and the heavier marls and clays in the west and southwest tend to be under permanent pasture. Gentle slopes with well-drained soils developed on the calcareous sandstones are devoted to arable, with strips under various crops, and in favoured areas to orchards and vineyards. Over the Bon Pays as a whole the land is divided more or less equally between grain crops, roots, and green fodder with permanent pasture. Oats for fodder make up almost half the grain crops, with winter wheat and some rye for human consumption. Potatoes, fodder beet, turnips and swedes comprise the root crops, the first occupying two-thirds of the total area, while red clover and lucerne are grown to supplement the permanent meadowlands which are cut for hay. The most significant changes which have taken place since the war of 1939–45 have been a marked decrease in arable land by almost a half, and an increase in pasture and meadowland by a third. While the area under cereals has declined but little, root crops occupied in 1967 only one-seventh of the area in 1938 and fodder crops have decreased by a third.

Both dairy and beef cattle, mostly Frisians, are kept in the Bon Pays; this is the most important aspect of agriculture. Every smallholding and farm has a few animals and large herds are rare. In 1966 there were about 34 000 cattle (almost double the 1937 figure), with a further 8 000 calves reared for veal and 150 000 pigs.

Milk is produced for the capital city and for the industrial towns in the south, as well as for sale to the dairy cooperatives which separate the cream to supply the butter factories at Saeul and Ettelbruck. The skimmed milk returned to the farms is fed to pigs, which share with dairy cattle the responsibility of being the 'cash crops' in the otherwise subsistence arable economy. There is not only a considerable demand within Luxembourg, for pork is an important item of diet, but also from neighbouring countries.

Many fruit trees are grown, including apples, cider apples, plums and damsons; most of these are scattered through the Bon Pays in every village for local needs, but some orchards are owned by commercial growers, mainly on the southeastern valley slopes. Rose-bushes are cultivated, notably on the heavy marls and clays of the Vallée de Mersch, though the area devoted to roses has considerably declined. About 75 ha (185 acres) were so used before 1914, producing six million bushes a year, but in the years before 1939 output fell to well below a million, and since the war less than half a million have been grown annually, though they are still exported.

The Moselle valley is famed for its vines, and although the bulk of the well-known Moselle wines are produced below Trier, Luxembourg yields quite a range both of light dry white wines and also of some sparkling wines.

The vineyards are situated on the southeast facing slopes of calcareous Keuper and Muschelkalk rocks, on natural or artificially constructed terraces above the river valley. The valley is very marginal for wine production, for the altitude is considerable, bitter winds from the uplands in the north are experienced despite the sheltered slopes, and both late frosts and wet summers with sunshine below average are regrettably common features. Both total yield and quality fluctuate considerably, but there has been a fairly steady increase from a mere 34 000 hectolitres in 1937 to 124 000 in 1967; about a third is exported.

## The iron and steel industry

The basis of the iron and steel industry of Luxembourg is the extension of the Lorraine *minette* field for a few kilometres across the French frontier into the Grand Duchy (Fig. 11.4). As a result of this grographical accident the country is the twelfth steel producer in the world.[13] Moreover, its economy is predominantly dependent on steel, for this accounts for from 65 to 75 per cent of the country's total productivity and exports by value. Even more eloquent is the fact that almost a quarter of the working population, were employed in the iron and steel industry in 1972.

ORE-MINING

The *minette* area in Luxembourg extends over little more than 36 sq km (14 sq miles), but the deposits are estimated to comprise 300 million tons of exploitable ore, with an iron content of 63 million tons. The field is divided into three basins (Fig. 11.15) by the river valleys. In the western basin, within the triangle of Rodange, Pétange and Differdange, and bounded on the southwest by the French frontier, the ore produced is mainly siliceous, with an iron-content of about 28 per cent. Between the rivers Alzette and Kayl lies the Esch field, and east of the Kayl the eastern field; these two deposits are calcareous, with an average iron content of only about 24·6 per cent. The average iron content of ore obtained is about 26·0 per cent, distinctly lower than that of French Lorraine; before 1939 the average varied between 30 and 31 per cent. This reduction over only thirty years indicates partly the working out of the richer upper beds, such as the 'Esch red bed', partly postwar technological improvements which have enabled the poorer ores to be utilised. There is wide variation in the colour and thickness of the individual beds, which are similar in nature and occurrence to those in French Lorraine. The 'grey' and 'yellow' beds comprise today the main exploited deposits; in the Esch basin the workable beds total 45 m (150 ft) in thickness.

In 1970 some 5·7 million tons were produced, of which just over half was calcareous. This output does not equal the highest ever, achieved in 1926 and again in 1957, when 7·8 million tons with an iron content of 30 per cent

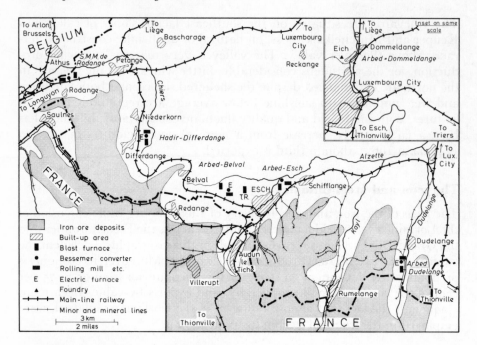

FIG. 11.15. The iron and steel industry of southern Luxembourg
Details of the French iron and steel works, not shown on this map, appear on Fig. 11.8.
The built-up areas are generalised. Only the active plants are shown.
 **TR** Terres-Rouges (a subsidiary within the Arbed group); **SMM de Rodange,**
Société Minière et Métallurgique de Rodange.

Based on: (*a*) *Carte de France au 50 000ᵉ*, sheets XXXIII/10, 11; XXXIV/10, 11; (*b*) *Carte topographique du Grande-Duché de Luxembourg*, sheets 11, 13, 14; (*c*) information derived from *Monthly Statistical Bulletin* (1952), vol. 27, no. 8, published by the British Iron and Steel Federation.

were obtained. Only seventeen individual mines are now in operation, indicating a steady reduction in number from eighty-one in 1926. About two-thirds are wholly opencast, where the ore is worked in large shallow quarries, but many of the former profitable opencast mines, particularly those in the upper 'Esch red beds', are now exhausted, for thirty-eight were being operated in 1937. The remaining mines are exploited by galleries driven more or less horizontally at different levels into the *minette* escarpment and into the sides of the river valleys. The dip of the strata is for the most part gentle and there is little structural disturbance, so that mining costs are relatively low. Nine of the mines, producing three-quarters of the total, are owned by three big Luxembourg steel companies, three others by Belgian steel companies, and the remainder are small independent concerns.

The calcareous ores are almost wholly self-fluxing, and the Luxembourg smelters blend them with siliceous ores in the proportion of two to one. Although rather more calcareous ore is produced this is still not sufficient, and moreover the more easily accessible calcareous 'grey' and 'yellow' beds are being rapidly worked out. A considerable amount of calcareous ore is therefore imported from French Lorraine, and in the postwar period some high-grade ore has been obtained from Sweden. Between 1946 and 1954 the latter sent a total of over 5 million tons, the peak of 1·3 million tons occurring in 1948, since when a considerable reduction has been effected; a mere 57 000 tons were imported in 1967.

Apart from the particular requirements of metallurgical practice, Luxembourg is unable to produce sufficient ore to feed her own furnaces; consumption totals 12 to 14 million tons, and about 6 to 7 million tons are imported annually from France. The Grand Duchy also exports a small amount, mostly to Belgium, the result both of geographical proximity and of industrial collaboration and financial relationships. In other words, the Luxembourg furnaces usually consume rather more foreign than home-produced ore, although in some years the balance is slightly in the opposite direction. The balance-sheet for 1967 is summarised in the following table:

*Luxembourg's consumption of iron ore (thousand tons)*

| CONSUMPTION IN BLAST-FURNACES | | | EXPORTS TO | | | | IMPORTS FROM | | |
|---|---|---|---|---|---|---|---|---|---|
| HOME-PRODUCED | FOREIGN | TOTAL | WEST GERMANY | FRANCE | BELGIUM | TOTAL | FRANCE | SWEDEN | TOTAL |
| 6 116 | 7 008 | 13 124 | — | 26 | 277 | 303 | 6 792 | 57 | 6 849 |

Source: Chambre de Commerce and Inspection du Travail des Mines, quoted in *Annuaire statistique*, 1969.

This table represents fairly adequately the postwar pattern, except that Luxembourg until 1957 exported some ore to West Germany and imported more from Sweden. In 1953, too, the Saar took over 600 000 tons but none in 1954. The table indicates both the central position of the Grand Duchy in Europe, and the present inadequacy of home production of the ore which was the basis of her iron and steel industry.

## Steel production

The industrial pattern, as in other west European countries, has been dominated by the gradual integration of individual enterprises. The largest is the Société Anonyme des Aciéries Réunies de Burbach, Eich et Dudel-ange, known generally as Arbed, which was created in 1911 by the merging of three independent companies. The Terres-Rouges company, incorporated in 1919 to take over various installations and properties owned and operated in Luxembourg by German interests, entered into association

287

with Arbed in 1926, and they have now merged to form one of Europe's largest combines.[14] Arbed has five plants in operation (Fig. 11.15), together with the Schifflange plant now closed down. These include blast furnaces and Bessemer converters at Belval, Esch and Dudelange, blast furnaces at Terres-Rouges to the northwest of Esch (from which molten iron is conveyed through conduits to the Belval and Esch converters), and electric furnaces at Dommeldange to the north of Luxembourg city which produce mainly alloy steels. Some of the Arbed plants are being modernised; efforts are in progress to remove the phosphoric content from the ore, so making basic pig, and allowing basic oxygen converters to be installed. This vast Arbed group has a total capacity of over 3 million tons of pig iron, the same amount of crude steel, and 2·5 million tons of rolled steel products. In addition to its ore mines in Luxembourg, Arbed owns others across the frontier in France, connected with its blast furnaces by electrified mineral lines and in places by overhead cables. It operates another integrated steel plant at Burbach near Saarbrücken in the Saar, it owns collieries and coking plant in the Aachen field, it has financial interests in the Kempen and South Limburg coalfields, and it controls a number of metal-using industries in Belgium, French Lorraine, the Saar and the Rhineland.

The second industrial corporation in Luxembourg was the S.A. des Hauts-Fourneaux et Aciéries de Differdange, St Ingbert et Rumelange, known as Hadir, formed in 1920 to take over and integrate a number of mainly German interests. The Rumelange works, comprising three small blast furnaces, stood idle during the interwar period, and was dismantled during the 1940–44 period by the Germans. Hadir's main plant was at Differdange (Fig. 11.15). While not of the industrial stature of the Arbed group, its interests were wide, and included iron-ore mines in the district and at Ottange in French Lorraine, and also a large rolling-mill at St Ingbert in the Saarland. In 1966, however, Hadir, owned by the French company of Pont-à-Mousson, was sold to Arbed.

Another company is a subsidiary of the Belgian Cockerill-Ougrée-Marihaye group, with works situated north of Rodange near the Belgian frontier, adjacent to the Luxembourg-Pétange-Paris railway line. Five blast-furnaces and four Bessemer converters are in operation, each with an annual capacity of half a million tons, several rolling-mills specialising in rails, iron and steel foundries, and a brick-making plant. The company owns ore mines both in the Grand Duchy near Rumelange and in French Lorraine, with which the works are connected by overhead cable.

In 1970 these steel companies, operating eight individual groups of plant (Fig. 11.15), produced 4·8 and 5·5 million tons of pig iron and of crude steel respectively. The industry consumed 13·2 million tons of ore, more than half of which was obtained from abroad, and used 3·5 million tons of coke in the blast furnaces. There are no coke ovens in Luxembourg, as it has always been considered more economical to import fuel in the form of coke; no outlet is afforded in the Bessemer steel converters for the use of coke oven gas. While Belgium and the Netherlands supplied some coke before the war of 1939–45, since then West Germany has provided almost all of Luxembourg's requirements.

A large proportion of Luxembourg's steel enters into world commerce, but it is difficult to give precise details since figures are published for the Union Economique Belgo-Luxembourgeoise as a unit.

## Steel-using industries

A number of important steel-using firms are active in the Grand Duchy. The largest is the Paul Wurth works at Hollerich in the southern suburbs of the capital; a proportion of its share capital is held by Arbed-Terres-Rouges. This firm has a wide range of interests, developed over the years from a small foundry and boiler works; it builds and erects bridges all over the world, it specialises in installations and equipment for iron and steel works, it has a high reputation for the construction of cranes, and it manufactures a variety of factory machinery and railway rolling-stock. A long-established firm, with its works at Wecker near Wasserbillig on the West German frontier, manufactures agricultural implements and machinery, serving the farming country of the Bon Pays and the Moselle valley. From its situation in the Moselle wine country, it has for long made wine presses for local use; this industry has developed so that the works now export wine presses to wine-making centres of central and southern Europe and also to the vine-growing areas in the southern hemisphere. The firm manufactures other presses and extractive machinery, as for cider and for vegetable oils. Lesser centres of engineering and metal manufacturing include Lintgen and Keispelt to the north of Luxembourg city, where tools and kitchen implements are made, and Hünsdorf which manufactures mining equipment for the Luxembourg orefields, for Lorraine and for further afield.

## Other industries

Other industries are much less important, most of them concentrated in the capital. They include textile factories (survivors of a widespread domestic industry) making woollen cloth, hosiery and knitted goods, leather-tanning for shoes and gloves, brewing and distilling, and the manufacture of cigarettes. Small brick works, cement works and saw mills are found in most towns and villages. Luxembourg city has many small-scale industries, particularly in the suburb of Hollerich to the south. In recent years efforts have been made to diversify the economy and more than fifty new industrial plants (many foreign owned) have been established. Luxembourg has also become an important European financial and commercial centre.

Finally, mention must be made of the tourist industry. This attractive little country, situated in the heart of western Europe and the focus of several transcontinental lines, is visited by a large number of tourists every year. Deliberate state encouragement and propaganda have fostered this. The chief tourist centre is the capital, partly because of its own interest as a charming and historic city, partly because it is an excellent centre for the country as a whole. Many small towns and villages cater extensively for visitors—Echternach for the Sûre valley and the 'Petite Suisse' district, Remich and Wormeldange for the Moselle valley, Vianden, Diekirch, Ettelbruck and Clervaux for the Ardennes, Mondorf-les-Bains in the extreme south for its mineral springs. The number of hotels, pensions, etc., has risen steadily, especially in Luxembourg city, Echternach, Berdorf and Vianden. In addition, the excellently organised youth hostels attract large numbers of younger visitors.

## Settlement

The density of population over the Bon Pays was about 140 per sq km (365 per sq mile) at the end of 1969, comparing notably with the Ardennes (48 per sq km (124 per sq mile)). This figure for the Bon Pays is as high as it is because the total population includes both the capital city (77 000 people) and the industrial area, notably Esch-sur-Alzette, the centre of the steel industry, which had a population of 27 000 in 1970. Differdange, Dudelange and Pétange were other towns almost exclusively preoccupied with iron and steel manufacture. The Bon Pays, occupying two-thirds of the area of the Grand Duchy, contains 93 per cent of its total population of 340 000, the result of a diverse agriculture and a highly developed iron and steel industry.

[1] A. Blanc, E. Juillard, J. Ray and M. Rochefort, *Les Régions de L'Est* (1960), in the series *France de Demain*, gives a well illustrated survey of Alsace and Lorraine.

[2] The estimates produced by the Economic Commission for Europe in 1949 gave the *iron content* of the total French reserves (of which about 10 per cent lie outside Lorraine) as 2 277 million tons, and of the Luxembourg *minette* field as 63 million tons. A later estimate gives the French total as 2 692 million tons.

[3] See A. Sömme, *La Lorraine métallurgique* (1938), chapter 17, 'Les Italiens et les Polonais sur le Plateau de Briey', pp. 146–50.

[4] A. A. Michel, 'The canalisation of the Moselle and West European integration', *Geogrl Rev.*, **52** (1962), pp. 475–91; and F. Chanrion, *Une Victoire européenne: la Moselle* (1964).

[5] There is an extensive literature on the Lorraine iron and steel industry. The 'classic' account is Axel Sömme, *La Lorraine métallurgique* (1938). See also J. Bichelonne and P. Angot, *Le Bassin ferrifère de Lorraine* (1939); J. Chardonnet, *La Sidérurgie française* (1954); and N. J. G. Pounds and W. N. Parker, *Coal and Steel in Western Europe* (1957). A very useful account is provided by J. E. Martin, 'Location factors in the Lorraine iron and steel industry', *Trans. Inst. Br. Geogr.* (1957), Publication no. 23, pp. 191–212. Two publications by the British Iron and Steel Federation are 'The French steel development plan', reprinted from *Monthly Statistical Bulletin*, **28** (1953), no. 2, and 'Steel developments in France', *ibid.*, **30** (1955), no. 8. The High Authority of the European Coal and Steel Community publish much statistical material, reports and bulletins from Brussels. See also C. Prêcheur, *La Sidérurgie française* (1963), a most valuable survey.

⁶ In 1970 the French total of crude steel was 23·77 million tons.

⁷ A review of the progress of industrial grouping and consolidation before the war of 1939–45 is provided by R. de Fou, *Le Mouvement de concentration dans la sidérurgie lorraine* (1943).

⁸ Modern methods of sintering, designed to utilise the fines and enrich the iron content, are overcoming this difficulty.

⁹ R. Frecaut, 'Les Agglomérations de Metz et de Thionville', *Rev. Géog. de l'Est*, **8** (1968), pp. 89–128.

¹⁰ R. Haby, *Les Houillères lorraines et leur région* (1965). The 1968 'run down' plan for the French coal industry envisages a national output of about 25 million tons by 1975 (cf. 55 million in 1964), of which the Lorraine field will contribute about 12 million from three mines only. But in 1971 its output was only 11.5 million (well below the peak of 15·7 million in 1964), partly because of a strike, mainly because of the competition of oil and natural gas piped from the Saarland and the Netherlands respectively. See D. I. Scargill, 'Energy in France: a Note on some recent Developments', *Geography* **58** (1973), pp. 159–63.

¹¹ R. Souchez, 'A propos de reliefs residuels gréseux au nord de Virton (Lorraine belge)', *Rev. belge Géogr.*, **87** (1963), pp. 171–6; and R. Souchez, 'Influence paléoclimatiques sur le modèle du plateau gréseux de Lorraine belge', *Annls Géogr.*, **75** (1966), pp. 401–9, with a detailed bibliography.

¹² '*L'aménagement du Sud-Luxembourg; aperçu des synthèses et conclusions de l'enquête préparatoire*', published by the Ministère des Travaux Publiques (1961).

¹³ A useful publication by the British Iron and Steel Federation is 'The Luxemburg iron and steel industry', reprinted from *Monthly Statistical Bulletin*, **27** (1952), no. 8. See also A. Kipgen, 'The Luxembourg iron industry', *Journal of the Iron and Steel Institute*, **130** (1934), no. 2, pp. 11–23. Historical aspects are dealt with by K. C. Edwards, 'Historical geography of the Luxembourg iron and steel industry', *Trans. Inst. Br. Geogr.*, **29** (1961), pp. 1–16. See also M. and G. Steffes, *La Sidérurgie luxembourgeoise* (Luxembourg, 1962), 181 pp.

¹⁴ *La Sidérurgie au Grande-Duché de Luxembourg et les origines de l'Arbed* (1960), published by the Arbed company.

# 12
# The plain of Alsace

The valley of the Rhine from Basel to Mainz consists of a broad trench bordered by parallel stepfaults which demarcate each edge of a rift valley.[1] The formation of this rift valley and in particular of its western containing wall, the Vosges, is described on pp. 512-13.

During much of Tertiary times the rift valley formed a long arm of the sea opening southward, which later became a brackish inland lake draining through what is now the Porte de Bourgogne (see p. 362) to the southwest. Vast amounts of sediment, chiefly Oligocene clays, were deposited on its floor. Probably during the Pliocene period, earth movements caused depression further to the north, and the proto-Rhine, which had previously formed a headstream of what is now the Saône draining to the plain of Bresse (see p. 366), was forced to develop a remarkable rightangle bend near Basel and to flow northwards through the rift valley. Thus not only was the river's direction reversed, but its base level was lowered and so its erosive power was increased; as a result it cut deeply into the Tertiary deposits. During interglacial and immediately postglacial times, great thicknesses of sands and gravels were deposited on the floor of the rift valley by torrents flowing from the Vosges, the Jura and the Black Forest. There were also considerable and very significant deposits of windblown loess, similar in origin and character to the limon of Picardy and southern Belgium (see p. 24). The Rhine and its tributaries have continued to deposit material on the present floodplain; in the neighbourhood of Kembs in the south this Recent alluvium is more than 10 m (30 ft) in thickness.

Only occasionally are the underlying rocks, mainly Oligocene clays, revealed in the floor of the valley by removal of the newer sediments. The most notable of some small outcrops of Jurassic rocks is a bar of limestone which crosses the Rhine transversely near Kembs, causing the Istein rapids.

## The physical features

The plain of Alsace forms the southwestern portion of this rift valley floor, extending northward for 150 km (90 miles) from the foothills of the Jura (the *Jura alsacienne*) to the West German frontier along the river Lauter, and varying in width from 15 to 40 km (10 to 25 miles) between the Rhine's regulated channel and the foothills of the Vosges. Three relief divisions may be distinguished: the higher terraces sloping gently eastward from 180 m (600 ft) above sea level along the Vosges foothills, the *Sundgau* in the extreme south of the rift valley, and the floodplains of the Ill and the Rhine in the south and of the Rhine alone to the north of Strasbourg.

## The higher terraces

The foothills of the Vosges, composed of Triassic and Jurassic sandstones, form stepped terraces (the so-called *collines sous-vosgiennes*), gashed through by deep, almost gorgelike, valleys of rivers descending eastwards or northeastwards from the High Vosges until they are picked up by the north-

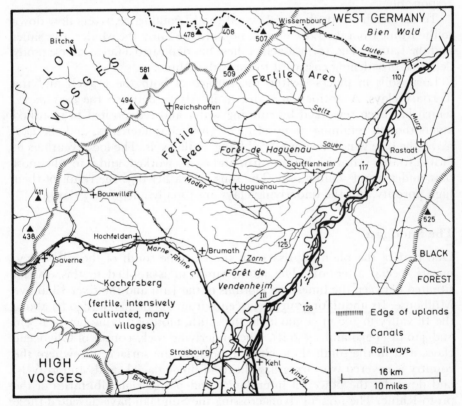

FIG. 12.1. The plain of Lower Alsace
The large number of minor streams and drainage channels flowing across the plain to the Rhine are omitted. The Franco-German frontier follows the centre of the Rhine. The Bien Wald, Forêt de Haguenau and Forêt de Vendenheim, developed on sheets of sand and gravel, separate the fertile loess-covered areas. Heights are given in metres.

Based on *Carte de France et des frontières au 200 000ᵉ*, sheets 19, 28.

293

wards-flowing Ill. These are torrential streams actively eroding into the flanks of the Vosges, and they are heavily laden with debris, particularly during the snowmelt floods of early summer and following late summer storms. As a result, extensive deposition takes place on the plain immediately beyond the foothills, where the gradient abruptly lessens and the rate of flow is checked. The confluence of each of these Vosges streams with the Ill forms an acute angle marked by the deposition of gravels, among which the waters flow in braided streams, sometimes below the surface.

Much of this area consists of marsh (where the watertable is high), alternating with dry pebble banks covered with scrubby vegetation. The Thur in particular flows across a large arid gravel fan (the Ochsenfeld), where it leaves its deeply cut valley below Thann. Parts of it have, however, been improved by irrigation to provide meadowland of sorts. North of Sélestat lies another area of gravels and marsh, for which the river Scheer is responsible.

To the north of Strasbourg, beyond the Ill confluence, rivers flow down to the Rhine from the Low Vosges, notably the Zorn, the Moder, the Sauer and the Lauter (Fig. 12.1). Each of these has deposited a fan of coarse sandy deposits, broadening eastward towards the Rhine.

Loess soils in places swathe the surface of both the gravels and the Tertiary clays. A distinction is drawn in Alsace between the *loess ancien*, which has been reworked by running water and redeposited in stratified layers though retaining many of its original characteristics, and the *loess récent*, the true windblown material lying at all levels. The loess weathers to form a friable yellowish loam, warm and easily worked, and is for the most part under arable cultivation. The soils are rather dry, the result of their high porosity, but the underlying clays are usually adequately damp.

## The Sundgau

One part of the plain of Alsace, in the extreme south of the rift valley, merits special attention. The name Sundgau is applied to this district situated between the limestone foothills of the Jura and the river Ill above Mulhouse. Its undulating surface ascends from about 260 m (850 ft) above the Ill valley to 400 m (1 300 ft) in the south, most of it lying between 370 and 410 m (1 250 and 1 350 ft). The underlying rocks consist of Oligocene clays, and in the south these clays appear on the surface. Elsewhere the country is covered with irregular sheets of fluvioglacial sands and gravels, laid down by the powerful interglacial and postglacial tributaries of the proto-Rhine. The present rivers crossing the Sundgau have dissected these sheets of gravels, forming broad shallow valleys in many places cutting down into the Oligocene clays, and leaving flat-topped interfluves still covered with the gravels. The present rivers are much smaller than those of late glacial times, and wander vaguely across their floors as misfits. Many of their tributary valleys are now dry, the result of a lowered watertable,

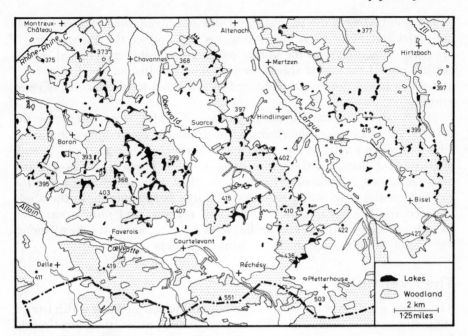

FIG. 12.2 The Sundgau of southern Alsace
Heights on the map are given in metres.

Based on *Carte de France au 50 000ᵉ*, sheets XXXVI/21, 22; XXXVII/21, 22.

others contain temporary streams which run down the valleys after heavy rain, to lose themselves in the gravel sheets where they open out into the more level plain. Small patches of good loam soils have developed on a sporadic cover of loess.

The western Sundgau is characterised by more than 200 lakes with an aggregate area of only about 4 sq km (1·5 sq miles) (Fig. 12.2). They occur in the flat valley bottoms, strung out in lines along depressions in the irregular gravel cover, their floors underlain by impermeable clays. Some are maintained artificially by dams.

## The Ill and Rhine floodplains

A distinct step (of 6 m (20 ft) or so) at the eastern edge of the river terraces marks the descent to the floodplains of the Ill and the Rhine. Especially in the south these floodplains are almost horizontal from west to east, but have a distinct northward slope. As a result the Ill, which rises on the flanks of the Jura, flows northwards for some 130 km (80 miles) almost parallel to the Rhine, until the easterly slope of the plain becomes rather more marked, causing the tributary to converge upon the Rhine and finally to join it 15 km (10 miles) north of Strasbourg.

The floodplains of the Ill and the Rhine were composed of gravel sheets deposited by the swollen rivers towards the end of the Pleistocene. A lowering of base level to the north (see p. 22) resulted in renewed down-cutting into these gravel sheets, and so now the Ill and the Rhine each occupies a broad floodplain separated by a distinct terrace formed of these gravels.

The floodplain of the Ill, 5 km (3 miles) in width, is intersected by the braided watercourses of the river and its gradually converging tributaries. This floodplain was formerly covered with swamp, interspersed with islands of gravel and clumps of trees, known as the *Ried*. Much of this *Ill-Ried* has been reclaimed, as evidenced by the network of drainage channels and the carefully maintained water meadows, though parts, notably in the angle between the Scheer and the Ill, are still marshy, and most areas even though protected with dykes are liable to flooding in winter. Settlements are notably absent, even in the reclaimed districts.

## The river Rhine

The Rhine winds over the floor of a floodplain which varies in width from a kilometre or so just below Basel to nearly 5 km (3 miles) near Strasbourg. Its current is swift, for between Basel and Strasbourg there is a fall in alti-tude of some 100 m (330 ft); during times of high water, particularly in early summer, the river swirls powerfully downstream. Much of this Rhine water comes from its Alpine headstreams, and the river carries an enormous amount of gravel, sand and silt. Much of this is deposited on the floor of the floodplain, largely as a result of the sudden decrease in gradient and hence in the speed of the current; at the Istein rapids at Kembs in the south the rate of flow is about 20 kmph (11 knots), but the average rate between Basel and Strasbourg is only 10–11 kmph (5–6 knots).[2]

Before extensive works of regularisation were carried out in the nine-teenth century (discussed below), the Rhine meandered over its floodplain among an ever-changing series of braided channels and gravel islets, and the floodwaters extended over an area several times as wide as at the pre-sent. The main river is now contained between reinforced banks, usually cutting across meanders to provide a more direct channel. But on either side of this channel remain part-silted backwaters, cutoffs and minor channels, where patches of alder, willow and poplar alternate with reed swamps. This area is known as the *Rheinwald* or the *Rhein-Ried*. Parts have been reclaimed to form tolerable summer pasture, particularly where the old gravels are overlain with sand and mud. But much of this *Ried* still remains unreclaimed, for the gravel sheets are too unrewarding to merit the effort involved. Sometimes the lower layers of the gravel banks have compacted into intractable conglomerates, which dry out into a concrete-like mass. Even in the main regularised channel, new gravel banks still form and change their positions during flood times.

The volume of Rhine water is exceedingly variable. The following graphic figures have been quoted[3] for three points within the rift-valley section:

*(Cu m per second)*

|  | LOW WATER | AVERAGE FLOW | HIGH WATER |
|---|---|---|---|
| Basel | 330 | 865 | 4 624 |
| Kehl | 380 | 956 | 4 685 |
| Lauterbourg | 465 | 1 106 | 5 010 |

During much of winter, the Alsatian Rhine experiences low water because of the freezing of its Alpine headstreams, and a further period of low water occurs in late summer, with a maximum in late May or early June. Floods may take place at any time, but they are most pronounced in early summer and can still be dangerous should there be a sudden and concentrated thaw. In the spring of 1972, by contrast, the Rhine was at its lowest level for many years, the result of an unusually snow-free winter in its headstream areas. This had serious effects on navigation, and on supplies of water for industrial, agricultural and domestic use, especially in the Netherlands (p. 98).

## Rhine navigation

The navigation of the Rhine is obviously handicapped by these many physical disadvantages. Yet because of its situation, the river has been used for centuries and much effort has been expended in schemes of regularisation. During the nineteenth century, as a result of works begun in 1817, the main river was gradually confined to a straightened dyked channel. This regularisation was completed as far upstream as Mannheim by 1866, and in the decade after 1906 the Mannheim-Basel section was also straightened and embanked. The dyked course between Basel and Mainz is about 80 km (50 miles) shorter than the natural channel, thus resulting in a steeper gradient, and this, combined with the confining of the waters to a narrowed channel, produced a much swifter current and made upstream navigation extremely difficult. In addition, the development of railways along the Rhine valley, linking Basel directly with the lower Rhineland and the North Sea ports, caused navigation above Mannheim virtually to cease until the twentieth century. From 1907 to 1914, however, further regularisation was carried out in the section between Mannheim and Strasbourg, and more improvements in the Alsatian section took place in the interwar years, notably in the Istein section below Basel. Developments by the French authorities involved the improvement of the river port of Strasbourg, and the construction of the initial section of the *Grand Canal d'Alsace*.

In 1928, moreover, the Swiss began a considerable development and extension of the riverport of Basel.

The result of these developments is that at the present time an effective minimum depth of about 2·5 m (8 ft) is maintained as far upstream as Strasbourg-Kehl, unless an exceptional period of low water should occur. Between Kehl and Basel the river is negotiable by barges of from 1 000 to 1 500 tons towed by powerful tugs and with expert pilotage, but this is normally only for about ninety days in the year between the beginning of June and the end of August.

### The Grand Canal d'Alsace

Since Alsace returned to France after the war of 1914–18, that country has been very interested in a left-bank lateral canal, with the dual function of overcoming the navigational difficulties of the Rhine and of utilising its hydroelectricity potential. In 1919 the state-sponsored Société des Forces Motrices du Rhin was formed, which produced an ambitious multi-purpose project involving a lateral canal of seven sections. One of the clauses in the Treaty of Versailles empowered France to divert water from the Rhine, providing that navigational facilities were not thereby impaired. France was in the strong position of having five members on the postwar Rhine Commission compared with Germany's four, and despite protests by Germany and also by Switzerland she decided to go ahead.[4]

The first stage was designed to overcome a serious obstacle on the river near Kembs below Basel, the transverse Istein Bar of resistant Jurassic limestone. The concentration of the current in a more direct channel had caused serious erosion below the bar, forming rapids extremely difficult of negotiation and impassable for much of the year. The French first constructed the Kembs barrage, completed in 1927, designed to raise the level of the main river and so provide water for a new lateral canal, as well as for the Huningue Branch Canal which links, with the aid of five locks, the riverport of Basel with the Rhône-Rhine Canal to the northwest (Fig. 12.5). The next stage was to cut a Kembs bypass loop of 6 km (4 miles), rejoining the Rhine below the Istein rapids by means of a locked connection. A power station was built at the northern end of this canal to utilise the head between the level of the canal and that of the river. The scheme was completed in 1933, and all traffic to or from Basel then utilised the canal, negotiating the sets of locks at each end; the section of the Rhine thus bypassed was in future neglected for navigation.

No further progress took place before the war of 1939–45, but in 1950 the French Government authorised the nationalised company of *Electricité de France* to go ahead with a second stage. The canal was extended between Kembs and Ottmarsheim; traffic then passed through the Kembs locks along both new sections, and so by a further set of locks to rejoin the Rhine, where a second power station was built. This stage was completed in 1952. The third section between Ottmarsheim and Fessenheim was then com-

PLATE 35. The Rhinau power-station, with navigation locks, on a short loop-canal from the Rhine, completed in 1964

menced, and the Fessenheim station was completed in 1956, followed by Vogelgrun in 1959. The whole position was, however, altered in June 1956, when agreement was reached in Luxembourg between West Germany and France concerning the future of the Saar (see p. 273), in which one of the terms involved the *Grand Canal d'Alsace*. The French Government agreed not to proceed with this canal beyond Vogelgrun. Below that point the Rhine itself is being jointly improved for navigation by France and West Germany, while four more stations have been constructed on derivation stops along the left bank: Marckolsheim (1960), Rhinau (1964), Gerstheim (1970) and south of Strasbourg (1970).

These Rhine power stations now afford a considerable contribution of electricity to the French grid. In 1969 the six in operation produced between them 5 980 gWh.

The importance of the postwar contribution of electricity to the French energy requirements is shown by these figures:

*Production of electricity in France ( 1 000 gWh)*

|  | 1938 | 1944 | 1949 | 1954 | 1958 | 1965 | 1969 | 1970 |
|---|---|---|---|---|---|---|---|---|
| Hydro | 10 | 10 | 11 | 24 | 32 | 44 | 53 | 56 |
| Thermal | 9 | 7 | 19 | 21 | 29 | 45 | 75 | 84 |

Source: *Direction de l'Electricité, Ministère de l'Industrie et du Commerce*, published in various volumes of *Annuaire statistique de la France*.

In 1969 the Grand Canal d'Alsace transported 2 100 million ton-km of freight; this is likely to increase appreciably when the Grand Canal du Rhin au Rhône (p. 311) is completed. The old Rhône-Rhine Canal north of Mulhouse is now disused, since traffic from the southwest joins the Grand Canal, hence the Rhine, via the Huningue Branch Canal.

## Land use and agriculture

### Climate

Climatically the plain of Alsace is well favoured for agriculture, at any rate compared with Lorraine to the west. The mean annual rainfall varies from 480 mm (19 in) at Colmar, which is very much in the rain shadow of the Vosges, to Strasbourg with 660 mm (26 in). The continental influences in this eastern part of France are manifested in a marked summer maximum of precipitation, July usually being the wettest month. The summers are warm, the mean monthly temperature at Strasbourg being 18°C (65°F), and sunshine hours are long. Strasbourg has in fact recorded a maximum temperature of 39°C (102°F), while the tendency to continentality is also indicated by a record minimum of −27°C (−16°F) and by the fact that the mean January temperature is −1°C (31°F). In severe winters the Rhine may freeze, as in 1952, and a navigable channel may be difficult to maintain even with ice-breakers. As many as eighty days with frost may be experienced.

The Vosges do, however, provide a surprising degree of shelter (see p. 516); spring comes appreciably earlier than in Lorraine, and the southeasterly aspect is of great importance to such crops as the vine. The fact that grapes and tobacco flourish, and that even peaches, apricots and almonds grow in favoured localities, is evidence of the pleasant summer climate.

### Agriculture[5]

The main agricultural variations in the gently sloping Alsatian plain are largely the result of differences in soil types—whether the soils are developed on *loess*, on recent alluvium, or on diluvial sands and gravels. The first tend to be under arable cultivation, the second under permanent pasture, the third under woodland, scrub forest or marsh.

The warm well-drained loess soils form an 'apron' over the lower slopes of the foothills and extend in places into the plain itself. To the south of Sélestat, in Haut-Rhin, the loess cover is uneven and patchy, but in Bas-Rhin it is quite extensive. To the north of Strasbourg these fertile loam soils occupy most of the Saverne 'embayment', which forms a broad re-entrant into the Vosges (see p. 520 and Fig. 19.2). From this, three 'promontories' of similar soils extend eastward, almost to the edge of the Rhine floodplain, between the 'sand deltas' of the Zorn, Moder, Sauer and Lauter (Fig. 21.1).

These undulating plains form a very fertile part of Alsace. The most prosperous district is that which lies to the northwest of Strasbourg, crossed by the main road and railway running westward to Nancy and by the old Marne-Rhine Canal; this district is known as the *Kochersberg*, after a prominent hill on which stood a castle built by the bishops of Strasbourg. Holdings have been subdivided through generations of *parcellement* and *morcellement*; indeed, in some cantons the average unit is a mere 700 sq m (840 sq yd) and cultivation is on an intensive garden scale. In recent years, however, *remembrement* has made some progress, enabling the extension of mechanisation, but much remains to be done; it is estimated that little more than a third of the available land has been consolidated.

Wheat, hybrid maize, barley (for brewing), sugar beet, tobacco, potatoes and oats (for fodder) are grown wherever these loamy soils occur. Dairying is widespread; in 1968 there were 186 000 dairy cattle in Bas-Rhin and 102 000 in Haut-Rhin. Large numbers are grazed in summer on the *Ried* pastures and stall-fed in the winter on locally grown trefoil, lucerne and fodder beet.

Hops are widely grown, usually on a small family holding; indeed, this is one of the world's chief producing areas, supplying the many Rhineland breweries in both France and West Germany. To the south of Strasbourg numerous orchards of apples, plums, cherries and even peaches and apricots flourish on the south-facing slopes covered with calcareous downwash; this fruit cultivation is a tribute to the long hours of summer sunshine and to a freedom from spring frosts on the slopes. The vineyards on the slopes of the foothills and in the valley re-entrants are described on p. 518, as they belong to the Vosges rather than to the plain; the vine-growing area is officially described as the *Zone sous-vosgienne du Vignoble*.

The reclaimed alluvium of the *Ried* of the Ill plain is mostly under permanent pasture, but in places there are market gardens, growing peas, potatoes, carrots and asparagus both for the urban markets and for the canning industry. In the northern part of the Rhine *Ried* tobacco and hops are grown on smallholdings cultivated by families.

## Woodland

Much of the Alsatian plain, especially in the south, is not reclaimed, and consists either of marshes along the Rhine floodplain and to a less extent along that of the Ill, or of forest on the loess-free gravels and coarse sands. In the Sundgau about a quarter of the surface is wooded (Fig. 12.2). In the south of the Rhine plain itself the forest of the Harth extends over the gravel-flats from northwest of Basel for nearly 30 km (20 miles) as far as Ensisheim. This is a poor scrub forest, of little value except for cutting vine- and hop-poles from the stunted oak coppice. Further to the west between the rivers Doller and Thur is the Forêt de Nonnenbruch (Fig. 12.3), an even poorer area of scrub woodland. Some smaller woodlands are found in Middle

Alsace, and on the sandy areas in Lower Alsace to the north of Strasbourg—the Forêt de Vendenheim in the Zorn valley, the extensive Haguenau forest which covers the 'sand-delta', seamed with distributaries, of the Moder and the Sauer (Fig. 12.1), and the Bien Wald in the lower Lauter valley, although most of this lies across the frontier in West Germany. These sandy areas have been carefully planted with pines, and provide timber of much better quality than does the scrub forest on the gravel sheets south of Strasbourg.

Some indication of the land use distributions which have been described is given by the statistics of the Alsatian *départements* of Haut-Rhin and Bas-Rhin. Admittedly the former includes the eastern flanks of the High Vosges and the latter a part of the Low Vosges, but they do provide some indication of the order of magnitude involved.

*Land use, 1968 (percentage of total area)*

|  | PASTURE | WOODLAND | ARABLE LAND |
|---|---|---|---|
| Bas-Rhin | 20 | 35 | 31 |
| Haut-Rhin | 22 | 36 | 30 |

Source: *Ministère de l'Agriculture*, published in the *Annuaire statistique de la France*, 1970–71.

## Mining and industry

Agriculture represents only one aspect of the economy of Alsace, for this is a considerable industrial region. Deposits of minerals include potash in the south and petroleum in the north, though production of the latter has now ceased (Fig. 11.11).

### Potash

In 1904, when this territory was in German hands, borings were sunk to the north of Mulhouse in quest of mineral oil. Deposits of potash in the form of *sylvite* (*KCl*) were discovered in the Oligocene strata, deposited when the rift valley was a gulf of the sea in early Tertiary times. One stratum of potash, about 1·2 m (4 ft) thick, lies at 627 m (2 057 ft), another nearly three times as thick is 21 m (70 ft) lower. The extent of the deposits, covering nearly 200 sq km (80 sq miles), was revealed by some hundreds of borings put down through the sandy soils of the Forêt de Nonnenbruch. The deposits contain between 12 and 22 per cent of pure potash, in places as much as 30 per cent, and the estimated reserves are 1 500 million tons, of which half are readily exploitable by present techniques. Before 1918 the great German *Kalisyndikat* was mainly concerned with the exploitation of its own vast deposits between the rivers Weser and Elbe, the chief centre being

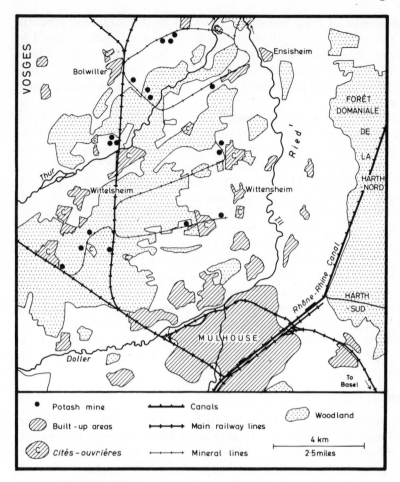

FIG. 12.3 The potash-mining district of southern Alsace
The outlines of the built-up areas and woodlands are generalised. The
large area of woodland northwest of Mulhouse is the Forêt de
Nonnenbruch.

Based on *Carte de France au 50 000ᵉ*, sheet XXXVII/20, with additional information.

Stassfurt; this was the only major potash resource worked in the world at
that time and the monopoly was jealously guarded. The Nonnenbruch
deposits were therefore exploited only slowly and the annual output was
deliberately limited to a mere 4 per cent of the German total, or about
50 000 tons of pure potash. As a result, until after the war of 1914–18
relatively little development took place. With the reacquisition of Alsace by
France the Stassfurt monopoly was broken, and within three years the
Alsatian output had trebled as compared with prewar figures. Several
companies are now operating the field, one of which (the Mines Domaniales
de Potasse d'Alsace) was acquired by the French state in 1924. Seven

303

individual groups of deep mines are situated in the angle between the Doller in the south and the Ill in the west (Fig. 12.3); each is served by mineral lines, branching from the main Strasbourg-Mulhouse railway, and a number of pleasant *cités-ouvrières* house the 10 000 workers. These mines and housing estates are dispersed among the woodlands of the Forêt de Nonnenbruch.

Development after 1919 proceeded apace, and by 1926 competition with German potash necessitated an agreement between the two countries concerning the amount which might be put on the world market, although several other countries (notably the USA and the USSR) were also increasing their output. This agreement was actually soon scrapped. By 1937 France was producing annually just over three million tons of crude potash, or 16 per cent of the world total, compared with Germany's 63 per cent and the USA's 9 per cent. After the end of the war of 1939–45, the enormous demand for fertilisers resulted in a considerable increase of output; in 1970 France produced 1·9 million tons (potash content), nearly four times her highest prewar output, of which 40 per cent was exported; this represents 10 per cent of the world output. Several processing factories have been built near the groups of mines. Much of this potash, crude and refined, is shipped from Strasbourg by barge down the Rhine to Antwerp, hence to the Benelux countries (her main customers), Great Britain and even the USA.

## Petroleum

Petroleum occurs on a small scale in northern Alsace. Oil seepages were known and utilised in this district as early as the fifteenth century, especially near the village of Pechelbronn (which means 'pitch spring'), and from 1735 small patches of oil sands occurring near the surface were worked. As late as 1888 these sands were mined by a German company by means of shafts and the oil extracted from the sands. In 1881 the first borings were sunk, and oil was pumped from depths between 200 and 900 m (650 and 3 000 ft). Until recently a series of oil wells operated along a line parallel to the Rhine. Further research and prospecting was carried out and a little oil was found elsewhere. The Alsatian output of oil was, however, only small. In 1969 the Pechelbronn and the Staffelfelden fields produced only 13 000 tons out of a French total of 2·5 million. This was but a small contribution to the 105 million tons through-put of French refineries, and in 1969 the field ceased production altogether.

## Industry

The most important aspect of industry is the manufacture of textiles, which began in medieval times on a domestic scale in the foothills of the Vosges, where it still continues (see p. 519). The introduction of steam power during the Industrial Revolution resulted in a certain degree of concentration in Mulhouse, Colmar and Belfort, and two-thirds of the operatives in this eastern textile region now live in and around these three towns. Although the emphasis is on the production of cotton cloth, a wide range of other textile products is made—sewing-thread, printed calico, woollens, silk and rayon.

As in many other centres, in recent years there has been an appreciable decline in the cotton textile industry. New activities have therefore been stimulated, including electrical and electronic engineering, general metallurgy, the manufacture of plastics and chemicals, the production of aluminium etc. Apart from the main cities, much activity has developed at new industrial estates near the Rhine power stations, as at Ottmarsheim and Neuf-Brisach.

## Population and settlement

The distribution of population and settlement shows some interesting features. Several areas are virtually uninhabited, notably the higher parts of the Sundgau among the lakes and woodlands, the *Ried* along the floor of the Rhine floodplain, the gravel sheets on the higher terrace plains, and the forested sandy 'deltas' of Lower Alsace. The aridity of the higher gravels and the waterlogged character of the lower gravels are alike inimical to anything but poor forest growth.

The loess-areas on the terraces are occupied by a quite dense agricultural population, spread out in a close pattern of prosperous villages and individual small holdings. This is particularly noticeable in the Kochersberg district to the northwest and west of Strasbourg. To the south of Strasbourg the pattern of settlement takes on a linear character, reflecting the parallel belts of land use. One string of villages lies on the higher ground between the respective *Ried* districts of the Rhine and the Ill, another follows the old Rhône-Rhine Canal, and a third is situated along the main-line railway between Strasbourg and Basel following the edge of the terrace to the west of the Ill. A further series of towns lies at the zone of contact between the Vosges and the Alsatian plains, where each upland valley opens on to the high terrace; many have textile industries, long-established because of water power, or are centres of wine production (see p. 518) and agricultural market towns. A few of these places, specially favoured as route centres, have developed a considerable urban life.

Mulhouse (116 000 people in 1968) is the commercial and industrial, although not the administrative, capital of Haut-Rhin and of southern Alsace. It stands on the northern edge of the Sundgau at an altitude of about 240 m (800 ft), overlooking the upper Ill valley. It has a basin, equipped with wharves and railway sidings, opening into the Rhône-Rhine Canal, now linked by the Huningue Branch to the Rhine system. As a railway route focus it has considerable importance, for the main line

305

following the left bank of the Rhine from Basel to Strasbourg passes through the town, from it a line proceeds westward through the Belfort gap to Besançon and Lyons, and another runs northeastward across the Rhine to Freiburg and West Germany. Mulhouse was only a small town of 5 000 people at the beginning of the nineteenth century; it had been an autonomous city in alliance with the Swiss Confederation until it became French in 1797. The industrial developments of the nineteenth century caused a rapid growth. Some pioneer efforts here in the housing of workers sought to cope with the increase of the industrial population in the mid-nineteenth century. In 1853 the mayor of the town, with the cooperation of the Société Industrielle de Mulhouse, inaugurated the Société des Cités-Ouvrières to build residential blocks in the northwest of the town near the Ill–Doller confluence. The society built about a thousand houses (together with schools, bath houses and other amenities) for sale to workers by means of long-term mortgage schemes. This district, known as the *Arbeiterstadt* during the periods of German sovereignty, represented a remarkable social achievement for the mid-nineteenth century.

The industrial life of presentday Mulhouse is varied, although there is still an emphasis on textiles—cotton cloth, sewing-thread, calico, linen, silk and nylon, together with ancillary industries such as printing, dyeing and finishing, and hosiery. The potash deposits to the north of the town have resulted in chemical industries, notably the production of refined potassium salts, dye-stuffs and explosives. Some of these factories lie outside Mulhouse along the main road between the town and Ensisheim. The several engineering concerns include a branch of the Société Alsacienne de Constructions Mécaniques (which has its main works near Strasbourg), manufacturing locomotives and rolling-stock, textile machinery and a Peugeot car assembly plant.

Colmar is the *chef-lieu* of Haut-Rhin, standing on the Lauch a few kilometres above its confluence with the Ill. The narrow irregular streets of the old Alsatian town, with its interesting timbered houses with fanciful façades, contrast remarkably with the unattractive industrial and residential suburbs. One feels, indeed, that this town has much of a German atmosphere, despite its undoubtedly strong pro-French sentiments. A German dialect is widely spoken, and place names and family names are mostly in the German forms. It is an important textile centre, with some factories in the town itself, particularly dyeing and finishing works, and many more along the Fecht and Logelbach valleys.

## Strasbourg

The dominance of Strasbourg in Alsace is indicated by the fact that the population of the city in 1968 was 249 000, which with its three contiguous communes of Bischheim, Hoenheim and Schiltigheim made up the official agglomération of about 335 000, or two-fifths of the total of Bas-Rhin.

The city now possesses the status of a '*métropole d'équilibre*' (p. 199), with many functions: a centre of commercial and industrial activity, a focus of road, rail and river communications, the headquarters of the Alsace planning region, the seat of the Council of Europe, a great Rhineland city near the frontier of West Germany. It stands at an altitude of between 140 and 150 m (450 and 500 ft), the inner part enclosed by the divided channel of the Ill, and situated about 3 km (2 miles) from the Rhine on the terrace above the flood-plain (Fig. 12.4).

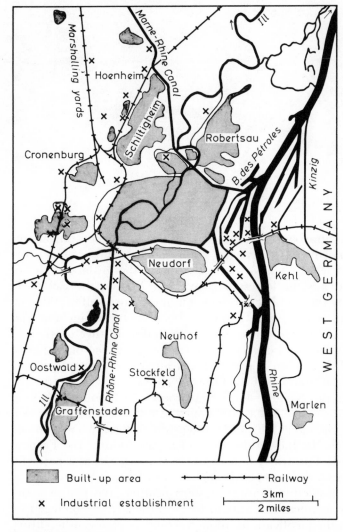

FIG. 12.4. Strasbourg

Based on (*a*) Plate 56, *Atlas de France* (1936); (*b*) W. Seghers, *Kaart der Binnen-scheepvaartwegen van N.-W. Europa* (n.d.); and (*c*) additional information derived from local town plans, etc.

PLATE 36. The Rhine and the port of Strasbourg

The location of Strasbourg is one of fundamental geographical importance. To the northwest, where the High and Low Vosges meet, the edge of the upland leans back to the west to form the lowland 'bay' of Saverne. Beyond this is the lowest pass over the Vosges, the Col de la Saverne, reached by the deeply cut re-entrant of the Zorn valley (Plate 56 and Fig. 19.2); this is the main 'gateway' between the Rhineland and Lorraine. Beyond the Rhine, some 65 km (40 miles) further north, is a similar gap, the Kraichgau, between the northern end of the Black Forest and the Odenwald. Here then is a transverse routeway crossing the Rhine valley (it is significant that one of the Orient Express routes between Paris and Istanbul used the Saverne-Kraichgau gaps). Strasbourg has long dominated these crossroads. It has functioned as a Gallic settlement, as a Roman military camp and as a Frankish town, and its history has been one of many vicissitudes, the inevitable result of its situation in the Franco-German marchlands. For nearly four centuries it prospered as a powerful imperial city until its annexation by France in 1681; then it became one of the fortress towns protecting France's eastern frontier, and like so many others was strongly fortified by Vauban. In 1870 the city was besieged by the German army; the fortifications, though strong by eighteenth-century standards, could not withstand a sustained bombardment which destroyed the citadel and other defensive works, and the city surrendered after six weeks' valiant resistance. During its German sovereignty, between 1871

308

and 1918, it was still more heavily fortified by concentric defensive works. It was returned to France in 1919. In 1939 many of its citizens were evacuated and it stood during the winter of 1939–40 as a silent outpost of France beyond the Maginot Line. A large part of the city was damaged before its surrender in the summer of 1940, but it was liberated in 1944. The German port of Kehl, on the opposite side of the Rhine, was captured and occupied by the French in 1944, and many of the returning inhabitants of Strasbourg were rehoused there until the destroyed portions of the French city were rebuilt. The riverport of Kehl was put under joint French and West German administration in July 1952, but in April 1953 it was returned wholly to West Germany.

The heart of Strasbourg lies on an island within the main branches of the Ill, dominated by the magnificent red sandstone Gothic cathedral whose spire rises to a height of 141 m (464 ft). Beyond the island, with the narrow streets and picturesque houses with carved gables, the suburbs of Strasbourg now spread for several kilometres. In the north are the industrial suburbs of Robertsau and Schiltigheim, and to the southwest is Graffenstaden, in each of which a wide variety of engineering industries has developed; others have grown up around the port district. Other activities include several chemical works (producing fertilisers, drugs, soap and perfumes), nylon-textile factories, and works which manufacture a variety of electrical equipment including refrigerators, radio and television sets. As a result of Strasbourg's position on the Alsatian plain it has many food-processing industries—the canning of fruit and vegetables, the production of the famous *pâté de foie gras Strasbourgeois*, tobacco processing, chocolate-making, brewing and distilling. Tanning, paper-making and printing have been carried on for centuries; Gutenberg made his first experiment in printing in Strasbourg in the year 1436, and the celebrated Johann Mentel established himself as a master printer in the city in 1458 only a few years after Gutenberg's Bible was published at Mainz. In recent years the emphasis has changed towards industries associated with advanced technology: electrical and electronic engineering, plastics, light metallurgy and petrochemicals.

Two large oil refineries, with petrochemical plants, in the suburbs of Strasbourg, at Reichstett and Herrlisheim, were completed in 1963. They are linked by the South European Pipeline with Lavéra and by a new pipeline (1971) with Fos on the Mediterranean (see p. 414). In 1969 these refineries had an output of 3·2 and 4·2 million tons respectively.

Strasbourg is an inland port of considerable importance (Plate 35).[6] It has been a small riverport for centuries, but the construction of the Rhône-Rhine Canal in 1832 and of the Marne-Rhine Canal in 1842 made it the chief canal-port in eastern France (Fig. 12.5). The first of these has a length of just over 320 km (200 miles), and links Strasbourg with the Saône at St Symphorien by a complex route necessitating no less than 166 locks. It is not a large waterway, although it was reconstructed after 1918 to accommodate 300 ton barges. A major project is in progress (with a com-

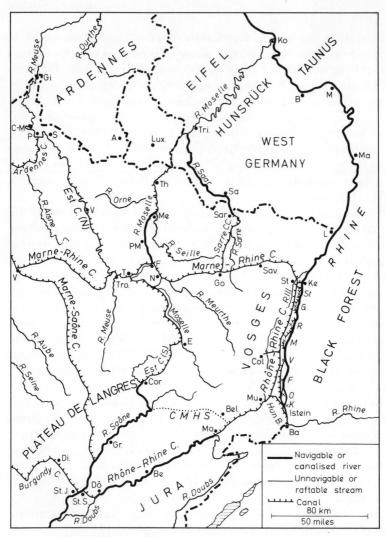

Fig. 12.5. The waterways of Eastern France

Towns are indicated by abbreviations, as follows: **A,** Arlon; **B,** Bingen;
**Ba,** Basel; **Be,** Besançon; **Bel,** Belfort; **C-M,** Charleville-Mézières;
**Col,** Colmar; **Cor,** Corre; **Di,** Dijon; **Do,** Dole; **E,** Epinal; **F,** Frouard;
**Gi,** Givet; **Go,** Gondrexange; **Gr,** Gray; **K,** Kembs; **Ke,** Kehl; **Ko,**
Koblenz; **L,** Lauterbourg; **Lux,** Luxembourg; **M,** Mainz; **Ma,**
Mannheim; **Me,** Metz; **Mo,** Montbéliard; **Mu,** Mulhouse; **N,** Nancy;
**O,** Ottmarsheim; **P,** Pont-à-Bar; **PM,** Pont-à-Mousson; **S,** Sedan; **Sa,**
Saarbrücken; **Sar,** Sarreguemines; **Sav,** Saverne; **St,** Strasbourg; **St J,**
St Jean-de-Losne; **StS,** St Symphorien; **T,** Toul; **Th,** Thionville; **Tri,**
Trier; **Tro,** Troussey; **V,** (Est Canal) Verdun; **V,** (Marne-Saône C.)
Vitry-le-François; **HunB,** Huningue Branch; **CMHS,** Canal de
Montbéliard à la Haute-Saône (projected).
The eight Rhine power stations are indicated.

Based on W. Seghers, *Kaart der Binnenscheepvaartwegen van N.-W. Europa* (Antwerp, n.d.).

pletion date of 1975) to turn the southern section of the Rhône-Rhine Canal into a modern waterway, forming a link between the North and Mediterranean Seas. The section of the old canal north of Mulhouse is now virtually disused, since traffic uses the *Grand Canal d'Alsace* (pp. 298–300) and the Rhine. An enlarged canal is under construction across the watershed through the Belfort gap, with a new Port de Bourgogne, near Belfort. The thirteen locks of this section of the old waterway will be replaced by a shiplift. The new waterway will be called the *Grand Canal du Rhin au Rhône*.[7]

The Marne-Rhine Canal, 317 km (197 miles) in length, runs westward from Strasbourg through the industrial districts of southern Lorraine and joins the Marne-Saône and Marne Lateral canals at Vitry-le-François. It was difficult to construct, since it has to negotiate first the northern part of the Vosges through the Saverne Gap (Fig. 19.2) and then in succession the Jurassic escarpments. This necessitated 178 locks, of which fifty-two are used between Strasbourg and the Vosges watershed, which it pierces in two tunnels. Maintenance of navigation is not easy, for the water supply is sometimes inadequate, and some sections supplied from torrential streams are liable as a result to silting. Nevertheless, this waterway links Strasbourg with Lorraine, and as a result conveys between 1 and 2 million tons annually.

As a Rhine port Strasbourg has developed only in this century. The improvement of river navigation before 1914 primarily benefited Mannheim, and while Alsace was still part of Germany constant demands came from the citizens of Strasbourg for further improvements upstream to their city. A port area has developed east and north of the town, facing Kehl across the river (Fig. 12.4). These developments have gone on since the *Bassin du Commerce* was opened in 1892; two link canals were built directly from the Rhine into the canal-port and several new basins have been constructed, including the *Bassin aux Pétroles* to the north of the port. The *Nouveau Port* to the south has been developed.

In 1969 the port of Strasbourg handled 13·2 million tons of freight, of which about 10 million moved along the Rhine, the remainder via the two canals. The city imports coal, cereals and timber by water, and exports potash from the Nonnenbruch mines (much of which goes directly by water to the fertiliser factories and chemical works of Antwerp), oil, chemical products and building materials. Though Strasbourg remains the second French inland waterway port, by reason of its industrial developments, it has suffered some relative decline, the result of the competition of the canalised Moselle (p. 262), the development of new ports at Colmar-Neuf-Brisach and at Mulhouse-Ottmarsheim, the construction of the South European Pipeline (p. 414), and the growth of Basle resulting from improvements in the Rhine navigation and the Grand Canal d'Alsace. The Strasbourg–Basle motorway is under construction. One important new function is as an inland container port, taking advantage of its central position in western Europe. For example, a weekly service to and from London was opened in 1971, also serving other Rhineland cities and Lorraine.

[1] Two sound, well illustrated accounts are E. Juillard, *L'Alsace: le sol, les hommes et la vie régionale* (1963); and A. Blanc, E. Juillard, J. Ray and M. Rochefort, *Les Régions de l'Est* (1960), in the series *France de Demain*.

[2] A. Demangeon and L. Febvre, *Le Rhin* (1935), p. 158.

[3] A Demangeon and L. Febvre, *op. cit.* (1935), p. 155.

[4] J. Ritter, 'L'Aménagement du Rhin français', *Annls Géogr.*, **62** (1953), pp. 365–8, gives an account of the installations at Ottmarsheim; see also J. Labadié, 'La Grand Canal d'Alsace', *Géographia*, **27** (1953), pp. 28–31; this includes a useful map.

[5] E. Juillard, *La Vie rurale dans la plaine de Basse-Alsace: essai de géographie* (1953).

[6] H. Nonn, 'Les Efforts de conversion du port autonome de Strasbourg devant les réalisations récentes de l'aménagement du territoire', *Rev. Géog. de l'Est*, **6** (1966), p. 351.

[7] R. Pilkington, 'Joining the Rhône and the Rhine', *Geog. Mag.*, **39** (1966), p. 214.

# 13
# The Basin of Aquitaine

The Basin of Aquitaine[1] forms a roughly triangular lowland occupying about one-seventh of the area of France. For long periods of geological time it was affected by extensive marine transgressions and the deposition that took place has contributed appreciably to the present surface features. The Jurassic sea extended over the basin and indeed over what is now the Central Massif, and so Jurassic limestones form a continuous outcrop from the Biscayan coast of southern Vendée as far south as the valley of the Aveyron. The Cretaceous sea, though less widespread, also covered the whole basin and was indeed continuous with the transgression over the Paris Basin by way of the straits now indicated by the 'Gate of Poitou' and with Languedoc by the 'Gap of Naurouze'. The Upper Cretaceous limestones now appear widely in the north and northeast and also again in the south along the Pyrenean flanks (Fig. 23.1), in each area dipping gently inwards under the Tertiary rocks. They are more sandy than the rocks of corresponding age in the Paris Basin, a result of the shallower waters in which they were deposited.

These Jurassic and Cretaceous rocks in the northeast are diversified by a number of minor folds running more or less from northwest to southeast, an apparent resurrection of Armorican trends as a result of the mid-Tertiary Alpine orogeny. The strata are also slightly inclined towards the west, the result of the *en masse* tilting of the Central Massif.

The still more reduced Eocene and Oligocene seas occupied most of the gulf between the edge of the Central Massif and the slowly uprising folds of the Pyrenees. Accordingly, extensive deposits of older Tertiary (particularly Oligocene) rocks form the surface cover over the northern part of the basin between the Garonne and the edge of the Cretaceous outcrop. They are also represented in the Gap of Naurouze, indicating the maintenance at that time of the marine link between Aquitaine and Languedoc. Unlike the Paris Basin, where these Upper Tertiary rocks mainly consist of limestones laid down in deep clear water, the seas in Aquitaine were shallow and the predominant deposits consist mainly of sands and clays, although frequently of a calcareous nature.

In mid-Tertiary times the Naurouze Gap was closed through a slight uplift, and the margins of the sea withdrew to what is now the south-western part of the Aquitaine basin. Great thicknesses of Miocene deposits worn from the uprising Pyrenees, forming a soft calcareous sandstone known as *molasse*, together with shelly sands, were laid down to the south of the Garonne. Occasional beds of limestone are intercalated among the *molasse*. In Pliocene times occurred the last stages in the infilling of this 'gulf of Aquitaine', the deposition of a fan of pebbles and coarse sand along the northern flanks of the Pyrenees, derived from their continued wastage.

Further diversification of a superficial character has subsequently occurred. The Quaternary Pyrenean glaciers, while not so extensive as those of the Alps, were responsible for the deposition of glacial drift over the northern foreland. More effective has been the continued work of the series of rivers flowing into the basin both from the Central Massif and from the Pyrenees, and (with the exception of the Charente in the extreme north and the Adour in the southwest) focusing on the Gironde estuary. On leaving the upland courses where erosion is still trenchant, their work has been primarily depositive and vast loads of alluvium have been laid down over the floodplains. The swollen rivers of the Pleistocene period did, however, cut down into the underlying rocks, thus forming broad valleys bordered with distinct terraces and separated by gentle interfluves. The rim of limestone plateaus in the northeast has been especially deeply trenched. The multitude of streams with their fluctuating regimes still modify the landscape. During the floods of winter and spring much erosion of the valleys takes place; vast loads of material are swept down, the coarsest gravels to encumber the floodplains, the finest materials to the Gironde or the Bay of Biscay.

Another contribution to the surface features of Aquitaine was the result of a minor Quaternary transgression of the sea, during which sheets of fine marine sands were laid down in the extreme southwest. These materials are the main source of the Landes, although additional sand has been derived from weathering in the Pyrenees by way of the Garonne and the Adour.

The net result has been the production of an extensive, rather monotonous, lowland of gently undulating hills and valleys, as D. Faucher expresses it, 'ce pays aux lignes molles, aux larges horizons'.[2] Though some low ridges appear in the east and southeast, the prominent concentric cuestas and vales which characterise the Paris Basin are absent.

Climatically this area is one of the most pleasant parts of France. Bordeaux has mean monthly temperature figures of 5°C (41°F) in January and 21°C (69°F) in August, an equability due in large part to the proximity of the ocean. Toulouse, though at a higher altitude and almost halfway between the Atlantic and the Mediterranean, has figures very little different −4°C (40°F) and 20°C (70°F) respectively. Rainfall is distributed throughout the year, and although Mediterranean tendencies are indicated by a July minimum, no month is really dry. Indeed, the basin is so open to the ocean in the west that Mediterranean influences are really slight. The

Naurouze Gap is in fact a climatic as well as a hydrographic divide; the olive is absent from Aquitaine and only appears as far east as Carcassonne. Bordeaux has a mean annual total of 760 mm (30 in), Toulouse of 660 mm (26 in), and both have quite humid autumns and springs. These figures do of course mask considerable variations; long periods of drought may be succeeded by rainfall of considerable intensity with widespread flooding, especially in the Pyrenean foothills and in the bordering low plateaus, where violent summer thunderstorms are experienced. Cases are on record of an annual total at various stations amounting to twice that received during the previous year. The basin is liable to the effects of wind, especially to cold, dry air streams from the Central Massif in spring, and to the *autan* which may blow northwards in the same season from Spain over the crest-line of the Pyrenees, in cause and character very similar to the *föhn*. These winds may have a desiccating effect during the critical spring growing season, particularly on the vine.

The way of life over most of Aquitaine is primarily rural and agricultural. The plains are traditionally the scene of cereal cultivation, and more than half of the arable is still so used; wheat and maize now occupying four-fifths of the cereal area are predominant, the latter being well suited by the damp springs and warm summers. In this century the area of temporary and irrigated grasslands, of fodder crops such as lucerne and red trefoil and of hybrid maize[3] has increased, and so have livestock. There has also been an appreciable increase in the area under sunflowers, colza and sorghum. In the northern part of the basin, in Charente, cooperation in the dairy industry (mainly for the production of butter) has developed more than anywhere in France. Horses, pigs and sheep are bred, many of the last involved in transhumance movements to and from the Pyrenean pastures, and small stock (especially geese and turkeys) are widely reared. The general character of the polyculture is emphasised by the market gardens on the lower valley terraces and by widespread orchards. Vineyards are extensive, and while *vin ordinaire* is produced almost everywhere, the superb wines of the Bordelais and the brandies of Cognac and Armagnac have a wide reputation.

The unit of cultivation tends on the whole to be small, much more so than in the Paris Basin, and rather resembling the pattern of things in the Rhône valley and along the Mediterranean coastlands. A farm is often still worked by a *métayer* or share tenant, with a few cows, poultry, some permanent pasture, an orchard and a vineyard, and a block of arable land under cereals and fodder crops. On the other hand, several large domains still exist, and *métayage* is rapidly decreasing.

Not all the land is under cultivation. The sandy surface of the Landes has little to offer, except on its margins where limited schemes of drainage and improvement have been effected, and it is now mainly under pinewoods. The southern fans of gravels, though often flooded after heavy Pyrenean rains or snowmelt, are for much of the year a scene of bleached aridity, and some of the river floodplains are encumbered with sheets of gravel and braided streams. The higher parts of the sandy or gravelly interfluvial plateaus carry heath and gorse, other areas once wooded with oaks are now fern brakes, and some of the limestones bear a scrub vegetation. The former forests now survive only as fragments, mainly along steep valley sides, though copses of evergreen oak and chestnut survive in the east, beech on the higher ground generally, and cork oak especially along the Garonne valley to the northwest of Toulouse. There are also scattered patches of other varieties of oak, groves of cypresses near villages, lines of poplars along the valleys, and willow thickets bordering the streams.

Aquitaine is one of the less densely populated parts of France, despite its prosperous and well-developed agriculture. Only the *département* of Gironde of the twelve occupying the basin has an average density (94 per sq km in 1968 (243 per sq mile)) exceeding that of France as a whole, and some districts are very scantily populated. Approximately a third of the population is concentrated along the lower Garonne and Dordogne valleys and the Gironde estuary, where Bordeaux and its agglomeration are situated, and the areas of denser population continue inland along the well cultivated valleys with their prosperous towns. The low overall average is mainly due to the absence of any large industrial regions, yet even so the rural population has been declining since the mid-nineteenth century. This is partly the result of a falling birth rate and an ageing population; between the wars deaths appreciably exceeded births in several *départements*, and even in the postwar years when the position has improved somewhat the balance is still precarious. In 1968 there were for example only 4 724 births in Dordogne compared with 5 181 deaths, and in Ariège (which includes part of the Pyrenees) there was likewise an adverse balance (1 663 births, 2 062 deaths). In five more favoured Aquitaine *départements* an overall excess of only about 2·3 per thousand of the population compares unfavourably with 5·7 per thousand for France as a whole. Other general causes of decline have been the attractions of urban life and of better paid employment in industry, and the increase in livestock farming at the expense of arable, which needs less labour. The decline has become so marked that paradoxically an appreciable shortage of agricultural labour has developed, remedied in part by an influx of Spanish and Italian workers. At times agricultural workers have even come from less favoured parts of France itself, such as Savoy, the Central Massif and Brittany.

This rural population lives in dispersed and sometimes widely scattered settlements. Small towns are distributed fairly evenly over the basin, each serving as a market and servicing centre for a particular district. Such are Angoulême and Périgueux in the northeast, Bergerac and Cahors in the east, Agen in the middle Garonne valley, Montauban and Albi in the Tarn lowlands, Tarbes and Pau in the south at the junction of mountain and plain, and Bayonne in the extreme southwest, towns of from 15 000 to 50 000 inhabitants. Most have a long history as bridge- or fortress-points, and have added to their market functions and old-established industries (mostly dealing with local agricultural products) a variety of modern manufactures, based on such factors as hydroelectricity and local natural gas and a deliberate location in the part of France furthest from her eastern frontier. Some discoveries of mineral oil and gas have been made in recent years.

One paradox is the fact that in this predominantly rural part of France are situated two of her six largest agglomerations, Bordeaux and Toulouse. The former had 555 000 people in its agglomeration in 1968; for long a great port, it is also the centre of a manufacturing district and of the Bordelais vineyards, and is indeed the commercial focus of southwestern France. Toulouse is a route centre at the other extremity of the axis of the Garonne valley, of 'la longue avenue garonnaise' (D. Faucher). It is the 'economic capital' of southeastern Aquitaine, a commercial and industrial centre with over 440 000 in the agglomeration.

## Regional divisions

Within the overall unity of these lowlands, with, at any rate to the casual traveller, a uniformity of aspect that seems to verge on the monotonous, it is possible to distinguish a number of *pays* with a certain individuality (Fig. 13.1). The *Garonne valley* itself, from the junction with the Ariège above Toulouse to the Gironde estuary, forms an axis lying diametrically across the lowlands. Between the Gironde and Vendée to the north is the *Charente*, drained by the river of the same name. The limestone margins in the east may be conveniently divided into the low Cretaceous plateaus of *Périgord*, and the Jurassic plateaus of *Quercy* crossed by the Lot. In the southeast are the low Tertiary plateaus of *Albigeois* and *Lauraguais*, leading via the Gap of Naurouze into Languedoc. Then to the southwest of the curve of the middle Garonne is an area of low plateaus covered with sediments and crossed by a fan of rivers, comprising the higher *Lannemezan* and the lower *Armagnac*. In the southwest, occupying the angle between the Pyrenees and the Bay of Biscay, is a region which, largely drained by the river Adour, is known generally as the *Pays de l'Adour*. Finally, to the southwest of the Gironde estuary is the sand region of the *Landes*.

## The Garonne valley

From above Toulouse to the Gironde estuary, the Garonne pursues its course more or less along the axial line of the Basin of Aquitaine. The valley floor lies at only 140 m (450 ft) above sea level near Toulouse, and the gentle descent of the river below this point contrasts with the markedly steep drop down the Pyrenean slopes in its upper course. The heavy winter rainfall and the rapid runoff from the impermeable rocks of the Pyrenean massifs can cause extensive winter flooding, with widespread deposition of gravel

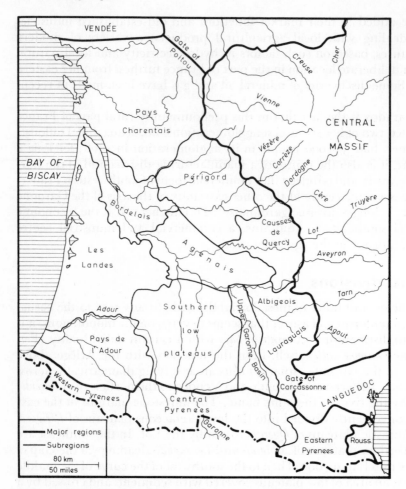

FIG. 13.1. The regional divisions of Aquitaine and the Pyrenees
**Rouss,** Roussillon.

Based on a variety of sources, notably the map *Régions géographiques de la France*; 1 : 1 400 000,
published by the Institut National de la Statistique et des Etudes Economiques.

and alluvium.[4] The record flood at Castets, 53 km (33 miles) above
Bordeaux, occurred in 1770 when the waters rose 13 m (42 ft) above mean
level. Floods still occur, despite measures of regularisation effected since
1830, when systematic efforts were first made to confine the river within a
single dyked channel. As a waterway, therefore, the Garonne is of little
value (see p. 329).

The valley of the Garonne comprises a shallow trench, within which the
river meanders among gravel banks and sheets of fine alluvium. Successive
phases of rejuvenation have caused the river to erode a series of terraces
standing above the present floodplain. Between Toulouse and the Tarn
confluence, for example, the terrace-surfaces are well defined at about

150, 180 and 200 m (500, 600 and 650 ft), and they are traceable downstream, decreasing in altitude, almost to Bordeaux.

The Garonne receives numerous tributaries, and the 'delayed' nature of their junctions, where the confluents flow almost parallel to the main river for some distance, helps to account for the width of the main valley floor. Above Toulouse, near the Ariège confluence, the valley floor is 20 km (12 miles) across between the lowest terrace bluffs. Further downstream below Castelsarrasin, where the Garonne turns westwards, it receives the Tarn (itself joined but a few kilometres higher by the Aveyron); their converging valleys form an extensive area of deposition, sometimes referred to as the *pays montalbanais* from the location of Montauban in the southeast of this lowland. Still further downstream are numerous other right-bank confluents, the largest being the Lot which joins the main river near Aiguillon. Most of the Garonne's left-bank tributaries rise on the higher parts of the Plateau de Lannemezan. These tributaries spread loads of silt over the plain of the Lomagne as they approach their successive confluences with the main river.

Below the Lot confluence the Garonne continues northwestwards through its floodplain, bordered by low Oligocene plateaus on either side; at times the limestone bluffs approach quite closely, as between St Macaire and Langon where they are only 800 m (half-mile) apart. Towards Bordeaux the valley widens again and is floored by marshlands now mostly drained. Twenty-five km (15 miles) below the city the Garonne unites with the Dordogne, at the beaklike tip (the Bec d'Ambès) of the Entre-deux-Mers peninsula.

The Dordogne, after crossing the Périgord plateau of Cretaceous limestone, enters the low Tertiary sandstone country near Bergerac. It too winds over its broad floodplain; its meanders are especially well developed above and below Libourne, where it receives the waters of the Dronne and the Isle from northern Périgord. The northern edge of its valley above the Garonne junction is bordered by a prominent though interrupted escarpment, known as the *Côtes de la Dordogne*. The régime of the Dordogne is extremely variable. In late summer the depth in the main channel below Bergerac may be little more than 0·5 m (1 ft), with bleached shingle banks separating the braided streams. In winter, by contrast, its surging waters may be 2 m (6 ft) or more in depth.

The estuary of the Gironde extends northwestward towards the Bay of Biscay for 80 km (50 miles); at its mouth between the Pointe de la Coubre and the Pointe de Grave it is 10 km (6 miles) in width. The river is bordered on the south by dyked and drained areas of alluvium known appropriately as *Petite Flandre*.[5] Along the north bank, however, cliffs of Upper Cretaceous limestone come right down to the shore. Near Royan at the Pointe de Vallière these horizontally bedded limestones have been worn into steep cliffs fronted by wavecut platforms from which rise rugged stacks.

The Gironde estuary is an immense area of deposition, for not only do the two main rivers contribute a continual aggregation of alluvium, particularly during the floods of autumn and winter, but much silt is brought in from the Bay of Biscay with each flow tide. Constant dredging is necessary to maintain a navigable channel to the port of Bordeaux.[6]

While the region of the Garonne valley possesses a distinct unity, the distance from Toulouse to the sea makes it inevitable that several individual *pays de Garonne* can be distinguished. The upper section is known as the *Garonne toulousaine*, then in turn downstream is the *pays montalbanais* in the neighbourhood of the Tarn junction, succeeded by the *Garonne agenaise*, the middle section of the river, and then above Bordeaux the *Garonne bordelaise*. Finally, the lands bordering the estuary are referred to as *les pays girondins*. The influence of the city makes it convenient and justifiable to describe the last two together as the Bordeaux region.

## The valley of the Garonne Toulousaine

In the Garonne valley, in the neighbourhood of Toulouse, sheets of quartzite pebbles alternate with layers of tough clay overlying the *molasse*. Percolating water has heavily leached these gravels, and in some areas this has caused the formation of an impermeable hardpan. Much of this area, particularly the upper terraces, is wooded.

Despite the not very favourable gravelly soils, agriculture is varied and quite prosperous. Some of the upper gravel terraces are vine-covered, and villages produce wines in considerable quantity, mostly for local consumption. Orchards of peaches, cherries and plums grow around the villages or in lines along the roads. On the broad middle terraces are hedgeless strips of arable cultivation, mainly of maize and wheat. The lowest damp terraces are usually under permanent pasture, often improved by the sowing of grasses and by the use of fertilisers, on which are reared dairy cattle (supplying milk for the urban population of Toulouse), beef cattle, and horses to be sold off in the markets of Toulouse. Sheep from the Pyrenean pastures are grazed during winter and spring. Along the valley terraces to the north and south of Toulouse market gardens cover a considerable area;[7] besides the usual vegetables interesting specialities include the production of gherkins, of which over 230 ha (600 acres) are grown; and, near Lalande, flowers, particularly violets. Tobacco is cultivated on the better soils.

## Toulouse

The *pays toulousain* is of course dominated by Toulouse, which (with its 370 000 people in 1968) is the fourth city of France,[8] though (with 440 000 people) only the sixth agglomeration. Most of the town stands on a low plateau above the right bank of the Garonne, although on the other side of the river have grown the suburbs of St Cyprien and the new Le Mirail planned development which when complete will house 100 000 people.

Toulouse is a striking example of a French city with well developed regional functions, emphasised by its new role as a *métropole d'équilibre* and as centre of the Midi-Pyrénées planning region. The town stands at the western approach to the Gap of Naurouze between the Montagne Noire and the foothills of the Pyrenees, in the corridor between Aquitaine and Languedoc. It is therefore an important road and rail focus; four main lines converge on the town, and the Canal du Midi joins the Garonne Lateral Canal. Toulouse has grown rapidly in the last century, for its population was only 83 000 in 1846. During the years of the war of 1939–45, when it was a refuge in southwest France, its population increased by some 50 000. The town centre is surrounded by a closely settled district of large villages, linked by an intensive autobus service, emphasising its importance as a market and servicing centre for a considerable region; the city has enormous markets and shopping districts, and a large number of apartment complexes.

Toulouse is also an industrial centre. Some of its activities are based on the processing of local agricultural produce, such as grain-milling, leather-tanning, fruit- and vegetable-canning, the making of pickles and tobacco-curing. In 1919 the French Government established a company, the Office National Industriel de l'Azote,[9] which took over the buildings of an explosives factory in order to manufacture a variety of nitrogenous materials from atmospheric nitrogen, with hydrogen obtained variously from coke-oven gas, later from the fractional distillation of mineral oil, and now from the natural gas found at Lacq and St Marcet (see p. 354). The installation, situated on the left bank of the Garonne in the southern outskirts of Toulouse, has expanded enormously; besides ammonia and nitric acid, it produces sulphate of ammonia, ammonium nitrate, nitrochalk and a wide range of other products. Several other factories make explosives and cartridges, some produce agricultural implements and electrical and electronic apparatus. Several branches of the textile industry have long been established, notably the production of ready-made clothing, *lingerie* and millinery. A small aircraft factory was established in Toulouse in 1917. Today France's largest aviation company, l'Aérospatiale (until recently known as Sud-Aviation), has three plants near the city; it makes the *Caravelle* jet liner, is cooperating with the British Aircraft Corporation in the *Concorde*, and makes numerous types of military aircraft. Toulouse, in fact, is described as 'the city of the space age'. The company employs about 11 000. Three other aircraft firms have plants near the city. In all, the commercial and industrial life of the city is varied, well developed and prosperous.[10]

This activity has been helped in recent years by the development of power supplies, and electricity is obtained by high voltage transmission lines from the Pyrenean stations. A most interesting development has been the piping of natural gas from a small field at St Marcet,[11] discovered in 1939 about 70 km (44 miles) to the southwest, and operated by the *Régie Autonome des Pétroles*. A pipeline was completed between the field and

Toulouse in 1942, and after the war this was extended westward to Pau and down the Garonne valley to Bordeaux, with branches to other towns.[12] The gas grid has been extended to include the very much larger Lacq field (see p. 354), and La Société Nationale du Gaz du Sud-Ouest has been formed to distribute the gas.

Finally, the importance of Toulouse as a regional centre is shown by its cultural life, for it has a famed university (with more students than any in France outside Paris), numerous academies and schools, libraries and museums.

## The Pays Montalbanais

The junction of the valleys of the Garonne, Tarn and Aveyron forms a broad lowland region sufficiently distinctive to be regarded as a *pays*, occupied largely by the modern *département* of Tarn-et-Garonne. The land varies in height from 75 to 60 m (250 to 200 ft) above sea level, and is covered with alluvium seamed by the meandering courses of the three rivers and their tributaries. The floodplains are liable to inundation; they are lined with willows and in places covered with plantations of poplars cut at intervals. The damp pastures are used for summer grazing.

About 30 per cent of the total area of Tarn-et-Garonne was under arable in 1968, and 11 per cent each under pasture and woodland. Most of these woods are on the higher interfluves, as between the converging Garonne and Tarn. The terraces away from the floodplain are characterised by a polyculture, with small fields of wheat, maize, potatoes, beans and lucerne, orchards of peaches and pears, vineyards both for wine and for table grapes on the higher gravel terraces, and market gardens producing asparagus, tomatoes, gherkins, melons and artichokes. Many of the labourers, both seasonal and permanent, and indeed some of the *patrons-propriétaires*, are Spaniards or Italians. There are many villages, neat and prosperous. Montauban (on the right bank of the Tarn some 13 km (8 miles) above its junction with the Aveyron), the capital of Tarn-et-Garonne, is essentially a rural centre, with large markets, widely radiating autobus services, and industries based on agricultural products.

## The Agenais

The Agenais in its broadest sense includes both the valley proper of the Garonne (the *Garonne agenaise*) and the low limestone plateau extending northward to the Lot valley, sometimes referred to as *Bas-Quercy*. The floodplain of the river is covered with gravel and alluvium, and in places the river forms complicated braidings, though the main channel is regularised. Above the floodplain rise three distinct terraces: the lowest covered with rich alluvium, the middle with quite fertile gravels, and the highest with poor leached gravels. In places occur some fertile patches of limon, and over the low plateau there is much clay soil with a high lime content, rather dry but quite productive.

As in the upper parts of the Garonne valley, market-gardening and fruit-growing have replaced to a large extent the traditional cultivation of hard wheat on the better soils and rye on the poor ones. Some smallholdings use irrigation, raising water from wells by electric pumps to ensure good crops on the dry soils. Thousands of tons of vegetables are sent to the markets of Bordeaux, Toulouse and Paris or to local canneries.

The limestone slopes descending gently towards the river are covered with orchards of peaches, apricots, cherries and plums, for these stone fruits do well on the calcareous soils. Much fresh fruit is exported, canning and the manufacture of *pâtes de fruits* and jam are carried on, and the drying of prunes is notable at Granges-sur-Lot.

Towns such as Agen (the *chef-lieu* of Lot-et-Garonne) are market- and processing-centres for this charming orchard country. This part of the Garonne valley contains a number of immigrants, not only from other parts of France where opportunities are limited but also from Spain and Italy.

### The Bordeaux region

The valley of the lower Garonne from St Macaire downstream to Bec d'Ambès can be called *la Garonne bordelaise*, a prosperous agricultural area. The lowest terraces and the drained marshes are the scene of intensive market-gardening,[13] which developed particularly after 1870 when phylloxera attacked the vines of the Bordelais. Again much specialisation occurs, notably on the former marshland of Grattequina to the north of Bordeaux, where 220 ha (550 acres) are under artichokes alone, and in the communes of Eysines and Le Taillan which grow early potatoes. Further away from the river valley, large fields of wheat and maize become dominant, and in fact 40 per cent of the whole arable area of Gironde was under cereals in 1968. The wheatfields to the south of the Garonne are especially important, supplying the flour mills of Bordeaux.

The demands of Bordeaux for milk are met by numerous though small herds kept on the permanent pastures of the floodplain; there were 106 000 dairy cattle in 1968 in the *département* of Gironde. The area of fodder crops has increased.

### The Gironde vineyards [14]

Notwithstanding this varied agricultural activity and despite the past ravages of phylloxera,[15] the proportion of Gironde under vines in 1968 (11 per cent) still exceeded that under general arable cultivation (9 per cent). In some communes, in fact, more than half of the total area is vine-covered, and the total of just under 110 000 ha (420 sq miles) of vineyards in 1968 was third to Hérault and Aude for an individual French *département*.

The Bordeaux region has been a major producer of wine for centuries. Output reached about 1·3 million hectolitres in 1870, but fell to about 0·8 million as the result of phylloxera during succeeding years. Recovery

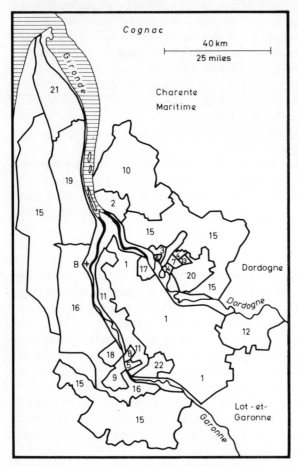

FIG. 13.2 The Bordeaux wine-producing area
The main *appellations* are numbered as follows:
1, Entre-deux-Mers; 2, Bourgeais-Côtes de Bourg;
3, Côtes de Fronsac; 4, Lalande de Pomerol; 5, Ste
Croix-du-Mont; 6, Côtes Canon Fronsac; 7, Pomerol;
8, Loupiac; 9, Région de Sauternes et Barsac;
10, Blayais: Côtes de Blaye; 11, Premières Côtes de
Bordeaux; 12, Ste Foy-Bordeaux; 13, Néac;
14, Sables-St Emilion; 15, *Appellation* 'Bordeaux';
16, Graves; 17, Graves de Vayres; 18, Cérons;
19, Haut-Médoc; 20, St Emilion; 21, Médoc;
22, Côtes de Bordeaux: St Macaire.

Based on *La France vinicole: carte publiée sous le haut patronage de l'Institut National des Appellations d'Origine*, in the *Atlas de la France vinicole L. Larmat* (80, Boulevard Haussmann, Paris, 8ᵉ).

has been steady, and in 1968 the yield amounted to about 4·9 million hecto-litres, nearly four times as much as in the pre-phylloxera period, a cir-cumstance which is unique in France.[16] More important is the fact that 90 per cent of this huge output consisted of quality wines, a quarter of the French output of these grades. The wines are of remarkable variety, partly the result of soils which vary from river alluvium to terrace gravels, calcareous clays and sandy marls, partly the result of different altitude and aspect, and partly the various traditions and age-old practices of individual producers; most famed are the *château* vineyards, some with world-renowned names. Many of the holdings are small; indeed, only 3 per cent of the total area is in units exceeding 30 ha (75 acres), and five-sixths of the estates are less than 2 ha (5 acres) each. The cooperative movement has made progress, especially since 1952, and over sixty cooperatives are now active in the Gironde with 8 000 members. These operate not so much in the areas of the individual high quality producers, but in the large-yielding districts of medium and lower quality wines.

Of the several main wine-producing districts (Fig. 13.2), three are out-standing. Along the left bank of the Gironde estuary, north of Bordeaux, is the *Médoc*, producing for the most part red wines, the southern part of which (the *Haut-Médoc*) yields the outstanding clarets. The second major district is *Graves*, extending along the left bank of the Garonne above Bordeaux as far as Langon. Two-thirds of these Graves wines are red, though the white varieties are particularly popular in England. Further south comes a group of five communes whose vineyards yield the sweet white wines known generally as *Sauternes*. The third famed district is *St Emilion* and *Pomerol*, situated near Libourne on the northern side of the Dordogne valley. Some three hundred vineyards produce considerable quantities of red wine of a heavier quality than claret.

Special mention has been made of these superlative districts, but other extensive vine-growing regions are found on the *palus* or riverside alluvial flats, on the gently undulating hill slopes or *côtes* in the Entre-deux-Mers (which produce quantities of dry white wine), and on the Côtes de Blaye along the right bank of the Gironde estuary. Quite apart from the amount consumed in France, large quantities of wine are shipped from Bordeaux, more than six times the amount before 1939 and nearly half the total French export.

## Bordeaux

Bordeaux is the sixth city and, in terms of tonnage handled, the fifth port of France.[17] Its long rather difficult estuary approach for large vessels, its position away from the main shipping routes, and its limited and primarily agricultural hinterland have made it progressively less able to compete with its rivals; Le Havre has taken most transatlantic traffic and is the gate-way for the Paris Basin, Marseilles dominates trade with North Africa and the Middle East, and Rouen and Dunkirk have outstripped it because of their large industrial hinterlands.

The city of Bordeaux lies mainly on the left bank of the Garonne at its lowest bridge point, 100 km (60 miles) up the estuary (Fig. 13.3). The river at this point makes a pronounced bend to the west (Plate 37), where firm banks overlook the deep water on the outside of the curve, and the town has gradually developed in a semicircle westward. Little urban growth took place along the right bank within the river curve until the beginning of this century, since when factories, power stations and marshalling-yards have been built.

Since Roman times Bordeaux has been the commercial metropolis of south western France. For three centuries it was the capital and outlet of the English possessions of Guyenne, and its trade (particularly in wine) throve exceedingly, but it suffered during the tribulations of the sixteenth and seventeenth centuries. The colonial activity of the eighteenth century gave the port a renewed prosperity similar to that of Nantes, but in the nineteenth century the town continued to grow more rapidly than the port, which suffered from competition with its more advantageously placed rivals. Its population reached 100 000 by 1841 and a quarter of a million by 1891, as a result of its multifarious commercial and industrial activities. Neighbouring communes to the west were gradually absorbed into the conurbation, so that by 1968 while the population of the *ville* itself was 267 000, the nine communes included in the official *agglomération* brought up the total to 550 000, a figure exceeded only by Paris, Lyons, Marseilles and Lille. It is the headquarters of the Aquitaine planning region, and has been designated a *métropole d'équilibre*.

Until the mid-nineteenth century the Gironde estuary, though requiring navigational care, presented no real obstacle to the ships of the time. In 1869 the first dock basin was constructed, succeeded by others, together with river quays and improved port facilities. Further developments were effected during the war of 1914–18, when the American forces in Europe made much use of the port. Plans were put forward in the closing years of the war for the extension of the dock system, linked by the projected Canal de Grattequina (shown on Fig. 13.3) to the river about 10 km (6 miles) below the city. But with the growth of outports, traffic using the port declined during the interwar period and these projects have never been realised. Although Bordeaux was spared the destruction suffered by many French harbours during the war of 1939–45, the channel between the city and Lagrange was blocked by the wrecks of eighteen vessels, some deliberately sunk by the Germans. The first ship managed to enter the port in August 1945, but it was two years before the main channel was clear.

The development of an outport is inevitable when a main port lies far up a difficult estuary. The first was Pauillac-Trompeloup, completed in 1894, situated halfway between Bordeaux and the sea. The Avant-Port du Verdon was constructed in 1933 just inside the Pointe de Grave, consisting

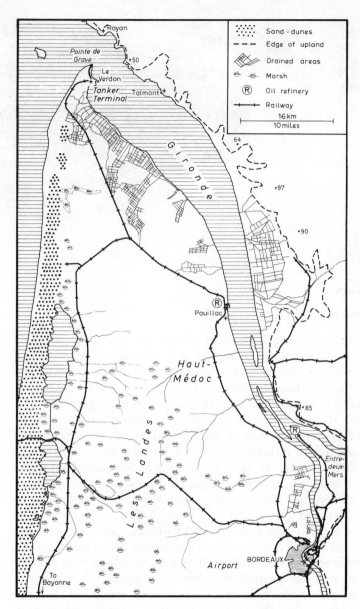

FIG. 13.3. Bordeaux and the Gironde estuary
The edge of the low Oligocene plateau in the northeast is
indicated approximately by a heavy pecked line; spot heights
are in metres. The built-up area of Bordeaux is shown by a fine
stipple. The Shell refinery at Pauillac and the Caltex and Esso
refineries at Bec d'Ambès are marked.

Based on *Carte de France au 200 000ᵉ*, sheets 50, 56.

PLATE 37. The Garonne and Bordeaux

of a liner pier with an approach channel affording a low-water depth of 13 m (42 ft), linked to Bordeaux by means of an electrified railway. The liner pier and other facilities were destroyed by the Germans during the occupation. An oil terminal accommodating 200 000 ton tankers was opened at Le Verdon in 1968; small tankers take the crude oil up the estuary. Other estuary ports include Mortagne and Blaye on the right bank, and the oil port at Bec d'Ambès at the apex of the Entre-deux-Mers peninsula.

The shipping and freight returns for *Le Port Autonome* of Bordeaux include these subsidiary estuary ports. In 1918 it was used by the American forces in Europe, and 6·9 million tons of freight passed through. In 1929 the total handled was 5·2 million tons, and after a marked decline during the depression years it rose again to 4·1 million tons in 1938. Following the war of 1939–45 it was not until 1947 that the channel had been cleared, but in that year the total freight handled recovered to the extent of 3·3 million tons, and by 1968 the figure totalled 8·68 million tons, of which 6·25 million consisted of imports. A big proportion consisted of crude oil handled at Le Verdon. About 77 000 tons of coal were imported, much less than the million tons annually before the war, mostly from Britain and Poland, although in the immediate postwar years American coal came in great quantities (in 1947 exceeding the prewar figure). About 900 000 tons of foodstuffs included wheat, sugar, coffee, rice, cocoa-beans, rum, bananas; other imports included timber, cellulose and chemical raw materials (mainly phosphates and pyrites). Exports are dominated by petroleum products, timber from the Landes, and wines and spirits.

The Garonne has few of the qualities of a navigable river, as might be deduced from the description of its physical characteristics above. It is officially classified as navigable for a distance of about 470 km (290 miles) up to Roquefort, but it is really only effectively navigable to Castets, where the lateral canal takes off (Fig. 13.4), to run parallel to the river for about 190 km (120 miles) to Toulouse. The *port fluvial de Bordeaux* nevertheless has some activity, and in 1969 the *Port Autonome* handled 4·46 million tons of riverborne freight[18] including small subsidiary ports upstream of the city (Cambes, Langoiran, Cadillac and others). Much of this is short-distance traffic. Rather more than half consisted of hydrocarbons, for Shell, Antar, BP, Caltex and Esso all have riverside oil-depots. The rest of the freight consists of sands and gravels, dredged from the river bed.

Bordeaux is an important industrial centre[19] with a variety of activities. Many are situated within the city to the west of the river, particularly those

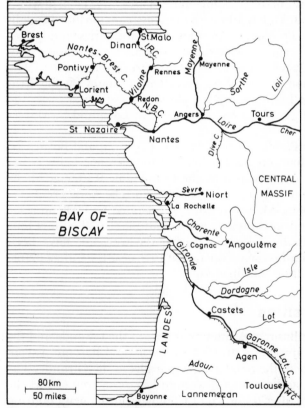

FIG. 13.4. The waterways of western France
Abbreviations are as follows: **IRC,** Ille-Rance Canal;
**MC,** Midi Canal; **NBC,** Nantes-Brest Canal.
Navigable portions of rivers are indicated by a heavy line;
some of these are used only seasonally, and are of little
importance.

Based on *Atlas de France*, sheet 56.

dealing with agricultural products—sugar-refining from beet imported coastwise from Boulogne, oil-seed-crushing (particularly groundnuts), chocolate and tobacco manufacturing, rum-refining, the distillation of liqueurs, and fruit- and vegetable-preserving. The specialised consumer goods include the processing and manufacture of leather, paper, wood (plywood, tropical veneers and furniture), electrical apparatus, glass bottles, corks, dyes and agricultural implements. The newer heavy industries are sited along the right bank opposite the city (an area developed when the first terminal of the railway from Paris was located there in 1852 before the rail bridge was constructed), on the left bank to the north of the dock basins, and at Bec d'Ambès. These include timber-yards, briquette plant, small shipyards and repair works, and flour mills. Recently installed factories include Siemens (electrical and electronic products), IBM (computers) and Ford (automatic transmissions). Three large cement works at Lormont on the right bank a few kilometres downstream use lime brought by rail from St Astier near Périgueux. An engineering works has foundries at Lormont, and several government sponsored aircraft, chemical and explosives factories are deliberately sited in the southwest of the country. The industries of Bordeaux use imported oil, electricity brought by the Grid from the Pyrenees via the Lannemezan transformer station, and (since the war of 1939–45) natural gas piped from the fields at Lacq and St Marcet (see pp. 321, 354).

Three oil refineries, at Pauillac, Bec d'Ambès (Fig. 13.3) and Bordeaux, are in operation.[20] The first, on the left bank of the Gironde halfway between Bordeaux and the sea, is owned by the Compagnie Raffinage Shell-Berre, and had an output of only 125 000 tons in 1969. The Ambès refinery, at the end of the Entre-deux-Mers peninsula, is operated by UIP, an associate of the big American firm Caltex; it had an output of 1·88 million tons in 1969. Both were virtually destroyed during the war, but have been rebuilt.[21] The Esso-Standard refinery, opened in 1960 near the Caltex plant, had an output of 2·53 million tons in 1969.

## The Pays des Charentes

The northern part of the Basin of Aquitaine, between the Gironde and the Vendéan margins of Armorica, is drained by the river Charente, except for the extreme south where the Seudre flows parallel to the Gironde. The Charente rises on the crystalline rocks of western Limousin, and crosses the *pays* known as *Confolentais* after the town of Confolens in the neighbouring valley of the upper Vienne. The river flows northwestwards towards Civray through the Lias vale flanking the edge of the Central Massif, then winds in loops southwards across low plateaus of Middle and Upper Jurassic limestones to Angoulême. It again changes direction to flow towards the sea beyond Rochefort. The main river and its tributaries thus drain a considerable area of these limestone and marl plateaus, and the general name of *Pays des Charentes* or *Pays charentais* is fully justified;[22] the region more or less comprises the two *départements* of Charente and Charente-Maritime. Several minor *pays* can be distinguished. In the east is *Angoumois*, the district around the city of Angoulême; in the centre is the *Champagne charentaise*, subdivided into the *Grande Champagne* to the south of Cognac and the lower *Petite Champagne* further west; bordering the coast between La Rochelle and Rochefort is *Aunis*, and in the southwest lies *Saintonge*.

In the northeast of Charente the Middle and Upper Jurassic limestones continue into the southwestern Paris Basin between the ancient uplands of Vendée and Limousin, through the broad 'Gate of Poitou', deriving its name from the province which extended westward to the sea. Poitou is in fact linked with Charente as one of the new planning regions, with its headquarters at Poitiers. The 'gate' forms a watershed at 200 m (650 ft) between the westerly-flowing Charente, the Sèvre Niortaise and their headstreams, and the Vienne's tributaries which ultimately join the Loire. The limestones in this area are purer than those to the southwest in Aquitaine, and furnish a freestone worked at a number of places, including the famous quarries of Tercé.

## The coast

The coastline between the mouth of the Sèvre Niortaise and the Pointe de la Coubre reflects the submergence of an irregular but low-lying land margin modified by subsequent deposition. The coastal scenery includes low rugged cliffs and isolated rock masses of limestone rising from sand- and mudflats, saltmarsh and sand-dunes.

The structural lines of Armorica can be traced southeastward across the Jurassic and Cretaceous limestone country. The anticline of La Rochelle forms a low ridge reaching the coast to the north of that port, and then continuing in a northwesterly direction as the 'back-bone' of the Ile de Ré. Similarly the anticline of Marennes is continued seawards as a string of rocks protruding from the tidal marshes, to form the nucleus of the Ile d'Oléron. Between these ridges, a rise of sea level contemporaneous with the Flandrian transgression along the North Sea coast (see p. 26) created broad estuaries and shallow bays. Protected by the islands, sedimentation has proceeded apace, helped by the development of vegetation, and thus creating extensive saltmarshes (Fig. 13.5).

Since the twelfth century the natural processes of saltmarsh accretion have been accelerated by the construction of dykes and palisades. Some of this effort has been devoted to creating the salt-pastures, and at times Dutch engineers have been employed in the work, as in the reign of Henri IV. Much of the reclamation was the indirect result of the flourishing salt industry; the Salines d'Aunis and Salines de Saintonge for many years provided salt for the fisheries of northern Europe, later for those of the Newfoundland Grand Banks. The marshes were subdivided by low dykes in-

331

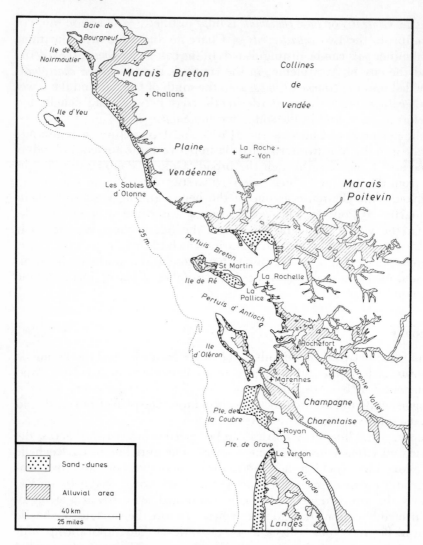

FIG. 13.5. The marshlands along the Biscay coast

Based on *Carte de France et des frontières au 1 : 200 000*, sheets 37, 43, 44, 50.

to a rectilinear pattern of 'pans' or *salines*, into which sea water was allowed to flow through sluices and left to evaporate during summer. By the beginning of the seventeenth century many of these *salines* had fallen into disuse, partly because of the extortionate methods of the gatherers of the notorious salt tax (*gabelle*), partly because of competition elsewhere. The neglected marshes became the home of malarial mosquitoes, and were commonly referred to as the *terres maudites*. Towards the end of the eighteenth century, efforts were made at reclamation by cutting a series of drainage channels;

the rivers were regularised, canals were constructed, and syndicates of landholders were established. Today much of the former marshland is under market gardens or pasture, though the river estuaries are still bordered by mudflats and sandbanks at low tide.

The honeycomb patterns of the enclosures surrounded by dykes still exist, for the marshes have in places been transformed into oyster-breeding grounds. This is notably the case at Marennes and La Tremblade on each side of the muddy estuary of the Seudre in the shelter of the Ile d'Oléron. Mussels are bred in the former *salines* on the seaward side of the Marais de Brouage and along the east coasts of Oléron and Ré, while eels are trapped in the canals.

## The interior

An area of low limestone plateaus slopes gently westward from 135 m (450 ft) on the borders of Limousin towards the coast. The landscape is open and somewhat monotonous, only slightly trenched into platforms by the rivers. In places, however, the limestones of differing degrees of resistance form low *côtes* and residual hillocks with quite steep slopes. Some of the towns, such as Angoulême and Rochefort, have taken advantage of these limestone bluffs and promontories as sites for defence.

Soils vary from lime-rich clays and marls to thin rather dry reddish soils on the plateaus formed by limestone disintegration. Some sandy soils are developed on residual patches of Oligocene sands to the northwest of Cognac and in the Saintonge. Along the floors of the valleys swampy and peat-filled areas of alluvium and marine sands thickly cover the underlying limestones. The calcareous soils are rather dry, but the water table is rarely far below the surface, and the light warm character of the soils is recognised by their name of *terres chaudes*.

## Land use and agriculture

The two *départements* of Charente and Charente-Maritime correspond so conveniently with the Pays des Charentes that their land use figures may be usefully quoted.

*Land use, 1968 (percentage of total area)*

|  | ARABLE LAND | PASTURE | WOODLAND | VINES |
|---|---|---|---|---|
| Charente | 45 | 18 | 19 | 7 |
| Charente-Maritime | 39 | 22 | 19 | 6 |

Source: Ministère de l'Agriculture, *Annuaire statistique de la France*, 1970–71.

The areas of woodland are small on these limestone plateaus, although patches of oak forest grow on areas of clay soils, the remnants of a more continuous cover. Maritime pines have been planted on the coastal sands, occasional lines of poplars form windbreaks, and juniper scrub covers part of the plateaus.

Pastureland includes water-meadows along the alluvium-lined valley floors, the *prés salés* bordering the sea coast and estuaries, and the poor grassland on some of the drier parts of the plateau (in parts used for military training grounds and racehorse stables). In 1968 about 28 000 horses and 169 000 sheep were in the two *départements*, the latter kept both on the limestone pastures of the interior and on the coastal salt-grazings. One of the most striking changes in the last thirty or forty years has been the increase in dairying in the Charente, replacing the arable systems. In 1968, of the 476 000 cattle 278 000 were dairy animals. This development has been furthered by the large-scale inclusion of short ley grass within the arable rotation and by the increase in the area under fodder crops. In 1968, 400 000 ha (1 million acres) were under clover, fodder beet, mixed grains, legumes and kale. The improvement in short-ley grassland has been made possible by increased supplies of superphosphate and other fertilisers from the factories near Tonnay-Charente and elsewhere, which the leached soils badly require. Water-meadows along the valley floors have been improved by both fertilising and irrigation. On the other hand, the dairy industry has been stimulated by the increase in cooperative methods, which are in fact better developed than anywhere else in France. Today the individual societies are organised within the Association Centrale des Laiteries des Charentes et du Poitou, handling nearly five million hecto-litres of milk each year. The emphasis is on the production of butter. In addition to dairying, young beef-stores are bought in Limousin and fat-tened in the Charente, and the pig population totalled 190 000 in 1968.

The ancient basis of agriculture in the Charente was the cultivation of cereals, and much of the plateauland grew wheat, usually with an alternate year's fallow. The poorer sandy soils were used for rye, while further south maize made its appearance. In 1968 the area under cereals had, however, fallen to under 40 per cent of the total arable, to be replaced by fodder crops and by potatoes.

Market-gardening has developed especially in the neighbourhood of Tonnay-Charente and on the sandy soils and reclaimed marshes along the coasts of the mainland and islands. The heavily fertilised soils yield excellent crops of asparagus, carrots, tomatoes, peas and garlic. The Tonnay-Charente district specialises in cauliflowers and early potatoes, and near Angoulême artichokes are cultivated.

## The vine

Before phylloxera struck the Charente in 1876, the vine occupied one-sixth of the farmed area. Since the sixteenth century grapes have been grown for the distillation of brandy, and the name *Cognac*, derived from the town of nearly 20 000 people on the south bank of the Charente in the heart of the *pays*, has become world-renowned. After the phylloxera attack, which caused almost economic disaster to the district, planting with imported American stocks using local scions proceeded slowly, and today 73 000 ha (185 000 acres) are under grapes, only a quarter of the pre-phylloxera area. Some grapes make red and white wines for local consumption and for the manufacture of vinegar, but the emphasis is on the production of high quality brandy. Organisation and control are rigorous to maintain the standards; in 1936 strict *Appellation Contrôlée* decrees were instigated, defining the specific districts with their soils, types of grape, and methods of distillation for each of the seven famous grades of *Cognac*. These districts are more or less concentric, with the *Grande Champagne* area in the centre between Cognac, Jarnac and Segonzac. The yields of the high quality *eaux-de-vie* are not great, but their value is considerable, especially as about three-quarters of the total is exported.

## Population and settlement

Numerous settlements are found along the coast, many of them fishing villages; others are pleasant resorts,[23] with sandy beaches backed by dunes and pines. The chief port is La Rochelle,[24] situated in the northeastern corner of a small bay sheltered by the Ile de Ré to the west and by a low limestone ridge to the north. It was one of the leading French seaports until the sixteenth-century wars of religion, during which as a centre of Protestantism it suffered several sieges (notably that of 1628 by Richelieu's forces) and much destruction. Its fortunes revived in the eighteenth century, for it became one of France's colonial ports, trading with her American possessions. In the nineteenth century, however, La Rochelle was faced with the problem of coping with the increased size of vessels; two wet docks were constructed, but rapidly became inadequate. In 1873 it was decided that the only solution was the construction of an outport where the limestone ridge on which the town stands ends abruptly at a deepwater roadstead, and between 1881 and 1890 the port of La Pallice was constructed, the works including a liner mole and a large dock basin. Its installations were heavily damaged during the war of 1939–45, but restoration was complete by 1950. Today La Pallice is the commercial port, while La Rochelle's chief importance is as a fishing harbour. The two ports (their returns are not separately distinguished) handle about 5 million tons of shipping, the ninth in France in this respect, though this activity is only half that of prewar years. La Rochelle is the fourth fishing port of France both by weight of catch and by value. A fish quay was built in 1925, equipped with storage sheds, refrigerator plant and railway-sidings, and 18 500 tons of fish were handled in 1969. The town in 1968 had a population of about 73 000, and forms the administrative centre of Charente-Maritime.

It has a variety of industries,[25] mostly connected with the processing of food products, the preparation of fertilisers from imported phosphates and fish residues, together with shipbuilding and repairing, the construction of aircraft and railway rolling-stock, and a Simca car assembly plant.

Further south, 16 km (10 miles) up the estuary of the Charente, Rochefort[26] was developed in the mid-seventeenth century by Colbert as a naval port and arsenal. It continued these functions until the Napoleonic wars, but as the size of warships grew, Rochefort, so far up a winding river, suffered by comparison with Brest and Toulon, and its functions slowly declined; in 1928 the naval dockyards and arsenal were finally closed. Its present population is about 40 000, some 12 000 more than before the war of 1939–45. Efforts have been made to introduce new industry, including chemicals, non-ferrous metals and aeronautical engineering. Further still up the river is Tonnay-Charente, the head of maritime navigation, whose wharves handle coal and phosphates for a large chemical factory nearby. It was for long one of the brandy-exporting ports, and until 1939 the spirit was taken by barge down the Charente to Tonnay, but during the war the river gradually became unnavigable through neglect and it has not been restored. Two-fifths of the cognac exported is railed or sent by road tanker to Tonnay.

The interior of the Pays des Charentes is a region of fairly uniform population dispersed over the countryside; the average density in Charente and Charente-Maritime in 1968 was 55 and 67 per sq km (142 and 173 per sq

PLATE 38. Jarnac in the Charente

mile) respectively. The larger towns are situated along the main river-valleys, notably that of the Charente itself; Angoulême, Châteauneuf-sur-Charente, Jarnac (Plate 38), Cognac and Saintes succeed downstream. Most are market towns and agricultural centres, situated where north–south routes cross the west–east lines of communication through the valleys. Cognac and Jarnac, as has been emphasised, have special functions 'grâce aux eaux-de-vie'.

The chief town of Charente is Angoulême,[27] with a population in 1968 of 48 000, or if the whole *agglomération* is included, of 92 000. It is situated in a strong defensive position on a low limestone plateau, partly surrounded by the Charente and its confluent the Arguienne. Today Angoulême is a pleasant city, very much the regional centre of the *pays*, 'le centre d'une région tres animée, un véritable entrepôt commerciale'.[28] Its industrial activity includes large paper mills, breweries, flour mills, leather works and metallurgical manufactures, including agricultural implements.

Further to the northeast, in the 'Gate of Poitou' (p. 313), several towns are strung out along the valleys of the upper Vienne and its tributary the Clain. These include the administrative centre of Poitiers, and the growing industrial town of Châtellerault, with aircraft engineering, the manufacture of machine tools and components, etc.

## Périgord

It is not easy to ascribe limits to Périgord, although on Fig. 13.1 an attempt has been made to do so. Structurally this region consists of a low plateau of Upper Cretaceous limestone, with cappings of Oligocene sandstones on the interfluves. These strata are separated from the crystalline rocks of Limousin by a narrow belt of Middle Jurassic limestone, by a depression floored with Lias clays, and in the neighbourhood of Brive by a low-lying Permian-floored basin occupied by the Vézère and its headstreams. These rocks were affected by the earth movements of early Tertiary times associated with the uplifting of the Pyrenees, and several folds and faultlines can be traced southeastward from the Charente.[29] Briefly, the anticline of Mareuil continues from near Angoulême into the Permian basin of Brive. Parallel to this and some 15 km (10 miles) to the south is the anticline of Périgueux, with folds represented most clearly in the *dôme de St Cyprien* where the limestone forms a broad ridge to the east of the angle of confluence of the Vézère and Dordogne. The folds are revealed in places as undulations in the limestone strata. Further south again is the anticline of Ribérac, which can be traced intermittently southeastward across the Lot valley near Fumel into Quercy.

The present relief of Périgord is the result of prolonged though interrupted periods of denudation, a 'relief cyclique périgourdin' in the words of P. Fénelon. He has determined six distinct erosion surfaces, ranging from the 'surface stéphanienne' of the Carboniferous age to that of the Mio-

Pliocene.[30] The heights of the individual peneplains vary considerably, since the late Tertiary uplift and tilting of the Central Massif affected these marginal areas also. Thus, for example, the Mio-Pliocene surface can be traced from about 400 m (1 350 ft) near the confluence of the Dordogne and the Diège to 180 m (600 ft) near Feugerolles, though most of it lies at 210 to 180 m (700 to 600 ft), sloping gently to the southwest.

Périgord is crossed by converging rivers flowing from Limousin and Cantal southwestwards to the Gironde estuary—the Dronne, Isle, Vézère and the Dordogne itself. The uplift and tilting of the Central Massif caused a complex series of rejuvenations of these rivers, so that they now flow in trenchlike valleys dividing the plateau into individual blocks. Several terraces can be distinguished, and Fénelon has proposed a classification (which accords well with the work of geomorphologists on the valleys of the western Central Massif), comprising four distinct erosional terraces and two aggradational terraces.[31] The rivers pursue extremely winding courses, with acute meanders enclosing meander cores, and limestone cliffs in places rise steeply on the outside of the curves.

The regime of the rivers is extremely variable. Many of the smaller tributaries are unable to maintain their courses across the permeable limestone during the long months of drought; even the Dordogne may shrink to depths of as little as 0·5 m (1 ft) as far down as Bergerac. In winter, however, the runoff from the crystalline rocks over which the headstreams flow may cause a rapid rise, producing extensive flooding lower down the main river.

The surface features of Périgord are thus varied. The limestone plateaus (which occasion the name *Périgord blanc*) show certain karstic features (hence another appellation of *le karst périgourdin*). Parts of the plateau are peppered with shallow solution hollows; at the most 45 m (150 ft) in diameter and 9 m (30 ft) in depth, they often lead by vertical shafts (*avens*) into complex cave systems below. Conversely, small elongated hummocks are the residual results of differential erosion of heterogeneous limestones, and from the fact that their long axes show a distinct alignment they may represent the dissected remains of once continuous ridges.

Several examples of subterranean rivers occur, and on the lower slopes of the valleys powerful resurgences burst out. Many cave systems have been dry for millennia as a result of the lowering of the watertable as the rivers deepened their valleys. Others are produced by differential solution; a much fissured but resistant horizontal cap of limestone commonly overlies a more soluble calcareous marl which has been eaten back under the overhanging hard stratum, forming caves opening on to the valley sides. Some of these are renowned as the homes of early man, as along the sides of the Vézère valley near Les Eyzies above its junction with the Dordogne, where occur the caves of Cro-Magnon, La Madeleine, Le Moustier, La Mouthe, Laugerie-Basse and -Haute, Font-de-Gaume, Lascaux and many more, with their remarkable wall-paintings, the legacy of primitive art.

By contrast with the limestone country, some areas of plateau are covered with Tertiary sands, sandy clays and gravels. These superficial deposits survive patchily on the interfluves in eastern Périgord and more continuously in the west and southwest. To the south of the Dordogne valley near Bergerac, the Tertiary siliceous sands, which are darker in colour than the limestones, have given to the district the local name of *Périgord noir*.

## Land use and agriculture

Périgord corresponds closely to the *département* of Dordogne, which was created with Périgueux as its *chef-lieu* more or less in the centre. In 1968 about 36 per cent of the total area was under woodland, 24 per cent under arable cultivation, and 19 per cent under permanent pasture.

This high proportion of woodland is at first sight surprising, but most of it is found on the Tertiary sands and clays. Chestnuts have long been widespread, and form part of the economy;[32] they are used for human consumption, they are fed to pigs and even sheep, and they are sent to the Bordeaux markets. Several varieties of oaks are found, sometimes growing in considerable though now reduced woodlands, others in copses on the plateaus or on the valley slopes. For centuries herds of swine have been pannaged in these oak woods. The trees yield the renowned Périgord truffles, which grow on their roots a foot or so beneath the ground, and are harvested during the winter with the help of pigs or dogs to locate them by the aid of scent. In addition to these deciduous woods, conifers (particularly maritime pine) have been planted on the sands since the mid-nineteenth century and especially since the war of 1914–18. These woodlands supply constructional timber and pit-props, tanning materials are obtained from the oaks, and much charcoal-burning is still carried on. This last was one of the bases of the long-established metallurgical industry; forges and furnaces, situated along the river valleys to utilise water-power, smelted the haematite ores found sporadically in the Tertiary sands.

The variety of relief, soil and aspect is reflected in the variety of agriculture; the polyculture is striking even for Aquitaine, a region of agricultural diversity. The countryside is a veritable *paysage mixte*, with patches of woodland and heath, small fields with hedgerows, occasional larger fields divided into hedgeless strips, orchards, groves of nut trees, and vineyards on sunny slopes. Almost half of the arable in Dordogne grows cereals (48 per cent), chiefly wheat with some maize and barley, and almost a third is under fodder crops. In 1968, 267 000 cattle were present, bred both for milk under the influence of the neighbouring Charente and for veal, and fed on the valley water-meadows and on fodder crops. About 170 000 sheep grazed on the poorer limestone pastures, and 119 000 pigs were reared on skim-milk from the dairies and in many places still pannaged on acorns and chestnuts in the woods. The breeding of capons, ducks, turkeys and geese is widespread, and fattened and truffle-stuffed birds are exported to the mar-

339

kets of Paris and elsewhere. The *foie gras de Perdrix* is considered by some to equal the product of Strasbourg.

Orchards are an important item in the economy, and the usual stone fruits are grown, particularly cherries, peaches, greengages and plums (the last especially in the Bergerac district where prunes are dried, and near Périgueux where the potent *eau-de-vie de prunes* is distilled). Apples rather unexpectedly are grown for cider-making. Chestnuts have already been mentioned, and another special item is the walnut, notably in the Vézère valley, of which more than 11 000 tons a year are produced.[33] Some of the nuts are crushed for oil, some exported green, others shelled and dried, others pickled, while the walnut wood is used by furniture makers in the local towns and in Bordeaux.

Finally, vineyards covered 3·5 per cent of the total area of the *département* in 1968; this is only half of the pre-phylloxera area. Still, 1·06 million hectolitres of wine were produced in 1968, of which a third was of *appellation contrôlée* quality; some, such as the white wines of Monbazillac and the Sauternes type wines of Brantôme, are widely known in France.

## Population and settlement

The population is rather thinly and unevenly distributed, with an average density for the *département* of Dordogne of only 41 per sq km (106 per sq mile). Small isolated farms and hamlets are found on the Tertiary sands and occasional larger nucleated villages on the limestone plateaus, but most settlements are situated along the valleys. On a larger scale are the attractive Bergerac, and the *chef-lieu* of the *département*, Périgueux, situated on gentle slopes rising from the banks of the Isle. Some industries are supplied with electricity from power stations in the neighbourhood (as at Tuilières a few kilometres above Bergerac, where a barrage has been constructed across the Dordogne, and at Manzac on the same river) or from the stations in the Central Massif. The processing of agricultural products includes the crushing of walnuts for oil, the milling of wheat and maize, the preparation of tobacco and the preserving of fruit. The manufacture is long established of footwear, textiles, paper, feltings and glassware. Timber-yards are situated along the river banks where water power is still used, and much sawn timber is exported. Numerous lime and cement works are also located along the rivers, where limestone can be worked in quarries on the valley-sides.

# The Causses du Quercy

The name Quercy is derived from a Gaulish tribe, the *Cadurques*, from which comes also the name of the main town of the region, Cahors. Its wider connotation as an ancient province of France included the districts of both Haut- and Bas-Quercy, although the latter to the south belongs to the Pays de Garonne. A small part of Haut-Quercy on the borders of Aurillac consists of the crystalline rocks of the Central Massif, known as the *Ségala du Quercy* (see p. 566). The greater part of Haut-Quercy proper comprises limestone plateaus of mainly Upper Jurassic age; indeed, these plateaus are sometimes known as the *Causses Aquitaines* or as the *Petits Causses* in contradistinction to the *Grands Causses* of the Central Massif. Four distinct *Causse*-units can be distinguished within this region, the names and locations of which are indicated on Fig. 20.2.

The limestone strata dip gently westward, the result of Tertiary tilting, from 450 m (1 500 ft) above sea level on the margins of the Central Massif to 260 m (850 ft) in the west and southwest, though the Causse de Martel has on the whole a rather lower elevation, sloping from 340 to 150 m (1 100 to 500 ft). The surfaces of the plateaus have been planed by the forces of subaerial erosion, and R. Clozier[34] has distinguished surfaces of three distinct ages, with traces of at least one still older in the extreme east.

The plateaus are deeply trenched by the steep-sided valleys of the Dordogne and the Lot; limestone cliffs drop abruptly in places to the river edge on the outer curves of meanders. The valley floors are, however, quite wide, sometimes as much as a kilometre, as the ingrown meanders swing from one side to another. A considerable extent of alluvium-covered flat usually lies on the inside of each meander, beyond which several gravel-covered terraces rise in low steps towards the bounding limestone bluffs.[35] There is an extraordinary ramification of valleys. Most of the higher ones are dry, while others contain seasonal streams draining from the individual plateau-blocks into the main rivers. Many complex systems of subterranean drainage occur, and powerful resurgences break out near the base of the valley sides; the flow from the Fontaine de Chartreux practically doubles the volume of the Lot within the town of Cahors.

The plateaus show in detail a diversity due to the differential denudation of the limestones, shales and marls, and to the solution features of the calcareous rocks. Broad shallow depressions often contain reddish *terra rossa* clays. Deep vertical chasms lead into extensive cave systems, and many of them have been explored. Perhaps the most famous is the Gouffre de Padirac in the Causse de Gramat not far from Rocamadour, descended by the *doyen* of French speleologists, E.-A. Martel, in 1889;[36] its mouth is about 30 m (100 ft) in diameter and its vertical shaft falls for 99 m (325 ft). The water-table in this cave-system fluctuates violently, and a vertical rise of 35 m (115 ft) above the usual low-water level has been recorded.[37]

## Land use and agriculture

The surface of the plateau reveals areas of bare limestone, greyish tracts of stony soil and residues of *terra rossa* in the depressions. Much scrubby vegetation consists of juniper, blackthorn and box. About 40 per cent of the total area of the *département* of Lot (which occupies the greater part of this region) was classified in 1968 as under woodland. Much of this consists of oak, usually forming a scrub forest, though in some parts a careful forest policy has produced a growth of well-developed trees. Areas of poor seasonal pasture, usually scorched and brown in summer, are found on the plateau, and meadows appear in hollows and valleys where the ground-water is not far below.

The arable lands, which amounted to only 20 per cent of the total area of Lot in 1968, are found in the depressions where a downwash of *terra rossa* has accumulated and along the floors of both the dry valleys and the river valleys. Much has gone out of cultivation in the last century; indeed, the official land use category of *territoire agricole non cultivé* occupied in Lot about 4 per cent in 1968, and none of this was deliberate fallow.

Nevertheless, a well-developed agriculture is found in more favourable areas, especially on south-facing slopes; it is interesting to find in this district the terms *souleillan* and *hiversenq*, which correspond to the *adret* and *ubac* in the Alps. The broad floors of the main valleys provide the most important arable lands; the Lot plain near Cahors, for example, presents a variegated pattern of fields of cereals, strips of improved pasture, and well-kept orchards and vineyards. More than half the arable produces wheat, grown either with an alternate year of fallow or in rotation with maize, potatoes and fodder beet. Small patches of rye can still be found, especially in the higher depressions, but the total area has declined. The vine is grown on south-facing slopes near Cahors, lavender on the plateaus south of the Lot,[38] walnuts in groves or as individual trees, and small orchards of plums, apricots and peaches on the river terraces near the villages, while straw-berries are a local speciality in the Dordogne valley. Tobacco is cultivated in small patches, and market-gardens are intensively worked on valley floors near the towns.

Pastoral farming is important, and about 239 000 sheep were in the *département* in 1968, mostly grazing on the high limestone pastures, although the animals are commonly turned on to the wheat stubble after the harvest. The richer valley pastures are the scene of dairying activity, especially along the Lot valley near Cahors. Of 112 000 cattle in the *département* in 1968, nearly half were dairy animals (some milk is used for cheese-making, notably the famous *Rocamadour* variety) and others were reared for farm work. About 74 000 pigs were kept, pannaged on acorns in the oak-woods for part of the year, and most farms kept poultry.

The agricultural scene in Haut-Quercy is therefore one of contrasts, ranging from poor grazing on the limestone plateaus to the varied and intensive activity on the valley floors and south-facing slopes of the more fertile depressions.

## Population and settlement

Although there are a few local concentrations, the population as a whole over Haut-Quercy is rather low; in 1968 the *département* of Lot had about 151 000 people, with an average density per square kilometre of only 29 (75 per sq mile), approaching indeed the sparseness of some of the Alpine and Central Massif *départements*. This is one of the regions where rural depopulation has proceeded steadily, for at the end of the eighteenth century the density in Quercy was probably of the order of 120 per sq km (300 per sq mile).

Most of the population in the Petits Causses proper live in villages and hamlets, clustered on the south-facing slopes or at the lower end of a dry valley near a permanent spring. Some large villages stand on the plateaus, acting as market and servicing centres; most contain two to four thousand inhabitants. The larger towns are situated in the valleys, although perched on the upper terraces away from the danger of flooding, or occasionally on the isthmus formed by a meander-neck, as in the case of Cahors around which the Lot swings in a sweeping curve. Rocamadour, in the valley of the Alzou, is an attractive little town clinging incredibly to the side of a steep limestone cliff crowned by a church. These towns—Cajarc, Puy-l'Evêque and Fumel, as well as Cahors, in the valley of the Lot, and Gourdon on the Bleu (a tiny Dordogne tributary)—are the main centres of Quercy's prosperity. Fumel on the borders of Périgord has old-established metallurgical works, originally based on local charcoal and iron ore, later on coke once brought by river from St Aubin, but now transported by rail from the Nord coalfield. It still makes a range of heavy machinery, tubes and pipes. But otherwise there is little industry except for saw mills and tanneries, a few limestone quarries and cement-works, and some food-producing activities such as the canning of vegetables, the milling of wheat, the processing of tobacco, and the manufacture of various macaroni-like *pasta*.

Cahors is the chief town of the *département*;[1] its function, as D. Faucher succinctly puts it, is as 'un marché et une petite ville de fonctionnaires'. It has long been a bridge-town, as its superb fourteenth-century bridge with three arch-pierced towers indicates, and the old walls across the Lot meander-neck testify to its rôle as a stronghold during the troubled past.

## Albigeois and Lauraguais

In the triangular area between the Aveyron on the north, the *Garonne toulousaine* on the west, and the Monts de Lacaune and Montagne Noire on the east lies a low undulating plateau region. The northern part, drained by the Tarn and centred on Albi, is given the *pays* name of *Albigeois*. To the south of the Agout (a left-bank Tarn tributary) a further series of plateaus extends southeastward into the Col de Naurouze; these include the *pays castrais* in the Agout valley around the town of Castres and the *Mirepésis* near Mirepoix in the south, but they are commonly referred to collectively as *Lauraguais*.

The rocks are varied in this region, testifying to the fluctuating conditions of deposition in early Tertiary times. Some of them are so similar to the true *molasse* of Miocene age that they are called *molasse gréseuse* and *molasse argileuse*, according to their content of sand and clay. The clays are occasionally interrupted by sheets of gravel, often of a quartzitic character, derived from the crystalline rocks of the Central Massif. Limestones intercalated among the *molasse* are widespread in the north of Albigeois, and elsewhere are deposits of coarse sandstones and conglomerates.

The present relief is largely the result of the differential erosion of these sediments by running water, for many streams flow westwards from the Central Massif and from the watershed in the Col de Naurouze further to the south. Most of their valleys form trenches 3 to 5 km (2 to 3 miles) wide, with the present rivers meandering across their clay-covered floors. The Tarn is particularly winding, especially in the section between Ambialet and Albi; near the former the river turns almost completely back on itself, leaving an attenuated meander-neck. In other places, by contrast, the rivers are contained in steep narrow trenches, particularly where they have cut through bars of resistant limestone to form small *cluse*like valleys; the valley of the Agout has in places a gorgelike character, as at Lavaur where the little town is perched on a steep hill overlooking the river. Dry valleys are common, cutting through the sheets of *molasse*, and probably eroded by powerful Pleistocene streams swollen by the heavier rainfall of those times and by the abundant meltwater from the Pyrenean glaciers.

The plateau landscape is subdued, sloping from 180 or 200 m (600 or 650 ft) in the east to 120 m (400 ft) as the Garonne valley is approached. Minor diversifications of the surface include long but irregular *côtes* of limestone in the south and east; near Fanjeaux, for example, overlooking the Col de Naurouze, appears a triple line of these *côtes*. Again, particularly in Albigeois, the Oligocene limestone sometimes forms low plateaus between the valleys, to which the name *causse* is given; they reveal narrow *crêts* of limestone, broader whalebacked ridges of calcareous sandstone, and occasionally flat-topped buttes where the interfluves have been cut into by transverse valleys.

The Quaternary rivers deposited over their valley floors vast amounts of gravel derived from the wastage of the Central Massif and the Pyrenees. The rapid runoff from the autumn and winter rains still brings down material, coarse and fine, to be deposited on the valley floors. Flooding is common, occasionally attaining serious proportions following heavy periods of rain, as in March 1930; near the confluence of the Tarn and Agout at St Sulpice the waters rose more than 18 m (60 ft) and caused widespread destruction among villages on the river-terraces.

**Land use and agriculture**

Both Albigeois and Lauraguais are prosperous agricultural areas, the result of reasonably fertile soils (especially where derived from the lighter clays and loams), the modest elevation, and the warmth of these southern latitudes. In the *département* of Tarn, which occupies much of the region, 38 per cent of the total area was under arable in 1968; of this about two-fifths was devoted to cereals, mainly maize and wheat, about a third to fodder crops, and a tenth was left fallow. Market-gardening is found especially in the Tarn valley near Albi and at Gaillac, Arthez and St Juéry where the terraces are intensively cultivated; specialisations include onions in the neighbourhood of Lescure and strawberries at Gaillac. Nearly a fifth of the *département* carried permanent pasture, including both poor winter pasture on the limestone and sandstone plateaus, and better meadows in the floors of the valleys. These pastures, supplemented by fodder crops, enabled 170 000 cattle (of which about 110 000 were dairy animals, the rest bred for beef or draught use), 180 000 sheep and 105 000 pigs to be maintained. The sheep, mainly the *Lacaune* breed, are kept both for wool and for milk to be made into cheese. Mules are bred in considerable numbers. Nearly 6 per cent of Tarn, 27 500 ha (70 000 acres), was occupied by vineyards in 1968. A large proportion of the wine output is *ordinaire*, both red and white, but the red wines of the Gaillac district and some white wines of a *graves* character in the Tarn valley have a certain reputation. Mulberries and orchard fruits are also widely grown.

The landscape is thus pleasantly varied, with low hills and gentle valleys, fields of maize and wheat, orchards and vineyards, and villages on the valley terraces. Probably much of the district was once tree-covered, and nearly 30 per cent of Tarn is still under woodland. Though some continuous stretches of forest still exist, most of the oak woodland, including also chestnuts, hornbeams, cypress and pines, occurs as small copses around villages, and there has been much recent planting of conifers.

## Industry and towns

Rather surprisingly, the district between Albi and Castres forms one of the minor industrial regions of France, an activity long established on a domestic basis, manufacturing cloth from local wool. Today Castres is still an important textile town, using electric power from Central Massif stations and manufacturing both woollen and cotton cloth. The wool-dressing and textile industries of towns in the Thoré valley, an extension of the lowland into the Central Massif between the ancient uplands of the Montagne Noire and the Lacaune, are described on p. 569. A large rayon factory operates in Albi. Tanning and leather-dressing, using local hides, is important at Graulhet on the banks of the Dadou, a tributary of the Agout. There is a considerable specialisation in furniture-making and cabinet work generally at Revel, and Castres has a number of engineering and metallurgical industries, including the manufacture of machine-tools, automobile bodies and parts, electrical machinery and equipment, and various types of pumps.

To the north of Albi and between the valleys of the Tarn and the Cérou is situated the coalfield of Carmaux-Albi, consisting of two small concealed basins separated by a barren area. This field is grouped administratively with Decazeville to the north as the *Houillères d'Aquitaine*;[39] the two produced jointly 1·61 million tons in 1968, though scheduled soon to close down. This coal is a valuable contribution to the economy of southwestern France, for it is used at the large Pinet power station near Carmaux and at a new one near Albi, in several local coke ovens, and in the glass, lime and cement works in the neighbourhood of Albi and Carmaux. Associated with the coke ovens are chemical works at the two last towns, making benzene, sulphate of ammonia and acids. Some coke is consumed at the steel works of St Juéry, situated on the banks of the Tarn a few kilometres upstream from Albi, which use pig iron from St Etienne and even from Lorraine, and supply the metal-using industries of Albi (notably tools and agricultural implements). The labour for this industrial activity is supplied partly by the local population (many men own small farms and work in a factory too, their womenfolk in the textile mills), partly by foreigners.

Albi and Castres have dual functions as market centres for a large agricultural area and as the foci of this industrial activity. Albi, as well as its administrative functions as *chef-lieu* of the *département* of Tarn, has several industrial neighbours, such as Carmaux and St Juéry. Castres is also the centre of the small industrial towns along the Thoré valley.

## The southern low plateaus

An undulating region of low plateaus slopes gently northward from a height of about 600 m (2 000 ft) in the foothills of the central Pyrenees to the margins of the Garonne valley at 180 m (600 ft). The *molasse* is covered for the most part with an alluvial fan crossed by a series of diverging rivers, each only a few kilometres from the next. Those in the east flow to the upper Garonne; those in the centre flow northwards to the *Garonne agenaise*; and the rivers in the west flow to the Adour (Fig. 12.11).

These streams laid down this joint alluvial fan in late Tertiary times, building out into the 'Gulf of Aquitaine' a delta of sand and gravel worn from the uprising Pyrenees. The apex of the fan consists of coarse Pliocene pebbles, forming the small triangular plateau of *Lannemezan*, deposited by the powerful river Neste which rises near the crestline of the Pyrenees. Further to the west are similar though smaller Pliocene fans—the *Plateau de Cieutat* in the neighbourhood of Bagnères-de-Bigorre, formed by the ancestor of the Adour, and the *Plateau de Ger*, the product of the streams which now join the Gave de Pau. These fans, or as the French geologists call them, *anciens cônes de déjections*, form in truth *les plateaux à débris*.[40]

To the north of these stony plateaus the lower *Plateau d'Armagnac* slopes away towards the Garonne valley. It too is crossed by many rivers, and although their valleys are cut down into the *molasse*, deposits of Pleistocene

FIG. 13.6. The drainage pattern in western Lannemezan and the
Pays de l'Adour
The map shows the extraordinary fan of streams flowing northwards
over the gravel plateau of Bigorre, situated about 30 km (20 miles) west
of Lannemezan. Long narrow ridges separate the valleys, their sides
furrowed with short rivulets. The asymmetrical nature of the valleys is
shown by the large numbers of these rivulets flowing down the gentler
east-facing slopes. Heights are in metres.

Based on *Carte de France au 200 000ᵉ*, sheet 70.

and Recent alluvium cover much of the interfluves and the river terraces.
Further variety is introduced by patches of glacial clay and of limon.

The southern plateaus therefore owe their present form primarily to the
past and present work of the multitude of rivers. The valleys are markedly
asymmetrical, with the steep side in each case facing the west; rivulets flow
down the longer east-facing slopes, as is evident on Fig. 13.6. Various theo-
ries seek to account for this asymmetry. Possibly exposure to the westerly
winds has caused more rapid weathering and erosion of the west-facing
valley sides as compared with the eastern slopes in a comparative lee.

Another suggestion is that fine windblown deposits, probably derived from the Quaternary sands of the Landes, have been blown eastwards, accumulating on the leeward side of each valley and thus compelling its stream to move further to the east, so cutting into and steepening the west-facing valley side.

The valleys are separated by gentle ridges, in the north composed of Oligocene limestone capped with *molasse* or sands, and known generally as *les coteaux de Gascogne*. In some of these limestone outcrops the gentle folds of the outer Pyrenean zone can be traced. For the most part, however, the Armagnac plateau is an area of only slight variations in relief.

## Land use and agriculture

The stony plateaus in the south consist for the most part of dreary moorlands, windswept and usually snow-covered in winter, and rather arid in summer. The soils are thin and coarse, leached and acid, and bear a poor pasture or a scrub of gorse, ling, broom and other shrubs. The valley sides and floors are wooded, especially in Cieutat where oaks and chestnuts grow. The chief value of Lannemezan and its neighbouring plateaus is as pasture for sheep and beef cattle, and some improvement of the moister valley pastures has been effected by irrigation and fertilisation.

Further north, with a milder climate, lower elevation and tractable soils, the countryside assumes a more genial aspect. A large part of Armagnac lies administratively in the *département* of Gers; in 1968 about 56 per cent of the total area was under arable, 16 per cent under permanent grassland, 14 per cent under woodland (oak and chestnut) and 6 per cent under vines. Here again is the polyculture so characteristic of Aquitaine, although the basis of life is the cultivation of cereals (principally quick-ripening hard wheats, maize and a little oats), which occupy almost two-thirds of the arable land. A further quarter of the arable is under fodder crops, which together with the improved irrigated pastures in the valley bottoms enable the *département* to maintain about 230 000 cattle, of which half are dairy animals. Others are bred for draught purposes (for which they are more widely used than horses) or for veal, and between 30 000 and 40 000 animals are shipped away each year to markets elsewhere in France. Pigs too are widespread, 76 000 in the *département* in 1968, fattened on maize and skimmed milk. Mules are reared, many of them to be sent over the Pyrenees for sale in Spain. Large numbers of poultry make Gers one of the main producers of eggs, and it is a famous rearing area for geese. Sheep, however, declined from about 100 000 in Gers at the turn of the century to 10 000 during the war of 1939–45, although by 1968 there were about 22 000. They are brought down in summer from the Pyrenean foothills or from Lannemezan to graze on the wheat stubble.

About 40 000 ha (100 000 acres) of Gers were under vines in 1968, yielding a large output of wine. Although none is of high quality, much pleasant *vin rouge* is produced in Haut-Armagnac, and white wines come from Bas-Armagnac. The district is best known for its brandy, regarded by many as little inferior to Cognac; around Condom are the specified zones which produce *Grand-Armagnac*, *Fin-Armagnac* and *Petit-Armagnac* in order of quality.

## Population and settlement

In spite of this agricultural prosperity, the density of population is well below that of France as a whole; the average for Gers was only 34 per sq km (88 per sq mile) in 1968, which represents a big decline since 1846, when the figure was 50 (130). Rural depopulation has proceeded steadily, and but for the fact that nearly 30 000 foreigners, mainly Italians and Spaniards, are settled on the land, comprising a sixth of the population of Gers, the density would be lower still. Towns are small, with few industries other than food-processing; their main function is as markets and shopping centres. One old-established feature is the frequent occurrence of fairs, each a focus not only of economic but also of social activity, and usually held in conjunction with religious festivals. The most important centre is the *chef-lieu* of the *département*, Auch (situated in the valley of the Gers at a height of about 120 m (400 ft)). The small town of Lannemezan stands on the northern edge of the gravel plateaus; it is the market centre for a considerable district and holds important sheep and cattle fairs. Here is situated the main transformer station for the central Pyrenean hydro-electric stations, from which transmission lines run to Pau, Dax and Bordeaux, and others to Toulouse, while a recently constructed 220 kv line runs to Verlhaguet (near Montauban) and beyond to link up with the main Dordogne transformer-station at Le Breuil.

## The Pays de l'Adour

The river Adour rises on the eastern flanks of the Massif du Néouvielle in the central Pyrenees, and flows northwards across Bigorre as one of the streams which have built up the detrital fan already described. It maintains this northward direction as far as Riscle, near which it turns westwards, and continues in this direction as far as Dax, then southwestwards to reach the sea 5 km (3 miles) beyond Bayonne.

The valley of the middle Adour is bordered on the south by gravels and coarse sands and on the north by the sheets of fine sand of the southern Landes. The river wanders among its deposits, with a maze of meanders, braided channels and gravel islets, the last especially pronounced during summer. In winter and spring, however, the headstreams bring down so much water that widespread flooding occurs, sometimes occupying the whole floor between the lowest terraces.[41] This zone of sand- and gravel-banks is known as the *graves* or *barthes*,[42] and is covered in places with alder thickets, willows and poplars, though drainage has improved the valley-pastures in some places. The main river is joined by a succession of tributaries flowing down in a northwesterly direction from the gravel plateaus of Bigorre and Ger which cover the frontal zone of the Pyrenean flanks. The chief confluents are the Gave de Pau and the Gave d'Oloron. A few right-bank tributaries drain the southern Landes, notably the Midouze, with its feeders issuing vaguely from shallow lakes and marshes.

This curve of the Adour encloses several subregions of considerable variety, though known collectively as the *Pays de l'Adour*. Along the northern edge of the Pyrenees are the low plateaus and ridges of *Béarn*, *Basse-Navarre* and *Labouard* (these three are sometimes referred to generally as the *Collines basques*), sloping gently northward and northwestward from 330 to 180 m (1 100 to 600 ft). These plateaus consist of Upper Cretaceous limestones, marls and conglomerates with occasional exposures of Upper Triassic sandstones, flanked on the north with varied Tertiary and newer rocks and an uneven layer of younger sands and gravels. The superficial cover is largely the result of the powerful action of the swollen rivers of glacial times, which have also cut into the underlying rocks and in part removed the newer deposits (even revealing in places the pre-Pyrenean fold trends). Several of the valleys form minor *pays*, such as the *Plaine de Tarbes* in the upper Adour valley and the *Pays de Soule* in the valley of the Saison (see p. 660). The rounded *coteaux* and *pays mamelonnés* forming the interfluves are of the order of 300 to 330 m (1 000 to 1 100 ft) above sea level.

To the north of these plateaus and within the curve of the Adour is the district of *Chalosse*,[43] very similar in character to Bas-Armagnac further east. In the east and centre lies a subdivision known as the *Chalosse de Geaune*, where the interfluves form whalebacked ridges scored by a multitude of rivulets, and the valleys are bordered by broad terraces at levels ranging from 9 to 60 m (30 to 200 ft) above the present rivers. The landscape is gentle, indeed D. Faucher describes it as 'les coteaux aimables'. The western part of the *pays*, the *Chalosse de Pouillon*, consists of sands of Miocene age.

## The coast

Between the mouth of the Adour and the Pointe-St Martin (just north of Biarritz) the coast is a continuation of that of the Landes, with a belt of forested dunes and a broad sandy beach. For a short distance to the south the Tertiary strata actually reach the sea, forming low cliffs subject to intense erosion, and at Pointe-St Martin the undercutting action of the waves has produced a steep cliff capped with an overhanging cornice from which falls are frequent. Further south the low cliffs of Eocene clays, gashed with ravines, are constantly receding as the result of *en masse* slumping on to the beach.

Still further to the south, however, the 'frontal zone' of the Pyrenees (see

p. 657 ), represented by the Upper Cretaceous limestone plateau of Labouard, reaches the sea, and the coastline cuts transversely across these structures. A slight marine transgression has produced an indented coast, and
limestone cliffs alternate with coves referred to as *les rias basques*. In some
places the strata dip seawards at an angle of about forty-five degrees, and
from a wavecut platform at the base of the cliffs project sharp sawtooth
ridges of the more resistant strata. The coves are being slowly filled in by
longshore drift of fine sand in a southerly direction, although groynes and
dykes have been built to protect the approaches to the harbour of St Jean-
de-Luz at the mouth of the estuary of the Nivelle. Hendaye is not backed by
cliffs, and its broad bay is flanked by sandy beaches.

## Land use and agriculture

Taking the *département* of Pyrénées-Atlantiques as an indication, 24 per cent
of the total area in 1968 was uncultivated, 22 per cent under arable, 21 per
cent under permanent pasture and 20 per cent under woodland. The
forested area was once much greater, but continued cutting and grazing
have converted much into scrub or rough pasture. A few continuous areas
of woodlands of oak, beech and chestnut still survive, and pine forests have
been established. Hedges of stunted oaks and lines of poplars are common
on the terraces and plateau.

The wasteland is still quite extensive, though it has been appreciably
reduced during the last decade; it includes bracken brakes covering former
woodland, poor grassland and heathland on some of the gravels and sands,
and the scrub-covered *graves* and *barthes* of the Adour valley. Along the
floodplains of the *gaves* are found scrubby thickets of willow, hawthorn and
alder.

The category of permanent pasture includes both poor grasslands on the
low plateaus between the rivers and on the rounded ridges of the Chalosse,
and also the verdant valley floors of the *gaves*, which in places are irrigated.
Feeders take off from the swiftly flowing streams and supply lateral irrigation canals running along the lowest terraces; in the plain of Tarbes the
Canal d'Alaric, for example, runs along the right bank. On these pastures
are kept cattle (which have increased rapidly in number during the last
half-century), horses, and large numbers of pigs. The most important
animal reared on the poor pastures is, however, the sheep; in 1968 Pyrénées-
Atlantiques had 310 000, and only Aveyron, Vienne and Haute-Vienne of
the other *départements* had more. In addition, Pyrenean sheep are brought
down to graze in the valleys during winter and spring. Poultry are widespread, especially turkeys and geese; a sideline is the manufacture from
goose down of *duvets* (down quilts, climbing jackets, etc.) at Hagetmau.

The traditional cultivation of the Adour basin has long consisted of
cereals—wheat, millet and barley; these are still important, especially on
the sandy loams, with the more recent addition of maize (see p. 358 n[3]) and

of oats for fodder, and the area under cereals in 1968 was still as high as 55 per cent of the arable. One major change has taken place in this century, for almost exactly a third of the farmland is under fodder crops, including lucerne grown with the aid of irrigation. The area under potatoes has also increased, there is much more market-gardening, and some tobacco cultivation. The area of vineyards has never recovered from the phylloxera ravages; only about 8 700 ha (21 000 acres) of vines were cultivated in 1968, producing almost entirely *vin ordinaire*, and brandy is distilled and sold in Bayonne, though not of a quality comparable with that of Armagnac to the east. Orchards of peaches and apricots are grown on the slopes.

## Population and settlement

The population of the Pays de l'Adour is unevenly distributed, with an average density of about 60 per sq km (155 per sq mile). The majority of people live in villages and isolated farms along the river valleys on the upper terraces away from flood-danger.[44] The way of life is pre-eminently rural, depending on a varied agriculture and the raising of stock. A few larger towns and some more densely populated rural areas are situated in the upper basins of rivers near the point of contact between the plain and the mountains to the south. Such is Tarbes, the chief town of Hautes-Pyrénées, situated in a basin on the upper Adour (Fig. 13.6). Its animal fairs are well known, and it is a commercial and industrial centre with old-established tanneries and leather-working industries, notably the manufacture of patent leather harness and footwear. Modern industries are based on natural gas piped from Lacq. There are also long-established furniture factories, and a specialisation in stone-carving, especially marble. As a result of the developments of Pyrenean power stations, some new industries have developed in recent years, including the manufacture of electrical apparatus and machinery, turbines, dynamos and locomotives.

Farther to the west is Pau, situated on the right bank of the turbulent Gave de Pau; with its 74 000 people it is the *chef-lieu* of Basses-Pyrénées. Not only is it one of the tourist gateways to the Pyrenees, but it is a prosperous market town. As an industrial centre it has grown as a result of the availability of hydroelectricity and, since the war, of natural gas piped from St Marcet. Numerous factories were built in the years before 1939 in this 'safe' area, including metallurgical and engineering works, tanneries and shoe factories, the manufacture of textiles and of the famous *bérets*, and the processing of agricultural commodities. Another important valley town is Oloron-Ste Marie, also with a diverse industrial activity: the manufacture of woollen, linen and cotton cloth, *bérets*, sandals and other footgear, wooden articles, and bells of all shapes and sizes. A few small towns are situated along the middle Adour valley, but the poverty of the *graves* along the valley-floor limits their importance.

The most important town on the Adour is Bayonne, situated at the confluence with the Nive, with a population of about 43 000. Much of the built-up area lies along the left bank of the Adour below the confluence, but the newer part of the town has been built on the triangular peninsula between the two rivers. Bayonne began life in the fifth century as a point on a main route into Spain, and in the twelfth and thirteenth centuries during English rule it became important for the wine trade. But situated 5 km (3 miles) from the open sea up a winding river with a difficult entry, the port of Bayonne was faced in the sixteenth century with serious problems of silting. By the beginning of the seventeenth century the river outlet had been stabilised at the southern side of Cap Breton (instead of as previously to the north), and further movement has been checked by the construction of moles on either side of its mouth. Regular dredging maintains a channel across the Barre shoal outside the estuary.

The modern port of Bayonne[45] includes quays at Le Boucau along the right bank midway between the town and the open sea, and others within the town as far upstream as the bridges at the Adour-Nive confluence. Its trade grew steadily in the late nineteenth century, particularly after the opening of the steel works at Le Boucau[46] in 1882, and a peak of a million tons of freight was handled in the years preceding the war of 1914–18. A considerable decline was experienced during the interwar years, particularly in the tonnage of exports, and by 1938 the figure was only about 610 000 tons. Bayonne is handicapped by its somewhat remote position in a corner of France and by the limited rail communications serving its own hinterland. Since 1945 the freight handled has fluctuated between 600 000 and 800 000 tons, predominantly imports, and in 1969 it accommodated 1 260 vessels with a net tonnage of about one million. The steel works at Le Boucau were formerly responsible for much of the freight handled, but these were closed down in 1965. The town has food-processing industries (notably wheat-milling), fertiliser factories and an aircraft factory established in the 'thirties, while a number of new industries have been introduced, during the last few years, to afford work for the thousand men formerly employed at the steel works.

Bayonne is a centre for the flourishing tourist industry of the extreme southwest, and especially for the attractive *Côte des basques*. A series of resorts extends from the Adour to the Spanish frontier, ranging from the sophisticated charm of Biarritz to villages such as the promisingly named Chambre d'Amour and Costa Aldia.

This coast was once one of the most active centres of the French fishing industry; Bayonne, Biarritz, Bidart, Guéthary, Ciboure and St Jean-de-Luz have been important for centuries. Fishing vessels from these ports went to Newfoundland and Arctic waters, and the Basque fishermen were second only to the Bretons, but since the mid-nineteenth century this activity has declined. St Jean is still the most important centre for the French sardine fisheries, and anchovy, tunny and mackerel are also caught. Along the coast at various towns are fish-preserving and canning factories.

353

**The oil and gasfields**[47]

The right to search for mineral oil over most of the Pays de l'Adour and adjacent areas in the upper Garonne basin was leased to the government-sponsored Société Nationale des Pétroles d'Aquitaine in 1941, although little was done until after the war, when in 1949 oil was located at Lacq, to the northwest of Pau; this field yields an oil with an asphalt base and a low petrol content. At first production rose steadily to 308 000 tons in 1954, but since then there has been a disquieting decline to only 61 000 tons in 1969, a probable indication of approaching exhaustion. The crude oil is sent by rail to the Shell-Berre refinery at Pauillac.

It seems that the major importance of Lacq lies in the production not of oil but of natural gas, which has been found below the oilfield at great depths.[48] The output during 1969 totalled 57·8 milliard cubic metres from numerous producing bores, the deepest of which exceeds 5 000 m (17 000 ft). The significance of this development is that by 1969 the gas furnished the equivalent of 10 million tons of coal or 6 per cent of France's total consumption of energy. A completely new town, Mourenx, has grown near Lacq, now with over 15 000 people. A vast amount of gas is stored underground at Lussagnet. About a third of the gas output is used locally in the nearby Artix thermal power station, opened in 1961–62; in 1969 it had the sixth largest output (277 million kWh) of any French thermal station. An aluminium refinery is now in operation at Noguères, supplied with power from the Artix station. A gas grid has been constructed in conjunction with the St Marcet field; mains have been built from Lacq to Bordeaux, Nantes, Vannes, Besançon, Lyons and Paris. The chemical works at Pierrefitte in Hautes-Pyrénées have been extended, and several factories for fertilisers, plastics and other byproducts have been made in both the Pyrenean and Bordeaux regions. The gas is highly sulphurous, and about 1·5 million tons of sulphur are extracted each year, making France the second world producer. Further discoveries of gas were made in 1965 at Meillon and Mazières, near Pau.

# The Landes

**The coast**

The straight coast of the Landes extends from the Pointe de Grave to the mouth of the Adour, unbroken for a distance of about 225 km (140 miles) save for the Baie d'Arcachon (Fig. 13.7). This shoreline has developed through the formation of an offshore bar by south-flowing longshore currents, thus straightening off former estuaries.[49] Extensive sand-dunes accumulated on this bar and so created a continuous barrier which has converted the indentations into a string of large shallow lagoons, for the most part reed-margined and dotted with islets and sandbanks.[50] The dune belt is so continuous that the northern lagoons are obliged to drain southwards,

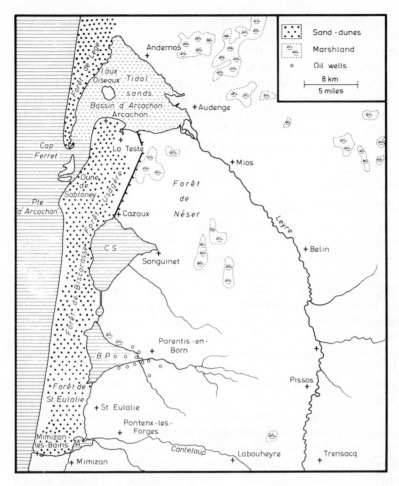

FIG. 13.7 Part of the Landes
The *étangs* are abbreviated as follows: **A,** Aureilhan; **BP,** Biscarosse-
Parentis; **CS,** Cazaux-Sanguinet.

Based on (a) *Carte de France et des frontières au 1 : 200 000ᶜ*, sheets 56, 63; (b) a map in the *Esso Magazine* (1955–56), vol. v, no. 1, p. 19.

each linked with the next by a channel roughly parallel to the coast and
leading ultimately into the Baie d'Arcachon. Some of the smaller southern
*étangs* do drain directly to the sea.

The dune belt, in places 10 km (6 miles) in width, consists of several longitudinal crest-lines separated by parallel depressions and fronted by shelving
beaches of fine white sand. Many of the dunes exceed 45 m (150 ft) in height,
and one, the Dune de Sabloney (or de Pilat), attains 90 m (300 ft), probably
the largest in Europe. The winds from the sea constantly blow sand inland,
and there is some movement within the dune belt,[51] although the *étangs*

check this, as does the planting of pines and marram grass, and the construction of wicker fences.

The Baie d'Arcachon forms the only major breach in the dune line. Across its mouth the long spit of Cap Ferret is still extending southward, built up by south-flowing currents. At low tide the water area of the bay shrinks to less than a third, leaving stretches of mud intersected by a labyrinth of channels separating mudflats and sandy islets, with areas of saltmarsh around the margins of the bay. Into its southeastern corner wanders the Leyre, the main drainage stream of the Landes. [52]

## The interior Landes

Behind the dune lagoon margin from the Gironde to the Adour lie the Landes proper, covering 15 500 sq km (6 000 sq miles) in the *départements* of Gironde and Landes. This area represents the Quaternary *dépression landaise*, into which marine clays and fine sands were deposited. The surface now consists of a gently undulating cover of fine siliceous sands, heavily impregnated with oxides of iron, which have been reworked and redeposited by numerous small streams, and sometimes even resorted by the action of the wind. They are underlain by a dark-coloured hardpan, in some places reinforced by an ironpan of complete impermeability formed by the leaching and downward percolation of water impregnated with ferruginous compounds. Shallow meres and swamps covered much of the Landes in the past, and despite measures of reclamation much remains as dreary reed-covered waste; in former days herdsmen on their stilts were a familiar sight and they are still occasionally to be seen. In their primitive state the Landes consisted of *étangs* and marshes,[1] thickets of broom and gorse, tangles of brambles, expanses of ling and coarse grass; at one extreme were small groves of evergreen oak and pine, at the other bare sand. The whole district comprised in fact *le grand désert landais*, and the word *lande* is used elsewhere in France and Belgium to denote a waste area.

The afforestation of the Landes began along the coastal dune-margin in the years immediately preceding the French Revolution.[53] During the first half of the nineteenth century, however, progress was slow, and it was only after 1857, when the government department of *Eaux et Forêts* took over, that any adequate drainage schemes were effected. Some of the marsh has been drained and the hardpan broken by deep ploughing. The main species used for afforestation is the maritime pine, of which many millions have been planted. The forest has to be carefully preserved, insect pests (particularly crickets) must be combated, and drainage systems maintained, while the tinder-dry nature of the woodland and the high resin content of the trees make fire a constant threat. Between 1930 and 1948 more than 360 000 ha (900 000 acres) of plantation were ravaged by fire; in the hot dry summer of 1949 occurred the grievous conflagrations which destroyed over 120 000 ha (300 000 acres) to the southwest of Bordeaux, with considerable

356

loss of life. Though the pine dominates, other trees have been deliberately planted, notably willows in the damper depressions, cork oak in the south, and in places groves of carob trees. In 1968, notwithstanding the fire damage of previous years, the Landes forests amounted to about 617 000 ha (2 400 sq miles), more than a third of the total area of the *département*.

Several subregions can be distinguished within the apparent uniformity of the Landes. In the centre are the *Grandes Landes*, still the wildest and most thinly populated part. This is bordered on the northeast by the rather higher *Petites Landes*, the *Pays d'Albret* and *la Marsan*, where the sand is less extensive and in many places replaced by Tertiary clays and limestones, wooded with evergreen oaks or covered with pasture. To the south of the Baie d'Arcachon is the *Pays de Born*, and to the south of this again the coastal region of *Marensin*, where grow extensive groves of cork oak. Finally, to the northeast of the Baie d'Arcachon is the *Pays de Buch*.

## Economic development

For long the Landes formed one of the most scantily populated, unproductive and unhealthy regions of France. As D. Faucher says, 'Le peuple, sous-alimenté, dévoré de paludisme, menait une vie chétive et précaire'. Agriculture was carried on in a humble way in clearings, forming minute *oases agricoles* where rye, later maize, melons and other vegetables could be cultivated. In the mid-nineteenth century considerable flocks of sheep were kept, indeed at that time Landes with 650 000 had more than any other *département* in France, and many more animals wintered there from the Pyrenees.

The reclamation and drainage measures intended primarily for the pine plantations also helped agriculture. So too did the extension of the railways into southwestern France, while numerous roads were constructed, and so the region was in some measure opened up.[54] By 1968 about 16 per cent of the *département* of Landes was under arable, but only 4 per cent was permanent pasture. Two-thirds of the arable grew cereals, chiefly maize, and 20 per cent was under fodder crops. Cattle (116 000) and pigs (39 000) have now largely replaced sheep (30 000). The same tendencies are discernible in the neighbouring *département* of Gironde.

The main economic importance of the Landes continues to be in the exploitation of the forests. For many centuries the poor woodlands were cut and burnt for charcoal to provide fuel for several small glass works (long since abandoned) and for furnaces which smelted local bog ores. Today the carefully grown trees are systematically cut for telegraph poles and sawn timber, much of which is exported from Bordeaux. In spite of the development of synthetic substitutes, the pines are still tapped for resin, from which terebenthine and other products are distilled at factories within the forests. But the annual production of resin is now of the order of 600 000 hectolitres, compared with a peak of more than twice as much; the fires of 1949

357

destroyed many mature trees and hit the industry seriously. Until recently the high resin content had precluded use of the wood for pulping, but technical improvements have made this possible, and paper mills have been built at Mimizan,[55] Bègles and Facture.

Lignite is extracted from large opencast workings near Hostens and Arjuzanx, yielding about 1·6 million tons annually. Near each field is a large modern thermal generator, producing together over 5 gWh annually.

There has been some development along the coast in respect of the tourist industry, making use of the fine sandy beaches and a pleasant sunny climate. Lacanau-Océan in the north, Arcachon, Biscarosse-Plage, Mimizan-Plage and Hossegor have grown considerably as resorts. In 1969 Arcachon landed 1 800 tons of fish, mostly sardines and also sole and turbot, though its chief importance is for oysters; with La Tremblade and Marennes further north it has virtual monopoly of the Portuguese variety, which is cultivated in vast numbers in small enclosed culture beds.

An extensive rocket range in the Landes is used to test missiles produced by the Bordeaux aerospace industry.

## The Parentis-Born oilfield

The Société Esso-Standard had considered developments in the area south-west of Bordeaux since before the war of 1939–45 and was granted an exploration permit in 1951, but serious development only started in 1954. Oil was reached in a bore sunk on the southern shores of the Etang de Parentis, and since then further wells have been drilled (Fig. 13.7), of which several have proved to be dry.[56] In 1954 only 132 000 tons of oil were produced, but in the following year this had increased to 576 000 tons and in 1969 it totalled just over 2 million tons, a slight decline on recent years, though an appreciable supplement to France's imported supplies. Exploration is continuing in the area and other discoveries have been made. The oil is piped to a small storage depot at Parentis, then conveyed by rail tankers to the Esso-Standard refinery at Bordeaux.

---

[1] Useful texts include P. Barrère and R. Heisch, *La Région du Sud-Ouest* (1962), a well illustrated volume in the series *France de Demain*; H. Enjalbert, *Les Pays aquitains, le modelé et les sols*, vol. i (1960), 618 pp.; and R. Brunet, *Les Campagnes Toulousaines* (1965).

[2] D. Faucher, *La France: géographie-tourisme* (1951), i, p. 423.

[3] S. Lerat, 'L'Introduction du maïs hybride dans les pays de l'Adour', *Rev. géogr. Pyr. S.-O.*, **34** (1961), pp. 97–117; the area of this high-yielding maize has doubled, its yield quadrupled, during the last decade, and this region produces a quarter of the country's output. It is used as feedgrain, is cut green as fodder, and maize-oil is extracted.

[4] M. Pardé, *Le Régime de la Garonne* (1935). See also H. Enjalbert, 'Les Inondations de Bordeaux en 1952', *Rev. géogr. Pyr. S.-O.*, **26** (1953), pp. 258–68, which describes the floods on the Garonne and the effects on the Bordelais in December of that year.

[5] H. Enjalbert, 'Les formations alluviales de la Gironde', in *Comptes-Rendus du Congrès International de Géographie* (Lisbon, 1949, published in 1950), ii, pp. 461–81.

[6] L. Glangeaud, 'Etudes océanographiques et géologiques pour l'aménagement de l'estuaire girondin', *Annls Géogr.*, **46** (1937), pp. 509–12.

[7] J. Odol, 'La banlieue maraîchère au nord de Toulouse', *Rev. géogr. Pyr. S.-O.*, **23** (1952), pp. 189–232. This is an immensely detailed account of the holdings, types of crops, methods of cultivation, etc. See also C. Couffin, 'L'influence de la ville de Toulouse sur l'agriculture des terrasses garonnaises de la rive gauché', *Rev. géogr. Pyr. S.-O.*, **28** (1957), pp. 359–72.

[8] J. Coppolani, *Toulouse: étude de géographie urbaine* (1954), affords an account of the origin, development, industrial activity and rôle as a regional capital of the city of Toulouse. A special edition of *Rev. géogr. Pyr. S.-O.* (1961) was devoted to Toulouse. See also P. Pechoux *et al.*, 'Les grandes villes françaises, Toulouse', *La Documentation française* (1966), 53 pp.

[9] A. Taillefer, 'L'Office National Industrial de l'Azote', *Rev. géogr. Pyr. S.-O.*, **28** (1957), pp. 5–34.

[10] J. Coppolani, 'Esquisse géographique de la banlieue de Toulouse', *Rev. géogr. Pyr. S.-O.*, **35** (1964), pp. 218–41, 347–67.

[11] D. Schneegans, 'Gas-bearing structures of southern France', *Bulletin of the American Association of Petroleum Geologists*, **32** (1948), p. 206.

[12] G. G. Weigend, 'The outlook for the gas and oil industry of south-west France', *Econ. Geogr.*, **29** (1953), pp. 315–18. See also R. Brunet, 'Lacq, le pétrole et le Sud-Ouest', *Rev. géogr. Pyr. S.-O.*, **29** (1958), p. 361.

[13] A detailed account of market-gardening in the Bordeaux area, with maps, plans and photographs, is provided by P. Barrère, 'La banlieue maraîchère de Bordeaux', *Cah. outre-mer*, **2** (1949), pp. 135–72; see also C. Castevert, 'Problèmes de la polyculture en Entre-deux-Mers', *Rev. géogr. Pyr. S.-O.*, **35** (1965), pp. 23–37.

[14] G. G. Weigend, 'The basis and significance of viticulture in southwest France', *Ann. Ass. Am. Geogr.*, **44** (1954), pp. 75–101; G. Lafforgue, *Le Vignoble girondin* (1947); and G. Mergoil, 'La structure du Vignoble girondin', *Rev. géogr. Pyr. S.-O.*, **34** (1961), pp. 119–40.

[15] The phylloxera is an aphid, of American origin, which first appeared in Languedoc in 1863, and had spread to the Bordeaux district by 1868. It multiplies prodigiously, living in galls on the leaves and the roots, where it cannot be reached by spraying. The affected vines become stunted and die. By 1884 every vine-growing part of France was affected, and no remedy had been found. In 1891 it was discovered that vine stocks from the eastern USA were almost immune, and a vast programme of grafting European scions on to these stocks was begun. While not wholly resistant, these vines are affected much less seriously. Other scourges of the vineyards are *oïdeum*, a white mildew, which can be checked by dusting with sulphur, and blue mildew, checked by spraying with copper sulphate solution.

[16] Unfortunately, the year 1956 was climatically very adverse for the Bordeaux vineyards. Cold chilling mists and frosts persisted in the valleys during almost the whole period from January to April, and only the vineyards on the upper terraces and slopes escaped. Many of the vines died, and vast areas have had to be replanted. Output fell by a third to 2·1 million hectolitres in 1957, but recovered somewhat to 2·98 in 1958, and by 1963 had reached as much as 5·0 million, a figure now normally maintained.

[17] The following articles on Bordeaux are useful: (*a*) A. Grange, 'Le Port de Bordeaux après la Libération', *Cah. outre-mer*, **1** (1948), pp. 14–27, containing photographs of vessels wrecked in the channel; (*b*) Y. Deler, 'Le Port de Bordeaux', *Information géographique*, **13** (1949), pp. 138–42; (*c*) G. G. Weigend, 'Bordeaux: An Example of Changing Port Functions', *Geogr. Rev.*, **45** (1955), pp. 217–43; (*d*) Y. Deler, 'Progrès et avenir du port de Bordeaux', *Information géographique*, **21** (1957), pp. 53–61; (*e*) M. Cassou-Mounat, 'Le port de Bordeaux', *Rev. géogr. Pyr. S.-O.*, **36** (1965), pp. 420–7.

[18] J. P. Sourbes, 'Le Port fluvial de Bordeaux', *Rev. géogr. Pyr. S.-O.*, **29** (1958), pp. 134–57; this contains several maps and tables of statistics.

[19] J. Dumas, 'Les zones industrielles de l'agglomération bordelaise', *Rev. géogr. Pyr. S.-O.*, **35** (1965), pp. 415–20.

[20] G. G. Weigend, 'The outlook for the gas and oil industry of southwest France', *Econ. Geogr.*, **29** (1953), pp. 307–19.

[21] P. Arqué, 'Bordeaux, port pétrolier', *Rev. géogr. Pyr. S.-O.*, **26** (1956), pp. 98–101.

[22] H. Enjalbert, 'La Vallée moyenne de la Charente', *Annls Géogr.*, **61** (1952), pp. 16–33, gives a full account of the physical features of the valley, with numerous maps and photographs.

[23] Mme (sic) Bordarier, 'Le Tourisme dans l'Ile de Ré', *Norois*, **13** (1966), pp. 453–72, gives a detailed survey of the development of tourism on the island, which now brings 50,000 holiday makers annually.

[24] See (*a*) F. Gay, *Le Port de La Rochelle-La Pallice: évolution récente* (1949); (*b*) Y. Deprez, 'Le Grand Port de La Rochelle-Pallice et la liaison routière Océan-Suisse', *Norois* (1955), vol. 2, pp. 419–22; and (*c*) C. Chaline, 'Le port de commerce de La Pallice', *Norois*, **3** (1956), pp. 427–38.

[25] T. Saint-Julien, 'La Rochelle et la decéntralisation industrielle', *Annls Géogr.*, **80** (1971), pp. 687–706.

[26] R. Renard, 'L'ensemble urbain Rochefort, Tonnay—Charente et ses industries', *Norois*, **18** (1971), pp. 615–31.

[27] J. Comby, 'L'agglomération d'Angoulême', *Norois*, **16** (1969), pp. 191–213.

[28] D. Faucher, 'Le Bassin d'Aquitaine', *La France: géographie-tourisme* (1951), i, p. 440.

[29] P. Fénelon, *Le Périgord* (1951), pp. 29–39, describes these structural features, with a number of detailed sections; the lines of folding are traced on a map on p. 113.

[30] Fénelon, *op. cit.*, has a detailed table (pp. 190–1) and a corresponding map (pp. 193–4) showing these surfaces. He indicates their correlation with the work of H. Baulig and others in the Central Massif and its western margins.

[31] These terraces are clearly tabulated, with the corresponding ones worked out by other authorities along other rivers in the western Central Massif, by Fénelon, *op. cit.*, pp. 275–6.

[32] M. Depain, 'La Châtaigneraie périgourdine', *Rev. géogr. Pyr. S.-O.*, **7** (1936), pp. 340–65.

[33] O. Lavaud, 'La Vallée périgourdine de la Vézère', *Annls Géogr.*, **40** (1931), pp. 144–52, gives a full account of walnut production. A more recent account is C. Laugénie, 'La culture du noyer en Périgord', *Rev. géogr. Pyr. S.-O.*, **36** (1965), pp. 135–58.

[34] R. Clozier, 'Les surfaces d'aplanissement des Causses du Quercy (Petits Causses)', *Comptes Rendus du Congrès Internationale de Géographie* (Paris) (1931), ii, pp. 461–8; and *Les Causses du Quercy* (1940).

[35] Terraces can be distinguished along the Lot valley (and very similarly along that of its tributary the Cère) at 290, 175, 140 and 95 m (950, 575, 460 and 310 ft), corresponding closely to those defined by Fénelon in Périgord, *op. cit.* (1951), pp. 275–6.

[36] E.-A. Martel, *Les Abîmes* (1894).

[37] N. Casteret, *Ten Years under the Earth* (English translation, 1940), p. 191.

[38] R. Lacaze, 'La Culture de la lavande dans le Quercy', *Rev. géogr. Pyr. S.-O.*, **35** (1965), pp. 39–52.

[39] L. Brunet-Le Roisic, 'L'évolution récente des houillères du bassin d'Aquitaine', *Rev. géogr. Pyr. S.-O.*, **36** (1965), pp. 193–201.

[40] An immensely detailed survey of these formations is given by F. Taillefer, *Le Piémont des Pyrénées françaises, contributions à l'étude des reliefs de Piémont* (1951).

[41] J. Fischer, 'Le régime de l'Adour et de ses affluents', *Rev. géogr. Pyr. S.-O.*, **1** (1930), pp. 75–97.

[42] M. Richard, 'Les Barthes de l'Adour', *ibid.*, **8** (1937), pp. 101–63 and 237–66.

[43] L. Papy, 'La Chalosse', *Annls Géogr.*, **40** (1931), pp. 239–58.

[44] See, for example, J. Loubergé, 'Villages et maisons rurales dans la vallée moyenne du Gave de Pau', *Rev. géogr. Pyr. S.-O.*, **29** (1958), pp. 21–50; he discusses the siting of villages relative to the river terraces and the valley edge, with a map.

[45] P. Duchemin, 'Le Port de Bayonne et les industries de l'Adour', *Rev. géogr. Pyr. S.-O.*, **25** (1954), pp. 144–56.

⁴⁶ S. Lerat, 'Le Sidérurgie du Boucau est-elle à la veille d'une reconversion?', *Rev. géogr. Pyr. S.-O.*, **31** (1960), pp. 113–22.

⁴⁷ (*a*) G. G. Weigend, 'The outlook for the gas and oil industry of south-west France', *Econ. Geogr.*, **29** (1953), pp. 307–19; (*b*) R. Brunet, 'Le Sud-Ouest et le problème pétrolier', *Rev. géogr. Pyr. S.-O.*, **28** (1957), pp. 60–78; (*c*) A. Guilcher, 'Le pétrole et le gaz naturel en France', *Tijdschr. K. ned. aardrijksk. Genoot.*, **73** (1956), pp. 245–59.

⁴⁸ S. Lerat, 'La mise en valeur du gisement de gaz de Lacq', *Annls Géogr.*, **66** (1957), pp. 260–7; J. P. Fouchier, 'Considerations économiques sur Lacq', *Revue française de l'Energie* (1955), p. 360; and K. Suter, 'Das Erdgas und Industriezentrum Lacq', *Geographica Helvetica*, **20** (1965), pp. 8–13.

⁴⁹ A. Guilcher, A. Godard and E. Visseaux, 'Formes de plage et houle sur le littoral des Landes de Gascogne', *Rev. géogr. Pyr. S.-O.*, **23** (1952), pp. 99–117; this deals with tidal and other influences on the form of the Landes beaches.

⁵⁰ J. Filliol, 'Aspects physiques de la région des étangs landais d'Arcachon à Soustons', *Rev. géogr. Pyr. S.-O.*, **26** (1955), pp. 28–43; this discusses the results of vegetation and sedimentation on the *étangs* of the Landes.

⁵¹ J. J. Wolff, 'The Dunes of Sabloney near Arcachon', *Geogr. J.*, **73** (1929), p. 453; this includes a series of interesting photographs illustrating the changing features of the dunes.

⁵² J. Weulersse, 'Le Bassin d'Arcachon', *Annls Géogr.*, **37** (1928), pp. 407–27, gives a full account, with numerous maps and photographs.

⁵³ A very detailed account of the reclamation of the Landes is provided by A. Larroquette, *Les Landes de Gascogne et la Forêt landaise. Aperçu physique et étude transformation économique* (1924). See also C. Angus, 'La Forêt landaise', *Géographia*, **28** (1954), pp. 25–31, which contains a detailed map of land-use.

⁵⁴ A detailed account, with maps, of the development of communications in the Landes and its effect on the economy is given by H. Cavaillès, 'Le Problème de la circulation dans les Landes de Gascogne', *Annls Géogr.*, **42** (1933), pp. 561–82.

⁵⁵ M. Preuilh, 'La papeterie de Mimizan (Landes), *Rev. géogr. Pyr. S.-O.*, **33** (1962), pp. 398–400.

⁵⁶ (*a*) 'Oil strike in France', *Esso Magazine*, **5** (1955–6), no. 1, pp. 15–19; (*b*) H. Enjalbert, 'Parentis', *Rev. géogr. Pyr. S.-O.*, **28** (1957), pp. 35–59; and (*c*) R. Brunet, 'Le Sud-Ouest et le problème pétrolier', *ibid.*, pp. 60–78.

# 14
# The Saône-Rhône valley[1]

The valley of the Saône, continued to the south of Lyons by that of the Rhône, forms such a distinctive elongated feature that it is often referred to as *le Fosse Saône-Rhône* or *le Couloir entre les Montagnes*. It consists of a structural depression, clearly defined in the west by the edge of the Central Massif. The Saône valley is demarcated on the east, though not quite so prominently, by the edge of the Jura. The eastern wall of the Rhône valley below Lyons is still less clearly defined, for the outlying uplands of the Fore-Alps project intermittently between the Rhône's left-bank tributaries.

The Plateau de Langres, which lies across the northern end of the corridor, is easily crossed from the Paris Basin and Lorraine by road, rail and canal. Another routeway leads into the valley from the Rhineland by way of the Porte de Bourgogne (the 'Gate of Belfort') between the Vosges and the Jura, and others, though more difficult, enter the corridor from the east from Switzerland and Italy. Thus despite the inadequacy of the Rhône as a waterway and the series of gorgelike sections within its valley, the corridor has formed for many centuries an obvious line of communication between northwestern Europe and the Mediterranean lands, or, as D. Faucher puts it, 'un vestibule du Nord pour le Midi, du Midi pour le Nord'. Roads and railways follow each bank of the river, although in places with considerable difficulty. The gorge sections had to be negotiated with the aid of cuttings and tunnels, as at Cruas where three roads, two railways and the river occupy a narrow valley. As most of the tributaries have braided their courses through broad gravel-fans across the main valley floor before they join the Rhône, each bridge is necessarily many times longer than the width of the stream (particularly in summer) would seem to require. It was not until 1855 that the Lyons-Valence left-bank railway was opened, and extended during the following year to Avignon. The right-bank line was completed even later, and the Lyons-Nîmes section was not finally opened until 1879. Today the left-bank railway is one of the most heavily used routes in France, carrying a considerable passenger and freight traffic between Paris and the lower Rhône-Marseilles-Riviera region. Freight traffic includes coal moving southwards, lime and cement going northwards from the large works along the valley, and wine from the Midi and Algeria. Many of the

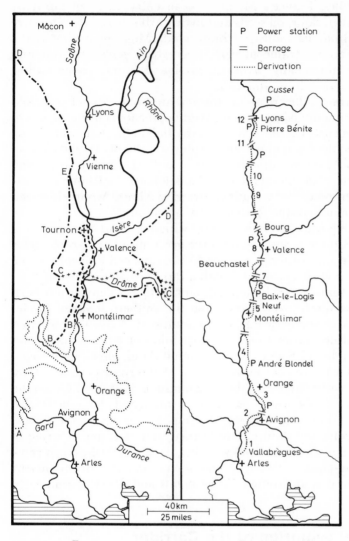

FIG. 14.1                    FIG. 14.2

FIG. 14.1 (left). Limits of critical botanical species in the Rhône valley
**A,** Northern limit of the olive and the holm oak; **B,** northern limit of the holm oak alone; **C,** northern limit of thyme; **D,** southern limit of pedunculate oak; **E,** southern limit of hornbeam.

FIG. 14.2 (right). The regularisation of the lower Rhône
The twelve schemes of derivations, barrages and power stations are shown.

Based on D. Faucher, *La France: géographie-tourisme* (1951), **i,** 14.

imports of Marseilles, France's Mediterranean entry, are sent north by rail, including wheat, flour, oil seeds and hydrocarbons, as well as a range of manufactures from its industrial hinterland. Most interesting is the specialised north-bound traffic in early vegetables (*primeurs*), fruit and flowers from the climatically favoured Midi and lower Rhône valley, carried in insulated or refrigerator vans.

The most important valley roads are the new autoroute N6 to Lyons, and N7 continuing from south of that city to Avignon, thence continuing south-east to Aix-en-Provence, Cannes, Nice and the Italian frontier, and via the N113 to Marseilles; these carry an immense tourist traffic of cars and coaches to the coastal resorts throughout the year, as well as lorries transporting agricultural produce. N86 along the right bank follows the Rhône to Pont-St Esprit, and then trends away southwestward to Nîmes, Montpellier and Perpignan as the mouth of the Rhône valley opens out.

The south-bound traveller is conscious within a short distance of a distinctive change in the landscape from the green meadows, arable fields and woodlands of western Europe to a bright sundrenched Provençal scene of bare limestones and silvery shrubs, with a rather harsh summer aridity. These changes are summarised botanically on Fig. 14.1, where the northern limits of certain Mediterranean species and the southern limits of species more characteristic of northern Europe are indicated. A diverse and often specialised agriculture varies from the cultivation of wheat, maize and fodder-crops in the broad Saône trough, to mulberries, olives, early vege-tables, subtropical fruits and flowers nearer the Mediterranean coast. Many of the valley slopes carry vineyards, the most famed on the Côte d'Or, on the east-facing slopes of the Central Massif further south, and along the Rhône terraces. An active industrial life has developed in many of the towns, particularly at Lyons, the third city of France, and at Dijon. A string of small towns is aligned along the Rhône valley, each in a fertile basin com-manding a crossing-point of the river, and often dominated by an ancient fortress; some indeed were Roman strong-points and developed an early civic life.

## The structural evolution of the Corridor

The structure of the Saône-Rhône valley is one of considerable complexity, since it forms a marginal region between the Hercynian uplands of the Central Massif and the mid-Tertiary folds of the Jura and the Alps, thus affected by both periods of earth movement. The resulting region has only, one might say, 'une unité de surface'.

It is probable that the depression was at any rate vaguely outlined by the end of the Hercynian earth movements of Carbo-Permian times. During the Jurassic and Cretaceous great thicknesses of limestone were deposited over much of what is now southern France. In Miocene times the earth move-ments which produced both the folding of the Alpine ranges to the east and also the bodily upheaval and tilting of the Central Massif to the west, defined the corridor in more or less its present form. Moreover, the gentle synclinal folding of the sediments laid down in what is now the Paris Basin, together with faulting along its southern margins, were responsible for the formation of the Plateau de Langres, a kind of bridge between the Morvan and the Vosges. The Saône-Rhône valley suffered down-faulting, although more unilaterally (along the edge of the Central Massif) than in the case of the Rhine depression. Geological borings have for example revealed a continuation of the coal basin of St Etienne away to the northeast, down-faulted progressively more deeply; at Torcieu in the Ain valley to the north-east of Lyons coal has been reached at 1 400 m (4 600 ft). In fact, beneath the sediments of the Rhône valley the surfaces of the Hercynian blocks lie at such varying depths that it has been said that 'le soussol profond était assez chaotique'. [2]

The lines of fracture are less defined on the eastern side of the Rhône valley in the Fore-Alps, although the lower courses of the Isère and the Drôme seem to follow groups of faults. Some small Hercynian horsts project through the newer cover, as in the Plateau de Crémieu to the east of Lyons where ancient igneous and metamorphic rocks form the 'prow' of a peninsula of middle Jurassic limestones. This happens again further up the Saône valley in the *petit massif de la Serre* to the north of Dole. Most of these faulting movements were completed by the end of the Miocene.

The history of the Saône-Rhône corridor also involved deposition under fluctuating marine and lacustrine conditions. Eocene deposits occur to the north of Montpellier and on the other side of the Rhône near Aix-en-Provence. Oligocene limestones and clays flank the edge of the Cévennes and overlie the Lower Cretaceous rocks to the east of Alès, and occur again on either side of the Durance. Many of these Eocene and Oligocene lime-stones have been gently folded, and the landscape is markedly undulating. Further north the limestones are buried by newer Tertiary rocks, but another considerable outcrop appears to the northeast of Dijon.

In late Eocene or early Oligocene times an eastward extension of the Pyrenean folding into Provence (see p. 615) probably confined a lake extending far to the north. These southern confining ridges, sometimes known as *l'isthme durancien*, were broken through in Miocene times by down-faulting movements which formed the Golfe du Lion. A narrow gulf of the sea thus extended during the Miocene along the valley to Lyons and north-eastward across what is now the Swiss Plateau, as evidenced by the present widespread Miocene deposits. Later in the Miocene or early Pliocene, changes of sea level substantially reduced this elongated gulf, so that the Swiss Plateau became first a lake, still draining southwards, and in due course dry land.

This reduced gulf of the sea in the lower Rhône valley was separated from the Saône valley by another transverse barrier, the 'sill of Vienne', to the south of Lyons. Here the southwesterly spur of the Plateau de Crémieu

365

approaches closely the Hercynian projection of Mont Pilat. To the north of the barrier, what is now the Plaine de Bresse was occupied by a large lake. A river flowed southwards from western Germany through the Porte de Bourgogne and approximately along the line of the present Doubs valley to 'lake Bresse', into which it poured vast masses of sediments. Almost the whole of the Saône basin from where the Jurassic rocks end near Vesoul is floored with these Pliocene deposits, except where still newer material has been laid down over them. 'Lake Bresse' drained southwards through a notch cut across the 'sill of Vienne' into the gulf of the sea occupying the lower Rhône valley.

Towards the end of the Pliocene occurred the subsidence of the floor of the Rhine rift valley and the creation of the rightangled bend in that river near Basel. For a time the upper Doubs probably continued northeastwards through the Jura to join the Rhine, until its remarkable capture by another river, now the lower Doubs, flowing southwestwards along the flanks of the Jura into the Plaine de Bresse (see pp. 603–5 and Fig. 21.1). The Porte de Bourgogne thus became a major watershed in central Europe. Finally, uplift to the south of Lyons converted the gulf of the sea into the valley of the lower Rhône. The rivers continued to deposit vast quantities of gravel worn from the uplifted ranges, in the form of 'stony deltas' around the edges of the retreating Pliocene gulf.

Alpine glaciers moved westwards from the high mountains at the maximum of the Quaternary glaciation, particularly down the upper Rhône and Isère valleys. They covered the marginal plateaus and coalesced to form piedmont sheets on the low ground of the main valley. At their maximum extent glaciers crossed the Rhône to the west of Lyons, and pushed north across the Pays de Dombes almost as far as Bourg on the river Reyssouze (Fig. 22.3). Much till was deposited, both as distinct morainic lines and as hummocky sheets of ground moraine, notably in the Pays de Dombes. Still more extensive were the outwash sheets of fluvioglacial gravels. As the Quaternary glaciation waned, the main tributaries continued to bring immense quantities of material, the heavier detritus forming cones beyond the valley exits, the lighter sandier material washed down into the Rhône valley. The Pays de Dombes and much of Bas-Dauphiné are covered with sheets of these gravels and coarse sands.

The postglacial Rhône and its tributaries have continued both their erosive and depositive activity. The snowmelt of early summer so much increases their volume and activity that vast quantities of material derived from the wastage of the Alps are brought down, ranging from 'rock flour' to gravel. Even the short but torrential tributaries from the west are responsible for masses of pebbles during their winter floods. The heavier grades are deposited in the lower courses; during the low water of late summer the Isère, Drôme and Durance twist in braided channels among banks of these bleached gravels. The finer sands and clays are swept downstream to their final resting place on the floodplain of the lower valley or in the delta. These marshy plains of the lower Rhône, often covered with reed swamps, contrast with the dry higher gravel terraces.

The Saône-Rhône corridor, although basically a low-lying reentrant between two major uplands, presents therefore a varied landscape. Its margins consist of limestones of a diverse character, of Jurassic, Cretaceous and early Tertiary ages; in the north they form well-cultivated south-facing slopes, but in the south increasing aridity results in a distinctive *garrigue* character with scrubby evergreen plants and much bare rock. The floor of the depression is filled with lacustrine, marine, glacial, fluvioglacial and fluvial deposits in great variety, including the sands, clays and marls of Bresse, the waterlogged clays of Dombes, extensive gravel sheets, banks of fine sediments and patches of limon. The changes of base level and course by the Rhône and its tributaries have helped to diversify the landscape by developing gorges, by leaving prominent residual hills, and by producing terraces with distinctive edges.

## The river Saône

The Saône is formed by a group of headstreams rising on the Triassic sandstones of the Monts Faucilles and on the southwestern flanks of the Vosges (Fig. 11.1). It flows southwestwards, with an exceptionally serpentine course, receiving a number of left-bank tributaries from the Vosges, notably the Ognon which rises on the southwestern flanks of the Ballon d'Alsace. Its major tributary from the Jura, the Doubs, joins some 30 km (20 miles) above Chalon (see p. 603 and Fig. 21.1). The Saône is not without right-bank tributaries, which flow down the steep southeastern edge of the Plateau de Langres on to the lowlands. The Saône then swings across to the western side of the Plaine de Bresse under the steep edge of the Mâconnais, the Beaujolais and the Lyonnais. Several clearly defined terraces border the floodplain on which the river wanders with braidings, cutoffs and shallow lakes. Its volume is increased by several left-bank tributaries which pick up water from springs issuing at the base of the Vignoble-Revermont ridges along the edge of the Jura. At Lyons the Saône is joined by the Rhône, enclosing within the angle thus formed the hummocky country of the Pays de Dombes.

The Saône has a more stable regime than that of the Alpine Rhône. It receives numerous large head-streams, many deriving their water from the extensive underground storage of the limestone Jura. In the Plaine de Bresse the gentle gradient of the long valley helps to even out the effects of protracted rain and late spring snowmelt, producing a steadily flowing river. As Dr H. Ormsby so felicitously expresses it describing the confluence of the Saône and the Rhône at Lyons, 'the two ill-assorted bedfellows occupy uneasily the same channel. The hurrying, often turbulent, Rhône is easily distinguished, with its milky waters, as it jostles the tranquil green flood of its companion from the north.'[3]

# The lower Rhône

The Rhône between Lake Geneva and the Ain confluence crosses transversely the ridges of the Jura (see pp. 602–3 and Fig. 21.1), then enters the Plaine de Bresse in the neighbourhood of Lagnieu. Until recently the section between the Ain confluence and the eastern outskirts of Lyons was liable to inundation; the river wandered in large loops over a floodplain 3 to 5 km (2 to 3 miles) in width, with areas of marshland, fluctuating lakes and reed swamps. Many disastrous floods have been experienced; the worst for several centuries was in 1840, which flooded the inter-riverine area and covered all the eastern parts of the city. Considerable regularisation has since taken place; the dyked Canal de Jonage was constructed in 1893 along the southern margin of the floodplain, with a large reservoir lake to draw off and hold up temporarily the floodwaters, and the Canal de Miribel follows the northern edge (Fig. 14.5). The former meandering course of the river, substantially reduced in volume, now lies between these two canals.

The Rhône, with its volume now greatly increased by the steady contribution of the Saône,[4] flows almost due south from Lyons for about 200 km (130 miles) to Arles, where the deltaic region begins (Fig. 14.6).

Between Lyons and the Isère confluence near Valence the effects of the Saône's regime are still dominant, and the winter rains on the uplands of west-central Europe result in a pronounced winter maximum. The Isère, which is a tributary of such importance that it increases the volume of the Rhône by a quarter, brings down early summer meltwater from the Alpine snowfields. Further south the drought and evaporation of the Mediterranean summer result in appreciable low-water conditions in late summer. The shorter tributaries from the Fore-Alpine hills and from the restricted catchment area of the steep margins of the Central Massif contribute little water in summer; some literally dry up. They can, however, produce sharp concentrated floods in autumn and winter, frequently spreading widely over the floodplain; the Ardèche, descending steeply from the Cévennes, is notorious in this respect.

The Rhône follows to the south of Lyons what is really an extension of the plain of Bresse, which ends in the neighbourhood of Givors where the river cuts through the 'sill of Vienne'. To the south of this narrow section is the first of the Rhône 'basins', the little plain of Vienne, formed by the coalescence of the Gère and several other small valleys. Next comes another narrow section, again succeeded by a more open valley where some small left-bank tributaries enter from the Plateau de Chambaran, and a further narrow section between St Vallier and the pleasant vine-growing centre of Tain-l'Hermitage. This in turn is succeeded southward by the basin of Valence, within which the Isère and the Drôme join the Rhône.

With its major headstreams, the Arc and the Drac, the Isère drains a large part of the French Alpine ranges (Figs. 22.1, 22.2). The Drôme, a much shorter river than the Isère, flows through a maze of shingle banks in the southern part of the Valence basin. It then cuts through a northward-projecting spur of the Diois in a fine gorge 8 km (5 miles) above its confluence with the Rhône.

To the south of the Valence basin the main valley narrows to form the Cruas gorge, steepsided though over a kilometre in width. At Baix, just above Cruas, the river swings against the limestone cliffs, and both road and railway are obliged to follow a series of tunnels and cuttings. Numerous islets, shingle banks and braided sections lie within the Cruas gorge, but the main stream is now confined between training-walls and embankments for much of its length. After the river leaves Cruas it passes into the Montélimar basin, and follows the edge of the Central Massif; the alluvium-floored basin, crossed by the Roubion and its tributary the Jabron from the Diois massif, lies almost wholly to the east of the river. Then the river enters the Donzère gorge, trenched through hard limestone for 5 km (3 miles). There is just room for the railways at the foot of the river cliff, and in places they are obliged to use cuttings and tunnels. Below the Donzère gorge, the Rhône enters the plain of Pierrelatte. A large loop canal has been completed across the eastern part of this plain from Donzère to Mondragon where it rejoins the main river (Fig. 14.6). To the south of the Mondragon couloir the plain of Orange opens out, next follows the Défilé de Roque-maure cut through the Tertiary rocks of the Collines de Châteauneuf-du-Pape and a narrow bar of Lower Cretaceous limestone, and then the broad triangular plain of Avignon to the north of the Chaîne des Alpilles.

The Fore-Alpine plateau country here swings away to the east, but long spurs project westward into the plains, separating the valleys of short tributaries such as the Eygues, Ouvèze and Nesque. To the west the undulating Cretaceous limestone country of the *garrigues* approaches closely the right bank of the river, except where Cévennes confluents such as the Ardèche and Cèze have eroded deep re-entrants.

A few kilometres below Avignon, the Rhône receives its last major tributary, the Durance, which rises far to the northeast in the Briançonnais, and drains the southern parts of the French Alps. The river emerges on to the lowland embayment between the westerly spurs of the Montagne de Luberon and the detached limestone Chaîne des Alpilles (Fig. 15.2). In Pliocene times the proto-Durance flowed to the south of the Alpilles into the Pliocene gulf, and built up an enormous delta of gravel debris, La Crau (see p. 405), but later the river abandoned this course for its present one along the northern side of the Alpilles. At Arles begins the Rhône delta.

## The Saône-Rhône navigation [5]

The nature of the river Rhône makes it manifest that considerable difficulties are presented to navigation. Although it is officially navigable from near the Swiss frontier to the delta, that is, for about 500 km (300 miles), the section above Lyons is as yet used little except for rafts and small pleasure craft, carrying a mere 70 000 tons of stone, gravel and sand.

The Saône has, however, been canalised as far upstream as Corre, where the southern branch of the Est Canal continues navigation over the water-parting of the Monts Faucilles into the Moselle basin (Fig. 12.5). About 150 km (100 miles) downstream from Corre, the Rhône-Rhine Canal (now being enlarged) (see p. 309) leaves the Saône at St Symphorien and begins its long difficult course to Strasbourg. Other northward links include the Marne-Saône Canal from Heuilly-sur-Saône to Vitry-le-François, the Burgundy Canal (Canal de Bourgogne) from St Jean-de-Losne to the river Yonne at Laroche, and the Centre Canal from Chalon-sur-Saône to Digoin, where it links up with the Loire navigation. This last waterway is most useful in spite of its sixty-three locks, since it serves the small but important Blanzy-Le Creusot and Nivernais industrial districts.

The Saône has achieved considerable importance as a waterway, since these five canals contribute an appreciable volume of traffic. The river between Chalon and Lyons carries about 2 million tons of freight; largely because of this Saône traffic, Lyons is the ninth inland port of France (see p. 384).

During the decade preceding 1939 there was constant discussion whether to regularise the middle and lower Rhône itself (a scheme favoured by the city of Lyons), or to construct a separate lateral canal (as supported by Marseilles). In 1931 the Government-sponsored Compagnie Nationale du Rhône was created to carry out a multipurpose utilisation of the Rhône for navigation, hydroelectricity production and irrigation, involving twenty major projects, twelve of which are below Lyons (Fig. 14.2). The first major scheme, at Génissiat (p. 608) was begun in 1937 and completed in 1948. Since 1950 most work has been carried out on the Rhône below Lyons. Twelve navigation loops (Fig. 14.2) are scheduled to bypass sections of the river, each with a power station, locks and barrage, and a ship lift.

So far completed are the *André Blondel* station at Donzère-Mondragon (1952) (Fig. 14.6 and p. 391); *Châteauneuf* near Montélimar (1957); *Baix-le-Logis-Neuf* above Montélimar (1960); *Beauchastel* below Valence (1963); *Pierre-Bénite* just below Lyons (1966); *Bourg-les-Valence* (1968); and *Vallabrègues* between Avignon and Arles (1969). Five others are under construction or projected; the master plan, when completed in fifteen to twenty years, will provide a looped lateral canal, each section supplying a head to a power station, and will also enable some 40 000 ha (100 000 acres) to be irrigated. The stations will generate an estimated 13 000 gWh. As yet traffic on the lower Rhône is light (about 4 million tons of oil, stone, cement, gravel, bauxite), but by 1976 it is expected to carry four times as much. Several industrial estates have been developed near the power stations.

# Climate

The Saône-Rhône valley forms a climatic transition between a regime in the north with continental tendencies and one in the south with distinctive 'Mediterranean' features, notably an increasingly marked summer drought. In the northern part of the Saône trough average temperatures in January are usually below freezing, although summer means may be in the neighbourhood of 19°C (66°F). Rainfall in this area varies from 690 to 1 020 mm (27 to 40 in) annually, according to aspect; thus Chalon, on the west of the valley and so to some extent in the rain-shadow of the Côte d'Or, has an annual mean of 700 mm (27·6 in), while Bourg on the east has as much as 970 mm (38·2 in). Throughout the Saône valley a distinct maximum is experienced in autumn (October), and a secondary maximum in May–June. Snow is often widespread in winter, even on the valley floor.

At Lyons there is still an appreciable range of temperature, with mean figures of 2°C (35°F) in January and 21°C (69°F) in July. The mean rainfall is 790 mm (31 in), quite well spread out through the year, but with a winter minimum between November and March and a hint of a drier summer between the secondary maximum in May–June and the main October maximum.

To the south of Lyons the climate shows increasing tendencies towards 'la transition méridionale'. As D. Faucher puts it, in the plain of Valence 'le ciel plus clair, l'horizon plus dégagé, la température plus douce, tout annonce l'approche d'une province climatique nouvelle'. At Avignon the mean January temperature is about 4°C (40°F), the July temperature 24°C (75°F), and daily maxima of 35°C (95°F) are frequent. The mean annual rainfall at Avignon is 640 mm (25 in), but summer is very dry, the bare 25 mm (1 in) received on an average in June being the result of short-lived thunderstorms. A distinct autumn maximum is experienced, and a third of the total usually falls between September and November, but a secondary spring maximum is the result of unstable pressure conditions in the western Mediterranean and the passage of depressions through the Golfe du Lion. Winds from the west and south, associated with the warm sectors of eastwards-moving depressions, may bring some winter rain at intervals, but this season is usually much drier than is autumn. This is the result of continental conditions, for much cold dry air moves from the Central Massif down the Rhône 'funnel', in its extreme form known as the *mistral*. This may originate as an air stream behind a depression moving eastwards through the Mediterranean, with all the characteristics of a cold front (turbulence, towering cumulonimbus clouds, and squally showers of rain or hail), and then the air flow becomes established as a strong, bitterly cold and extremely dry wind. The true *mistral* exceeds 40 kmph (20 knots), but considerably higher forces, occasionally as much as 130 kmph (70 knots) have been recorded; its effects are most marked in winter and spring. Trees are sometimes damaged and even uprooted, houses deroofed, telegraph poles snapped off at the ground and motor-cars overturned. Even without the destructive gale force results, the wind can do much harm in spring to fruit trees, vines and flower gardens, both by direct physical damage and by its desiccating effects. The landscape of the lower Rhône valley is diversified by long windbreaks of poplars, dense cypress hedges and hurdle fences, erected in an effort to mitigate the worst effects of this unpleasant wind.[6]

## Regional divisions

The Saône-Rhône valley can be divided into a number of subregions. In the north is the upper Saône valley, including both the actual *Val de Saône* and the lowland flanking it to the northwest, the plain of Burgundy. The east-facing slopes overlooking this valley also comprise a distinct subregion, for although they are the edges of the Jurassic uplands and of the Central Massif, they clearly belong to the Saône region, forming the *rebord viticole* which has made the name 'Burgundy' world-famous. To the south succeeds the main valley between the Mâconnais and the Jura, known as the Plaine de Bresse. Further south again in the angle of the Saône-Rhône junction lies the *Pays de Dombes* or *la plaine dombiste*, with its flanking terraces along the Rhône, Ain and Saône, and then follows the Lyons district. Below the junction, the Rhône valley may be divided into three—the middle section between Lyons and Donzère, together with the flanking hill-country of Bas-Dauphiné, the lower section between Donzère and Arles, and the delta (see pp. 399–407).

## The upper Saône valley

This subregion includes the valley of the Saône as far downstream as Chalon, together with the portions of the valleys of its almost parallel headstreams, the Ognon and the Doubs (Plate 39), below where they leave the Jurassic country of the Porte de Bourgogne.[7] This 'gateway', the scene of a remarkable major reversal of drainage towards the end of the Pliocene (see p. 366), lies at a height of about 350 m (1 150 ft). The Jurassic rocks which floor most of this gap have been faulted and feebly folded, 'pincés entre la retombée méridionale des Vosges et les plissements du Jura' (E. Juillard), and now form low limestone plateaus with occasional higher ridges, and with the surface diversified in places by Tertiary rocks and by patches of sands and gravels of recent deposition. Although the gap is one of the major European watersheds, the divide is really very indeterminate; the Largue and its many small confluents drain northeastwards across the Sundgau (see p. 294) to the Ill, while the Doubs receives the Rapine, the Savoureuse (on which stands Belfort) and the Luzine from the southern slopes of the Ballon d'Alsace in the Vosges, and the Allaine from the flanks of the Jura. To the west of the Porte de Bourgogne the Jurassic limestone

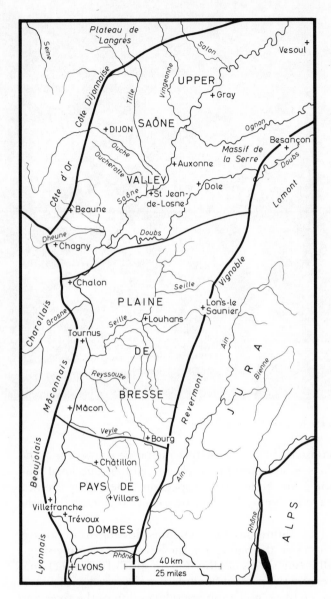

Fig. 14.3 Regions of the Saône basin

country forms undulating country crossed by the Doubs, Ognon and Saône itself, known generally as the *plateaux de la Haute-Saône*.

The land slopes gently to the west and southwest to the valley proper of the upper Saône, known as *le Pays-bas bourguignon*. Broad terrace steps rise from the floodplain of the river to the foothills of the Côte d'Or to the northwest. These terraces are covered with sheets of Pliocene, Pleistocene and

373

PLATE 39. Besançon within the loop of the river Doubs

Recent deposits, with consequent variety of soils, including coarse sands and gravels, and sandy clays which become sticky in winter but hard and cracked in summer. Some are quite fertile, especially where they are of a loamy character and have been enriched by calcareous downwash from the *côtes*.

This plain is crossed by numerous short streams flowing from springs near the base of the *côtes* to join the Saône. On the lower terraces tiny sheets of water lie among undulating sheets of alluvium, in spite of some reclamation. The lowest terraces and the present floodplain are covered with watermeadows, marsh and osier-thickets. Despite regularisation of the river and the building of continuous embankments, these lands are liable to winter flooding.

To the east of the Saône, the plains of the lower Ognon and Doubs (separated by the ancient rocks of the Massif de la Serre) have much the same characteristics as those to the west. The soils tend to be richer, partly because of the greater amount of limy downwash from the Jura, partly because of a limon-like covering on the higher terraces.

The diverse land use of the upper Saône region is summarised by the

374

figures for the *département* of Haute-Saône, which occupies the valley as far downstream as the Ognon confluence. About 42 per cent was under woodland in 1968, 31 per cent under pasture, and 16 per cent under arable. These proportions are broadly similar in the contiguous lowland portions of the neighbouring *départements* of Côte-d'Or, Saône-et-Loire and Jura.

This high proportion of woodland is not surprising, since considerable areas of the coarse sandy soils are forested. In the plain of Burgundy forests total about 350 sq km (135 sq miles). Further east, in the plain between the gradually converging Loue and Doubs, is the Forêt de Chaux covering 200 sq km (80 sq miles), and much of the Serre massif is also forested. These forests are dominated by oaks, but coniferous plantations have been established, and along the rivers grow osiers, willows, poplars and alders.

The most fertile lands are found on the lower clay-covered terraces of the main river and of its tributaries, and on the limon-covered higher terraces bordering the Jura. Almost half of the arable is devoted to cereals, both wheat and maize, together with sugar beet, fodder beet, potatoes, lucerne and trefoil. Tobacco, hops and mustard are also grown, and vineyards occur on the slopes, though much less extensively than a century ago. The less fertile soils to the northwest of the Saône are also assiduously cultivated, the result of centuries of effort, often originated by clearance schemes of the Cistercian houses in the Middle Ages. In some districts a period of fallow is introduced into the rotation. Some of the *étangs* are drained, cultivated for a few years, flooded and used for pisciculture for a few more years before being drained again. The most prosperous and intensively cultivated districts are the market gardens on the lower terraces of the Saône. Here the light soils, heavily fertilised and cultivated in strip holdings, produce early potatoes and carrots, asparagus, onions and cauliflowers, which find ready markets in Belfort, Besançon, Montbéliard and Dijon.

As nearly a third of the upper Saône valley is under pasture, dairying is of importance. Water-meadows along the rivers are irrigated during the summer by means of a network of channels filled through sluices in the river dykes; these also help drainage during winter flooding. Temporary grassland enters into the rotation systems, and fodder crops are grown. Many riverine meadows are owned by the communes and grazed in common by the herds of the proprietors. The quality of the animals has been improved by the gradual substitution of the good milk-yielding *tachetée* breed for the small red *Bressane* type. Much milk is sold in the industrial towns, and there is an appreciable output of both farmhouse and factory-made butter and cheese.

Thus the Saône valley presents a pleasantly diverse landscape. The population in this primarily rural area is not dense, of the order of 35 to 40 per sq km (90 to 100 per sq mile). Numerous villages, with their clustered red roofs among the trees, are mostly situated on the terraces or on small eminences away from the floodplain. A few larger towns stand at river crossings, for the Saône lies athwart the routeways from the north. Gray is the bridge town on the important N67 between the Paris Basin and Switzerland via Langres and Besançon, and Auxonne is situated at the crossing of N5 between Dijon and Geneva. These towns are among the market and servicing centres, with various food-processing industries, such as the flour mills of Gray. Agricultural implements are manufactured at Vesoul (the *chef-lieu* of the *département* of Haute-Saône) and at Arc, an industrial suburb of Gray. Lure has some small anciently established textile factories. Dôle, once a capital of Franche-Comté, on the right bank of the lower Doubs, dominates the crossing of the river. It has a small port on the Rhône-Rhine Canal (which here utilises the channel of the regularised Doubs), and industries have developed—flour mills, the manufacture of agricultural implements and of electrical heating apparatus, and a large chemical factory using as raw material rocksalt and brine from the Salins area (see p. 609). Other long-established industries include cooperage and wood-working generally in this region of extensive woodlands, and some small specialised metallurgical industries are survivals of forges formerly using alluvial ores and charcoal. Fraisans also has a small glass works. This industrial activity is on a small scale, and emphasises the essentially rural and agricultural economy of this countryside of small scattered villages and large farms.

Three towns dominate the valleys of the upper Saône and its tributaries the Ognon and the Doubs, leading to the Porte de Bourgogne (p. 362): Belfort, Montbéliard and Besançon, though the last belongs primarily to the Jura region (p. 611). Belfort is situated at an altitude of 350 m (1 150 ft) on the banks of the Savoureuse near the northern edge of the Porte de Bourgogne. It has served as a fortress town since the thirteenth century, but was tremendously strengthened by Vauban. Its situation in this routeway from the Rhineland into central France is responsible for this strategic importance, and the town is known as the *ville aux trois sièges* from the three outstanding sieges it sustained, the last during the winter of 1870–71. Today the city has about 53 000 inhabitants, but it is the capital of its own territory of 608 sq km (235 sq miles) with a population of 118 000; this was left to France in 1872 when Germany annexed the rest of the *département* of Haut-Rhin, and on the return of Alsace it retained its administrative independence. Belfort is one of a group of towns—the others being Montbéliard, Mulhouse and Basel—which form the industrial region of the upper Rhineland. The great Société Alsacienne has works there, manufacturing electrical and electronic machinery, turbines and locomotives, and other activities include several large textile factories.[8] Its position inevitably makes Belfort an important route centre; the Calais-Basel and Arlberg-Orient expresses pass through the town, and five *routes nationales* meet there.

Montbéliard (agglomeration population, 115 000), barely 10 km (6 miles) from Belfort, is situated on the Rhône-Rhine Canal. A wide variety of engineering industries is carried on in the town and its satellites (Sochaux,

Valentigny and Audincourt), including the manufacture of machine tools, cycles, aircraft engines, agricultural implements, hardware, typewriters and watches. The dominant enterprise is the great Peugeot works at Sochaux, with its cluster of component factories.

## The northwestern côtes

The Saône is bounded to the northwest in succession by the slopes of the Côte d'Or, the Chalonnaise, the Maconnais and the Beaujolais, known collectively as the *Côte bourguignonne*. These slopes rise irregularly from 210 to 230 m (700 to 750 ft) in the foothills to summits of over 600 m (2 000 ft) in the Côte d'Or and to 1 012 m (3 320 ft) (the summit of Mont-St Rigaud) in the Beaujolais. The Côte d'Or[9] consists almost entirely of Jurassic limestone, although the ancient igneous and metamorphic rocks of the Central Massif are in evidence further south. The lower slopes are veneered with downwash and have been under the vine since pre-Roman times.

If one drives for 50 km (35 miles) along the foot of the Côte d'Or from Dijon through Beaune to Chagny in the Dheune valley, at a distance of some 20 to 30 km (15 to 20 miles) from the Saône, one can see rows of vines tiered on the hillsides. From these are produced the superlative Burgundy wines,[10] though not in great quantity; the *département* of Côte-d'Or produced in 1968 only 304 000 hectolitres of wine out of a French output of 66 million. A third of the 3 600 ha (9 000 acres) of vineyards grow in the northern part (known as the *Côte de Nuits*) as far south as the small town of Nuits-St Georges, and the rest further south along the *Côte de Beaune*. A list of the vineyards and the wines produced reads like a high-class wine-merchant's catalogue; some are indicated on Fig. 14.4. As D. Faucher expresses it: 'Les subtiles différences de terrains, les impondérables variations d'atmosphère, les procédés et le savoir-faire des hommes depuis des générations, tout s'y traduit en une gamme infinie de qualités.' Output varies immensely from year to year, both in quantity and quality; another glance at the wine-merchant's catalogue will reveal the 'vintage years'. The names of the famous wines are sometimes derived from a neighbouring town or commune, sometimes merely from a small château with a few hectares of carefully tended vineyards.

To the south of the Dheune valley vineyards continue along the slopes of the *Côte Chalonnaise*, and again to the south of the Grosne valley along the *Côte Mâconnaise*. Both these districts are in the *département* of Saône-et-Loire, whose vineyards yielded 523 000 hectolitres in 1968, of which a third was of quality wine. To the south again is Beaujolais, extending as far as the Azergues valley in the *département* of Rhône. These three districts, bordered closely by the Saône at the foot of the cuesta, are included within the Burgundy district, although sometimes they are differentiated as Lower Burgundy.

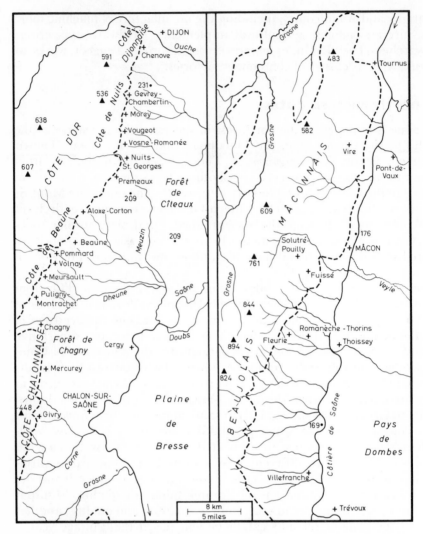

FIG. 14.4. The Saône plain and the Côte de Vignoble

The edge of the Côte is shown diagrammatically by a heavy pecked line, while spot heights in metres on the valley floor and on the ridges indicate the steep rise between them. The righthand map shows the country immediately to the south of that in the lefthand map. Only a limited number of the important wine-producing communes are named.

Based on (*a*) *Carte de France au 200 000ᵉ*, sheets 24, 41; and (*b*) *La France vinicole: Carte publiée sous le haut patronage de l'Institut National des Appellations d'Origine*, in *Atlas de France vinicole L. Larmat*.

The vine-growing districts of the *côtes* represent a remarkable example of monoculture. The large owners and firms, and the thousands of small growers who sell their produce to the *caves coopératives*, depend alike on their vineyards, whether they produce the *bourgogne ordinaire*, the more select

378

*bourgogne grand ordinaire*, or the individually renowned and highly profitable (in a good year) *vins fins de Bourgogne*. Many of the villages have indeed sought to introduce other fruit cultivation,[11] blackcurrants for making *cassis*, raspberries, and orchards of cherry and peach, while on the lower slopes grow fields of wheat, maize, sugar beet and even hops. The vine, however, remains dominant almost everywhere.

Along the lower slopes of the *côtes*, usually where valleys open out through the hills, are prosperous attractive villages, with what might be called an *opulence joviale*. The centre of the wine industry of Côte d'Or is Beaune, an old walled town. Chagny is a route junction where the Dheune valley opens into the Saône plain, with roads, a railway and the Canal du Centre leading southwestward to the industrial region of Le Creusot and Montceau-les-Mines, so into the upper Loire basin. Further south the chief towns are at Saône bridge points, for the river swings close under the edge of the uplands. At Chalon the Canal du Centre joins the Saône, and it is a road centre through which N6 runs southward to Lyons. Chalon has developed into a prosperous town, with engineering industries, barge-building, the processing of food products (notably sugar-refining), textile industries, and photographic materials (Kodak). Further down the river is Tournus, with metallurgical industries (notably using aluminium). Mâcon is the commercial centre of both the western Plaine de Bresse and the Mâconnais wine-producing region, and also is the *chef-lieu* of Saône-et-Loire; it has a range of light industries, including the manufacture of motor-cycles and motor-scooters. Villefranche is the 'capital' of Beaujolais and the centre of its wine trade. It manufactures presses, tuns and other apparatus for the wine industry, agricultural implements, pharmaceutical chemicals, and (an indication of the influence of Lyons to the south) some silk textiles. Trévoux, once the capital of the principality of Dombes (incorporated in France as late as in 1762), has factories specialising in rich cloth of silver.

The most important town of this region is Dijon,[12] with about 145 000 inhabitants in 1968, the *chef-lieu* of Côte-d'Or and one of the most important route centres in France. Almost every main railway-line from south and southeast France, Switzerland and Italy converges here on its way to Paris, and moreover the transverse lines linking the Rhine valley and Lorraine with western and southwestern France also pass through. Seven main roads, including the Paris–Geneva (N5) and the Sarreguemines–Montceau (N74) routes, converge on it, though the autoroute N6 passes some 30 km to the southwest. Finally, it has a port, a barge-repairing yard and a coal dépôt on the Burgundy Canal.

Dijon has grown rapidly during the last century as a result of its dominating position and the expansion of rail communications, for in 1866 its population was only 39 000. Many of the wine organisations have their central administrative offices in the town. Modern factories have been built in the suburbs, leaving the attractive old town within quadrangular boulevards which occupy the site of the former moat and defensive works needed when the city was the fortress capital of the Dukes of Burgundy. Its industries are diverse, including the processing of foodstuffs, for which its annual *Foire Gastronomique* is a great advertisement—confectionery, biscuits, tobacco and liqueurs (such as *cassis* made from blackcurrants). Particular mention must be made of its mustard, for which the town is famous. Its metallurgical industries include the production of motor-cycles, pedal-cycles, machine tools and a wide range of aluminium articles (notably foil), and other activities comprise the manufacture of cement, lime, chemicals, and boots and shoes.

## The Plaine de Bresse

This part of the Saône valley lies between the Doubs in the north and the Veyle in the south. It is covered with sheets of clay, although in the north are also considerable areas of sand, while on the eastern slopes good loamy soils have developed on the limon deposits. The Saône flows along the western edge under the foot of the *côtes*, and several long tributaries wander leisurely across the plain from the edge of the Jura to the main river. In the north there are many small lakes, some artificially maintained behind barrages and used for carp-breeding. Marshland borders the floodplains of the rivers, their courses usually lined with willows. Small groves and copses of trees occur in places, with some oak forests, particularly in the north.

Bresse presents a varied landscape, devoted to mixed farming, though with an emphasis on livestock. Much permanent pasture is found on the damp heavy soils, as well as fields devoted to fodder crops including lucerne, fodder beet and a variety of maize, grown in rotation. Dairy cattle provide · milk for the urban populations and for the cheese factories in such towns as Bourg-en-Bresse and Louhans. Pigs consume the skimmed milk and also acorns from the oak woods, and horses and poultry are reared. The last are very important both as a sideline on the dairy or mixed farms and as a main preoccupation on large poultry farms, using modern intensive methods of production and fattening; plump Bresse capons are famous throughout France, and vast numbers are sent to Paris. On the higher terraces away from the rivers areas of vine yield *vin ordinaire*, while wheat is grown on the limon soils nearer the Jura edge.

This predominantly rural and agricultural region is somewhat thinly populated. Small though prosperous villages and individual farms stand on the terraces above the floodplains, while the western part is served by the Saône towns already mentioned, notably Chalon and Mâcon. The regional centre for Bresse is Bourg on the upper Reyssouze, which is well served as a road focus (eight main roads concentrate on the town) and as a railway junction. Bourg is the *chef-lieu* of Ain, a very busy market and despatching centre for agricultural produce, especially for poultry. The only other place of importance in Bresse is Louhans to the north, also a market centre.

# The Pays de Dombes

This region is enclosed within the angle of confluence of the lower Saône and the Rhône, and is bordered on the east and north by the Ain and the Veyle respectively. It consists of a gently sloping plateau between 290 and 300 m (950 and 1 000 ft) above sea level, diversified as a result of an uneven covering of glacial ground moraine, terminal moraines, and sheets of fluvioglacial and postglacial sands and gravels. Hummocky eminences alternate with marshy hollows, many of which contain small lakes. In the eighteenth century these covered an aggregate of about 20 000 ha (50 000 acres), but today their area has been reduced to about two-fifths as the result of drainage. Most of the *étangs* are sheets of stagnant water with no inlet or outlet, bordered by reedy marshland; some have been surrounded by ring dykes of clay, with channels to facilitate draining; others are interconnected by wandering streams converging on the Chalaronne, the main drainage outlet of the *pays*, which joins the Saône near Thoissey.

For centuries this was a scantily populated area, liable to flooding and somewhat malarious in summer. Fishing and wild-fowling were the main pursuits, indeed considerable *territoires de chasse* were maintained by wealthy citizens of Lyons. Reclamation proceeded slowly around the margins, particularly on the better drained slopes bordering the rivers—the *Côtière d'Ain* on the east, the *Côtière de Saône* on the west and the *Côtière du Rhône* on the south. Along these edges run the lines of communication. Here have grown up numerous villages, prosperous farms, attractive parks, villas and even châteaux, forming a rural residential area for Lyons. Orchards, vineyards and a patchwork of market gardens, meadows, dairy and poultry farms form a *ceinture d'or* around the Dombes.

As indicated by the reduced area of the *étangs*, much reclamation has been effected even in the *plaine dombiste* itself. Lonely sheets of water and dreary wastes of reeds and alder are still found, but much has been improved, and a considerable area has been forested with both deciduous trees and coniferous plantations. Here again systematic use is made of many of the *étangs*. For two years they form *étangs piscicoles*, during which time carp and pike are reared; the lakes are then netted and drained, the floors cultivated for two or three years, and then reflooded and restocked with fish. This practice has declined of late, for much permanent drainage has been effected to supply land for market gardens, poultry (especially duck) farms and orchards. Further north larger farms possess permanent damp pasture on the heavy clay soils, and a mixed economy with a predominance of livestock has developed, yielding milk, butter and veal. Pigs are reared in large numbers, and in some parts flocks of sheep are still kept for meat rather than for wool. Arable cultivation has likewise extended; fodder crops, potatoes and wheat (which has replaced the former dominance of rye) occupy an appreciable area. The major factor in this improvement is of course the constant demand for produce in the Lyons agglomeration.

381

Population is nevertheless still scanty. Most towns and villages are situated marginally along the *Côtières* near the main rivers. Châtillon-sur-Chalaronne is the centre for the northwestern Dombes, by virtue of its road connection with Lyons. Finally, the influence of the neighbouring Lyons region is again revealed in the development of several silk thread and textile mills at Meximieux, Miribel and Montluel.

## The Lyons district

The Romans built *Lugdunum* on a prominent hillock, the Fourvière, rising to 295 m (968 ft), overlooking the right bank of the Saône about 3 km (2 miles) above its confluence with the Rhône (Plate 40). This remains the heart of Lyons, for the old town clusters around these hills. The strategic position of the city, more or less halfway along the Saône-Rhône corridor, made it a commercial centre from early times although it inevitably experienced many vicissitudes under the rule of Burgundy, Provence, the Holy Roman Empire and the Bourbons in turn. Much of the city was destroyed during the French Revolution as a reprisal for its support of the royal cause. But in the nineteenth century its prosperity and size increased apace. The town successively expanded on to the hilly interfluve of La

PLATE 40. The city of Lyons

Croix-Rousse, which rises some 90 m (300 ft) as a peninsula above the rivers, then in the nineteenth century to the east of the Rhône (Fig. 14.5); this last development has necessitated considerable measures against flooding.[13] Along the east bank of the Rhône developed the residential district of Les Brotteaux and the extensive working-class quarters of La Guillotière and La Mouche, and since 1870 the city has expanded still further east into the industrial suburbs of Montchat and Montplaisir. The commune of Villeurbanne is now a contiguous industrial town.

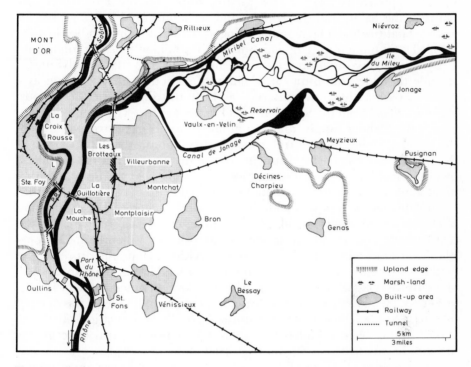

FIG. 14.5. Lyons
The steep bluffs which bound the valley floors are indicated by hachuring. The built-up area is shown in generalised form.

The abbreviations are as follows: **L,** *Lugdunum*; **PR,** Port Rambaud.

Based on *Carte de France au 50 000ᵉ*, sheets XXX/31, 32, with later information.

Lyons is the third city of France.[14] Its population, which was about 120 000 before the French Revolution, has steadily grown to about 527 000 in 1968. This figure refers only, however, to the *ville* itself; if the 8 contiguous communes be included, the total population of this *agglomération urbaine* amounted in 1968 to about 1·07 million, nearly 110 000 greater than that of the Marseilles agglomeration. The city has a wide range of functions, administrative, commercial and industrial; it is a centre of life and thought, of religion and education, the focus not only of the *région lyonnaise*, but of the Rhône-Alpes planning region, and is the most important of the *métropoles d'équilibres* (with St Etienne). Its nodal position has made it a vital road and rail centre, and despite the limitations of the lower Rhône the river port is the ninth in France. The building of the Port Rambaud along the Saône and of the Port Edouard Herriot (or Port du Rhône) to the south of the city has provided a series of quays, with sidings, coalyards, warehouses and oil tanks. Port facilities in Lyons were considerably improved when the *Pierre-Bénite* derivation canal and power station were completed (p. 370). This greatly improved the navigation link between the Saône and the Rhône, and reclaimed land is being used for storage facilities and a large marshalling yard. The freight handled in 1969 totalled 1·66 million tons, of which nearly 1·4 million tons was unloaded.

Lyons is a very important and diversified industrial city; its advantages include the long establishment of many of its activities, its position as a centre for obtaining raw materials and for distributing finished goods, supplies of coal from the St Etienne field to the southwest, a vast skilled and semi-skilled labour supply, and an unlimited supply of electric power from the Rhône, Alpine and Central Massif hydrostations. About 40 per cent of the workers are engaged in branches of engineering, and in the chemical, metallurgical and electrical industries. The *Berliet* heavy vehicle assembly plant alone employs about 15 000. One special activity is the manufacture of tinplate and the supply of containers for local canneries. The production of chemicals (pharmaceutical, photographic, explosives, and dyes for the textile trade) is carried on at several factories at Villeurbanne, Montplaisir, St Fons and Vénissieux. Other activities include the processing of leather and leather products, the refining of vegetable oils, the manufacture of foodstuffs, glassware and paper. About 16 km (10 miles) south of Lyons, at Feyzin, an oil refinery, with a throughput of 3·7 million tons, was opened in 1964. On the Rhône below Lyons the *Pierre Bénite* derivation canal and power station were completed in 1960. Great new suburbs have grown around the city, each serving an industrial estate or complex.

About a third of the gainfully employed workers of Lyons are occupied in the silk industry or in the manufacture of synthetic textiles. The former was introduced into Lyons in the fifteenth century, when numerous Italian *émigrés* were encouraged to settle, and in 1450 Charles VII gave the city merchants a complete national monopoly. The white mulberry was introduced into the Rhône valley, and silkworms have since then been reared in the neighbourhood and along the valley to the south; sericulture affords a supplementary cash reward to the small farmers, the tedious work being done by women and children. Silkworms are still reared on this cottage basis, but most thread is now imported. The manufacture of silk thread and cloth grew up as a domestic industry, though organised by wealthy merchants, and the *canuts* or handloom weavers established themselves in blocks of flats and workshops, particularly in La Croix-Rousse. Large modern factories are now responsible for an increasing proportion of the output, particularly in Villeurbanne. In 1969 France produced 509 tons of silk thread and 34 000 tons of cloth, of which half was exported, mostly to America; the rest went to the haute-couture and the lingerie industries, and a large proportion of these finished products was also exported. The Lyons area was responsible for some 80 per cent of this French output.

Rayon, nylon and other synthetic textiles have developed greatly in France, and of twenty-two major units active in 1969, eleven were situated in the *région lyonnaise*; five were in the city itself or the suburbs, and others were at Izieux, Péage and La Voulte to the south. A large plastics factory is at Feyzin.

Some 50 km (30 miles) southeast of Lyons, a new town (in fact France's newest) is being developed. Called L'Isle d'Abeau, it is located on the main Lyons—Grenoble railway line, on a motorway, and near the expanding Satolas airport. On an extensive site landscaped industrial zones with full facilities are being laid out, together with areas designated for housing, shopping and business. Five thousand houses are scheduled for 1976, and by the end of the century this will be a city of 200 000 people.

## The middle Rhône valley

The course of the Rhône, flowing alternately through narrow gorges and open basins[15]—Vienne, Valence and Montélimar—is shown on Fig. 14.6. Smaller areas of lowland along the river with individual names include *Valloire* in the northern angle between the Rhône and the Isère, *Bayane* to the south of their confluence, and *Livron* occupying the embayment of the lower Drôme. These lowlands are covered with sheets of gravel, ancient and recent; indeed, during each early summer flood period, the Alpine tributaries renew their contributions of rounded pebbles. These deposits, as a result of complex changes in the base level of the main river, have been eroded into terraces separated by prominent edges, the *Côtes du Rhône*. Streams flowing westwards to the Rhône have dissected the terraces, forming a most uneven margin to the floodplain. While gravels are predominant, areas of coarse sand lie on the higher interfluves, and much fine alluvium is on the present floodplain. Some of the upper terraces, notably in the plain of Valence, are limon-covered,[16] producing good loamy soils often with a high calcareous content due to downwash from the Fore-Alpine foothills. Thus while much of the soil covering the terraces is poor and stony, there are some better favoured areas; centuries of effort, moreover, have done much to improve the soils for agriculture.

Some of the higher terraces and interfluves are forested with oaks or in places with pines, while the floodplain is lined with poplars. The middle and lower terraces, the slopes between them, and the floors of the larger basins are intensively cultivated, for the most part on a garden-scale; even the fields of wheat and maize seem to consist of tiny strips. Market gardens occur especially on the lower terraces near Lyons in the neighbourhood of

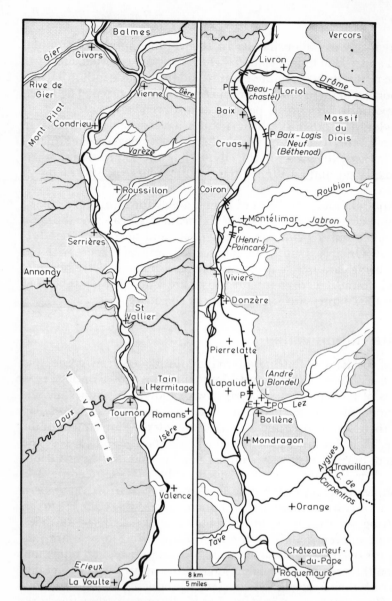

Fig. 14.6. The Rhône valley between Givors and Orange
The righthand section of the maps lies to the south of the lefthand
section, with slight overlap.

The upland area is indicated generally by stipple, which emphasises
the alternation of gorges and basins.

The derivations are shown by barbed lines, the short underground
section of the Canal de Carpentras (used for irrigation' by a pecked line.

The power stations are indicated by **P**. In the neighbourhood are
several newly built *cités-ouvrières*; these are: **E,** Cité de l'Ecluse; **L,** Cité
du Lauzon; **PO,** Cité Pierre Ollivier; and **U,** Cité de l'Usine.

Based on *Carte de France au 200 000ᵉ*, sheets 53, 59, 66, with recent revisions.

Vaulx-en-Velin, and in the plain of Valence where irrigation is used, more particularly on the accessible lands lying just above the wet water-meadows. Water cannot easily be applied to the upper terraces, and they are occupied by field crops such as winter wheat. Local specialisations include the cultivation of melons and strawberries in the plain of Valence. Flowers are grown for the cut flower trade, large quantities being sent to Paris. Early potatoes are cultivated in the sandy soils, but other roots are not grown on any scale because of the problems of drought. Dairy cattle are reared on the water-meadows.

Orchards extend almost continuously along the terraces from south of Lyons to Montélimar, growing peaches, cherries and apricots which flourish in the stony soils and sunny climate. The most renowned peach-growing district lies along the east bank of the Rhône to the south of Vienne; St Rambert-d'Albon is said to have the largest peach market in France and several hundred tons are sent off by rail each season. Some hundreds of hectares of dessert pear orchards flourish along the valley between the Drôme confluence and Montélimar. Groves of mulberries provide leaves for the domestic sericulturists, and these trees line most of the roads.

Vineyards once covered a much greater extent of the Rhône terraces than they do now; the phylloxera attacks in the late 1860s, together with the completion of the railway from Lyons, made the development of orchards more profitable. Nevertheless vineyards still extend over much of the Côtes du Rhône[17] along each side of the river, producing both *vin ordinaire* and better qualities known generally as *ordinaires Côtes du Rhône*, though not bottled and sold under the name of any individual vineyard. The Rhône vineyards are fortunate in that really poor years for climatic reasons, so common in the marginal wine areas further north, are rare in this sunny climate. A certain amount of high quality wine is obtained from a few special districts. One of the most famous is along the steep right bank of the Rhône near Ampuis, a few kilometres downstream from Vienne. This is the *Côte Rôtie*, where the vineyards perch on tiny terraces apparently cut in the solid granite, reached by steep rock staircases; here are produced what are considered to be the best of the Rhône red wines. Immediately south of the *Côte Rôtie* are the vineyards of Condrieu, again steeply overlooking the river; from them come the finest Rhône white wines. No more quality vineyards are found until the granitic spur of the *Coteau de l'Hermitage* rises above the left bank of the river opposite Tournon. The two well-known villages, Tain-l'Hermitage near the river and Crozes-l'Hermitage on the hillside further north are the centres of vineyards producing both red and white wines.

A journey from Lyons to Montélimar thus produces an impression of a rural way of life, with a succession of *jardins d'opulence*, orchards, vineyards and red-roofed villages on the terraces above the floodplains, with châteaux perched on higher spurs; green in the winter, with magnificent blossom in spring, and a sundrenched, rather dusty appearance in summer.

387

Nevertheless a good deal of industrial activity is evident, partly the result of its ancient establishment in riverside towns, partly the influence of Lyons, partly because of the modern availability of electric power. Small specialised industries, established in the Middle Ages in the towns, contrast with modern large-scale enterprises with their neighbouring *cités-ouvrières*. Large chemical factories are at St Fons to the south of Lyons and at Péage-de-Roussillon 20 km (12 miles) south of Vienne; at the latter is the extensive *Usine de Produits Chimiques Rhône-Poulenc*, making a wide range of pharmaceutical chemicals, situated alongside the main railway and road, and with a well laid out housing estate. Further south, in the neighbourhood of the Cruas gorge where limestone outcrops border the river, large-scale lime and cement works have been built. In many towns along the river the silk industry functions as part of the Lyons activity. Small factories and domestic workshops produce raw silk, despite a large decline in the late nineteenth century as a result of Far Eastern and Levantine competition, and also the disastrous effects of disease. A certain amount of silk thread and cloth is made in such towns as Vienne and St Vallier and in many villages.

Towns and villages succeed each other along both banks of the Rhône, carefully sited on knolls or terraces away from the river floods, at strategic points guarding the approaches to the gorge sections, and where outcrops of hard rock and a narrowing of the main stream have enabled the river to be bridged. Most are market and servicing centres for the individual basins, linked by railways and roads along either side of the river. After passing through several small towns with industries due to the proximity of Lyons, one comes to Givors, at the exit of the industrialised valley of the Gier (see p. 541). The ease of obtaining coal (formerly by a now disused canal, today by rail) has led to the establishment of coke ovens, engineering works, and glass manufacture, particularly of wine bottles. Vienne, the *Vienna Senatoria* of the Romans (of whom many remains survive), stands on the outer curve of a prominent meander near the confluence of the Gère. It has had a long history as the residence of the rulers of Burgundy and then of the Dauphins. Today it retains little of its former administrative importance, since it is overshadowed by Lyons to the north, but it forms a useful servicing centre. Vienne has long been an industrial town, famous for leather since the thirteenth century, for sword steel in the fifteenth and sixteenth, and for woollen and silk cloths; several of these activities are still prosperous. Further south is St Vallier, also with a variety of industries, including the manufacture of pottery, porcelain and tiles from local kaolin deposits quarried around the flanks of the granitic hills, and of silk cloth.

The twin towns of Tournon and Tain-l'Hermitage are linked by a graceful suspension bridge. Tain is a wine-exporting centre, while Tournon is a town of merchants and craftsmen with a range of interests—tanning, dyeing, the making of furniture, cardboard and straw hats. Valence, also a Roman town, stands in the centre of a broad bay to the south of the Isère junction, at a point where the north–south corridor is joined by the route from Grenoble and further east; it is the *chef-lieu* of the *département* of Drôme, and a busy commercial centre for the prosperous agriculture of the surrounding basin. Its industrial activities if small-scale are multifarious, including the manufacture of rayon, silk, cartridges and furniture (particularly from local walnut), and food-processing—flour-milling, the canning of vegetables, and confectionery. Three canal derivations and power stations have been completed in this section (Fig. 14.6): Beauchastel, Baix-le-Logis-Neuf, and Montélimar (p. 370). Montélimar stands at the convergence of the Roubion and Jabron before they enter the Rhône. This attractive fortified town is a regional market for agricultural products, and has a variety of small industries, mostly food-processing (including the manufacture of the well-known nougat). Finally Viviers, the ancient capital of Vivarais, clusters round its Gothic cathedral on a prominent eminence guarding the northern entrance of the Donzère gorge.

## The hill country of Bas-Dauphiné

This undulating hill country,[18] situated in the angle between the Rhône and the Isère, rises to form the Plateau des Terres-Froides in the north and the Plateau de Chambaran in the south, where it culminates in summits at about 730 m (2 400 ft). The superficial deposits are extraordinarily diverse, but clays tend to predominate. Many streams flow from shallow lakes lying on the uneven clays, particularly in the Terres-Froides, or from marshy peat-filled hollows; some have been drained but many remain. The valley of the Bourbre, crossing the northern part of the Terres-Froides, was formerly a vast marsh. A main drainage canal was constructed between 1809 and 1814, which with the help of some 200 km (120 miles) of minor canals converted this valley floor in the neighbourhood of Morestel into fertile land, most of which is now under pasture; about 5 000 ha (12 000 acres) were thus reclaimed.

The valley trenches divide up the hill country into a chaos of gently swelling eminences and more pronounced ridges, whose slopes descend by terrace steps to the floodplains. Along the lower Isère valley, for example, terraces can be distinguished at about 370 m, 260 m, 230 m and 200 m (1 250, 850, 750 and 650 ft).

This diversity of relief, drainage and soils has resulted in a varied land use pattern. In the Middle Ages Bas-Dauphiné was extensively wooded, but long continued depredations for fuel, charcoal and building, and to obtain oak bark for tanning, cut deeply into the ancient forests, while the naval wars of the eighteenth century removed many fine oaks for shipbuilding. Grazing by flocks then prevented natural rehabilitation. As a result, by the mid-nineteenth century much of this woodland cover had been removed; there was, for example, virtually no trace of the large medieval Forêt de Mantaille. Some areas now form scrubby heath, providing little more than poor grazing, and a tract near Grand-Serre has been occupied for many years by a large military training camp. During this century much of Bas-Dauphiné has been forested with both deciduous and coniferous trees, some converted into improved pasture, and some put under arable.

The naturally poor soils have been improved in places by drainage, liming and chemical fertilisers. The districts which have benefited most are the margins of the hill country in the west along the Rhône valley, and along the sides of the trenches of its tributaries. The better soils, such as those developed on limon or on the sandy clays which veneer the terraces, are under arable, growing wheat, sugar beet, potatoes, and fodder crops (such as lucerne) with the help of irrigation. Specialisations include tobacco, hemp and flax in the Valloire (the broad valley between the Terres-Froides and the Chambaran), and asparagus, gherkins and other market garden produce in the northwest. Vineyards, orchards (particularly of peaches and cherries), mulberries and nut groves are carefully tended on the gravel-covered lower terraces. Walnuts are a speciality and thousands of trees grow in the neighbourhood of St Marcellin and St Quentin; nut-picking affords a profitable seasonal industry. Along the damp pastures and irrigated meadows of the valley floors and in the higher depressions cattle, horses and pigs are reared.

The small towns of Bas-Dauphiné have for centuries fostered local craft industries. The growth of Lyons as a regional centre, the development of communications such as the Lyons-Grenoble railway line which crosses Bas-Dauphiné diagonally through Bourgoin, La Tour-du-Pin, Voiron and other small towns, and the widespread transmission of electric power, have served to bring Bas-Dauphiné within the industrial *grande banlieue* of Lyons. Old industries have survived in a modernised form, new ones have been introduced. The manufacture of silk is carried on at some hundreds of establishments, many producing raw silk, silk thread or cloth for working up in Lyons, others specialising in various finished materials such as satin, cloth of gold or silver and embroidered velours. Linen is manufactured at Voiron and St Jean-de-Bournay from locally grown flax, and hemp is made into cordage, ropes and netting at Voiron. The long-established but small-scale metallurgical industry, based on alluvial ores and charcoal, survives as the manufacture of files and rasps at St Laurent-du-Pont and of edged tools at La Fure, while electrical machinery is made at Pont-de-Chéruy to the east of Lyons. Fine papers are produced at Renage, Apprieu-Fures and Rives, with the original advantage of a plentiful supply of pure water; the last of these makes bank-note paper for the Banque de France. Tanneries and leather factories have been established in Bas-Dauphiné since Roman times, using local hides and oak bark for tanning; boots and shoes are made in Romans-sur-Isère and at Bourg-de-Péage on the opposite side of the river. Glass is made at Grand-Serre and pottery at St Uze.

The population is thus scattered over Bas-Dauphiné in small towns and villages of 1 000 to 2 000 inhabitants, with a few larger places, notably Bourgoin. Their activities are based on a variety of both agricultural and industrial pursuits. That no prominent regional centre has grown within Bas-Dauphiné is because of the powerful influence of Lyons at the north-western corner.

## The lower Rhône valley

The Rhône between Donzère and the apex of the delta at Arles flows in turn through the plains of Pierrelatte, Orange and Avignon, each separated by a prominent defile. To the west rises the upland country of the limestone *garrigues*, forming the foothills of the Cévennes. To the east the marshy alluvial plain of the Rhône widens to form the *Plaines vauclusiennes*, into which spurs project from the Lower Cretaceous Fore-Alpine plateaus.

Across the plain of Pierrelatte the Donzère-Mondragon derivation canal has been completed by the Compagnie Nationale du Rhône since the war of 1939–45.[19] A barrage was constructed at the southern end of the steep-walled Donzère narrows, with six sluices to control the water level of the Rhône. A derivation canal, 30 km (18 miles) in length, takes off through a

PLATE 41. The Donzère-Mondragon by-pass canal and power-station

locked connection above this barrage, and follows the eastern edge of the Pierrelatte plain to rejoin the Rhône where it swings eastwards again to the south of Mondragon (Plate 41). Eighteen kilometres (11 miles) along the canal at Bollène, where a mass of rock beneath the alluvial cover afforded a solid foundation, the André-Blondel power station was built; its production in 1969 was 2·1 million kWh, France's largest hydroproducer, though several stations have a greater installed capacity. There is a fall at this point of 26 m (85 ft), and a navigation lock with the world's highest ship lift was constructed. The derivation canal is wider in fact than Suez, and it has obviated the braided rapids and steep gradient of the Rhône through the western margin of the Pierrelatte plain. Several housing estates have been built for workers at the power station and neighbouring factories (including a plutonium plant), shown on Fig. 14.6.

Below Mondragon the valley floor of the Rhône is marshy and the river braids to form backwaters and elongated reed-covered islands; one of the largest lies just above Avignon, the Ile de la Barthelasse. The floodplain is seamed with drainage channels, which have improved the state of the higher terraces, but along the river itself there are still marshes liable to inundation.

The edge of the floodplain is indicated approximately by the 100 m (330 ft) contour, beyond which rise distinct erosion surfaces at about 150, 200 and 270 m (500, 650 and 900 ft), worn in the Tertiary sediments. These are much dissected by gravel-floored valleys of the various rivers flowing down from the higher Fore-Alpine plateaus. The upper terraces are dry and rather bare, covered in places with scrubby woods of oak and box, and like the southern Fore-Alps they have suffered deforestation for firewood, charcoal and tanning bark, though some deliberate planting of pines has been carried out in recent years. Limestone spurs and knolls rise from the Tertiary alluvium, including the long rugged Chaîne des Alpilles rising to over 500 m (1 600 ft) and projecting within 3 km (2 miles) of the Rhône near Tarascon. These limestone outcrops afford valuable sites for settlement clear of the floodplain; the nucleus of Avignon (the cathedral and the Palais des Papes within the fortifications), is built on the Rocher des Doms overlooking the divided channels of the Rhône which enclose the Ile de la Barthelasse (Plate 42).

Despite the disadvantages of too much water on the low-lying parts of the plain and too little on the higher areas, together with the poor stony soils, the lower Rhône valley has been an agricultural region for centuries. The basis of life was cultivation of the Mediterranean triad—wheat, vines and olives, the first of these as a winter crop using long periods of fallow. From the fifteenth century the breeding of silkworms led to the planting of some millions of mulberry trees. Tobacco was later introduced and grown profitably until the eighteenth century. Madder-root was another valuable cash crop introduced in the eighteenth century; this flourished until its cultivation was killed by the discovery in 1869 of a method of extracting substitutes from coal tar. Almost simultaneously the phylloxera scourge made its appearance. These agricultural disasters, succeeding one another, brought the region to near poverty.

Since the latter part of the nineteenth century a diverse agricultural economy has developed, capitalising the long hours of sunshine, and helped by efficient rail communications with distant markets and by the development of irrigation. The last is no recent introduction, however; there are records of canals constructed as early as the eleventh century. In the seventeenth and eighteenth centuries several new distributaries were built, including the northern branch of the Canal des Alpilles from the river Durance to Orgon, completed in 1783 and extended to Châteaurenard in 1849. After the unfortunate vicissitudes of the 1860s and 1870s, the irrigation system was extended. The Canal de Carpentras was constructed from Mérindol on the Durance along the 100 m (330 ft) contour northward to the Eygues at Travaillan. It picks up water from many rivers and springs, including the Fontaine de Vaucluse (which has given its name to the *Vauclusian* type of resurgence), and with many kilometres of distributaries running westward into the plains it serves the districts around Carpentras and Cavaillon. To the south of the Durance the Canal de Craponne has been constructed, with branches running west to Arles and south to the Etang de Berre. The Canal des Alpilles and its branches now supply the Tarascon and Châteaurenard districts, and the Canal de Vaucluse and the Canal de l'Isle provide for the Avignon area. The total area irrigated, both by gravity from these feeder-canals and by artesian and subartesian wells, is over 300 sq km (120 sq miles) (Fig. 15.2).

Much of the cultivation of these plains is in the form of market gardens;[20] tiny plots of land are exploited assiduously by hand, protected by shelters (see p. 371) from the biting blast of the *mistral*, an enemy second only to drought. The most important market-gardening area is a triangle enclosed by Avignon, St Rémy and Cavaillon (Fig. 15.2), including the collecting centre of Châteaurenard. The constant succession of produce includes cauliflowers and lettuce during the winter, new potatoes as early as March, artichokes from March to June, early peas, spinach, onions and carrots throughout the spring and early summer. Tomatoes occupy a considerable area. In some districts specialisation is practised; thus Cavaillon is renowned for melons and Carpentras for strawberries, and flowers are grown for seed in the neighbourhood of St Rémy on the northern flanks of the Alpilles. But more usually the *patron-propriétaire* grows a variety of items to spread his risks and to provide some continuity of output. His holding, small though it may be in aggregate, is normally divided into a number of scattered 'parcels'.

Not all the crops of the lower Rhône are irrigated. In Vaucluse the lavender grows in long rows on the dry gravel surface. Olive-groves straggle up the limestone slopes, almond, peach, apricot, cherry and quince orchards on the terraces, and walnuts and chestnuts along the sides of fields. The most extensive orchards are on the slopes to the east and south of

PLATE 42. Avignon, with the Palais des Papes overlooking the Rhône

Carpentras and along the southern flanks of the Durance valley between Châteaurenard and Cavaillon.

Although phylloxera dealt a damaging blow in 1865, vineyards have been re-established with near-immune American grafts. Their extent is only about 9 per cent of what it was (the actual area in 1968 in Vaucluse was 54 700 ha (134 000 acres) ), yet the *département* produced over 1·85 million hectolitres of wine in 1968. Most of this was *vin ordinaire*, but a group of vineyards on the hill slopes overlooking Châteauneuf-du-Pape, near the left bank of the Rhône above Avignon, yield a quality wine. More than two hundred individual firms produce wines, red, white and *rosé*, which are entitled to the *appellation* of *Châteauneuf-du-Pape*. 13 km (8 miles) to the northwest of Avignon the vineyards of Tavel produce a wine usually regarded as the best of the French *rosés*. It is a reflection on the decline of these Vauclusian vineyards that the little town of Roquemaure was once a busy port, shipping wine in bulk to many European countries. Table grapes are also cultivated: hundreds of tons are sold at the markets of Cavaillon, Châteaurenard and Tarascon and despatched, carefully packaged, to Lyons, Paris and Britain.

Villages and small towns are widely dispersed among these areas of cultivation. One line of towns extends along each bank of the Rhône at suitable points for bridging, defence and flood protection; such are Pont-St Esprit, Roquemaure, Avignon itself, and the towns of Beaucaire and Tarascon linked by a long suspension bridge. Others are situated within the plain on the lower slopes of hills above flood level, such as Mondragon, Orange, Châteaurenard and St Rémy. A third string of settlements stands at the foot of the uplands on the eastern edge of the plain, including

394

Carpentras and Cavaillon. Most are market towns from which agricultural produce is shipped by road and rail, and many preserve rich legacies of their historic past.

The only town of any size is Avignon, the *chef-lieu* of Vaucluse, with over 86 000 people in 1968 and about 140 000 in the conurbation;[21] its site has already been mentioned. Today Avignon is the regional and commercial centre for the lower Rhône valley, its silk industry has been revived and a large rayon factory built, several factories manufacture packaging for market garden produce, there are canneries for fruit and vegetables, and cement works. The first French nuclear plant was opened in 1953 at Marcoule near Avignon, mainly used for the production of plutonium.

[1] D. Faucher, *L'Homme et le Rhône* (1968), deals with all aspects of the river and its valley from source to delta.

[2] D. Faucher and A. Gilbert, 'Le couloir entre les Montagnes', *La France: géographie-tourisme* (1951), i, p. 206.

[3] H. Ormsby, *France: a regional and economic geography* (1950), p. 281.

[4] M. Pardé, *Le Calcul des débits du Rhône et de ses affluents* (1925), gives details of the régime of the Rhône; see also M. Pardé, *Le Régime du Rhône; étude hydrologique* (1925).

[5] M. Laferrère, 'Le projet de liaison fluviale Rhine-Rhône', *Rev. Géog. Lyon*, **37** (1962), pp. 113–29; and I. E. Jones, 'The development of the Rhône', *Geography*, **54** (1969), pp. 446–51.

[6] D. Barsch, 'Les arbres et le vent dans la vallée méridionale du Rhône', *Revue de Géographie de Lyon*, **40** (1965), pp. 35–45.

[7] A. Journaux, *Les Plaines de la Saône et leurs bordures montagneuses: Beaujolais, Mâconnais, Côte d'Or, Plateaux de la Haute-Saône, Jura occidental: étude morphologique* (1956); this is a monumental work of 526 pages.

[8] B. Dézerl, *La Croissance industrielle et urbaine de la Porte d'Alsace* (1970).

[9] M. Dubois, 'Les plateaux méridionaux de la Côte d'Or de Nuits à Chagny', *Annls Géogr.*, **59** (1950), pp. 336–45, provides detailed maps of the faults (p. 338) and erosion surfaces (p. 339) of the Côte d'Or.

[10] G. Chabot, 'La Côte et le vignoble', *La Bourgogne* (1945), pp. 88–136; and P. Marres, 'Le Vignoble bourguignon', *La Vigne et le vin en France* (1950), pp. 91–9.

[11] R. Gadille, 'Les Cultures de petits fruits en Côte d'Or', *Rev. Géogr. de l'Est*, **9** (1969), pp. 127–48, stresses the avoidance of a vine monoculture by growing other bush fruit.

[12] J. Gerbault, 'Le Développement industriel de l'agglomération dijonnaise', **80** (1971), *Annls Géogr.*, pp. 534–53, discusses the introduction of new factories decentralised from the Paris area, and the creation of new industrial zones around the outskirts of the city.

[13] H. Villien, 'L'endiguement du Rhône et de la Saône: les quais de Lyon et leur efficacité contre les inondations', *Etudes rhodaniennes*, **13** (1937), pp. 5–21.

[14] A detailed account of the city and region of Lyons, with thirty-eight maps in a separate portfolio, is provided by *Lyon et sa région: analyse et enquêtes pour l'aménagement du territoire*, published by the *Comité pour l'Aménagement et l'Expansion économique de la Région lyonnaise* (1955). See also Ph. Russo and A. Audin, 'Le site de Lyon', *Rev. Géogr. Lyon*, **36** (1961), pp. 296–346; M. Laferrère, *Lyon: ville industrielle* (1960); and J. Labasse and M. Laferrère, *La Région lyonnaise* (1960), in the series *France de Demain*.

[15] D. Faucher, *Plaines et bassins du Rhône moyen entre Bas-Dauphiné et Provence* (1927).

[16] Suen Tang-Yuet, *Le Loess de la vallée du Rhône* (1934), provides a detailed map (p. 24) of the distribution of limon.

[17] P. Marres, 'Les Côtes du Rhône', *La Vigne et le vin en France* (1950), pp. 103–11.

[18] Y. Bravard, *Le Bas-Dauphiné: recherches sur la morphologie d'un piémont alpin* (1963), 504 pp.

[19] See (a) G. Kish, 'Hydroelectric power in France: plans and projects', *Geogr. Rev.*, **45** (1955), pp. 84–7; (b) R. Dugrand, 'L'aménagement du Bas-Rhône', *Annls Géogr.*, **62** (1953), pp. 368–73, which provides details and a map of the Donzère achievement; (c) J.-B. Suchel, 'L'hydraulique agricole dans le couloir rhodanien entre Vienne et Bollène, projets et réalisations', *Rev. Géogr. Lyon*, **32** (1957), pp. 201–26.

[20] R. Pélissier, 'La Production maraîchère et fruitière et le marché de Cavaillon', *Méditerranée*, **5** (1964), pp. 279–97; and J. Bethemont, 'Progrès technique et réactions paysannes; l'irrigation dans la plaine de Montélimar', *Rev. géogr. Lyon*, **36** (1961), p. 347.

[21] E. Delaruelle, 'Avignon capitale', *Rev. géogr. Pyr. S.-O.*, **23** (1952), pp. 233–64.

# 15
# The Mediterranean coastlands
# I. Provence

The coastline of southern France between the Spanish and Italian frontiers is bordered by a region often known simply as the *Midi*. From the point of view of structure and relief it exhibits great diversity. There are coasts bordered with lagoons and sand-dunes, others with lofty cliffs and deeply cut bays from which the land rises steeply inland. A great expanse of sand and mud forms the ever-growing delta of the Rhône, while by contrast ancient crystalline massifs abut on to the coast in the east. Widespread outcrops of limestone, mostly of Mesozoic or early Tertiary age, form blunt headlands, prominent ridges and deeply dissected plateaus. Huge sheets of gravel vary in age from the Pliocene to those brought down by the floods of last autumn. The region has had a complex geomorphological history. Much of the western and central Midi suffered marine transgression in early Pliocene times, forming gulfs in which sedimentation took place. Considerable oscillations of level have since taken place, and periods of high sea level in which deposition was active have alternated with low sea level stages when the rivers cut down into these sediments, forming a series of terraces.

Upon this area of physiographical diversity the climate has imposed a unifying stamp reflected in both the landscape and the way of life.[1] The summer drought, emphasised by the widespread occurrence of limestone and of highly permeable gravels, has resulted in a vegetation cover with xerophytic characters. Holm oak and cork oak forests once covered large areas, but the region has been occupied by man since early times, and the gradual inevitable clearance of these forests exposed the terrain to the rains of autumn and the heat of summer; much soil was removed by erosion, and in places vegetation deteriorated into scrubby aromatic *garrigue*. For millennia the economy was based on the typical Mediterranean crops—wheat, vine and olive, utilising both the terraces of better soil and the alluvial plains where irrigation water was available. Early settlements grew into cities, for the accessible coastlands have attracted seafarers since the days of the Phoenicians. For over six centuries the Romans impressed their cultural mark, as many of the cities testify. Although interrupted by the vicissitudes of more than a millennium of troubled history, an important agricultural, industrial, commercial and urban life has developed. In modern times the advent of the railway has encouraged a profitable agricultural economy, capitalising the sunshine, the mild winter temperatures and the early springs, and the same factors have allowed the development of a highly organised tourist industry.

But even with these unifying features, there are some remarkable land use contrasts.[2] The *garrigues* and the dusty gravels, offering sustenance only to goats, contrast with the luxuriance of intense cultivation in the vineyards, orchards and market gardens, and with the groves of holm oak or cork oak. The lonely, now virtually landlocked, ports of medieval times contrast with the activity of Marseilles. The ancient Provençal cities contrast with the new *cités-ouvrières* near the huge oil refineries and modern factories around the Etang de Berre. The beaches and dunes of the western and central coastlands, with their modern tourist developments, contrast with the *plages*, promenades, villas and hotels of the fashionably thronged Côte d'Azur in the east. Yet all these form ingredients in the cultural landscape of *le Midi méditerranéen*.

## Regional divisions

Two main divisions may be made to assist regional description (Fig. 15.1), divisions recognised by many centuries of some degree of provincial autonomy (see p. 1). In the east lies Provence, in the west Languedoc (Chapter 16).

In its broadest sense, Provence includes the land to the north of the Mediterranean between the Rhône on the west and the crestline of the High Alps in the east. Its northern margin is more difficult of definition; politically it is demarcated by the northern boundary of Vaucluse and Basses-Alpes, yet geographically there is no clearcut limit, rather a zone of transition as the characteristics of the Mediterranean climate gradually change to those of a more continental régime. The basins of the middle Durance, the Verdon and the upper Var, together with the uplands of the limestone Fore-Alps and the ranges of the Maritime Alps, are often referred to as *Haute-Provence*. Though undeniably the Mediterranean climate exerts an influence upon this landscape, from a geomorphological point of view it is more convenient to include these parts of Haute-Provence in the French Alps (see p. 622 and Fig. 22.1).

Even the more limited *Basse-Provence* represents an area of extraordinarily varied structure and relief. In the west is the delta of the Rhône. Then to the east of the Etang de Berre appears a succession of ridges and plateaus of Mesozoic rocks, separated by Tertiary basins and deep river valleys floored with recent deposits; this is known generally as *la Basse-Provence calcaire*. Two crystalline Hercynian massifs comprise *la Basse-Provence cristalline*, Maures between the Aille valley and the sea, and Esterel to the northeast of the Argens valley. Finally, in the extreme east, where the

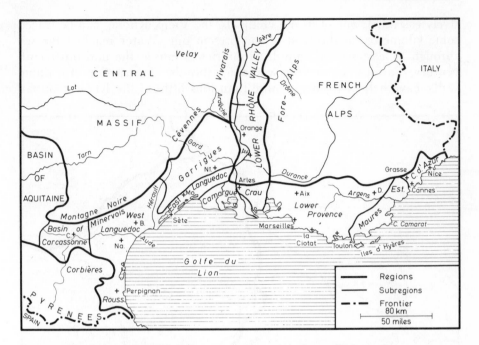

FIG. 15.1 The regions of the Mediterranean coast and the lower Rhône valley
The other major regions shown—the French Alps, the Central Massif, the Basin of
Aquitaine and the Pyrenees—are not subdivided (see Figs 22.1, 20.3 and 13.1
respectively).

Abbreviations used are as follows: **Av,** Avignon; **B,** Béziers; **C,** Carcassonne; **D,**
Draguignan; **Est,** Massif of Esterel; **Mo,** Montpellier; **Na,** Narbonne; **Ni,** Nîmes;
**Rouss,** Roussillon.

limestone Alps closely approach the sea, lies a narrow coastal margin
known as the *Côte d'Azur*.

## The Rhône delta

The delta of the Rhône (Fig. 15.2) begins 5 km (3 miles) above Arles, where
the river, flowing between massive embankments, is about 160 m (170 yd)
in width. Here it divides to form its two chief distributaries, the Grand
Rhône which flows in a southeasterly direction to the Golfe de Fos, and the
Petit Rhône which wanders in circuitous meanders more to the southwest.
The two mouths, 40 km (25 miles) apart, have changed considerably in
position, and the main exit has been displaced successively to the east.[3]
The Petit Rhône once reached the sea much further to the west at Aigues-
Mortes, a medieval port now only linked to the open sea at Le Grau-du-Roi
by a canal 6 km (4 miles) in length. Later the Petit Rhône entered the Golfe
du Lion through a mouth further to the east, a course now followed by the
Canal de Peccais. Similarly the Grand Rhône's mouth has moved succes-

sively eastward; one of its old channels, the Vieux Rhône, can be traced some kilometres to the west of the present one. Water reached the sea through at least six separate distributaries as late as the mid-nineteenth century. Various engineering works, notably the construction of training walls, have helped to divert more than four-fifths of the Rhône's outfall

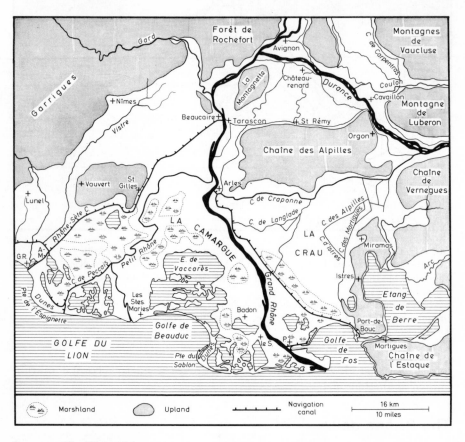

Fig. 15.2. The Rhône delta

The areas of *étang* and marsh are generalised, and the vast complicated pattern of drainage channels is necessaily omitted. The stipple indicates the higher areas, approximately over 60 m (200 ft).

The abbreviations are as follows: **A-M,** Aigues-Mortes; **GR,** Le Grau-du-Roi; **P,** Port-St Louis-du-Rhône; **le S,** Le Salins-de-Giraud.

Based on *Carte de France au 200 000ᵉ*, sheets 66, 67, 73, 74.

through a single main channel, thus concentrating the deposition of much of the river's vast burden of sediment, with the result that the extreme south-eastern corner of the delta is growing outwards at an average annual rate of about 40 m (45 yd). The present delta is known as *La Camargue*. To the east of the Grand Rhône and in the angle of the limestone hills of lower Provence extends an immense triangular plain of gravel, the Pliocene 'dry delta' of the Durance, *La Crau*.

## The Camargue

The seaward face of the delta, nearly 80 km (50 miles) in length, consists of a series of bays bordered by a sweeping curve of sandspits backed by low dunes. The westerly direction of longshore drift has developed two rounded sandy 'points', the Pointes de l'Espiguette in the west and du Sablon in the east. Behind the line of dunes lies a vast expanse of marshes and shallow brackish *étangs*, connected with the open sea through shallow channels or *graus*, a term derived from the Latin *gradus* (a passage); the mouth of the Grand Rhône is known as the Grau de Pégoulier, that of the Petit Rhône as the Grau d'Orgon.

The central and southern part of the Camargue consists of marshes, covered with sedge reeds and stretches of *Salicornia* and *Phragmites*, and interlaced by winding channels and irregular shallow *étangs*. The largest of these, the Etang de Vaccarès, extends to 150 sq km (60 sq miles), but is nowhere more than a metre in depth; it connects with a maze of more than twenty other named *étangs* to the south. Occasional clumps of tamarisk and cypress stand above the general level on long low banks of alluvium which represent silted-up and abandoned distributaries; these raised their beds above the surrounding marsh by accretion, then breached their banks at a time of flood and so occupied new channels. The dreary marshes are the haunt of bird life and in fact a nature reserve of about 15 000 ha (37 000 acres) has been created in the Ile du Plan du Bourg in the southeast, where wild duck, herons and storks congregate and even flamingo come seasonally.

This southern part of the delta is thinly populated, although here and there on slight eminences stand villages, whose people fish in the open sea and in the lagoons; the *étangs* are netted, and large quantities of fish are dried in the sun. The only other activity is the exploitation of salt by solar evaporation in the saltpans or *salins*. This is done near Aigues-Mortes, at Badon to the southeast of the Etang de Vaccarès, and at Le Salins-de-Giraud; between 80 000 and 100 000 tons of common salt are produced annually from Bouches-du-Rhône, and the gleaming white pyramids in late summer stand out above the marshes. Ancillary chemical industries, including the production of magnesium and potassium chloride and of carbonate of soda, have been established at Badon, and also at Le Salins-de-Giraud where Solvay have a large factory. Near to these towns stand regular rows of houses in which live the *saliniers*.

For many centuries schemes of reclamation have slowly pushed into the Camargue. Progress has, however, been slow, for the disadvantages are great. Flooding has always been a menace, both from the sea breaking through the *cordon littoral* of dunes and from the rivers. The latter are especially dangerous, because their beds, built up by sedimentation, stand a metre or two above the surrounding land, and the Rhône with its irregular regime is liable to sudden rises of level. Numerous drainage channels intersect the land. The soil of newly reclaimed areas is impregnated with salt, difficult to remove and to maintain clear since saline solutions constantly rise to the surface by capillarity during the summers, and irrigation also tends to increase the salt content. Other drawbacks are the scarcity of drinking-water since wells are mostly brackish, the breeding of malarial mosquitoes on the stagnant marshes, and the difficulty of access through inadequate communications.

In the mid-nineteenth century, following a disastrous decade of flooding between 1840 and 1850, ambitious plans were discussed for integrated schemes of reclamation with state financial assistance. These envisaged the construction of a number of coastal and riverine dykes, and a systematic network of canals leading to a reduced Etang de Vaccarès, which would function as an intermediate drainage reservoir, with pumping stations to maintain a determined water level. Some opposition was inevitably met from fishermen, wildfowlers and *saliniers* who feared for their livelihoods. Certain parts of this programme were, however, slowly carried out, notably the development of drainage canals in the north leading to the Etang de Vaccarès, but disputes of various kinds among interested parties and then the war of 1914–18 prevented the full implementation of the scheme.

For many centuries, the northern Camargue offered only poor pasture for cattle and sheep, notably for the black Camarguais bulls bred for the Provençal rings and herded by *gardians* on horseback. Cultivation progressively spread along low ridges on which farms and then settlement clusters were gradually established, while the intervening hollows were drained to furnish rather rank pastures.

During the last half century, the area of reclaimed land has appreciably increased. As a result, the northern Camargue, with its arable fields, vineyards, improved pastures and market gardens, contrasts markedly with the reed-covered swamps and meres of the south. The pastures are used both for Camarguais cattle and for the more recently introduced Andalusian breed, and merino sheep have also been imported. Wheat and fodder crops are grown, and over 30 000 ha (74 000 acres) are now under rice, cultivated by modern methods;[4] it is interesting to see large combine harvesters at work in the ricefields. Yields of cereals are not high, admittedly; the amount of wheat produced in 1968 averaged 26 quintals per hectare compared with 41 in Nord and 44 in Aisne. Vineyards now cover about 30 000 ha (74 000 acres), yielding large quantities of *vin ordinaire*.

Communications have gradually been improved, and so helped the progress of settlement. A single-track railway was constructed between Arles and Port St Louis-du-Rhône along the left bank of the Grand Rhône, and another skirts the northern edge of the western Camargue and then runs south to Aigues-Mortes and Le Grau-du-Roi. Roads constructed along the low ridges link up the small settlements and the individual farms,

PLATE 43. Aigues-Mortes

each standing within its shelter belt of trees.

Several canals have been constructed in the delta region. The Arles-Bouc Canal follows the left bank of the Rhône, then cuts across to Bouc on the coast near the entrance to the long channel of the Etang de Caronte; it is, however, only 2 m (6 ft) in depth, and carries a mere 100 000 tons of freight annually. Its future is tied up with the development of the Marseilles-Rhône Canal (see p. 413) and of Rhône navigation generally. The Rhône-Sète Canal, completed in 1934, runs from Beaucaire on the Rhône southwestward to Aigues-Mortes, and then is enclosed in a dyked channel through the coastal *étangs* to the harbour of Sète. It carries only about 300 000 tons of freight, two-thirds of which consist of petroleum and oil products.

Some attractive little towns stand in the Rhône delta, but their former importance as ports has disappeared, and they survive in a peaceful yet romantic decay. Three, Aigues-Mortes (Plate 43), Les Stes Maries-de-la-Mer and Port St Louis-du-Rhône, are situated near the mouths of past or present distributaries, while the largest, Arles, is near the apex of the delta. Aigues-Mortes, surrounded by thirteenth-century rectangular ramparts, is reached by both road and rail on causeways across the marsh. This was the port at which Crusading armies once embarked, but today, although at the junction of the Canal Maritime (leading to Le Grau-du-Roi) and the Rhône-Sète Canal, and furnished with wharves and railway sidings outside

403

PLATE 44. Arles

the walls, its commercial importance is negligible. There are neighbouring salt-works, and like most of these little towns it receives a considerable tourist traffic. Les Stes Maries-de-la-Mer stands just east of the mouth of the Petit Rhône. It is reputedly the site of the landing from the Holy Land of the two Marys and their servant Sarah, whose bodies lie in the massive thirteenth-century church; to the town each May come large numbers of gypsies, for Sarah is their patron-saint. Port St Louis, the only harbour today actually within the Rhône delta, is linked with the Golfe de Fos by the St Louis ship canal, built in 1871 to bypass the bar which obstructs the mouth of the Grand Rhône. The port is overshadowed by Marseilles, but as it has rail connection with Arles it acts in some measure as its outport, importing oil, timber, phosphates and other fertilisers, Algerian wine and wheat, and exporting some cement; it has a large salt-refining industry. New developments around the Golfe de Fos are discussed below (p. 413) in connection with the port of Marseilles.

Arles is situated on the left bank of the Grand Rhône at its lowest bridging point (Plate 44). The town was founded on a small mass of limestone projecting above the surrounding marshlands, and it became a Roman centre, of which ample evidence survives in its magnificent amphitheatre (said to have held over 20 000 spectators) and theatre. Today it is a market focus for

404

both Crau and Camargue, a packing and despatching point for the rail shipment of their agricultural produce, and a very attractive venue for tourists.

## The Crau

The 'dry delta' of the Crau is composed of a pair of alluvial fans covering a gentle infilled syncline of Miocene *molasse*, which appears on the surface in the east along the margins of the Etang de Berre, rising to over 120 m (400 ft) as a chain of rugged hillocks. One alluvial fan was laid down in the west by the Pleistocene Rhône, and slopes southward from about 9 m (30 ft) to near sea level. The second, larger fan was the work of the Pleistocene Durance, which at that time pursued a course much further to the southwest through a prominent gap known as the Cluse de Lamanon between the Alpilles and the Provençal uplands. This fan has its apex at a height of about 70 m (230 ft) and slopes very gently southwestward towards the Grand Rhône. The Durance later abandoned this course and now flows to the Rhône below Avignon. Its varied regime is shown by the fact that its mean discharge is 350 cu m (12 260 cu ft) per second, as compared with a recorded minimum of 54 cu m (1 906 cu ft) and a maximum of 920 cu m (32 600 cu ft) per second.[5]

The Crau consists therefore of extensive sheets of water-worn stones of all sizes,[6] from small pebbles to masses of limestone and sandstone 150 to 200 mm (6 to 9 in) and occasionally 300 mm (12 in) in diameter, a veritable *désert de pierres*. Much of this gravel surface is loose, but in other parts it is cemented into a hard though much fissured conglomerate. It is for the most part dry because of its extreme permeability, but by contrast in some places an underlying pan has allowed the formation of saline marshes and even a few saline lakes. The soil cover is thin, consisting merely of a dusty layer formed by the decomposition *in situ* of limestone and sandstone pebbles, and of patches of coarse sandy material.

This not very attractive environment is further handicapped by the climatic regime. Scorched by the sun in summer to a bleached dusty aridity and swept by the blasts of the *mistral* in winter, as the few windbent trees testify, the effectiveness of its scanty winter rains is still further reduced by rapid evaporation and percolation. Much is covered by a *garrigue*-like vegetation of scrubby plants—cistus, rosemary, thyme, juniper, coarse clumps of grass, occasional patches of dwarf evergreen oak and thorny bushes. In summer the vegetation is dry and silvery-grey, but in response to autumn and winter rains an intermittent covering of coarse grass spreads between the stones, with a rather attractive though shortlived profusion of such flowering plants as asphodel.

For centuries the only importance of the Crau was to provide winter grazing for flocks of sheep which spent their summers on the Alpine pastures, moving slowly up and down through Provence on regular stock routes. Sheep are still important, indeed the total of 280 000 in the *départe-ment* of Bouches-du-Rhône in 1968 was fifth to Aveyron, Vienne, Haute-Vienne and Hautes-Pyrénées. The breeds have been improved by crossing the Crau animals with merinos; transhumance is still carried out, but by rail transport; and the *'prairies artificielles'* have been extended both by irrigation and by the sowing of drought-resistant varieties of grass. Lucerne and sainfoin are grown with the help of irrigation. The sheep arrive in the Crau towards the end of November and graze on the natural pastures until mid-February, after which they spend a month or so on the cultivated meadows before returning to the foothills, the first stage of their summer journey to the alpine pastures. The flocks are carefully maintained and organised; a proportion of the lambs born in December is sold off at the Arles sales in spring.

Cultivation has gradually pushed its way into the margins of the Crau since the sixteenth century, when the first irrigation canals were constructed. Since that time the system has been extended (Fig. 15.2). From the main derivations branches a network of minor channels. Even so, great areas in the centre and south of the Crau are untouched by irrigation because the return would hardly merit the vast initial expense of canal construction. Moreover, the supply of water from the Durance, whence these derivations originate, is not sufficient for much extension of the irrigated area, and it is in addition fluctuating and unreliable. Water has been diverted from the Durance below the Verdon confluence into a canal which runs into the Etang de Berre, providing both for irrigation and hydroelectricity require-ments.

Irrigation water is used for market gardens, protected by fences from the mistral, and for the cultivation of hay, fodder crops such as lucerne and sainfoin, and melons. Drought-resisting varieties of winter wheat are grown without irrigation, using periods of fallow. On the edges of the Crau olives, almonds, apricots, peaches and vines appear, the first particularly on the bordering limestone slopes, and there are some large fields of laven-der, which does well in the dry stony soils.

The Crau is scantily settled and thinly populated. There are isolated large farms, known in the district as *mas*, surrounded by windbreaks of planes, elms and cypress, and noticeably without windows or doors on the north; some have formed the nuclei of small agricultural settlements. Others, such as Grand Mas de Pillier, are located along the railway which runs straight across from Arles to the important junction and marshalling-yards at Miramas near the northwestern corner of the Etang de Berre. Most of the larger settlements are situated around the margins of the Crau. Salon has industries connected with local products: the refining and bottling of olive oil, the packing of olives, soap-making, fruit-preserving and the manufacture of boxes for the export of vegetable produce.

The wastes of the Crau are used for other purposes, such as the enormous sewage works serving Marseilles, a large explosives dépôt at Entressen, a motor-racing circuit at Miramas, a military airfield at Istres and in recent years for an oil refinery, petrochemical plants and other large-scale industry. These uses, of a non-productive character, emphasise the limitations of this desolate but spacious region.

## Lower Provence

The country of Lower Provence to the east of the Rhône delta is one of very considerable complexity. It consists of a series of limestone ridges, the origin of which is due to the west–east Pyrenean folding projecting westward towards the delta. The Massif de la Ste Baume, for example, to the east of Marseilles, consists of a series of parallel folds, with the main crestline extending for about 11 km (7 miles) as a vertical rock wall rising from the swathing woodlands to culminate in a prominent peak at 1 154 m (3 786 ft). Further north is another striking series of Jurassic ridges between the parallel valleys of the Arc and the Durance. There are many more ridges and plateaus, with sharp crests, bare crags, deep gullies and flanking sheets of scree. The torrential rains form torrents which have deeply gashed this mountain country, although in summer their courses are mostly dry and boulder-strewn.

Many deeply cut valleys and a few quite extensive basins separate these limestone uplands. Behind the port of Marseilles lies a depression floored with varied Oligocene rocks, drained by the Jarret and the Huveaune; the western part, in the angle to the south of the Chaîne de l'Estaque, has subsided and forms the deepwater Golfe de Marseille. The most extensive basin is that of the Arc, floored for the most part with Eocene rocks. Around its margins are scarped ridges, formed by the differential denudation of the flanking Upper Cretaceous and Lower Eocene rocks.[7] The river Arc flows through the basin and then crosses an alluvial plain to enter the Etang de Berre. Other depressions drain eastward to the Argens or southward directly to the coast. Bordering the limestone country on the east is a distinct structural depression, filled with varied Permian rocks, which can be traced northeastward from the neighbourhood of Toulon to the valley of the Argens; the last occupies another west–east structural depression of Triassic rocks between Barjols and the coast near Fréjus and St Raphael. The railway route from Toulon via Le Luc to Fréjus indicates clearly the line of these depressions.

The coast bordering *la Basse-Provence calcaire* is very indented, since the margins of this alternation of ridge, valley and basin, submerged by the sea, form a series of bays and promontories. Some of the bays (known as *calanques*),[8] such as the Calanque de Sormiou and Calanque de Morgiou, are long deep winding inlets, between steep cliffbound *becs* and *pointes*. This type of *calanque* seems to comprise ancient fissures enlarged by marine erosion, not just ria-like gulfs due to submergence alone. Others, such as the Baies de Cassis, de la Ciotat and de Bandol, are more open, rounded in outline and with low-lying hinterlands fronted by sandy beaches; these seem to be submerged portions of marl-floored depressions. J. Chardonnet, in fact, classifies these openings into *calanques-criques* and *calanques-estuaires* respectively.[9]

## Land use and agriculture

The basis of life in much of this part of Provence[10] consists of small-scale though varied agriculture, making use of the basins and valleys where 'pockets' of more fertile clay and alluvial soils are concentrated. The limestone ridges and plateaus are *garrigue*-covered, although some poor patches of evergreen oak and Aleppo pines, occasionally of beech, are the remains of the forests cleared before the nineteenth century; much wood, for example, has gone to the shipyards of Toulon, La Ciotat and Marseilles. With the reduction in the number of sheep and goats, woodland is now increasing in area.

In the clay-floored basins and in the Permian depression, wheat is grown biennially with an intervening season of fallow, though rarely on an extensive scale. The usual holding includes a piece of irrigated land in the valley bottom near a village, growing vegetable crops. Further up the terraced slopes are patches of wheat or maize, then fruit trees such as peaches, followed by vines and finally groves of olives and sweet chestnut. In the depression behind Marseilles this intensive polyculture supplies the local urban market. In some districts cooperation is practised in the processing and marketing of both wine and olive oil.[11] At the southern end of the Permian depression to the east of Toulon, the clay soils and the availability of irrigation water have made the Plaine d'Hyères an 'oasis de cultures arbustives, maraîchères ou florales', as E. Bénévent puts it. Special features are the cultivation of choice varieties of cherries, which are sent to markets in Paris, England and Belgium, and of figs. The development of the Riviera flower industry has encouraged here also the cultivation of flowers, particularly roses. Despite the limitations of relief and soil, agriculture in this part of Provence, small-scale though it may be, exhibits a diversity and an intensity in marked contrast to the vine-covered *pays* of Bas-Languedoc.

## Industry and mining

Industrially this part of Provence is not of any great importance, with the outstanding exception of Marseilles and its *banlieue*. There are, of course, flour mills, olive oil mills and wine presses in most villages. Some of the small towns, such as Barjols and Brignoles, have tanneries; the former also has potteries and a paper works, the latter a small silk factory. At Aubagne, in the Huveaune valley behind Marseilles, and at Roquevaire, 8 km (5 miles) further up the same valley, a dozen works make bricks and glazed tiles from local Oligocene clays. The widespread occurrence of calcareous rocks provides raw material for large-scale cement manufacture; several works are in the Marseilles area, and others are at Valdonne, near Gréasque in the Fuveau lignite-basin (which provides fuel for the kilns), and in the south near the coast between Cassis and La Bédoule, using coal from the Alès field. Nearly 2 000 Italian workers are employed in the cement works, living in *cités-ouvrières*. At Aix is a variety of industries on a small scale: the manufacture of matches, agricultural implements, fertilisers, and equipment for olive oil mills. Shipbuilding is carried on at La Ciotat, its facilities modernised and extended since 1950, and a dry dock is used for repair work. The varied industrial development in and around Marseilles, and the naval shipbuilding at Toulon, are described below.

A certain amount of mining and quarrying is active in this part of Provence. The deposits of the main commercial ore of aluminium, hydrated oxide of alumina (known as bauxite from its occurrence near the now almost deserted town of Les Baux, where it was discovered in 1821), are exploited in the valley of the upper Argens and its tributaries. Here the ore is preserved in synclinal pockets among Lower Cretaceous limestones, and is worked in shallow quarries which form red scars on the flanks of the wooded ridges. About 3·0 million tons of bauxite were produced in France in 1970, (some increase from 2·2 in 1961), of which 94 per cent came from this

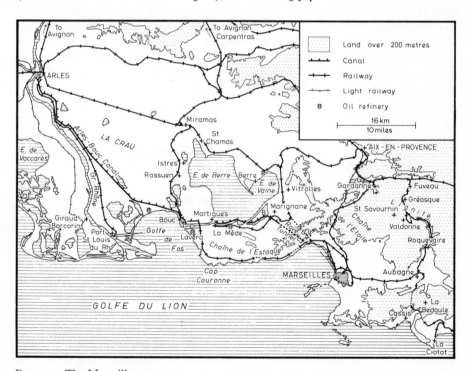

FIG. 15.3. The Marseilles area

Based on *Carte de France au 50 000ᵉ*, sheets **XXIX/43, 44, XXXI/44, 45**.

*département* of Var. This represents a big increase on prewar days, for in 1938 the output was only 680 000 tons. France is no longer the world's chief producer, however, a position which she held until the war of 1939–45, for consumption has risen so considerably that even with her greatly increased output she is behind Surinam, Guyana and the USA. The bulk of the bauxite production of Var is sent by rail to Gardanne to the east of Marseilles, where it is reduced to alumina, and this is sent by rail to the refineries of the Arc and Isère valleys where it is smelted electrolytically (see p. 647). About 148 000 tons of alumina were exported in 1969, two-thirds of it from Toulon, the rest from St Raphaël.

Considerable deposits of lignite occur in Basse-Provence,[12] the most important being the Fuveau field in the upper part of the Arc basin. The lignite occurs in thick beds among lacustrine deposits of Cretaceous age, and forms France's only worked field (Fig. 15.3). The annual production topped a million tons during the war of 1914–18, when the northern coalfields were fought over. It fell to 600 000 tons in the interwar years, but has been stepped up again in the postwar period; 1·61 million tons were produced in 1969. Much of the lignite is used locally by a large power station at Gardanne, and at the cement works. The lignite mines are drained of water, which has caused much trouble, by a tunnel nearly 16 km (10 miles) long from near Gréasque to Gardanne, then passing under the ridge of l'Etoile to the northeastern corner of the Golfe de Marseille at L'Estaque. The recent extension of the lignite mines has necessitated the importation of much foreign labour, since the local population can supply only about half the required personnel. Most of the foreigners are Italians, living in *cités-ouvrières* near the collieries.

## Marseilles

With a population of 889 000 in 1968, Marseilles[13] is the second largest city in France, and is the largest port; in 1969 it handled just over a third of the total tonnage entered and cleared through the country's ports, though dominated by oil. Marseilles has an important regional administrative function as headquarters of the Provence: Côte d'Azur: Corse planning region and (with Aix) forms one of the *métropoles d'équilibres* (p. 199). It presents the paradox of being one of the oldest settlements in the Mediterranean while its real growth is of the late nineteenth and particularly of the twentieth centuries. The town was founded at the end of the seventh century BC by the Phoceans, and so it became a Greek colony and port; a small rocky basin was the original harbour, known today as the *Vieux-Port*, while the settlement was called *Massilia*, from which the present name is derived. It was of some importance throughout classical times, but in the great period of the Mediterranean city-states Marseilles failed to rival Pisa, Genoa or Venice. What trade used the Rhône valley went through the harbours to the west of the delta, which had more direct contact with Lyons

PLATE 45. The port of Marseilles

and the Rhône valley than had Marseilles, tucked away and isolated to the southeast of the Chaîne de l'Estaque. Some development took place in the sixteenth and seventeenth centuries, including the building of new quays, but still the port was far behind Nantes and Bordeaux.

Several factors contributed to the rapid growth of Marseilles in the nineteenth century, notably increasing French interests in North Africa which followed the conquest of Algeria in 1830. The development of railways afforded vastly improved access to central and northern France, although the link with Arles and Lyons involved the construction of a difficult line from Miramas along the shores of the Etang de Berre and then the penetration of the Chaîne de l'Estaque by a tunnel. A second rail link (the *Corniche* line) was created as a result of the development of Port-de-Bouc, running south to this from Miramas, then crossing the Etang de Caronte by a swing bridge and viaduct, and rounding the Chaîne de l'Estaque on the west and south by a difficult route involving several cuttings and short tunnels. Perhaps the most important factor was the opening of the Suez Canal in 1869, which transformed the Mediterranean from being a *cul-de-sac* into a world highway. Marseilles has suffered competition with Genoa, especially as a result of the construction of the Alpine tunnels which drew off much Swiss

PLATE 46. The city of Marseilles

traffic, and has also suffered during the last few years from the closure of
Suez, but the French commercial interests throughout the Mediterranean
provide much activity. In the last forty years, with the immense development of the Middle East and North African oilfields, the Mediterranean
has become Europe's chief oil route, and Marseilles with its four nearby
refineries has formed one of the main oil terminals; in 1969 the port and its
annexes handled 50 million tons of crude oil (nearly half of France's total
imports), and also exported by sea 5·1 million tons of refined hydrocarbons.
Most of the other imports consist of oil seeds, wheat, sugar, timber, hides,
some coal, raw cotton, phosphates, oil seeds and other foodstuffs and raw
materials. The tonnage of exports is far less; apart from refined hydrocarbons, the chief items are cement, chemical products (especially fertilisers). flour, wines and liqueurs, and textiles and metallurgical goods for
North Africa. Indeed, Marseilles mostly re-exports her imports in refined or
manufactured form, since the port is not an outlet for the produce of the
Rhône valley, which being perishable, non-bulky and valuable travels
directly by rail.

All this development has not been achieved without considerable difficulty, for Marseilles has hardly a good natural harbour and there are con-

siderable physical obstacles between it and the Rhône valley. Moreover, development inland to the east has been cramped by the encroaching limestone hills. The coast does, however, form a right angle, sheltered by these hills from the north and east, with deep water offshore, virtually no tidal range, and with a complete absence of silting, unlike the delta and the Languedoc coast to the west. The tiny rock basin of Lacydon has long been left to fishing boats, and the modern port lies behind a breakwater mole (Plates 45, 46) running parallel to the coast for 5 km (3 miles) northwestward, along which basins and quays have been constructed. The basins have been gradually extended, and developments are still going on to the north in the Bassin Mirabeau and at Mourepiane. The damage caused during the war of 1939–45, involving the destruction of many port facilities and the blocking of several basins by sunken vessels, took some time to restore. No locks or dock gates are required with the negligible tidal range, and the only impediments between the various basins are the necessary swing bridges. A road-tunnel has been constructed under the Vieux-Port.

Both Lyons and Marseilles have long desired a major waterway between them, preferably of ship canal dimensions. A canal penetrates the Chaîne de l'Estaque to the north of the port by means of the Rove Tunnel (Fig. 15.3), 6 km (4 miles) in length and 22 m (72 ft) in width. Started in 1911 and interrupted by the war of 1914–18, it was not completed until 1929. It can accommodate thousand-ton barges, and not only shortens considerably the distance from Marseilles to Bouc but also enables barges to avoid the crossing of the Golfe de Fos, which can be very stormy, particularly in winter when the mistral is blowing. The canal continues along the southern shores of the Etang de Berre to Martigues, then through the Etang de Caronte to Port-de-Bouc (Plate 47). From here the smaller Arles-Bouc Canal runs northwest along the left bank of the Grand Rhône to Arles. This continuous waterway enables small barges to pass through from Marseilles to Arles; larger barges can move between Marseilles and the Etang de Berre; and shipping drawing 8 m (26 ft) can use the ship canal through the Etang de Caronte from Bouc to Martigues and so proceed to the tanker and other berths in the Etang de Berre.

Considerable development has taken place around the shores of the Etangs de Berre, de Vaine and de Caronte, and the Golfe de Fos; the new ports are included within the administration of Marseilles (Fig. 15.3). These integrated plans on a massive scale imply the creation of a great 'Europort South', a vast growth centre for the Mediterranean, akin to Rotterdam-Europoort (p. 68) in the north. Ship channels have been dredged from Port-de-Bouc on the shores of the Golfe de Fos to Martigues, with a depth of 9 m (30 ft), and across the Etang de Berre to its northeastern shore. The development of these channels, quays and tanker-terminals has progressed steadily, and several large schemes are under construction at Fos-sur-Mer (with a 20 m (66 ft) deepwater channel) and Port St Louis-du-Rhône. The reason for this progress has been the need to cope with large-

PLATE 47. Port-de-Bouc, with the Lavéra oil-terminal in the foreground

scale industries requiring considerable space which could not be accommodated in the immediate neighbourhood of the old port and town. The areas of shallow water and marshland around the margins of the *étangs* are easy to reclaim, and afford extensive sites, as does the plain of La Crau.

The most important of these 'new' industries is oil-refining, forming a quarter of France's capacity. Four large refineries have been built in the district. On the south side of the entrance to the Etang de Caronte, opposite Port-de-Bouc, is the petroleum basin of Port-de-Lavéra (Plate 47), behind which is the Lavéra refinery[14] with an output of 4·5 million tons of refined oil (Plate 48), owned by the Société Française des Pétroles B.P. Further to the east in the Etang de Berre is an offshore tanker mooring berth, connected by underwater pipeline to the La Mède refinery (with an output of 8·57 million tons), owned by the Compagnie Française de Raffinage. In the northeast of the Etang de Berre is the Berre tanker terminal, linked by a 5-km (3-miles) pipeline with the Berre-l'Etang refinery (output 5·77 million tons) owned by Shell-Berre. A pipeline has been built along the southern shore of the Etang de Berre to La Mède, and another one right round the eastern shores to Berre, which the large tankers cannot reach. The Lavéra terminal is linked by the South European Pipeline, of 750 km (468 miles) in length, with Mannheim in West Germany via Strasbourg (see p. 309).[15]

An Esso refinery was opened at Fos-sur-Mer in 1965, with an output of 2·76 million tons, and in 1968 the Golfe de Fos became a deep water port taking 250 000 ton tankers, with pipelines to Lyons and to Karlsruhe. France's third largest container terminal (after Dunkirk and Le Havre) was opened at Fos in 1970.[16]

The Etang de Berre first became an extension of Marseilles during the war of 1914–18, when explosives factories were built at St Chamas. Since 1950 the whole area is being developed as a great industrial complex in a part of France which has suffered considerable unemployment and resultant economic and social problems from lack of industrial opportunity. As yet, there is perhaps an undue dependence on oil-refining and the associated petrochemical industry. Several plants have been put into operation,[17] at L'Estaque (owned by Standard-Kuhlmann), at Berre (Shell-St Gobain), at Lavéra (Naptha-chimie), and at La Mède (Cie Française de Raffinage). They make a wide range of products—detergents, plastics, carbon black and many more hydrocarbon derivatives. ICI have built a polyethylene plant, which came on stream in 1972. Chemical works are in operation at Port-de-Bouc, cement works at Istres, Martigues and Fos-sur-Mer, engineering works at St Chamas, railway workshops at Miramas and Rognac, oil seed crushing at Croix-Sante. One of the most important developments will be the enormous Sacilor steel plant, on which construction began in 1971. Several *cités-ouvrières* have been built to house the workers, many of them foreigners. Finally, there are port and canal works, railway marshalling yards, the rapidly developing Marignane airport and the Istres military airfield. In fifty years much of the desolate wastes of the *étangs* and marshes has become a region of activity.

Marseilles itself, a cosmopolitan city with a quarter of its population of foreign origin, has spread upwards on to its confining slopes. From the narrow rather furtive streets around the old port[18] to the villas among the olives and orchards on the hill slopes, there is a bewilderment of contrasting characteristics. Quite apart from the Berre exclave, the city is an important industrial centre. Vegetable-oil refining, soap-making, the manufacture of fertilisers from North African phosphates, flour-milling, sugar-refining, the making of corks, a large ship-repairing industry and several marine engineering plants, timber industries and miscellaneous metallurgical industries have developed, as might be expected in a great port. In addition, some large cement-works use local limestone, and two outlying chemical factories are in the northern (L'Estaque) and northeastern (Septèmes-les-Vallons) outskirts of the city. Considerable development has progressed eastward along the lower valley of the Huveaune since 1876, particularly in the fifteen years before 1939, and now extending to Aubagne. Industrial suburbs have grown along each side of the valley. Numerous factories have been built, making furniture, glass, pottery, chemical products, paper and cardboard, biscuits and foodstuffs generally, and miscellaneous metallurgical items. Modern housing estates contrast with old villages.[19]

PLATE 48. The oil-refinery at Lavéra, near the Golfe de Fos.

## Toulon

Toulon has been a Mediterranean naval base for many centuries, important since Henri IV founded the arsenal and developed the harbour works. A west–east inner *rade* on the eastern side of the prominent peninsula of Cap du Sicié is almost enclosed by the crystalline ridges of Mourillon on the east and La Seyne on the west. Further south again, affording further protection from the south and enclosing the outer *Grande Rade*, is the peninsula of St Mandrier, made of Permian rocks, which projects eastward to end in Cap Cépet. Five kilometres (3 miles) east of this headland is the Cap de Gard de Carqueiranne, and as a result both outer and inner roadsteads are protected from strong gales, while the several hilly peninsulas provided sites for defensive shore batteries. The limestone hills behind the town, rising to over 450 m (1 500 ft) within 4 or 5 km (2 or 3 miles) of the port, afforded excellent sites for a perimeter of fortresses, as well as providing shelter from northerly winds. Toulon has experienced critical phases of naval history; it has been blockaded on many occasions, notably in the French Revolutionary and Napoleonic wars, but perhaps its most tragic hour was when a large part of the French fleet was scuttled there in November 1942. Both port and town were grievously damaged during the war, and the population dropped from about 150 000 in 1938 to 125 000 in 1946. Much reconstruction has taken place, and Toulon is once again France's main Mediterranean naval base, as well as being one of the NATO bases, with a population of 175 000, and a conurbation total of 340 000. At La Seyne, in the western angle of the inner roadsteads, are both naval and civil shipbuilding yards and repair shops.

Toulon has a small commercial harbour, which exports bauxite from the producing centre of Brignoles, 50 km (30 miles) away to the north, with which the port is connected by a circuitous railway; about 138 000 tons were shipped in 1969, rather less than in 1938. Imports included 318 000 tons of oil for the base and 21 000 tons of machinery and steel for the repair shops, but little else. It has a weekly shipping service to Corsica in summer.

## The Maures-Esterel massifs

Massifs of crystalline rock reach the Mediterranean coast between Cap du Sicié, to the south of Toulon, and the Golfe de la Napoule. The massifs belong structurally to the Hercynian core of the Alps (see p. 626) and form part of a foundered continental mass. The Iles d'Hyères and western Corsica comprise similar structures, and were probably once continuous with the mainland, now separated by a fractured and sunken area forming part of the Ligurian Sea. The rocks are complex, consisting of granite, gneiss and crystalline schist, for the most part of Pre-Cambrian age.[20]

These crystalline massifs can be divided into three unit areas. In the

417

southwest the small Massif du Sicié rises to 351 m (1 152 ft) within a kilometre of the coast, and is separated from the upland of Maures by the
submerged southern end of the Permian depression, which forms the
harbour of Toulon. The Massif des Maures is much larger, extending
inland for 30 km (20 miles). These uplands are interrupted only by the
broad Golfe de St Tropez, cut in less resistant slates, and by its continuation
to the southwest as a valley across which a cluster of streams converges
towards the gulf. The northeastern part of Maures, known as the Massif du
Tanneron, consists in part of granitic rocks. The Permian depression swings
eastward around the northern edge of Maures, reaching the sea at the
broad Golfe de Fréjus. Beyond this, between the valleys of the Argens and
the Siagne, is the compact Massif de l'Esterel; along the coast the rocks are
again mainly granitic.

These massifs are not lofty, the highest point being only 780 m (2 550 ft),
but they are rugged and gashed with steepsided river valleys. Their impermeable rocks contrast with the limestones which form so much of Provence.
The hills, while rocky, have not the near-karstic aridity of much of the limestone; they bear woodlands of cork oak and chestnut on their lower slopes,
and coarse pasture, bracken and scrub higher up. Esterel is particularly
well wooded.

The coast of Maures and Esterel is bold and massive, with prominent
headlands, rocky islands, occasional broad bays and deep narrow indentations. Submergence of the margins of the crystalline rocks formed the bay
of Hyères and the several outlying Iles d'Hyères.[20] One of these, Giens, has
been converted into a peninsula by the formation of two parallel sandspits
from the mainland to the island, 8 km (5 miles) long and over a kilometre
apart, enclosing areas of salt-marsh, *étangs* and pans from which salt is
extracted. The several rivers flowing into the Rade d'Hyères and into the
Golfe de Fréjus have collaborated with longshore drift to build out broad
coastal plains fronted with sandy beaches and low dunes, with spits across
the river mouths enclosing several *étangs* and areas of saltmarsh. Fréjus itself
was a port in Roman times but is now nearly 3 km (2 miles) from the sea; a
small airport, serving St Raphaël, has been developed on the alluvial flats
between Fréjus and the sea. The plentiful material available for this coastal
accretion is an indication of the eroding capacity of the short rivers flowing
to the sea over the impermeable crystalline rocks. Further to the northeast,
prominent capes of resistant igneous rocks alternate with bays worn in less
resistant slates. Beyond the Golfe de Fréjus the Esterel coast is less interrupted by large bays but consists of an alternation of deepwater *calanques*
and bold yet short promontories.

Apart from the towns in the Permian depression (Toulon, Hyères,
Le Luc and Fréjus), few settlements are of any size. Along the coast, with its
magnificent *Corniche* road and parallel railway, occur villages from which
small-scale tunny-fishing is carried on. Some tourism has developed, but
this coast, overshadowed by the Côte d'Azur further east, tends rather to

encourage individual villas and occasional hotels delightfully situated in secluded bays.

In spite of the greater surface water supply, the agricultural economy of this part of Provence differs little from the rest. On the terraced sides of the valleys vines, olives, fruits (such as peaches) and vegetables are cultivated, and chestnut groves are widespread, while the higher pastures in the interior are grazed by sheep and cattle. The forests play an important part in the economy, as apart from timber and tan bark, the cork oak is carefully tended to provide corks for the millions of wine bottles filled every year in the Midi and elsewhere in France. This industry has however suffered considerably from competition with North Africa, Spain and Portugal.

## The Côte d'Azur[22]

The granitic and metamorphic rocks which compose the Massif de l'Esterel end abruptly at the Golfe de la Napoule and are replaced by rocks of Mesozoic age. From Cannes to the broad valley of the Var the coast cuts transversely across a sequence of Triassic and Jurassic rocks; a mass of resistant Middle Jurassic limestone forms the prominent Cap d'Antibes, and some Lower Jurassic fragments comprise the two offshore Iles de Lérins. Torrential streams flow southwards to the sea in narrow ravines, separating steepsided limestone *collines*. To the east of Antibes the lower ranges of the calcareous Maritime Alps trend southward towards the coast, which consists accordingly of prominent white headlands alternating with broad valleys reaching the sea as roadsteads. The largest of the rivers is the Var, whose lower valley is floored with an extensive talus of Pliocene gravels. The Paillon enters the sea in the Nice roadstead, and further east the Rade de Villefranche lies between the ridge culminating in Mont Boron and the prominent Cap Ferrat. Further east still the Cretaceous limestone hills come close to the sea, with many rocky spurs separating bays each with its resort. Complex movements of sea level have occurred in geologically recent times, resulting in the features of a submerged upland coast. Much deposition results from the efforts of the sea to straighten out the coastline; in some parts fine sand grains worn from the crystalline rocks accumulate to form the superb *plages*, as at Cannes and Juan-les-Pins, but in others (notably near the mouth of the Var) the fluvioglacial gravels provide less attractive stretches of shingle beach.

### The agricultural economy

Neither along the coast of Alpes-Maritimes nor in the interior is the terrain suitable for agriculture, except in some small clay- or marl-floored depressions among the limestone and along the lower valleys of the rivers. The *département* has in fact the lowest proportion of arable land in France; this

419

amounted in 1968 to little more than 3 per cent of its total area, though the cultivation of fruit, vines and vegetables added another 15 per cent. Twenty-nine per cent was under permanent pasture (much of this in the higher ranges of the Maritime Alps, the rest consisting of scrubby limestone pasture), and about the same proportion carried woodland, mostly thin pinewoods and rather poor holm oak and cork oak forests. The region shares the general summer aridity of the Midi; both July and August have an average of less than 25 mm (1 in) of rainfall, frequently none at all, and what there is comes in the form of torrential showers.

Until the mid-nineteenth century, the pattern of the economy resembled that of the Midi generally; on small pockets of favourable land wheat, olives, vines, figs and other fruit were cultivated, sheep and goats were grazed on the limestone pastures, cattle in the higher valleys and on summer alpine pastures, and some fishing was active along the coast. Then began the gradual development of the tourist industry; this revolutionised the agricultural economy. Much more produce was required for local consumption, while conversely better communications allowed perishable crops to be produced for distant markets. The cultivation of flowers achieved an outstanding place, both for the cut flower trade and for perfume. A remarkable *ceinture fleurie* developed along the coast, with concentrations at Vallauris (between Cannes and Antibes), along the valley of the Loup behind Cagnes-sur-Mer, in the adjoining Valvan valley at Vence, and in the Var valley at St Laurent. There is some specialisation, notably in mimosa at Nice, but usually a variety of flowers, choice fruit and early vegetables, maturing in sequence, is grown by each *propriétaire*. Competition to produce earlier crops has forced the use of glass (cloches and greenhouses) even in this favoured climate, especially for carnations. While the luxury resorts consume some of this produce, three-quarters is sent away by train; this tendency developed during the early 1930s, when the world depression drastically reduced the number of visitors, and the cultivators were obliged to seek wider markets.

Some 13 km (8 miles) to the northwest of Cannes, in a basin drained by a number of headstreams of the Siagne, is situated Grasse, where since the end of the eighteenth century the cultivation of flowers for perfume has provided a prosperous livelihood. At one time between four and five thousand *petits-propriétaires* grew roses, jasmine, violets, orange blossom and other herbs and flowers to supply the small factories in and around the town. The production of cheap synthetic perfumes by industrial processes and the great decline of high price luxury markets during the world depression hit the Grasse area badly. While today some cultivation[23] still produces the really expensive perfumes requiring the natural essence of flowers, much of the Grasse district has fallen into line with the Côte d'Azur generally, and is producing early vegetables, fruit (particularly peaches) and flowers. 'Après une brillante carrière, la culture des plantes à parfum, née de l'industrie, semble tuée par l'industrie.'[24]

## The Riviera resorts

Between the Golfe de la Napoule and the Italian frontier lies an almost continuous line of resorts catering for an enormous annual influx of visitors. The Riviera has capitalised its mild sunny climate,[25] its south-facing aspect and its protection from the *mistral* by the surrounding hills, its attractive subtropical vegetation of palms and mimosa, and the general charm of the coast. It can offer sunny beaches, magnificent inland scenery, and snow-covered hills in winter but a few hours away. From being merely the winter home of the wealthy, with their villas and large yachts, the Riviera has become one of the playgrounds of Europe, catering both for the fashionable and the sophisticated and increasingly also for the ordinary visitor. It is estimated that half a million people visit the Riviera between Christmas and Easter and 2 million during the summer. Its main drawback is its lack of space and facilities for providing cheaper holiday accommodation and camp sites; it seems that many tourists now go to the new resorts west of the Rhône (see p. 442). The main line of the *Région-Sud* from Paris, via Dijon and Lyons, was opened to Nice in 1865, and now a heavy traffic of *rapides* leaves the Gare de Lyon every evening for this Côte d'Azur. The last section, from Fréjus round the edge of the Esterel massif to the Italian frontier, is a superb train journey, with the line following a sinuous course near the sea and using tunnels, cuttings and viaducts to negotiate the difficult terrain. The busy Nice airport on the shingle flats to the east of the mouth of the river Var, with the end of the runway but a few metres from the sea, affords a rapid means of access from most of the cities of Europe.

There are four *grands centres*—Cannes, Nice, Monte Carlo and Menton,[26] and innumerable others which form coastal fringes of hotels, luxury shops, villas and casinos behind the *plages* and tiered up the hillsides. Cannes, Juan-les-Pins and Antibes comprise virtually one continuous resort from the Golfe de la Napoule, round Golfe Juan and along both sides of the Cap d'Antibes. Beyond the alluvial flats at the mouth of the river Var are Nice, Villefranche, Beaulieu-sur-Mer, Eze and Cap d'Ail. Then the famous group of Monte Carlo and La Condamine in the principality of Monaco are succeeded by Beausoleil, Roquebrune, Cap Martin, Carnolles and Menton. Thus the permanent population of Alpes-Maritimes, despite its considerable area of rugged limestone mountains, totals 700 000, three-quarters of whom live along or near the coast, a population which is swollen by the seasonal influx of visitors.

## Nice

The most famous Mediterranean resort is Nice,[27] *chef-lieu* of the *département* of Alpes-Maritimes and 'capital' of the Riviera. For long it was merely a small port and fortress, situated on a bay where the river Paillon reaches the sea to the west of the sheltering peninsula of Cap Ferrat. Its growth really started when France acquired the County of Nice in 1860, and was particularly stimulated when the coastal railway reached the town in 1865. During this century its population has increased by more than 100 per cent. As the Riviera became increasingly fashionable, Nice grew rapidly. Villas and hotels spread upwards on the south-facing hillsides and along the coast to the west in the contiguous suburbs of Ste Hélène, St Jean and La Californie. It so dominates the Côte d'Azur that the district is in fact sometimes referred to as *la Côte niçoise*, and Nice is now the fifth city of France in size, with a population in 1968 of 322 000. Roads, autocar routes, the electric tramways, the railway opened in 1928 over the Col de Tende (using a series of fine spiral tunnels) to Cuneo (Coni) in north Italy,[28] and its busy international airport all contribute to its becoming 'la grande métropole de la Côte d'Azur'. Some light industries have been introduced, notably a large IBM computer factory.

Nice has a small harbour situated to the east of the town, below the old château, with a jetty protecting an *avant-port* and three open basins. There are regular sailings to Corsica and Italian ports, and the port is also used by pleasure yachts, coasting vessels, and a small amount of commercial trade, mainly the export of cement and lime from works near the town, and the import of some coal. The port handled about four times as much trade before 1939 as at present, but there was a certain amount of wartime damage, and although reconstruction is now complete it has not recovered its prewar position.

[1] J. Sion, *La France méditerranéenne* (1934); and P. Carrère and R. Dugrand, *La Région méditerranéenne* (1960), in the series *France de Demain*.

[2] A useful summary, with examples, is given by A. Perpillou, 'Types d'évolution de quelques paysages agricoles méditerranéens', *Mélanges géographiques offerts à Ernest Bénévent* (1954), pp. 289–309. See also R. Livet, 'Les elevages provençaux', *Méditerranée*, **6** (1965), pp. 185–200.

[3] An immensely detailed and well documented piece of work is R. J. Russell, 'Geomorphology of the Rhône delta', *Ann. Ass. Am. Geogr.*, **32** (1942), pp. 149–254. The author includes a bibliography of 129 references. Much of the article deals with progressive changes in the main Rhône exits, using both geomorphological and historical evidence, including some fascinating old maps.

[4] Two interesting accounts of rice-growing in the delta of the Camargue are (*a*) J. Girod, 'La culture du riz en Camargue', *Bulletin de la Société de Géographie et d'Etudes coloniales de Marseille*, **64** (1948–50), pp. 55–60; and (*b*) V. Prévot, 'La culture du riz de Camargue', *Informations géographiques*, **17** (1953), no. 1, pp. 13–20. In 1970 about 91 000 tons of rice were produced in Bouches-du-Rhône and the margins of the neighbouring *départements*.

[5] R. J. Russell, *op. cit.*, p. 159.

[6] H. Baulig, 'La Crau et la glaciation würmienne', *Annls Géogr.*, **36** (1927), pp. 499–508, provides a detailed account of the deposition of the gravels.

[7] R. Livet, 'Le peuplement des cuestas du bassin d'Aix-en-Provence', *Annls Géogr.*, **62** (1953), pp. 133–6, has a map and several photographs of these cuestas.

[8] J. Chardonnet, 'Les calanques provençales, origine et divers types', *Annls Géogr.*, **57** (1948), pp. 289–97; there are several detailed maps and photographs.

9 It should be pointed out, however, that J. Nicod, in 'Le problème de la classification des calanques parmi les formes de côtes de submersion', *Revue de Géomorphologie Dynamique*, **2** (1951), pp. 120–7, disagrees with Chardonnet's suggestion that *calanques* are due to submergence, but suggests that they are the result of karstic collapse without invoking submergence.

10 R. Livet, *Habitat rural et structures agraires en Basse-Provence* (1962).

11 J. Nicod, 'Grandeur et décadence de l'oléiculture provençale', *Rev. Géogr. alp.*, **44** (1956), pp. 237–95; this contains some detailed maps.

12 J. Nicod, 'L'Essor des houillères du bassin de Provence', *Bulletin de la Société de Géographie de Marseille*, **65** (1954), pp. 39–50, provides some detailed maps and a number of photographs.

13 The following articles on Marseilles are useful: (*a*) D. Tomkinson, 'The Marseilles experiment', *Tn Plann. Rev.*, **24** (1953), pp. 193–214; (*b*) F. A. Dufour, 'The industrial growth of Marseilles', *Progress*, **44** (1955), pp. 270–6; (*c*) L. Pierrein, 'Sur l'expansion économique de Marseille et de sa région', *Bulletin de Géographie d'Aix-Marseille*, **66** (1955), pp. 81–90; (*d*) L. Pierrein, 'Marseille et le Canal de Suez', *ibid.*, **67** (1956), pp. 73–94; (*e*) C. Barrilon, 'Le port de Marseille et le delta rhôdanien', *Urbanisme*, **95** (1966), p. 26.

14 L. Pierrein, 'Le bassin pétrolier du Port de Marseille; Marseille-Lavéra', *Bulletin de la Société de Géographie de Marseille*, **65** (1954), pp. 51–9.

15 H. Debrabant, 'Le Pipeline sud-européen: aspects techniques et économiques', *Rev. Navig. intér. rhén.* (1963), pp. 377–83.

16 H. D. Clout, 'Expansion projects for French seaports', *Tijdschr. econ. soc. Geogr.*, **59** (1968), pp. 271–7, gives maps of Marseilles, with a plan of the Golfe de Fos project. See also F. Pasqualini, 'Giant harbour complex in South France', *Dock & Harbour Authority*, **574** (1968), p. 142.

17 The petrochemical industries which have developed in conjunction with the oil-refineries are described, with numerous illustrations, by R. Guglielmo, 'Principaux aspects de développement de la pétrochimie en France', *Annls Géogr.*, **65** (1956), pp. 123–39; and B. S. Hoyle, 'The Etang de Berre', *Tijdschr. econ. soc. Geogr.*, **51** (1960), pp. 57–65.

18 Much of this area was demolished by the Germans during the war, and there has been considerable rebuilding in recent years.

19 A detailed account, with maps and photographs, is given by M. Roncayolo, 'Evolution de la banlieue marseillaise dans la basse Vallée de l'Huveaune', *Annls Géogr.*, **61** (1952), pp. 342–56.

20 Y. Masurel, *La Provence cristallin et ses enveloppes sédimentaires* (1965).

21 A full account, with maps and photographs, is given by Y. Masurel, 'Observations sur la structure et la morphologie des Iles d'Hyères', *Annls Géogr.*, **62** (1953), pp. 241–58.

22 B. Kayser, *Campagnes et villes de la Cote d'Azur* (1958).

23 O. Beniamino, 'Grasse, centre mondial des matières premières aromatiques', *Rev. Géogr. alp.*, **45** (1957), pp. 763–74; and D. Balducchi, 'La Répartition des actionnaires de la parfumerie de Grasse', *Annls Géogr.*, **69** (1960), pp. 462–76.

24 E. Bénévent, 'La Basse-Provence', *La France: géographie-tourisme*, edited by D. Faucher Faucher (1951), i, p. 300.

25 L. Gorczynski, *Climat solaire de Nice et de la Côte d'Azur. Mémoire IV de l'Association des Naturalistes de Nice et des Alpes-Maritimes* (1934).

26 L. Guéron, 'Le tourisme à Menton', *Méditerranée*, **7** (1966), pp. 51–64.

27 R. Blanchard, *Le Comté de Nice. Etude géographique* (1960).

28 This railway line was destroyed during the war of 1939–45, but is now again in full operation.

# 16
# The Mediterranean coastlands
# II. Languedoc and Roussillon

The plains extending from the Rhône to the outlying masses of the Pyrenees are referred to generally as *Languedoc*[1] (see p. 1), or sometimes more specifically as *Bas-Languedoc*. Various distinctive zones can be recognised—the coastal dunes, marshes and *étangs*, the alluvium-covered lowlands and lower terraces, the upper gravel terraces, the limestone *garrigue* country extending to the foothills of the Cévennes, and the outlying upper Aude valley or basin of Carcassonne. The small semicircular plain of Roussillon in the extreme south is sufficiently individual to be described separately.

## The coast

The coastline of Languedoc sweeps round the Golfe du Lion as two intersecting arcs, the first from the prominent headland of Cap Leucate to Cap d'Agde (enclosing the Golfe de Narbonne), the second continuing to the western wing of the Rhône delta fronted by the Golfe d'Aigues-Mortes. In mid-Pliocene times the sea stood about 50 m (160 ft) higher than at present, so that the coast was indented by several irregular-shaped shallow lagoons, extending far inland up the valleys of the Aude and the Hérault. Various masses of limestone and basalt (the capes mentioned above, together with the hills of La Clape and the Cap de Sète) stood out as islands. By the time of the Romans, sea level had fallen more or less to its present position, but shallow lagoons still remained between these coastal hillocks. The plain in which Narbonne stands was occupied by the *Lacus Narbonensis*, the Etang de Vendres covered what is now the mouth of the Aude, and the several *étangs* to the northeast of Sète were then continuous and much more extensive.

A long process of coastal straightening by natural means has since gone on slowly but steadily. The rivers of Languedoc, often affected by violent floods in autumn and spring, bring down vast amounts of sediment; the Aude, for example, contributes an annual load estimated to be 1·8 to 2·0 million cubic metres. The rapid gain of the land has been helped also by the shallow nature of the water offshore and the gently shelving sea floor; the ten-metre submarine contour is 3 to 5 km (2 to 3 miles) away, the 50 m

(55 yd) contour as much as 11 km (7 miles) out. Longshore drift assisted in the building of offshore bars, on which wind-blown sand has established a rampart of dunes, aligned in sweeping curves from one rocky island to the next.

Behind the bars the lagoons were slowly filled in by river sedimentation and by the mud-accretion of halophytic saltmarsh plants such as *Salicornia*, succeeded by reeds, rushes and salt grasses. Slowly the *étangs* became marshes, and the marshes became pastures. The work of man collaborated in the planting of sand-binding grasses on the dunes, and the building of causeways to carry railways, of dykes enclosing the Rhône-Sète and Midi Canals, and of dykes against river-flooding. The former Etang d'Ingril to the south of Montpellier has been reduced to four interconnected *étangs*—along the seaward edge of which runs the Rhône-Sète Canal. The river Lez has built an isthmus of its own alluvium to the sea right across a former large *étang* (through which the Lez itself is endyked to its outlet at Palavas). Parts of the *étang* now form the Marais de la Joncasse, de la Grande Palude and de la Grande Maïre, other areas in the southwest near Frontignan provide saltpans, and parts have been drained and now grow vines. Similarly the *Lacus Narbonensis* is now a plain, at the southern end of which are the much reduced Etangs de Sigean[2] and de l'Ayrolle. The Etang de Vendres, into the southern end of which flows the Aude, is really no longer a lagoon of open water but a saltmarsh. The largest remaining lake is the Etang de Thau, 20 km (13 miles) in length; it lies in a distinct synclinal hollow, and with a maximum sounding of 25 m (82 ft) it is the deepest of these lagoons, most of which vary from only about 2 to 6 m (6 to 20 ft).

## The lowlands of Languedoc

The term 'lowlands' is used in a general sense to denote the area between the dune-bordered coast and the edge of the limestone *garrigue* country. It is, however, a district of considerable physical variety, and several regional names emphasise this diversity: the *Costière* in the Nîmes district and elsewhere, the *Vistrenque* or alluvial plain of the Vistre between the Costière and the *garrigue* country, the alluvial plains of the *Lunelois* and those around Montpellier, the *Plaine de Montbazin* between the *garrigue* country and the outlying ridge of Gardiole, the lower basin of the river Hérault, the *Biterrois* to the northwest of Béziers, and the *Plaine Narbonnaise* or the basin of the lower Aude.

This diversity is largely due to the fact that the region represents an ancient gulf of the sea, several times covered by marine transgressions alternating with periods of emergence and denudation. It was, moreover, affected by the earth movements and volcanic activity associated with the building of both the Central Massif and the Pyrenees. Several different rocks and structures are thus involved. Lower, Middle and Upper Jurassic

425

limestones to the southwest of Montpellier form the upland ridges of the Montagne de la Mure and the Montagne de la Gardiole, separated by the Miocene-floored plain of Montbazin; the Gardiole is a ridge trending northeast to southwest which rises steeply to 228 m (748 ft) within a few kilometres of the coastal lagoons. Sète is built on and around an Upper Jurassic limestone knoll, which culminates in a summit 180 m (591 ft) above the sea. A mass of Lower Cretaceous limestone comprises the dissected hill country of La Clape rising to 210 m (700 ft) between Narbonne and the coast. Oligocene limestones outcrop as low hills between the Orb and Aude valleys.

One interesting contribution to the geology and relief of Bas-Languedoc is the result of Pliocene volcanic activity characteristic of the Central Massif. Outcrops of basalt can be traced interruptedly southward from the Escandorgue hills on the margin of the Causse du Larzac to the coast near Agde. To the northwest of Béziers appears a series of these small volcanic eminences; the rounded mass of St Thibéry rises to 88 m (289 ft) from the western side of the valley floor of the Hérault, and the prominent Cap d'Agde is backed by the eminence of Mont-St Loup 115 m (377 ft), and fronted by the rocky island of the Roches de Brescou.

Elsewhere Tertiary and newer sediments of varying character cover the undulating surface.[3] One feature is the presence of gravels of Pliocene age, similar in character to La Crau to the east of the Rhône delta. To them is given the name of *costières* after the Costière de St Gilles to the northwest of Arles where they are extensively developed. These gravel sheets, from 30 to 75 m (100 to 250 ft) above sea level, were laid down by the Pliocene rivers in the form of fans. A former westerly course of the Rhône, represented now only by the little river Vistre, was responsible for the deposition of the gravels of the Costière de St Gilles. Other similar *costières* occur to the south of Montpellier, and again between the valleys of the lower Hérault and Orb to the northeast of Béziers. Finally, many rivers continue to deposit fine alluvium along their lower valleys and floodplains, while along the coast both fluvial and marine sands and clays are continually accumulating.

## The *garrigue* country

The country between the edge of the Cévennes and the trench of the Rhône, bounded on the northeast and southwest by the valleys of the Ardèche and the Hérault respectively, consists mainly of limestone. The greater part is of Lower Cretaceous age but much Jurassic appears in the valleys of the upper Hérault and the upper Ardèche, and to the west of Montpellier. Lower Tertiary limestones are also represented as Eocene rocks between the valleys of the middle Hérault and the Vidourle, and Oligocene further to the northeast in the valley of the middle Gard and the Alès basin.

These rocks underwent gentle folding in early and mid-Tertiary times, associated with the Pyrenean earth movements; the folds trend roughly southwest to northeast. Long periods of planation in late Tertiary times produced widespread erosion surfaces. While there is therefore a general fall in altitude from nearly 600 m (2 000 ft) at the foot of the Cévennes to 100 m (350 ft) between Nîmes and Montpellier, three dominant levels can be distinguished: a higher surface at 370 to 400 m (1 250 to 1 300 ft) in the north between the rivers Gard and Ardèche, an intermediate one at 270 to 300 m (900 to 1 000 ft), and the most extensive at 180 to 210 m (600 to 700 ft). These planations cut right across the structures, and the influence of the numerous small anticlines and synclines on the present relief is therefore emphasised. The less resistant anticlines have been heavily eroded, revealing the underlying clays and marls in broad open valleys and basins, overlooked by white crags. The more resistant synclines, where the carapace of hard limestone has been preserved, form upstanding summits and crests, many of them orientated from southwest to northeast.

Numerous rivers flow down from the edge of the Central Massif, both to the Rhône (Ardèche, Cèze and Gard) and directly to the Golfe du Lion (Vidourle and Hérault). Their valleys are superimposed across the different structures, and differential erosion has produced diverse relief features. The clay and marl outcrops form basins, while the limestones are cut through in gorges reminiscent of the Grands Causses. The Ardèche leaves the basin of Vallon (floored with Upper Cretaceous clays) and crosses a continuous area of limestone in a cliffed gorge over 30 km (20 miles) in length. The most spectacular feature is the limestone arch of the Pont-d'Arc, with an opening 60 m (194 ft) in width through which flows the river; this arch is a surviving piece of roof of the river's former underground course. The Chassesac, the main confluent of the Ardèche, has also eroded a magnificent gorge in almost horizontally bedded limestone; this too was a subterranean channel, and the top of the gorge is in places only a few metres wide. The Cèze and the Gard flow in their middle courses across basins of Oligocene rocks before crossing the Lower Cretaceous limestones in winding steep-sided gorges; the former rushes down as a series of cascades (*Les Chutes du Sautadet*) among innumerable large potholes. There is much complicated underground drainage, large sinkholes, powerful resurgences and cave systems. The regimes of the streams are variable; in late summer they diminish to trickles among boulder-strewn beds or even vanish altogether. Numerous dry valleys occur, some permanently waterless because of a lowered watertable, others sometimes swept by torrential floods in autumn and spring.

The vegetation is characteristic of the word *garrigue*, for this is in fact the type region which has given its name to xerophytic scrub growing on limestone in a climatic regime of summer drought. The varieties of aromatic shrubs and rockplants include thyme, cistus, broom, heaths, arbutus, thickets of kerm oak, and for a few weeks in early spring a profusion of annual flowers and bulbous plants such as asphodel. The exotic prickly pear has spread considerably. This vegetation cover is partly the result of man's past depredations; a former continuous forest of evergreen oaks (ilex or holm), beech and Aleppo pine has been removed, and its regeneration was precluded by the grazing of sheep and goats and by the frequent disastrous fires during the dry summers. Much careful planting has been effected, especially during the last fifty years.

## The basin of Carcassonne

The Narbonne plain narrows to the west between the foothills of the Montagne Noire and the Massif de Mouthoumet, the northern part of the Corbières. It leads up to the Col de Naurouze, which at an altitude of 191 m (627 ft) forms the watershed between the Bay of Biscay and the Mediterranean. Because this broad col leads over into the basin of Aquitaine it is sometimes given the name of *La Porte d'Aquitaine*, but as Carcassonne dominates the approach from the east the corridor is also called the Gate of Carcassonne.

At the end of the Mesozoic era, the depression was open to the west and so formed part of the 'Gulf of Aquitaine' (see p. 313), though it was closed to the east. During Eocene times the character of the deposition varied as the transgression waxed and waned, so that deep-sea, lagoon and lacustrine deposits succeeded each other. This period of predominant transgression lasted at least until the end of the Oligocene, by which time the Pyrenean folds were being uplifted to the south. The development of the Mediterranean basin in mid-Tertiary times and the *en masse* subsidence of the Golfe du Lion wrought a profound change, for the rivers which previously flowed to the proto-Garonne were drawn into an eastward-draining system. The Aude became the master stream; rising in the Carlitte uplands of the eastern Pyrenees, it flowed first northwards into the depression, and then turned at right angles towards the Mediterranean. To it numerous streams came from the Montagne Noire, and as the main valley was lowered by this powerful river, its left-bank tributaries (notably the Fresquel) cut back westwards, and the watershed between the Garonne and Aude systems became defined.

Denudation has been active on the eastern side of the col, and the surface rocks of the middle and upper Aude basin consist of a variety of Eocene deposits—sandy limestones, blue marls, red clays and conglomerates, for the Oligocene rocks (which cover the eastern flanks of the Basin of Aquitaine almost to the summit of the col) have here been completely removed. Subsequent denudation has produced a diverse relief of sharp ridges and deep valleys, elevated platforms and basins isolated except for gorgelike exits, and along the Aude and its tributaries at least four clearly defined terraces can be distinguished. In addition, torrential tributaries, particularly from the Montagne Noire, brought down material, forming gravel-fans along the northern edge of the Aude floodplain and depositing fine material on the floodplain and in the coastal lagoons.

As a result of this diversity of land forms, within the middle and upper Aude basin several distinctive units can be distinguished. In the north along the flanks of the Montagne Noire are the ridges and valleys of *Minervois*, so called after the little town of Minerve, tucked in a steepsided basin where the valley of the Cesse opens out between level-topped limestone plateaus. To the west of Minervois is another limestone plateau, *Cabardès*. The actual valley of the Fresquel and the Aude, the axis of the depression, contains a series of *pays* — the basins of *Castelnaudary* at the western end, of *Carcassonne* in the centre, and of *Lézignan* in the east; the last two are separated by a *cluse*like valley at Argens, cut through one of the southwest to northeast ridges which are characteristic of these marginal areas of Pyrenean folding. To the south of the main axis are the dissected limestone *pays* of *Piège* in the west, and of *Razés* in the angle between the Fresquel and the upper Aude. The valley of the upper Aude itself, below where it leaves the Cretaceous limestones of northern Corbières, is known as *Limouxin*, after the town of Limoux situated in a basin where several tributaries join the Aude.

## The climate of Languedoc

While diversity is the keynote of the land forms of Languedoc, the climatic regime is the unifying feature of the whole region, with a marked seasonal rhythm. As R. Plandé puts it:[4] 'Sur tous ces paysages bas-languedociens règne la même luminosité du ciel, le même rythme des saisons.' The chief contrast is between the almost completely dry summer (save for an occasional brief thunderstorm) and the rains of autumn and spring. Rainfall totals vary from about 500 mm (20 in) at Narbonne, situated away from the coast and partly in the rainshadow of the hills of La Clape, to 630 mm (25 in) at Nîmes and 750 mm (30 in) at Montpellier. The rainiest month at the last of these is October (with a mean of 100 mm (4 in)), but July averages less than 25 mm (1 in) and in many years is wholly rainless. Most of this precipitation falls in a few showers of considerable intensity, causing the rivers to flow torrentially.[5] These heavy showers are associated with the onset of the *marin* (known also as the *autan* further west in the upper Aude valley), a humid wind from between southwest and southeast, which may be experienced on sixty to seventy days during the winter months. It is caused by the eastward passage of low pressure systems through the western Mediterranean, or from the Bay of Biscay through the Gate of Carcassonne, producing a southerly inflow of humid air in the warm sector. By contrast, strong, cold and extremely dry air streams from a northerly direction are frequent features; the wind is here known as the *cers*, which blows on an average on 140 days at Montpellier and 160 at Narbonne, mostly between November and April, but it can be experienced at any time of the year. One other characteristic wind is experienced, the humid, blustery and rather cool *grec*, blowing in spring from the east. Local sea breezes known as the *labech* are experienced in summer along the coast, and help to modify temperatures and to freshen the atmosphere.

The mean temperature figures for Montpellier vary between 5°C (41°F) in January and 23°C (73°F) in July, giving a quite high range of 18°C (32°F) for a near-coastal situation. On an average, frost is experienced on forty days per annum at Montpellier, again a high figure. Late frosts and cold northerly winds in spring may do much harm, especially if an exceptionally mild spell has occurred earlier in the year which has caused fruit-trees to blossom. Market gardens are intersected with frameworks of laths over which woven mats can be drawn as a protection against night frosts.

## Land use

The lowlands of Languedoc broadly correspond to the three *départements* of Gard, Hérault and Aude, and it is helpful to examine their land use categories.

*Land use, 1968 (percentage of total area)*

|        | ARABLE | PASTURE | VINEYARDS | ORCHARDS | WOODLAND | AGRICULTURAL LAND NOT CULTIVATED |
|--------|--------|---------|-----------|----------|----------|----------------------------------|
| Aude   | 19     | 15      | 19        | —        | 20       | 19                               |
| Gard   | 9      | 18      | 16        | 3        | 31       | 10                               |
| Hérault| 8      | 15      | 28        | 1        | 23       | 11                               |

Source: Ministère de l'Agriculture, *Annuaire statistique de la France*, 1970–71.

This region, with its areas of limestone, gravel, saltmarsh and sand-dune, together with the rather arid climate liable to temperature extremes and to sudden inclement spells, is obviously subject to agricultural limitations, and the figures in the table bear this out. The low proportion of pasture is to be expected in a region of summer drought; what there is consists of salt pasture around the *étangs*, irrigated meadows along the streams or in clay-floored basins among the limestone, and upland pasture in the foothills of the Cévennes; much of the last is fit only for sheep and goats. As a result, in the three *départements* there were a mere 39 000 cattle (Hérault had only 6 400), but 279 000 sheep and 20 000 goats. Most of these flocks are kept in the *garrigue* country and in the foothills, and many move into the Central Massif during the summer. The ewes' milk is made into cheese, much of it 'finished' in the caves of Roquefort in the Central Massif (see p. 564). Sheep-rearing has, however, declined during the last century.

The percentage figures for the woodland cover are as high as they are partly because the *départements* include the rather better wooded foothills of

PLATE 49. The Canal du Bas-Rhône-Languedoc

the Central Massif, partly because much scrubby evergreen oak is included in the land use classification, and partly because of some progress in the planting of pines behind goat-proof fences. Some areas of forest occur to the northwest of Avignon, in the middle Cèze valley, on the *garrigue* to the north of Uzès, and within the basin of St Martin-de-Londres. In addition scattered clumps of evergreen oaks or chestnuts surround villages and farms, isolated pines survive incredibly on limestone slopes, planes line roads and village squares, poplars and cypress form windbreaks.

The Mediterranean triad—wheat, olive and vine—have been the staple crops for millennia, in fact this was one of the granaries of Imperial Rome, but this is now being modified. The three *départements* in 1968 had 62 000 ha (153 000 acres) under wheat, mostly 'hard' drought-resisting varieties grown in small fields (surrounded by dry stone walls) on the terraces and in clay-floored basins, using a period of fallow. Along the canals, where irrigation water is available, lucerne, sainfoin and vetches provide fodder (Plate 49).

A scheme was started in 1955 by the Compagnie Nationale d'Aménagement du Bas-Rhône-Languedoc (in which are represented state and

431

private interests) for a unified system of irrigation, using water brought through a Canal du Bas-Rhône-Languedoc, taking off from the Rhône 4 km (2·5 miles) above Arles, and running along the southern edge of the *garrigue* westward for 170 km (108 miles) to the Hérault river.[6] Some 15 km (10 miles) west of the Rhône take-off, water is lifted at the huge *Aristide Dumont* pumping station, to enable the higher lands to be served by gravity flow. Further west, water is also taken from the Orb, Hérault and other rivers. The overall scheme envisages not merely the application of irrigation to agriculture, but a complete reorganisation of the rural way of life: reclamation of land, the *remembrement* of divided holdings, diversification away from viticulture to other fruit, vegetables, poultry and flowers, and the building of new farms, cooperatives and processing plants.

Olives are still grown but less now for their oil than for preserving and bottling, notably at Gignac and Aniane in the middle Hérault valley. They do well in the gravelly soils of the *costières* and on the limestone slopes bordering the *combes* and river valleys among the *garrigues*. Mulberries have been grown since the seventeenth century, and in spite of the calamitous silkworm disease in the mid-nineteenth century and the vast increase in silk imports (see p. 384), occasional groves of trees and lines of them along the roads and between fields can still be seen. Table grapes, apples and apricots have been introduced on to some of the better lands, supplying distant markets. Cooperation has been widely developed enabling efficient methods of grading, packing, shipping and selling to be used. While in 1954 the vine yielded 60 per cent by value of the region's agricultural produce, by 1970 this had fallen to 45 per cent.

## Viticulture

The dominant crop since the mid-nineteenth century has been the vine; over a quarter of Hérault is now covered with vineyards, and between a fifth and a sixth of the other two *départements*. Here is monoculture carried to its extreme.[7] The three *départements* produced in 1968 over 24 million hectolitres of wine, or a third of the total French output. Significantly, however, only a minute proportion of this enormous yield consisted of *vin à appellation contrôlée*. The wines are mostly sold under the general name of *vins du Midi*, although sometimes they are known under individual *crus*, as *Corbières*, *Biterrois*, *Minervois* and *Costière*. Some of the red wines seem harsh and sour to the unaccustomed palate, but occasional wines are of great charm.

Vines have been grown since classical times, but until a century and a half ago they were cultivated in association with other crops. Gradually the vine became dominant; from the limestone *côtes*, the little stone-walled fields among the *garrigues*, and the *costières*, the vineyards have spread downhill on to the floodplains and the coastal plain. This is exemplified in the basin of the Aude; the former Etang de Marseillette, 6 km (4 miles) across, lying in the valley between Lézignan and Carcassonne, has been drained, and forms one vast vineyard with rows of vines separated by irrigation channels.

This dependence on a single crop has its dangers. From 1850–55 the Midi was swept by *oïdium* (the vine mildew), which did much damage before the efficacy of spraying with sulphur or copper sulphate was discovered. Far worse was the phylloxera which appeared in 1863, and within twenty years had devastated much of the Midi; the area under vines decreased to one-fifth. When the American *Riparia* stocks were at last introduced, the extent under vines first slowly then more rapidly increased, and gradually the coastal plain between the dunes and the *garrigues* became the major producing area. Other crises were the result of the first large-scale imports of cheaper Algerian wine, of overproduction and price slumps, of laws against distillation (as in 1903), and of some post-1950 half-hearted government efforts at discouragement of wine-drinking in France. Nevertheless, this monoculture has persisted.

Cooperation has become the basis of production; the first *coopérative viticole* was founded in western Biterrois in 1901, and the movement increased particularly in the 1930s after the world economic depression, when the need for organisation became critical. The 180 000 *vignerons* are grouped into a *Confédération Générale des Vignerons* to protect their interests. The many small proprietors (about 95 per cent of all growers) belong to one of the five hundred cooperatives situated in the large villages and towns, owning fleets of wine tanker barges, lorries and rail tankers. By contrast, a quarter of the land under vines consists of holdings of from 25 to 250 ha (60 to 600 acres) owned by a few proprietors, self-contained and usually operating independently of the cooperatives.

Much work in Languedoc is afforded by occupations ancillary to vine cultivation: in the *caves collectives*, in cooperative distilleries, in the making of non-fermented wines known as *mistelles*, in making barrels, bottles and corks, printing labels, and distributing fertilisers and insecticidal sprays.

One area where there is less dependence on monoculture is the upper Aude basin, from Lézignan up past Carcassonne to Castelnaudary. While the vine is still dominant, wheat, maize, oats and fodder beet are also cultivated in rotation with lucerne, clover and vetch. There are extensive orchards of fruit trees, especially the famous *Reine Claude* plums, and of sweet chestnuts. More livestock is kept, not only cattle but pigs, poultry and bees. Prosperous villages and towns are dotted about this pleasant landscape, which contrasts in its green diversity with the sunbaked coastal plains and the harsh *garrigue* country further east.[8]

## Fishing

The long stretch of coast, the waters of the *étangs*, and the many little harbours and coastal villages would seem to indicate the possibility of fishing.

In point of fact, the Mediterranean littoral is not of any great importance in the French fishing economy; in 1969 only 31 800 tons of fish was landed here out of a total of 421 000 tons around the whole French coast. Of course, these figures refer only to fish sold commercially, and much Mediterranean fishing is on a part-time and subsistence basis. The little fishing ports along the coast of Languedoc—Palavas, Sète, Marseillan, Agde, Gruissan and Leucate—do not land sufficient even to supply the towns of the hinterland. Still, about 6 900 men are engaged full-time in fishing, and many others fish occasionally, including Italians who come for the summer, living in camps among the sand-dunes, before moving on to the Midi vine harvest. Red tunny, sardines, anchovies and mackerel are caught in the open sea. The Etang de Thau has oyster and mussel fisheries; almost wiped out by too thorough dragging before 1907, they are now carefully conserved. Eels, lobsters and crayfish are also caught in the lagoons.

Some of the fishing is done by curious methods. Fishermen from the villages among the lagoons work with their families, using complex nets, some fixed permanently in place as fish traps, others pulled into position to net a large area; some fishermen even use harpoons and tridents. The Sète fishermen have a system of working their boats in pairs, behind which a long net with wide wings is towed to catch sardines and anchovy. All this is on a small scale; nevertheless, along the lagoon coast the little huts of the fishermen, the boats hauled up on the sands, and fish drying in the sun are part of the Mediterranean scene.

## Population and settlement

In 1968 the average density of population in the three *départements* of Aude, Gard and Hérault was 44, 81 and 95 per sq km (114, 210 and 246 per sq mile) respectively; approximately 1·35 million people lived there. These average densities mean little, however; some of the *garrigue* country within a few kilometres of Montpellier is one of the most scantily populated parts of France, and the sand-dune *cordon-littoral* and the marshy areas around the lagoons are little better. The population is grouped in hamlets among the basins in the *garrigue*, and in small fishing villages or on eminences among the marshlands.

The mean densities are as high as they are because of intensive cultivation on the terraces and lowlands, forming a longitudinal belt of dense population between the coast and the *garrigues*, with a 'tongue' extending up the Aude valley into the basin of Carcassonne. This rurally employed population lives not dispersed among the vineyards, but in large villages which have usually been nuclei of settlement for many centuries. Their sites take advantage of minor eminences, knolls and ridges rising from the formerly marshy plain, chosen both for defence and to avoid floods;[9] many have protecting ramparts surrounding a church or château. Another reason for the quite high density is the number of fair-sized towns, in common with the lower Rhône valley and Provence, for here are some of the most attractive towns in France, centres of civic life since Roman times, although some are indeed decayed in comparison with their past glories. From the little ports[1] the tide of commerce has receded as the accretion of mud and sand extended into the shallowing sea. Agde stands near the mouth of the Hérault river among the vineyards, with wharves on the Canal du Midi.

Sète is the one coastal town of any size; grievously damaged during the war of 1939–45, it has only just regained its pre-1939 population of nearly 40 000. Compared with most towns of Languedoc, Sète is a newcomer; the port was deliberately created during the reign of Louis XIV. The limestone knoll of Mont-St Clair rises to over 75 m (250 ft) on the southern shore of the Etang de Thau, which is otherwise separated from the sea only by a long narrow beach crowned with sand-dunes. Moles were built on the southeastern side of the hill to afford shelter from the open sea and to provide an *avant-port*. Several basins and quays have been constructed, particularly during and after the war of 1914–18. A channel is maintained by dredging across the eastern end of the *étang* to the Frontignan oil refinery near its shores. In 1839 the railway line between Montpellier and Sète was opened, with sidings on the northern side of the port.

The town of Sète grew up originally on the lower slopes of Mont-St Clair but has since spread ribbonwise eastward along the sandspit, following the main road to Frontignan and Montpellier. During this century its industries have developed in much the same way as those of Marseilles, although on a much smaller scale. The reclaimed land along the eastern shore of the Etang de Thau has provided spacious factory sites for chemical and cement works, yards building canal barges, cooperage factories and distilleries producing various spirits, including Vermouth for which the town is well known. The Frontignan oil refinery, owned by a French associated company of Mobil-Oil, and supplied with crude oil from tankers moored offshore by a submarine pipeline, had an output in 1969 of 1·7 million tons. The refinery is linked by pipeline with storage tanks along the quays of the Bassin aux Pétroles on the eastern side of the *avant-port*, and there are petrochemical and fertiliser plants.

In 1969 Sète was the ninth port of France in terms of tonnage of shipping entered and cleared; it was used by 3 047 vessels of a net tonnage of 4 millions. Its chief imports were crude oil (1·9 million tons, or over six times the 1938 figure), phosphates, sulphur, Algerian wine, and smaller amounts of North African wheat, copper sulphate (for vine spray), timber and wool. Its exports, only a quarter of the volume of imports, consisted of refined hydrocarbons, cement, bauxite, liqueurs, wines and spirits, various chemical products, and live sheep and cattle to Algeria.

Sète is also an inland waterway port, for the Rhône-Sète and Midi Canals open into the Etang de Thau. The former, completed only in 1934, runs from Beaucaire on the Rhône to Aigues-Mortes (Fig. 15.2), then in a dyked channel through the coastal *étangs* to Sète. The Canal du Midi, completed in 1681, runs for 240 km (150 miles) between the southwestern end of the Etang de Thau and the city of Toulouse, crossing the Col de Naurouze by means of sixty-five locks and a tunnel. With the continuation of navigation along the Garonne Lateral Canal and the Garonne itself (Fig. 13.4), the canal thus negotiates the watershed between the Mediterranean and the Atlantic. In the latter part of the nineteenth century, the canal concession was bought by the Midi Railway Company in order to divert traffic from the waterway to the railway; this succeeded so well that the former ceased to be used and fell into disrepair. The Government bought it in 1898 and tried to revive navigation by freight rate reduction, while after 1921 considerable expenditure was incurred in an effort to make it navigable to 300 ton barges. But even so only a depth of 1·8 m (6 ft) can be maintained, so that the canal is still used merely by 120 ton barges. The main cargoes consist of wine moving in both directions (including Algerian wine imported via Sète), wine casks, corks, coal, cement and petroleum.[10]

In spite of the limited use and value of the present Midi Canal, the concept of a *Canal des Deux Mers* is obviously attractive. The project of a ship canal was raised several times in the nineteenth century, and in the 1920s the scheme was seriously considered. A congress held at Toulouse in 1932 produced plans for a ship canal about 300 km (190 miles) long between Bordeaux and La Nouvelle; it was to be nearly 150 m (500 ft) in width, of sufficient depth to accommodate ocean-going vessels, and equipped with modern ship lifts. But in view of the immense expenditure involved, the French Government showed little interest until February 1939; at this inauspicious time it was announced that the preliminary consent of the Government had been obtained. But no further action has so far been possible.

The largest town of Languedoc is Montpellier, with a population of 162 000 in 1968. It stands on low hills (the Buttes de Montpellier and Montpellieret) rising from the coastal plain between some right-bank tributaries of the Lez. For long Montpellier has been the administrative and commercial centre of Languedoc, as it is now of Hérault. Spaciously laid out with squares and broad avenues, it was for a time a fashionable tourist centre. It is the second wine-market of the Midi, it has light industries (food-preserving, perfumes, soap, pharmaceutical chemicals, electronics and computers), and is an attractive intellectual and cultural centre with a celebrated university.[11] During the intercensal period, 1962–68, it had the highest percentage growth (37·7) of any French agglomeration.

The *chef-lieu* of Gard is Nîmes, with 123 000 people in 1968. It stands on the edge of the *garrigue* country overlooking the plain of the lower Rhône; indeed, it was on a spur of the limestone hills that the Romans built the dominating *Tour Magne* and from the foot of this ridge issued the thermal spring which supplied the famous bath systems. It became one of the finest cities of the Roman empire, of which many remarkable remains survive, including its superb arena. Today, with its nodal rail and road position,

Nîmes is an important commercial centre, it has silk and wool textile and clothing industries, factories producing consumer goods such as shoes, and metallurgical industries (including agricultural machinery and the repair of SNCF rolling-stock and locomotives). It is also an important market for agricultural produce.

In southern Languedoc two smaller towns, Béziers and Narbonne, have populations of about 80 000 and 40 000 respectively. The former is situated where the Orb valley opens into the coastal plain. The narrow streets of the old town ascend steeply to the summit of a prominent hill on which stands a massive fortresslike church, while the modern commercial and residential suburbs have spread out on to the plain. Béziers is the main centre of the Languedoc wine industry, and the town's growth during the last century has been closely related to the prosperity of this dominating product. In 1850 its population was only 16 000 but during the expansion in vine cultivation the total increased to 43 000 by 1866. There followed forty years of virtual stagnation while the phylloxera and other troubles which beset viticulture affected the whole economy of the district, but today the wine industry is again all-important in its life; apart from processing, blending and shipping, Béziers is the main despatching centre of rail tank wagons, and it makes barrels, metal containers, bottles, corks, wine presses and insecticides.

Narbonne too owes much of its growth during the last hundred years to the vine. For long the town strove to maintain an outlet to the sea, for it was once a port on a broad inlet, but today the Canal de la Robine (to La Nouvelle at the southern end of the residual string of *étangs*) is the sole connection and is but rarely used; it has, however, a link with the Canal du Midi. Narbonne is an important rail junction for routes from Béziers, from Perpignan and Spain, and from Carcassonne and Toulouse, and serves as the market and servicing town for the lower Agde valley.

Finally, there is a series of towns up the fertile Aude valley on the route through the Porte d'Aquitaine to Toulouse, followed by roads, rail and the Canal du Midi. Some, such as Roquecourbe, Marseillette, Carcassonne, Bram and Castelnaudary, stand in the floor of the main valley, usually on a terrace above the Aude floodplain. Others are situated where tributaries open out into the plain or in these valleys themselves. Neat, compact and prosperous-looking, each is the centre of a thriving agricultural life, and many have factories specialising in textiles, shoes and leather work, cooperage, and the processing of foodstuffs (milling, olive-preserving, liqueur-distilling). The chief town is Carcassonne, the *chef-lieu* of Aude and an important point on the Biscay-Mediterranean through-route. It stands in a basin where converge several rivers, dominated by the castle on a steep-sided plateau within a meander of the Aude. For long a vital strongpoint, the castle fell into ruin, but was restored in the middle of the nineteenth century; today stands a double rampart with fifty towers surmounted by conical roofs, the old buildings within the walls and the newer town spread outside. Carcassonne is the centre of the upper Aude wine industry, and many of its occupations are ancillary to this function.

## Roussillon

The semicircular *Plaine du Roussillon* is enclosed on the north by the uplands of Corbières and on the south by the Albères ridges, both of which project eastward almost to the Golfe du Lion. On the west lies the upland country of Capcir and Canigou, broadly part of the Pyrenean system. The longitudinal valleys of the Agly, the Têt and the Tech provide re-entrants of lowland far into this hill country, known respectively by their *pays* names of *Fenouillèdes*, *Conflent* and *Vallespir*. The three main rivers, joined by a multitude of torrential tributaries (many of which dry up in summer), flow eastwards across the plain to the sea (Fig. 16.1).

Roussillon was in Pliocene times a marine gulf, which has since been infilled with masses of alluvium worn by torrential streams from the bound-

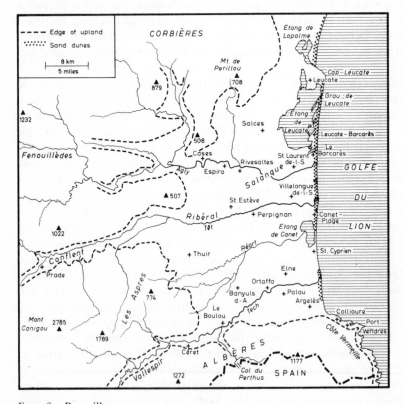

FIG. 16.1 Roussillon
The edge of the uplands (at about (230 to 300 m) (750 to 1 000 ft)) is generalised. Heights are given in metres.

Based on *Carte de France et des frontières au 200 000ᵉ*, sheet 78.

ing massifs. Much of the surface is covered with sheets of Pliocene gravels, forming plateaus on the edge of the uplands at altitudes of 90 to 230 m (300 to 750 ft), flanked on the seaward side and in the river floodplains with newer materials—fine alluvium, sand and gravel. Recent changes of sea level have caused the rivers to cut down their present valleys into the older gravel sheets, forming distinct steps and terraces, and they have also resulted in marine transgressions on to the seaward margins of the plain. The material brought down by the rivers, combined with longshore drift, has created an almost complete *cordon-littoral* from the Silurian rocks of the coast near Collioure, where the Albères uplands reach the sea, to the Oligocene headland of Cap Leucate. A line of sand-dunes forms a gentle arc, interrupted only by the mouths of the three rivers and by the *graus* opening seawards from the lagoons. Many smaller *étangs* have been reclaimed, either naturally by accretion of alluvium and vegetation or by man, but three remain (Fig. 16.1). They are surrounded by marshes, glistening white with salt encrustations, or green with stretches of *Salicornia* and other halophytes, or brown and dreary with reed beds. Further inland, as the salt-content becomes less, poor pastures appear, green in winter but brown and arid in the dry heat of summer. The importance of *les terres salées* is shown by the common use of the salt element in place names now well inland from the coast, such as Salses, Rivesaltes and Saleilles.

## Climate

The climate exemplifies the Mediterranean regime in its most emphasised form in France. The summer drought is virtually complete in July and August, and the sunbaked plains shimmer in the heat. Perpignan has a mean rainfall of 560 mm (21·9 in), falling on only sixty-four days in the year. Salses, with 440 mm (17·3 in), is perhaps the driest place in France, and the mean number of days with rain is only thirty-four. Most of the rain is due to the moist *marins* blowing in from the Golfe du Lion, bringing short-lived but intense downpours. The tendency to dryness is emphasised both by the porous gravel sheets and by rapid evaporation, the result of high temperatures and strong drying winds. The *tramontane roussillonnaise* occasionally blows down from the surrounding uplands as a dry chilly wind with some of the features of the *mistral*, though rarely so violent. Temperatures are higher in both winter and summer than almost anywhere else in France; Perpignan has a January mean of 7°C (44°F), and a July mean of 23°C (73°F), and indeed the maximum shade-temperature ever recorded in the country was 42°C (108°F), experienced there in 1871.

## Land use and agriculture

With the exception of areas of recent alluvium along the floodplains of the larger rivers, the plain of Roussillon is not naturally a favourable agricultural district. The scrubby tracts among the western gravel plateaus, the stony interfluves between the river valleys, the saltmarshes flanking the inner side of the *étangs*, and the dunebelts of fine sand are all unsuited to cultivation, and the sunbaked aridity of summer can only be alleviated where irrigation is possible. Considerable areas consist of poor *garrigue*, thickets of stunted holm oak or cork oak, and poor winter pasture (grazed by the flocks brought down from Capcir and Cerdagne).[12]

Agriculture, however, flourishes wherever the physical disabilities can be overcome. The lower gravel plateaus and terraces have long been cultivated in the traditional way—hard wheat with a biennial period of fallow, olives, almonds, stone fruits such as apricots, peaches and cherries (notably on the terraces above the Tech valley near Céret) and mulberries. Most of these flourish on the dry warm slopes, despite the stony soils. This polyculture was still more diverse in the past, when such industrial crops as hemp, saffron and madder were grown.

In the nineteenth century, however, the cultivation of the vine increased on the gravel plateaus and terraces, and such wines as *malvoisie* and *maccabéo* achieved a certain fame. The area of vineyards in Pyrénées-Orientales grew to a maximum of 80 000 ha (200 000 acres) before the phylloxera crisis, and after the inevitable resultant decline has slowly increased again. Even today, when orchards have developed at their expense, the vineyards occupy more than 66 000 ha (163 000 acres), and in 1968 the *département* produced 2·8 million hectolitres of wine. While much of the yield is of *ordinaire* grade, there are several quality wines. In the neighbourhood of Thuir, to the southwest of Perpignan, alcohol-rich wines are produced from which is prepared the celebrated liqueur '*Byrrh*'. Many of the vineyards of the Agly valley concentrate on the production of high quality table grapes.

Where irrigation water can be obtained, an intensive cultivation of vegetables on a market garden scale has developed. Since the Middle Ages water has been taken from the rivers through derivation canals to supply orchards and vegetable gardens similar to the *huertas* of the east coast of Spain. The main difficulty is the fluctuating regime of the rivers; they are at a low level at the very time of year when water is most required, and they lose so much volume that even the three large ones can hardly sustain their flow to the sea. Some supplementary well irrigation has been developed, using wind pumps and in modern times diesel pumps, to exploit the water from the uplands around which has sunk into the rocks of the alluvial basin. These irrigated lands are found on the lower terraces and floodplains along the three main rivers, where villages and small towns stand among gardens and orchards. The chief districts are in the Tech valley (the *Bas-Vallespir*, with centres at Elne, Palau, Ortaffa and Céret), in the lower Têt valley (known as the *Ribéral*, especially at Perpignan, St Estève and Ille-sur-Têt), and further north in the Agly valley (at Espira and Cases). The vine and fruits such as apricots, figs and peaches are widely grown, but the cultivation of vegetables is most important. The methods of cultivation and types of vegetables are much the same as in the lower Rhône, but the growers in Roussillon can produce salads and other *primeurs* several weeks earlier, owing to the virtual freedom from frost and strong winds; the *tramontane* does not approach either the frequency or violence of the *mistral*, as is shown by the usual absence of windbreaks, and the mild winters make cloches and glasshouses unnecessary. Marketing is organised in cooperatives, and at Perpignan station cold stores have been built to accommodate the produce before its northward shipment by rail.

Cultivation has extended seawards on to reclaimed marshlands where the salt content has been reduced either by years of 'flushing' by the annual floods of such rivers as the Réart and by systematic irrigation, or by cultivating salt-absorbing plants. The main areas of such improvement are known as *salanques*, the most important district being La Grande Salanque between the Agly and the Têt. Here are found vineyards, often with beds of asparagus, artichokes and other vegetables on the rather sandy soils between the rows of vines, and patches of barley and of irrigated lucerne.

## Settlement

The plain of Roussillon is studded with small towns and villages, usually on the terraces well above the river floods. The rural density of population is of the order of 80 per sq km (210 per sq mile), in some places (notably along the Ribéral) rising to over 200. Many towns were fortified, the result of their 'marchland' situation, and at some the walls and towers are still standing, as at Salses.

The only port of any significance is Port-Vendres,[13] situated not on the sand-dune coast, but 14 km (9 miles) north of the Spanish frontier, where the ranges of the Albères reach the coast. What was little more than a creek along the rocky coast was developed by Vauban, and the main port now consists of a rectangular basin. It handles 100 000 tons of freight a year, mostly imports of cereals, wine and fruit from Algeria, but its chief importance is as a packet port. Rail connections from the north serve this nearest port to Algeria, though since the latter attained independence the number of passengers has greatly declined.

Perpignan of course dominates the plain. The old town clusters around a low hill (*le Puig*) near the Têt, 11 km (7 miles) from the sea. It was for long a fortress town, guarding the land-route from Spain into Languedoc and beyond to the rest of France. The town developed industries, including the manufacture of silk cloth, and became the economic capital of this rather isolated region. This rôle was increasingly important after the railway reached the city, and with the development of intensive cultivation Perpignan became the chief administrative, marketing and despatching centre for Roussillon. In the last fifty years the town has grown considerably; with a population of 20 000 at the beginning of the nineteenth century and still of less than 30 000 at the outbreak of the war of 1914–18, the total had increased to 102 000 by 1968. At Quillan (between Perpignan and Carcassonne) a recently built plastics factory is owned by a subsidiary of British Formica.

About 200 000 people in Roussillon speak Catalan, the linguistic features of which are in some ways transitional between Spanish and the Provençal form of French. The French form of Catalan does differ in a number of ways from that spoken by some millions of people across the Pyrenees in northeastern Spain.

## Recent tourist developments

Until recently most resorts in this part of France were situated along the rocky coastline in the south of Roussillon between Collioure and Cerbère, known as the *Côte Vermeille*. Farther north the few small resorts on the 150 km (93 miles) of sweeping sandy shoreline included Canet-Plage, St Cyprien-Plage and Le Barcarès, visited mostly by people from Perpignan. There were few settlements other than the huts of fishermen and *saliniers*. Though this coastline afforded vast sandy beaches and dune areas, it was backed by *étangs* and mosquito-infested salt swamps, with so few access roads that much was virtually inaccessible. In recent years there has been a concerted effort, as part of the whole integrated plan for the economic reconstruction of Languedoc, to develop the tremendous tourist potential of sea, sand and sunshine. The existing N86 motorway between Nîmes and Montpellier is being extended northeastward to join the Rhône valley motorway south of Orange, and southwestward via Béziers and Perpignan to the Spanish frontier and the Barcelona motorway.

The first stages were undertaken by the government agency, the Languedoc-Roussillon Commission, which carried out the comprehensive and integrated work of drainage, mosquito eradication, construction of main roads and afforestation. The responsibility was then passed to a series of consortia, on which were represented the *départements* and local chambers of commerce, to create internal roads and services, and blocks were then sold off to private developers, to create within the overall master plan what has been termed 'a planned tourist environment': hotel, apartment and bungalow complexes, several new 'tourist townships', a dozen yacht marinas and extensive camp-sites. At Le Barcarès the former P & O liner *Lydia* has been embedded in concrete to serve as a headquarters. The new or extended resorts are St Cyprien, Leucate-Barcarès, La Grande Motte and Cap d'Agde.

---

[1] D. Faucher, *Visage du Languedoc: géographie humaine* (1949); and R. Dugrand, *Villes et Campagnes en Bas-Languedoc* (1963), a massive monograph of 638 pp., with an immense bibliography.

[2] Ch. Cavériviète, 'L'Exploitation des étangs de Sigean', *Rev. géogr. Pyr. S.-O.*, **21** (1950), pp. 61–80, gives an account of the exploitation and partial reclamation of the *étangs*, with a detailed map of the reclamation stages, and accounts of fishing, salt extraction, etc.

³ P. Demangeon, *Contribution à l'étude de la sédimentation détritique dans le Bas-Languedoc pendant l'ère tertiaire* (1958).

⁴ R. Plandé, 'Le Bas-Languedoc', in *La France: géographie-tourisme* (1951), ed. D. Faucher, i, p. 302.

⁵ The heavy rains of late autumn and winter in Languedoc, and their resultant floods are described by M. Pardé, 'Les crues languedociennes en décembre 1953', *Annls Géogr.*, **65** (1956), pp. 140–2; see also G. Viallet, 'Les crues du Lez', *Bulletin, Société Languedocienne de Géographie*, **26** (1955), pp. 389–432; and S. Laborde, 'La crue du Lez (nov.-déc., 1955)', *ibid.*, **26**, pp. 433–69.

⁶ A discussion of the scheme, with a map giving the possible line of the canal, is given by P. George, 'Problèmes agricoles de l'aménagement hydraulique du Bas-Rhône', *Mélanges géographiques offerts à Ernest Bénévent* (1954), pp. 223–33. See also P. Carrère and R. Dugrand, *La Région Méditerranéenne* (1960), pp. 118–19, which gives a detailed map; N. J. Graves, 'Une Californie française. The Languedoc and lower Rhône irrigation project', *Geography*, **1** (1965), pp. 71–3; and J. Richez, 'Les transformations des structures agraires sous l'influence de l'irrigation sur le plateau de Garons (Gard)', *Méditerranée*, **6** (1965), pp. 201–18.

⁷ S. Agnew, 'The vine in Bas Languedoc', *Geogr. Rev.*, **36** (1946), pp. 67–79. See also G. Galtier, *La Viticulture du Languedoc méditerranéen et du Roussillon* (1947).

⁸ The contribution of cooperation to the agricultural economy is discussed by B. Derousseau, 'La coopérative agricole lauragaise', *Rev. géogr. Pyr. S.-O.*, **35** (1964), pp. 214–20.

⁹ S. Agnew, 'Rural settlement in the Coastal Plain of Bas Languedoc', *Geography*, **31** (1946), pp. 67–77.

¹⁰ R. Brunet, 'Expansion et problèmes des canaux du Midi', *Rev. géogr. Pyr. S.-O.*, **35** (1964), pp. 207–13.

¹¹ G. Galtier, 'Les Conditions géographiques de Montpellier', *Mélanges géographiques offerts à Ph. Arbos* (1953), pp. 237–46; published by the Faculté des Lettres de l'Université de Clermont.

¹² This diversity of land use is well shown by the beautifully produced Perpignan sheet of the *Carte de la végétation de la France (1 : 200 000)* (1950), the second of the series to be issued, compiled by H. Gaussen.

¹³ An account of Port-Vendres, in immense detail, is given by S. Laborde, 'Port-Vendres, études de géographie humaine', *Bulletin, Société Languedocienne de Géographie*, **28** (1957), pp. 3–108.

# Part II
# The Hercynian Uplands

# 17
# Armorica

The term Armorica is derived from the Celtic words *Ar-Mor,* 'the country of the sea', which refer to the long indented coastline and hinterland of a triangular peninsula projecting westward into the Atlantic Ocean, the ancient province of *Bretagne.* The term is commonly applied more widely to a geographical region,[1] the basis of whose identity is structural, for it consists of a massif of Pre-Cambrian and Palaeozoic rocks, together with some large intrusive masses of granite and some smaller areas of newer rocks preserved in depressions. This geological definition is shown on Fig. 17.1. This larger area includes not only *Bretagne,* but also the western parts of the former provinces of *Maine, Anjou* and *Normandie* (Fig. 1.1).

## General features

### Structure and relief

Armorica has experienced a complex structural history of successive alternations of folding, peneplanation, *en bloc* uplift and renewed denudation. An early period of folding, corresponding to the Caledonian orogeny in northwestern Europe, probably affected the Pre-Cambrian rocks, but it was the widespread earth movements of Carbo-Permian times that were responsible for the basic structures. The fold mountain ranges produced by this orogeny, known as the '*Altaides*', once extended across central Europe from southwestern Ireland to southern Russia. Fragments of these ancient ranges now project as upland blocks from the surrounding sedimentary plains. The folds in the west are referred to as 'Armorican', those further east as 'Hercynian', although occasionally they are known collectively as 'Variscan'.

The trendlines of the folding in Armorica are complex, but a central synclinorial 'furrow' can be traced eastward from the bays which deeply indent the west coast through the Carboniferous-floored basins of Châteaulin in the west (now followed longitudinally by the river Aulne) and of Laval in the east (now crossed transversely by the Mayenne). Between these two basins the downfold is indicated by a narrow band of Carboniferous strata to the south of the Landes du Menez and on the northern edge of the Rennes depression. To the north and south of this synclinorium are the trendlines of upfolds, running from west-southwest to east-northeast in the Pays de Léon (hence the term *direction de Léon*), and from northwest to southeast in Cornouaille. The latter trend is known as *la direction de Cornouaille*, but as it continues southeastward beneath the Jurassic rocks of the Gate of Poitou to reappear in the western part of the Central Massif, the wider term *direction armoricaine* is usually applied. The Léon anticlinorium is broken into by the roughly quadrangular Golfe de St Malo, its fragments forming the islands of Jersey, the Minquiers and Chausey, and reappears in the southern part of the Cotentin peninsula. Further north, beyond another synclinal depression of Silurian slates in part floored with Tertiary rocks, a further broken anticlinal ridge can be traced through Guernsey and Alderney into the northern part of the Cotentin.[2] These Armorican folds become increasingly complex in the east and southeast, where they vanish under the Mesozoic and Tertiary cover. Although the original folds have been largely destroyed by denudation, their trendlines impose a clearly defined 'grain' (Fig. 17.1). A large number of faults demarcate both horst-like uplands and distinct basins,[3] and account for the presence of long 'slices' of different rocks in close juxtaposition.

A long period of denudation in early Mesozoic times wore down the folded region into a peneplain cutting across the various structures. Within this general peneplanation a number of individual erosion surfaces at different heights can be distinguished.[4] Over this peneplain then spread the fluctuating marine transgressions which covered much of western Europe, and a widespread cover of Mesozoic and Tertiary rocks was laid down. These now form the surface rocks of much of the lowlands of northern France and Belgium, but they have vanished from Armorica except on the eastern and southern margins and in a few depressions. One result is the presence of ferruginous ores preserved in the shales and sandstones of the Silurian synclines, a relic of the vanished overlying Jurassic beds. These are the *Gisements d'Anjou* in the *départements* of Ille-et-Vilaine and Mayenne, extending in an interrupted series northwestward from Angers (Fig. 11.7). The ore is found in ridges of sandstone lying among the Palaeozoic slates and shales. Before the war of 1914–18 just over a quarter of a million tons was mined annually; this was raised to a record production of 788 000 tons in 1955, but there has since been an appreciable decline.

In mid-Tertiary times the repercussions of the earth movements associated with the Alpine orogeny further south were such that the massif suffered some uplift, with a slight tilt towards the south. This movement was not as marked as in the other Hercynian massifs, possibly because it lay more on the margins of the orogeny, but the uplift was sufficient to inaugurate a new phase of denudation. The newer cover was almost wholly removed and the ancient peneplain more or less exhumed. The resistant granites and granulites were exposed as elliptical domelike masses, their

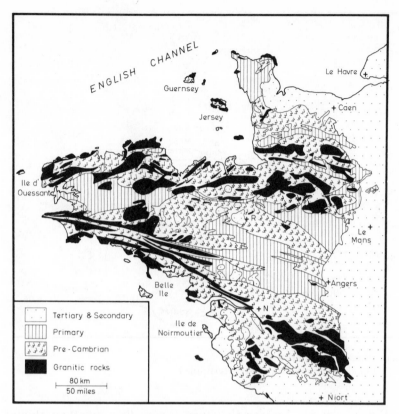

Fig. 17.1 Simplified geological map of Armorica
Minor areas of Quaternary and Recent deposits in bays and estuaries are
omitted. **N**, Nantes; **R**, Rennes.

Based on (a) folding map in L. de Launay, *Géologie de la France* (1921); and (b) *Carte géologique de
la France*, 1:1 000 000, published by the Service de la Carte géologique détaillée de la France
(1933).

axes also orientated from west to east, for they represent the deepseated
cores of the destroyed anticlines. The crystalline schists form extensive
plateaus over much of central Armorica.

Finally, small patches of Tertiary rocks are preserved in depressions and
basins. Eocene rocks occur near Mayenne in the east, areas of Oligocene
and Miocene limestone and clay to the west and southwest of Rennes and
in La Vendée, and scattered Pliocene outcrops survive in the south between
Redon and Angers.

The rivers were superimposed across the varied rocks of the peneplain,
although their courses reveal in detail an adaptation to the structure.[5]
The Devonian and Lower Carboniferous slates and shales preserved in the
synclinorium across the centre of the massif were worn into a long narrow
depression (the basin of Châteaulin), now occupied by the river Aulne.

449

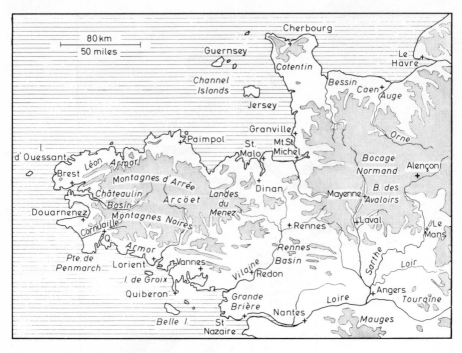

FIG. 17.2. General map of Armorica
**Q,** Quimper. Land above 100 metres (328 ft) is stippled.

Again, on Fig. 17.3 it can be seen that two streams flow due west along valleys partly the result of faulting, partly due to weak Silurian slates, in a direction almost parallel to the orientation of the Crozon peninsula, even though it is long and narrow. The same west–east trend is shown even more strikingly further south in Le Cap.[6] Where slices of resistant sandstone, quartzite and grit alternate with clayey shales and slates, the former now form prominent though narrow ridges, the latter the intervening valleys. The Vilaine below the Rennes basin, for example, occupies several narrow valley sections eroded across outcrops of Silurian sandstone, but between these it flows through broad basins into which come tributary strike streams wherever shales or slates occur.

## The coast

Perhaps the most remarkable feature of Brittany is its magnificent rugged coast, the edge of a rocky peninsula projecting boldly into the Atlantic. It has been calculated[7] that the total length of coastline around the Breton peninsula is no less than 3 480 km (2 160 miles), of which a fifth comprises islands. Its characteristics are the combined result, first, of a slight marine transgression in late Quaternary times which inundated the margins of the irregularly dissected peneplain; second, of the marine denudation of rocks of varying degrees of resistance lying in close juxtaposition; and third (less marked but in places quite appreciable), the complementary processes of deposition in the sheltered bays.

The marine transgression was responsible for the drowning of the lower portions of river valleys cut deeply into the peneplain, so forming a typical *ria* coast with long winding indentations. This is particularly marked in the west, where the trend of the coast runs transversely to the 'grain' of the structure. The Rade de Brest and the Baie de Douarnenez penetrate eastward on either side of the Crozon peninsula (Fig. 17.3). The first represents

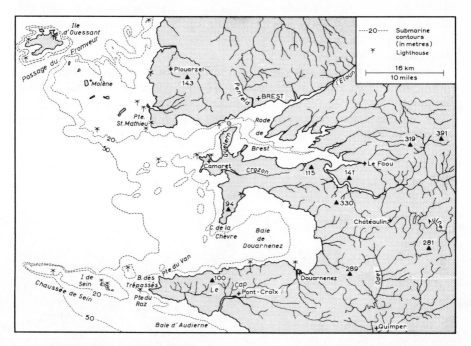

FIG. 17.3. The coast of Western Brittany
The large numbers of islets and tidal rocks which cover the submarine banks west of Pte St Mathieu and the Pte du Raz are not shown. The drainage pattern indicates the irregularly dissected margins of the ancient peneplain, but the west-east 'grain' is clearly noticeable, particularly in the Crozon and Le Cap peninsulas. Note the acute meanders of the Aulne, deeply incised in the slates of the Châteaulin basin. The submarine contours and spot-heights are in metres.
**G**, Goulet de Brest.

Based on (*a*) *Carte de France et des frontières au 200 000ᵉ*, sheet 21; (*b*) various British Admiralty charts.

the drowned lower portion of the basin of Châteaulin, and the river Aulne enters the Rade through a long winding inlet. The Baie de Douarnenez represents the inundated portion of a basin worn subaerially in weak slates, into which flow a dozen short rivers instead of a single master stream, so that the bay is more open and rounded than the usual *ria* type of inlet. The trend of the structure lines in the south of Brittany runs more or less parallel to the coast, but the lower courses of the larger rivers have been submerged to form long *ria* estuaries, as in the case of the Odet below Quimper, the Ellé below Quimperlé, the Blavet and the Vilaine. By contrast, the broad island-studded inlet of Morbihan, into which flows the Auray and other small rivers, represents the submergence of a basin so shallow that large parts dry out at low tide to form mudflats. The northern coast also lies roughly parallel to the main structural trends, but even here so many short rivers flowing northwards from the Montagnes d'Arrée and Landes du Menez have cut deep winding valleys across the various rocks that the submergence of their estuaries has resulted in some striking indentations. The estuary of the Rance, for example, runs inland for about 27 km (17 miles) from St Malo to Dinan.

Long ridges project seaward between the various inlets (Plate 50), ending in cliff-fronted promontories. Their former prolongation is indicated by the patterns of the submarine contours and the strings of offshore rocky archipelagoes and submerged rock banks (Fig. 17.3). Thus the granitic ridges of Cornouaille end in the Pointe du Raz, while the Ile

Plate 50. Brittany: the Breton coast near Potspoder

de Sein and its surrounding islets and reefs extend seawards for over 30 km (20 miles).

A further result of submergence has been the formation of islands, the higher outliers of the irregularly dissected margins of the peneplain. Many are little more than rocky stumps or submarine shoals, others are of larger dimensions. In the right angle of the Cotentin peninsula are the Channel Islands, the Minquiers and the Iles Chausey. Near the coast is the fascinating granitic pyramid of Mont St Michel, some 270 m (300 yd) in diameter at the base, and rising to a height of 78 m (256 ft) from its surrounding low-water sandbanks (crossed by a causeway). Further west some granitic fragments comprise the Ile Bréhat and the cluster of Les Sept Iles, and Les Héaux is made of rhyolite. Off the coast of the Pays de Léon are rocky islets which culminate in the famous Ile d'Ouessant, known to English seamen for centuries as 'Ushant'; it rises to 65 m (213 ft) but is only about 20 sq km (9 sq miles) in area.

Along the south coast of Brittany are many more islands, several lying some distance offshore. Some are granitic fragments, such as the Iles de Glénan, Houat and Hoédic. Belle-Ile is a massive piece of schist, with a coast of alternate steep cliffs and sandy bays. Groix, lying nearer to the mainland, consists of Pre-Cambrian schists and Silurian slates, while Yeu, off the Vendéan coast, is a mass of granite rising to 35 m (115 ft), surrounded by low but steep cliffs. The isolated granite masses of Quiberon and Le Croisic were once islands, but were converted into peninsulas by marine deposition.

The second contribution to the present Breton coastline is marine denudation, which operates unceasingly on the irregular margins of the peninsula. The resistant granites form bold steep cliffs; Pte St Cast to the west of St Malo rises almost vertically to 50 m (160 ft), while Pte Plouha on the western shores of the Baie de St Brieuc is nearly twice as high. Similarly, in the south the granulitic rocks form the rugged headlands of Penmarch and Quiberon, and many of the islands have steep cliffed margins. Not only granite forms near-vertical sections of coast. Cap Fréhel and Cap d'Erquy, to the east of the Baie de St Brieuc, are of hard Devonian sandstone, and the Crozon peninsula (Fig. 17.3) consists of a number of headlands of quartzites and grits, notably Cap de la Chèvre of Lower Carboniferous grit. But for the most part granitic rocks dominate along the Breton margins, and castellated cliffs, caves, arches and stacks form a most striking coastline to which the name *Côte sauvage* is justifiably applied. It is a dangerous one for shipping, as evidenced by the number of lighthouses in the west (Fig. 17.3). A rock platform or reef, worn by wave abrasion, extends seaward in places for a distance exceeding 800 m (a half-mile). These platforms are partly caused by submergence, partly by wave action; they are well developed off the northern coast near Roscoff, and again between the mainland and the Ile de Batz. Marine erosion has worn embayments from less resistant slates and shales to form bays; half a dozen are eroded out of the shales along the Crozon peninsula, and to the west of Roscoff the bays of Plestin, Morlaix and Goulven are formed from schists. Similarly in the southwest the curving outline of the Baie d'Audierne is worn from schists between the granitic promontories of the Pte du Raz and Pte de Penmarch.

While submergence and erosion have combined to produce this diversified coastline, deposition seeks to smooth out the irregularities. In the more sheltered bays and gulfs accumulate first bay-head beaches of gravel and sand backed by dunes and marsh, then more extensive tidal flats of sand and mud. The attrition of the crystalline rocks produces an abundance of pebbles and ultimately of fine sand, and some fine beaches occur even on quite exposed coasts. The Baie d'Audierne, though facing southwest, is fronted by a sweeping curve of sand, and the equally exposed but smaller Baie des Trépasses between the Ptes du Van and du Raz (Fig. 17.3) has a beach and a dune cordon behind which lies a tiny *étang*. Even in the Rade de Brest dredging is constantly necessary.

A striking example of sedimentation occurs along the coast of the Baie du Mont St Michel, within the angle of the Cotentin peninsula where a waste of quicksands, uncovered at low tide, is crossed by creeks and channels, for the sea goes out for 13 km (8 miles) at spring-tides (Fig. 17.4).

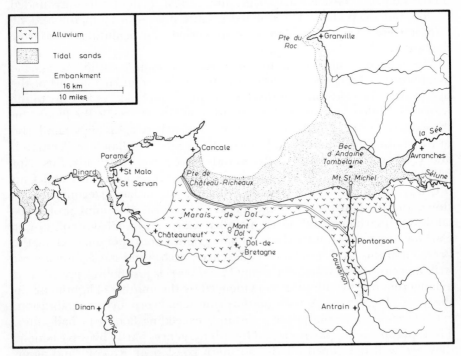

FIG. 17.4. The Baie du Mont St Michel

Based on *Carte de France et des frontières au 200 000ᵉ*, sheets 22, 23.

The deposits are of fine clay sands with an admixture of finely comminuted shells, producing a slimy sand known as *tangue*. The edge of the coast now lies some km north of its former position. Three crystalline masses project above the general level: Mont Dol (rising to 65 m (213 ft)), Mont St Michel and Tombelaine. A marsh fronted by a sandbar accumulated along the south side of the bay, and was for long liable to inundation during storms. To protect this a dyke, over 30 km (nearly 20 miles) in length, was built as long ago as 1324 from the Pte de Château-Richeaux eastward to the valley of the Couesnon near Pontorson. It was soon afterwards breached and much land was inundated until the end of the eighteenth century. Then the dyke was rebuilt, and the Marais de Dol was drained by a network of channels, administered by a syndicate of proprietors. From 1849 to 1870 further developments reclaimed the triangle of marsh between the eastern part of the dyke and the causeway carrying the road and railway to Mont St Michel. This celebrated eminence is crowned by an eleventh-century abbey church, and has houses and cobbled streets clustered around its steep flanks.

A further result of sedimentation can be seen along the south coast where several sandspits have been built between islands and the adjacent mainland, particularly at Quiberon and Le Croisic. Quiberon was a granitic island rising to 38 m (125 ft), but now it is 'tied' to the mainland by a sandbar 6 km (4 miles) in length, flanked by tidal sands. The bar is now artificially protected, and a road and railway run along it to Quiberon. Le Croisic further to the south was also a granitic island 11 km (7 miles) in length, lying parallel to the mainland at a distance of 8 km (5 miles). A spit extended westward from the mainland at Pornichet to the eastern end of the island at Le Pouliguen, thus forming a rectangular bay, and another bar developed southward from La Turballe, although this has not quite reached the island. An extensive area of tidal marsh was thus naturally enclosed, and a considerable part has been drained by a close network of channels to form salt pasture, leaving the tidal flats of Le Grand Trait and Le Petit Trait.

Finally, it must be remembered that weathering greatly modifies the varied rocks of a steep coast.

## Climate

Brittany is a peninsula experiencing what might generally be termed 'a western oceanic type of climate', though of course differences are apparent between the coastlands and the higher interior, and again between the north and south coasts. Armorica is subject to strong onshore winds; thus Cap de la Hague and the Ile d'Ouessant have on an average 122 and 144 days in the year respectively when rough seas are experienced, and during winter it is likely to be rough on one day in two. At Brest the average number of calm days during each of the four seasons spring, summer, autumn and winter is only 3, 4, 6 and 4 respectively.[9] Gale-force winds are experienced mainly during the winter months, mostly from directions between northwest and southwest and just occasionally from the south. Along the coast of Brittany names are given to the dominant winds—the *suroît* from the southwest and the *noroît* from the northwest. Further east a distinction is drawn between the southwesterly sea-wind (the *solaire*) and the northeasterly land-wind (the *galerne*).

The Breton peninsula, exposed to moist air-masses from the ocean, is characterised by high humidity, cloudiness and much fine drizzling mist. Because of its not very considerable altitude, however, precipitation totals are by no means as high as at places much further from the sea in the Central Massif, Alps or Vosges. Even the limited range of altitude within Armorica has an effect on precipitation. Thus at the Pte St Mathieu station near Brest, just over 30 m (100 ft) above sea level, the mean annual total is 810 mm (32 in), a figure characteristic of most Breton coastal stations. On the exposed moorlands totals are somewhat higher; La Feuillée (in the Montagnes d'Arrée at a height of 280 m (922 ft)) has 1190 mm (47 in), and Edern (in the Montagnes Noires at 207 m (679 ft)) receives 1170 mm (46 in). As would be expected, places in the more easterly valleys and basins receive less rain; Guipry in the Vilaine valley to the south of Rennes has 690 mm (27 in), and La Flèche on the eastern margins in the lower Loir valley only 560 mm (22 in).

This precipitation is well distributed throughout the year; at St Mathieu the least rain experienced on an average in any one month is 40 mm (1·7 in), the highest is 100 mm (3·9 in). Summer is nevertheless appreciably drier, a season when fewer disturbances cross the peninsula and when anticyclonic conditions spreading northeastward from the Azores tend to establish themselves. The period from May to August receives a mean total at St Mathieu of 180 mm (7 in), compared with twice as much in the four months from October to January. At the same station twelve days with measurable rain (0·1 mm) may be expected on an average in June, but as many as eighteen in November and nineteen in December. Finally, as an indication of the nature of the rainfall, the average amount per rainy day in January at St Mathieu is less than half that experienced during the same month at Nice.

The other main characteristic of the Breton climate is its moderate temperatures near sea level along the coast. The lowest range of temperature between the mean warmest and coolest months experienced in all France is about 9°C (17°F), at Roscoff; the warmest and coolest months there are not July and January, but August and February, an indication of the effects of the sea in retarding the cooling of the atmosphere in winter and its heating in summer. The most striking fact is that the mean January temperature for St Mathieu is 7°C (45°F), only about 1°C (2°F) lower than that of Nice. The Breton coast experiences frost on about the same number of days as does the Riviera, roughly a dozen. The moorlands in the interior have naturally a more severe winter, being both further from the sea and higher, with more days of frost, a snow cover of from fifteen to twenty days, and quite bleak conditions.

In summer mean temperatures approximate to 17°C (62°F) along the northern and western coasts, and 1 or 2 degrees C higher along the southern coasts near the Loire estuary. This slight difference is nevertheless critical as far as the successful cultivation of the vine is concerned, for the northern limit runs eastward from the coast near Lorient. R. Dion has suggested that this line corresponds to the 15°C (59°F) actual isotherm for the period April to September.[10] The long summer hours of sunshine and clear bright days are one of the charms of the Breton coast, but sea breezes modify the actual temperatures and hot days are rare. One important factor in the agricultural economy is the early spring, indeed in many years the temperature rarely falls below 6°C (43°F), and meadow grass hardly ceases to grow.

Here then near the coast is a soft mild climate characterised by equability and humidity. On the interior uplands, much bleaker conditions occur— raw, windswept and cloudy, and with frost and snow.

## Land use and agriculture

It is useful to summarise the main categories for each of the seven *départements* which comprise Armorica (excluding the three which make up La Vendée, dealt with separately below) to give some indication of the pattern of land use.

*Land use, 1968 (percentage of total area)*

| DÉPARTEMENT | ARABLE | PERMANENT PASTURE | WOODLAND |
|---|---|---|---|
| Côtes-du-Nord | 54 | 14 | 11 |
| Finistère | 58 | 13 | 5 |
| Ille-et-Vilaine | 53 | 27 | 8 |
| Loire-Atlantique | 46 | 27 | 5 |
| Manche | 10 | 70 | 5 |
| Mayenne | 35 | 51 | 7 |
| Morbihan | 46 | 22 | 9 |

Source: Ministére de l'Agriculture, *Annuaire statistique de la France*, 1970–1.

The small proportion of woodland is evident from these figures, indeed Manche has the lowest percentage of any *département* in France. These humid lands were covered with ancient forests of oak and beech, but once the woodlands had been destroyed regeneration became difficult. The humus-rich soils which had developed under deciduous woodland, thus left unprotected, were removed by denudation and gradually replaced by thin gravelly and acid soils, the product of *in situ* weathering of the granites, schists and quartzites. The solid blocks of ancient forest once provided their own shelter, but after these were removed the winds which sweep the peninsula were inimical to regeneration except in sheltered hollows and valleys. Some forests of oak and beech are carefully preserved. Along the ridge of the Landes de Lanvaux are coniferous plantations, and some small woodlands occur around the margins of the Rennes basin and on the Montagnes Noires. The rest of the woodland occurs as copses around villages and farms, or along the hedgerows in the form of pollarded oaks and ash. The last, incidentally, give an impression of a much more wooded character than is actually the case.

Some of the higher, bleaker uplands are covered with moorland. The impermeable acid rocks, mantled with a thin layer of either coarse gravelly soils or sticky clays, carry a vegetation of gorse, broom, patches of hawthorn and bramble scrub. On the better-drained slopes grow vast sheets of ling, with heather on south-facing aspects, and especially on the clays flourish considerable areas of bracken fern. In spite of the general humidity, the impermeable rocks and the rapid runoff induce xerophytic characters; after a spell of drought the moorlands assume a bleached and arid appearance.

On some of the flatter moorlands and in the high depressions flourish expanses of bog grass, sphagnum moss, reeds, bilberry and hard fern, sometimes producing an appreciable accumulation of peat.

Around the coast saltmarshes have developed in the angles of sheltered bays or along the margins of estuaries. Large parts of these have been reclaimed, both naturally and by man's efforts, to furnish rich pastures and arable land. In the western angle of the Cotentin the Marais de Dol lies along the coast of the Baie du Mont St Michel (Fig. 17.4), on the northern shore of the Loire estuary is the Grande Brière, and on the coastal plain of Vendée the Marais Breton and Marais Poitevin[11] (Fig. 13.5).

It can be seen from the table that between 70 and 80 per cent of Armorica is under either arable[12] or permanent grassland. Manche has the highest proportion of permanent pasture in France. By contrast, it is perhaps surprising to find such a low proportion of permanent pasture in the *départements* of Finistère, Côtes-du-Nord and Morbihan, but there the economy is an arable one. There is a certain amount of short ley grass, and in addition some of the arable fields are left as fallow for a number of years, affording some pasture.

Most of this farmland is enclosed in small fields by banks, crowned with a thick hedge, often containing pollarded oaks and ash, though in the west these banks are replaced by dry-stone walls. This is the *bocage* country so characteristic of northwestern France, and contrasting markedly with the open hedgeless *plaines, campagnes* and *champagnes* of the Paris Basin. The term *bocage* is widely used; there is the *Bocage Normand* in the east, the *Bocage Manceau* of the upper Mayenne basin, the *Bocage Breton* of the west, and the *Bocage Vendéen* to the south of the Loire estuary.

PLATE 51. Granville on the coast of the Cotentin

The small fields are the basic agricultural units of Brittany, whether under arable cultivation, temporary or permanent grass, market gardens or cider-apple orchards. The arable fields are located near the sea, and in the Châteaulin and Rennes basins. From the coast shelly sands can be obtained for sweetening the acid soils and for lightening the clays, and seaweed is used as a fertiliser. Here are the sheltered pockets of *primeurs* cultivation, now more profitable than cereals, capitalising the relative freedom from frost and the early springs.

Once cereals were the chief agricultural products, and grain and flour were exported by sea round to the Seine estuary and Paris. Little fields of cereals are still grown, usually oats and barley near the coast, rye and buckwheat in the interior, and wheat in the eastern districts of Maine and Anjou. Sometimes *méteil* (a mixture of wheat and rye) is grown, and also a mixture of oats and buckwheat which forms the basis of the widely eaten *pain de mêlée*. But *primeurs*, permanent pasture and fodder crops now afford a much more lucrative use of the land. Further inland less cultivation is found on the poorer soils and under the bleaker climatic conditions,

459

consisting merely of some patches of potatoes, cabbages, rye and buck-wheat.

Armorica is one of the main dairying districts in France; in 1968 there were 4·03 million cattle in the seven *départements*, or about 17 per cent of the French total, and the most important *département* was Manche with over 745 000 head. Many of the cattle are the particoloured *vaches bretonnes*, small-boned as a result of the inherent shortage of phosphates and lime in the soil, although Jerseys and Jersey crosses are increasing in number, particularly in Manche. One great advantage of the mild climate is that except during the worst weather on the uplands cattle can be left out of doors through the year. On many small farms one or two cows are kept as part of the subsistence economy; *caudelée*, a kind of curdled milk, is made and eaten by the producer or sold in the regional markets. The rearing of cattle for beef is increasing, particularly in the uplands, where the poor pasture is usually supplemented with fodder crops. Large numbers of young bullocks are shipped from the Cotentin and the Bocage Normand to the plains of Lower Normandy, to the eastern Paris Basin and even to Belgium, and from the Bocage Vendéen to Poitou and the Charolais.

In this region of mixed agriculture, other animals afford an important contribution to the economy. About 2·81 million pigs were in the seven *départements* in 1968, or over a quarter of the French total, fattened for local slaughter and also bred for shipping away as stores; there are some famous markets, notably the *Marché aux Porcs* at Pont l'Abbé. Nearly a quarter of all French horses are reared here, mainly for ploughing, indeed Finistère with 20 000 and Côtes-du-Nord with 22 000 animals were the two most important *départements*, though recently there has been a big decline. Little more than a quarter of a million sheep indicates a big reduction during the last century; they are kept both on the rougher pastures in the interior and on the coastal salt-marshes.

## Regional divisions

Within this general setting it is evident that a number of subdivisions can be distinguished. The coast and its immediate hinterland is *Ar-mor* itself, the *pays de la mer*. The upland area of the interior is often referred to as *Arcoët* (variously spelt *Argoat*, *Archoat* or *Arcoat*), which means literally 'the country of the woods', another indication of the former forest cover, but now occupied by expanses of *bocage* interrupted by the *landes* on wind-swept eminences and in damp depressions. The three basins, Châteaulin, Rennes and Laval, merit separate treatment, as does the northward-projecting Cotentin peninsula. The lower Loire crosses on to the ancient Armorican rocks just above the Maine confluence, and its valley with the estuary forms a distinctive unit. Finally, to the south of the Loire are the rather dreary moorlands of the *Collines de Vendée*, flanked on the north by the lower plateau of *Les Mauges* and on the south by the pleasant *Bocage Vendéen*.[13]

# Armor

Armor comprises the coast and its hinterland from the base of Cotentin right round the peninsula to the mouth of the Loire. The north coast is higher and more rugged than the south, and consists of an alternation of sheltered bays into which lead narrow, winding and deeply incised valleys, with massive cliffed promontories where the peneplain ends abruptly. The south coast, though frequently cliffed, is generally lower, the 50 m (150 ft) contour commonly lies 30 km (20 miles) inland, and the estuaries and bays are broad and open. Climatically the south coast is milder and not quite so humid as the north. Yet paradoxically the north coast has a more prosperous agricultural life, the result of centuries of effort.[14]

Nearly three-quarters of the population of Brittany live in Armor. Although the term '*ceinture dorée*' is sometimes used to describe the coastal zone, it indicates a peripheral continuity which does not actually exist; the alternation of valley and inlet with ridge and peninsula has resulted in the growth of small towns and villages, each with a closely settled but limited hinterland. Most of them are fishing ports, some with a small harbour exporting agricultural produce and importing coal, fertilisers and oil. Others lie at the heads of the estuaries: on the north coast stand Dinan[15] on the Rance, St Brieuc[16] (the biggest town in the north) on the Gouet, and Morlaix on the Rivière de Morlaix. The last although well inland has a little port with a dock. A new deepwater port, equipped for the speedy and efficient export of vegetables, has been constructed at Roscoff. Quimper, placed far inland at the head of the Odet ria, is the administrative centre of Finistère and a prosperous market town. Vannes, the *chef-lieu* of Morbihan, is situated where a group of valleys open into the northern angle of the large Baie de Morbihan. The only concentrations of population on the Breton coast are at Brest and Lorient, mainly the result of their function as naval bases.[17]

The emphasis in Armor is on agriculture, both dairying and the production of *primeurs*, utilising 'pockets' of land around the bays and the larger areas of reclamation, as on the former marshes of Dol which provide both pasture and excellent soils for vegetables. Early potatoes, cauliflowers, onions and salad vegetables are exported, both by rail to Paris and by boat from St Malo, Morlaix, Roscoff[18] and other small ports to Great Britain.

The tourist industry is an additional source of employment, capitalising the magnificent coastal scenery, the secluded bays and picturesque harbours, the general charm of the Breton landscape.[19]

Industry is restricted, with some notable exceptions, to the processing of the produce both of the land and of the sea—the preserving of vegetables, the making of butter, the canning of sardines and tunny, and the making of cider and apple liqueurs. A Michelin tyre factory has recently been opened at Vannes. A few local industries include a tobacco factory at Morlaix, a pottery at Quimper, and some small tanneries. Formerly

PLATE 52. The tidal power scheme (*Usine Maremotrice*) on the Rance estuary

spinning and weaving of linen and wool produced homespun clothing at a time when Brittany was remote and of necessity largely self-sufficing. Both flax and hemp were grown, the latter for ropes and cordage. Only a small textile factory survives at St Brieuc. At two of the larger centres, Brest and Lorient, shipbuilding and repair work for the French navy are carried out, and near the latter the steel works of Hennebont make tin plate for the canning industry. The building and repairing of boats is carried on at many of the harbours around the coast.

In the estuary of the Rance near St Malo, a 250 mW power station operated by the tides was opened in 1966; its capacity is 544 million kWh annually, or about 1 per cent of total French hydro production. A barrage 750 m (2 500 ft) long was constructed across the Rance estuary, in which are set twenty-four reversible bulb turbines. These can generate power during both the filling and emptying of the estuary above the barrage. While of course the tidal range varies considerably (with a maximum of 14·6 m (48 ft) at equinoctial springs), off-peak current is used to pump up water behind the barrage and so increase the head at non-productive periods (Plate 52).[20]

**Fishing**

The sea may either provide the farmer with a supplementary occupation or offer full-time employment as a fisherman or in the French navy and merchant marine. About 23 000 people in the six coastal *départements* are full-time fishermen, of whom half live in Finistère. This figure represents 60 per cent of all the personnel in the French fishing industry, and it must also be remembered that many of the 5 000 men employed in the trawler fleets of Boulogne are Bretons.

Many fishing harbours are scattered around the coast,[21] indeed almost every bay and inlet has a few boats; the four most important are:

*Total catch, 1969 (thousand tons)*

| | |
|---|---|
| Concarneau | 59·3 |
| Lorient | 54·1 |
| Douarnenez | 22·7 |
| Le Guilvinec | 19·3 |

Source: Comité Central des Pêches
Maritimes, *Annuaire statistique*, 1970–1

It must be remembered that these figures do not include the less important fishing harbours which each land a few hundred tons of fish either for local sale or to despatch via the larger centres. The table does not include subsistence fishing, nor the quite valuable catch of crustaceans and shellfish.[2]

The fishing industries of northern and southern Brittany are markedly different. At many harbours in the north the men engage in coastal fishing for herring, mackerel, skate, turbot and mullet, a scattered and unorganised industry on a subsistence or part-time basis, where each *patron-propriétaire* owns his boat. Some shrimps and shellfish are gathered, mainly by women, there is sporadic fishing for crustaceans, and the cultivation of oysters at Tréguier. At Roscoff lobsters caught off the Moroccan and Portuguese coasts are stored alive in tanks. Once seagoing schooners operated from St Malo, St Servan, Paimpol and Cancale. Indeed, as late as 1937 St Malo was the third fishing port of France in terms of shipping tonnage; the *terreneuviers* sailed every March for the cod fisheries off Newfoundland, where they were based on St Pierre and Miquelon, or for Icelandic waters, and the port handled a quarter of all cod landed in 1937 in France. Today much of this activity has passed to the trawlers of Boulogne and Fécamp, though a new fishing port was opened in 1965.

One associated industry along the north coast is the collection of seaweed, cut at low spring-tide by long-established custom from barges or collected in carts from the waveworn platforms. It is used as manure, particularly on the potato fields, or for the extraction of iodine.

On the south coast fishing is organised on a larger scale. The waters of the Bay of Biscay are warmer than those of the English Channel, and sardines and white tunny provide the main varieties; in point of fact the

463

total French catch of each of these species is exceeded only by that of cod. The sardine-fishing season starts in the Golfe de Gascogne in February, and the fleets work gradually northwards during summer, ending for the year off Finistère in November. The fish are caught in fine-meshed drift nets. The white tunny is fished between July and October, using rods fixed to the base of the mast.[22] Miscellaneous fish are caught by steam trawlers based on Lorient, which operate as far afield as the waters off southwest Ireland for hake and skate, and drifters fish for mackerel and whiting.

Lorient is the second fishing port of the Breton coast. A modern fish dock was built in the years following the war of 1914–18 at Keroman,[23] to the south of the main commercial and naval port of Lorient, where the river Scorff enters the Blavet river. As a result, while Lorient handled only 8 000 tons of fish in 1913, this had increased to 33 000 tons before the war of 1939–45, a figure which was soon attained again after a war-time decline, and in 1969 reached over 54 000 tons, third in France to Boulogne and Concarneau. The facilities include two large basins, fish warehouses, a cold store, an ice-making plant, and coal- and oil-fuelling facilities for trawlers. Railway sidings alongside the fish market enable refrigerator cars to be loaded for express despatch to Paris. Concarneau and Douarnenez are the bases of most of the sardine- and tunny-boats. Each of these has factories where the fish are canned.

Crustaceans and shellfish provide an important item along the south coast. Lobsters are caught either in wicker pots or in heavy nets dragged along the bottom. Some vessels go for three months to the coasts of Portugal, Morocco and Mauritania, returning with their catch of live spiny lobsters to be stored in tanks at Concarneau, Audierne and elsewhere until required for market. Oysters are cultivated at Auray, La Trinité and Carnac, but on a smaller scale than further south at Arcachon. Mussels are reared in the Vilaine estuary near Penestin, where large culture beds are enclosed between long palisades.

## The ports

The port and naval base of Brest[24] is situated on the northern side of the Rade de Brest, a sheet of water nearly 160 sq km (60 sq miles) in area, reached from the open sea through the rocky channel of the Goulet de Brest, 5 km (3 miles) long but only a little over 1 km wide between the mainland and the northerly part of Crozon (Fig. 17.3). The town has grown up on either side of the Penfeld estuary, which is spanned by the largest lift bridge in Europe, opened in 1954. Quays and basins line this estuary and the shores of the Rade itself, protected by moles. Most of the port is accessible at the lowest tides to vessels drawing 10 m (32 ft), and the only locks are for entry to the dry dock; in places least depths exceed 18 m (60 ft). The naval port occupies the Penfeld river and the Laninon quays to the west of its mouth, where dredging enables large carriers to berth.

The Port de Commerce occupies the quays and basins to the east of the Penfeld estuary.

The growth of Brest dates from the rise of France as a naval power in the seventeenth century, and Richelieu and Vauban carried out works to develop both the naval base and the arsenal, so that the heavily fortified shores of the Goulet made the base virtually impregnable from the sea. In the late nineteenth century the outer harbour in the Rade was developed, following the building of the moles. During the war of 1939–45 the port was used by the Germans as a submarine-base, and in addition the *Scharnhorst*, the *Gneisenau* and the *Prinz Eugen* lay there for many months. The installations were heavily damaged from the air, and at the date of the liberation (17 September 1944) the port was hardly usable; nearly 2 000 vessels were sunk in and around the waters. The work of reconstruction was badly set back in July 1947 by the explosion of a cargo vessel laden with ammunition. By 1949, however, nearly 90 per cent of the quays and basins were usable, and the naval port was once again functioning.

The commercial harbour handled just under a million tons of freight in 1938, of which about one-third was coastal. Trade was of course at a standstill during and immediately after the war, but in 1946 shipments of American coal were directed through the port; in 1947 some 857 000 tons of freight, most of which consisted of coal, was handled. In 1968 the freight amounted to 2·20 million tons, 90 per cent of which comprised imports, out of a French total of 143 millions.

Brest is very isolated for passenger traffic as compared with Cherbourg and Le Havre, the railway route from Paris is long and quite difficult, the hinterland is restricted, and the commodities produced (mainly perishables) can move more conveniently eastwards by rail or directly from Channel ports such as St Malo. Finally, although it has a splendid harbour, the approaches are difficult, and are endangered by rocks, fogs and storms. In 1970, however, it was officially announced that Brest was scheduled to become an oil terminal for large tankers, and that a refinery was to be built in the near future.

The shipyards situated along the Penfeld river have turned out many warships, including the *Richelieu* and the *Dunkerque,* and numerous submarines. In recent years the carriers *Clemenceau* (1961) and *Foch* (1963) have been launched. Most of the repair and machine shops have been rebuilt since the war, and there are ancillary engineering industries and chemical and explosive factories. As a result of these activities, together with its function as a market and servicing centre for western Brittany, Brest had a population of 154 000 in 1968.

Lorient has already been mentioned as the third fishing port of France, and it possesses various fish-processing and fish-preserving industries. Lorient, a creation of the Breton merchants in the seventeenth century as a base for ships trading with India, was established on a creek where the Scorff enters the Blavet estuary. The Compagnie commerciale des Indes orientales named it L'Orient, and developed it as an *entrepôt*, with large storehouses and repair yards. Lorient declined after the virtual disappearance of the French empire in India, and when the company ceased to function the port passed to the French Government. Shipbuilding and repairing yards were then created. Several cruisers were launched there in the interwar years, although destroyers and submarines were the chief vessels handled. During the war, when it was used by the Germans as a submarine base, the town and port were badly damaged. Its population fell from 46 000 in 1936 to 12 000 ten years later, although by 1968 it had risen to 66 000. Lorient's importance is now almost wholly as a fishing port, for much of the arsenal has been closed and its activities transferred to Brest. A new Renault plant makes car components. The commercial port, which before the war of 1939–1945 handled annually half a million tons of freight, has increased its activity to 950 000 tons in 1969. Hennebont, 10 km (6 miles) further up the Blavet river, has a small tinplate works, serving the fish and vegetable canneries along the Breton coast.

## Arcoët

The Breton peninsula[25] rises inland to two areas of upland standing above the general level, separated by the east–west valley of the Aulne. The larger mass in the north is the Montagnes d'Arrée, mostly consisting of granite and Devonian sandstone; much is above about 260 m (850 ft) and the highest point, the Signal de Toussaines, reaches 384 m (1 260 ft). This upland continues eastward as the Landes du Menez, whose swelling eminences just exceed 330 m (1 100 ft), and beyond as the hills of Alençon overlooking the Sarthe valley; here the Butte des Avaloirs attains 417 m (1 368 ft), the highest point in Armorica. This elevated country in the east includes stretches of moorland, peaty swamps and woodland, but much is the typical *Bocage Normand*. While the summits are usually rounded and smooth, here and there rise tor-like masses of granite, and in some places narrow ridges of resistant sandstones have weathered to form groups of crags. This line of upland forms the main longitudinal watershed of Armorica; short streams flow directly northwards in deeply cut valleys to the Channel, while others drain west and south to the Aulne, directly to the Bay of Biscay, to the Vilaine system, and in the east to the Loire via the Sarthe and Mayenne.

The southern ranges of hills are much lower and less continuous than those in the north, and in places are broken through completely by such streams as the Blavet. In the Montagnes Noires,[26] the ridge to the south of the Châteaulin depression, the highest point is 326 m (1 070 ft) but elsewhere the inconspicuous summits rarely exceed 180 m (600 ft), covered with moorland and peat bogs, and diversified only by occasional granite tors.

The limitations of Arcoët, the result of its upland relief, its poor acid soils and the bleak climate, have already been indicated; the farms among the *bocage* country grow rather poor crops of buckwheat, rye and potatoes, and maintain some cattle and sheep. The density of population averages about 40 to 60 per sq km (100 to 150 per sq mile), only from a third to a quarter that of the coastal strip. Settlement is widely distributed in the form of hamlets and isolated farms, usually sited on gentle slopes below exposed hilltops but above the marshy valley floors and depressions. Often these farms are accessible only by deeply sunk muddy lanes. This is one of the areas which has seen much emigration from the rather hard rural existence to the towns—to Rennes, Nantes, Angers and Paris.

The few towns of note are Fougères in the upper Couesnon valley in the east, Guingamp and Loudéac in Côtes-du-Nord, and Pontivy and Ploërmel in Morbihan. Most of these are market centres, situated at road junctions where the few north–south transverse roads make their way over the moorlands to link up with the three east–west routes: the main N12 along the northern edge of the Montagnes d'Arrée through St Brieuc and Morlaix, a secondary road along the central depression, and a road from Nantes via Quimperlé skirting the southern margin of the Landes de Lanvaux and the Montagnes Noires. The two main railway lines follow approximately the trend of the northern and southern roads, and another single-track line runs along the central depression from Rennes to Carhaix before it cuts northwestward to Morlaix. Only two transverse lines make their way across the peninsula, a central one from St Brieuc via Loudéac and Pontivy to Quiberon, and an eastern one from St Malo to Rennes, from which one line continues via Redon to St Nazaire, another directly to Nantes. The line south from St Malo to Nantes carries through trains to La Rochelle, Bordeaux and Bayonne (including the *Côte d'Emeraude-Pyrénées* express). It is a reflection of the scanty population and limited resources of interior Brittany that the large area enclosed by the main lines is served only by motor-bus.

The long Nantes-Brest Canal (Fig. 13.4) wanders northwestward from Nantes via Redon and Pontivy (where a short branch continues to Lorient), thence to the canalised Aulne below Carhaix. The difficulty of this route between Pontivy and Carhaix is shown by the fact that 201 locks are required.

## The basins

Three distinct basins are contained within the uplands: *Châteaulin* (the lower Aulne valley) in the west, *Rennes* occupied by a series of rivers converging on the Vilaine, and *Laval* in the east (the valley of the middle Mayenne).

The valley of the Aulne, between the Montagnes d'Arrée and the Montagnes Noires, opens westward into the Rade de Brest. The lower Aulne itself forms a series of deeply incised meanders (Fig. 17.3). The basin is floored with Lower Devonian shales which have weathered to form rather wet clay soils. In spite of its low altitude compared with the uplands to north and south, this basin is not densely populated, though a string of villages and small towns, including Châteaulin itself, lies along the main road and the Nantes-Brest Canal. It is a dairying region, and potatoes are grown.

The basin of Rennes stands out as the largest area of lowland in Brittany, where a number of streams converge before flowing southwestwards to the Bay of Biscay. Faulting has contributed to the formation of this basin; the southern edge is defined by the Faille de Pontréan, which in places forms a quite distinct faultline scarp.[27] It is floored with areas of Tertiary rocks, for the depression seems to have been occupied by a lake, certainly in mid-Tertiary times. Various Oligocene, Miocene and Pliocene deposits have accumulated, including patches of distinctive shelly sands. Most of these newer materials have been removed, so exposing tracts of schists, shales and sandstones, and even in some places (as to the northeast of Rennes) masses of granite. The result is that both relief and soils are diversified. Rennes itself lies near the confluence of the Ille and the Vilaine at a height of 54 m (175 ft), but the interfluves rise to 120 m (400 ft).

The surrounding uplands are mostly moorlands, although some pines have been planted, while the valleys are chequered with meadows and arable land. The lower and more sheltered basin experiences a climate appreciably drier and less windswept than the uplands to the west, and it is the scene of a prosperous mixed agriculture—dairying, stock-raising, cereal cultivation and market-gardening.

Many small towns occur in the valleys, but Rennes is pre-eminent, for with its population of 181 000 in 1968 it contained nearly a third of the total of Ille-et-Vilaine.[28] Its central position has been appreciated for two millennia, for it was the capital of one of the main Celtic tribes, then a Gallo-Roman town, and later the chief town first of the duchy then of the province of Brittany, where the Breton *parlement* met. It was largely destroyed by fire in 1720, and the new town was attractively laid out with spacious streets and fine squares. In the nineteenth century Rennes expanded rapidly as a communications centre; eleven radial roads now converge and two railway lines cross here—the transverse line from St Malo to Nantes and the longitudinal line from Paris and Le Mans to Brest. Quays line the banks of the Vilaine (which is navigable to the sea) and of the Ille-Rance Canal, which provides a minor and little used water link across the peninsula (Fig. 13.4). The modern industrial development of Rennes has been a major feature of the economic plan for Brittany.[29] New light industries, such as the manufacture of electronic apparatus, clothing, photographic film, pharmaceutical chemicals, footwear, hosiery, brushes and printing, have been introduced, notably on new industrial estates. In 1951 a *Citroën* works was opened outside the town which has grown into a large, highly automated plant. It is a commercial and servicing centre, the market for the surrounding agricultural lands, and an administrative,

judicial and cultural centre; there is a famous university with a distinguished school of Celtic studies. Near Rennes at Vern-sur-Seiche an oil
refinery has recently been completed, with an output in 1969 of 1·4 million
tons of hydrocarbons.

Further east, on the borders of Armorica, is the basin of Laval, a depression floored mainly with Lower Devonian and Lower Carboniferous rocks,
diversified on the one hand by outcrops of granite and a long narrow ridge
of rhyolite, on the other by tracts of Pliocene sands and gravels. The basin is
crossed transversely by the well defined valley of the Mayenne, which,
rising in the Avaloirs upland to the north, flows southwards to join the
Loire below Angers. At Laval the floor of the valley lies at 45 m (150 ft)
above sea level, and its clay soils result in a varied agriculture of dairying
and market-gardening. Laval (45 000) is the market town for the middle
Mayenne valley, a route centre halfway between Le Mans and Rennes,
and a small industrial district. At dairy factories in the town and in neighbouring villages the famous *Port-Salut* cheese is processed. On the original
basis of wool from the moorland sheep and locally grown flax and hemp,
Laval became a thriving textile town, and today it has factories making
cotton cloth and drills of cotton-linen mixtures, together with various
branches of hosiery manufacture. Attractive marbles are obtained from
neighbouring quarries. Mayenne, higher up the river, shares on a smaller
scale the industrial development of Laval.

## Cotentin

The Cotentin peninsula and its 'roots' consist of three distinct structural
regions. In the north granite massifs and Pre-Cambrian schists form the
northwestern (Cap de la Hague) and northeastern (Pte de Barfleur)
headlands of the peninsula, and the same type of rock comprises the little
massif of Les Pieux projecting towards the west coast. The moorland hills
rise above 180 m (600 ft), interrupted by the wide valley of the Divette
worn in Silurian slates and shales, and opening into the broad north-
facing bay on which stands Cherbourg. To the south of these granite hills,
the Silurian and Lower Devonian rocks give rise to undulating country,
with occasional summits rising to over 120 m (400 ft), dissected by streams
mainly flowing eastwards.

The central and eastern part of Cotentin consists of the lowland basin of
Valognes and Carentan, drained by the rivers Douve and Taute into the
broad Baie des Veys. Geologically this basin is most varied; outcrops of
Triassic and Jurassic rocks in the northeast and of Permian rocks in the
south are separated by lowlands covered with Pliocene deposits and recent
alluvium. The flat plain of Carentan, formerly marshy along the river
valleys, is still liable to flooding as a result of the convergence of so many
meandering streams towards the Baie des Veys. In the centre of the
peninsula, forming the heart of this lowland belt, lies a circular depression,

6 km (4 miles) in diameter, the *Prairies marécageuses de Gorges,* partially drained by the Canal du Plessis, and to the southeast of Carentan the land is seamed with drainage channels. The main line northward through Carentan to Cherbourg is carried on an embankment because of liability to flooding.

To the south of this central lowland the ancient rocks once more appear, rising southward to the hill country of the Collines de Normandie and reaching heights of well over 300 m (1 000 ft). These uplands form the watershed between northwards flowing rivers, such as the Vire, Aure and Orne, and the Mayenne and its headstreams.

The coast of Cotentin[30] differs markedly from that of Brittany, except in the north where there are some cliffed promontories and at two places in the west where the granitic Cap de Flamanville rises steeply to over 75 m (250 ft) and the Pte du Roc projects sharply into the Baie de Mont St Michel. Elsewhere by contrast the coast is low and rather featureless; on the west are the sweeping curves of several bays, bordered with broad sandy beaches and backed by dunes, while on the east behind a similar littoral lie marshes seamed with drainage channels. Some of the dunes are 15 to 18 m (50 to 60 ft) in height; at places along the west coast the sand blows inland, but most of the dunes are planted with pines to prevent any further movement.

It has already been stressed that Manche, which comprises the whole of the peninsula and its 'roots', is the most important *département* of France for dairy cattle, that about 70 per cent of its surface is under permanent pasture and a further 10 per cent under rotation grassland. The cattle, gradually improved by careful maintenance of pedigree, are bred both for milk and meat. Milk, butter and cheese are sent to Paris, and live bullocks and heifers are sold out of the district. Sheep are reared on both the upland grazings and on the saltmarsh pastures in the southwest along the shores of the Baie de Mont St Michel and in the east between Montebourg and Ste Mère-Eglise. Horses and poultry, particularly geese, are also reared.

Despite the dominance of livestock, some arable cultivation is found. As in the *bocage* generally, barley and oats are grown for animal feeding, root crops such as potatoes, and vegetables, and there are pleasant orchards of cider apples. As a result, nearly half the working population in Manche is employed in agriculture.

No *ceinture dorée* has developed along this Cotentin coast as in Brittany, and most of the rural population lives inland, spread over the countryside in villages among the *bocage*. Occasional larger towns are market centres for agricultural produce, such as Valognes in the north, Carentan in the centre, Coutances in the west and St Lô in the south; the last was so grievously damaged in 1944 that its population was then reduced to half its prewar total of 12 000. The industries consist of the processing of agricultural products, such as making butter and cider.

Few settlements are found along the coast itself, since except in the west it offers small attraction to holiday-makers, and the exposed shallow anchorages are of little value as harbours. One exception is Granville (Plate 51), perched on the southern side of the cliffed Pte du Roc, from which a breakwater projects southeastward to give some shelter to a basin and to a wet dock. A few resorts in the west make use of the sandy beaches, such as Granville, Carteret (where the bathing is superb in the Atlantic rollers on the shelving sandy beaches) and Le Bec de Carolles. Fishing is carried on from a few ports and oysterbeds are cultivated at St Vaast-la-Houge in the northeast.

The port of Cherbourg stands on the northern shores of the Cotentin peninsula where a broad open re-entrant appears in the coast. As a natural harbour the site is poor, but its modern advantage lies in its virtual mid-Channel position, only 134 km (83 miles) south of Southampton. It was a minor naval port for centuries, but its value was limited because of its exposed situation. A few years before the French Revolution the immense work began of constructing the Digue Centrale, a breakwater 5 km (3 miles) in length running west–east and enclosing the Grande Rade within its shelter; this was not completed until 1853. Flanking moles project from either side, the eastern taking advantage of the rocky mass of the Ile Pelée. Work progressed steadily, and several basins and docks have been excavated from the slate rocks on the western and southern sides of the harbour. In the interwar period, the decision to make Cherbourg a transatlantic terminal and port of call was implemented by the construction of two inner moles enclosing the Petite Rade, within which a large basin, the Darse Transatlantique, was completed, with liner berths providing least depths of 12 m (40 ft). On the east of the liner-basin is the recently completed Quai de Normandie.

The port was seriously damaged in the later stages of the war, although captured speedily by the American forces. But most of the port installations and the Gare Maritime were destroyed, the two main quays were completely unusable, and the *rades* were encumbered with wrecks. However, Cherbourg was used as a supply port for the American forces in Europe, and temporary facilities were rapidly installed. After the return of the port to the French authorities in October 1945, ambitious schemes of restoration and improvement were steadily pushed ahead, a new Gare Maritime was built, and the Darse Transatlantique was reconstructed. Cherbourg briefly resumed some of its functions as a liner port, though not for French vessels (which use Le Havre), but as a port of call for foreign liners. In 1963, for example, Cherbourg disembarked about 17 000 passengers from the North Atlantic services, compared with Le Havre's 50 000. But even this function has dwindled as the great liners have been withdrawn, and in 1969 fewer than 2 000 ocean passengers disembarked. However, in 1964 a car ferry with Southampton was inaugurated, and the port has thus acquired a new importance, as shown by the fact that it handled 128 000 passengers and their cars in 1969. Cherbourg has modern naval dockyards, from which in 1967 was launched the *Redoutable,* France's first nuclear submarine, and there has been some recent development of general engineering, including the manufacture of agricultural machinery.[31]

## The lower Loire valley and estuary

The Loire enters its lower section at Les Ponts-de-Cé, a few km above the confluence of the Maine; at this point the river is only 14 m (46 ft) above sea level, yet it is still 150 km (90 miles) from the sea. A sudden change occurs in the geology of the valley, for the river leaves the Upper Cretaceous area of Touraine and Anjou and crosses obliquely the ancient rocks of the southern part of the Armorican massif, which here forms a subdued peneplain. Between Les Ponts-de-Cé and the Maine confluence the flat-floored valley is trenched into Lower Palaeozoic slates, which are worked near Angers at Trélazé, France's largest quarries. Then the valley widens out across Coal Measure shales between Montrelais and Ancenis, but near Champtoceaux it is again constricted almost to a gorge through a narrow outcrop of Pre-Cambrian schists. From here to Nantes the valley widens out once more across soft shales, thickly covered with marine clays, sands and river alluvium. The floodplain consists of marshlands extending for several km along both sides of the river, seamed with drainage ditches and crossed by embankments. At Nantes, where the Loire is joined by the Erdre from the northeast and the Sèvre from the southeast, the river splits up to enclose several large islands. A long narrow heath-covered ridge of granite, rising to about 90 m (300 ft) and known as the *Sillon de Bretagne,* almost reaches the north bank of the Loire; on its south-facing bluff stands the city of Nantes.

From Nantes the Loire estuary extends for 50 km (30 miles) to the Bay of Biscay. The bed of the estuary as far downstream as Couëron is cut in schistose rocks upon which quantities of alluvium have been deposited; this section of the river is dyked and the shipping channel is constantly dredged. Below Couëron, where the estuary opens out, the branches of the river flow between elongated islands and ever-changing sandbanks, despite dredging and the construction of groynes and training walls. Before the river's final entry into the *Embouchure de la Loire* the valley once more narrows, for a low interrupted granitic ridge, trending almost parallel to the Sillon de Bretagne, forms steep rocky headlands on either side of the river. The town of St Nazaire is built on the granite outcrop on the right bank, while the port has been developed to the east where downfaulted slates afford easier ground for dock excavation.[34]

Both banks of the estuary are bordered with marshlands. On the north side, between the Sillon de Bretagne and the granitic ridge on which stands St. Nazaire, is the Grande Brière,[32] an ancient gulf of the sea partly filled with alluvium and still sometimes inundated in winter. Parts have been drained, but there are still reed-covered wastes, shallow *étangs* and bogs from which peat is cut.[33] The estuary marshes on the south have been dyked and for the most part drained. Further west the marshes between Le Croisic and the mainland are covered with rectangular pans where salt is recovered by evaporation.[3]

A varied agricultural economy is found along the lower Loire valley. The area around Nantes and along the Erdre and Sèvre valleys is important for market-gardening,[35] especially for the production of *petits pois* and haricot beans, to be consumed in Nantes, sent to Paris, or used for preserving. Some dairying on the reclaimed meadowlands supplies Nantes, while on the higher terraces away from the floodplain, particularly on the south- and east-facing slopes of the Sillon de Bretagne, are orchards and vineyards.

Several towns and villages stand along the terraces of the lower Loire, minor centres of agricultural activity, occasionally of quarrying. Between Nantes and Couëron are several small subsidiary ports—La Martinière, Le Pellerin, Indret and Basse-Indre, and near the mouth of the estuary St Nazaire, Donges and Paimboeuf; these serve the Nantes industrial region. At Donges is the refinery of Raffineries françaises de Pétrole de l'Atlantique,[36] with a throughput in 1969 of 3·9 million tons of crude oil, and a small BP refinery. It passes various hydrocarbon byproducts to the Progil-Electrochimie works at Pont-de-Claix. Paimboeuf imports phosphates and pyrites for nearby chemical works, Couëron has the Port-Gibaud nonferrous metallurgical plant (lead, copper and brass), another large chemical factory is served by Basse-Indre, and on the north bank between the last named and Couëron are steel works.

St Nazaire,[37] near the northern entrance to the estuary, was only a fishing village of 3 000 inhabitants a century ago. Its development began in the mid-nineteenth century, when a basin was constructed as an outport to accommodate shipping unable to negotiate the estuary to Nantes. Even though a channel is now carefully maintained for the benefit of Nantes, St Nazaire has continued to flourish. Its basins have increased in number and size and indeed the Bassin de Penhoët, entered by a huge entrance lock, provides one of the largest docks in Europe; this lock served as a dry dock, and was used to accommodate the *Normandie*. The strategic significance of St Nazaire was such that the occupying Germans made considerable use of it, and concrete submarine pens were built. The port suffered severe damage as a result of the raid in April 1942, when the outer gate of the lock to the Penhoët basin was wrecked by the *Campbeltown*, and by heavy Allied air bombardment. Although many installations were ruined, the other quays and locks which the Germans had planned to destroy were saved by the capitulation. Nevertheless, it was four years before the port was restored to full service (Plate 53).

St Nazaire still acts as an outport for Nantes, and oil, mineral ores and other raw materials are landed. Its chief importance is, however, as an industrial centre, especially for shipbuilding; the *Normandie* was built in

473

PLATE 53. The port of St Nazaire

1935 and later the 35 000 ton battleship *Jean Bart*. In 1961, the *France*, the world's longest ship, was completed. Tankers up to 200 000 dwt and bulk-carriers are constructed. Unfortunately, shipbuilding is feeling acutely the competition of Japan, Sweden and West Germany. The steel-works to the northeast of St Nazaire at Trignac have been closed, but a large plant produces a third of France's tinplate. Other activities include ship-repairing, marine engineering, the making of ships' cables, the large plant of Fabrique Air-Liquide which produces liquid oxygen, a chemical factory for processing North African phosphates, a refrigeration plant, breweries and vegetable canneries, and a factory building caravans. L'Aérospatiale has a large plant on the edge of the town. A large chemical plant has recently been built at the nearby town of Montoir. The population of the town, over 40 000 in 1938, fell to less than 10 000 in 1945, but by 1968 it had reached 63 000.

## Nantes

In spite of the rise of St Nazaire and of the other estuary harbours, Nantes is still an important port, and with a population of about 259 000 is the seventh city of France. Its situation on the southern edge of the Sillon de Bretagne has already been mentioned. The Loire flowed below the bluffs through a maze of channels, and successive schemes of reclamation have united several of these islands to the mainland to provide building land; the Erdre is now led through a tunnel into the main river.

Nantes has long been a port at the junction of maritime and fluvial navigation. In the eighteenth century it was the leading French port, its many wealthy merchants trading with India, Madagascar and especially the West Indies. Constant work was necessary to maintain and improve the navigable channel, and the experiment was even tried between 1869 and 1892 of building a Canal Maritime along the left bank between La Martinière and La Gruaudais, but this was little used and was finally abandoned in 1911. Dyking, the construction of training walls and dredging have steadily continued, and ships drawing about 9 m (31 ft) can dock at any time, a substantial improvement since the war. When the German forces evacuated Nantes in August 1944, they deliberately damaged much of the port; most of the bridges were blown up, 150 wrecks lay in the river, and practically all quays were unusable. Within four years, however, the port was in virtually complete working order.

While in 1937 about 2·7 million tons of foreign freight and 0·6 million· tons of coastal freight were handled at Nantes and its subsidiary ports, in 1945 this had sunk to under 200 000 tons. The revival of industry, the restoration of port facilities, and the increase in oil-refining capacity produced a rapid recovery (9·6 million tons in 1969). Crude oil (5·7 million tons), phosphates, wine and pyrites are the main imports, and refined oil-fuels (1·6 million) are the dominant exports. The crude oil supplies not only the Donges refinery and petrochemical plants, but is piped to the Vern refinery at Rennes.

A range of industries is based on imports (sugar-refining, rice-milling, tobacco-processing and oil seed-crushing), and on local market-gardening (the canning of vegetables, the manufacture of tinplate). Consumer industries include the manufacture of furniture and wooden articles, glassware, paper, brushes, carbon-paper and typewriter ribbons. There has been a great development in petrochemicals (notably plastics and synthetic fibres). Nantes has been made the headquarters of the Pays de la Loire planning region, and with St Nazaire has been designated a *métropole d'équilibre* (p. 199).

## La Vendée

The region to the south of the lower Loire, comprising more or less the present *départements* of Vendée and Deux-Sèvres, was formerly known as *Bas-Poitou*.[38] The term Vendée came into use in the eighteenth century, and the individuality of the region was manifest in 1793 when the peasants rose in a counter-Revolutionary rebellion, to be later ruthlessly crushed by

Napoleon. Today the term is used in a geographical sense to include also the *bocage* country of Les Mauges, now in the *département* of Maine-et-Loire but once part of the ancient province of Anjou, which (centred on Angers) straddled the lower Loire valley. Geologically Vendée clearly belongs to Armorica (Fig. 17.1), and its landscape too is similar, for the familiar *bocage* country is much in evidence, although lower altitude and a more southerly position induce features of land use progressively more characteristic of southern France.[39] Maize, for example, begins to appear instead of wheat and oats.

Vendée consists of the dissected and much-faulted remnants of one of the more southerly Armorican anticlines; its 'grain' trends distinctly from northwest to southeast.[40] Four individual units can be distinguished: in the northeast is the country of Les Mauges, in the centre the high upland area, the low-lying Plaine Vendéenne, and the coastal margins which include several tracts of marshland.[41]

## Les Mauges

This area, lying immediately to the south of the Loire valley between the Maine confluence and Nantes, is a plateau of Pre-Cambrian schists. Its general level varies from 45 to 140 m (150 to 450 ft), but it is much dissected by the winding valley of the Evre which flows northwards to the Loire, and by streams joining either the Sèvre-Nantaise on the west or the Layon on the east, both Loire tributaries. One or two gentle eminences stand above the general level, but the highest is only 176 m (575 ft). The Mauges landscape is essentially one of *bocage*.

## The central uplands

The uplands of central Vendée consist of a series of gentle ridges orientated along the usual northwest to southeast trend. This same trend is followed by the main drainage system, the Sèvre-Nantaise, which divides the central uplands into two parallel ridges. The eastern flanks of the uplands are drained by streams which ultimately join the Thouet and so the Loire at Saumur. The higher central ridges consist of rounded masses of granite. The highest points form gentle eminences mantled with gritty or sandy soils; the summits are usually called *puys*, such as the Puy Crapaud (the highest point 295 m (968 ft)) and the Puy Papin. They have a vegetation of ling, gorse, bramble, coarse grass and stunted trees, with many shallow lakes.[42] Occasionally tor-like masses of crags diversify the rather dreary moorlands.

The lower schist country flanks the granite on the west, and on its clay soils has developed a *bocage* landscape very similar to that of Mauges but lower in altitude. An interesting geological feature is the presence of a long narrow inlier of Carboniferous and Jurassic rocks within the schists to the east of La Roche-sur-Yon, orientated along the usual Armorican trend between Les Essarts and St Laurs. These newer rocks form the pleasant *Plaine de Chantonnay*, with many of the *bocage* characteristics, but lower and more sheltered.

## The Plaine Vendéenne

The Pre-Cambrian schistose rocks continue westward towards the coast, though masked in places by patches of Eocene and Miocene sediments and to the south of Challans by an outcrop of Upper Cretaceous clays and limestones. Granitic rocks still appear on the surface as small massifs surrounding the basin in which stands La Roche-sur-Yon, but the highest point is only 78 m (256 ft) and most is below 45 m (150 ft). It is gently undulating country, drained by a multitude of winding streams. In the north, the Boulogne flows into a shallow depression containing three or four small lakes and a large extent of unreclaimed marsh, frequently flooded in winter. To the northwest of this depression the undulating country continues into the broad peninsula between the Loire estuary and the Baie de Bourgneuf, a district known as the *Pays de Retz*. Most of this *Plaine Vendéenne* differs little from the *bocage* to the west and is often known as the *Bas-bocage*; it tends, however, to be under cereals rather than permanent pasture.

## The coastal margins[43]

The ancient schistose rocks extend westward to and beyond the coastline, as shown by the low dark-coloured cliffs flanked by rocky waveworn ledges and platforms;[44] near Les Sables-d'Olonnes a lighthouse is perched on a dark fang of rock about 3 km (2 miles) offshore. Offshore are more fragments of Armorica—the granitic Ile d'Yeu and the schistose cliffs and reefs at the northern end of the Ile de Noirmoutier. Just south of Les Sables the limestone cliffs of the Pte du Payré indicate that the Jurassic border of Armorica, curving around its southern edge, has been reached.

Most of the Armorican margin of Vendée is, however, masked with lines of dunes fronted by sandy beaches through which protrudes an occasional mass of Pre-Cambrian rock. The dunes have been planted with marram grass and conifers, and again in a solid block to the north of Les Sables-d'Olonnes. The low-lying Ile de Noirmoutier consists of sand-dunes and saltmarshes which have accumulated on a mass of Pre-Cambrian rocks, revealed only in the north. A causeway runs across the tidal flats of sandy mud.

On the northern and southern flanks of the *Plaine Vendéenne* lie two large tracts of marsh, the *Marais Breton* or *Marais de Bourgneuf* and the *Marais Poitevin* (Fig. 13.5). Smaller areas of marsh lie between the dunes and the edge of the *bocage* country. The marshes are the result of the infilling of shallow embayments in the edge of the massif with both fluvial and marine sediments.

Frequent attempts have been made to reclaim these areas,[45] the earliest probably in the twelfth century. The Marais Breton is separated from the Baie de Bourgneuf by a dyke, behind which close patterns of canals cover the surface, and the drainage systems are regulated by syndicates, some of them established for well over a century. About three-quarters of the reclaimed area is under pasture, the remainder forms arable land. From the general level of the marshland rise former small islets, now the sites of settlements.

Many rivers debouch on to the Marais Poitevin, principally the Sèvre-Niortaise, the Vendée and the Yon, and drainage was accordingly very difficult. An elaborate system of canals has been gradually constructed; the Canal de Luçon, draining the western marshes, was cut as early as the beginning of the twelfth century and subsequently several times enlarged. Later the rivers were dyked and regularised, and the Marans Canal was constructed from the Sèvre to an outlet much further south at La Rochelle. The drainage pattern thus evolved is of several main radial canals leading to the sea, fed by concentric canals draining a series of polders.[46] As a result, almost two-thirds of the total area of 650 sq km (250 sq miles) is now drained, mostly under arable cultivation, the remainder consisting of improved pasture.

## Land use

It is useful to summarise the main land use categories of the three *départements* that comprise broadly the region of La Vendée.

*Land use, 1968 (percentage of total area)*

|  | ARABLE | PERMANENT PASTURE | WOODLAND |
|---|---|---|---|
| Vendée | 46 | 33 | 8 |
| Deux-Sèvres | 53 | 31 | 7 |
| Maine-et-Loire | 38 | 36 | 12 |

Source: Ministère de l'Agriculture, *Annuaire statistique de la France,* 1970–1.

La Vendée resembles the rest of Armorica in the small extent of its woodlands. Oak woods grow in the valleys and in the basins of the *bocage,* and poplars and willows flourish along the rivers, around depressions, and in the coastal marshlands. Coniferous plantations have been established on some of the granite moorlands and along the belt of coastal sand-dunes.

The fields are bordered with a ditch (essential in the lower *bocage* for drainage), a bank made of the earth excavated from the ditch, and a close hedge of oak and ash, sometimes pollarded, sometimes including trees of considerable size.

Mixed farming is practised all over La Vendée, but with differing local emphasis. Large proprietors own massive châteaulike buildings and magnificent estates, with some of the land often rented out as smaller holdings. Some farmers have units of 10 to 20 ha (25 to 50 acres), and there are many *petits propriétaires*, notably the market-gardeners on the reclaimed marshlands. In the lower *bocage* the emphasis is on cereals, particularly wheat; about 11 per cent of the area of each of the three *départements* is under wheat, though in the higher parts rye (grown with intervening years of fallow) is common. About 22 per cent is under fodder crops, notably clover, turnips and kale. La Vendée is an important livestock area; in 1968 there were about 1·5 million cattle, about 455 000 pigs, and even 328 000 sheep kept both on the moorland pastures and on the salt-grazings. Some dairying is practised but the emphasis is on meat production; fat cattle appear in the local markets and are then sent to the Paris abattoirs. Fruit is widely grown, including the vine in the valleys of Mauges and of the Sèvre-Nantaise.

La Vendée, with the exception of the moorland country of the Gâtine, presents a cheerfully pleasant and prosperous appearance, rather milder and softer than Brittany but with its same rural character. There are many individual farms and isolated hamlets, together with larger market towns at conveniently central points, such as Niort (the *chef-lieu* of Deux-Sèvres) and Cholet. Nantes, Angers and La Rochelle tend to act respectively as regional foci for the northwestern, northeastern and southwestern parts of Vendée. Angers[47] has food-processing industries, the manufacture of electric cable and television sets, and computer assembly activities. La Roche-sur-Yon is the *chef-lieu* of the *département* of Vendée, an almost artificial administrative centre created by Napoleon I and actually known as Napoléon-Vendée in its early days. Some of the towns have servicing industries, particularly for agricultural implements, processing industries for agricultural products, and some small rather specialised textile manufactures of cotton and linen, a legacy of a once quite considerable rural industry. Several new factories have been built in Les Mauges since the war; at St Pierre-Montlimart in the Evre valley, for example, the Cie des Lampes has opened a factory for making electronic tubes. Another small town with rapid industrial growth in recent years is Cholet; it is the centre of a number of factory estates, making footwear, textiles, machine tools and vehicle components.

The marshes and sand-dunes along the coast do not encourage much settlement, providing another contrast with Brittany. A few small towns are situated on 'islands' in the marshes as centres of market-gardening. Some little fishing harbours and rapidly developing resorts are tucked in behind the dunes, such as St Gilles-sur-Vie and Les Sables-d'Olonnes, centres of tunny- and sardine-fishing, and with fish-canning factories.

[1] See R. Musset, *La Bretagne* (1937); M. Gautier, *La Bretagne centrale* (1947); M. le Lannou, *Géographie de la Bretagne* (1952); W. Diville and A. Guilcher, *Bretagne et Normandie* (1951); P. Flatrès, *La Région de l'Ouest* (1964); and H. Elhaï, *La Normandie occidentale* (1963), 624 pp., with many maps and an extensive bibliography.

[2] P. Morin, 'Le golfe Normand-Breton', *Annls Géogr.*, **40** (1931), pp. 1–23.

[3] See, for example, a map, section and much other detail in A. Guilcher, 'Observations sur la formation du relief de la Bretagne méridionale', *Annls Géogr.*, **50** (1941), pp. 255–65. See also maps showing the faults bounding the Bassin de Rennes and those in north-eastern Brittany in A. Meynier, 'Influences tectoniques sur le relief de la Bretagne', *Annls Géogr.*, **56** (1947), pp. 170–7.

[4] The classic study is E. de Martonne, 'La pénéplaine et les côtes bretonnes', *Annls Géogr.*, **15** (1906), pp. 213–36 and 299–328. See also the detailed articles by R. Musset, 'Le Relief de la Bretagne occidentale', *ibid.*, **36** (1928), pp. 209–23; and A. Darté, 'Les abrupts asymétriques du Massif armoricain', *Norois*, **50** (1966), pp. 157–63.

[5] Some of the complexities are discussed by R. Musset, 'La formation du réseau hydrographique de la Bretagne occidentale', *Annls Géogr.*, **43** (1934), pp. 561–78.

[6] See R. Musset's study of the valley of the Loc'h and its 'fossil ria', 'Les rias fossiles de la côte occidentale de la Bretagne', *Annls Géogr.*, **35** (1926), pp. 360–2.

[7] R. Musset, 'La Bretagne péninsulaire', *La France: géographie-tourisme* (1952), ii, p. 141.

[8] A. Guilcher, 'Formes de décomposition chimique dans la zone des embruns et des marées sur les côtes britanniques et bretonnes', in *Cinquantième Anniversaire du Laboratoire de Géographie, 1902–52, volume jubilaire* of the Université de Rennes (1952), pp. 167–81, with a useful bibliography.

[9] Figures obtained from J. Rouch, *Météorologie aéronautique* (1933), and the Admiralty *Channel Pilot*.

[10] It seems, however, that the limit is in part an economic one, for the vine was grown quite widely in Brittany throughout the Middle Ages and up to 150 years ago. When communications improved so that better wines could be easily brought into Brittany, and with the spread of cider-drinking, these marginal lands ceased to grow the vine.

[11] A. Bouhier, 'Les communaux de la partie orientale du Marais Poitevin', *Norois*, **49** (1966), pp. 5–58.

[12] A. Meynier, 'La modernisation de l'agriculture bretonne', *Tijdschr. econ. soc. Geogr.*, **48** (1957), pp. 37–42.

[13] A discussion of Brittany's engrained problems is by M. Phlipponeau, *Le Problème breton et le programme d'action régionale* (1960).

[14] Y. Poupinot, 'Bretagne Nord et Bretagne Sud', Université de Rennes, *volume jubilaire* (*op. cit.*) (1952), pp. 350–7.

[15] J. Stéphant, 'Dinan: étude de géographie urbaine', *Chronique géographique des pays Celtes* (1948), (no vol. numb.), pp. 17–24.

[16] M. Simon, 'Les Fonctions industrielles de St Brieuc', *Norois*, **48** (1965), pp. 449–58.

[17] A. Meynier, 'Villes de Bretagne', *Annls Géogr.*, **55** (1946), pp. 178–87.

[18] Mme (sic) Aubry, 'Le Port de Roscoff', *Norois*, **16** (1969), pp. 520–35, discusses the evolution of the port at various stages in its history, especially the present trade based on the export of cauliflowers and other vegetables to the United Kingdom.

[19] J. Givier, 'Le Tourisme finistérien', *Norois*, **18** (1971), pp. 573–60.

[20] I. E. Jones, 'The Rance tidal power station', *Geography*, **53** (1968), pp. 412–15.

[21] M. Gautier, 'L'evolution récente des principaux ports de pêche bretons', *Norois*, **13** (1966), pp. 59–71. This discusses the individual ports, the introduction of deep-freezing methods, the opening of a new fishing port at St Malo in 1965, and the organisation of co-operative marketing at Concarneau; it has a full bibliography.

²² C. Robert-Muller, 'La pêche et la conserve du thon dans la Bretagne de l'Atlantique', *Annls Géogr.*, **45** (1936), pp. 375–98; see also *Pêches et pêcheurs de la Bretagne Atlantique*, by the same author (1944).

²³ C. Robert-Muller, 'Le nouveau port de pêche de Lorient', *Annls Géogr.*, **36** (1927), pp. 193–212; see also M. Gautier, 'L'évolution récente des principaux ports de pêche bretons', *Norois*, **49** (1966), pp. 59–71.

²⁴ L. Chaumeil, 'Sur l'emplacement de Brest et de Lorient', Université de Rennes, *volume jubilaire op. cit.* (1952), pp. 358–64.

²⁵ M. Gautier, *La Bretagne centrale, étude géographique* (1947).

²⁶ G. Mareschaux, 'Les Crêtes de la Montagne Noire centrale (Massif Armoricain)', *Norois*, **14** (1967), pp. 6–20; this stresses the tectonic (rather than erosional) origin of the Montagne Noire, as a set of blocks tilted to the south.

²⁷ A. Meynier, 'Influences tectoniques sur le relief de la Bretagne', *Annls Géogr.*, **56** (1947), pp. 170–7, examines some of the geomorphological complications inherent in the formation of the Rennes basin.

²⁸ A. Meynier and Chr. Loscun, 'Rennes', *Annls Géogr.*, **65** (1956), pp. 259–69, is an account of 'les fonctions urbaines' of 'la capitale de la Bretagne'. See also *Les Grandes Villes françaises, Rennes, Notes et Etudes Documentaires, La Documentation Française* (1966), no. 3257.

²⁹ H. Granier, 'La Zone industrielle de la route de Lorient, à Rennes', *Norois*, **17** (1970), pp. 199–215, discusses the establishment of an industrial zone on the western side of the town, which was started in 1954; however, it has attracted few factories, but consists mainly of warehouses and commercial depots for wholesalers.

³⁰ F. Joly, 'Le littoral du Cotentin', *Annls Géogr.*, **48** (1939), pp. 225–34.

³¹ A.-M. Seronde, 'L'agglomération Cherbourgeoise', *Norois*, **50** (1967), pp. 158–66.

³² A.-M. Charaud, 'L'habitat et la structure agraire de la Grande Brière et des Marais de Donges', *Annls Géogr.*, **57** (1948), pp. 119–30.

³³ Ph. Decraene and P. Moreau, 'L'exploitation de la tourbe en Grande Brière', *Géographia*, **40** (1955), pp. 23–7.

³⁴ A very detailed study of the salt industry of western France from Morbihan to the Gironde, with detailed maps of pans, etc., is afforded by W. Gehlhoff, 'Die Salzgartenlandschaften an der französischen Atlantikküste', *Petermanns geographische Mitteilungen*, **92** (1948), pp. 134–54.

³⁵ M. Oliviero, 'Les cultures maraîchères de la banlieue nantaise', *Chronique géographique des Pays Celtes* (1952), (no vol. numb.), pp. 272–83, which includes a detailed map.

³⁶ A.-M. Pavard-Charaud, 'Le Développement de Donges, centre pétrolier de la Basse-Loire', *Annls Géogr.*, **52** (1953), pp. 259–70, affords a full account of the development of the *Raffineries françaises de Pétrole de l'Atlantique*, established in 1948 by the merging of two firms. The name of the company has recently been changed to *Antar P.A.*

³⁷ A very detailed account is provided by M. Barbance, *Saint-Nazaire* (1948).

³⁸ M. Gautier, *La Vendée (Bas-Poitou): esquisse géographique* (1949).

³⁹ A.-M. Charaud, 'Bocage et plaine dans l'ouest de la France', *Annls Géogr.*, **58** (1949), pp. 113–25, analyses the agrarian structure at the meeting-place of *plaine* and *bocage* in the *départements* of Loire-Inférieure and Vendée.

⁴⁰ See a detailed map of folds and faults within the Vendéan massif, and a list of named anticlines, synclines and faultlines, in R. Facon, 'La formation de la Sèvre Niortaise', Université de Rennes, *(op. cit.)* (1952), pp. 365–71.

⁴¹ J.-M. Bourdeau, 'La Morphologie de la bordure atlantique du Massif Vendéen', *Annls Géogr.*, **40** (1941), pp. 81–93. See also M. Ters, 'Permanence et ancienneté des grandes lignes du reseau hydrographique et du relief en Vendée côtière occidentale', *Annls Géogr.*, **67** (1958), pp. 1–11.

⁴² R. Bobin, *La Gâtine, étude de géographie* (1925).

⁴³ A detailed geomorphological study is provided by M. Ters, *La Vendée littorale* (1961), of 578 pp., with numerous maps and plates.

[44] M. Gautier, 'Etude morphologique de la côte rocheuse du Pays de Retz', Université de Rennes, (*op. cit.*) (1952), pp. 147–66.

[45] *Aménagements des eaux des marais de l'Ouest*, published by the Ligue Générale pour l'Aménagement et l'Utilisation des Eaux (Comité régional des Charentes et du Poitou) (1928–29). F. Verger, *Le Marais de monts* (1946), deals with the marshland along the Vendéean coast, its physical features, reclamation, agricultural patterns, fishing and oyster cultivation.

[46] J. Huguet, 'Un polder du marais poitevin', *Norois*, **2** (1955), pp. 19–39.

[47] J. and E. Soppelsa, 'L'évolution récente d'Angers', *Annls Géogr.*, **80** (1971), pp. 554–75.

# 18
# The Ardennes and the Sambre-Meuse valley

The term Ardennes is applied to the western part of a group of uplands lying across the basin of the Rhine, known as the Middle Rhine Highlands or the *Schiefergebirge*. The Ardennes[1] are situated for the most part in southeastern Belgium, although a small tract extends into France as far west as Hirson, and they also comprise the northern third of the Grand Duchy of Luxembourg. The upland areas continue eastward into West Germany as the Eifel, in the angle between the Moselle and the Rhine below Koblenz.

## Structural evolution

The 'core' of the Ardennes consists of Lower Palaeozoic rocks, mainly Cambrian and Silurian slates and quartzites. These outcrop in the higher northeastern parts (the Stavelot massif), again over a very small area in the centre near Serpont, and in the southwest, extending into France as the Rocroi massif. These basement rocks are exposed further north in the deeply cut valleys of the plateaus of central Belgium (see p. 160). Otherwise the greater part of the surface of the Ardennes consists of varied Devonian rocks (Fig. 18.1); the lower series are mainly sandstones and quartzites, the upper limestones and shales. The Carboniferous rocks have been denuded from the higher parts and now survive only in the northern Ardennes near Dinant and in the major structural 'furrow' extending from Mons to Liège, where in addition to Lower Carboniferous rocks the Coal Measures of Upper Carboniferous age are preserved in discontinuous basins. These two areas of Carboniferous rocks are separated by a narrow outcrop of Silurian and Devonian rocks which form a plateau lying at 200 to 340 m (650 to 1 100 ft) above sea level, diversified by low parallel ridges, dominating the Famenne depression.

The Ardennes owe their structural features to the Hercynian orogeny of late Carboniferous-Permian times. This folding was extremely complex, but certain major trendlines (Fig. 18.2) can be traced; the Meuse valley, trenched across the 'grain' of the country, is most helpful in determining the location of these structures.

483

In the south ancient rocks of the Ardennes rise prominently from beneath the Jurassic rocks of the Lorraine scarplands, a prominence emphasised by the valleys of the Sûre-Attert in Luxembourg and of the upper Semois in Belgium which lie along the margins of the upland. The most southerly structural feature is an upfold known as the anticline of Givonne in southern Belgium. This anticline is succeeded to the north by the two major thrust faults of the Faille d'Aiglemont in France and the Faille de Herbeumont extending across Belgium into the Grand Duchy. Then again to the north appears a much contorted synclinorium, known in Belgium as the Neufchâteau, in Luxembourg as the Wiltz or sometimes as the Eifel synclinorium.

The main Ardennes anticlinorium lies next to the north, forming a series

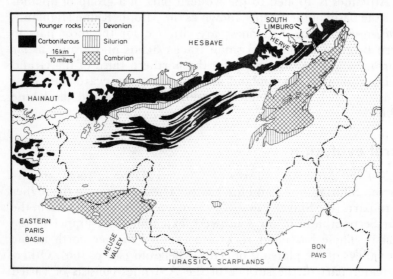

Fig. 18.1. Simplified geological map of the Ardennes

Based on *Atlas de Belgique*, sheet 8.

of broadly parallel major folds; its core, consisting of masses of overthrust Cambrian and Silurian rocks, has been exposed in the Stavelot, Serpont and Rocroi massifs already mentioned, because of the greater denudation of these more sharply folded and prominently uplifted areas. Part of its southern flank runs eastward across northern Luxembourg as the Bastogne anticline.

An interruption to the outcrop of Cambrian-Silurian rocks in the north of the Stavelot massif is provided by the so-called *Fenêtre de Theux*, to the south of Verviers. It is a small massif, consisting mainly of Devonian rocks, outlined by perimeter faults, the *Failles de Theux*. It is possibly a piece of a nappe revealed through the removal of the overthrust Cambrian-Silurian rocks by denudation, hence the term *fenêtre*. It is associated with past volcanic activity, and some rhyolites and kindred rocks occur in the neighbourhood of Spa; the famous mineral springs are another symptom.

To the north of the Ardennes anticlinorium is the broad synclinorium of Dinant, comprising at least a dozen minor synclines and anticlines, and involving Middle and Upper Devonian, Lower Carboniferous and some Coal Measures strata. This Dinant synclinorium narrows in the east to form the Massif de la Vesdre, lying between the Cretaceous plateau of the Pays de Herve and the *Fenêtre de Theux*. From the western end of this

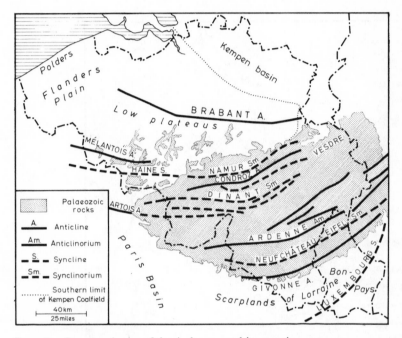

Fig. 18.2. Structural map of the Ardennes and its margins

Based on (*a*) J. Halkin, *Atlas classique* (1934), plate 16; and (*b*) *Atlas de Belgique*, sheet 10.

synclinorium, near Hirson, emerges the anticline of Artois, trending west-northwest to the English Channel.

Next to the north succeeds the narrow but intensely contorted Condroz anticline.[2] This is represented by a narrow outcrop of Silurian rocks (Fig. 18.1), flanked on the north by Middle Devonian and on the south by Lower Devonian, both, however, resting on the same basement strata of Cambrian and Silurian. The folding has been so severe that thrust faults have developed, the best defined of which is the *Grande Faille du Midi* on the southern side of the anticline, with others, notably the *Faille de la Tombe*, on the north. As a result, the Devonian and Carboniferous rocks have been thrust northwards, partly over the Namur synclinorium. The Coal Measures are preserved in this complex downfold as a narrow

485

'furrow', now followed by the lower Sambre and the Meuse. The synclinorium of Namur is continued westward under a cover of Chalk and newer rocks as the Haine syncline into northern France; here is the 'concealed coalfield' of the Mons, Valenciennes and Douai basins. The Coal Measures are exposed to the east in the Namur synclinorium from west of Charleroi. The complexity and intensity of the folding and associated faulting have caused difficult mining conditions; in extreme cases Devonian, Carboniferous Limestone and Lower Coal Measure strata have been thrust over the younger coal-bearing Upper Coal Measures, and as a result deep shafts

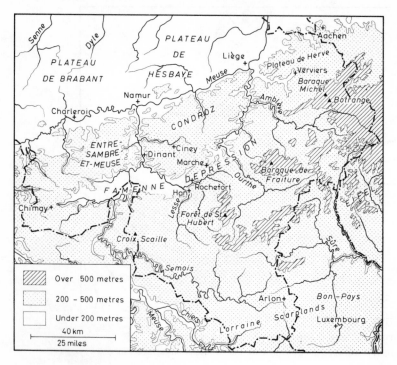

FIG. 18.3. General map of the Ardennes
Based on *Atlas de Belgique*, sheet 6.

are sunk through the older rocks to reach the underlying coal. This 'coal furrow', then, may be regarded as the northern edge of the Ardennes.

The next phase was one of prolonged denudation, lasting until the Cretaceous period, that is, for approximately a hundred million years; during this long span the Hercynian mountain ranges were gradually worn down to a peneplaned surface. In the Cretaceous came the extensive marine transgression of the Chalk Sea, partly caused by the *en bloc* sinking of this worndown upland; indeed, some geomorphologists claim that marine erosion contributed appreciably to its final planation. In this sea, which covered so much of western and central Europe, was deposited the

Chalk, and later still during further transgressions rocks of Tertiary age.

The third major phase was renewed uplift and resultant denudation of the peneplain, during which the newer rocks were almost completely removed, although a few small patches of Triassic and Cretaceous rocks survive, especially on the high eastern uplands. In some places residual Clay-with-flints rests on the Devonian rocks, testifying to the now vanished Chalk cover. This sequence of uplift and denudation was by no means continuous throughout the Tertiary. During the Oligocene period a renewed marine transgression left its deposits in the Ardennes in the form of marine sandy clays lying both on Cretaceous and Palaeozoic rocks, showing that denudation was well advanced before this renewed transgression. These Oligocene deposits are found in several localities in the west, and again in the northeast, at heights exceeding 550 m (1 800 ft). Further uplift followed, probably associated with the mid-Tertiary Alpine folding to the south, and so denudation again became active. Finally, late Tertiary uplift and tilting produced the long northward slope towards the North Sea Basin (see p. 162).

The net result of these alternations of uplift and denudation is an upland area, standing prominently above the surrounding lowlands. The Palaeozoic rocks and the ancient structures have been resurrected and their 'grain' revealed. Along the axis of the Ardennes anticlinorium, where the original elevation and resultant denudation had been most pronounced, the Cambrian-Silurian rocks are exposed as gently rounded summits exceeding 600 m (2 000 ft) in altitude; these High Ardennes proper are the 'roots' of the Hercynian fold ranges.

The effects of the various periods of denudation and uplift are shown by distinct continuous surfaces at several heights; such surfaces can be distinguished both to the south and to the north of the High Ardennes, at about 550, 450 and 400 m (1 800, 1 500 and 1 300 ft), and another at 300 m (1 000 ft) on the northern side only. These surfaces are worn mainly from the Devonian formations.[3]

## The rivers

Many of the present features of the Ardennes landscape are the work of rivers, which usually rise in swampy depressions on the plateau surface, and then flow rapidly outwards over the impermeable rocks, becoming increasingly incised within narrow and sinuous valleys. This tendency has been emphasised by phases of rejuvenation associated with the successive uplifts. For the most part the river valleys are entrenched across the different rock formations with little regard to their boundaries, the results of the superimposition of the drainage. In detail, however, the valleys show minor features which are the result of differential denudation, particularly in the Condroz, where compact sandstones alternate with less resistant shales and limestones.

PLATE 54. The Meuse at Monthermé, with the steep valley-sides rising to the Ardennes plateau

The High Ardennes form a major watershed between streams draining west and north to the Meuse, and those flowing east and south to the Moselle (Fig. 18.3). This watershed is, however, very indeterminate; thus only a gently swelling ridge at about 600 m (2 000 ft) separates the neighbouring headwaters of the Ourthe Occidentale (a Meuse tributary) from those of the Sûre and the Wiltz flowing eastwards across Luxembourg.

## The Meuse system [4]

After crossing the Liassic clay vale in the scarplands of the eastern Paris Basin, the Meuse continues northwards across the Ardennes into Belgium and so to its junction with the Sambre at Namur (Plate 55). This course is transverse to the general trend of the structure, superimposed on the pre-existing cover of Cretaceous and Tertiary rocks now almost wholly removed. The valley forms three distinct sections. In the south, from below Mézières to Givet, the river flows over Cambrian and Lower Devonian rocks in a tortuous gorge, 90 to 150 m (300 to 500 ft) below the surface of the High Ardennes plateau. Then from Givet to just above Dinant it crosses the more low-lying Famenne of Upper Devonian rocks, receiving tributaries from both west and east along this depression. From Dinant to Namur the Meuse once more cuts transversely across the plateau, and the valley is in places spectacular, particularly where the river cuts across bands of compact limestone, forming gorge sections which alternate with

488

more open valleys. The river meanders considerably, forming acute loops whose necks have been sometimes cut through by the river, leaving isolated meander-cores, as at Profondeville, about 13 km (8 miles) south of Namur, and again at Anhée, just north of Dinant (Plate 54).

At Namur the Meuse undergoes a marked change of direction as it enters the west-southwest to east-northeast line of the 'coalfield furrow' flanking the edge of the Ardennes. The river, in fact, follows the trend of its main tributary, the Sambre, coming in from the west (Plate 55). This direction, at right angles to the consequent drainage lines originally established, must have been initiated after the cover of younger rocks had been removed, thus revealing the structural line of the Namur synclinorium, now followed by the lower Sambre and the Meuse. Probably a left-bank tributary of a northward-flowing consequent river (represented now by the line of the Ourthe and the Meuse below Liège) cut back and captured the Meuse at Namur. Erosion would then be rapid in the Coal Measure shales in the floor of the furrow, particularly as this is confined on the north by the Cambrian and Silurian rocks of the Brabant massif.

The Meuse thus continues eastwards to Liège through a broad open valley, though with a distinct steep edge to the north. It receives numerous tributaries, in contrast to its isolation in the Lorraine scarplands (see p. 248). The southern Ardennes are drained by the Semois, which rises near Arlon and flows at first over the Jurassic rocks, but near Florenville like the main stream it crosses on to the Devonian and incises an even more striking succession of meanders. The Semois picks up most of the southwards-flowing drainage from the High Ardennes. The other Meuse tributaries—the Lesse, the Ourthe and the Amblève—developed their courses transversely across the Palaeozoic rocks in which they too are now deeply incised. The middle sections of both the Lesse and Ourthe systems have, however, developed longitudinally in Upper Devonian shales, and the two headstreams of the Ourthe, in fact, are wholly longitudinal rivers (Fig. 18.3), converging near Houffalize from the southwest and the northeast respectively. In the Condroz plateau further adaptation to structure is revealed by the many minor tributaries, which have eroded shallow valleys in the less resistant limestones and shales, leaving between them rounded ridges of more resistant sandstone. The limestone areas, both the more extensive Devonian and the Carboniferous, reveal underground drainage features (see p. 498).

## Meuse navigation

After the Meuse enters Belgium, despite some difficult sections through the Ardennes it is navigable for a distance of about 190 km (116 miles) to Lanaye, near the Dutch frontier south of Maastricht. The river in this section has a variable régime, much more so than the upper French portion, as a result of receiving numerous torrential Ardennes tributaries.

Below Namur, in fact, the flow may vary from 35 cu m per second at low water to as much as 3 000 cu m per second at flood. Since about 1852 the Government has carried out regularisation schemes, and has constructed locks, sluices and stabilising barrages (Fig. 18.4) in an effort to maintain an adequate navigational depth; this, however, still fluctuates from 2 to 3 m (7 to 10 ft). A master barrage has been completed at Neuville-sous-Huy, 14 km (9 miles) above Yvoz-Ramet, which has replaced the three barrages at Amay, Ampsin and Huy (numbers 17, 16 and 15 on the Meuse).

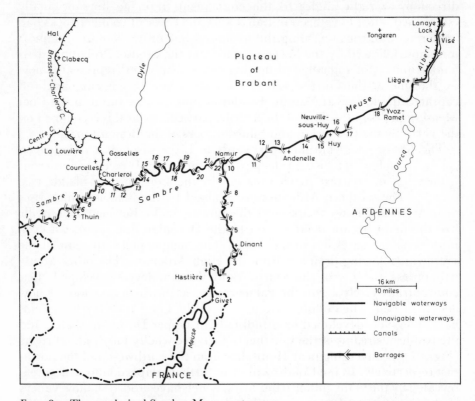

FIG. 18.4. The regularised Sambre-Meuse waterways

Based on information received from the *Institut National de Statistique de Belgique*. The figures indicate the official numbering of the barrages.

The effective limit of downstream navigation is the Monsin barrage just below Liège, completed in 1930 near where the Albert Canal branches off. The regularised river is navigable for barges of up to 2 000 tons between Liège and Huy, and for barges of up to 1 350 tons between Huy and Namur, while the section from Namur to the French frontier can now also accommodate barges of 1 350 tons.

The Meuse is joined at Namur by the Sambre, which affords 93 km (58 miles) of navigable waterway in Belgium and another 55 km (34 miles)

490

in France as far upstream as Landrecies (Fig. 9.5). A navigational depth of 2 m (7 ft) is maintained on the river by means of thirty-one locks, of which twenty-two are in Belgium. Work is in progress to improve still further the section of the river between Namur and Charleroi.

Some indication of the navigational importance of the two rivers within Belgium is provided by the following figures:

*Million tons (1969)*

|  | MEUSE | SAMBRE |
| --- | --- | --- |
| Tonnage carried | 19·04 | 5·60 |
| Loadings at river ports | 6·11 | 2·03 |
| Unloadings at river ports | 7·21 | 1·99 |

Source: *Annuaire statistique de Belgique*, 1970.

Loadings on the Meuse in 1969 included 4·4 million tons of building stone from Ardennes quarries and 1·1 million tons of metallurgical products, while unloadings included 2·60 million tons of coal and 1·60 million tons of building materials. On the Sambre, too, 0·81 million tons of steel, etc. were loaded. Thus the rivers contribute notably to the industrial life of the Charleroi-Namur-Liège industrial region.

## The Moselle drainage

The drainage of the eastern Ardennes finds its way ultimately to the Moselle and so to the Rhine. There is a remarkable convergence of drainage waters towards the southeastern angle of Luxembourg. The river Our rises in the High Ardennes near Monderfeld and then wanders southwards, forming for much of its length the Luxembourg-West German frontier, to its confluence with the Sûre. The Clervaux from the north, and the Wiltz and the Sûre from the High Ardennes to the west, converge across the Luxembourg Ardennes, their combined waters reaching a well-marked west–east depression along the southern margin of the uplands, and then flowing in a general easterly direction to join the Moselle near Wasserbillig. The gradients of these rivers are steep and their upper courses are torrential; the Sûre, for example, rises at an altitude of 550 m (1 801 ft) to the southwest of Bastogne and leaves the Ardennes near Ettelbruck at 200 m (640 ft), a fall of nearly 350 m (1 200 ft) in only about 65 km (40 miles). Still more strikingly, the Blees, a tributary of the Sûre, descends from its source at 500 to 180 m (1 640 to 600 ft) in little more than 20 km (12 miles). These eastern Ardennes rivers are deeply incised, flowing several hundred metres below the plateau surface in deep winding valleys, hemmed in by steep forested slopes or by rock cliffs. Prominent spurs are sometimes only a few hundred metres across at their necks, round which the river swings in a tight loop.

In 1964 the canalisation of the Moselle, to take 1 500 ton barges, was completed by means of fourteen locked barrages, of which three are on the Luxembourg section of the river. A modern riverport and a hydrostation have been constructed at Grevenmacher. [5]

The Ardennes may be divided into a number of subregions (Fig. 18.5), which will be described in turn.

## The High Ardennes

The upland of the High Ardennes is more or less defined by the 300 m (1 000 ft) contour both on the north and south. In the northeast the plateau continues over the West German frontier as the Eifel, while in the southeast the general level falls gradually to the Luxembourg Ardennes. Almost the whole of the High Ardennes consists of Devonian rocks, except where the Cambrian and Silurian rocks outcrop. The main summits are marked on Fig. 18.3; the highest point is actually the Botrange at 694 m (2 277 ft), but it is of no great prominence. The broad line of highest

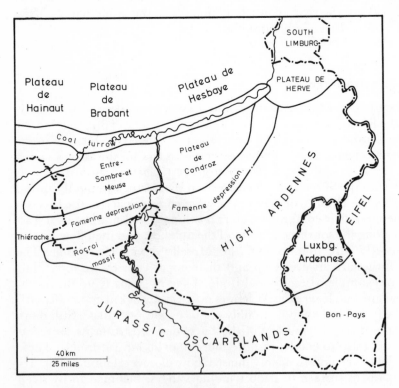

Fig. 18.5. The regions of the Ardennes and its margins

elevation trends southwestward, interrupted by the valleys of the Amblève, Ourthe and Lesse, and gradually diminishing in altitude. Thus the highest point of the Plateau des Tailles (between the Amblève and the Ourthe) is the Baraque de Fraiture 652 m (2 140 ft). Most of these plateau areas form rounded summits separated by shallow depressions, often containing peat bogs or wet moorland, notably the Plateau des Hautes-Fagnes in the northeast which is continued into West Germany as the Hohe Venn. The drier eminences are often heath-covered, but there is also much woodland (Fig. 18.6) covering about half of the total area, and occurring both in the deeply cut valleys and also on the plateau surface. The southern portion along the French frontier is heavily wooded; from the Meuse valley the dark forest-wall can be seen in the distance. In the valleys are some attractive oak-birch and beech forests, but the plateau surface also bears plantations of spruce and Scots pine. The Belgian province of Luxembourg, in which much of the High Ardennes lies, contains almost exactly a third of the total wooded area in the country. Some of the best-maintained forests are in the Eupen-Malmédy districts, acquired from Germany in 1919.

Physical conditions are somewhat adverse for agriculture. The thin, acid soils developed on the slates, quartzites and sandstones are for the most part infertile, and waterlogging is common on the plateau surface, especially in the depressions. Precipitation is heavy: Baraque Michel has a mean annual precipitation of 1 210 mm (47·7 in), and Chiny, in the Semois

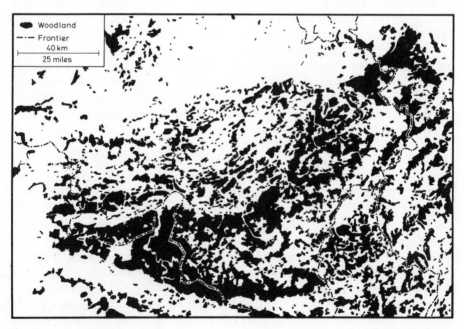

Fig. 18.6. The Ardennes forests

Based on *Atlas de Belgique*, sheet 29.

valley to the southwest (officially the wettest place in Belgium), has 1 260 mm (49·6 in). Some of this precipitation is in the form of snow, which lies above 600 m (2 000 ft) during an average year for over fifty days, and at an altitude of about 300 m (1 000 ft) for about thirty days. The final German offensive in the Ardennes in January 1945 drove westwards over snow-covered country. Low cloud, frequent hill fogs, and a frost occurrence on an average of about 120 days all combine to make the Ardennes uplands distinctly bleak.

At the last official agricultural census only 2 per cent of the arable land of Belgium was recorded within the *région agricole* of the *Haute-Ardenne*. Within this region 89 per cent of the small area classified as farmland was under permanent grassland. Beef cattle are bred on the uplands to be sent to lowland areas for fattening and some dairy-farming is practised, mainly for butter and cheese making as a result of the limited market for liquid milk in the scantily populated district. Arable farming, mainly the culti-vation of oats, rye, trefoil and potatoes, is carried on in the valleys and basins, particularly in the lower southwestern parts. The area around Bastogne, though at an altitude of nearly 500 m (1 600 ft), has more arable land than any other part of the Ardennes, for it lies to the east of the massif and has a lower rainfall and a southeastern aspect. The deeply cut, sheltered Semois valley in the south has a specialised production of tobacco, the chief cash crop of the farmers. Smallholdings devoted to it are found on little alluvial flats below the steep sides of the valley between Bouillon and Bohan, each with its drying shed. The crop is grown intensively year after year on the same land with heavy fertilising.

The density of population is well below 40 per sq km (100 per sq mile) and much is quite unpopulated. A few small towns stand on the plateau, mainly along the railway lines which cross it—Butgenbach and Bullange in the extreme northeast, St Vith, Bovigny, Bastogne and Libramont. St Vith was almost completely destroyed during the Ardennes offensive of 1945 and has been attractively rebuilt.

Several railway lines negotiate this barrier between central Belgium and the Rhineland; one important international line (Brussels-Namur-Arlon-Luxembourg) crosses the watershed at Libramont at a height of 490 m (1 608 ft). Bastogne is particularly important as a route centre, lying in the upper valley of the Wiltz, for seven roads converge on it; it was as a result the focal point of the German offensive in 1944–45. These small towns are minor market centres for the higher plateau areas. Some are tourist centres capitalising the attractive wooded valleys and pleasant walking country. The most famous resort is Spa, once called 'the café of Europe'; situated on the northern edge of the Hautes-Fagnes, at a height of 250 to 300 m (800 to 1 000 ft) in a wooded valley, its mineral springs have made it a health resort since the sixteenth century, and in the eighteenth it was at the height of European fashion.

Industry is of no great importance in the High Ardennes. Some woollen

494

factories survive in the villages on the northern side of the Hautes-Fagnes within the orbit of Verviers. The leather industry is carried on in valley towns such as Malmédy and Stavelot, using tan bark from the local oak forests and the hides of cattle bred in the uplands. This industry has been long established in the Ardennes, indeed Roman tanning pits have been identified. Quarrying, particularly of quartzite for road metal, is widespread; about fifty quarries are in operation, four in the neighbourhood of Bastogne.

The High Ardennes then consists of bleak monotonous uplands, covered with heath, peat bog or pine forest, with scanty agriculture, small isolated market towns, and the lowest density of population of any part of Belgium.

## The Rocroi upland

A small part of the High Ardennes plateau extends west of the Meuse valley between Mézières and Givet, forming the triangular massif of Rocroi (Fig. 18.7), with its apex projecting towards Hirson. The core of this massif consists of Cambrian rocks along the axis of the Ardennes anticlinorium, while the northern part is composed of Lower Devonian rocks. A few surviving patches of newer rocks rest on the Palaeozoic base—some Eocene sands near Signy-le-Petit and Oligocene clays to the west of Rocroi.

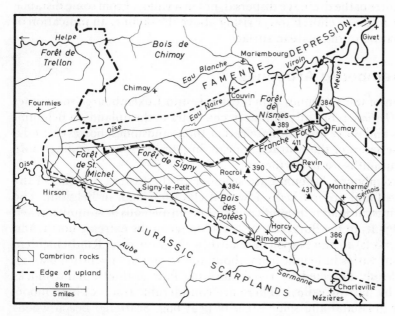

FIG. 18.7. The Rocroi massif
The approximate edge of the massif is shown by a pecked line. Heights are given in metres.

Based on (*a*) *Carte de France au 200 000ᵉ*, sheet 10; and (*b*) *Carte géologique de la France*, 1 : 1 000 000, published by the *Service de la Carte géologique détaillée de la France* (1933).

495

The plateau is demarcated approximately by the 300-m (1 000-ft) contour; the highest point, a few kilometres west of Monthermé, attains 413 m (1 355 ft). It is exceptionally cut up by river valleys, forming in effect a radial drainage pattern, as Fig. 18.7 shows. The Oise itself, so definitely a French river and one of the great Seine 'family', flows for its initial 15 km (10 miles) within the Belgian portion of this upland.

The plateau presents the usual Ardennes appearance—monotonous, with a few unobtrusive summits separated by shallow depressions, poor acid soils weathered from the shales and slates, peat moors and bogs in the waterlogged depressions, and sombre woodlands. Some cultivation takes place on the gentle outside slopes of the meanders and on small alluvial terraces. The only other activity is the quarrying of Palaeozoic slates at Monthermé, Fumay and Haybes in the Meuse valley, and at Rimogne and Harcy in the Sormonne valley. These quarries were flooded and their surface installations destroyed during the war of 1914–18, but were re-opened and re-equipped in the following years. At Chooz near the Belgian border an underground atomic energy plant has been built jointly by France and Belgium as part of the *Euratom* programme.

The plateau is thinly populated and few roads ascend on to its higher parts. Some small towns are market centres for agricultural districts. Rocroi stands at a height of almost 400 m (1 300 ft), on the open plateau at the very centre of the drainage dispersal, not in a valley. From some distance away one can see its church tower rising above the skyline, an indication of the even nature of the plateau surface.

## The Luxembourg Ardennes

The section of the Ardennes which extends into Luxembourg (sometimes called the *Oesling*) is broadly similar in character to the uplands in Belgium. Quartzites and slates predominate rather than sandstones, however, and a remarkable series of these strata appears in parallel zones trending more or less from southwest to northeast.

The Luxembourg Ardennes are situated on the eastern margins of the whole massif and are markedly lower in elevation than in Belgium. The highest points, although insignificant and inconspicuous as summits, reach 559 m (1 835 ft) in the Burgplats near Huldange in the extreme north, and 545 m (1 788 ft) in the Napoléonsgaard in the west near Rindschleiden. The plateau varies in height from about 400 to 500 m (1 300 to 1 650 ft), but it is deeply dissected by rivers, forming four distinct upland blocks separated by narrow valleys. There are considerable tracts of high moorland, poor grassland and some areas of peat bog. Scattered beech woods and some solid coniferous plantations occur on the plateau, with thickly wooded valley slopes.

The climate is neither so bleak nor so wet as that in the Belgian Ardennes, since it is considerably lower and also to some degree lies in the rainshadow of the higher plateau to the west; Clervaux in the north, for example, has a mean rainfall of about 810 mm (32 in). Few meteorological stations are situated on the plateau, but mean figures do not apparently attain 1 000 mm (40 in). Nevertheless, the elevation and exposure of the uplands, while less than in Belgium, result in bleakness, cloudiness and a snow cover of twenty to thirty days.

The Luxembourg Ardennes, therefore, is not a favourable agricultural area. Potatoes and oats are grown on the plateau as subsistence crops and rye is still cultivated. One result of the harsh climate is that seed potatoes are grown for export to the milder south of the Grand Duchy. The rearing of livestock has recently become more important, particularly cattle and pigs, and even today draught oxen can be seen. Since 1927 developments in cooperative livestock breeding and dairying have been effected in an effort to improve the standard of animal farming. *Syndicats d'élevage* have been created by voluntary associations of farmers, and cooperative dairies have been organised which send cream to the main butter factory for northern Luxembourg at Hosingen, or to another at Ettelbruck on the southern edge of the Ardennes. The main agency operates a fleet of lorries to collect cream and despatch butter to retailers. In the last few decades the plateau pastures have been improved, the result of ploughing and seeding with better grasses and the use of lime and fertilisers on the sour soils. The valleys are of little value for arable agriculture because of their steep walls and winding narrow floors, although some of the alluvial flats produce hay crops; in places these flats are intersected with irrigation channels, producing two crops of hay during the summer.

Despite these activities, the average density of population is low, the result of large unpopulated areas of moorland, woodland and pasture, and people live in isolated villages and hamlets. In the three Ardennes cantons of Clervaux, Wiltz and Vianden, the average density of population in 1960, the date of the last available census, was 46, 45 and 49 per sq km (120, 117 and 128 per sq mile) respectively, compared with 114 per sq km (295 per sq mile) over the Grand Duchy as a whole. The Ardennes support only 15 per cent of the total population of the Grand Duchy, although the upland occupies 32 per cent of the area. Furthermore, the population of some of the rural cantons of the Ardennes is declining. The attractions of better-paid employment in the industrial area of the south have caused many to leave the more rigorous uplands.

The only town of any size in the Luxembourg Ardennes is Wiltz. The old town (*Oberwiltz*) grew up around a castle on a meander spur, then spread over the river to the valley floor on the other side (*Niederwiltz*). It is situated on the railway line running westward to Bastogne in Belgium and is the focus of a number of roads, so that the town acts as a market centre for the eastern Ardennes and is also a pleasant little tourist resort. Vianden is a tourist centre in the Our valley near the West German frontier, and Clervaux grew up around a castle in the wooded valley of the river of the

497

same name, a tributary of the Wiltz. A few other large villages are situated along these valleys, and others such as Bourscheid, Heiderscheid and Putscheid are on the plateau itself.

In 1964 the world's largest pumped storage hydrostation, with a 900 mW capacity, was completed, with a dam across the river Our at Vianden.

## The Famenne depression

A broad depression, parallel to the main structural trend of the Ardennes, runs from the neighbourhood of Chimay in a northeasterly direction towards Liège; the section lying west of the Meuse is sometimes known as *La Fagne*.[6] Most of the Famenne lies below 180 m (600 ft), and it forms a distinct trough eroded in the Upper Devonian shales and schists, less resistant than the sandstones and quartzites to the north and south. As the original consequent streams developed their northward courses, subsequents cut back along these Upper Devonian rocks. In the west the Viroin with its two headstreams, the Eau Noire and the Eau Blanche, flow to the Meuse itself in broad valleys (Fig. 18.7). The section east of the Meuse is occupied by the Lesse and its confluents, the Lhomme and the Wamme. These each have the usual northward course until they reach the less resistant rocks of the depression, whereupon they abruptly change direction and flow westwards to the Meuse master stream. A distinct divide, attaining about 300 m (1 000 ft) to the northeast of Han, separates the western part of the Famenne from the valley of the lower Ourthe, which turns abruptly eastwards along the eastern section of the Famenne near Noiseux.

The Famenne is mostly an area of gently undulating relief, interrupted by limestone hills rising more prominently to 200 to 250 m (700 or 800 ft), while the valley floors are in places as low as 90 m (300 ft). The hills are often wooded, and forest covers nearly two-fifths of the total area. In many parts occur outcrops of Upper Devonian limestone, with underground stream courses, grottoes and resurgences.[7] A tract of limestone appears in the neighbourhood of Rochefort, where there are numerous caverns. One of the best known series of caverns is the Grottes de Han. The Lesse formerly occupied a large loop to the northeast of Han, the abandoned valley of which is clearly visible, but the river now disappears as a cascade into the Perte de la Lesse, to reappear a kilometre away at the Trou de Han after a complex subterranean passage. The grottoes consist of inter-connected caverns representing a former underground course of the river at a still higher level, now abandoned except during extreme floods.

The Famenne is rather more densely populated than the higher country to north and south, for it is lower and milder, with considerable areas of calcareous loams and heavy clays. A particularly prosperous district lies in La Fagne to the east of Chimay, where oats, fodder crops and vegetables are grown. This is the 'calcareous corridor', where a band of Devonian limestone, only 5 km (3 miles) wide, has weathered to form loamy soils of considerable fertility, and as a result the prosperous, well populated agricultural country contrasts markedly with the forested sandstones to north and south. In the agricultural census of 1961, 70 per cent of the Famenne's farmland was under permanent pasture, a proportion rising to 90 per cent in the Fagne, and it forms a dairying region with some production of beef cattle. Most of the hills and the steep valley sides are, however, wooded.

Many of the little towns are route centres where the trans-Ardennes routes cross the diagonal line of the Famenne, and the attractive landscape has a certain tourist interest. Marche, in the centre of the Famenne on the watershed between the Lesse and the Ourthe, Rochefort on the Lhomme, and Durbuy on the Ourthe, are the main resorts and market towns.

## The Condroz

The plateau contained to the southeast of the Meuse rightangle is known as the Condroz, where the complexity of the 'graining' of the Lower Palaeozoic rocks is well shown. The plateau here has a general elevation of between 180 and 300 m (600 and 1 000 ft), but it rises towards the southern edge overlooking the Famenne to 342 m (1 122 ft) near Durbuy. There are many parallel ridges, formed mainly of sandstone, some quite steep and prominent, others with rounded crests. Between them long parallel valleys are developed in the less resistant Carboniferous and Upper Devonian shales and limestones. The most prominent (although not the highest) ridge is in the extreme north, where outcrops a narrow belt of Lower Devonian and Silurian rocks. Numerous streams have developed longitudinal courses, but the deeply cut Meuse valley to the north has caused many northward flowing streams to break through to the main river across the 'grain' in steepsided transverse valleys.

The sandstone ridges are mostly wooded, while the valley floors are used for mixed farming, although the soils are not particularly good, and farms tend to be large. They usually possess arable land under oats, winter barley, rye, potatoes, trefoil and even a little wheat, but the proportion of permanent pasture has increased rapidly during this century. Dairying to provide milk for the industrial towns of the Meuse valley, and cattle-rearing for beef, are the main farming occupations, though horse-rearing is still important.

The population is nucleated in large often isolated villages, situated at intervals along the roads which exhibit the same parallelism to the 'grain' of the country, for naturally they follow the valleys. Where the occasional transverse road, climbing over the plateau from the Meuse valley to the Famenne, crosses these longitudinal routes, there is usually a village, and settlements follow the line of the Namur-Arlon railway line. Such is Ciney, a railway junction and the focus of eight roads; it is a market town, with a small factory making stoves. The chief town is, however, Dinant, which owes its importance to its position in the Meuse valley, the chief transverse corridor through the Ardennes, where the important longitudinal highway from Valenciennes via Maubeuge and Philippeville to Liège crosses the river. It was for long a fortress town, with its citadel perched on steep limestone cliffs overlooking the river. Once also it was an industrial town, renowned for its chased copper and brass ware, but today it functions as a centre for the tourist industry of the Meuse valley; a *téléferique* takes one swiftly from the river-side to the citadel, steamers make river excursions, and coach tours radiate through the wooded hills and valleys.

## Entre-Sambre-et-Meuse

To the west of the river Meuse, the structural features revealed in the Condroz are continued in the district of Entre-Sambre-et-Meuse;[8] the eastern part of this is given the *pays* name of *Marlagne*. As far west as Philippeville the alternating ridge and valley structure can still be seen, although it is more interrupted by transverse valleys than is the Condroz. The land gradually decreases in altitude to the west of the frontier, forming a region known in France as the *Plateaux préardennais*.

This is a thinly populated area, contrasting markedly with the numerous small towns along the Sambre valley to the north. Much of the country is wooded, particularly the ridges, though some farming is practised in the valleys, mainly the rearing of cattle and horses, and the cultivation of fodder crops such as oats. Industries are few and related to local needs, including the long-established manufacture of tubs, wine casks and clogs at Philippeville from local timber.

## The Sambre-Meuse valley

The valley of the Sambre-Meuse extends parallel to the structure lines along the northern edge of the Ardennes. In this belt, more than 150 km (100 miles) in length but only 5 to 15 km (3 to 10 miles) wide, live approximately a quarter of the people of Belgium. This is the 'industrial crescent' based on the southern coalfield or *Bassin Sud*. There is a series of large towns—Liège, Namur and Charleroi, with Mons situated in the western part of the 'coal furrow' though not on the Sambre, which enters the industrial area a few kilometres above Charleroi. These towns are surrounded by large sprawling satellite villages, and here is situated the greater part of Belgium's heavy industry—iron and steel, chemicals, glass and non-ferrous metallurgical industries, for which the coalfield provided the initial momentum, and it still helps to sustain them. The importance of the waterways is emphasised by the fact that in 1969 about 1·9 million tons of metallurgical products and 5·4 million tons of building materials were loaded at points along them, and 3·0 million tons of coal were unloaded. Most of the last came from the Kempenland or from the Netherlands and West Germany, consisting of coking coal.

## The southern coalfield (Fig. 18.8)

The southern Belgian coalfield forms part of an elongated series of Coal Measures which extend from the *départements* of Pas-de-Calais and Nord across the French frontier. The structural complexities make this field extremely difficult to work, for faulting and overthrusting interrupt the continuity of the seams (there is a classic example near Mons where a single shaft 340 m (1 115 ft) in depth passes through the same seam six times), some seams dip at a high angle particularly on the southern side of the fields, and minor anticlines divide the districts into individual basins. Thus in the Liège district there are three distinct basins where mining is

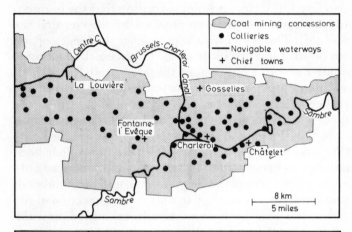

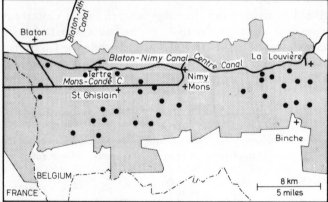

FIG. 18.8. The coalfield of southern Belgium
For the location of collieries on the French side of the frontier, see Fig. 7.3. Since this map was drawn, a large number of collieries has been closed; only 21 are still active in the whole southern field (including the Liège section).

Based on *Atlas de Belgique*, sheet 37 (*Charbonnages* I), with revisions from official information.

concentrated, separated by less productive or even barren ground. Sometimes the coal is so shattered that it has to be briquetted, or used in thermal generators, or burnt *in situ* for underground gasification. The fractured seams hinder mechanisation, and firedamp is prevalent, contributing to a very high accident rate. Further disadvantages are that the exploited seams are thin, though numerous; in the Mons district few of the 157 seams are thicker than a metre, and at Charleroi there are about fifty, the thickest of which is 1·2 m (4 ft). Many mines are deep, particularly those in the west where the productive Coal Measures are covered by Cretaceous and Triassic rocks; near Mons the mines exceed 1 000 m (3 300 ft) and are among the deepest in the world.

With these adverse physical factors it is not surprising that the southern field is difficult and expensive to exploit, emphasised by the fact that the mining region is now 'old'. This is literally the case, since the Liège portion of the field vies with South Limburg in its claim to possess the first mine worked in continental Europe. Long before the Industrial Revolution, vertical shafts were sunk to provide coal for the smiths and metal-workers of Liège, while the deeply cut valleys of the Meuse and its tributaries enabled horizontal adits easily to be driven for drainage. The nineteenth century saw the removal of the most accessible coal—output reached 23·5 million tons in 1900—and many parts of the field have now either been worked out or abandoned as uneconomic. In 1969 the field produced only 5·19 million tons, about 31 per cent of the Belgian total, and the number of active collieries has fallen from 271 in 1875 to only 21. One section of the field, the Namur basin, has long been economically exhausted, and the Mons and Centre basins almost so.

The southern coalfield is divided into five districts; the most easterly is the Liège area, the second most productive, geologically separated by barren strata from the exhausted basin around Namur, while the Charleroi district, the Centre district (with its focus La Louvière), and the rapidly declining Couchant de Mons or Borinage[9] district extend westward to the French frontier.

The nature and quality of the coal vary greatly from place to place; in

*Coal output in the southern field (million tons)*

|  | 1938 | 1952 | 1964 | 1969 |
|---|---|---|---|---|
| Couchant de Mons (Borinage) | 4·90 | 4·80 | 2·84 | 1·14 |
| Centre | 4·26 | 3·71 | | |
| Charleroi | 7·98 | 7·21 | 5·25 | 2·62 |
| Namur | 0·39 | — | — | — |
| Liège | 5·52 | 4·96 | 3·08 | 1·43 |
| Total | 23·05 | 20·68 | 11·17 | 5·19 |

Source: *Annuaire statistique de la Belgique*, 1970, and Institut National de Statistique by correspondence.

general the volatile content of the seams is higher in the upper strata and on the southern side of the field. The long-flame coals, with over 25 per cent volatile matter, are found mainly in the extreme west in the upper strata of the concealed part of the field near Mons; such coals, used for gasification, are known as *Flénu*, after the colliery of that name which closed down just before the war of 1939–45. The other categories are the bituminous coals (*gras*) used domestically, in gas works, and for steam raising; the semi-bituminous coals (*demi-gras*) burnt in coke ovens to produce hard metallurgical coke; and short-flame semi-anthracites (*maigre*) of low volatile content. The bulk of the Liège district's production is *maigre*, a regrettable fact from the point of view of the iron-masters, who are obliged to use Kempen or Ruhr coking coal; the best southern coking coals are in fact worked in the Centre and Charleroi fields. Notwithstanding the limitations of this coalfield, it formed the basis of the industrialisation of southern Belgium, though output is rapidly declining and it is expected that under EEC direction the whole field will be phased out before 1983.

### The iron and steel industry

In 1970 the country produced 10·84 million tons of pig iron and ferro-alloys, 12·61 million tons of crude steel, and 9·30 million tons of finished steel; more than 90 per cent came from this southern industrial region (Fig. 18.9). Much rationalisation and modernisation have been effected in recent years, and a third of the steel is now made in huge BOS converters.

Liège had been an industrial centre of European pre-eminence long

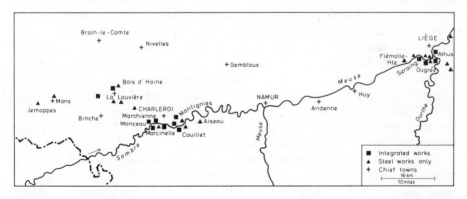

Fig. 18.9. The major iron and steel-works in southern Belgium
Only the major establishments are shown. The chief concerns are the *Cockerill-Ougrée* plants at Seraing, Ougrée, Grivegnée and Tilleur; *Hainaut-Sambre* at Couillet and Montignies; *Forges de la Providence* at Marchienne; *Espérance-Longdoz* at Seraing, Chertal, Jemeppe and Genk (Kempen); and *Gustave Boël* at La Louvière.

Based on *Carte du bassin houiller belge et des voies navigables* (n.d.), with details of industrial establishments revised to 1970.

503

before the Industrial Revolution had developed. In 1817 John Cockerill, son of an English mechanic who migrated to Belgium at the end of the eighteenth century, established workshops at Seraing, a few kilometres upstream of Liège within a northerly loop of the Meuse. Supplies of pig iron were at first used from the charcoal-fired furnaces of the Condroz and the Famenne to the south. But Cockerill from the beginning was attracted by the possibility of smelting his own pig iron and so establishing on a single site a large-scale self-contained metallurgical unit, and his first coke-fired blast furnace was built in 1823. On his death in 1840 his industrial empire was reorganised as the Société Anonyme John Cockerill, in which the Belgian government held 50 per cent of the shares. The name of Cockerill has been pre-eminent in Belgian industry for a century and a half, and the vast Seraing works still stand on the original though greatly enlarged site. The western part of the Sambre-Meuse coalfield also rapidly developed during the first half of the nineteenth century, and although the Charleroi district did not possess the industrial antecedents of Liège, the metallurgical industry grew following the erection of the first coke-burning blast furnace at Hauchies near Charleroi soon after that at Seraing. Later still furnaces were installed at La Louvière, using the good coking coals of the Mons-Centre basins.

Today most of Belgian steel is produced by a few large integrated concerns situated (with the notable exceptions of SA d'Angleur-Athus near the French-Luxembourg frontiers and of the works at Clabecq 24 km (15 miles) south of Brussels) in the southern industrial region. For many years two of the largest companies, both in the Liège area, have been the SA John Cockerill already mentioned and the SA d'Ougrée-Marihaye also on the banks of the Meuse; in 1955 these two companies were merged to form one of the largest metallurgical combines in Europe, producing about 5 per cent of the ECSC steel output; later Forges de la Providence also joined the combine. The SA Métallurgique d'Espérance-Longdoz also operates steel works in eastern Liège; their new plant at Chertal, 11 km (7 miles) north of Liège between the Meuse and the Albert Canal, was completed in 1963, and other works are at Seraing, Liège and Jemeppe. The Charleroi district (Fig. 18.11) contains several large-scale combines, situated along the banks of the Sambre, including SA Hainaut-Sambre, the second largest in Belgium, formed in 1955.

The heavy engineering industries are also located on the southern coalfield, and particularly near these sources of steel; in fact, many of these industries are integrated with the iron- and steel-producing units, frequently on the same or an adjacent site. The output includes boilers, girders, bridges, diesel engines, electrical apparatus, locomotives and rolling-stock; the first Belgian locomotive was built at Seraing by SA John Cockerill in 1835, and was used on the Brussels-Mechelen railway, the first European line to be operated with steam locomotives. They are still constructed at Seraing, and also at Couillet, Tubize and Haine-St Pierre.

Most big towns mentioned along the Sambre-Meuse valley have heavy engineering works.

Numerous establishments concerned with light industry are located on the southern coalfield, many with age-old traditions. Liège and its satellite towns are of major importance (Fig. 18.10); in the Herstal region to the north of the conurbation are many medium sized and small firms engaged in the production of hardware, motorcycle, bicycle and aircraft parts (including jet engines), electrical goods and small-arms. Liège has had an international reputation for weapons since the fourteenth century, and

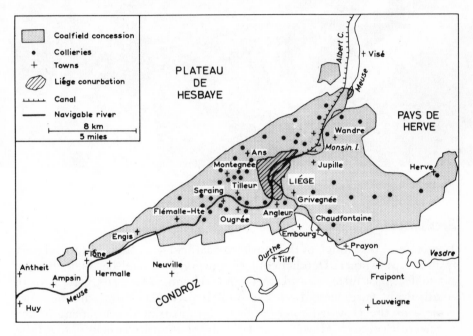

FIG. 18.10. The Liège industrial region
See note to Fig. 18.8 (p. 501).

Based on (*a*) *Atlas de Belgique*, sheet 38 (*Charbonnages* II); (*b*) T. H. Elkins, 'Liège and the Problems of southern Belgium', in *Geography* **41** (1956), p. 91; and (*c*) J. A. Sporck, *L'Activité industrielle dans la région liègeoise* (1957).

until recent years small-arms were made by highly skilled craftsmen in workshops on virtually a domestic scale. A number of separate firms are grouped within the Union des Fabricants d'Armes de Liège, with a specialised production of sporting weapons of jealously guarded reputation. But the dominant producer is the SA Fabrique nationale d'Armes de Guerre, which makes the FN rifle now adopted by the armies of the NATO countries. Wire, nails and screws are produced in the Charleroi area at Fontaine-l'Evêque and Anderlues, and machine tools, electrical apparatus, nuts and bolts.

## Settlement

It is obvious that much of the southern coalfield is an 'old' industrial area from its appearance. Derelict collieries, overgrown spoil-banks, a chaos of pit shafts, blast furnaces and steel works, chemical factories, long rows of small, drab, gardenless dwellings built in irregular rows—all these are typical of the crowded and haphazard industrial development of the nineteenth century. However, not all the southern coalfield is like this; new housing estates, and (particularly in the western part of the field) more open industrial villages, smallholdings and farmland intermingle in a manner characteristic of so many parts of Belgium. To the north of Mons, away from the cramping bounds of the Meuse valley, extend the fertile limon-covered arable lands of the Hainaut plateau. But elsewhere the very concentration of industrial activity along the narrow line of the Sambre-Meuse valley leaves little space for planned development.

Liège (Fig. 18.10) is the fourth city of Belgium,[10] with a commune population in 1970 of 147 000; with the adjacent communes the total population of the official agglomeration exceeded 445 000. The city stands in the deep alluvium-floored trench of the Meuse at the point where the trend of the valley markedly changes, and near the junction of the Ourthe, with its tributaries the Vesdre and the Amblève, which have cut their valleys transversely across the Ardennes. The Ourthe valley provides one of the few routeways from the Meuse valley into the Famenne and the southern Ardennes. Liège therefore stands at the point of contact between the Hesbaye in the north, the Pays de Herve in the east, and the Condroz to the south, and it has long been a centre of communications in western Europe. The Sambre and the Meuse upstream of the city are useful waterways, although they have required much regulation (Fig. 18.4). Some kilometres below the city the Meuse becomes an international river, for it is followed by the Dutch-Belgian frontier, though virtually unnavigable; it was not until 1940 that the long-desired major waterway link between Liège and Antwerp was established with the completion of the Albert Canal (see pp. 128–31 and Fig. 6.8). The city has been a road centre since the early Middle Ages; routes converged from the Flemish ports in the west, from Paris in the southwest, from Lorraine and Burgundy to the south, and from the Rhineland in the east. The modern road system shares this focus character, which will be further emphasised when the Belgian contributions to the European motorway network are completed, for six motorways (including the Brussels-Köln through route) will converge upon the city. As a railway centre it has its difficulties; the main line from Brussels is obliged to negotiate the Ans bank over the edge of the northern plateau (see p. 160), and routes southward through the Ardennes are difficult. Nevertheless Liège is crossed by several international routes (Paris-Charleroi-Köln following the Meuse valley, Amsterdam-Luxembourg-Basle and Ostend-Brussels-Leuven-Köln), and it is the focus of five other lines.

It is not surprising therefore that the city should have long nurtured a flourishing commercial life. Its industrial activities, based at first on local iron ore, charcoal from the Ardennes forests, and water power from the many streams, have long been of major importance, and the coalfield has been worked since the twelfth century at least. Since the Industrial Revolution the development of the Liège mining and metallurgical industries has been on a very considerable scale, as described above. In addition to these basic industries, it is one of the largest producers of refined zinc in the world, and it has a range of other nonferrous refining and consuming industries. Many factories produce heavy chemicals, glassware (notably at the long-established Val-St Lambert works at Seraing), rubber tyres, leather, pottery, and the lighter consumer goods.

Namur is a much smaller town (32 000 people in 1970), although with the neighbouring communes of Jambes and St Servais the population of the agglomeration was just over 50 000. It has an important position at the junction of the Meuse and the Sambre, 'the gateway to the Ardennes'. As a result, it has been a fortress-town for centuries, and has suffered many sieges, right down to 1914 when the Germans finally captured it after destroying its ring of outer forts. It has developed a flourishing tourist industry under its progressive Syndicat d'Initiative. Although Namur's economically exploitable deposits of coal are now exhausted, its heavy industries are well established, using coal brought in by waterway. In addition to its steel-using industries, ranging from cranes and boilers to cutlery, it has many miscellaneous manufactures—cement, glass, paper, leather, glue, soap, tobacco and even pianos. It is also an important market town and the centre of considerable areas of market gardens on the limon-covered area within the southeastern angle of the Meuse.

Charleroi forms the heart of a considerable urban agglomeration (Fig. 18.11). The populations of the commune itself in 1970 was only 23 000. But with the satellite towns of Jumet, Gilly, Montignies, Marcinelle

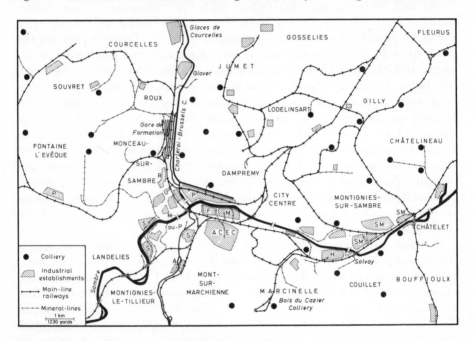

Fig. 18.11. The Charleroi industrial district
The names of the communes in the Charleroi conurbation are shown.
  The main iron and steel works are as follows, indicated on the map by initials:
(1) *S.A. Laminoirs, Hauts Fourneaux, Forges, Fonderies et Usines de la Providence* (**P**), at Marchienne-au-Pont (M.-au-P.) and Fontaine-l'Evêque; (2) *S.A. Société Métallurgique Hainaut-Sambre* (formerly *S.A. Sambre-et-Moselle* (**SM**) and *S.A. Métallurgique du Hainaut* (**H**) at Couillet; (3) *S.A. Hauts Fourneaux, Forges et Aciéries de Thy-le-Château et Marcinelle* (**M**), at Marcinelle; (4) *S.A. Aciéries et Minières de la Sambre* (**S**), at Marchienne-au-Pont; (5) *S.A. Fabrique de Fer de Charleroi* (**F**), at Marchienne-au-Pont; (6) *S.A. Laminoirs et Boulonneries du Ruay* (**R**), at Monceau-sur-Sambre; (7) *S.A. Usines et Aciéries Allard* (**A**), at Mont-sur-Marchienne.
  There are many other factories in the Charleroi neighbourhood. They include the *Ateliers de Constructions Electriques de Charleroi* (**ACEC**) at Marcinelle, the *Solvay* chemical works at Couillet, and two large glass-works at Courcelles (*Glaces de Courcelles* and *Glaver*). The Bois du Cazier colliery at Marcinelle, the scene of a major disaster in August 1956, is named. Since this map was drawn, a number of collieries has been closed (see p. 501).

Based on *Plan de Charleroi et de la grande banlieue* (1 : 15 000), *Carte No. 61* of the *Editions R. de Rouck* (Bruxelles).

508

and Marchienne-au-Pont and with the additional small towns and villages around, there is a continuous conurbation (the *agglomération carlorégienne*) officially created in 1942, with a population of 217 000. Charleroi is the centre of one important basin of the southern coalfield, and it has metallurgical industries and two of Belgium's largest glass factories.

Mons is the centre of the most westerly part of the southern coalfield, known generally as the Borinage. Numerous mining villages and collieries spread beyond the town to the southwest, but coalmining is a rapidly declining industry; by mid-1969 only three collieries remained in activity. Unlike the large towns already described, the Mons district has few heavy industries except for coke ovens, briquetting plant and chemical by-products. Other new factories, opened recently to help combat industrial unemployment, make chemicals, electrical equipment, aluminium ware, and pottery and refractory ware. There are also soap works, textile mills manufacturing cotton and rayon (for it is not far from the Flanders textile region), tobacco factories, breweries, a rope works and a cement works. Several large sugar refineries process beet grown on the limon-covered plateau of Hainaut to the north.

Thus Belgium's chief industrial area, producing a third of her coal and much of her steel, lies as a long narrow zone along the northern margin of the Ardennes, the country's least productive and most thinly populated region. In fact large numbers of work-people live in the small towns and villages of the Condroz and Entre-Sambre-et-Meuse and travel in daily to their work in the industrial crescent.[11]

[1] G. Hoyois, *L'Ardenne et l'Ardennais*, 2 vols. (1949, 1953), is a vast reference work of 983 pp., in remarkable detail.

[2] It must be noted that some Belgian geomorphologists do not regard this as an anticline, but as the complex *failles de charriage de Condroz* separating the structures of the Dinant and Namur synclinoria.

[3] The erosion surfaces of the Ardennes are discussed in detail by P. Macar, 'L'évolution géomorphologique de l'Ardenne', *Bull. Soc. belge Géogr.* (1954), fasc. 2–4, pp. 9–33. See also C. Stevens, 'La géomorphologie ardennaise', *ibid.* (1955), fasc. 1–2, pp. 7–17; and P. Macar, 'Aperçu synthétique sur l'évolution géomorphologique de l'Ardenne', *Travaux géographiques de Liège* (1965), no. 150, pp. 3–11.

[4] J. Vereerstraeten, 'Contribution à l'étude hydrologique du Bassin de la Meuse en Belgique', *Bull. Soc. Belge Et. géogr.*, **21** (1952), pp. 269–318; this gives a very full account of the Meuse and its tributaries, their flow, seasonal variations, etc.

[5] A. A. Michel, 'The canalization of the Moselle and West European integration', *Geogrl. Rev.*, **52** (1962), pp. 475–91; and F. Chanrion, *Une Victoire européenne: la Moselle* (1964).

[6] A. Gamblin, 'Quelques aspects de la morphologie de la Fagne de Chimay', *Bull. Assoc. Géogr. franç.* (1954), nos 241–2, pp. 68–78.

[7] Much detail about the caves and underground streams is given in E. van den Broeck, E.-A. Martel and E. Rahir, *Etudes hydro-spéléologiques sur le calcaire dévonien du bassin de Dinant* (two vols., 1910); it includes many maps and plans; see also J. Corbel, 'Les Karsts de Belgique', *Les Karsts du Nord-Ouest de l'Europe* (1957), pp. 381–429.

[8] P. Bourguignon, 'Contribution à la géographie régionale de l'Entre-Sambre-et-Meuse condrusien', *Bull. Soc. belge Et. Géogr.*, **22** (1953), pp. 223–59.

[9] R. C. Riley, 'Recent developments in the Belgian Borinage', *Geography*, **50** (1965), pp. 261–73.

[10] For a full description of Liège, see (a) T. H. Elkins, 'Liège and the problems of southern Belgium', *Geography*, **41** (1956), pp. 83–98; (b) J. A. Sporck, *L'Activité industrielle dans la région liègeoise: étude de géographie économique* (1957), which provides much statistical material, plates and maps; (c) L. E. Davin, L. Degeer and J. Paelinck, *Dynamique économique de la région liègeoise* (1959); and (d) *L'Economie de la Région liègeoise* (1962), published by the Conseil Economique Wallon.

[11] For a full analysis of this situation in Belgium and the Netherlands generally, see R. E. Dickinson, 'The geography of commuting: The Netherlands and Belgium', *Geogr. Rev.*, **47** (1957), pp. 521–38.

# 19
# The Vosges

The Vosges form an upland area rising impressively along the western side of the broad rift valley of the Rhine, then falling away more gradually towards the scarplands of Lorraine. The uplands are at their widest in the south, becoming narrower and lower in the vicinity of the 'Saverne Gap', and continuing northward to the West German frontier (Fig. 11.1). The term 'Vosges' was used originally in a general way to denote forested lands. In this sense it survives as a *pays* name, *La Vôge*, which refers to a small wooded district of the upper Saône basin; probably the name was first given to this, and later transferred to the whole of the uplands to the east.

Various regional subdivisions may be defined. Because the *département* boundary (which was actually the Franco-German frontier in 1871–1918 and again in 1940–44) between Vosges and Moselle on the west and Haut- and Bas-Rhin on the east closely follows the crest-line, the western and eastern sections are sometimes known as the *Vosges lorraines* and *Vosges alsaciennes* respectively. Again, a fundamental difference in structure is recognised in the terms *Vosges cristallines* applied to the southern part and *Vosges gréseuses* to the hills in the north. From the point of view of altitude, there are the southern *Hautes-Vosges* (Plate 55) and the more northerly *Basses-* or *Petites-Vosges*.

## Structure and relief

The core of these uplands consists of ancient crystalline gneiss, schist and granite (Fig. 11.2). The gneiss appears to be of Pre-Cambrian age, and occurs as three distinct massifs; one lies to the east of the Col du Bonhomme in the neighbourhood of Ste Marie-aux-Mines, another to the north of Gérardmer, the third to the northwest of Remiremont. Associated with these gneissic rocks are varied schists about whose age there is some doubt, although they are commonly ascribed to the Cambrian. The main mass of the Vosges comprises intrusions of early Palaeozoic granitic rocks of varying composition. In the southeast and south appear several extruded masses of trachytes and andesites.

These rocks, together with some Lower Carboniferous slates, were involved in the Hercynian orogeny and were very complexly folded; the structural trends can be traced from northeast to southwest. Several distinct faultlines form troughlike depressions, parallel to the structural 'grain', in which newer rocks are sometimes preserved. The Vosges share the tectonic character of the Black Forest to the east, in fact until late Tertiary times the two were probably a structural unit.

The Hercynian orogeny was succeeded by a long period of denudation which reduced these mountains to a gently undulating peneplain. This denudation seems to have continued into Permian times, but it was in turn followed by a long-sustained period of deposition. Some Permian rocks still survive on the surface, preserved in the downfaulted St Dié basin.

During extensive submergence by the inland Triassic sea, really widespread deposition took place, and over great areas of what is now Alsace and Lorraine, as well as in the Haardt and the Pfälzer Wald of western Germany, Lower Triassic sandstones were laid down to a thickness of approximately 500 m (1 600 ft). These comprise fine-grained sandstones, clays and limestones of Lower Bunter age, followed by much more extensive coarse-grained Upper Bunter Sandstones (known as *grès-vosgien,* or sometimes where their colour is particularly vivid as *grès-rouge*). Then follows the mid-Triassic *Muschelkalk* or Shelly Limestone, a hard yellow fossiliferous limestone which now appears as an interrupted outcrop 8 to 16 km (5 to 10 miles) wide along the western edge of the sandstone uplands, in places forming a quite distinct cuesta, notably to the east of the Sarre valley and to the west of Epinal. Elsewhere the Muschelkalk rises little above the general level, but forms a strip of rather dry but often well cultivated country, differing markedly from both the forested sandstone to the east and the clay lands of Lorraine to the west. Sedimentation continued throughout Triassic and Jurassic times.

Towards the end of the Jurassic, the Vosges–Black Forest massif was bodily uplifted, and it must then have stood above the waters of the widespread marine transgressions to the north and west, in which were deposited Cretaceous and Lower Tertiary rocks. The next phase developed during mid-Tertiary times, when the massif formed part of the Hercynian foreland of the central European orogenic zone and so contributed to the alignment of the Alpine arcs. On the other hand, the effects of the orogeny were experienced by the massif itself, so that it was bodily uplifted and at the same time strongly faulted. Some of these faultlines are associated with mineral springs.

The most drastic modification of the unit-massif was caused by the formation of the Rhine rift valley, outlined by two broadly parallel lines of stepped faults now reflected in the terracelike descent to the floor of the rift valley. The faults involved the crystalline basement rocks, the overlying Triassic sandstones, and even in places surviving Jurassic limestones; indeed, some of these rocks now outcrop in places on the actual floor of the rift valley (see p. 292). It may be that the formation of this rift valley began as early as Eocene times, and continued through the Tertiary period; certainly Oligocene strata are preserved on its floor. However, it is probable that the actual fracturing of the uplifted block took place in the late Tertiary. Although these rift valley faultlines are the most clearly defined, there are others to the west with a roughly parallel trend but with a smaller throw, so that the westward slope is also broken into broad terraces separated by low but distinct steps. Some associated volcanic activity produced minor results, including the formation of the Kaiserstuhl, a mass of basalt protruding from the rift valley floor in West Germany to the northwest of Freiburg. In the Vosges, however, only a few small basalt flows are to be seen to the north of the High Vosges in the valley of the Bruche.

As a result of this parallel fracturing, the former massif was separated into two. The highest summits in both the Vosges and the Black Forest occur near their steep inner edges overlooking the rift valley, from which the land descends more gently westward into the Lorraine scarplands and eastward into the Swabian scarplands respectively.

Perhaps during the period of renewed late Tertiary uplift which tilted the Ardennes (see p. 487), further movements elevated the southern part of the Vosges. This was responsible for the greater eminence of the High Vosges, outlined by a number of well-defined faults along the southern margins overlooking the Belfort depression. The final result forms what was called by a French geologist [1] 'une sorte de grand dôme à noyau hercynien'.

Since mid-Tertiary times denudation has proceeded relentlessly, and the Triassic and newer rocks have been completely removed from the central parts of the High Vosges, revealing the core of granite and gneiss and in the extreme southeast some Lower Carboniferous slates. The newer rocks form a frame—a broad rim to the west covering most of Lorraine, a narrow one in the east where outcrops of Triassic and in places Jurassic rocks are preserved between the stepped faults, the *zone sous-vosgienne*. In the north the Jurassic limestones have completely vanished, but the Triassic sandstones survive over the Low Vosges as far north as the Saar Basin. Here then are the basic differences between the High and Low Vosges—altitude and structure.

## The High Vosges

The surface of the High Vosges has an average altitude of about 900 m (3 000 ft), rising in places to individual summits known as *ballons* [2] (or in German *Belchen*). The highest point is actually the Ballon de Guebwiller 1 423 m (4 669 ft), with the Hohneck further north (Fig. 19.1), and the Ballon d'Alsace stands prominently on the southern edge of the massif overlooking the Porte de Bourgogne. A motor road passable for nearly half the year actually leads to the summit of the last-named. In the northern part of the High Vosges the uplands are of sandstone, with prominent

PLATE 56. The Vosges near Gérardmer

tabular summits flanked by steep slopes; the forest-covered Mont Donon
1 008 m (3 307 ft), for example, is a mass of sandstone rising from its
exposed granitic base. Further north still the sandstone cover is uninterrupted, even in deeply cut valleys.

The summits of the granite peaks have been worn by denudation into
massive rounded humps (hence the name *ballon*) (Plate 56). Occasional tors
diversify the plateau surface, rising from broad spreads of granite boulders
and pebbles surrounded by a gritty clay, the product of *in situ* decomposition
of the granite.

The numerous Moselle headstreams drain lengthily northwestwards
across Lorraine, while the shorter eastern tributaries are soon picked up by
the Ill a few kilometres to the east. There is in effect a pattern of radial
drainage from the main mass of the High Vosges culminating in the
Hohneck, as shown on Fig. 19.1.

These torrential headstreams, fed by rapid runoff over the granite
surface, are powerful eroding agents, and deep valleys have been worn.
Several of the *ballons* reveal steep rock slopes falling away sharply from
their rounded summits, especially on the east where gradients are steep,
and gorgelike valleys open out into the *région sous-vosgienne* and the rift
valley. To the west the Moselle system has worn a form of 'scarp-and-vale'
structure in the westerly dipping rocks. East-facing escarpments can be

514

distinguished, each paralleled by a river which in due course breaks through the ridge in a *cluse*-like valley. Thus on Fig. 19.1 the Collines de Vologne lie to the west of the Moselotte, and parallel to it but still further west are the valley of the Chajoux and its bordering Collines de Chajoux. Thus although the general trend of drainage on the western side of the High Vosges is to the west and northwest, the rivers have alternate sections flowing parallel to the ridges and short transverse sections.

During Quaternary times the higher parts of the Vosges were covered with small ice caps from which glaciers moved outwards along the pre-glacial river valleys. The impress of ice on the physical landscape is revealed by the profiles of over-deepened valleys, sometimes containing moraine-dammed 'ribbon lakes'. The Vologne, for example, rises on the northwestern flanks of the Hohneck, flows torrentially down to the small Lac de Retournemer, and then descends into the steep-sided flat-floored valley in which lies Lac de Longemer (Fig. 19.1). Further west is Lac de Gérardmer, which drains into the Vologne; this lake actually stands on a col with a low watershed 800 m (a half-mile) to the west. It seems that the

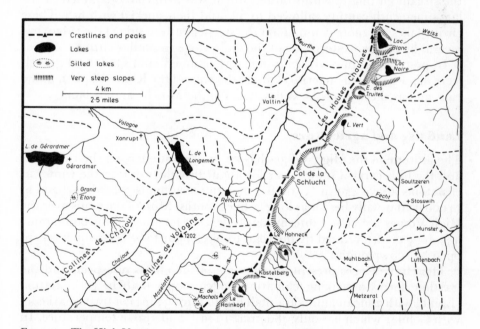

FIG. 19.1. The High Vosges
The relief is so complex that this map is largely diagrammatic. The main crestline (the former Franco-German frontier) runs across the east-centre of the map (Les Hautes Chaumes, Le Hohneck, Kastelberg), marked by a heavy pecked line. The steep eastern slopes, notably where cirques have been cut back into them, are indicated by hachuring. The minor crestlines indicate the complexity of river erosion in this dissected crystalline massif.

Based on *Carte de France au 50 000*, sheets XXXVI/18, 19.

Vologne once flowed directly westwards through the lake, but it was captured by a more active stream which had cut a deep gorge into which the upper Vologne was diverted, so that it now flows down through this gorge to the Moselle at Jarmenil. As a result, the Lac de Gérardmer now drains northeastwards to the Vologne, a complete reversal of direction.

Glaciation also accounts for a series of fine cirques and cirque lakes below the central crestline (Fig. 19.1). Seven cirque lakes lie in deep hollows along the eastern side of the Chaumes-Hohneck ridge, as well as swampy hollows which were once obviously lake-filled. Two of the most striking are Lac Blanc and Lac Noire; both have been artificially deepened with small dams, but they are true rock basin lakes, lying in steep craggy-walled hollows and separated from each other by an impressive granite arête. Lac Blanc is in fact a double basin, separated by a submerged rock bar. Further to the south are Lac Vert (so called because of the prolific growth of green weed in summer), where depths of over 60 m (200 ft) have been sounded, and the Lac des Truites, enclosed on its eastern side by a small but distinctive moraine. This hollow was once quite dry, the result of the stream cutting down its outlet, but it was artificially dammed in the late nineteenth century, allowed to fill, and then stocked with fish. These cirque lakes are more common on the steeper eastern side of the ridge, but several lie on the western side of the main ridge in similar cirques.

In postglacial times river erosion was resumed, and sands and gravels were deposited both on terraces along the edge of the Rhine-Ill plain in the east, and as sheets over the valley floors of the Moselle and its family.

## Land use and agriculture

The altitude of the High Vosges has an important effect on their climate, and the hills carry a snow cover for about fifty days during the winter at elevations above 450 m (1 500 ft), though on summits exceeding 1 200 m (4 000 ft) it usually lies for as long as five months. Most of the roads over the High Vosges are closed intermittently, except for the Col du Bonhomme 953 m (3 127 ft), crossed by the road from Colmar to St Dié, which is kept open by snowploughs.

The High Vosges present an example of the effects of aspect, and the crestline forms a striking climatic divide, shown both in precipitation (Epinal with a mean annual rainfall of 940 mm (37 in) contrasts markedly with Colmar which has only 480 mm (19 in) ) and also in temperature. In the western valleys snow lies longer, spring comes later and the summers are less sunny than on the eastern slopes. The difference is illustrated by the fact that vineyards are rare in the west, but widespread on the southeast Alsatian slopes; in 1968 the *département* of Vosges on the west yielded a mere 23 000 hectolitres of *vin ordinaire*, while Haut-Rhin on the east produced 649 000 hectolitres of better quality wine.

The granite summits of the High Vosges are covered with moorland, with occasional peat bogs in the depressions, and with nearly level stretches of granite rubble among which grow scrubby plants. Considerable areas consist of rough pasture, dotted with stunted shrubs and rather bleak, although in places they have been improved for summer grazing. The summit plateaus bear few trees, except where plantations of conifers have been deliberately established. Possibly these bleak uplands were naturally devoid of tree cover owing to exposure, for the more sheltered valley slopes are commonly covered with beech and spruce and on the eastern side of the uplands with chestnuts. It is more probable that a former forest cover, once destroyed, could not naturally regenerate because of the thin gravelly soil and also because of the destructive grazing of sheep and goats.

It is possible to give some indication of the land use in the High Vosges. The figures are on a *département* basis, and Vosges includes land well to the west while Haut-Rhin includes the western side of the Rhine valley floor, but the two *départements* do include the High Vosges, and their figures are indicative.

*Land use, 1968 (percentage of total area)*

|  | PASTURE | WOODLAND | ARABLE LAND |
|---|---|---|---|
| Haut-Rhin | 20 | 36 | 32 |
| Vosges | 31 | 43 | 16 |

Source: Ministère de l'Agriculture, *Annuaire statistique de la France*, 1970–1.

The limitations of the summits are obvious, but agriculture is surprisingly important in the valley margins, and arable crops such as rye and barley are grown as high as 840 m (2 750 ft) on the Alsatian side. The upland villages and isolated farms on both sides of the range concentrate on dairy farming, the arable crops being used mainly for supplementary stockfeed. The high pastures graze dairy cattle during the summer months, and patterns of transhumance between them and the valley villages are long established. In 1969 292 000 dairy cattle were in the *départements* of Vosges and Haut-Rhin. The milk is used mainly for cheese production, either at the farmhouses or at small cooperative dairies; the *marcaires* (literally 'milkers') spend summer at the high pastures and make cheese at the dairies. Several distinctively named cheeses are produced, the most renowned being *Gérômé-Munster*, which rather resembles Camembert. Sheep and goats are not kept in their former numbers, but in 1968 25 000 and 9 300 of these animals were in Vosges and Haut-Rhin respectively.

Further down the slopes on either side of the ridges farming assumes a more mixed character. In the east dairying is associated with the cultivation of patches of cereals and vegetables, and there are orchards of chestnuts, walnuts, cherries and even peaches. In the west, where rather coarse hungry soils are developed on the sandstones, less farmland and much more woodland is found. Some varied cultivation appears around Epinal, and areas of orchards are maintained, notably of cherries from which is distilled the *Kirsch* liqueur for which the town is famed.

On the foothills of the High Vosges grow some 10 000 ha (25 000 acres) of vineyards;[3] although these extend northward along the flanks of the Low Vosges and across the West German frontier into the Palatinate, the most important area is in the south, with Colmar as its centre. The output of wine is small, totalling in 1968 for the *départements* of Haut- and Bas-Rhin only 1 046 000 hectolitres (less than 1 per cent of the French total). The vineyards too are small, owned by a large number of *vignerons* who sell their wine to merchants for blending, bottling and marketing. The grapes are grown on pockets of calcareous downwash soils from the Jurassic outcrops, usually on south-facing slopes of valleys such as the Thur, Fecht and Weiss. The most popular varieties of grape are *Riesling, Sylvaner* and *Traminer,* from which are produced light white wines generally marketed under the name of the grape rather than that of the locality. There are a few estate-bottled wines, such as *Clos du Maquisard,* which is produced from a vineyard near Riquewihr. Many delightful villages, picturesquely situated in the foothills, are centres of these vineyards, notably Riquewihr (to the north-west of Colmar), Ribeauville, Turckheim and Hunawihr (which was completely destroyed in the latter stages of the 1939–45 war but has been attractively rebuilt).

## Industry and settlement

The villages and small towns in the High Vosges valleys have an air of quiet prosperity, partly the result of their function as market towns, and partly because of the tourist industry, for the High Vosges are extremely popular, with their delightful scenery of hill, forest and stream, and afford magnificent walking country. Gérardmer is said to receive 120 000 visitors each year. In addition, the Vosges has for long been an important industrial area, so affording alternative and supplementary sources of livelihood to agriculture. Admittedly it is not always easy to distinguish between these categories, since many agricultural labourers are employed in the factories in winter while some industrial workers go to the land for the harvest and the *vendange.*

While textile manufacturing, the most important branch of industry in Alsace, is now concentrated at Mulhouse, Colmar and Epinal, many small factories in the towns and villages in both the Alsace and the Lorraine sections of the Vosges still contribute to the output. Such towns as Thann, Ste Marie-aux-Mines, Ste Croix-aux-Mines (the mines refer to long-exhausted deposits of silver ore), St Amarin and Guebwiller in Alsace, and St Dié, Gérardmer and Remiremont in Lorraine, possess many factories, both within the towns and along neighbouring valleys. The industry began in medieval times on a domestic scale with the advantages of local wool, pure soft water from the granitic uplands, and fast-flowing streams for power; the long winters and the need for supplementary employment were additional incentives. In the eighteenth century small-scale calico and muslin weaving and printing works were established, then a little later the spinning of cotton was introduced as a cottage industry. As the nineteenth century brought the steam power of the Industrial Revolution, the textile industry began to concentrate in Mulhouse and Colmar, but many small factories and domestic producers continued to function, either supplying part-finished material or undertaking contract piecework for the large centres. Today the distribution of electric power through the French grid has helped the survival of these small producing units, though as in other textile districts recent years have seen a disquieting decline in the industry.

With the exception of St Dié, most of the industry, both domestic and factory, was situated in Alsace until after the Franco-Prussian War, when workers migrated across the new frontier into the western Vosges valleys. Epinal on the Moselle owes its considerable increase in population to this migration and resultant industrialisation. This increase has not been sustained; in fact, the population of Epinal reached 30 000 by 1911, had declined to 29 000 in 1954, though it has since reached about 36 000. These western textile factories are widely dispersed, but the majority are located along the railway from St Dié to Epinal, and down the Moselle valley towards Nancy in Lorraine. As one looks from a ridge towards a little town clustering in a valley, a characteristic sight is the tall chimney of a single small mill. Local specialisations are often of long establishment: Gérardmer still produces fine linens, Soultz spins silk thread, and Barr is a hosiery centre.

Minor industrial occupations include forestry; numerous saw mills and pulp mills are directly powered by fast-flowing streams, others by electricity from the grid. In some forests wooden runways are used, down which timber is conveyed on sledges. Pit props and constructional timber are extracted from the carefully preserved forests, and many wood-using domestic and small factory industries produce barrels for the Alsatian wine industry, furniture, toys, sabots, and tourist bric-à-brac. Even charcoal-burning still survives in places. Several paper mills near Epinal use local pulp and pure water from the Moselle.[4]

The High Vosges is then a region of remarkable contrasts—of bleak moorlands and dark forests, of snow-covered uplands and sun-bathed valley slopes, of rich dairy herds and productive vineyards, of prosperous farms and active textile mills. There are many small villages, and a few rather larger towns situated in Lorraine well back from the ridgeline, such as Epinal and Remiremont. In Alsace they are much closer, both high up in the steep valleys and lower down where these open into the rift valley.[5]

These towns and villages are quite well served by roads, many of which were built for strategic purposes when the crest-line was a vital frontier, and maintained today largely for the tourist industry. The famous *Route des Crêtes*, for example, runs along what was the frontier ridge, reaching a maximum altitude of 1 360 m (4 450 ft); though snow-blocked from November to the end of May, it is a popular summer road with magnificent prospects. Another tourist road ascends to the top of the Ballon d'Alsace. A few roads cross the High Vosges—the Col du Bonhomme from Colmar to St Dié, the Col de la Schlucht 1 139 m (3 737 ft) between Gérardmer and Colmar, and the Col de Bramont 967 m (3 173 ft) between Gérardmer and Thann in the Thur valley; these are blocked by snow, continuously or intermittently, for much of the winter, except for the Col du Bonhomme. Two railway lines cross the uplands, both built since the war of 1914–18 to tie Alsace more closely into the rest of France. Formerly the line from Epinal terminated at St Dié, but it was extended up the Fave valley to Saales, then by means of tunnels through the Vosges watershed into the Bruche valley and so to Strasbourg; this affords a useful through route for express trains between Dijon and Strasbourg. In 1937 a second line was completed, also from St Dié; it tunnels due east, emerging in the Lieporette valley near St Marie-aux-Mines, and continues down the valley to Sélestat on the edge of the Rhine valley.

## The Low Vosges

The High Vosges really end at the 'Saverne Gap' to the northwest of Strasbourg, where a prominent embayment in the side of the rift valley (Fig. 12.1), together with a narrowing and decrease of elevation of the Bunter Sandstone, forms a gap affording a line of communication between the Rhineland and Lorraine. The lowest part of the gap, dominated by the old fortress town of Phalsbourg standing on a steep Muschelkalk ridge, is crossed by the Strasbourg-Nancy road. The main Paris–Strasbourg railway and the Marne-Rhine Canal both prefer a route further south along the narrow Zorn valley (Fig. 19.2). Both require tunnels to negotiate the watershed, the narrowest part of the Vosges, and the canal ascends from Strasbourg by means of fifty-two locks (Plate 57).

The Upper Bunter Sandstone extends northward beyond the Saverne Gap, though only the southern part comprises the Low Vosges, for beyond the West German frontier the uplands are continued as the Haardt and the Pfälzer Wald. The sandstone cover is still complete, despite erosion by the west-flowing headstreams of the Sarre and by short Rhine tributaries such as the Moder and the Sauer. The valleys are winding and deeply cut, separating irregular tabular sandstone summits and sharp ridges, the highest of which is the Wintersberg 581 m (1 906 ft) near the West German frontier; in many places these summits are weathered into fantastic crags and pinnacles. The average altitude of the upland surface varies from only 400 to 500 m (1 300 to 1 600 ft), but its dissected nature makes it difficult to negotiate.

PLATE 57. The Zorn valley, followed by the river, the Marne-Rhine Canal, and the railway between Strasbourg and Nancy

The Low Vosges are extensively forested and only in the valley-floors is the forest cover interrupted by strips of pastureland; the *département* of Bas-Rhin, which includes much of the Low Vosges, had 34 per cent of its total area under forest in 1968. Far less population and settlement is found here than in the High Vosges, despite the appreciably lower altitude. There are a few small towns and the railway line from Strasbourg to Sarreguemines crosses the hills, utilising the upper part of the Moder valley. Some of these towns once had iron works and a few outposts of the textile industry survive, but the chief occupations are now dairying, forestry and the manufacture of wood products. The Low Vosges stand out prominently as an area of scanty population, for some communes have a density of about 20 per sq km (50 per sq mile).

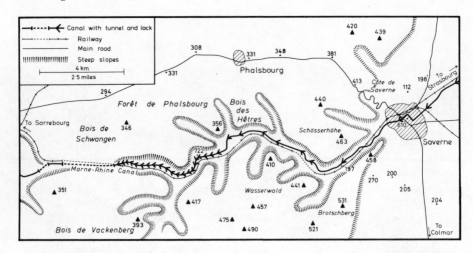

FIG. 19.2. The Saverne Gap

Relief is shown in a generalised way by means of hachures and spot heights in metres. In the east is the edge of the Vosges, fronting the Rhine rift-valley.

The main road from Strasbourg to Sarrebourg zigzags up the edge of the Côte de Saverne on to the plateau surface at about 400 m (1 300 ft), some 60–90 m (200–300 ft) lower than the hills to north and south; the fortress-town of Phalsbourg stands in this shallow gap. Minor roads are omitted.

Based on *Carte de France au 50 000ᵉ*, sheets XXXVI/15, XXXVII/15.

[1] L. Bertrand, *Les Grandes Régions géologiques du sol français* (1934), p. 146.

[2] This is sometimes spelt *bâlon*, but *ballon* is used on the *Carte de France au 50 000ᵉ* and on other recent maps.

[3] P. Marres, 'Le Vignoble alsacien', *La Vigne et le vin en France* (1950), pp. 85–9.

[4] M. Thouvenin, 'L'industrie papetière dans les Vosges lorraines', *Rev. Géog. de l'Est*, **10** (1970), pp. 35–64.

[5] J. Dion, 'Etude des peuplements forestiers: quelques vallées alsaciennes des Vosges', *Rev. Géogr. de l'Est*, **5** (1965), pp. 141–55.

# 20
# The Central Massif

The Central Massif[1] is an upland area, more or less bounded by the 300 m (1 000 ft) contour, and composed of varied rocks among which ancient crystalline rocks are dominant. It covers about 85 000 sq km (33 000 sq miles), or a sixth of the total area of France. Although its average height is about 900 m (3 000 ft), the maximum altitude is only 1 886 m (6 188 ft), attained in the Puy de Sancy in Auvergne. In places there are deep gorges and rugged pinnacles, it is true, but much of the Massif consists, in the words of Ph. Arbos, of 'ondulations lentes ou . . . surfaces planes'. Its geomorphological history has been one of great complexity, the details of which are by no means wholly unravelled.

## General features

The foundations of the Massif consist of a crystalline *socle* of granite, gneiss, schist and mica-schist.[2] Some of these rocks are of Pre-Cambrian age, others consist of highly metamorphosed sediments (described on the official *Carte Géologique de la France* as 'cristallophylliens d'âge indéterminé'), and some of the granites may be Carbo-Permian intrusions since they cut across the schists and gneisses. Areas of indisputable Palaeozoic rocks are small in extent, but Silurian rocks occur in the extreme southwest, others of Devonian age also in the southwest and again in the Morvan, and Lower Carboniferous rocks near Lyons and in small patches further west.

The whole area may have been peneplaned before the end of Carboniferous times (the so-called 'pre-Hercynian Peneplain'), but the evidence for this is decidedly scanty, and the first major event in the geological evolution of the Central Massif was the Carbo-Permian (Hercynian) orogeny. Two main trendlines of folding can be distinguished, the Armorican orientated from northwest to southeast, the Variscan from northeast to southwest; there must have been a complex structural apex where these met in the south-centre of the Massif. This orogeny has not left such clear results on the ultimate 'grain' of the Massif as in some of the other Hercynian uplands, mainly because of the uniform resistance to subsequent denudation of the granites, gneisses and mica-schists. However, the trend of the northeast to southwest folding can be seen in the eastern uplands of Lyonnais and Vivarais, where different crystalline rocks appear in succession in broadly parallel bands.

More striking is the pattern of Coal Measure synclines and Permian inliers (Fig. 20.1). The little coal basin of Ahun in northeastern Limousin lies on the line of a northwest to southeast fault and the Permian basin of Brive with several tiny coalfields is orientated similarly. The Autun-

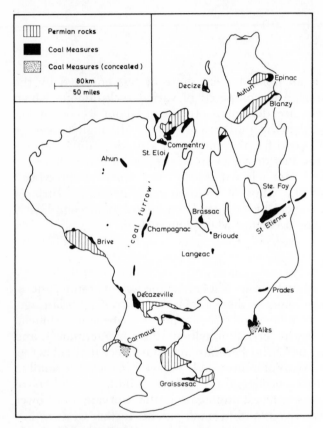

FIG. 20.1. The coal basins of the Central Massif
The approximate edge of the Central Massif is shown.

Based on the *Carte géologique de la France*, 1 : 1 000 000, published by the Service de la Carte Géologique détaillée de la France (1933).

Epinac and Blanzy basins enclose between them the crystalline upland of Autunois; the St Etienne 'furrow' (traced by the Furens-Gier valleys) separates Lyonnais and Vivarais; the smaller fields of Prades and Alès on the southeastern flanks reveal the same trend. The outstanding Hercynian line is the *sillon houiller* or 'coal furrow', which can be traced diagonally for a distance of 300 km (180 miles). In the extreme southwest, between

Villefranche-de-Rouergue and Najac, it forms the structural boundary of the Massif and is followed closely by the river Aveyron. This 'coal furrow' represents a distinct line of infolding associated with down-faulting, hence the preservation of several long coal basins, never more than about 15 km (9 miles) in width.

This orogenic period was long continued, not one of violent folding and sudden cessation, for both the surviving Upper Carboniferous and Permian rocks show evidence of folding. Then followed a long period of planation, which produced the first of the traceable major erosion surfaces. This probably started well before the end of the Carboniferous, since in places the Permian rocks lie unconformably on a surface already worn in Upper Carboniferous rocks. The result was an extensive peneplain which can still be traced in the higher parts of the Cévennes and Limousin, and around the margins of the Massif. This planation may be in part marine, slowly worn as the Mesozoic seas gradually transgressed, but other evidence is suggestive of subaerial weathering under semi-arid tropical conditions.

Deposition, mainly of limestones, went on slowly during the Triassic and Jurassic periods, though these deposits formed for the most part only a thin layer over the crystalline *socle* and indeed were soon to be removed, with one notable exception. In the south a synclinal depression or local 'deep' in the Jurassic sea projected northward between the crystalline promontories of the Montagne Noire-Ségalas uplands and the Cévennes; here deposition went on to a thickness of at least 1 400 m (4 500 ft) as downwarping continued. When later denudation removed the limestones from most of the Massif (though remaining an important element on its flanks), they survived in this depression as the Grands Causses. It is not known how much of the Central Massif was covered by this Mesozoic transgression, since so little of the rocks survive, but it probably did not cover Limousin, then the highest part of the Massif. By the end of the Jurassic the whole of the region had emerged, and the Cretaceous sea merely 'lapped' it around; a glance at a geological map shows the wide-spread Cretaceous deposits on the margins.

Denudation probably began to remove the Jurassic deposits during Cretaceous times, but the main period of activity was Eocene and Oligocene, and this produced another distinctive surface, called by French geomorphologists the *Eogéne*. This can be traced widely within the Central Massif, especially in Limousin, and on the borders it cuts across both the Mesozoic and the ancient crystalline rocks. This surface is characterised in places by a veneer of residual deposits known as the *dépôts sidérolithiques*.[3] These vary in character, sometimes consisting of Clay-with-flints, at other times of bedded sands and gravels, or of reddish clays, which according to H. Baulig are indicative of erosion and deposition under renewed semi-arid conditions.

During Middle and Upper Oligocene times, deposition was once more widespread. Rocks of this age, deposited under freshwater or brackish lacustrine conditions, are preserved in the south on the flanks of Margeride, in the northern Ségalas, on the margins of Cantal near Aurillac (where they are part-covered with lava flows), and much more extensively in the basins along the valleys of the Loire, Allier and Cher. In Limagne they accumulated to an appreciable thickness, indicating that the Eogene planation, which provided the detritus, was long continued.

In mid-Tertiary times the Central Massif was greatly affected by the Alpine orogeny. In point of fact, the southwestern parts had experienced faulting since the Jurassic, and this had increased in severity during early Tertiary times in association with the Pyrenean folding movements. The rigid structure of the crystalline block resisted these movements, and indeed it acted as one of the stable bastions which directed the alignment of the folding of the geosynclinal sediments to the south. The Massif however was affected both by associated *en masse* uplift and by faulting. It may be that the Pyrenean movements in effect 'revived' some of the Armorican trendlines in the south, and that the Alpine movements 'revived' some of the Variscan lines in the east and southeast. The net result was an uplift which inclined the massif both from east to west and from south to north, so that the main watershed now lies on its southeastern margins. The faulting was mostly experienced in the south (where the lines run from west to east), on the east (where multiple stepped faults form the edge overlooking the Rhône valley), and in the centre where the rift valleys of Limagne, Forez, Roanne and several others were created. Thus the broad outline of the Central Massif was defined.

There were two other major contributions, however, to the pattern of things; one was vulcanicity, the other further stages of denudation. Most of the volcanic activity can be attributed to the Pliocene, although some flows in Velay and Vivarais are clearly Miocene and the trachytes and andesites of Cantal and Mont Dore are Pleistocene. In some districts, notably the last two mentioned, at least three phases of volcanic accumulation can be discerned. One effect was to move the point of maximum altitude; from its position in Limousin in the Jurassic it shifted to the Cévennes as a result of the mid-Tertiary orogeny, and now although the highest foundation rocks are in the tilted southeast, the superimposition of volcanic rocks has located the highest individual eminences in Auvergne. The effects of vulcanicity are seen most markedly along a north–south line through Auvergne. Further east they appear in both Limagne and Forez, in the lava tablelands of Aubrac and the Le Puy basin, and in Vivarais where high peaks rise from the ridgeline and lava flows extend down the marginal slopes almost to the Rhône near Montélimar. The effects are seen also in the southern part of the Grands Causses, extending as an interrupted line of basalt buttes to the Mediterranean coast near Agde (see p. 426). Almost the only part of the Central Massif unaffected by vulcanicity is Limousin, another indication of its prolonged stability.

The uplift and tilting of mid-Tertiary times began a new cycle of erosion. An individual Mio-Pliocene surface has been determined in Ségalas at about 300 to 315 m (1 000 to 1 050 ft) by A. Meynier,[4] and again in Limousin at about 280 m (920 ft) by A. Perpillou.[5] According to H. Baulig's views,[6] the Central Massif consists not merely of a single warped peneplain, but of several surfaces intersecting each other at low angles; in other words, there has been a series of cycles or partial cycles, producing in fact a polycyclic relief. Some are ancient surfaces, subsequently covered with newer deposits and later still resurrected, while others belong to the period subsequent to the late Pliocene, and he attributes their origin to eustatic changes of sea level during which the land mass remained stable. The main erosion surfaces distinguished by Baulig in the southeast of the Massif are at 180, 280 and 380 m (590, 920 and 1 250 ft), with others less clearly defined at 150 and 250 m (490 and 820 ft).

Rivers were markedly rejuvenated as a result of these changes in base level. The remains of the erosion surfaces are preserved as lofty gently sloping plateau interfluves, contrasting with the steepsided valleys with their fragmentary benches. These valleys are most clearly developed in the south where the mid-Tertiary uplift was greatest, so that the long rivers flowing west and north have formed gorgelike valleys. In the northwest the gorge sections occur more on the margins, beyond the plateau surfaces where the rivers still flow in their shallow old-age courses.

The general drainage pattern of the Central Massif has developed as a result of the mid-Tertiary uplift. The main north-flowing arteries are the Loire and the Allier, originating near the southeastern edge and following elongated tectonic basins to the margins of the Massif. The western and southwestern rivers, notably the Dordogne, Lot and Tarn, were superimposed on the Eogene peneplain; the Tarn, for example, rises on the crystalline rocks and passes on to the limestones and marls of the Grands Causses, crosses the crystalline rocks again in the south of Ségalas, and then flows over Cambrian limestones and slates into the Basin of Aquitaine (Fig. 20.2).

In detail, however, some of the Tertiary structures are expressed in the courses of the rivers; the Aveyron, for example, turns abruptly southwest for 40 km (25 miles) at Villefranche-de-Rouergue along one of the major marginal faults. In the south the Thoré and the Jaur, though flowing in directly opposite directions, follow the Pyrenean fault trend between the Lacaune and Montagne Noire massifs. The Tertiary uplift and tilt were responsible for the many short streams, furrowed in the steep upland edge, which flow southeastwards to the Rhône or directly to the Mediterranean. The Gard rises on the ancient mica-schists on the flanks of Mont Aigoual, crosses an outcrop of granite on to the mica-schists once more, and descends over Lias marls and in turn over Jurassic, Cretaceous and Oligocene limestones to the Rhône floodplain. These steep and powerful streams have by headward erosion pushed back the main watershed to the northwest; the Chassesac for example has captured streams that once flowed either to the Lot or to the Allier.

Volcanic activity has also induced a number of drainage modifications. The huge cones of Cantal and Mont Dore became centres of radial drainage, and down their flanks torrents flowed both to the Dordogne and the Allier. The Truyère possibly once flowed northwestwards, continuing the direction of its present headstream between Margeride and Aubrac to the river Alagnon, hence to the Loire. Lava-flows issuing southeastwards from Cantal blocked its course and forced it to turn at rightangles towards the southwest, so cutting a deep gorgelike valley to the Lot. The lava plateau of Aubrac thus became a centre of radial drainage; the headstreams of the Truyère and the Lot rise on the slopes of Margeride only a few kilometres apart, flow parallel to each other towards the west, and then diverge at right angles in diametrically opposite directions around Aubrac (Fig. 20.2), to unite at Entraygues.

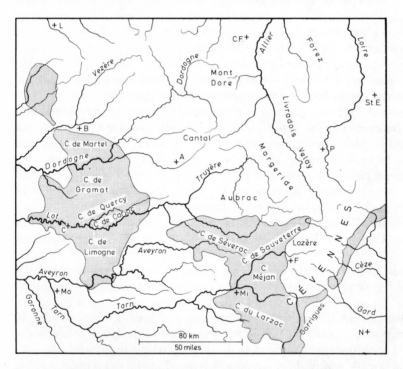

FIG. 20.2. The drainage dispersal of the southern Central Massif
Only the names of the more extensive *Grands Causses* are given; further details can be obtained from Fig. 20.7.

The outcrops of Jurassic rocks are stippled.

Some towns are indicated by abbreviations, as follows: **A,** Aurillac; **B,** Brive-la-Gaillarde; **C,** Cahors; **CF,** Clermont-Ferrand; **F,** Florac; **L,** Limoges; **Mi,** Millau; **Mo,** Montauban; **N,** Nîmes; **P,** Le Puy; **StE,** St Etienne.

Based on (*a*) *Atlas de France*, sheets 4, 5; (*b*) *Carte géologique internationale de l'Europe*, 1 : 1 500 000, sheet 30.

River erosion has continued during Quaternary and Recent times, accentuated by rejuvenation. Resultant deposition has taken place in the bordering basins of Aquitaine and Paris, in the form of sheets and cones of débris on the western flanks of the Rhône valley, and in the basins of Limagne, Forez and Roanne.

One more element, if on a relatively minor scale, enters into the pattern, the effects of glaciation. The volcanic cones and the higher parts of the crystalline uplands nurtured small snowfields from which glaciers moved outwards, and as a result cirques, U-shaped valleys and terminal moraines were formed. The increased floodwaters of the rivers towards the close of the Quaternary glaciation also exercised pronounced effects, trenching radially the major volcanic cones. Nivation processes were effective on the crystalline massifs, particularly in Margeride and Limousin. Mass movements of decomposed granites and coarse sands charged with water from the melting snows bared the upper slopes, filled broad depressions and sometimes obliterated breaks of slope. The more severe periglacial conditions formed blockspreads on these uplands.

The net results of this complex geomorphological history involve four distinct structural elements. There is (i) the Hercynian *socle* or crystalline basement; (ii) a covering of Mesozoic rocks, mostly removed from the Massif except in the Grands Causses, but contributing an essential element on the marginal plateaus and edges; (iii) the Eocene and particularly Oligocene deposits that accumulated under lacustrine conditions in the downfaulted basins of the Loire and Allier; and (iv) the volcanic rocks, including both cones and basalt flows.

Superimposed on this diverse structure and relief is an equally varied climate. The lofty upland is characterised by bleakness, by winter cold both on the higher parts and often as a result of inversion in the deep valleys and depressions also, and by a precipitation which in places exceeds 2 000 mm (80 in) but exhibits great variability. The winter cold is emphasised by the facts that over 900 m (3 000 ft) only about three months are frostfree, and the snow cover may lie for three or four months, even for six months in Cantal and on the Mézenc.[7] No permanent snowfields exist, although after a snowy winter some of the high cirques in Cantal may contain a snow patch sufficiently large to survive the following summer.

Within the Massif appear considerable climatic variations, both in a general way because it lies intermediately between Atlantic, Mediterranean and continental influences, and in detail because of altitude and aspect. South-facing slopes in the south of the upland grow olives, mulberries, figs and even pomegranates; maize appears in the southwest in place of the rye and buckwheat of Limousin. Some areas in the west and north are too damp and bleak for anything but moorland, conversely others in the south and east are too dry and too sun-scorched in summer for anything but *maquis* or *garrigue*.[8] While drainage is necessary in some places, paradoxically irrigation is required in others.

Soils too are very diverse. Those derived from the granitic and schistose rocks are base poor, coarse and infertile, while the warm soils developed on limestones can if adequately watered support excellent crops. The surfaces of the newer basalt flows are rocky and arid, while by contrast the older ones have decomposed to form dark base-rich soils. Some of the Tertiary and Quaternary sediments consist of coarse sands and gravels, others yield clay soils of good texture and rich in calcium salts. Areas of deficient or impeded drainage occur both on the uplands where shallow depressions are underlain by impermeable rocks and also in lowland basins where clays or sands are underlain by a hardpan. The multitude of rivulets on the crystalline uplands (the term *Millevaches* means a thousand springs, not a thousand cows), the springs bursting out among the basalts, and the wandering streams of Limagne and Forez, contrast with the near-karstic aridity of the surface of the Grands Causses.

As a whole, then, the Central Massif affords a limited *milieu*, though by no means a negative one, for human use. Population is thinly spread except in a few favoured localities, and the emphasis is on a stock-rearing economy which can utilise the upland pastures. In the centre and north cattle are dominant, while in the south (and particularly in the Grands Causses) sheep are important, although not on the scale of a century ago. Well-defined seasonal movements of stock still take place; sheep from Languedoc move up to Aigoual and Lozère or from the Causses to Aubrac, and cattle from the lower pastures of Limousin transfer to the uplands of Millevaches. A steady supply of calves and mature beasts leaves the Central Massif for the lowland pastures or moves directly to the markets of Paris and Lyons. Despite factors of remoteness and difficult communications, dairying is widely carried on, and results in such products as the *fromages bleus* of Auvergne. The arable economy is necessarily subsidiary to livestock, growing fodder crops and short-ley pasture, but cereals and potatoes are cultivated widely.

A further contribution is provided by the forests. The former woodlands which swathed all the Massif but for the highest uplands (these carry in fact a sub-Alpine flora) have been largely removed by centuries of cutting for fuel (including charcoal-burning) and for construction, and by burning and clearance to increase the area of pasture. Vestiges of former oak and beech woods remain, and chestnut groves occur widely on the southwestern and southeastern margins, contributing to their economy. During the last seventy-five years the area under forest has once again increased in the form of beech woods and of pine, spruce and fir plantations. This is largely due to official encouragement in the direction both of the creation of State forests (as in the Cévennes) and of subsidising private planting of small wood lots (as in Millevaches); there has been a marked increase during the last decade.

One would hardly call the Central Massif an industrial region, yet there are some industrial centres of importance. Advantages are indeed few;

they include the tiny coal-basins, some small-scale deposits of metals (still mined sporadically) and of kaolin, other local materials such as timber, skins and hides, available labour which seeks to supplement agricultural production, and water power. The last, used for centuries to work mill-wheels, has been capitalised since 1920 in the Dordogne, Truyère and Lot valleys, where barrages pond up reservoirs to supply power stations linked into the grid.[9] Although the rivers experience low water in summer, their winter maximum is complementary to the minimum of those in the Alps and Pyrenees which suffer from freezing.

For centuries various craft manufactures have been carried on at the small towns, including enamels, leather, textiles, lace, paper and wooden articles of all kinds. With the help of hydroelectric power, many of these activities still flourish, and some specialisations survive in a modernised form. Numerous centres of iron and steel production are found within the Central Massif, usually associated with the coalfields (Fig. 20.1). They grew up near small ore deposits, now exhausted or economically unworkable. In 1876 the forty-two blast furnaces in operation produced over 400 000 tons of pig iron, a quarter of France's total. They survived through sheer inertia, through the development of specialised industries based on steel, through the utilisation of the coalfields for steam-raising and some coke production, through the labour supply available in the isolated upland valleys and basins, and more recently through the development of hydro-electric schemes which afford current for electric furnaces. They have concentrated on the production of highly fabricated articles, mostly importing pig iron from Lorraine to make the special grades of steel required. Before the 1914–18 war, the obvious vulnerability of the north and northeast of France stimulated the armament industry in the centre, and the later military devastation of the frontier areas caused a boom.

Three towns have become the centres of considerable modern industrial agglomerations, and as a result are included among the thirty-two French towns with populations of over 100 000. These are St Etienne, Clermont-Ferrand and Limoges. Other industrial towns, smaller but still of importance, include Le Creusot and Montceau-les-Mines in the northeast, Alès in the southeast, Decazeville and Rodez in the southwest, and Montluçon and Moulins on the northern margins. The varied attractions of tourism are expressed in the growth of Vichy as a fashionable spa, of Le Puy in the upper Loire basin, and of Millau as a centre for the Grands Causses.

By contrast, however, to these centres with specially favourable circumstances, much of the Central Massif is an area of low and in places decreasing density of population. This has been emphasised since 1870 by a rural exodus from the hard and unrewarding labour of the uplands for the attractions of the towns. More people migrate from Lozère, Cantal, Ardèche and Corrèze than from any other *département* in France; they go to Paris, Lyons and the towns of Bas-Languedoc. The age structure of the

531

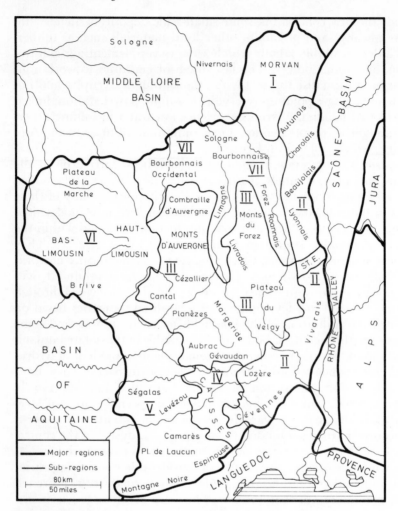

FIG. 20.3. The regions of the Central Massif
The Roman numerals (**I** to **VII**) correspond to the main sections of the
text, as follows: **I,** The Morvan; **II,** The eastern margins; **III,** The central
uplands; **IV,** The Grands Causses; **V,** The southwestern uplands; **VI,**
Limousin; **VII,** The northern basins and margins.

population is changing as a result of this exodus of many young people, of
a resultant declining birth-rate, and of the losses of manpower in two wars.
In the two *départements* of Lozère and Corrèze, there were only 4 005 births
in 1968, compared with 4 222 deaths. If the few larger towns are excluded,
the total population of these *départements* is less now than a century ago.
Indeed, if one considers the four *départements* which constitute the Auvergne
planning region (Allier, Cantal, Haute-Loire and Puy-de-Dôme), their
combined population has fallen from 1 479 000 in 1861 to 1 312 000 in

1968. In individual communes in the uplands the number of people has halved, as indicated by the many deserted farms and hamlets.

It seems most practicable to distinguish seven individual areas (Fig. 20.3). In the northeast projects the distinct block of the Morvan. Then along the eastern edge of the Massif for a distance of nearly 400 km (250 miles) are the high marginal uplands, from Autunois in the north to the Cévennes in the southeast. The heart of the Massif, though consisting of both crystalline basement rocks and of volcanic outpourings, constitutes a third subregion, flanked on the south by the limestone plateaus and valleys of the Grands Causses. The crystalline uplands of the Montagne Noire, Lacaune and Ségalas form the southwestern margins, and the plateau of Limousin the northwestern. Finally, it is convenient to group together the low-lying basins of the Loire and Allier valleys and the marginal lands of Bourbonnais into which these valleys gradually merge.

## The Morvan

This upland[10] of ancient crystalline rocks projects boldly from the northeastern corner of the Central Massif into the Mesozoic rocks which cover the southern part of the Paris Basin, and forms, in J. Beaujeu-Garnier's apt phrase, 'un môle de terres crystallines au milieu des terrains sédimentaires'. The Morvan is defined by a series of clearcut faults on both its western and eastern margins.[11] On the west sometimes occurs a single fault, as near Bazoches where the crystalline rocks lie directly against the Mid-Lias marls, sometimes by two or more broadly parallel faults, while the eastern faults are much more confused and less continuous. On the south the upland is separated from *Autunois* by a downfaulted depression trending from southwest to northeast; this is occupied mainly by Permian rocks and the narrow Autun-Epinac coalfield (Fig. 20.1), and drains southwestwards by the river Arroux to the Loire.

Around the western, northern and eastern margins of the crystalline rocks lies a band of Mid-Lias marls, continuous except in the northwest where the faulted edge of the Archaean rocks lies directly against Middle Jurassic limestones. Elsewhere the marls have been worn down to form a distinct peripheral depression, to which is given several *pays* names (see p. 229). Beyond this depression a prominent limestone scarp faces inwards towards the Morvan, its continuity interrupted only by the valleys of streams draining northwards to the Yonne and the Armançon.

Geologically the Morvan massif is one of great complexity. Most of its rocks are crystalline, of Pre-Cambrian age, but areas of Devonian and Lower Carboniferous slates also appear in the south. In the extreme north within the long syncline of Sincey-les-Rouvray lies a narrow exposure of much metamorphosed Upper Carboniferous rocks where anthracite has been worked in the past. Structurally too there are many complex features;

J. Beaujeu-Garnier traces seven distinct anticlinal axes and four synclinal axes of Hercynian age,[12] and faulting has introduced further structural problems. Peneplanation has cut right across these various rocks and structures. The post-Hercynian surface, which is still apparent in the north and northeast, has been subjected to a series of peneplanations, the relics of which are fragmentary. The net result is a gently undulating surface sloping from 260 m (850 ft) in the north (*Bas-Morvan*) to over 750 m (2 500 ft) in the south (*Haut-Morvan*). The highest summits, the rounded culminating points of two granitic bosses, are the Bois du Roi 902 m (2 959 ft) and Mont Beuvray 810 m (2 658 ft). The massive homogeneous rocks, especially the granites and gneiss, for the most part weather into gentle surfaces, although occasionally differential erosion does produce more striking features, such as the granulitic crags of the Roche du Chien in the valley of the Cure to the west of St Brisson, and the porphyry cone of Mont Genièvre in the southwest.

The drainage of the Morvan is radial, and from the impermeable gently sloping rocks a myriad of rivulets flow outwards, their upper valleys but slightly incised. In the more deeply cut main valleys, terraces at approximately 15, 30 and 70 m (50, 100 and 230 ft) above the present floodplain can be distinguished, related by Beaujeu-Garnier to the various erosion surfaces. The streams on the north find their way to the Serein, the Cousin and the Cure (themselves tributaries of the Yonne) or to the Yonne itself which rises on the northwestern slopes of the Bois du Roi. Another group from the southwestern margins of the Bois du Roi and Mont Beuvray work their way to the Aron, a right-bank tributary of the Loire, and others from the south and southeast of the massif flow down into the Autun depression to the river Arroux, another Loire tributary.

The impermeability of the rocks, the gentle gradients and the superficial depressions have resulted in the formation of a multitude of shallow *étangs*. Some have been transformed by the accumulation of sphagnum peat into upland bogs, some have been artificially drained, others have been dammed and deepened for water supply or for pisciculture. The largest sheet of water is the Etang des Settons in the upper valley of the Cure. Another large reservoir has been created by damming the Yonne above Montreuillon; the water now fills the main valley for 8 km (5 miles) upstream, extending also into tributary valleys.

## Land use and agriculture

Much of the surface of the Morvan is wooded, although not as continuously as in the past because of agricultural colonisation schemes on the one hand and of exploitation for timber on the other. About a third of the *département* of Nièvre is under woodland, and some fine forests still exist. The beech is the dominant tree over the uplands, with oaks on the northern margins and chestnuts on the lower slopes, while the area under plantations of conifers has greatly increased during the last thirty years.

For many centuries the Morvan's woodlands have been exploited for fuel and constructional timber, much of it being sent to Paris. Until just before the war of 1939–45, the timber was mostly rafted down the head-streams; it was stacked at certain points to await the deliberate releasing of floodwaters from *étangs* dammed higher up the valleys for that purpose.[13] It was floated downstream to collecting points on the Yonne, and then sent by barge along the Nivernais Canal and the canalised Yonne to Paris. Today much of the timber travels by lorry, although pit props are still transported by canal. Saw mills, timber yards and pulp mills are in operation at such towns as Clamecy and Prémency.

About 10 per cent of the surface of the Morvan is covered with moorland and upland bog. This area of waste is less than in the past, partly because of afforestation, partly because the area under permanent grassland has increased. Some cultivation is practised, mainly of wheat (which has largely replaced rye and buckwheat) and potatoes, helped by heavy liming and fertilising of the coarse acid soils. Farming activity is, however, mainly concerned with livestock; the rather poor *race morvandelle* has been supplanted by Charolais cattle, young stores being grazed on the hill pastures and then sent down to the lowlands for fattening. Pigs are reared and allowed to pannage in the beech woods.

## Population and settlement

Inevitably this upland area has suffered depopulation, as shown by ruined farms and even some abandoned hamlets; in fact, it is estimated that the Morvan has lost half its population during the last hundred years. The attractions of employment in the towns around in the Loire and Saône valleys, in the Le Creusot industrial district, and in Paris have drawn off much of the younger population. Château-Chinon in the southwest and Saulieu in the northeast are the only places of any size within the Morvan, and (unusually) they are situated high on the upland rather than in valleys; Château-Chinon rises in tiers up the slopes of a hillside, culminating in the church at a height of exactly 600 m (2 000 ft). A single-track line, the only railway to penetrate the Morvan, climbs circuitously from the Yonne valley line at Tamnay-en-Bazois to its terminus at Château-Chinon. Most of the other Morvan settlements are however in the valleys. The chief market towns for the region are in the marginal depression.

Some hamlets and small villages are found surprisingly high among the uplands, usually in a depression where surrounding hills afford protection from the winds. But the forest-covered heart of Haut-Morvan is virtually unpopulated, except for a few hamlets along the winding road between Château-Chinon and Autun, the only main road to cross the upland.

# The eastern margins

The eastern edge of the Central Massif overlooks the lowlands of the Saône-Rhône valley and of Languedoc for a distance of nearly 400 km (250 miles). The main rivers—Loire, Allier, Lot and Tarn—rise near this edge and trench their valleys across the whole Massif. With the exception of the volcanic peaks of Auvergne and the Mézenc, the highest points in the Central Massif are on this southeastern margin, notably Mont Lozère 1 702 m (5 584 ft) and Mont Aigoual 1 567 m (5 141 ft). The height of this rim decreases northward; to the west of Lyons it just attains 900 m (3 000 ft), and in the Mâconnais and Charolais overlooking the Plaine de Bresse it is 530 m (1 750 ft) or less.

While it is broadly true to say that this eastern margin represents a faultline scarp, the dislocations are multiple and complex. Some of the faults are associated with the original Hercynian structures, thus trending from northeast to southwest. In several downfaulted depressions Permian and Carboniferous rocks have been preserved among the crystalline rocks, including workable Coal Measures (Fig. 20.1). This faulting has caused diverse rocks to lie in close juxtaposition, so affording full scope for differential denudation. Some of the rivers have developed their valleys in downfaulted areas of less resistant rock, so forming distinct northeast to southwest depressions; one such is occupied by the Dheune flowing to the Saône and the Bourbince flowing in the opposite direction to the Loire.

## Autunois and its margins

The small massif of Autunois consists of a block of granite in the west and of more complex granulites and schists in the east, partly covered with Triassic and Liassic sandstones and marls. It is of no great altitude, the highest point being only 684 m (2 244 ft) and the greater part under 600 m (2 000 ft). The river Arroux, draining the depression containing the Autun-Epinac coalfield, cuts across the western part of the granite in a broad valley to join the Bourbince just above its confluence with the Loire. Like the Morvan to the north, much of Autunois is forested; the rest is under moorland, rough grazing and some arable. Many of the shallow lakes are artificial, and are used to maintain the level of the Centre Canal.

Paradoxically, the main significance of the Autunois massif lies in the depressions which flank it to north and south. The former is floored with Permian and Upper Carboniferous rocks, and the Autun-Epinac field produced annually about a quarter of a million tons of *gras* coal, consumed in a thermal station at Epinac. This depression forms a routeway between the Loire and Saône valleys, avoiding a lengthy détour around the forested uplands of the Morvan. The Romans appreciated this fact, and sited Autun (*Augustodunum*) on a prominent hillock near the south bank of the Arroux. This is a busy town, with several fairs and markets, hotels catering

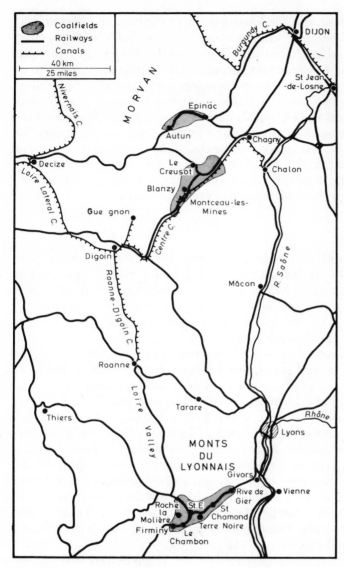

Fig. 20.4. The St Etienne and Le Creusot coalfields
**St E,** St Etienne. Mining ceased in these coalfields during 1973.

Based on *Carte de France et des frontières au 200 000ᵉ*, sheets 41, 47, 53, with areas of
the coalfield taken from the *Carte géologique de la France*, 1 : 1 000 000, published
by the *Service de la Carte géologique détaillée de la France* (1933).

for a tourist activity, and a number of manufacturing industries, notably
of furniture and other wooden articles from the timber of the Morvan and
Autunois. It is a route focus, and nine major roads converge on it.

More important is the southern depression, which forms a quite densely
populated industrial re-entrant, lying diagonally across the uplands,

between the Autunois and the Charolais. This contains the Blanzy coal-field, which produced 1·87 million tons of coal in 1969, with the busy towns of Blanzy, Montchanin and Montceau-les-Mines, and the steel works of Le Creusot, Gueugnon, Breuil, and Montchanin (Fig. 20.4). Pig iron is no longer made, but steel forgings and castings are produced, together with stainless steel, cables, agricultural machinery and a wide variety of mechanical and electrical engineering products. Other industries have developed along the banks of the Centre Canal, which utilises this depression, including the making of bricks, tiles, earthenware pipes and sanitary ware. Montceau-les-Mines and Le Creusot[14] now form agglomerations of steel works, factories, nineteenth-century housing and modern *cités-ouvrières*, though the coal-mines have recently closed.

## Charolais[15]

The Monts du Charolais form an upland mass between the Blanzy depression and the broadly parallel Grosne, which joins the Saône below Chalon. Structurally Charolais and Mâconnais to the southeast are part of a single ancient Hercynian anticline, and the valleys of the Grosne on the northeast and of the Sornin on the southwest represent its axis, denuded at an early date and infilled with Mesozoic rocks.

Charolais can therefore be divided into two. There is *Charolais cristallin*, the uplands of granite and gneiss, rising to such eminences as the Roche de Montmélard 772 m (2 533 ft) in the extreme south and Mont St Vincent further north. Much of it once was forested, but now this has been largely replaced by pastures, heavily limed and fertilised to make good the deficiencies of the thin acid soils. In contrast *Charolais sédimentaire*, sometimes called the '*bon pays*', is an area of varied Jurassic rocks—Lias clays and marls and Middle Jurassic limestones, lying on the western flanks of the crystalline rocks in the valley of the Sornin, a district known as the *Pays de Charolles* after the town of that name. The Mesozoic rocks occur too on the east in the Grosne valley, further diversified with patches of Triassic sandstone and Pliocene sands. These sedimentary rocks form a gentle country of limestone hills and clay-floored vales.

Charolais is famed for its large white beef cattle; there were over 553 000 cattle in Saône-et-Loire in 1968. About 40 per cent of this *département* consists of permanent pasture, both on the Jurassic limestones and Lias marls, and on the crystalline uplands. Another 10 per cent is under fodder crops—trefoil, lucerne, mixed grains and legumes, and roots. Animals are bred mainly for meat; mature animals are despatched directly to the abattoirs of Paris and Lyons and young stores are sent to other districts of France for fattening—for example, to the Paris Basin where they are fed on fodder beet and on sugar beet pulp. Stock fairs are held at Charolles and several other places, attended by buyers from a considerable distance. While this emphasis is on beef cattle, most of *Charolais sédimentaire* forms a prosperous mixed farming area; horses, pigs and poultry are also reared, wheat and potatoes are grown on the arable land, and vineyards (see p. 377) cover the limestone slopes overlooking the Saône valley.

## Mâconnais

The upland of the Mâconnais projects in a north-northeasterly direction into the Plaine de Bresse. The Saône flows closely along its eastern margins, and in fact makes a right-angle bend near Chalon around its northern extremity. A narrow 'slice' of granite overlooks the Grosne valley to the northwest; this rises for much of its length to over 450 m (1 500 ft), with one summit (la Mère-Boîtier) reaching 734 m (2 408 ft). A few other granite outposts appear to the northwest of Mâcon, but the rest of Mâconnais consists of Jurassic limestone and Lias marls. These rocks are banded in a direction parallel to the granitic 'slice', the result of profound faulting. There are even narrow exposures of Eocene clays and sands downfaulted among the limestones.

These varied rocks suffered the usual phases of peneplanation, but subsequent erosion has had full play. Several sharp-edged limestone edges overlook the Saône valley, each dropping as a step to the next marl terrace. Some parts of the limestone country form rather bare plateaus, with solution hollows, caves and disappearing streams. By contrast, the marl- and clay-filled depressions are damp and usually under grass, while the rounded granitic ridges to the west are forested.

The chief feature of the economy is the vine, grown on the *côtes* over-looking the Saône valley (see p. 377). The proximity of these uplands to Charolais has also induced a considerable development of cattle-rearing on the hill pastures.

## Beaujolais

A much higher group of uplands, the Monts du Beaujolais, extends south-ward from the high valleys of the Grosne headstreams as far as a distinct west–east structural depression, known as the Seuil de Tarare. This southern limit is emphasised by the river Reins draining westwards to the Loire and the Tardine eastwards to the Azergues, with between them a col through which pass the main road (N7) and (in a tunnel) the railway between Roanne and Lyons. The higher parts of Beaujolais, culminating in the rounded summit of Mont St Rigaud 1 012 m (3 321 ft), consists of porphyries and granulites, while outcrops of Lower Carboniferous lime-stones and shales are preserved within downfaulted zones which extend westward across the Loire valley to the south of Roanne. As in the case of the northern massifs, Jurassic and Tertiary rocks appear on the eastern flanks, a feature particularly evident on the slopes rising from the Saône valley near Villefranche.

Beaujolais is much dissected by a well developed pattern of valleys; the upper sections of many of these run north–south, following the faultlines, and leaving between them smooth-topped ridges orientated in the same direction. The long valley of the Azergues, for example, forms a broad gently sloping re-entrant into the heart of the uplands. Other streams drain more directly eastwards to the Saône or westwards to the Loire. This radial pattern leaves a substantial upland area, the Plateau de Poule, in the heart of Beaujolais.

A marked contrast is presented by the granite uplands (*La Montagne*), the Jurassic slopes descending in steps to the Saône (*La Côte*) and the broad valleys. The uplands, covered with thin soils, carry rough grazing, considerable tracts of gorse scrub, and pine plantations. The *Côte* on the east has long been devoted to the production of the celebrated red Beaujolais wines (see p. 377), although this has been less of a monoculture since the phylloxera ravages. Orchards, fodder crops and even small fields of cereals diversify the agricultural landscape.

The main valleys are quite densely inhabited; large farms and hamlets can be seen far up their heads to about 750 m (2 500 ft). Vaux-en-Beaujolais is situated to the northwest of Villefranche, on the slopes overlooking the valley of the Vauxonne at a height of 530 m (1 750 ft); wooded or pasture-covered slopes rise to rounded ridges, while the sheltered village is surrounded by orchards, vineyards, little fields of arable and patches of meadowland. One reason for this relative density of population is the surprising industrial activity. For centuries textiles have been made on a domestic basis, first wool, then silk and cotton. Today many small towns have factories, usually subsidiary to the big concerns in Lyons. Special cotton fabrics are made, and numerous local specialisations are evident.

## Lyonnais

The Monts du Lyonnais extend southward from the Seuil de Tarare to the well-defined coal basin of St Etienne. This is perhaps the most massive of the marginal uplands, for it consists solidly of mica-schists, gneiss and granite. On the west the faulted edge ends abruptly at the Tertiary-floored Plaine du Forez, in the east it terminates even more abruptly, so that just to the north of Lyons the Saône actually cuts into the crystalline rocks. The flanking Jurassic rocks are here absent, with the exception (to the northwest of Lyons) of the little outlying mass of Mont d'Or culminating in the 625-m (2 051-ft) summit of Mont Verdun, a limestone plateau resting on a foundation of crystalline rocks; these limestones have long been quarried to provide stone for the buildings of Lyons.

Much of the plateau of Lyonnais exceeds 600 m (2 000 ft), the highest point reaching 1 004 m (3 294 ft) near St Héand in the west. The gently swelling and rather bare ridges alternate with shallow depressions, sometimes marshy and peat-filled, though other parts are wooded, the higher areas with pine and beech, the lower slopes on the east with oak and chestnut. Agricultural activity is evident on the eastfacing slopes and valleys, largely owing to demands of the Lyons markets. Cattle are reared for both milk and meat; vines and orchards (particularly of peaches) grow on the terraced slopes; and lower down near the main valley floor heavy fertilising has helped to create productive market gardens.

As in the case of Beaujolais, the proximity of Lyons has influenced the development of a considerable textile industry, mostly connected with silk. Moreover, workpeople from the eastern Lyonnais villages travel daily considerable distances into Lyons. Other industrial activities were the result of fortuitous geological circumstances. In the heart of the crystalline massif, a narrow strip of Upper Carboniferous coal-bearing rocks is preserved in the syncline of Ste Foy-l'Argentière, formerly yielding from 20 000 to 50 000 tons of coal a year, though now closed.

## The St Etienne region

Lyonnais is bounded on the south by a depression through which the Furens flows westwards to join the Loire, and the Gier follows one of the characteristic structural lines in a northeasterly direction to the Rhône at Givors; their headstreams are separated by a watershed at a height of about 450 m (1 500 ft). The St Etienne field (Fig. 20.4) lies mainly in the Furens valley and was worked near St Etienne itself and at Roche-la-Molière, but it was also exploited over the watershed to the east near Terre Noire, St Chamond and Rive-de-Gier, and again to the southwest near Le Chambon and Firminy in the valley of another Loire tributary, the Ondaine. The coal seams are much disturbed by faulting and were difficult to work, but the mines were vigorously exploited during the war of 1914–18. St Etienne is linked with Lyons by a railway following the Gier valley, and about a quarter of the coal was consumed in the Lyons industrial district. About 330 000 tons of metallurgical coke were produced in 1969 in pit-head cokeries. The rest of the coal output (which totalled 1·6 million tons in 1969) was used for steam-raising in the St Etienne industrial district, for gas-making, for thermal-electric generators (notably the huge Centrale le Bec) to supplement the hydrostations, and for domestic consumption, though the field closed down during 1973.

The steel manufacturing region [1] extends from Firminy over the watershed into the Gier valley. Pig iron is no longer made locally, but imported from Lorraine. At Rive-de-Gier is a large steel plant, modernised in 1952, and numerous steel works are at St Etienne itself, St Chamond, Assailly and Firminy. Compared with Lorraine, the actual output of steel is small (of the order of 200 000 tons per annum), but there is an important production of special alloy steels for armaments, tools, parts of cars, cycles and aircraft, nuts and bolts, machinery, and a range of other metal articles.

An application of the postwar principle of 'readaptation' has taken place in the St Etienne district. Underinvestment, the restrictive independence of small producers, and wartime stagnation had resulted in this area becoming in the post-1945 years what M. Monnet had called 'a backward pocket' when in 1946 he urged a merger of the four major steel plants in order to effect modernisation and reconstruction. This was then turned down, but after the formation of the ECSC action was taken; the four plants were merged into the Compagnie des Ateliers et Forges de la Loire, and modernisation, conversion and concentration have been effected.

There are many specialised textile manufactures, mainly of silk and manmade fibres; St Chamond makes ribbons, laces, hosiery and elasticated cloth, and St Etienne, St Chamond and Izieux have plastics and rayon factories. Glass works have been long established at St Etienne and Rive-de-Gier, and pottery is made at these two towns and at Lorette and La Grand-Croix. Chemical works are associated with the coke ovens, producing tar, benzine, methanol, sulphate of ammonia and dyes. A considerable industry of textile dyeing was based originally on the availability of pure water from the rivers.

The district has been helped by its communications, although St Etienne is situated at a height of 500 m (1 600 ft). The railway between the city and Andrézieux, 14 km (9 miles) to the northwest in the Loire valley, was actually the first line to be opened in France (in 1828). Lines run down the Gier valley to Givors and Lyons, northward to the Loire valley and Roanne, and southwestward to Le Puy.

St Etienne is an important industrial centre and the economic capital of the eastern margins of the Central Massif. It is a market and shopping focus for a widespread rural district, for it is situated in one of the main routeways by which the eastern rim of the Massif can be negotiated. As an educational centre it is especially famed for its Ecole Nationale des Mines, founded in 1816. The population, which totalled 45 000 in 1830, by 1968 had reached 213 000. With a total population of over 330 000 people, this industrial belt lying diagonally across the eastern rim of the Central Massif affords a marked contrast with the uplands to north and south. St Etienne is linked with Lyons as a *métropole d'équilibre*, though as yet their complementary functions are but little developed.

## Vivarais

The name Vivarais[16] is applied somewhat widely to the uplands along the east margin of the Central Massif from the St Etienne depression to the Cévennes. It is difficult to define the boundary between Vivarais and the Cévennes, and in point of fact the name *Cévennes vivaroises* is bestowed upon that part of Vivarais overlooking the upper Ardèche valley. It is convenient, if a little arbitrary, to take the line of the Chassesac–lower Ardèche valleys as the boundary between Vivarais and the '*Cévennes proprement dites*'. A distinction must also be drawn between the crystalline upland (*la Montagne vivaroise*), and the lower plateau region (*le piémont vivarois*), lying between the high edge and the Rhône. The *piémont* is commonly known as the Plateau d'Annonay, and is much dissected by many short streams which flow down between projecting spurs. These distinctions are mainly the result of altitude, for Vivarais as a whole is made up of solid masses of granite and gneiss which continue westward into Velay. The watershed between the headwaters of the Loire and Allier and those of the Ardèche really forms the division between Vivarais and Velay.

The plateau surface is smooth and uniform, mostly between 900 and 1 200 m (3 000 and 4 000 ft) in height, with occasional swelling summits rising to 1 500 m (5 000 ft). By contrast their eastward slopes are gashed with ravines worn by the torrential streams making their way to the Rhône. Between them project ridges, at first broad and uniform, but narrowing eastward as the ravines widen into valleys; these are the *serres*, which become still more prominent further south in the Cévennes.

Another group of features is due to the effects of vulcanicity. The remains of basaltic lava flows form the highest summits of the Mézenc (1 754 m (5 754 ft)) and the Gerbier de Jonc (1 551 m (5 088 ft)), a neat little peak on the southern slopes of which rises the Loire. Small craggy cappings of basalt survive here and there to form prominent summits, contrasting with the smooth granitic slopes.

Finally, two quite individual uplands project prominently towards the Rhône, the Massif du Pilat in the north and the Coiron in the south. The former comprises a spur of gneiss and granulite surrounded on three sides by the Gier valley and the Rhône, culminating in the massive rounded summit of the Crest de la Perdrix and the more craggy ridge of the aptly named Crest des Trois-Dents. The Coiron is by contrast a much dissected spur of Upper Jurassic limestone capped with an escarpment of phonolitic lavas of Pliocene age, forming a narrow tableland running for 24 km (15 miles) in a direction south of east almost to the banks of the Rhône. Its sides are deeply scalloped by the valleys of torrential streams. Fantastically eroded piles of dark basalt often form ragged cornices overhanging the valleys.

A distinct zoning of vegetation and land use is apparent from the ridges to the Rhône valley. The higher summits are covered with rough pasture, moorland and in places plantations of pine, larch and fir, with the remains of more continuous beech woods, and lower down chestnut. The greater part of Vivarais falls within the *département* of Ardèche; just under a third of its total area was under woodland in 1968, and over a third was under permanent pasture, utilised mainly by cattle in the north and by herds of sheep in the south, many of which are brought up in summer from the limestone country of the Rhône valley. But nearly a third was waste, and only a tenth was returned as arable, most of which occurs on the lower terraced slopes just above the floor of the Rhône valley and in valley depressions. On the lower terraces fruits are grown (notably peaches, cherries, plums and in favoured localities figs), vines and mulberries, although the last are now much less important than in the past. Irrigation is commonly used, and water is led from rivulets in channels along the terraces. Small fields of wheat, potatoes, fodder crops and vegetables of various kinds are grown, and even quite high up under the crest of the uplands are patches of rye and potatoes.

Vivarais is not an area of dense population, and parts of the high uplands are virtually uninhabited. Nevertheless, over the whole of Ardéche the density averages about 46 per sq km (120 per sq mile) in 1968, a figure achieved without any major urban centre to swell the total, for the largest town is Annonay and the *chef-lieu* is the little town of Privas. Most of the population of Vivarais live in small towns and villages in the valleys, many of them situated where the slope of its valley becomes markedly gentler and the walls recede. A few small villages, often consisting of high-storeyed stone buildings clustered on the terraced slopes, are found far up the valleys, some as high as 1 200 m (4 000 ft).

Little industrial activity is found in Vivarais. Annonay, centrally situated in the valley of the Cance, is a market town, and has tanneries, glove-making works and a paper mill. Around the flanks of Mont Pilat are villages which come within the Lyons industrial orbit and possess small silk mills. Vals-les-Bains on the southern flanks of the Coiron has utilised the numerous mineral springs which burst out of the sides of the valley to become a pleasant little spa.

## The Cévennes

On a clear day one can see from viewpoints in Nîmes or Montpellier a dark blue line of hills 50 km (30 miles) away to the northwest. Here the edge of the Central Massif is defined most clearly by a fault line scarp trending from northeast to southwest. The ridgeline consists of a broad upland of crystalline rocks, more or less continuous with Margeride to the north and flanked by the Grands Causses on the west and south. It forms a rolling tableland at a height of between 1 200 and 1 400 m (4 000 and 4 500 ft), gently incised on the northwest by streams that find their way westwards to the Lot and the Tarn. Above this general level, rounded summits rise merely thirty metres or so, described by E.-A. Martel as *croupes mamelonnées* and *gibbosités de granit*. A northern group culminates in the mass of Lozère (1 702 m: 5 584 ft), the highest point on the whole eastern margin of the Central Massif, and a more southerly group of summits has its highest point in Mont Aigoual (1 567 m: 5 141 ft), crowned with a meteorological observatory. In places occur great piles of rectangular granite blocks, with sometimes curious pinnacles. Elsewhere the slopes are covered thinly with coarse granitic gravels, so smooth that in winter they form pleasant ski-fields. Much of the upland consists of less resistant metamorphosed slates (mostly phyllites), which also weather to form gentle slopes; Mont Lozère is so called from the *lozes* or plaques of slate which occur commonly on its flanks. The ridge is at its narrowest to the northeast of Mont Aigoual, where it is actually trending from west to east; the lowest point is the col of the Barre des Cévennes, at only 930 m (3 051 ft), while a little to the northeast another gap, the Col de Jalcreste, is crossed by the motor-road between Florac and Alès via the little town of Anduze, known as *la Porte des Cévennes*.

Numerous depressions occur on the uplands where Mesozoic rocks (mostly Lias clays) have been downfaulted along lines running from west to east. Even occasional patches of Upper Triassic sandstone survive. Generally speaking, therefore, the ridgeline and the western slopes and valleys of the Cévennes, planed by the various cycles of erosion, are gentle and mature in appearance, as A. Meynier describes them, 'très réguliers, très étendus, très monotones'.[17]

The eastern slopes of the Cévennes present a very different appearance. Deep steepsided ravines run up to the edge of the ridgeline, separated by narrow crumbling rocky ridges. These valleys, again in the words of Meynier, are 'profondes et escarpés', by comparison with their westerly neighbours which are 'douces et évasées'. The tilting of the Central Massif left a steep edge facing the Mediterranean; from the summit of Mont Aigoual the land falls 1 200 m (4 000 ft) in a direct distance of only 6 km (4 miles). The major part of the steep face is eroded into the crystalline rocks themselves; both the beds of the ravines and the rocky sides of the ridges show this quite clearly. The slates tend to form wider and less rugged valleys than do the granitic rocks.

A series of nearly parallel torrential streams flows southeastwards to join the Cèze, the Gard and the Hérault. Their sources are working back rapidly through headward erosion, the result of rapid runoff and steep gradients. The rain tends to fall in concentrated downpours; the most notable record in this area was the 990 mm (39 in) received in forty-eight hours at Valleraugue in September 1900, which gashed and scoured the landscape.[18] In the words of Ph. Arbos, 'Le relief . . . manifeste la violence de l'érosion méditerranéenne'. These easterly headstreams (known as *gardons*) interlock with the more gentle rivulets which form the Tarn and the Lot (Fig. 20.2); indeed, in several places the Hérault source streams have captured former headstreams of the Dourbie in the depression between Mont Aigoual and Mont Lingas. The Hérault is a particularly active river, for the main stream rises on the southern slopes of the Aigoual well to the west of the actual summit, and flows southwards first over the crystalline rocks, then crosses a southeasterly extension of the limestone Causses; one of its headstreams, the Vis, in fact drains the eastern margins of the Causse du Larzac. The gorges of the Hérault (in places 400 m: 1 300 ft deep), the Vis, and its left-bank tributary the Lamalou, are on a dramatic scale; the lower Lamalou gorge, known as the Ravin des Arc, with its waterworn cliffs, potholes, arches and cascades, surpasses anything in the Grands Causses to the north.

These contrasts between the relief of the crestline and western slopes of the Cévennes on the one hand and of the steep eastern flanks on the other is reflected in the land use and the economy. On the uplands a pastoral way of life has been dominant for many centuries. The hill slopes carry pasture of variable quality, in places improved by liming and fertilising, elsewhere either so overgrazed or conversely so neglected that it has degenerated into rough grazing or still further into heath, covered with ling, broom and coarse grasses.[19] Along the valleys of some of the west-flowing rivulets appears better meadowland, in places improved by the trenching of irrigation channels over the surface. Patches of arable land near the occasional settlements grow rye, buckwheat, oats and potatoes, and vegetables are cultivated in carefully tended gardens (often protected from winds by high stone walls) for local needs. But the area of arable is small, usually less than 5 per cent of any commune, and moreover half of that in any one year is under fallow.

The animals reared are chiefly sheep, and cattle are rarely seen. Some flocks live permanently in the Cévennes, moving from hamlets in the valleys to the upper slopes, but most sheep come up from Bas-Languedoc, following an age-old pattern of transhumance. The routeways winding up from the plains of Languedoc can be seen from far away as white ribbons on the hillsides; they are potent causes of soil erosion, since their worndown surfaces become runnels which readily develop into ravine gashes. During the last sixty years sheep-rearing has markedly decreased, together with transhumance. It is difficult to give exact figures, since only parts of three *départements* fall within the Cévennes region, but to use Lozère as an indication, there were 300 000 sheep in 1890 and only 209 000 in 1968. This decline is due to the deterioration of upland pastures, to the increase in woodland, to the tendency towards rural depopulation with resultant shortage of workers, and to the generally unprofitable character of upland farming.

A long struggle has taken place on these uplands between the pasture and the woodland. Except perhaps for the highest summits of Aigoual and Lozère, where relics of a sub-Alpine flora can be discerned (the tree-line lying at about 1 500 m (5 000 ft)), thick beech woods with some ash probably covered most of the slopes; in the local *patois* the term *Cebenno* indicates a wooded slope. Rainfall is everywhere adequate, indeed plentiful, for tree-growth; at the Aigoual observatory the mean annual total is 2330 mm (92 in). But people of the upland villages have cut gradually into the woodland cover for fuel or building material or to increase the extent of pasture, and uncontrolled burning and close grazing by sheep and goats for long prevented any natural forest regeneration. In the third quarter of the nineteenth century a counteroffensive began, carried on both by individuals with financial assistance from the state and by the state itself. Though rainfall is adequate, the chief climatic disadvantages are the wind, for the *mistral* blows over the exposed ridges towards the Mediterranean with icy force, and the summer drought, which together make the early years of plantation establishment difficult. In addition summer fire hazards are grave. However, both state forests and privately owned plantations now cover most of the available land, and postwar planting has made good the inevitable heavy inroads of 1939–45. Large compact blocks of beech and spruce, together with the native pine, some Douglas and silver fir, and larch on the lower slopes, have been planted. Most of the high communes now have a quarter of their land under forests, some more than half. The state forests are carefully managed and a system of gradual thinning and progressive planting rather than complete felling is employed. In some communes the widespread progress of rural depopulation has been checked by forestry employment; some men are whole-time forestry workers, others work on a part-time basis, providing a useful supplement to the limited income derived from a small farm. Even so, the shortage of labour is such that it is necessary to bring in labour gangs for felling and removal, to supplement the labour of permanent employees.

Population is scanty and settlements few. Some small villages lie in the high valleys and depressions well above 900 m (3 000 ft); one of the most elevated hamlets in the whole Central Massif must be Salarials, on the southern flanks of Lozère at a height of 1 412 m (4 632 ft). A few other settlements are situated in the high valleys of the Lot and the Tarn, some with hotels, notably Bagnols-les-Bains with its thermal springs, others the centres of a sporadic mining activity. But except for a line of villages along the main road down the Lot valley, other settlements are few and widely separated.

The southeastern slopes of the Cévennes present a very different aspect. On a diverse terrain of steep rugged ridges, deeply cut valleys, and, lower down, gently inclined but stepped slopes, are imprinted many of the characteristics of a Mediterranean climatic régime and an intensive polyculture. On the lower south-facing terraces are mulberries (now much less important than they were) and olives, long rows of vines, patches of wheat in narrow fields enclosed by dry stone walls, orchards of peaches, apricots, cherries and higher up apples, market gardens commonly irrigated by rivulets led along the terraces, and huddled villages of tall stone houses among the cypresses. On the rugged slopes of the ridges between the terraced valleys flourishes the *garrigue* in all its variety, with scrub oaks among the aromatic shrubs.

Still higher, from about 400 to 750 m (1 350 to 2 500 ft), appears a zone of carefully tended chestnut groves, degenerating among the rocky slopes into scrubby semiwild trees. Villages and large farms are located on the floors of the valleys, their occupants depending on this mixed agricultural economy, though for long the basis of subsistence has been chestnut porridge and goats' or ewes' milk cheese. Some of the high basins contain meadows of good quality, often irrigated, and here cattle have increased in numbers, supplying milk for the towns of Languedoc. On this Mediterranean side of the Cévennes there is again evidence of rural depopulation in the part-ruined hamlets and abandoned farms, with the chestnuts and fruit trees degenerating into the *garrigue* that has spread around them.

Roads push their way, sometimes by incredible loops and zig-zags, up through these valleys. A few motor roads cross the ridge, improved for the ubiquitous autobus services which link remote hamlets with civilisation, for the lorries carrying timber and produce, and for the cars of tourists. Rail communications are difficult and limited. One remarkable main line (the chief longitudinal rail route in the Central Massif) works its way north from Nîmes and Alès via Villefort, crossing transversely the ridges and ravines by means of innumerable viaducts and tunnels to penetrate the uplands to the Allier valley, hence to Clermont-Ferrand. A branch from this line at La Bastide runs westward to Mende and Millau, thus affording a complete crossing of the Cévennes.

Many villages and hamlets are situated along these railways and roads, others are reached only by tracks into *cul-de-sac* valleys. Little towns at the mouths of each valley form servicing and market centres, with their periodic fairs. Some contain small specialised silk industries.

Along the margins of the Cévennes occurs a series of depressions in the Lias marls, forming an area of prosperous agriculture; the many streams down the slopes are used for irrigation. A string of towns forms a linear 'paysage minier jusque dans la châtaigneraie' (Ph. Arbos). The basis of their industrial activity is the Alès coalfield, which produced about 1·4 million tons in 1969, which however is now being run down and is scheduled soon to close. A small-scale steel industry, originally using local ores, produces a small amount of high-grade steel, and a variety of specialised engineering and metallurgical industries has developed. Other activities include the manufacture of chemicals and the reducing of bauxite into alumina at Salindres and of silk at several towns. Mulberries are widely grown, and silkworms are reared domestically.

## The central uplands

The term Auvergne, derived from a Gaulish tribal name *Arverni,* is often applied, if rather loosely, to the central uplands as a whole,[20] more narrowly as a modern planning region comprising the *départements* of Allier and Puy-de-Dôme. Some geographers restrict the term to the line of volcanic uplands lying west of the Allier valley from the Puy de Dôme to Aubrac. Others include the western part of the Allier valley, centred on Clermont-Ferrand, as *la grande Limagne auvergnate.* The granitic uplands to the south-east are sometimes described as *la Margeride auvergnate* in distinction to the more outlying *Margeride du Gévaudan.* On the northern margins are the crystalline uplands of the *Combraille d'Auvergne.* In this section, however, the usage of the term Auvergne is restricted to the line of volcanic hills, one major ingredient in these central uplands.

The central uplands may be divided into two main groups (Fig. 20.3):
the crystalline massifs of Margeride, Livradois, Forez and Madeleine, and
the volcanic hills of Auvergne proper and of the Plateau du Velay. The
last of these is complicated by the fact that it includes the Bassin du Puy,
the most southerly of the basins through which the Loire pursues its northward course; it is, however, so much part of the volcanic uplands, with its
lava flows and plugs and much of it above 600 m (2 000 ft), that it is
desirable to include it in this region of central uplands.

## Margeride

Delimited by the headstreams of the Truyère and the Lot in the west and
by the long line of the Allier in the east, lies the massive upland of Margeride
(Fig. 20.2). In general outline it consists of broad planated plateau surfaces,
1 200 to 1 400 m (4 000 to 4 500 ft) in altitude, with rounded '*sommets
mamelonnés*' rising barely 90 to 120 m (300 to 400 ft) above this level and
cols sinking only 60 m (200 ft) or so below. The highest point, in fact, the
Truc de Randon in the south, only attains 1 554 m (5 098 ft). In the southern
*Margeride du Gévaudan* the rock consists predominantly of well-jointed
granite, which has weathered to form a surface diversified with large
rectangular blocks, culminating at intervals in torlike mounds, columns
and obelisks. Sometimes these granitic masses project irregularly from a
coarse vegetation cover, elsewhere from bare granite pavements. In the
northerly *Margeride auvergnate* the rock is predominantly gneiss and mica-
schist, and the relief is smoother and more monotonous; its higher surfaces
are only gently furrowed by many rivulets flowing in a northeasterly
direction to the Allier, and southwesterly to the Truyère and the Lot.

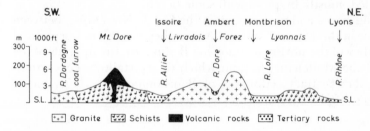

FIG. 20.5. Geological section across the Central Massif
The length of the section is about 201 km.

Based on A. Cholley *et al.*, *La France* (n.d.), p. 240.

The surface of Margeride is one of the most desolate in the whole Central
Massif, with vast extents of poor upland grazing, ling-covered heathland,
bilberry moors and peat bogs, snow-covered and bleak in winter. In the
words of Ph. Arbos, 'une atmosphère de mélancolie, de tristesse même,
baigne cette montagne, une des régions les plus désertes de l'Auvergne'.[21]

## Livradois, Forez and Madeleine

This group projects boldly northward between the downfaulted Limagne on the west and the series of Loire basins on the east. It forms, in fact, the middle 'prong' of hills for those who visualise the uplands of the Central Massif as a trident, providing a remarkably continuous line of high-level uplands; it is possible to walk northwards, if one is so disposed, for a distance of over 150 km (90 miles) without ever descending below 900 m (3 000ft).

Livradois is separated from the Monts du Forez by the downfaulted valley of the Dore. Both consist of granites and granulites, with some masses of gneiss and of mica-schist in the southwest. Their relief is even more subdued than that of Margeride. The highest point in *Haut-Livradois* in the southeast is Notre-Dame-de-Mons, a rounded eminence attaining 1 210 m (3970 ft). *Bas-Livradois*, sloping gently towards Limagne, represents the surface of an early Tertiary peneplain, diversified only by a few tiny downfaulted depressions (such as that of St Dier) containing Oligocene sediments.

The Monts du Forez consist largely of the surface of a peneplain at about 900 m (3 000 ft) from which swell the rounded vestiges of higher levels.[22] The highest point, Pierre-sur-Haute, attains 1 640 m (5381 ft), formed by a chaotic pile of weathered rectangular boulders. Some features on the eastern slopes of Forez are the result of volcanic activity, especially to the west of Montbrison; these include basalt flows, culminating in Mont Semiol, and small cones. The flanks of the Forez are diversified with striking boulderstrewn gorges. In the higher southern parts distinct U-shaped valleys, cirques (notably that of Valcivières), and terminal moraines afford traces of the former glaciers. Most of the plateau is covered with coarse pasture or with a heath vegetation of myrtle and bilberry, though large areas are wooded, mostly by pines with some beech.

The Monts du Forez end in the north at the Col de Noirétable, between the headstreams of the Durotte and the Auzon. Beyond this col, separated by the deep valley of the northward-flowing Besbre, are the uplands of the Bois-Noirs and the Madeleine, beyond which the crystalline rocks vanish steeply below the Tertiary sediments of Bourbonnais. As the name of Bois-Noirs would imply, they are thickly wooded.

## The Puys

In contrast with the monotonous crystalline uplands, the volcanic landscapes present a variety of physical forms, ranging from peaks and extensive lava flows to minute cones and residual plugs. In the north is the remarkable landscape of the *Chaîne des Puys*. From a uniform plateau surface varying in height from about 800 to nearly 1 000m (2 700 to 3 250 ft), worn both from the crystalline basement and the products of ancient periods of vulcanicity, about seventy little cones, mostly of Pleistocene age, rise for a further few hundred metres. The majority are ash and cinder cones, with a thin vegetation cover in places, but much of the surface is covered with rough black cinders. Other cones consist of solidified siliceous lavas. The cones are strung out in chains from north-northeast to south-southwest, 'une véritable galerie des divers types de cônes'; indeed their forms are so varied that they form in truth 'un musée de reliefs éruptifs' (Ph. Arbos). The Puy de Jumes and the Puy de la Coquille have regular craters with circular rims; the Puy de Pariou has a cone with a crater 180 m (200 yd) in diameter within an outer partly destroyed crater ring; the Puy de Louchadière forms a miniature caldera; the Puy de Côme has a double crater with a cone on the outer rim. Some circular depressions are the result of explosive activity without any extrusion of lava, notably the Gour de Tazenat. Some of the volcanoes are of the 'Peléean-dome' type, in which the siliceous lavas were so highly viscous that they formed craterless extrusive domes. The best example of these, and the largest of the individual volcanic peaks, is the Puy de Dôme (Plate 59), 'une gigantesque pustule' (A. Meynier) which attains a height of 1 485 m (4 872 ft). It was long thought to be either a small granite boss or a laccolith revealed by denudation, but it is clear that it was built up by slowly extruded trachytic lava (known as *domite*). An interesting *puy* of a different character is the Chopine, about whose origin there has been much discussion; it consists of a mass of granite, a fragment of the *socle cristallin* which probably stuck in the 'throat' of the volcano and was subsequently exposed by the removal of the surrounding cone.

A striking feature of the landscape is the number of basalt lava flows, which have penetrated neighbouring valleys.[23] They are exceedingly numerous, both in space and time; on the flanks of the Puy de Dôme, for example, seven different lava flows are superimposed. The newest flows are of fissured lavas, and form desolate rocky regions with an irregular wrinkled surface. Some of these flows have blocked valleys; the lava from the twin Puys de la Vache and Lassolas moved down towards the narrow Veyre valley, and blocked the mouths of several valleys, so creating a number of lakes. Some, such as the former Lac Randamme, are now peat-filled, others, notably Lac d'Aydat, still form sheets of water.

## Mont Dore

To the south of the *puy* country occurs the complex volcanic structure of *Mont Dore*. Its present height is 1 886 m (6 188 ft), but at the time of its maximum activity it probably exceeded 2 400 m (8 000 ft), and it is about 27 km (17 miles) in basal diameter, considerably bigger than Vesuvius. The original cone has been so much dissected by fluvial and glacial action that the crater has disappeared and the inner structure of the volcano is revealed. Volcanic activity probably began in the Miocene, associated with the dislocations responsible for the downfaulting of Limagne, and continued until the late Pliocene. A variety of trachytes, andesites and basalts was poured out, probably from several different vents, forming both vertical plugs and gently inclined flows. Radial drainage was succeeded by the Quaternary glaciation; the Dordogne actually rises in a large cirque on the northwestern side of the massif. The resistant trachytes and andesites now form sharply pinnacled residual peaks, notably the Puy-de-Sancy which forms the highest point, the Aiguiller, and a number of other peaks, while a massive basalt flow in the northwest comprises the plateau summit of the Banne d'Ordanche.

## Cantal

Further south still is the huge cone of Cantal, noteworthy both for its regularity and its size. About 80 km (50 miles) in diameter, its base covers an area of just over 2 600 sq km (1 000 sq miles), approximately the same extent as Mount Etna, resting on a basement of both crystalline and Oligocene rocks; the latter are visible in the southwest and also in deeply trenched valleys in the northeast. Its origin is still a matter of conjecture; some authorities attribute its vast size to two major vents, others to three, though one theory postulates a much denuded gigantic single caldera. Whatever the origin may be, the result is a mass of volcanic rocks of Miocene and later age, mainly andesitic breccias and conglomerates, with also masses of scoriae, metamorphosed mud flows, and layers of fine ash. The forces of denudation have had full play on such heterogeneous materials, and a preglacial radial drainage system developed which trenched the slopes. Probably the huge broken-rimmed crater nurtured a Quaternary *névé*, from which glaciers flowed outwards, enlarging the valleys, forming cirque basins and depositing moraine. Many of the valleys have a distinct U-section, and numerous lateral hanging valleys or *gouttières* can be seen. Several small lakes (the Lacs de Guéry, de la Crégut and des Bondes) occupy some of these glacial hollows, others are now filled with peat.

Postglacial river action has continued the work of destruction; head-streams of the Truyère flow down the southern slopes, the Cère, Jordanne, Doire and Maronne down the western slopes to the Dordogne, and the Rhue on the north also to the Dordogne. Between these gashed valleys inclined plateaus (*planèzes*) narrow upwards into rocky peaks. The largest of these spreads out towards the east as the Planèze de St Flour, forming an extensive level lava-plateau, while others radiate towards the northwest, the northeast, and southeast.[24]

The result of these several processes is a magnificent irregular pyramid with four curvilinear faces culminating in three major and numerous minor summits. These main peaks are quite different in character; the Puy Mary (1 787 m: 5 863 ft) in the west is an ice-rounded dome of andesite, the Plomb du Cantal (1 858 m: 6 096 ft) on the east consists of a rather unimpressive rounded mass of basalt where several *planèzes* converge, and, most striking of all, the Puy Griou (1 694 m: 5 558 ft) is a pinnacle of phonolitic trachyte which projects steeply for about 60 m (200 ft). The last may represent a near-vertical dyke exposed by denudation. Some subsidiary cones occur on the flanks, notably Puy Violent in the west.

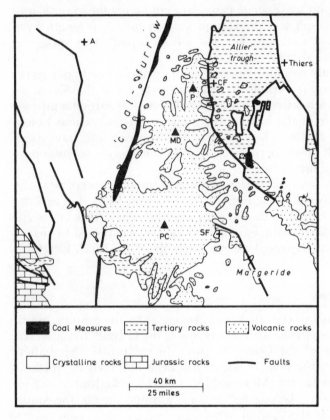

FIG. 20.6. The major volcanic areas of the Central Massif
The three main volcanic peaks are shown by initials as
follows: **MD,** Mont Dore; **P,** Puy de Dôme; and **PC,**
Plomb du Cantal.
  The towns shown are **A,** Aubusson; **CF,** Clermont-
Ferrand; and **SF,** St Flour.

Based on *Atlas de France,* plate 7 (1939).

The surfaces of the lava flows are extraordinarily weathered, on the lower slopes providing rich black soil, higher up forming a rough surface of bare rock. Some of the basalts are so permeable that water penetrates them, forming sinkholes, subterranean drainage systems and copious springs at the margins.

553

## Aubrac and Cézallier

Less striking than the volcanic peaks, but making a considerable contribution to the relief, are the basalt plateaus of Aubrac (to the south of Cantal) and Cézallier (between Cantal and Mont Dore). Aubrac[25] is composed of lava flows varying in age from late Miocene to Pliocene, with the basal ones resting on the Eogene peneplain cut across the granitic and schistose rocks. The result is a plateau 40 km (25 miles) in length from northwest to southeast and 130 km (80 miles) broad. The surface is remarkably uniform at about 1 300 m (4 250 ft).

Cézallier is an equally monotonous area, with a general height of 1 100 to 1 200 m (3 500 to 3 900 ft), rising to 1 555 m (5 101 ft) in the Signal du Luguet. It represents a relatively thin accumulation of basalt on a gneissic basement. At the base of the basalts, lying on the gneiss, various much-altered lignites and diatom clays of possibly Miocene age have been discovered. The basalt flows are probably of Pliocene age, the topmost ones consisting of large tabular masses.

The surface of these lava plateaus is uniformly smooth, except near the margins, where the rivers flowing radially from Aubrac to the Lot and the Truyère, and from Cézallier to the Alagnon and the Allier, have cut steep-sided valleys. The surface of the basalts here too has weathered to yield a good soil, largely pasture-covered except where there are beech forests.

## The Plateau du Velay

An area of volcanic rocks, separated from Auvergne by the granitic massif of Margeride, lies across the headstream region of the Loire.[26] In the west is the plateau-like ridge of the *Chaîne du Devès,* in the centre the shallow Tertiary *Basin du Puy,* the floor of which has been modified by volcanic activity, and in the east the Mézenc-Mégal-Gerbier de Jonc group of peaks. The last, however, belong to Vivarais, forming part of the south-eastern marginal rim of the Central Massif.

The Chaîne du Devès, nearly 65 km (40 miles) in length and culminating in the Montagne du Devès (1 463 m: 4 800 ft), forms a distinct range separating the Allier and the Loire. This upland is the product of a series of Pliocene fissure-eruptions, and comprises for the most part a basalt plateau, slightly inclined towards the margins, with a central line of low volcanic hills. These are geologically older than the *puys* of Auvergne, and have suffered more denudation, but they survive as gentle cones, some with quite distinct craters; one explosion crater contains the almost circular Lac du Bouchet. The surface of the lava has been much weathered to form a thick black soil, and the plateau is covered with quite good upland pasture, together with beech and pine woods.

In the centre of the Plateau du Velay the granite basement has been downfaulted to form a shallow basin, sometimes referred to as the *Creux du*

PLATE 58. Le Puy. The basin of Le Puy, with the town clustered around the Rocher de l'Aiguilhe

*Puy.* The Loire enters this basin from the south by way of a valley deeply cut through the granitic plateau, and leaves it in the north through a series of fine gorges across another granite horst. Three diverse elements enter into the composition of the basin of Le Puy: the underlying granitic floor, an incomplete veneer of Tertiary sediments, and volcanic accumulations overlying both granitic and Tertiary rocks. The granite floor is exposed as a low ridge extending diagonally across the basin from northwest to southeast, and also as several isolated masses. The incomplete Tertiary cover consists of Oligocene limestone, marls, clay and gypsum, and of Pliocene sands. The volcanic contribution includes Miocene basalt flows in the south and east, Pliocene flows in the west, and many small cones. All these have been much dissected by the Loire and its numerous tributaries converging towards the centre of the basin in deeply trenched valleys. The clays and marls form small basins and depressions, the limestones in places stand out as low hills.

Many of the basalt flows have been eroded into steepsided tablelands, with some fantastic columnar or 'organ-pipe' structures around their margins. The more resistant basalt forms a horizontal cap rock so that a vertical cornice falls away from the summit, succeeded by an abrupt change of slope where the less resistant underlying Tertiaries appear.

555

Sometimes the lava flows are quite thick; the plateau of Polignac, for example, forms a small flat-topped eminence, rising sheer from the floor of the basin. The most striking relief features occur near Le Puy itself, where several isolated rock pinnacles diversify the landscape. The Rocher de l'Aiguilhe rises sheerly for 85 m (279 ft), crowned by the church of St Michel reached by a winding rock staircase. The town of Le Puy stands on the lower slopes of Mont Anis, culminating in the craggy mass of the Rocher Corneille surmounted by a large statue of Notre Dame de France. These and other rock pinnacles may be erosional survivals of dissected basalt flows, or they may be resistant plugs that have remained after the surrounding cones have been removed (Plate 58). In the east and south of the basin numerous small cones of phonolite sometimes reveal well-developed craters.

## Land use and agriculture

It is not easy to describe in general terms the features of the economy of such varied upland region, although its limitations are obvious. The three *départements* of Puy-de-Dôme, Cantal and Haute-Loire cover a considerable part of the region, and afford some indication of the pattern of land use. During the last decade a regional improvement plan has been worked out for Auvergne, with State financial assistance. The main integrated projects are concerned with forestry, livestock farming and tourism.

The woodland areas are found chiefly on the northern crystalline uplands of the Madeleine and the Bois-Noirs, on the slopes of the Forez, in the valleys which dissect the volcanic district of Auvergne, on the flanks of the volcanic hills of the Devès, in Livradois where there are several State forests,[27] and on the eminences within the basin of Le Puy. The natural woodland was probably beech, and this is still the most common tree, although pines have been planted. Sweet chestnut grows well on the crystalline slopes. The chief areas of forest occur between about 600 and 850 m (2 000 and 2 750 ft); although the upper treeline on sheltered slopes is as high as 1 200 m (4 000 ft), most of the bleak windswept plateau surfaces are devoid of trees and form dreary moorlands, peat bogs and areas of grazing. During the last decade there has been a big increase in the wooded area under coniferous plantations; about a third of the three *départements* is now wooded, compared with a fifth ten years ago.

The area of arable land is surprisingly high in this upland region. Haute-Loire of course contains the upland basin of Le Puy with its areas of quite fertile calcareous loams enriched with volcanic débris, while the figures for Puy de Dôme include the *terres noires* of Limagne (see p. 582). But agriculture pushes its way far into the uplands, making use both of the deep valleys that dissect the edge of the volcanic region of Auvergne and of the surfaces of the *planèzes,* where the fields are enclosed by black dry-stone walls made of basalt blocks. Arable farming occupies great areas of

*Land use, 1968 (percentages of total area)*

| | ARABLE | PERMANENT PASTURE | WOODLAND | WASTE AND NON-CULTIVATED LAND |
|---|---|---|---|---|
| Cantal | 16 | 47 | 26 | 7 |
| Haute-Loire | 19 | 33 | 33 | 10 |
| Puy de Dôme | 22 | 34 | 27 | 7 |

Source: Ministère de l'Agriculture, *Annuaire statistique* (1970–1).

the basaltic plateau surface of Devès, and is even found in sheltered depressions high up on the crystalline uplands, as evidenced by the little village of Estables near the source of the Loire at a height of 1 350 m (4 430 ft), with its tiny walled fields. Rye, once universally grown, is still found, but it has been largely replaced by wheat (grown as high as 1 200 m (4 000 ft) on the volcanic plateaus of Velay), barley, oats, potatoes and increasingly fodder crops. Favoured slopes in Auvergne and Velay are covered with vineyards and orchards.

PLATE 59. The Central Massif: the Puy de Dôme and the crater of the Puy de Côme

Considerable areas of permanent or temporary pasture and of fodder crops are used for stock-rearing; these include the poor moorland pastures of the crystalline massifs and the better pastures of the well-watered volcanic soils. They are, however, snow-covered for several months, and so seasonal movement of animals necessarily takes place. The chief element in the economy is cattle, and 856 000 animals were in the three *départements* in 1968, of which over half a million were dairy beasts. The animals move seasonally between villages and farms in the valleys and depressions up to the high *montagnes*. Stall-fed in the winter on fodder crops (which now occupy about a third of the arable), they spend a month or two in spring on the irrigated water-meadows, and then move on to the high pastures. The emphasis is on milk production, although calves for veal are sent away in early summer to the markets of Paris and Lyons. Cheese is produced in large quantities; the *fromages bleus* of Auvergne are made at centres such as Thiézac in Cantal and Laqueille near Mont Dore, and several well-known varieties (*Cantal, Bleu St Nectaire, Laguiole* and *Fourme*) are produced. Sheep have declined in numbers, but in 1968 there were still 255 000 in the three *départements*. Many come up from Bas-Languedoc for the summer months, or move across from the Grands Causses on to the high pastures of Aubrac and Margeride when the summer aridity becomes pronounced. Much ewes' milk is turned into cheese which is processed in Roquefort.

## Population and settlement

Population is dispersed widely though somewhat thinly over much of this region, and villages and hamlets are found at high altitudes in sheltered valleys and depressions. The summits of the crystalline uplands are largely deserted, except for shepherds' huts; Margeride must be one of the most extensive unpopulated areas in all France.

There are obviously few large towns, and the regional foci are actually situated on the margins. Thus Clermont-Ferrand (see p. 584) is the regional centre for the uplands of northern Auvergne, Thiers on the eastern edge of Limagne for the Madeleine, Ambert and Montbrison on either side of the Forez. In Cantal several market towns are situated in the radiating valleys, notably Aurillac in the valley of the Jordanne to the west, Murat in the Alagnon valley to the northeast, and St Flour in the upper Truyère valley to the southeast. Similarly Marvejols on the upper Colagne is the centre for southern Aubrac, and Mende is the focus for three distinct regions—Margeride, Lozère and the northeastern Causses. Le Puy is the *chef-lieu* of Haute-Loire, and an administrative, commercial and tourist centre. This town has been famous for its lace for centuries, and once employed over 10 000 women, but the industry has sadly declined, although some quality lace is still sent to the Paris fashion-houses. Other small industries include paper-making and the distillation of liqueurs.

# The Grands Causses

The geological map of the southern part of the Central Massif shows an extensive area of Jurassic limestone, a curious Z-shape enclosed between Ségalas and the massifs of Lozère and Aigoual. This region is known as the *Grands Causses*,[28] or as the *Causses Majeurs*. Structurally this limestone region is the result of the accumulation of sediments in a basin within the crystalline rocks, trending approximately north to south, as described above (p. 525). Most of these deposits consist of limestones of Middle and Upper Jurassic age, the latter appearing on the surface in the extreme east. The limestones rest on and largely cover the Upper Lias marls, which now occur on the surface only around the margins.

The Causses region underwent planation in early Tertiary times, then it was uplifted, tilted and fractured in mid-Tertiary times; vast faults can be discerned in the strata forming the walls of some of the gorges, with throws of hundreds of metres.[29] Most of the faults which affected the Causses trend from west to east. Two major faultlines in this direction, to the south of the Lot and Aveyron valleys, enclose a rift valley containing Jurassic rocks which form a westerly prolongation of the limestone plateaus, the Causses de Rodez and Séverac. This, incidentally, is a structural feature of great age; it probably represents a gulf of the sea in late Palaeozoic times, for it contains several small coalfields (Fig. 20.1) and deposits of Permian shales and sandstones, over part of which lie the Jurassic rocks.

The cycles of erosion inaugurated by the mid-Tertiary uplift and tilting have cut across the varied structures, and a series of surfaces at various levels from 1 200 m (3 900 ft) down to 600 m (2 000 ft) has been recognised by P. Marres.[30]

The rivers which rise on the crystalline rocks near the high southeastern rim of the Central Massif flow westwards over the limestone and then again on to the crystalline rocks before escaping into the Basin of Aquitaine (Fig. 20.2). Their valleys have divided the peneplaned surfaces of the Causses into a number of individual blocks (Fig. 20.7); the valleys and the plateaus therefore form two main relief elements. Differential erosion has resulted in a third; the less resistant Lias clays now form a series of depressions, known as *vallons*, around the margins of the Causses between the limestones and the crystalline rocks.

## The valleys

The northern margin of the Causses is roughly defined by the valley of the Lot; only a few small outliers of limestone appear to the north of it. The main river of the Causses is the Tarn, with its two tributaries the Jonte and the Dourbie; it rises on the granitic uplands of Mont Lozère at a height of about 1 500 m (5 000 ft), but descends nearly 450 m (1 500 ft) down the western slopes in less than 16 km (10 miles). At Florac the river enters a deep gorge, and for nearly 80 km (50 miles) between Florac and Millau the valley sides rise for heights of 450 to 600 m (1 500 to 2 000 ft) above the river bed. In places these precipitous cliffs fall sheer to the water's edge, elsewhere the walls recede and leave shingle banks and a strip of meadow. Thus in 'the Narrow' (*Le Détroit*) near La Malène the walls approach closely, to widen out into the broad vale of the steeply walled Cirque des Baumes a few km downstream, below which a northwestern spur of the Causse Méjan projects boldly to form an overhanging beaked promontory, narrowing the valley once again.

Even more striking is the valley of the Jonte, where vertical walls of resistant limestone are separated by sloping terraces or ledges worn in the narrow bands of shale or marl, producing a steep stepped effect. This river flows intermittently underground for a considerable distance from below Meyrueis to its final resurgence at Les Douzes. The Bonheur, one of the headstreams of the Dourbie, which rises on the western slopes of the Aigoual, plunges down the Perte du Bonheur into a labyrinthine underground course 11 km (7 miles) long, part of which has been exposed as a gorge by the collapse of the roof. The water finally issues from a vertical rift in a limestone cliff as a fine waterfall, the Abîme de Bramabiau.[31]

The regime of these rivers is variable. Heavy rains on the crystalline uplands to the east supply their headstreams with a runoff which contrasts with the waterless character of the limestone plateaus through which they flow. The main streams receive much underground water by way of resurgences, the most prominent of which are plotted on Fig. 20.7.[32] The Tarn receives no surface tributaries between Florac and the confluence of the Jonte, but its flow is maintained by five major and about twenty-five minor underground affluents; just below Le Détroit, for example, a powerful torrent bursts from a cave on the right wall of the valley. During autumn and winter the concentrated rains can produce sudden flooding. It is recorded that during the floods of 1876 the water level of the Tarn rose in 'the Narrow' 20 m (65 ft) in a mere eight hours; immense destruction was wrought in riparian towns as far downstream as Montauban. By contrast, in summer the volume of the rivers is much reduced; shallow but still fast-flowing, the playground of canoeists, the numerous branches of the current flow between shingle banks.

### The plateaus

These valleys divide the limestone into individual blocks which are named on Fig. 20.7. The plateaus form an extensive area of limestone karst; when one stands on a slight prominence the wide nature of the erosion surfaces is abundantly evident. The general level does, however, swell to a number of gentle eminences, as Ph. Arbos expresses it, 'un moutonnement de mamelons'. The highest point of the Causses in fact attains 1 278 m (4 193 ft) in the east of Méjan.

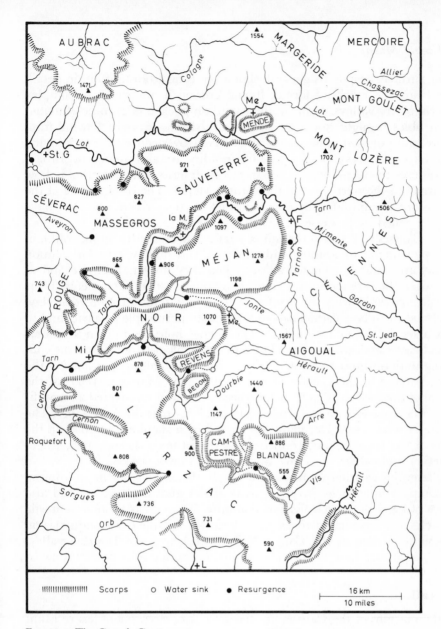

Fig. 20.7. The Grands Causses

The abbreviations represent towns, as follows: **F,** Florac; **L,** Lodève; **la M,**
La Malène; **M,** Mende; **Me,** Meyrueis; **Mi,** Millau; **St G,** St Geniez.

The main *Causses* are outlined by hachuring; Aubrac in the north, although
flanked by a prominent edge, is, of course, a lava plateau. The higher granitic
and crystalline uplands to the east of the *Grands Causses* are named. A number
of spot heights (in metres) is given to emphasise the general altitudes. The
Causse de Rodez lies to the west of Séverac.

The relations of the *Grands Causses* to the wider dispersal of Central Massif
drainage, together with the position of the lower *Causse Aquitain*, are shown on a
smaller scale on Fig. 20.2.

Based on: (*a*) *Carte de France au 200 000ᵉ*, sheets 58, 65; (*b*) E.-A. Martel, *Les Causses majeurs* (1936),
folding map; and (*c*) P. Marres, *Les Grands Causses: étude de géographie physique et humaine* (1935), vol. i,
Plate XXX, 'Carte hydrographique des Grands Causses', p. 93.

The surface, despite its general planation, is far from uniform in detail, for it bears the marks of former fluvial erosion in the shape of complex patterns of dry valleys. Many of these contain pockets of granitic alluvium and pebbles brought down by now vanished streams once flowing from Lozère and Aigoual. The *combes* are flanked by steep even overhanging cliffs. Larger depressions of a *polje*-like quality are also numerous. In fact Marres uses the term *les poljes caussenards* to describe the elongated hollow of Carnac in the northwest of the Causse Méjan. The original line of the depressions was initiated by now vanished Tertiary rivers, and they have been deepened by processes of solution.

The Causses well reveal the minor karstic features of limestone solution. Rock pavements are seamed with crevices, and shallow circular solution hollows are common, known as *cros* when they are small in size and as *sotchs* when they are more than 30 to 45 m (100 to 150 ft) in diameter. Their floors are covered with the residue of limestone solution, *terra rossa* clay, sometimes in sufficient thickness to form an impermeable covering and so allow a small lake to accumulate. The deeper holes lead down to underground caves and grottoes well known to speleologists, some systems containing underground rivers and lakes. The most famous 'pot-hole' is the Aven Armand in the Causse Méjan, explored by Martel in 1897; at the bottom of this, 200 m (650 ft) below the surface, was discovered a magnificent series of caves with stalagmite columns known as the *Forêt Vierge*. The celebrated Grottes de Dargilan, discovered by a shepherd in 1880 on the flanks of the Causse Noir, consist of a series of magnificent caves, where stalactites and calcite 'curtains' are present in profusion.

Differential weathering helps to diversify the surface, for in addition to the compact limestones, layers of weak shales and marls occur, and also masses of hard but much fissured dolomite. The last form some fantastic pinnacles and castellated rocks, notably in the Cirque des Rouquettes on the southern edge of the Causse Noir, overlooking the Dourbie valley. As Arbos puts it, there is 'une forêt de piliers et d'aiguilles dolomitiques'.

## The vallons

On the margins of the Causses are the *dépressions marneuses* of less resistant Liassic marls. On the east their outcrop is narrow, but the depression can be traced southward from near Mende in the Lot valley through the Valdonnez. Then it is followed to the south of Florac by a left-bank tributary of the Lot, the Tarnon; this latter section is sometimes referred to as the Sillon de Florac. Further south again, on the western flanks of Aigoual, is the depression of Meyrueis, occupied by the headstreams of the Jonte. On the north of the Causses the Lias outcrop is followed closely by the Lot valley between Mende and Rodez, and on the south headstreams of the Hérault occupy the basins of Bédarieux and Lodève.

The Lias outcrop is at its most extensive in the west, where the basins of

Millau and St Affrique form broad fertile lowlands lying between the Causses and the crystalline uplands. These marginal lands, with their lower elevation and good marly soils, are favoured for agriculture and settlement compared with neighbouring districts.

## Land use and agriculture[33]

The Grands Causses and their margins occupy the greater part of the two *départements* of Aveyron and Lozère.

*Land use, 1968 (percentages of total area)*

| | ARABLE LAND | PERMANENT PASTURE | WOODLAND | WASTE AND NON-CULTIVATED LAND |
|---|---|---|---|---|
| Aveyron | 23 | 29 | 23 | 18 |
| Lozère | 9 | 48 | 30 | 9 |

Source: Ministère de l'Agriculture, *Annuaire statistique*, 1970–1.

It is probable that the area of woodland was formerly very much greater, but as in other uplands once clearance had started natural regeneration and maintenance proved to be virtually impossible. The protective cover of vegetation was removed, soil was then washed away revealing much naked limestone, and even where young trees could start to grow, grazing soon destroyed them. In favoured areas, such as the floors of the depressions and some of the sloping valley sides, appear groves of evergreen oak and beech, and clumps of *Pinus sylvestris*; the western part of the Causse de Sauveterre is particularly well wooded. Since 1945 many plantations, mainly of Austrian pine, have been established, and their area has been doubled during the last decade. Considerable areas are covered with a patchy scrub of box, juniper, dwarf oak, lavender, blackthorn and small lime-loving plants growing in crevices among the bare limestone pavements.[34]

The areas of arable are confined mainly to depressions on the plateau surface floored with *terra rossa*, to small tracts in the river valleys, and to the Lias clay districts of the *vallons*. More than half the arable in Lozère, usually enclosed by dry-stone walls (*clapas*), is under cereals, either wheat or oats, though in Aveyron the proportion drops to a third, while a quarter of Lozère and two-fifths of Aveyron are devoted to fodder crops of various kinds. Orchards and vineyards cling to south-facing slopes on natural or manmade terraces; the shelter, the quite high summer temperatures, and the sunshine which seems doubly bright reflected from the limestone cliffs behind, combine to create a remarkable impression of subtropical luxuriance. In many places water is led from springs in channels along one terrace, then on to a lower one. As a result apricots, peaches and plums all flourish, and even figs, almonds and pomegranates do well. Vegetable gardens and patches of maize and tobacco are also patiently cultivated.

A large part of the Grands Causses and their margins is covered with permanent pasture. The limestone plateau carries much sweet though scanty grass, and the Lias marls grow a rich pasture. For many centuries sheep have been grazed in large herds; in 1968 Aveyron had 572 000 sheep, Lozère 209 000 (between them over 8 per cent of the French total), while other flocks come up from the Mediterranean coast during the summer months. The sheep are kept principally for their milk, from which *Roquefort* cheese is made, so called after the town which clings to the sides of the valley of the Soulzon on the western edge of the Causse de Larzac, with cliffs towering above the highest houses. The famous caves, part natural, part artificially hollowed out and supported with columns, maintain a temperature and humidity constantly favourable for the maturing of the cheeses, with the beneficial aid of *penicillium glaucum*. The development and commercialisation of cheese production have been helped by the development of cooperation. The first cooperative dairy was opened in 1887, and now over 500 individual firms are grouped within the several societies. Ewes' milk is processed not only from the Grands Causses, but also from the surrounding crystalline uplands, from the Pyrenees and even from Corsica.

Cattle are not as important as sheep, but the extension of fodder crops, of improved temporary pastures on the Lias marls, and of irrigated water-meadows on the valley floors, has contributed to the fact that there are now some 418 000 cattle in the two *départements*, of which nearly half are dairy animals.

## Population and settlement

The Grands Causses are among the most sparsely populated parts of France. The population of Lozère in 1968 was 77 600, the lowest total of any *département* in France, and with a density of only 16 per sq km (41 per sq mile) it had the second lowest average after that of Alpes-de-Haute-Provence. In places, notably in the west along the Lias clay margins, the average per square kilometre goes up to about 30 (80 per sq mile), but some parts of the limestone plateau are virtually uninhabited except for shepherds during the summer living in their scattered stone cottages. Occasional large but isolated farms stand in sheltered depressions surrounded by trees, with small arable fields of *terra rossa* enclosed by stone walls and from 400 to 600 ha (1 000 to 1 500 acres) of rough grazing. Apart from these, few settlements are found on the surface of the Causses, and most of the villages occur along the valleys, clinging to a terrace at the foot of a steep cliff, linked by roads which follow the banks of a river, sometimes along a terrace blasted out of the limestone cliffs or tunnelled through projecting spurs of rock.

The larger towns are all in the flanking *vallons*; they are peripheral market towns and route centres for both the Causses and the neighbouring districts. The largest town is Rodez, the *chef-lieu* of Aveyron but lying to the west of the Grands Causses proper, and serving as a market town both for the Causse de Rodez and for a large part of Ségalas (see p. 566). It is the focus of a number of roads and of a well-developed autobus service, and holds numerous markets and fairs.[35] The chief town of the *Causses* region proper is Millau, situated in a broad basin surrounded by gentle slopes culminating in limestone edges. Here converge the Tarn and Dourbie, while below the town the Tarn valley leads westward to Albi and ultimately to the Gironde. It is a pleasant town, set among orchards and gardens, a gateway to the Tarn valley for tourists, and with small-scale industries such as glove-making from the skins of local sheep. St Affrique in the southwest is the market town for neighbouring areas of the Causses, and for parts of Ségalas and the Montagnes de Lacaune. Séverac-le-Château in the Lot valley serves as a centre both for the northern Causses and for Aubrac. Mende, the *chef-lieu* of Lozère, is situated on the banks of the Lot in the northeast of the Causses on the borders of Margeride. Behind the town rise gentle slopes of pasture, steepening and becoming forest-covered, to the dissected limestone crags under the edge of the Causse de Mende. It has some small textile industries. Florac, on the banks of the Tarnon just before it joins the Tarn, is a tourist resort. Roquefort, as already mentioned, is primarily concerned with the processing and export of cheese. In all, these little towns indicate that this is one of the least urbanised parts of France.

Communication links are difficult; indeed no railway crosses the area from west to east, though one line, using tunnels, spirals and viaducts, runs southward from Montluçon through Auvergne by way of St Flour, Marvejols and Séverac-le-Château to Millau (up which steep section the trains are double-headed) and then on via Bédarieux to Béziers. The road system is well engineered despite physical difficulties, and has been developed largely for the tourist industry, though many parts are roadless and served by little more than mule tracks.

## The southwestern uplands

The southwestern uplands include first the plateau of the *Ségalas*, so-called from the former dominance of rye (the *pays de seigle*), lying between the Dordogne and the Tarn, and second the Pre-Cambrian massifs of the Lacaune and the Montagne Noire, flanked to north and south by considerable outcrops of Cambrian schists and limestones and on the east by a varied series of minor uplands and depressions in the neighbourhood of Lodève. These southwestern uplands are characterised by a number of major faultlines, which in the north trend in the characteristic Armorican way from northwest to southeast, forming a clearcut boundary between the crystalline massifs and the Jurassic rocks of the Causses du Quercy. Further south another longitudinal fault (but with an orientation more from north-northeast to south-southwest) separates Ségalas proper from the Causse de Limogne; the Aveyron below Villefranche-de-Rouergue flows along the line of this fault for 30 km (20 miles). Most of the other faults in this region trend from west to east. Several parallel faultlines enclose a long down-faulted depression enclosing the Causse de Rodez, the Permian basin of Marcillac, and the coal basin of Campagnac-Aubin-Decazeville (Fig. 20.1). Other faults trending more or less from west to east define the southern margins of Ségalas and both edges of the Montagne Noire.

## Ségalas

This name, applied originally to the upland projecting westward between the Aveyron and the Tarn, now signifies the wider *pays siliceux*. In a broad way there is a certain uniformity; distinct erosion surfaces (notably the Eogene) cut right across the slates, mica-schists, gneisses and the occasional granite intrusions.[36] The land slopes gently from 670 m (2 250 ft) in the northeast to 400 m (1 300 ft) on the margins of Albigeois and Lauraguais. In detail, however, much more diversification is apparent. Bordering the Millau Liassic depression on the northwest are gneissic rocks which culminate in the broad ridges of Lévezou and Palanges, forming swelling summits, separated by deeply notched cols. Further north the peneplain is interrupted by buttelike eminences, the residuals of a former erosion cycle. Further north still, between the Cère and Cèle valleys, the land rises to the bleak summit of La Falzinde.

Conversely, many parts of Ségalas sink below this general level. The river valleys are prominently incised across the crystalline rocks, especially the Lot and the Truyère, which, with their main confluents (mostly rushing torrents with numerous cascades), dissect the plateau into a number of independent fragments, some of which form the most isolated and remote districts in the whole Central Massif. The middle Tarn crosses the Permian rocks which lie to the west of the Grands Causses, forming a broad depression floored with red Permian soils which flanks Ségalas on the south.

The diversity in the physical landscape of Ségalas is reflected in the number of individual *pays* names: the *Ségala du Quercy* which borders the Jurassic lands of Quercy in the north between the Cère and Cèle valleys; the *Châtaigneraie* to the south of Aurillac; the *Veinazes* bordering the northern side of the Lot valley below its confluence with the Truyère; the *Viadène* in the extreme east on the edge of Aubrac; the *Ségala rouergat* to the south of Rodez; and the *Ségala tarnais*[37] to the north of the Tarn valley.

The bleak uplands of Ségalas are covered with tracts of heath and gorse-covered scrub, while much consists of poor scrubby pasture. The thin acid soils weathered from the siliceous rocks are not very fertile, and much of Ségalas was for centuries a poor agricultural region, with an economy based on rye, chestnuts and sheep. An area of heath was burnt off, cropped with rye for four or five years, and then allowed to revert; a privately owned grove of chestnuts, or communal rights in one, provided nuts for porridge meal; and sheep were reared on the scanty pasture. That was the basis of life, perhaps supplemented by charcoal-burning, tanning, and the domestic spinning and weaving of cloth. Some parts of Ségalas are still poor areas with a scanty population; the upland of the Ségala de Quercy grows much rye, and the Châtaigneraie is so limited that to neighbouring districts the name is synonymous with poverty—'ce pauvre pays de Châtaignes'. But over much of Ségalas, particularly in the south, the agricultural economy has been transformed as a result of improvement of the soils by lime and fertilisers. Lime became available when kilns were built in 1820 at Carmaux, fired by coal from local collieries, and later better road and rail communications enabled fertilisers to be brought in. Several west–east railway lines now cross the region, and an important longitudinal line works its way northward from Toulouse to Aurillac. These enable produce to be exported from the region. As a result, rye has almost disappeared from many parts, replaced by wheat, potatoes and fodder crops and in the south by maize. Some of the basins have become important for fruit (peaches, apricots, cherries, pears), almonds, and even near Marcillac and Camarès for figs. The number of cattle has increased greatly, bred both for veal and dairy produce,[38] and pigs also. Much of the lower Ségalas landscape now has a *bocage* appearance, with small fields of permanent pasture or arable surrounded by hedges from which rise occasional oaks. Some small woods of oak and beech still survive, mainly on private estates, and there has been afforestation with conifers, mostly in Lévezou.

On these well-watered uplands, the population is widely dispersed in individual farms and small hamlets. Many are remarkably isolated, especially those in the north away from the railways; some indeed are reached only by rough tracks 11 or 12 km (7 or 8 miles) from the nearest autobus route. By contrast large villages and small towns are located in the valleys (many of them with the rectilinear street plan of the medieval *bastide*) which have served as commercial centres for centuries. The railway which curves across Ségalas from Figeac via Rodez to Carmaux links dozens of these little towns, each ' une petite agglomération commerciale, entrepôt, lieux d'expéditions, siège de magasins coopératifs ou particuliers' (Meynier). Some of the towns on the little coalfields have associated metallurgical and textile industires. At Viviez, a few kilometres west of Decazeville, the Belgian firm SA des Mines et Fonderies de Zinc de la Vieille-Montagne built a refinery to smelt local zinc ores. A modern refinery, using electric power from the grid, now smelts a quarter of France's output of zinc metal, and also refines cadmium.

On the borders of Ségalas stand two more important towns. Villefranche-de-Rouergue is situated on the Aveyron, on the margins of the Causse Limogne and Ségalas; of *bastide* pattern, it has long been a market centre, and at one time had a variety of metallurgical industries based on local iron and lead mines, and some flourishing textile manufactures. Rodez, the *chef-lieu* of Aveyron, is another marginal town lying between Ségalas and the Grands Causses.

## Lacaune

This crystalline upland projects boldly westward to the south of the Tarn valley, separated from the Montagne Noire to the south by a remarkable through-valley drained westwards by the Thoré, eastwards by the Jaur, each flowing along a clearcut faultline and separated by an indeterminate watershed. The more active erosion of the steeper torrential Jaur and its tributary torrents is pushing the watershed westward at the expense of the Thoré.

The Monts de Lacaune form the highest point (1 266 m: 4154 ft) of a gneissic plateau flanked with Cambrian slates; as the river Agout forms a deep re-entrant far into the upland, it is sometimes known as the Massif de l'Agout. It consists of rounded bosses swelling inconspicuously from damp depressions, covered with poor pasture and some forests of oak and beech. In the depressions and valleys a limited amount of arable land produces rather meagre crops of rye, buckwheat and potatoes. Both sheep and cattle are reared, but not in large numbers.

More striking is the southwestern part of the massif, a small oval boss of granite between the Agout and Thoré valleys, known as the *Sidobre*. The well-jointed rock forms in places a chaos of huge blocks, individual monoliths and torlike masses project from the gravelly soil, sometimes balanced precariously on each other. Some granite is quarried, but otherwise the economy is limited; in the words of Ph. Arbos, these are 'pays rude . . . d'agriculture archaïque'.

The Lacaune massif is defined on the southeast by a clearcut faultline, where the gneissic rocks are downfaulted to considerable depths, so bringing less resistant Cambrian, Devonian and Lower Carboniferous slates and shales against the crystalline rocks. Differential erosion by the Jaur and the Orb has worn a deep valley bounded by the steep faultline scarp of the *Espinouse*; its sides are fantastically eroded. Some cultivation is practised on the terraced slopes, and the grazing of animals, but the main features are rugged gorges, steep slopes of bare rock and scree, and scrubby woodland of oak and beech.

A few towns and villages are situated in the lower valleys on the flanks of the massif and along the Agout valley. The regional centre for Lacaune is Castres, situated on its margins where the Agout leaves the uplands for Lauraguais. On the northeastern flanks lies the small down-faulted Carboniferous basin of Graissesac, where some coal is mined (Fig. 20.1). A number of small but long-established industries (glass works, brick works and textiles) thrive at the town of Lodève.

## The Montagne Noire

This prominent massif of Pre-Cambrian rocks (mostly gneiss and mica-schist, with several oval bosses of granite along its structural axis) forms the southwestern culmination of the Central Massif. It has suffered the usual vicissitudes of peneplanation, and of uplift and tilting associated with the past orogenies. The surface of the plateau forms a monotonous upland, from which rounded summits project but slightly; the highest point is the Pic de Nore (1 210 m: 3 970 ft). Its flanks are more accidented; short streams flowing north to the Thoré have cut steepsided gorges, while the longer rivers descend the southern margins towards the Aude, crossing flanking limestones (varying in age from Cambrian to Eocene) and pro-ducing a rather confused relief of ridges and valleys known in the east as *Minervois*.

The higher parts of the Montagne Noire consist mainly of poorly drained moorlands, diversified by plantations of conifers. A remarkable contrast is apparent between the northern and southern flanks, for apart from the obvious difference in aspect the upland forms a climatic boundary between Atlantic and Mediterranean influences. The northern and northwestern slopes are wooded with chestnut, oaks and beech, and some plantations (including state forests) of pine, spruce and occasionally evergreen oak); seen from the Thoré valley, these forested slopes present a distinctly sombre aspect, hence the name bestowed on the massif. The main features of the economy consist of cattle-rearing (which has increased in importance of late at the expense of sheep), and the cultivation of wheat, rye and potatoes on the lower slopes and in the valleys. In favoured places irrigation is used for the improvement of the valley meadows.

On the southern and southeastern slopes rainfall is appreciably less and the summer aridity more pronounced. As a result, the poor pasture is scorched brown in summer and there are considerable areas of *maquis*-like scrub and bare limestone, relieved only by occasional woodlands of ever-green oak and chestnut. The economy has a Mediterranean character; terraces enclosed by dry-stone walls grow vines, olives and fruit trees, irrigation is used for vegetable gardens, and sheep and goats increase in number at the expense of cattle.

The character of the settlement changes too. While in the north isolated farms and small hamlets are found, in the south occur the typical Mediter-ranean agglomerations of high-storeyed houses clustering around a church on a hillside, sunbaked and drowsy. The southern flanks belong to the basin of the Aude and to the Mediterranean; its regional centres are Carcassonne and Castelnaudary, and indeed in the southeast Béziers. The only town of importance in the north is Mazamet in the Thoré valley, which carries on a long-established industry of separating wool from sheep-skins by special techniques. Based originally on local sheep, the factories in the Thoré and Arnette valleys now import skins from the southern hemisphere; both the rough and washed wool is sent to the textile-manufacturing areas of France, Switzerland, Belgium, and even to Great Britain and America. Some wool is used locally in the textile and clothing factories, and leather working (including footwear) is active at Mazamet.

Finally, mention must be made of some sporadic mining activity on the southern slopes of the Montagne Noire, producing copper, arsenic, gold, silver, bismuth and pyrites in small quantities. A small refinery is in operation at Lastours.

## The eastern margins

Between Lacaune and the Montagne Noire to the west and the prolongation of the Causse du Larzac in the east lies the rather complex region of *Escandorgue, Bédarieux* and *Lodève*. Geologically this comprises a *mélange* of outcrops ranging from Cambrian to late Tertiary, resulting in a most varied relief, including karstic limestone uplands (the Monts du Pardailhan), and basaltic buttelike hills, the product of Pliocene volcanic activity. Several depressions, notably that of Bédarieux (drained by the river Orb), are floored with Permian and Triassic marls and sandstones, and the larger Lodève depression is covered with fertile red Permian marls.

The countryside has a Mediterranean character—terraces with olives, vines and fruit trees, patches of hard wheat in fields enclosed by walls, irrigated gardens, groves of evergreen oaks and chestnuts, irrigated meadows, and extensive poor upland pasture grazed by sheep whose milk is mostly destined for Roquefort. In the larger depressions agriculture is likewise on a larger scale.

There are many nucleated villages, and a few larger towns with old-established industries now using Graissesac coal or electricity from the grid, such as textile manufacturing at Bédarieux and Lodève. Lamalou-les-Bains has exploited its waters to become a small spa town.

## The development of hydroelectric power

One of the most important contributions of the Central Massif in general and of Ségalas and its margins in particular to the French economy is the generation of hydroelectricity. The installed capacity of Central Massif generators at the beginning of 1970 was 3 090 mw, just over a quarter of the French total, and in 1969 they produced 12 090 gWh, nearly a quarter of the total output. Most of the large stations are situated in the valleys of the Dordogne, Cère and Truyère, with a few outlying ones on the Lot and the Tarn. These rivers, rising in the centre and east of the Central Massif where rainfall exceeds 1 200 mm (50 in), with a host of headstreams and gorgelike valleys cut in impermeable rocks, offered obvious sites for the construction of power stations. Their disadvantages are the rapid torrential runoff over the crystalline rocks, and the frequent periods of summer drought and thus uneven flow; at Bort-les-Orgues on the Dordogne the ratio between minimum and maximum rates of flow is of the proportion of 1 to 780.[39]

The solution has been the creation of huge barrages at carefully selected points to impound reservoirs far back up the valleys.[40] The first major scheme was completed between 1932 and 1934, when the Sarrans and

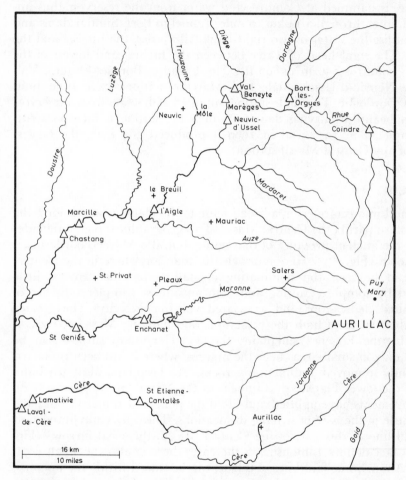

FIG. 20.8. Hydroelectric installations in the western valleys of the Central Massif
Only major stations are shown, marked by an open triangle.

Based on *Atlas de France* (1952), sheet 46, '*Energie*', with additions.

Bromme barrages were built across the Truyère to supply the Sarrans and the underground Brommat power stations.[11] Later the Couesque and Lardit stations were constructed, supplied with water from the rivers Selves and Selvet. This group has a total output of 1 100 mwh. The Marèges dam and power station on the Dordogne were completed in

571

1935. Since the war a great concerted scheme has been worked out (Fig. 20.8), and in all a series of fifteen high-head barrages has been built on the Dordogne and its tributaries.[42] The largest, at Bort-les-Orgues, is 121 m (394 ft) high, ponding up between the walls of the gorge (on which columnar basalts are exposed) a reservoir 24 km (15 miles) long and from 3 to 6 km (2 to 4 miles) in width. To supplement this, a left-bank tributary, the Rhue, is dammed at Coindre, and water from the reservoir thus impounded flows through a 14 km (9 mile) tunnel to Bort. Similar dams and tunnels utilise the water of two right-bank tributaries, the Luzège and the Doustre. The total head of water between the highest and lowest of the Dordogne dams is 550 m (1 800 ft). The Coindre, Bort-les-Orgues, Val-Beneyte, Neuvic-d'Ussel, Aigle and Marcille stations have been built along the Dordogne. The Aigle station, supplied with water from a reservoir behind a beautiful curving dam (in which the station is incorporated), was completed in 1947 and in 1969 it produced 584 gwh, the biggest output of any Central Massif station.

## Limousin

The name Limousin refers in a broad sense to the plateaus which form the northwestern part of the Central Massif. This geographical region includes not only the ancient province of that name, but also Marche bordering it on the north (Fig. 1.1). Here more clearly than anywhere in the Central Massif can be seen the dominating crystalline basement rocks, little disturbed by complex faulting and with an almost complete absence of downfaulted depressions and associated volcanic activity. The greater part of the surface of both the crystalline and flanking Mesozoic rocks is formed by the Eogene peneplain; the post-Hercynian surface can be detected only in small areas near the margins where it has been protected by recently removed sedimentary rocks. A. Perpillou also attributes much of the lower Plateau de Limoges to the Mio-Pliocene surface.[43] *En masse* movements have uplifted and tilted the peneplaned massif, but have caused little in the way of striking dislocations. The only really important structural line in this part of the Central Massif, the 'coal-furrow' (Fig. 20.1), in fact defines Limousin on the east; there is also the small coal-basin of Ahun. Some faultlines, it is true, can be traced within the uplands, such as that separating the granites and granulites of the centre and east from the mica-schists of the west, and marginal faults in the west bring the crystalline rocks abruptly against the Jurassic rocks of Périgord and Charente. But these structural lines in no way resemble the violent riftings of Auvergne, the Loire and Allier valleys, and the southeastern uplands.

A broad distinction can be drawn between the higher uplands in the east-centre above 600 m (2 000 ft), referred to as *La Montagne*, and the lower plateaus on the flanks, sometimes known collectively as *Besse*. The latter is much dissected by diverging river valleys, for Limousin is the centre of a remarkable radial drainage system, the result of its heavy rainfall (mostly over 1 000 mm (40 in) per annum), impermeable rocks and rapid runoff.

## La Montagne

The term *La Montagne* is bestowed by the people of Limousin on all the uplands in a general sort of way, and this is reflected in many place names; it refers in fact to what might conveniently be termed *Haut-Limousin,* as on Fig. 20.3. The greater part is usually known as the Plateau de Millevaches, flanked on the north by the Plateau de Gentioux, on the south by Les Monédières, and on the southwest by the Plateau d'Ussel. La Montagne forms in fact a rough quadrilateral, 100 km (60 miles) from west to east, 50 km (30 miles) from north to south.

La Montagne culminates in rounded summits, the remnant of a peneplaned surface, presenting the familiar *croupes mamelonnées* and *larges bombements,* the *lignes molles* and the *contours arrondis,* the highest of which attains 978 m (3 209 ft). They are covered with heath and rough grassland. Between these hillocks are shallow depressions filled with the gritty residue of granitic decomposition, from which project torlike masses of granite. The granitic residue overlying the impermeable bed-rock is usually saturated with water, sometimes forming shallow *étangs* and peat bogs, from whose edges ooze rivulets to form the headwaters of several large rivers. The fact that much of the surface of the high plateau is so damp may explain the derivation of the place name Limousin from the Latin word *limosus,* meaning marshy. It is dreary country, covered with snow in winter and bleak even in summer, but with a certain charm for the walker. In the classic words of A. Demangeon, 'ces étendues infinies contemplées le soir du haut d'un sommet laissent dans l'âme une sensation inoubliable de grandeur et de tristesse'.

The diverging rivers (Indre, Creuse, Vienne, Vézère, Corrèze and on the southern margins the Dordogne) flow placidly in open valleys across the plateau, separating broad interfluves. For the most part they ignore structural differences, being superimposed across the Hercynian structure lines, although occasionally they adapt themselves to lines of weakness; the Creuse below Aubusson, for example, flows northwest along the downfaulted Ahun coal-basin.

## The marginal plateaus and valleys

The *plateaux inférieurs* surround La Montagne on the north, west and south, and here again many regional names are apparent: the *Plateau de la Marche* on the north, the *Plateau de Limoges* on the west (sometimes called *Bas-Limousin* or *Limousin Occidental*), the *Plateau d'Uzerche* on the southwest and the *Plateau de Xaintrie* on the south. The dwellers on the plain of Aquitaine refer generally to these lower plateaus as *La Montagne,* though the inhabitants of Millevaches describe them as *Les Pays-Bas.*

These lower plateaus present a more diversified landscape than La Montagne because the streams, flowing from high depressions through shallow, hardly noticeable valleys, lower down dissect the several erosion surfaces. Some distinct breaks of slope can be distinguished, and numerous impressive gorges and incised meanders occur, notably on the Corrèze and the Vézère. These rivers and their many affluents have so strongly dissected the edges of the Limousin plateau that where the valleys widen out towards Berry, Poitou or Charente, residual *petits monts* stand up prominently. Their summits sometimes partake of the character of La Montagne, with heathcovered surfaces. In the north, between the Cher and Creuse valleys, fragments of the Plateau de la Marche form the Buttes de Royères and the Pierres Jaumâtres. To the west of the Creuse rise the granite hummocks of Guéret, and to the northwest of Limoges the isolated Monts de Blond and Monts d'Ambazac. To the southwest of Limoges is another much dissected outlying fragment, the Monts de Châlus, wooded and gently undulating. These more varied margins of Limousin do in fact emphasise the essential monotony of relief of the region.

## Land use and agriculture [44]

Limousin is covered conveniently by three *départements,* Haute-Vienne, Creuse and Corrèze. Each, however, contains part of La Montagne, of the lower plateaus and river valleys, and of the surrounding marginal lands, although the bulk of the Plateau de Millevaches lies in Corrèze and southern Creuse.

An appreciable distinction is apparent between the agricultural economy of La Montagne and of the lower plateaus. On the uplands a rainfall exceeding 1 000 mm (40 in), strong winds and a long-lying snow cover combine with thin acid soils and poor drainage to limit the agricultural possibilities. Much consists of heath and rough grazing; the distinction

*Land use, 1968 (percentage of total area)*

|  | ARABLE LAND | PERMANENT PASTURE | WOODLAND | WASTE AND UNCULTIVATED |
|---|---|---|---|---|
| Corrèze | 16 | 26 | 42 | 4 |
| Creuse | 32 | 30 | 25 | 8 |
| Haute-Vienne | 28 | 34 | 42 | 7 |

Source: Ministère de l'Agriculture, *Annuaire statistique,* 1970–1.

between the two is not always clear. Heath certainly occupies more than half the area of most of the upland communes,[45] a figure which has increased during the last century. This is caused by the unprofitability of a hill-farming existence, the consequent migration of rural workers, the decline in the number of sheep, both of permanent and transhumant flocks, which enables the heath to creep forward, and the unchecked leaching of the soil. Farms and hamlets are found on the flanks of valleys and depressions, away from the marshes but with some degree of shelter, and increase in number with diminishing altitude. Patches of land improved by liming and fertilising surround each farmstead, growing subsistence crops of rye (which still occupies more than half the arable), buckwheat, potatoes and vegetables in small strips. The basis of the economy is sheep, though reduced in number, and hill cattle. Animals from the lower plateaus are brought up to graze during summer, and then sold off at fairs held in autumn on the flanks of La Montagne.

Another possibility of some economic return from these uplands is afforded by afforestation. Conditions are far from favourable, owing to exposure to wind, heavy snowfall which can break branches, and long periods of frost. Since 1870 planting has made progress (helped by the completion of the railway across the plateau from Montluçon to Brive in 1881), mostly by private individuals and communes with state assistance, though greatly accelerated during the last decade by the planting of extensive state forests; the wooded area of the three *départements* now approaches two-fifths of their total extent. Many farms and holdings have wood lots, and the area of scattered copses among meadowland has also increased. Larger patches are found on better drained hill crests and more sheltered southeastern slopes. The trees most commonly used are pine, spruce and Douglas fir.

Conditions are more favourable on the marginal plateaus to the north and the west. The climate is less severe, soils are fertile owing to the accumulation of downwash, and drainage is better. While areas of heath-land still survive, much of the land presents a *bocage*-like aspect of fields of arable land and improved pasture, surrounded by thick hedges, with occasional copses of oak, chestnut and birch. In some of the communes of Corrèze woodland occupies as much as a third of the total area. Exploitation both of mature timber and of coppice contributes to the economy, and provides firewood, constructional timber, and wood for barrel-making, vine and hop poles, and trellis work. Oak bark is used in the tanneries, pigs feed on acorns and beechmast, and chestnuts form a supplement to the economy. Arable land has not increased much in extent, though with the use of lime from the kilns of Berry and Charente and of fertilisers there has been a distinct improvement in quality. Rye and buckwheat on the higher lands, wheat and barley lower down, even maize on the south-western plateaus, are grown. Oats has increased in importance as a fodder crop, and potatoes are grown and shipped to the Paris markets. In the neighbourhood of Limoges and other towns are extensive market gardens.

The main progress in the economy of Limousin has been in the direction

575

of cattle-rearing. The three *départements* had in 1968 a total of 812 000 cattle, and not only did permanent pasture occupy more than a quarter of their total area, but temporary pasture and fodder crops comprised nearly a half of the arable; much of the former fallow is now utilised profitably in these ways. A striking development has been effected in irrigation practice; two local sayings, *Le Limousin ne pourra périr de sécheresse* and *C'est l'eau qui fait l'herbe*, illustrate the outlook. A network of irrigation channels seams the broad valley floors, usually leading from a storage reservoir. The water is used both for water-meadows, enabling two crops of hay to be taken each summer, and for crops of trefoil and sainfoin. Even in the more deeply worn valleys near the plateau margins, water-meadows occupy much of the valley floors and meanderflats.

The Limousin cattle are one of the outstanding French breeds, and the markets in Limoges and elsewhere attract buyers from far afield. Though an ancient breed, only a century ago it was not a particularly good type of animal; since 1850, and especially since 1886, when the Limousin herd book was established, careful breeding has produced great improvements, as evidenced by the export of bulls to many parts of the world. Their primary value is for beef and veal, although they are also used for draught purposes, but they are not particularly good milkers. Another contribution to the agricultural economy is the rearing of pigs, and large numbers are sold off at the annual fairs.[46]

## Towns and industries

La Montagne is scantily populated; small farms and isolated hamlets are situated in sheltered positions, but considerable areas are quite uninhabited. Some of the large communes contain a dozen or twenty hamlets, each a kilometre or so from the next, the centre of the commune being marked merely by one larger hamlet containing the church and *mairie*. A few larger villages stand high up in the river valleys.

Small market towns are situated in valleys on the flanks of the central upland, forming minor route centres—Aubusson in the Creuse valley (with light electrical and electronic industries), Ussel on the opposite (southern) side of Millevaches in the valley of the Diège, and Eymoutiers in the valley of the Vienne. On the lower plateau small towns are more frequent, while an outer ring of towns stands on the margins of Limousin, serving parts of that region and its borders—Argenton on the borders of Berry, Montmorillon of Poitou, Confolens of Charente, Thiviers of Périgord, Brive[47] of Quercy, Bort-les-Orgues of Auvergne and Chambon of Bourbonnais. The function of these towns is primarily commercial, and most hold fairs and markets for their rural districts. Some have small-scale industries, such as paper mills at St Léonard. There has been striking recent development at Brive, including light engineering, electronics, the manufacture of paper cartons, domestic appliances and clothing. St Junien is an important centre of glove manufacturing.

Considerable developments of hydroelectricity have taken place along the valley of the Vienne and of its tributaries. A small station was built at Bussy as early as 1910, and in 1920 a company was set up to construct barrages and stations, the most important of which is Eguzon on the Creuse, completed as early as 1926; this forms one of the main nodal points on the French grid, with a transformer station from which radiate power lines. Nine barrages and eighteen stations are now in operation in the Vienne basin, with three more on the Maulde.[48]

The largest city of Limousin is Limoges,[49] which contained 133 000 people in 1968. The ancient *cité* with its thirteenth-century cathedral stands on a bluff at a height of about 290 m (950 ft) on the right bank of the Vienne. Limoges has been a route-centre since Gallo-Roman times. A ford is said to have crossed the river; today there are five bridges, and nine roads converge there. The Vienne valley is narrow and steepsided and no main road follows it, so that the town is essentially a focus of roads radiating across the plateau. The old town developed a most interesting duality; the *cité* was under the bishop's jurisdiction, the *ville* under that of the Counts of Limoges, each unit enclosed by walls. Today these two nuclei, though surrounded by the newer industrial and residential districts, are still distinguishable, with boulevards occupying the sites of the walls.

Limoges has been an industrial centre for more than a thousand years, in spite of stormy vicissitudes during the Hundred Years War and at other times. Its medieval craftsmen were famed for their metalwork, especially of gold, enamel, cloth (notably flannel) and leatherwork. The kaolin deposits near St Yrieix to the south of Limoges were first exploited in 1755, and have nurtured an industry which has made the name of Limoges synonymous with fine porcelain. The first factory began operation in 1774, and in the nineteenth century progress was rapid as numerous establishments and workshops were opened. By 1898 the industry employed about 10 000 workers, and the manufacture of pottery, tiles and bricks about the same number. The population growth in the nineteenth century as a result of these activities was rapid; from 25 000 inhabitants at the time of the French Revolution it increased to 46 500 in 1856 and to 92 000 in 1911. The pottery industry has had its setbacks—the 1914–18 war, the competition of such new countries as Czechoslovakia, the world economic depression which reduced the demand for high-class luxury products (only 2 000 workers could find employment in 1934), and the war of 1939–45. Since then the industry has contributed to France's export drive, though the proportion of ordinary to high-class products has increased; however, only about 3 000 are employed in the pottery industry, the result of modern automated methods. In addition it has developed ancillary trades such as the manufacture of electrical porcelain. Other industries are tanning and shoe-making (another legacy of the past developed on modern lines), the making of coachwork for cars (hence the origin of the word *limousine*) and accessories for motorcycles, the processing of tobacco, paper-making, brewing and specialised textile industries (cloth for uniforms and flannel). A Renault factory has recently been opened. The city still indeed maintains its rôle as one of France's major regional centres.

## The northern basins and margins

The upper Loire and its major headstream the Allier flow from south to north through lines of downfaulted basins more or less parallel to the eastern edge of the Central Massif. The general tilt of the uplands ensures that the drainage of most of the northern and eastern parts of the Massif must find its way northwards or northwestwards to the lower Loire by way of the Allier, Cher (occupying in part a similar though smaller down-faulted basin), Indre, Creuse and Vienne. The upper valley of the Loire belongs to the central uplands, below which the river enters first the Plaine de Forez and then the Bassin du Roannais. Further to the west, beyond the granite uplands of the Forez and Livradois, the Allier leaves its steep upper valley, cut through the crystalline rocks, and traverses first the small basins of Brioude and Issoire and then the more extensive Limagne. The two rivers converge beyond the northern margins of the crystalline rocks in Bourbonnais.

### The Plaine du Forez

The Plaine du Forez forms an oval of lowland about 20 km (12 miles) from east to west and 40 km (25 miles) from south to north, lying between the Monts du Forez and the Monts du Lyonnais, its margins sharply defined by faults, especially on the east. The basin itself slopes gently northward from about 400 to 330 m (1 300 to 1 100 ft). It has been filled in both by Oligocene sediments laid down under lacustrine conditions, and by deposits of more recent alluvium brought down by the Loire and its torrential tributaries, which gully the uplands on either flank. Into these deposits the Loire has trenched itself, forming a series of terraces. Some masses of Pliocene basalt project through the Oligocene sediments and form prominent little summits.

The sedimentary infilling yields soils of no particular fertility, since they are derived from the flanking granite uplands. The compact clays which cover much of the surface are heavy, cold and frequently waterlogged, with shallow *étangs* lying on their uneven surface. Since the middle of the nine-teenth century several *syndicats de dessèchement* have drained and reclaimed about a third of their former total area of 3 000 ha (7 500 acres). Some, however, are periodically flooded, and used for breeding carp and tench. In contrast to these clay soils are the light siliceous sands, formerly of little use other than for pine woods. The best soils, of limited extent, are loams, developed on the recent alluvium along the floodplain of the Loire.

Improvements during the last century have appreciably modified the economy. Mixed farming is practised, with an emphasis on stock-rearing, especially of Salers and Charolais cattle, pigs and fowls, and the former unproductive system of rye alternating with fallow has been replaced by a rotation of wheat, potatoes, fodder beet, lucerne and legumes. The construction of the Canal du Forez and about 200 km (120 miles) of distributaries since 1865 has facilitated the cultivation of lucerne, trefoil and meadow grass under irrigation.

As a result of these improvements, the population has increased by 50 per cent during the last century and the density now averages about 60 per sq km (155 per sq mile). Several small towns are situated around the margins of the basin and in the south a group is situated on either side of the Loire. The influence of the St Etienne region to the southeast is felt, for people from these southern towns travel to work in the factories, and moreover some manufactures have spread to the Forez—the making of cycles at Sury, textiles at Montrond, lace at Montbrison, and glass at Andrézieux, St Romain and St Just. St Galmier, Montrond-les-Bains, Sail-sous-Couzan and one or two other little towns have a certain tourist activity, due to the thermal springs; St Galmier even exports bottles of mineral water. The largest town is Montbrison, but has only about 10 000 inhabitants, so that the rural way of life is clearly dominant.

### Roannais

The Loire on leaving the northern end of the Forez basin cuts through a rather confused upland area of Lower Carboniferous slates and associated ancient igneous rocks, known as the Plateau or '*seuil*' de Neulise, to the Plaine de Roanne.[50] The gradient is steeper than in the Forez basin, and the river, enclosed in a steepsided valley, forms picturesque cataracts.

Roannais is bounded on the west by the granitic Montagnes de la Madeleine, the edge of which is defined by one of the most continuous faults within the Central Massif, trending from north-northwest to south-southeast for 50 km (30 miles). An abrupt change occurs between the steep granite slopes and the Oligocene sediments of the basin floor, partly covered with Pleistocene and Recent gravels and alluvium. The eastern margin of Roannais is less clearly defined, for stepped faults have allowed the preservation of Triassic and Jurassic sandstones, marls and limestones from which small masses of granite protrude. A much more gradual ascent leads from the floor of the basin to the uplands of Beaujolais and Charolais than on the west.

The basin slopes gently northward from about 270 to 200 m (900 to 650 ft). Like Forez, it has been infilled with lacustrine and alluvial deposits, but there is less clay and more gravel and sands. The basin is not 'dammed' at its northern end, so that there is a steady downfall through a deeply trenched valley. As a result, the surface of Roannais is much better drained and has few *étangs* and areas of marshland.

Its landscape and economy are, however, much the same as that of Forez, although being lower, better drained and with more fertile soils the agriculture is more prosperous. Between the hedges and rows of poplars are fields of arable and permanent pasture, with orchards and vineyards on the slopes, for the keynote is mixed farming with an emphasis on livestock. Some of the areas of sand and the outlying granitic hills are thickly wooded.

Small towns and villages are aligned along the foot of the Madeleine, and more dispersedly in the broader valleys of such tributaries as the Arconce and the Sornin on the east. Some are market towns with large fairs, and there are some spa towns. Individual farms and prosperous little villages are widely dispersed. By contrast, the town of Roanne in the south is the centre of a prosperous industrial region; for some centuries textile industries, based on local wool, flax and hemp, have flourished. In the late eighteenth century cotton manufactures developed, especially the production of dyed cloth and yarn introduced by the merchants of Lyons. The industry received a boost in 1871 when the Treaty of Frankfurt removed Mulhouse and the Alsatian cotton industry from France. New mills were built and installed with mechanical looms, and the textile industry spread from Roanne up the neighbouring valleys of the Trambouse and the Reins. A variety of cotton goods is produced, also cotton-silk mixtures, and there is a small rayon factory. Other industries include light engineering, hosiery and millinery, wrapping paper, tanning and leather goods, and tiles and drainpipes made from local clay. This varied industrial activity has resulted in the rapid growth of Roanne during the last seventy years. It had long been a centre on which routes converged from the Paris Basin up the Loire, from the upper Saône by way of the Bourbince-Dheune depression, and from Lyons by the Seuil de Tarare between Beaujolais and Lyonnais. The opening in 1838 of the Roanne-Digoin Canal (a lateral canal along the left bank of the Loire) resulted in the growth of a busy little port at Roanne, handling coal from Montceau-les-Mines for local industries. The construction of a main line railway over the Col des Sauvages has improved links with Lyons, while direct rail communication to the south with St Etienne is a further advantage. The population of Roanne, which was under 7 000 at the beginning of the nineteenth century, had increased to 40 500 in 1931; there has been a less rapid growth since that date, but if the contiguous communes of Riorges and Coteau are included the agglomeration totals over 78 000. It forms therefore a considerable urbanised area in the middle of the *paysage rural* of the middle Loire basin.

**Limagne** [51]

Several small Tertiary basins are aligned along the course of the upper Allier, forming indeed 'un chapelet de dépressions' (Meynier), known generally as the *Petites Limagnes*. They are bounded by crystalline rocks, their margins defined by faultlines complicated by small volcanic masses and outlying granitic hillocks, and their floors for the most part are infilled with Oligocene lacustrine sediments. The first of these depressions (excluding the Bassin du Puy) is Langeac, though this is not one of the *fossés tertiaires* but a rift of Hercynian age, floored with Upper Coal Measures which, however, have yielded but little coal. After another steep valley section through the crystalline rocks, the Allier enters the larger basin of Brioude, floored with Oligocene limestones and a veneer of alluvium, continued again to the north by the basin of Brassac where another small coalfield has been preserved (Fig. 20.1). Then follows the basin of Issoire, diversified by basaltic masses rising above the Oligocene limestones and marls, and by a mass of granite trenched across by the Allier.

This group of small basins, together with several others along the tributary valley, affords a striking contrast in land use and economy with the bleak uplands which surround them. Their milder climate, earlier springs and lower rainfall, their quite fertile alluvial soils and gentle slopes, allow a prosperous agriculture—wheat, malting barley, fodder crops for the cattle, market garden produce, fruit and vines on the slopes. The small towns, each of about 5 000 inhabitants, situated on the higher margins of the basins away from flood dangers (which are very real because of the rapid runoff from the surrounding uplands), are market centres, though several have industries; Brassac and Ste Florine are the centres of small-scale coalmining and some metallurgical activities. Brioude manufactures furniture, an occupation based on local walnut, and other wooden articles. Brassac possesses specialised textile industries, such as embroidery and ribbons. The coalfields will close in 1975.

The *Grande Limagne* occupies the largest of the Tertiary depressions, known sometimes as the Bassin de Clermont-Gannat, and extending from south to north for 100 km (60 miles). Though narrowed in the south by a prolongation of Livradois, the Limagne basin opens out further north to a width of about 40 km (25 miles). A long curving fault on the west marks the edge of the high uplands of Auvergne, although to the west of Gannat other faults define the Horst de Jenzat which projects boldly eastward into Limagne, partially enclosing to its northwest the little Bassin d'Ebreuil. Another series of faults on the east defines the margins of the Monts du Forez. The basin is enlarged by the fact that into it opens the broad valley of the Dore in the southeast. This river flows through an Oligocene-floored downfaulted depression (in which stand the towns of Marsac and Ambert) between the mountains of Livradois and Forez, and its lower course (the basin of Courpière) is likewise enclosed by faults.

581

The sedimentary infilling consists of Oligocene limestones and marls, with a veneer in places of coarse granitic and basaltic débris, elsewhere of clays. This superficial material, including also clay sands derived from disintegration of the surrounding granite, covers much of the basin to the east of the Allier, and is referred to collectively as the *varennes*. The darkish clays are found mainly in the southwest and also to the northeast of Vichy as the Sologne bourbonnaise is approached. A variety of gravels and alluvial deposits occurs along the terraces of both the Allier and the Dore.

The plain of the Grande Limagne exhibits considerable diversity in its relief features. In the west low limestone ridges and buttes, orientated more or less from south to north, and sometimes defined by prominent scarp faces, rise above the intervening marl-floored depressions, in places marshy. The name *Pays des Buttes* is usually applied to this western zone. In the centre of the basin, between the Pays des Buttes and the Allier, is the clay-floored and rather damp *plaine marneuse*, which once consisted of marshlands, though parts are now drained.

Volcanic activity of both Pliocene and Pleistocene age contributes diversification to parts of the basin lying west and south of a line from Riom to Billom. On the northwestern margins of Livradois, protruding into the southern Limagne, a continuous volcanic cover forms the Plateau de la Comté, where the remnants of at least fifty individual cones and lava flows can be traced, orientated in three lines from northeast to southwest; 'le relief est morcelé en minuscules coulées et en pointements isolés' (Derruau). Lava flows project eastward from the Chaîne des Puys, crossing the fault scarp and overlying the Oligocene limestones and clays. Some basalt masses have been eroded into steepsided 'tables', so contributing a distinct element to the Payes des Buttes. The Montagne de la Serre comprises a ridge projecting several kilometres into the Limagne plain. The dark-coloured andesitic lavas are quarried; much of Clermont-Ferrand (including the cathedral) is built of this stone from the quarries at Volvic, which have been worked for eight centuries. There are also numerous little cones and hillocks, some of them are probably small laccoliths.

The net result is that the Grande Limagne can be divided into three distinctive regions—the *paysages de buttes volcaniques ou sédimentaires* in the south and west, *la plaine marneuse* in the west-centre (the Allier to the north of Pont-du-Château swings well to the east), and the *varennes*.[52]

The soils of Limagne are thus variable, ranging from near sterile sands underlain by a hardpan (here known as *mâchefer*) and gravels to calcareous marls frequently enriched by the products of basalt disintegration. Some of the poorer soils are forested. Many of the volcanic *puys* have a fringe of woodland around their upper slopes, and pollarded willows, poplars and aspens stand in lines among the marshes.

By considerable effort Limagne has been made into a productive agricultural region. Climatically there are difficulties, for much of the basin receives only about 500 to 600 mm (20 to 24 in) of rainfall, and its winters are cold. Parts (the sands) suffer from an inadequacy of water, paradoxically others (the marshlands) have an excess of it, and so both drainage and irrigation have their place; indeed, the same channels frequently serve each function at a different season. Much of the better soil is under wheat, the *blé dur* similar to that grown along the Mediterranean coastlands, which is made into various *pâtes* in the factories of Clermont-Ferrand. Rye, formerly grown on the poorer soils, has virtually disappeared, but malting barley, oats, sugar beet (the second most important crop to wheat), maize and fodder beet have increased in area during the last fifty years. Market gardens and orchards appear near towns such as Clermont-Ferrand, Vichy and Riom, and form tongues of intensive cultivation projecting into the western Limagne from the basalt hills.

Limagne is pre-eminently an arable region, but the number of livestock (cattle, pigs and poultry) has increased during this century, and the area both of permanent and temporary pasture and of fodder crops has likewise expanded. In 1890 the vine covered about 45 000 ha (110 000 acres) and in places formed a profitable monoculture, but although phylloxera arrived later than in many parts, it wrought great destruction between 1895 and 1899, and in the first decade of this century mildew caused further havoc. Now the cultivation of the vine is restricted to the southern slopes of the ridges, along some of the higher Allier terraces, and on the western terraces overlooking the Sioule valley in the extreme north, where a pleasant white wine is made at St Pourçain.[53] Most *vignerons* are now employed only part-time in their vineyards, and usually own livestock or a plot of arable land.

One feature of the agricultural economy of Limagne is the extraordinary degree to which *parcellement* has been carried out among a large number of small proprietors. As Coutin expresses it,[54] 'une parcelle de propriété est parfois divisée en plusieurs parcelles de culture; d'autres fois, plusieurs parcelles de propriété ne forment qu'une seule parcelle de culture'. A certain amount of grouping and consolidation (*rémembrement*) of holdings has been effected, however, during the last twenty years, partly as a result of wartime legislation.

In this predominantly agricultural area small towns are dispersed as market centres. A few stand on the banks of the Allier, such as Pont-du-Château and Vichy. The latter is a spa of considerable repute, the result of its alkaline springs; others are found near by at St Yorre and Cusset. Though known since ancient times, it was not until the reign of Napoleon III that Vichy became really famous; now it is a town of 33 000 permanent inhabitants, 'la reine des villes d'eaux', and with its parks, hotels and shopping streets supplementing the therapeutic qualities of its waters, it attracts many visitors, exceeding 100 000 annually. Certain associated industries have developed—the bottling of Vichy water, and the making of pharmaceutical chemicals and toilet articles. Royat and Châtel-Guyon have similar thermal establishments on the western faultline of Limagne.

Apart from the perhaps declining attractions of the thermal resorts, tourism in this area is now much more broadly based, including winter sports and summer holidays, generally in the uplands; seven winter sports complexes have been developed in recent years. Other small market towns of 5 000 to 7 000 people are situated at intervals over the plain. Riom was once the capital of the Dukes of Berry, and is encircled by boulevards occupying the site of the former fortifications; situated at the edge of a basalt spur, its position was naturally strong. Many towns have industries, sometimes long established. As centres of prosperous agricultural regions, some possess canning and preserving factories. Local heavy clays supply raw material for the brick and tile works of Varennes-sur-Allier, St Amand-Tallende has paper mills, Martres-de-Veyre has a large printing works, Courpière, Billom and Lezoux have pottery and earthenware works, Riom processes tobacco and has a large modern factory making electrical apparatus. Thiers is the Sheffield of France, with an ancient cutlery industry originally based on water power, and now highly specialised.

### Clermont-Ferrand

While there is this widespread diversity of small-scale industry over a preeminently rural region, most of the urban and industrial activity is concentrated at Clermont-Ferrand, which dominates the economic life of at least the western Limagne. It stands on the slopes of one of the volcanic buttes at a height of 400 m (1 350 ft), overlooking the valley of the Tiretaine, its suburbs even spreading on to the eastern slopes of Puy de Dôme. It is at the crossing-point of the north–south (Paris-Nîmes) route through the Allier valley with an east–west (Lyons-La Rochelle and Bordeaux) route crossing the Monts du Forez via Thiers and the Col de Noirétable and the Chaîne des Puys by the Col de la Moréno. The town is a commercial and marketing centre, and for centuries has possessed minor industries such as the tanning of leather, the making of paper, flour-milling and the processing of other local agricultural products, and wool-weaving.[55] But it was not until the nineteenth century that the real industrial expansion took place. In 1832 a small factory for making rubber was established, but little development occurred until the invention of the pneumatic tyre and the growth of the cycle and automobile industry; after 1890 progress was immense, associated with the name of *Michelin*, now France's largest single company, though it has many other factories elsewhere in the country. The three local factories cover a great expanse of land to the north-east of the city; badly damaged by aerial bombardment in March 1944, they have been rebuilt and re-equipped, and in fact have gained by this compulsory modernisation. Other modern industries include the making of sulphuric acid, the construction of railcars, mining equipment and of engineering machinery generally, textiles (notably readymade clothing), printing, chemicals, footwear, and confectionery (particularly chocolate, jams and preserves). The town still has a wide sphere of influence, both in Limagne as a market and servicing centre and in central France generally.[56]

Thus Clermont-Ferrand has become second only to St Etienne in the Central Massif. In 1872 its population was 37 000, by 1911 it was 63 000 and by 1968 it had reached 149 000. The city includes the ancient town of Montferrand, a kilometre to the northeast, a medieval *bastide* which has changed little for centuries; in the apt words of Arbos, it forms 'un fossile médiéval incrusté au milieu de l'alluvion urbaine du XX$^e$ siècle'. Montferrand was joined administratively to Clermont in 1731. Today the agglomeration with its contiguous towns has a population of 205 000. Large blocks of *cité-ouvrières* have been built to house the industrial population, and the cathedral and the old town on the 'Plateau Central', bounded by boulevards, are now surrounded by several square kilometres of built-up area.

## Bourbonnais

As Limagne widens to the north, the river Allier flows in a broad valley, bordered by a distinctive series of terraces, parallel to the Loire, before the two rivers converge near Nevers. Further to the west the much-faulted crystalline rocks of northern Auvergne gradually give way to newer rocks as the land sinks towards the *Champagne berrichonne*. In spite of this diversity, it is logical to regard this as a unit area on the northern margins of the Central Massif. The name *Bourbonnais* is justified in that it formed one of the provinces (Fig. 1.1) before 1789, with its capital at Moulins on the banks of the Allier. Today it coincides quite well with the *département* of Allier, and Moulins is its *chef-lieu*. For convenience, however, the region may be subdivided into three: the *Sologne bourbonnaise* in the east, the *Bourbonnais occidental*, and the small downfaulted basin of the upper Cher known as the *région montluçonnaise*.

The *Sologne bourbonnaise* forms a gently undulating plateau, sloping northward from 300 to 200 m (1 000 to 600 ft) between the converging Loire and Allier. The greater part is covered, like the Sologne proper to the north, with a sheet of Miocene sands, diversified with layers of quartz gravel and sheets of clay, and frequently underlain by a hardpan. The rivers have cut down through these deposits, exposing in places the Oligocene limestones, and their terraces and floodplains are covered with Pleistocene and Recent gravels, sand and fine alluvium. The low gradients, the sheets of clay and the underlying hardpan do not make for adequate natural drainage, and until the nineteenth century it was a poor area of *étangs* and marshes, alternating with heathland. A considerable amount of reclamation and improvement has been accomplished—the drainage of marshes, the fertilising of impoverished sands, the planting of trees, and the improvement of roads and rural housing, but there remain many *étangs* (some used for pisciculture) and much heathland.

585

The pattern of the geology and the relief is more complex in *Bourbonnais occidental*. The southern part consists of gneiss and granite, dominated in the south by the well-named Signal de la Bosse (774 m: 2 539 ft). The crystalline rocks are cut through by the northeastern part of the 'coal furrow' (Fig. 20.1), containing the small Noyant field, while half a dozen others, including that of Commentry, lie on the northern flanks. In succession northward appear an area of Permian rocks, a band of Trias, and then Jurassic marls and limestones as the lowland of Berry is approached. The whole region is much faulted and several outlying masses of granite and gneiss project through the newer rocks. In all, this part of the Bourbonnais forms 'sur la carte géologique un bariolage qui témoigne de sa diversité de nature' (Arbos). The many streams flowing to the Allier and the Cher trench boldly through these rocks, often forming gorges, as in the valley of the Aumance, where the striking relief due to differential erosion gives rise to the somewhat affected appellation of *la petite Suisse*. Elsewhere the peneplaned surfaces form a series of monotonous plateaus descending to the north.

The Cher rises to the south on the granite plateau of Combrailles, and flows northwards into the downfaulted basin of Montluçon. It is bordered by cleancut faults, and floored as it is by Oligocene marls in the south and Miocene sands in the north, it partakes of the general character of the other Tertiary basins of the Central Massif.

It is not easy to summarise the character of this variegated region; an impression is given by the fact that in 1968 just under a third of the *département* of Allier was under arable, about 35 per cent under permanent pasture, and 15 per cent under woodland. The woodland (much formerly preserved in domanial forests) has been somewhat reduced from 100 000 ha (250 000 acres) in 1840 to a little under 80 000 ha (200 000 acres), but some fine forests of oak and beech still exist.

Much of the country has a rather *bocage*-like character (in fact the term *bocage bourbonnais* is sometimes used), the result of the patchwork of fields surrounded by hedgerows and the extent of permanent pasture, especially in the *Sologne bourbonnaise*. Though many holdings are small, farmed by individual proprietors, some large estates still survive, created through the colonising activity of the nineteenth century, some growing wheat, others divided into smaller units and farmed by *métayers*, a method of sharetenancy which has declined appreciably. Wheat occupies more than half the total arable area, but fodder crops have increased during the last half-century. Curiously, this is the most important part of France for the cultivation of artichokes. Livestock are important, and 459 000 cattle were present in the *département* in 1968, including both dairy animals (about half) and the Charolais breed for meat, and about 210 000 pigs.

Bourbonnais is pre-eminently a rural region with an agricultural economy, and individual farms and hamlets are widely peppered over the landscape. The density of population is about 50 per sq km, or more than double that of a century ago. The little market towns are usually situated on a river and serve one of the valley re-entrants into the upland, while a few towns were concerned with coalmining. Three larger towns are Montluçon in the Cher valley, Commentry in the valley of the Oeil (a Cher tributary) and Moulins on the Allier. The last is primarily an administrative town and has not grown much during the last century. It has a few small industries of leather-tanning, hosiery and furniture-making, but it can hardly be called an industrial town. It is a notable railway junction where north–south and west–east lines cross; it is said that one can get direct trains to more cities from Moulins than from any other town in France except Paris and Lyons, a measure of its centrality. Commentry is a busy industrial town, with small steelworks.

Montluçon has become the major industrial centre of this rural area. Situated on the margin of the Paris Basin and the Central Massif, it has long stood at a crossroads; today it is a focus of four railways and the terminus of the Berry Canal by which raw materials such as Lorraine pig iron are brought. The neighbouring coalfields are small, but they helped the industrial development of the town in the nineteenth century; blast furnaces and glass works were set up in the 1840s, and thereafter progress was rapid. The former steel works, though modernised after 1945, are now largely closed down except for the finishing of special steels. Armaments, motor-car parts, and special tools are manufactured, and there is a long-established industry of iron pipes and, more recently, steel tubes. Rubber manufacturing, introduced in 1920, is carried on at the Dunlop works. Glass, pottery, chemical fertilisers and commercial waxes are made, leather is processed, and a large rayon factory was built between the wars. Various light precision engineering and electronic industries have been recently introduced. In all, its flourishing industrial development is shown by the fact that its population, only 4 500 in 1840, increased tenfold in a century, and today is nearly 60 000.

[1] S. Derruau-Boniol and A. Fel, *Le Massif Central* (1963); and R. Joly and P. Estienne, *La Région du Centre* (1961), both in the series *France de Demain*.

[2] R. Calalp, 'Connaissances sur le socle cristallin du Massif Central français', *Annls Géogr.*, **74** (1965), pp. 68–72.

[3] The origin and character of these deposits are discussed in detail by P. Fénelon, *Le Périgord* (1951), pp. 131–6.

[4] A. Meynier, *Ségalas, Levézou, Châtaigneraie* (1931).

[5] A. Perpillou, *Le Limousin: étude de géographie physique régionale* (1940).

[6] H. Baulig, *Le Plateau central de la France et sa bordure méditerranéenne: étude morphologique* (1928), especially pp. 432–50, 'Les Grandes Surfaces d'aplanissement cyclique'.

[7] P. Estienne, 'La neige dans le Massif Central', *Mélanges géographiques offerts à Ph. Arbos* (1953), i, pp. 197–200.

[8] A. Fel, 'Le climat agricole et les limites altitudinales de l'occupation du sol dans le Massif Central', *Annls Géogr.*, **44** (1955), pp. 401–12, considers the relationship, *inter alia*, between the index of aridity and the yield of rye, and hence the possibility of settlement. He

includes a map (p. 405) which distinguishes between *montagnes humides* and *montagnes sèches*; see also A. Fel, *Les Hautes Terres du Massif Central* (1962), a detailed study of the agricultural economy.

[9] G. Veyret-Verner, 'L'evolution de l'équipement hydro-électrique du Massif Central', *Mélanges géographiques offerts à Ph. Arbos* (1953), i, pp. 211–17; and G. Kish, 'Hydroelectric power in France: plans and projects', *Geogr. Rev.*, **45** (1955), pp. 88–91.

[10] J. Bonnamour, *Le Morvan, la Terre et les Hommes* (1966), of 454 pp.

[11] J. Beaujeu-Garnier, *Le Morvan et sa bordure: étude morphologique* (1951), has several large-scale maps on which these faults are traced.

[12] J. Beaujeu-Garnier, *op. cit.*, particularly the map facing p. 160.

[13] An interesting account of these operations is given by J. Levainville, *Le Morvan: étude de géographie humaine* (1909), pp. 99–128, including a map (p. 102) of saw mills.

[14] The development of industry in Le Creusot before the last war is given by M. Perrin, 'Le Creusot', *Annls Géogr.*, **43** (1934), pp. 255–74.

[15] This district is sometimes referred to as *Charollais*, after the town of Charolles. French practice is to use the term *Pays de Charolles* for the area around Charolles, but to use *Charolais* for the wider upland region.

[16] E. Reynier, *Le Pays de Vivarais* (1947); and P. Rozon, *La Vie rurale en Vivarais. Etude géographique* (1961).

[17] A. Meynier, *Géographie du Massif Central* (1935), p. 144.

[18] Meynier, *op. cit.*, p. 145.

[19] J. W. House, 'A comparative study of the Landscapes of the Plateau de Millevaches and the Western Cévennes', *Trans. Inst. Br. Geogr.*, **20** (1954), pp. 159–80, gives some interesting land use statistics for sample communes, and emphasises changes that are taking place.

[20] The standard monograph on this part of France is Ph. Arbos, *L'Auvergne* (1932, with several subsequent editions); see also L. Gachon, *L'Auvergne et le Velay* (1949). A detailed account of the volcanic features is by A. Rudel, *Les Volcans d'Auvergne* (1962, new edn 1963), a monograph of 166 pp. See also H. D. Clout, 'Rural Improvement in Auvergne', *Geography*, **53** (1968), pp. 79–81.

[21] Ph. Arbos, 'La Margeride', *Mélanges géographiques offerts à Ph. Arbos* (1953), i, p. 66.

[22] B. du Rosselle, 'Les Monts du Forez: recherches morphologiques', *Annls Géogr.*, **59** (1950), pp. 241–58, plots on a map (p. 243) four distinct surfaces, together with major faultlines and the extent of the Quaternary glaciation.

[23] L. Gachon, 'L'evolution morphologique des coulées volcaniques en Auvergne', *Annls Géogr.*, **53** (1945), pp. 254–73.

[24] The *Carte de France et des frontières au 200 000ᵉ*, sheet 58 (Aurillac), shows these features admirably by means of contours and hill-shading.

[25] M. Ayral, 'Le Plateau d'Aubrac', *Annls Géogr.*, **37** (1928), pp. 224–37.

[26] An interesting account of the volcanic elements in the relief of Velay is given by P. Bout, 'L'erosion des reliefs phonolitiques et basaltiques de la Haute-Loire depuis le dernier Glaciaire', *Mélanges géographiques offerts à Ph. Arbos* (1953), i, pp. 91–102.

[27] L. Gachon, 'Géographie de la végétation arbustive et arborescente dans le Massif du Livradois', *Mélanges géographiques offerts à Ph. Arbos* (1953), i, pp. 113–29.

[28] E. Coulet, 'Morphologie des Grands Causses', *Bull. Soc. Languedoc Géog.* (1962), *fasc.* 1, 2, pp. 3–62.

[29] Nine distinct major faultlines have been distinguished by P. Marres, and are shown and named on a folding map in *Les Grands Causses* (1935), vol. i (frontispiece).

[30] Marres, *op. cit.*, i, pp. 24–42.

[31] A detailed account, with many maps, diagrams and photographs of the caves and other phenomena of the Grands Causses is given by E.-A. Martel, *Les Causses majeurs* (1936).

[32] Marres, *op. cit.*, has a map (p. 93) on which the resurgences are named.

[33] Volume ii of Marres's work (*op. cit.*) entitled *Le Labeur humain*, provides a detailed analysis of the features of agriculture, industry and settlement.

[34] Marres, *op. cit.*, i, pp. 148–98, 'La végétation des Grands Causses', goes into con-

siderable detail, with long lists of species found in various localities.

³⁵ Y. Pomarède, 'L'Essor d'un petit centre régional: Rodez', *Rev. géogr. Pyr. S.-O.*, **35** (1954), pp. 243–59; and *ibid.*, pp. 271–3, 'Le rôle de la route dans les vicissitudes d'un petit centre régional: Rodez'.

³⁶ These various surfaces are discussed by A. Meynier, *Ségalas, Lévezou, Châtaigneraie* (1931).

³⁷ G. Bertrand, 'Société rurale et réaménagement agricole dans le Ségala tarnais', *Rev. géogr. Pyr. S.-O.*, **33** (1962), pp. 163–82.

³⁸ J. Vayron, 'L'elevage dans le Ségala du Quercy', *Rev. géogr. Pyr. S.-O.*, **33** (1962), pp. 163–82.

³⁹ G. Kish, 'Hydroelectric power in France: plans and projects', *Geogr. Rev.*, **45** (1955), p. 90.

⁴⁰ G. Veyret-Verner, 'L'évolution de l'équipement hydro-électrique du Massif Central', *Mélanges géographiques offerts à Ph. Arbos* (1953), i, pp. 211–17.

⁴¹ Brommat, the sixth largest hydrostation in France, produced 950 gWh, and Sarrans 349 gWh.

⁴² V. Prévot, 'Les Aménagements hydroélectriques en France. I. Le Bassin de la Dordogne', *Acta Geographica* (1952), pp. 68–97.

⁴³ A. Perpillou, *Le Limousin: étude de géographie physique régionale* (1940).

⁴⁴ G. Bouet, 'La Production agricole du Limousin', *Norois*, **18** (1971), pp. 477–89, makes the point that Limousin has the lowest gross profit per worker of any French region, and imputes this to old-fashioned methods, the slow development of co-operation and the general lack of organisation. See also H. D. Clout, 'Limousin: Regional crisis and change', *Tijdschr. econ. soc. Geog.*, **61** (1970), pp. 288–99.

⁴⁵ J. W. House, 'A comparative study of the landscapes of the Plateau de Millevaches and the western Cévennes', *Trans. Inst. Br. Geogr.*, **20** (1954), pp. 159–80.

⁴⁶ An interesting account of the rural economy of part of Limousin, and of changes which have taken place in the last century, is given by G. Beis, 'Transformation de l'économie rurale dans les plateaux limousins du Sud-Est', *Annls Géogr.*, **55** (1946), pp. 164–77.

⁴⁷ A. Meynier, 'Les Activités urbaines du bassin de Brive', *Rev. géogr. Pyr. S.-O.*, **33** (1962), pp. 49–71.

⁴⁸ P. Garenc, 'Les aménagements hydroélectriques du bassin de la Vienne', *Annls Géogr.*, **61** (1952), pp. 106–22.

⁴⁹ R. Lazzarotti, 'Limoges, capitale régionale, peut-elle devenir une métropole d'équilibre', *Norois*, **17** (1970), pp. 57–80. He discusses the decline of porcelain and the resulting economic crisis, and describes the efforts to revive and modernise the town.

⁵⁰ A very full account of Roanne and the *Pays Roannais* is given by J. Labasse, 'Queliques Aspects de la vie d'échanges en Pays Roannais', *Annls Géogr.*, **63** (1954), pp. 193–218.

⁵¹ M. Derruau, *La Grande Limagne* (1949), pp. 8–9, has an interesting discussion on the origin of the name. It is related etymologically to *limon*, and it is regarded by Derruau as '*synonyme de terre grasse*'. The name is used for the adjacent parts of Bourbonnais to the north, as the *Limagne bourbonnaise*.

⁵² These divisions form in fact the basis of M. Derruau's detailed study, *op. cit.* (1949). Of considerable interest is a detailed study by the same author, 'L'occupation humaine dans la Varenne de Lezoux (Limagne)', *Annls Géogr.*, **56** (1947), pp. 178–91.

⁵³ Derruau, *op. cit.*, pp. 207–35, has a full account of the problems of viticulture in Limagne, including a detailed map.

⁵⁴ P. Coutin, 'La remembrement des terres en Limagne', *Mélanges géographiques offerts à Ph. Arbos* (1953), i, pp. 149–56.

⁵⁵ A most interesting account of the industrial development of Clermont-Ferrand is given by Philippe Arbos himself, *Mélanges géographiques offerts à Ph. Arbos* (1953), i, pp. 28–44.

⁵⁶ Meynier, *op. cit.* (1935), has an interesting map (p. 220) showing its spheres of influence; see also Arbos *et al.*, 'Clermont-Ferrand et sa région', *Association française pour l'Avancement des Sciences*, 68th Congress (1949).

# Part III
# The Fold Mountains

# 21
# The Jura

The Jura form a crescent-shaped mass of uplands extending for 240 km (150 miles) from the southern end of the Rhine rift valley to the middle Rhône near Lyons.[1] The maximum width is 50 km (30 miles) between the valley of the Saône to the west and the Swiss Plateau to the east, but tapering to 10 to 12 km (6 or 7 miles) at each extremity. The frontier between France and Switzerland crosses the upland area obliquely from Basel to Geneva, leaving all the southwestern Jura in France and the greater part of the northeastern Jura in Switzerland. The name Jura is derived from a Celtic word meaning forest, probably akin to the Slavonic word *gora*. The term *Jurassic* has passed into geological usage from the excellent development of limestones and associated mid-Mesozoic rocks in this type region.

## Structure and relief

The basement rocks consist of biotite gneisses similar to those appearing on the surface in the Vosges; though these crystalline rocks never actually outcrop in the Jura, their presence is known through deep borings. After the peneplanation which succeeded the Hercynian orogeny, a long period followed of extensive though intermittent marine transgressions which covered most of central Europe. Permian conglomerates and sandstones were laid down on the crystalline basement rocks, and were succeeded by a considerable thickness of the Trias, comprising the Bunter Sandstone, the Muschelkalk and the Keuper Marls. The last are overlain by Rhaetic marls and limestones, which indicate a renewed marine transgression following a regression during the Keuper. These Triassic rocks appear on the surface only on the flanks of the Jura—in the extreme northeast in Switzerland, along the northern margins near Montbéliard, again near Besançon, and as a narrow outcrop between Poligny and Lons-le-Saunier. In the Muschelkalk occur salt-beds which have long been exploited, as the names Salins and Lons-le-Saunier would indicate.

These rocks were succeeded by great thicknesses of Jurassic strata deposited during another prolonged period of marine transgression. At the base are Liassic marls and shales, varying in thickness from 30 to 90 m (100 to 300 ft), and invariably resting on the Triassic formations. The Middle Jurassic deposits, 150 to 400 m (500 to 1 300 ft) thick, consist of oolitic and marly limestones; these form the surface rocks extensively in the west and stand out as long ridges in the east. The Upper Jurassics, varying in thickness from 90 to over 900 m (300 to over 3 000 ft), comprise coralline and dolomitic limestones and some marls. Almost all these are of marine origin, although at the end of the period freshwater beds (the Purbeck Limestones) indicate a temporary regression of the sea.

The Jurassic rocks make up the great mass of the Jura, but some deposits of younger rocks survive in places. Lower Cretaceous marls, chalky limestones and glauconitic sandstones once probably covered the whole area, but have been preserved only in the downfolds. Particularly in the northeast appear outcrops of Eocene ironstones, Oligocene limestones, gypsum, clays, freshwater and marine Molasse sandstones, and Pliocene pebbles and sands. These Tertiary rocks are represented only to a very small extent in France.

The formation of the Jura was associated with the earth movements responsible for the Alps. The Hercynian horsts exercised less controlling effect in the central Jura, where the folds were able to splay out, hence the folding is less strongly developed, but further to the east pressure was concentrated against the southern edge of the Black Forest and the folding is more intense. The long arc of folds lying along the northwestern margin of the Swiss Plateau is given the name Folded Jura (the *Jura plissé*), but only its western and southwestern portion lies in France.

The term Jura is not restricted to this folded zone, for to the west lies a distinctive area of Jurassic rocks known as the Plateau Jura (*Jura tabulaire*), which forms the greater part of the French Jura. The result of tangential pressure from the south has been the formation of a series of faultlines which divide the plateau into a number of blocks. Along the outer (northwestern) margins of the plateau further folding combined with faulting has formed a boundary flexure, so producing a prominent sharp edge.

A long period of denudation succeeded the Alpine folding, and it is estimated that the Jura are now less than half as high as they once were. The Tertiary and Cretaceous sediments were removed except in some of the synclines in the east. The extent of the denudation has of course varied; in parts of the plateau where the Upper Jurassic is still the surface rock, probably as little as 90 m (300 ft) of sedimentary rocks have gone, while in the extreme northeast, where Triassic rocks now appear on the surface, more than 900 m (3 000 ft) must have been stripped from the former folds.

It is possible, as some French geographers have done, to divide the whole upland area latitudinally into *le Jura septentrionale* or *le Jura du Doubs*, *le Jura central*, and *le Jura méridional*. Undoubted differences in landscape and economy are apparent between north and south, mainly the result of distinct variations in climate, but this division cuts across the obvious longitudinal structural lines. It is preferable to distinguish (i) the Folded Jura proper (*le Jura plissé*), otherwise known as *les hautes Chaînes du Jura central*; (ii) the *Jura méridional*, the extreme southern wing where the Rhône cuts across the packed folds, forming the distinctive regions of Haut- and Bas-Bugey and Crémieu; and (iii) the Plateau Jura, known as

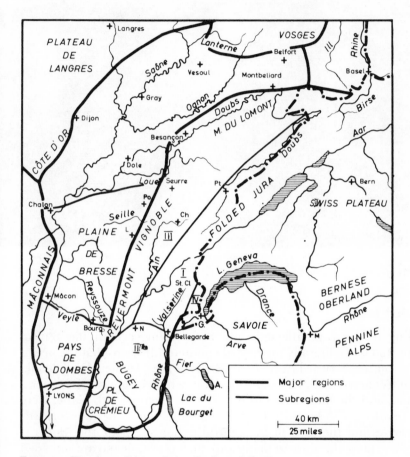

FIG. 21.1. The upper Rhône-Saône Basin and the Jura
The abbreviations are as follows: **A,** Lake Annecy; **Ch,** Champagnole; **G,** Geneva; **L,** Lons-le-Saunier; **M,** Martigny; **N,** Nantua; **P,** Poligny; **Pt,** Pontarlier; **St Cl,** St Claude.
The numbers **I** to **IV** refer to the four physical units of the Jura, described in the text.

*le Jura tabulaire* or *les Plateaux jurassiens*. There remains a small unit area, (iv) the Pays de Gex, tucked in a corner to the west of Lake Geneva between the high easternmost Crêt de la Neige and the Swiss frontier (Fig. 21.1).

Plate 60. Ridges and valleys in the Jura

## The Folded Jura

The folding of the Jura affected only rocks younger than the Bunter Sandstone, and is of a literally superficial character. It seems that the newer rocks were pushed forward over the saltbeds of the Middle Muschelkalk, which in effect acted as a plane of lubrication, while the gneissic basement, the Permian and the Bunter Sandstone, all lying beneath this plane, were virtually unaffected. A large number of individual anticlines was formed; some estimates put the total in the central region as about 160, but it is difficult to calculate this since so many anticlines pitch out and are succeded by others appearing from a neighbouring syncline; this pitching out is a further indication of the superficial nature of the folding. The most pronounced folding is found along the inner (Swiss) edge of the Jura, especially in the northeast where the fold zone is at its narrowest and most compressed.

The majority of the anticlines are more or less symmetrical in character. Nevertheless, in places more complicated fold forms can be found; thus the main arch of an anticline may contain two or more secondary anticlines, or pressure may have been intensified locally to form steeplimbed 'trunk anticlines', asymmetrical anticlines, and even occasionally fanfolds and overfolds. It seems from the evidence of railway tunnels that even clean-cut

596

thrusts are present. In fact, these not only occur in the heart of the folded zone, but the outer anticlines have been thrust on to the Plateau Jura to the northwest, and some outlying portions have been isolated by denudation to form *Klippen*, prominent hillocks rising from the plateau surface 5 to 6 km (3 to 4 miles) beyond the outer ranges of the Folded Jura.

In most cases the anticlines still correspond to the upstanding ridges and the synclines form the valleys. The latter are usually floored with sandstones and clays of the Molasse and Cretaceous, and are followed by longitudinal sections of rivers. Nevertheless, as long periods of denudation have worn away part of the original upfolds, the form of these valleys and ridges is far from simple or regular. Torrents, flowing down the sides of the anticlines, furrow deeply into the limestone, and erode headwards into the less resistant underlying clays and marls. Sometimes a torrent may cut right back into an anticline and so form a high-lying depression (*combe*) along its crest (Fig. 21.2). These *combes* are usually both short and narrow, but occasionally denudation has proceeded so far that a basinlike depression of appreciable size has been created. This process has rarely gone on so far in the Jura, however, as to produce synclinal ridges, a complete reversal of the relief.

The *combes* are walled with infacing escarpments (*crêts*), which form the high summit lines. A *crêt* commonly culminates in a vertical limestone cliff (the *corniche calcaire*), below which a gradual slope, covered with scree and in parts wooded, descends to the floor of the *combe*. Although most of the folded zone lies in Switzerland, by an odd trick of the frontier the highest point of the Jura is actually in France, the Crêt de la Neige (1 723 m : 5 653 ft). This fine ridge runs southward to culminate in the Grand Crêt d'Eau, overlooking a gorge occupied by the Rhône above Bellegarde (Fig. 21.3).

Another prominent feature of the Folded Jura is the transverse valley or *cluse* which cuts across an anticline, often as a precipitous gorge. The existence of these *cluses* involves an antecedent drainage system; the rivers existed before the anticline was upraised, and then maintained their courses by erosion as uplift progressed. There are between sixty and seventy of these *cluses* in the Folded Jura, of which a quarter are in France. The drainage as a result reveals a complex alternation between the longitudinal valleys and the transverse *cluses*, with sudden changes of direction, elbowlike bends and frequent river captures (Figs. 21.2, 21.4).

## The Jura Méridional [2]

Between the Rhône and its parallel tributary the Ain on the west, the folding is more tightly compressed than in the central Jura, and sheafs of parallel ridges trend southward. The prominent *crêt*-lines culminate in such peaks as the Grand Colombier (1 537 m : 5 043 ft), which rises steeply for more than 1 200 m (1 000 ft) above the Rhône to the east in its *val*

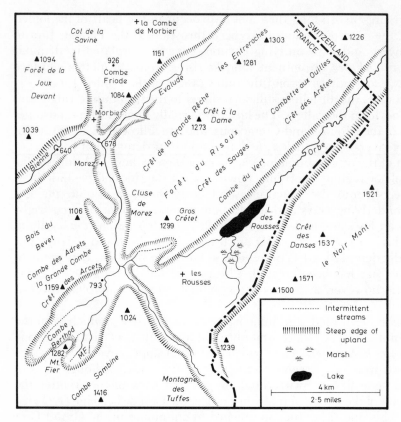

Fig. 21.2. *Créts* and *combes* in the folded Jura
The edge of the upland is shown by hachures in generalised form, in order
to bring out the broad pattern of ridges and valleys. Heights are given in
metres.

Some of the headstreams of the Bienne rise in a group of *combes*, Berthod
and Mont Fier **(MF),** with sharp infacing *créts*, notably on the north (the
Crêt des Arcets). The Bienne then cuts northwards through the Cluse de
Morez, and makes a rightangled bend, before following a rocky steepsided
valley to the southwest. The Lac des Rousses lies in a broad *val* trending
northeastward, drained by the Orbe. The Risoux ridge, cut through by the
Cluse de Morez, has been dissected into a series of long narrow *combes*
separated by *créts*.

Based on *Carte de France au 50000ᵉ*, sheet XXXIII-XXXIV/27.

between Seyssel and Culoz. This area is given the name of Bugey, sometimes divided into *Haut-Bugey* to the north of the Albarine-Seran valleys,
and *Bas-Bugey* between these valleys and the most southerly elbow of the
Rhône.

The low *Plateau de Crémieu*, to the south of the Rhône, is the most southerly
manifestation of the Jura proper. Actually the Jurassic limestone, concealed for the most part beneath late Tertiary deposits of the Rhône valley,

PLATE 61. The valley of the Arve near Cluses

makes a final brief appearance along the left bank of the Rhône in the Plateau de Balmes.

## The Plateau Jura

The Plateau Jura has been considerably faulted, and there are several distinctive blocks, although the strata for the most part remain horizontal. Three major levels can be distinguished, separated by steps, descending towards the Saône valley. The highest surface, bordering the Folded Jura, and sometimes called the Plateau de Noseray, lies at about 840 to 900 m (2 750 to 3 000 ft), consisting mainly of resistant Upper Jurassic limestones. Then comes the second step, the Plateau de Champagnole at 600 to 750 m (2 000 to 2 500 ft), of Middle Jurassic Oolite, although in places the Oxford Clay has been preserved in depressions. In this hollow is situated Champagnole, a flourishing little town at a height of 550 m (1 800 ft), while Mont Rivel on the mountain wall to the north of the valley rises to 789 m (2 589 ft). The lowest section of the plateau, developed on the Keuper and flanked by the Muschelkalk, lies at 500 to 600 m (1 600 to 2 000 ft).

The northwestern edge of the Plateau Jura is characterised by boundary flexures, forming a distinct edge overlooking the Saône valley. In the north the western bounding fault of the Black Forest trends southwestward as a flexure, and forms the Mont Terrible ridge in Switzerland, continued by the Montagnes du Lomont; the highest point on the latter attains 837 m (2 746 ft). The northern edge of the Mont Terrible ridge just projects into France as the *Jura alsacien*, which descends northward towards the Sundgau in southern Alsace. To the southwest of the Lomont, from the neighbour-hood of Besançon to near Poligny, the edge of the Jura is less sharply defined, but further south it reappears as the Vignoble in the neighbour-hood of Lons-le-Saunier, and is continued southward as the Revermont until it reaches the Ain valley (Fig. 21.1). The edge of the Revermont rises to about 640 m (2 100 ft), while a few kilometres to the west the Plaine de Bresse is at only 230 m (750 ft). In places this marginal ridge is remarkably continuous, although scalloped by deeply cut gullies and hollows; else-where, as near Besançon where the Doubs winds along the margin of the plateau, erosion has broken the edge into individual summits and pro-jecting spurs.

## The Pays de Gex

This little unit area does not belong geographically to the Jura at all, but to the Swiss Plateau. The Franco-Swiss frontier makes a rectangular salient to the east, almost reaching Lake Geneva, and thus enclosing a small portion of the Swiss Plateau between the frontier and the most easterly Jura ridge. The area is covered with glacial material, although the under-lying Oligocene clays are revealed in places, and it drains southwards to the Rhône by the river Journan. The *pays* lies in the Geneva region, and has had special customs arrangements with that city since 1815.

## Glaciation

The Quaternary glaciation had quite an appreciable effect on the Jura,[3] and at its maxima several local glaciers were nurtured by tiny snowfields. More important was the effect of the main Alpine ice moving outwards from the Swiss Plateau; it probably covered the eastern and southern parts of the Jura, and from it tongues projected westward through the cols. Erratics of undoubted Alpine origin have been found in the Jura as high as 1 500 m (5 000 ft) on the southern ridges. Till lies in sheets and undulating mounds over some of the higher depressions on the plateau and between the ridges. Many small lakes are dammed up by crescentic mounds or lie in uneven depressions in the clay. On a larger scale some of the main synclinal *vaux*, similarly floored with till, contain lakes; the Doubs, for example, flows in succession through the Lacs de Remoray and de St Point (Fig. 21.4), 8 km (5 miles) above Pontarlier. The Orbe flows through the Lac des Rousses (Fig. 21.2) and then in Switzerland through the long narrow Lac de Joux. Occasionally the *cluses* contain lakes; the Lac de Nantua lies in a broad *cluse* cut across the Montagne de Chamoise.

## Drainage patterns

The Jura receive a considerable rainfall, and despite the dominance of limestone there is a plentiful supply of surface water. The presence of beds of Jurassic clays and marls among the limestones, of the Cretaceous and

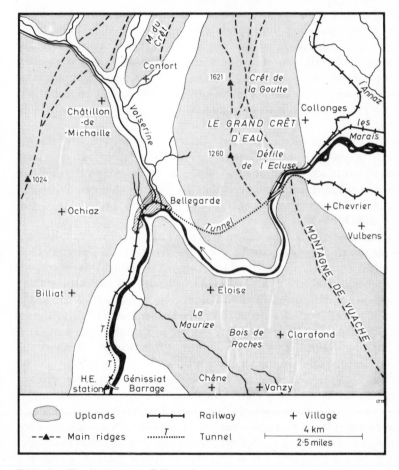

FIG. 21.3. The Rhône near Bellegarde
The upland area, approximately over 530 m (1 750 ft), is generalised.
Heights are given in metres.
    This exemplifies the transverse *cluses* by which the Rhône and other Jura rivers break through a ridge from one *val* to another. The line of the Valserine and the Rhône below Bellegarde indicates a major synclinal valley.

Based on *Carte de France au 50 000ᵉ*, sheets XXXIII/29, 30, with revisions.

Tertiary clays in the synclines, and of the considerable patches of till contribute to the permanent character of the rivers. Springs are common, even up in the high *combes*. Of course intermittent streams appear in the valleys, which may vary from a torrent to a trickle or even dry up altogether, and complex subterranean drainage systems have developed. Some parts of the higher plateaus consist of monotonous expanses of almost bare limestone, reminiscent of the *Causses*, displaying irregular solution hollows, dry valleys,[4] deep chasms, watersinks and resurgences, with irregular steepsided summits rising above the general level.

The varied nature of the Jurassic rocks, where resistant limestones lie in close juxtaposition to weaker shales and marls, produces remarkable effects both in the cross profiles of the valleys and in the nature of the streambeds. In places steep cliffs fall almost to the water's edge, in others the valley sides open out, with gentle meadow- or tree-covered slopes. Stepped falls, where a river crosses a succession of horizontal resistant strata, are common. The Loue, for example, leaves its cave as a powerful resurgence down such a 'staircase'.

Most of the drainage of the southern Jura finds its way to the Rhône either directly or via its right-bank tributary the Ain. In the extreme west and northwest, short streams flow down through the steep gorges that fret the edge of the Vignoble and Revermont to join the Saône's left-bank tributaries. The waters of the central and northern French Jura are collected by the Doubs.

The Rhône leaves the southwestern wing of Lake Geneva (*Lac Léman*), which lies at 375 m (1 230 ft) above sea level; the river has already descended 1 500 m (5 000 ft) from its glacier source in central Switzerland. The abrupt checking of the gradient as the river leaves the Alpine tract causes considerable deposition in the lake; the milky colour of the laden current can be traced from the air far out into the clear waters as it extends its lacustrine delta. The lake therefore serves a valuable purpose as a filterbed, and the Rhône issues as a sediment-free stream through the sluices in the barrage controlling the lake level.

The Rhône negotiates the fold ridges of the southern Jura by a series of *vaux* alternating with the usual *cluses* through the ridges. Below Pougny, 40 km (25 miles) from Lake Geneva, the turbulent river surges through the well-named Défilé de l'Ecluse (Fig. 21.3). The valley is so steepsided that the railway from Geneva to Bellegarde tunnels through the spur to the north rather than attempt to follow the gorge. A few kilometres further downstream, the river negotiates a lower and less sharply defined ridge by means of a double rightangle bend; Bellegarde stands on the northern abutment of this ridge overlooking the river.

Then the Rhône follows a long synclinal *val*-section, continuing the trend of its tributary the Valserine from the north. Although this is a *val*, it is deep and steepsided, with limestone hills rising for nearly 300 m (1 000 ft) above the river. This offered a firstrate site for a reservoir, and the huge Génissiat dam, 50 km (31 miles) downstream from Lake Geneva, and rising for 80 m (260 ft) above its base, has ponded up a narrow lake extending 23 km (14 miles) upstream almost as far as Bellegarde.

The river continues southwards, its valley enclosed by the ridges of the Montagne du Grand Colombier to the west and the forested Montagne du Gros Foug to the east. In this flat-floored valley deposition has caused extensive braiding (Fig. 22.4) among shingle-islands and marshes. The valley opens out southward into the main Sub-Alpine Depression (see p. 624), although the Rhône, hugging its western side, leaves this for another parallel Jura syncline, and the depression itself is occupied by the Lac du Bourget and by extensive marshlands; the lake, fed from the south by the Leyesse, is connected to the Rhône by the Canal de Savières. The Rhône proceeds southwards to Tenne, turns abruptly west through another transverse gorge, follows a further synclinal valley, and then crosses the last main Jura ridge to St Genix-sur-Guiers. This is in point of fact the most southerly point reached by the river in its midsection between Geneva and Lyons. It meanders and braids its channel; a few kilometres downstream from St Genix its streams extend in width over the flat valley floor for about a kilometre, enclosing gravel- and sandbanks such as *les Iles Molottes, les Iles des Sables,* and *les Graviers Grand Jean.* The river then crosses the narrow southerly extremity of the Plateau Jura for about 30 km (20 miles), swings round the northern abutment of the Plateau de Crémieu, and enters the Plaine de Bresse.

Above Lyons the Rhône has a predominantly Alpine régime, and high water occurs in late spring and early summer because of snowmelt in the French Alps; the Arve is a major contributor, draining as it does the north-western side of the Mont Blanc massif and the Alps of Haute-Savoie, while the Jura tributaries add their quota. Lake Geneva, however, acts as a stabilising reservoir, damping down the floodwaters of Alpine Switzerland, though the sluicegates in the controlling barrage are necessarily open in early summer and the riverflow is much increased. A marked low water period is experienced in late summer, and then a secondary maximum follows the increased rainfall of the autumn months. The winter freeze materially reduces the outflow for several months until the spring snow-melt begins.

The Ain, the major tributary of the middle Rhône, is the chief drainage artery of the southern Jura. Its headstream, the Bienne, rises not far from the Valserine (which flows directly to the Rhône) and the Orbe (which flows in a northeasterly direction to Lake Neuchâtel and so to the Rhine); this is a striking drainage dispersal (Fig. 21.2). The upper Ain and the Bienne both reveal the rectilinear pattern of Jura rivers. The greater part of the course of the Ain is trenched in a southwesterly direction across the Plateau Jura.

The Doubs, which joins the Saône about 30 km (20 miles) above Chalon, has a most remarkable course. It rises in the *Hautes Chaînes* of the Folded

Jura on the slopes of Mont Risoux, and pursues a northeasterly direction into the Lac de St Point (Fig. 21.4), which once extended further to the southwest along the floor of a *val*. The Doubs built up a marshy alluvial flat, which in due course cut the original lake into two, separating St Point to the northeast from de Remoray to the southwest. Areas of marsh still cover the valley floor. Below the Lac de St Point, the Doubs turns abruptly

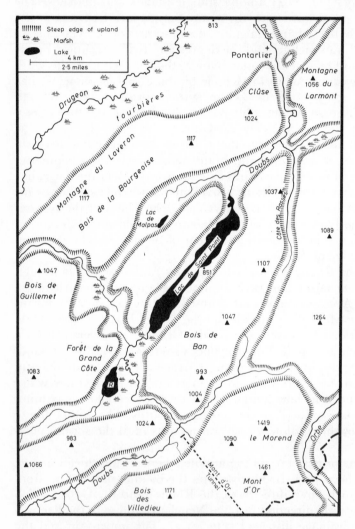

FIG. 21.4. The valley of the upper Doubs
The edge of the upland is shown by hachures in generalised form, in order to bring out the broad pattern of ridges and valleys.
Heights are given in metres.
　**R,** Lac de Remoray.

Based on *Carte de France au 50 000ᵉ*, sheets XXXIV/25, 26.

through a magnificent *cluse* to enter a basin in which stands Pontarlier at a height of 800 m (2 600 ft). This synclinal depression is drained by the Drugeon, joining the Doubs a few kilometres below the town. The floor of this basin is so flat that areas of peat bogs (*tourbières*) have accumulated. After forming the Franco-Swiss frontier for more than 50 km (30 miles), the Doubs passes into Switzerland for a short distance, and then makes a striking reversal of direction by means of an acute bend. It seems that the upper northeasterly section of its course is a legacy of a former continuation to the proto-Rhine. River-capture caused this change of direction; the beheaded trunk flows as a misfit to the Rhine just above Basel as the tiny river Birse (Fig. 21.1).

The Doubs bends northwards yet again, crossing the Plateau Jura, but near Montbéliard it flows southwestwards along the margin of the Mont-agnes du Lomont through Besançon and Dole into the Plaine de Bresse and hence to its junction with the Saône.

Both the Doubs and the Saône receive left-bank tributaries from the Jura, many of them the product of complex underground systems developed in the limestone. The Loue, for example, emerges as a seething resurgence from a cave near Mouthier, only 8 km (5 miles) from the Doubs but 357 m (1 170 ft) below. E. de Martonne describes how the *absinthe* factory at Pontarlier suffered damage from fire; the liquor from the damaged vats escaped through the limestone joints, and its unmistakable odour was in due course traced far below in the waters of the Loue. The Loue then flows through a magnificent gorge where vertical cliffs of limestone alternate with tree-covered terraces. It approaches within 5 or 6 km (3 or 4 miles) of the Doubs below Besançon, but swings away again, and does not make its confluence for another 50 km (30 miles), below Dole.

## Land use

Many contrasts are evident in the climates of the Jura, as between the northern end where a distinct bleakness is apparent, and the southern part which possesses a certain brightness, almost of a Mediterranean quality. There are contrasts too between the high ranges and the south-facing valley slopes, and altitude ranges from 450 to over 1 500 m (1 500 to over 5 000 ft). The region as a whole lies in the east of France and so is subject to continental influences. The winters are quite severe; at Rousses, near the frontier to the east of Morez, the lake is frozen on an average for 130 days per annum, while frost is experienced on the *Hautes Chaînes* on an average for a hundred days and for about eighty on the plateau.

Precipitation is heavy, averaging 990 mm (39 in) on the plateau and as much as 1 650 to 1 800 mm (65 to 70 in) on the crest-lines. Much falls as snow; at Mouthe, in the upper Doubs valley at an altitude of 950 m (3 100 ft), the average accumulated depth of snow is about 3 m (10 ft), and several high villages have developed as winter sports centres, notably

Gilley on the eastern slopes of Mont Chaumont, Morteau and Pontarlier. The expectancy of the number of days during which snow may lie around 600 m (2 000 ft) is about 55, increasing to 125 at 1 200 m (4 000 ft). No road passes are sufficiently high to suffer regular snow-blocking, although the Col de la Faucille between St Claude and Geneva may be intermittently closed. On the other hand summer days are sunny, although continental influences may reveal themselves in considerable August-September rain. Mean July temperatures of 19°C (66°F) occur in the southern valleys.

The Jura occupy the greater part of the three *départements* of Doubs, Jura and Ain, although the western part of the last extends into the Plaine de Bresse. However, the official returns for these three *départements* are indicative of the land use in the Jura generally.

*Land use, 1968 (percentages of total area)*

|       | ARABLE | PASTURE | WOODLAND |
|-------|--------|---------|----------|
| Doubs | 14     | 39      | 41       |
| Jura  | 15     | 33      | 43       |
| Ain   | 15     | 33      | 26       |

Source: Ministère de l'Agriculture, *Annuaire statistique de la France*, 1970–1.

## Woodland

Woodland covers almost two-fifths of the Jura. Indeed, the characteristic landscape of the *Hautes Chaînes* comprises steep sides swathed with dark conifers (notably spruce), interrupted by near vertical limestone cliffs too steep to support vegetation, rising from the fresh green meadows in the *vaux*. In some of the gorges, such as the Loue, where the river has cut deeply into horizontal strata of varying resistance, a striking alternation is apparent between treeclad terraces and precipitous limestone walls. Many parts of the Plateau Jura have been planted with blocks of conifers. Deciduous trees increase on the lower slopes—beech, mountain ash, plane, maple and (particularly in the south) sweet chestnut and oak. On lower slopes and in the valleys patches of green meadowland alternate with clumps of trees. The state is not an important owner of forests; in fact only 4 per cent of the woodlands in the *département* of Doubs and 13 per cent in Jura are state owned. It is estimated that 15 000 private proprietors own small 'parcels' of woodland in Jura and nearly as many in Doubs. Most of the remaining woodland is the property of the communes, as much as 68 per cent of the total in Doubs.

## Agriculture

Though there is a varied agricultural life, the emphasis in the Jura is on pastoral activities. Many of the valleys and depressions contain tolerable soils; sometimes Jurassic marls appear in depressions on the plateau, Lower Cretaceous clays in the *vaux*, sheets of till in the *combes* and recent alluvium along the valley floors, and these carry a detailed patchwork of cultivation. Along the rivers, stretches of water-meadow afford one and sometimes two crops of hay for winter feed; some are irrigated by a network of artificial channels. They are succeeded away from the rivers by strips of cultivation, many small scattered 'parcels' growing wheat and oats, potatoes, turnips and other vegetables, and maize and tobacco in the south. Local specialisations include the cultivation of peas near Frasne, cauliflowers around Hautepierre, herbs for the distillation of liqueur at Pontarlier, and flowers for perfume between Culoz and Seyssel. Then on the slopes are orchards of apples, plums, medlars and cherries; fruit is also grown along the sides of the roads. Peaches and even figs are cultivated in favoured places.

Vineyards cover a considerable area of the more favoured south-facing slopes. Admittedly the Jura are not an outstanding wine-producing district, although grapes have been grown since at least the tenth century. The region was badly affected by phylloxera in the late nineteenth century, and the area under vines is now only a sixth of that in 1868. Not much quality wine is produced, though *Arbois* is a rich golden wine of long renown,[6] produced around the little town of that name (where Louis Pasteur lived and died) in the valley of the Cuisance, which flows to the Loue and so to the Doubs. The *département* of Ain has a considerable output of *vin ordinaire* on the northwestern slopes of the Revermont, although here large areas of vineyards have been abandoned during the last thirty years.

Most of this Jura agriculture then is of a subsistence character, a *petite culture*, pleasant, comfortable, varied, and in places quite specialised. It is, however, concentrated in the valleys and in the depressions, for on the higher surfaces of the plateaus there is naturally little cultivation, merely rough grazing and plantations of conifers.

The chief agricultural emphasis is on dairying; in the three *départements* in 1968 were 399 000 head of dairy cattle out of a total of 694 000 cattle. Before 1914 cattle-rearing was restricted to the high pastures (the *alpages*), often owned in common by members of a valley commune, for little of the valley floor could be spared for grazing. These upland pastures are still used, indeed much has been considerably improved by fertilisers, but the pastoral economy is now emphasised in the valleys as well, where about half the arable was converted between the wars into pasture lying near each village. Moreover, there has been greater concentration on fodder crops (oats, beet, trefoil) and on the improvement of hay meadows. Between the wars, as a result, the output of milk in the Jura doubled. Transhumance is still practised, families taking the animals up to the *alpages* from May to September, but many cattle are now kept permanently in the valleys.

Some of the milk is destined for chocolate factories at Geneva, Pontarlier and Morteau, and much is consumed in liquid form in towns such as

Montbéliard and Besançon or sent further afield to Lyons and even to Paris. But the chief product is cheese, and the term *Gruyère* had been applied to Jura produce for centuries. These magnificent cheeses are made in small dairy chalets, in larger *fromageries*, and in recent years at factories in Pontarlier, Dole and Lons. Some highly organised cooperative societies have been developed, which collect the milk, deliver it to the *fromageries*, and then sell cheese to the merchants. Gruyère is not the only Jura cheese, although pre-eminent; there are the delicate blue-veined '*bleu de Jura*' and '*bleu de Gex*', the 'parsley-cheese' and goats'-milk cheeses. Other dairying industries include the production of processed cream-cheeses, cream, butter and casein for some local industries. Pigs are fed on skim-milk returned from the factories to the farmers, and poultry are bred in huge numbers, particularly in the Ain valley, where these poultry farms are on a considerable scale, rearing birds for the Paris and other markets. But the production of cheese has been justly called '*la première richesse du Jura*'.

## Power and industry

### Power

The industries of the Jura have long made use of water power; the tumbling streams were harnessed to drive water mills to provide power for saw mills, grain mills and lathes. But the development of hydroelectric power has gone on apace in France, especially since 1946 under the nationalised Electricité de France. Before 1939 only a few small stations were in operation in the Jura, including two on the Ain and several on the Rhône and the Doubs. Since then France's biggest hydrostation has been built on the Rhône below Bellegarde at Génissiat,[7] the famous Léon Perrier undertaking (Fig. 21.3), by the Government-sponsored public corporation, the Compagnie Nationale du Rhône, established in 1931 as a multipurpose planning authority for the development of hydroelectricity, navigation and irrigation along the river. The *val* below Bellegarde offered an obvious site for a reservoir, and work began in 1937. The first task was to drive a tunnel parallel to the river as a temporary bypass, and a coffer dam was built at the diversion to enable construction to proceed in the dry bed. In 1939 the Rhône was diverted into this tunnel, but in 1940, on the fall of France, the coffer dam was opened and the site flooded. In 1942 the Germans allowed work to be continued and the immense project went forward until the completion in 1948 of the main barrage. The river was returned to its bed, and water backed up behind the barrage almost to Bellegarde to form a 23-km (14-mile) long reservoir. The installed capacity of the main power-house is 405 mW, with an output of 1 660 gWh out of a French hydro total (1969) of 52 000 gWh. A smaller plant of 45 mW capacity was opened in 1952 downstream at Seyssel. The Génissiat plant is linked to the main French grid; a 220 kv line and a more recent 380 kv line run direct to Paris via Vielmoulin and Creneye. It represents a major achievement in the overall Rhône plan; in fact, with the other new stations (see p. 370), the French have already harnessed over half of the Rhône's potential. Apart from the Génissiat and Seyssel stations, plants of smaller capacity are in operation along the Rhône. The station at Cusset, on the Rhône above Lyons, has been enlarged in recent years, and produced 406 gWh in 1969.

## Industry

What are commonly called '*les petites industries du Jura*' make an appreciable contribution to the economy.[8] They are legacies of long-established 'chalet industries', which occupied winter leisure and still afford on a piecework basis a useful supplementation of the family incomes. Although still organised in small specialised units, industry is now, however, more concentrated in the many towns and villages, using electric power.

It must be remembered, however, that the distinction between industrial and agricultural employment is difficult to define, indeed, there is much seasonal work in both spheres.

Industry is extremely varied, and includes the activities associated with agricultural products, such as the factory-manufacture of cheese, butter, cream and casein, the distillation of various liqueurs (absinthe, *Pernod*, plum- and cherry-brandy), brewing at Besançon, the production of chocolate, and the processing of tobacco. Several small metallurgical works are still active, which once derived their ores from Liassic strata in the valleys, their fuel from charcoal, their power from running water; the place names Ferrière and Forges bear testimony to the antiquity of these iron works. Today the industry survives in steel foundries and electric furnaces at Pontarlier and Bellegarde, forges for special steels at Champagnole, rollingmills at Syam, wire mills at Lods and Vuillafans, and nail and bolt factories at l'Ile-sur-Doubs, Ornans, Jougne and Clerval.

The Triassic saltbeds along the northwestern flanks of the uplands in the neighbourhood of Salins, Grozon and Montmorot have been the basis of a flourishing salt trade since the Middle Ages. It has declined in importance, but salt is still extracted by brine pumping at Poligny, from which a pipeline runs northwest to the Solvay works at Dole. About 40 000 tons of salt are produced each year, employing 250 workers. Limestone is quarried at several places for building stone, notably an attractive free-stone with rose-coloured veins in the Rhône valley between St Genix and Lagnieu. Cement is manufactured in the Rhône and Ain valleys. Lime is worked and crushed for agricultural and other purposes.

Wood-using industries have long been established, now centred at St Claude in the valley of the Bienne. For centuries workshops in the neighbourhood manufactured buckets, tubs and vats, tool handles, wooden utensils, clock cases, cheese presses and furniture. One specialisation is the carving of rosaries and religious statuettes, for which St Claude became famous in the eighteenth century, as also for the fashionable carved snuff-boxes. Another item comprises pipes for smokers, originally made from box wood growing on the Jura slopes, now from cherry wood or heath roots (*bruyère*) imported from Corsica, Algeria and the eastern Pyrenees; the pipes of St Claude have a worldwide reputation. In addition to these specialised wood-using industries, larger scale manufactures include butter- and cheese-boxes, furniture, ladders and wine-casks, and a large amount of sawn timber and pit props is sent away.

The development of these varied industries has led to the introduction of others requiring similar techniques, but with different media. The manufacture of articles in bone and horn in the nineteenth century has developed into similar activities using celluloid, casein and plastics, making combs, toilet articles such as hand-mirror frames, electrical apparatus and fountain pens.

Watch- and clock-making, so famous in the Swiss Jura, was introduced into France in the mid-seventeenth century by refugees from Geneva who settled in the valley of the upper Bienne. The small towns of the Pays de Gex manufacture individual watch parts, still sent into Geneva for assembly. In 1793 watch-making was introduced into Besançon, and today this has become the chief individual centre, with a number of factories. Another specialisation is the cutting and polishing of precious stones, both for watches and for jewellery.[9] Workshops are engaged in this industry in the Pays de Gex, in the hills between the rivers Valserine and Bienne (where Septmoncel is the centre), and at St Claude and Morez. Aspects of the glass industry include the manufacture of spectacles and watch-glasses at Lons-le-Saunier and Morez.

In the extreme south of the Jura, in the district of Bugey, the industrial influence of Lyons makes itself felt, and the electric power available in the Rhône valley is utilised by the textile industry. Thrown silk and silk thread are made in small factories at Argis, St Rambert, Ambérieu and Pont-d'Ain, silk cloth is woven at Nantua, Bellegarde and Maillat, linen at Belley, lace and net at Ambérieu and Nantua. Similarly, the influence of Mulhouse has spread into the northern Jura and textile factories are active in Besançon, producing mainly rayon, hosiery and cotton-elastic fabrics.

The Jura therefore is an industrial area of some importance and interest, partly the result of long-established local skills and specialisations and partly the influence of three neighbouring industrial regions—southern Alsace, the Swiss Plateau and the Lyons district, from each of which people and ideas have migrated to the Jura at various times. A few marginal towns —Besançon and Montbéliard in the northwest (p. 376), Lons-le-Saunier in the west—have grown into larger industrial centres; their factories have drawn workers from both agriculture and from domestic industry, and the development of the grid has enabled power to be used on a large scale.

The industries which are aptly called 'de luxe ou de demi-luxe' still employ 40 000 workers, or a quarter of the total industrial personnel. But in recent years there has been a great diversification, including the manufacture of typewriters, electric locos, motors and turbines, and general hardware.

## Population and settlement

Population is remarkably dispersed throughout the Jura, though with concentrations in the valleys and scanty areas on the forested plateau and along the *monts*.[10] Much of the plateau has a density of less than 20 per sq km (50 per sq mile), and the only town there is Pontarlier, lying in a depression crossed by the Doubs. The towns of the western Jura are situated on its margins—in the Doubs valley where stands the industrial centre of Besançon (113 000 people), and at the foot of the Vignoble-Revermont escarpment, notably Lons-le-Saunier and Bourg. Besançon formed one of Louis XIV's frontier fortresses, for it lies to the west of one of France's main eastern gateways, the Porte de Bourgogne. The Doubs at that point makes a bend of almost 300 degrees, leaving a meander spur with a precipitous 'neck' where Vauban built one of his then near-impregnable fortresses; it was later necessary to tunnel right through this neck to afford passage for the Rhône-Rhine Canal. This tunnel has been enlarged for the new Grand Canal du Rhône au Rhin (see p. 311). Many small villages are situated at considerable altitudes; the highest are Lajoux (1 180 m: 3 871 ft) and Septmoncel (1 175 m: 3 855 ft), the latter of which produces a local speciality, a delightful blue cheese.

Although the Folded Jura would seem less propitious for settlement, with its lofty wooded ridges and steep slopes, nevertheless its population is considerably greater than that of the Plateau Jura, over 60 per sq km (150 per sq mile) in many parts. Settlement is concentrated in the valleys where small but prosperous towns and villages have grown up—St Claude, Oyonnax, Bellegarde, Belley and many more. They have a distinct charm, and many are examples of what the French guidebooks call *villes gracieuses*. The villages are centres of a flourishing and varied agriculture with some local industry, the towns of an equally varied industrial life. Finally, the Jura, with their hills and valleys, forests and meadows, rivers and lakes, and in fact their general charm, attract large numbers of visitors.

The upland arc of the Jura does not attain any great altitude, but its succession of parallel ridges and *vaux* make it quite difficult to cross transversely. In spite of these physical difficulties, the Jura afford major passageways between central France and the Swiss Plateau, and beyond to Italy, Austria and the Balkans. Several important transcontinental lines run southeastward from Basel, Belfort and Dijon. These lines were expensive to build; tunnels, cuttings, viaducts and avalanche galleries are required, but they are important international routeways and carry a heavy tourist traffic.

The Jura road system is remarkably adequate. There are three main road passes, Les Verrières (760 m: 2 500 ft) between Pontarlier and Neuchâtel, the Col de St Cergue (1 235 m: 4 051 ft) from Les Rousses to Nyon, and the Col de la Faucille (1 321 m: 4 331 ft), between St Claude and Geneva. These passes may be intermittently blocked by snow in the winter, usually on the Swiss side, but rarely for any length of time. Many minor roads and light railways penetrate the hills to link up the small towns and villages.

[1] E. de Margerie, *Le Jura* (1922), is one of the classic French regional monographs.

[2] M. Dubois, *Le Jura méridional: étude morphologique* (1959); and M. Dubois and R. Lebeau, 'Le Jura méridional', *Annls Géogr.*, **71** (1962), pp. 337–8.

[3] J. Tricart, 'Quelques aspects particuliers des glaciations quaternaires du Jura', *Revue géographique de l'Est*, **5** (1965), pp. 499–527.

[4] S. Daveau, 'Vallées sèches des plateaux du Jura', *Revue géographique de l'Est*, **5** (1965), pp. 461–72.

[5] I. Trautsolt, 'Recherches sur les climats du Jura français', *Annls Géogr.*, **78** (1969), pp. 405–34.

[6] R. Dion, 'Le vin d'Arbois au Moyen-Age', *Annls Géogr.*, **64** (1955), pp. 162–9.

[7] A. Blanchard, 'Les travaux de la Compagnie Nationale du Rhône: Génissiat, Donzère', *Rev. Géogr. alp.*, **38** (1950), pp. 189–92. It must be noted, however, that although the installed capacity of Génissiat is greater than that of Donzère, the output of the latter is usually appreciably higher.

[8] A. Mathieu, 'Les petites industries de la montagne dans le Jura français', *Annls Géogr.*, **38** (1929), pp. 439–59.

[9] P. Antoine, 'L'industrie de la pierre précieuse dans le Jura', *Annls Géogr.*, **58** (1949), pp. 126–31.

[10] Some interesting features of the Franco-Swiss frontier region are discussed by S. Daveau, *Les Régions frontalières de la Montagne jurassienne: étude de géographie humaine* (1959).

# 22
# The French Alps

The mountainous region of southeastern France between Lake Geneva and the Mediterranean forms part of the fold mountain system of the Alps, which sweeps in a curve around the western and northern margins of the North Italian Plain. The frontiers of France, Switzerland and Italy meet at a pinnacle on the summit ridge of Mont Dolent, in the northeast of the Mont Blanc massif. From this point the Franco-Italian frontier runs away southward, following the main watershed between the tributaries of the Rhône and those of the Po. This leaves four-fifths of this part of the Alps, 190 km (120 miles) in overall width, within France.[1] Because these uplands receive heavy precipitation on their western slopes they carry extensive snowfields and numerous glaciers, though of much more limited extent on the Italian side of the ranges.

## General features

The Alps are primarily the result of mid-Tertiary earth movements which upfolded vast thicknesses of Mesozoic and Tertiary sediments; these had accumulated in the geosyncline between the ancient Hercynian foreland of Europe and the plateau continent of Africa. The direction, nature and degree of this folding depended both on the compressive forces affecting the geosyncline and the positions of the rigid 'outer horsts' of the Hercynian continent—the Central Massif, the Vosges, the Black Forest and the Bohemian Plateau. The outer margins of the folded zone, affected only superficially, are represented by the Jura and further south by the limestone Fore-Alps which lie east of the Rhône valley. Within the main orogenic zone the folding was exceedingly complex, involving the formation of recumbent folds and the carrying forward of several series of *nappes*, that is, overthrust masses that have been forced far away from their 'roots'. One series of these nappes comprises the Pre-Alps, most of which are in Switzerland to the east of Lake Geneva, but one group to the south of the lakes lies mostly in France. Of the six major nappes which are developed so well in the Pennine ranges of the Swiss-Italian Alps, one (the Great St Bernard nappe) is extensively represented in the French Alps.

Involved in the folds, which consist mainly of metamorphosed sedimentary rocks, are several blocks of crystalline rock, the so-called 'inner horsts', which represent portions of the 'splintered edge' of the Hercynian continent overwhelmed by and caught up in the folding. Other crystalline masses may represent the deep-seated cores of the folds, or they may be

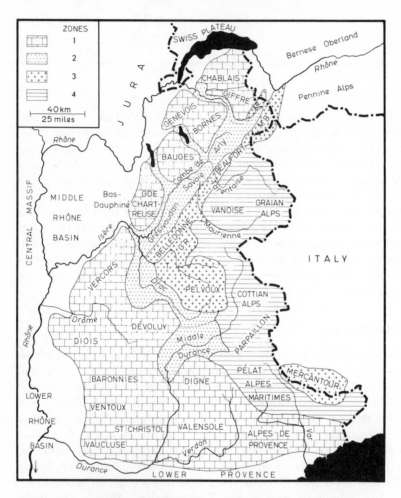

FIG. 22.1. Structural divisions of the French Alps

The divisions are described in the text, under the following headings:
**I,** The Fore-Alps, together with the Pre-Alps of Chablais; **II,** The Sub-Alpine Furrow, including the *Pays de la moyenne Durance*; **III,** The Hercynian Massifs; and **IV,** The Sedimentary Zone of the High Alps, including the upper valleys of the Isère, Arc and Durance.

The abbreviations are as follows: **AR,** Aiguilles Rouges; **MB,** Mont Blanc; **GR,** Grandes Rousses; **T,** Taillefer.

The extension of the Mont Blanc massif into Italy and Switzerland and that of Mercantour into Italy are indicated.

batholithic intrusions over-run by the folds. In either case, these crystalline rocks have been exhumed in places by long-continued denudation.

One other structural complication has affected the southern part of the Alps. The earlier earth movements which produced the Pyrenees, probably in late Eocene times, induced a west–east direction in these fold systems, what the French geomorphologists call '*la direction pyrénéenne*', in contrast to the predominant north–south trend of the French Alps. The ranges of Lower Provence, although separated from the main Pyrenean region by the Golfe du Lion and the lower Rhône valley, are a structural continuation of the Pyrenees. The same west–east trend is revealed in the Provençal

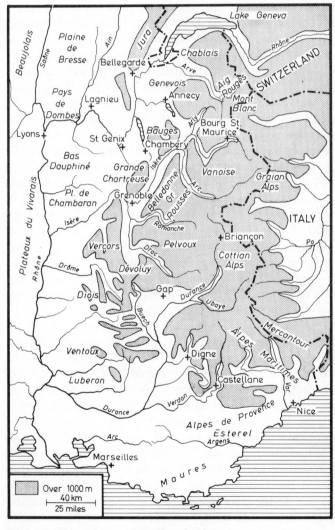

Fig. 22.2. General map of the French Alps

Alps and in the southern sections of the Fore-Alps (Baronnies, Ventoux, Lure, Luberon), spurs of which project into the Rhône valley. The zone of contact in the southeast between the Pyrenean and Alpine trends is therefore complex.

The rocks of which the Alps are composed are thus of great diversity. Granite, gneiss and crystalline schists form the Hercynian massifs; Cretaceous and some Jurassic limestones, together with Tertiary *Flysch* sandstones and marls comprise the outer zone of the Fore-Alps; while in the inner folded zone appear Carboniferous, Permian and a wide range of Mesozoic and Tertiary rocks. What is more, many of these have been metamorphosed into schistose rocks of quite different character; these notably include the *Schistes lustrés*, for the most part metamorphosed Mesozoic rocks. The varied rocks have been intensely modified through long-sustained denudation, for the diverse nature of the rocks has allowed differential weathering full scope in producing the present land forms.

The prime fact about the major drainage systems (Fig. 22.2) is that they have developed across the longitudinal structural zones, for the frontier ridge forms the main watershed between the west-flowing drainage to the Rhône and the east-flowing Po tributaries. In their transverse sections across the structures, the rivers have adjusted their courses wherever possible to belts of less resistant rock, sometimes utilising portions of the various longitudinal zones, and emphasising the more resistant rocks. Two rivers, the Isère and the Durance, have become the master streams; between them they drain all the French Alps, except for a small part in the north which drains by the Arve, and another area in the south which drains directly to the Mediterranean by way of the Var. Most tributaries of these rivers consist of immature torrents and cascades, frequently flowing in gorges. The steep gradients, heavy precipitation, considerable snow-melt and torrential runoff over the crystalline rocks combine to make the rivers powerful agents of sculpture. They bring down loads of rock waste, most of which ultimately reaches the Rhône valley. The evidence of the ravages of these mountain torrents is everywhere; hillsides are gashed with gullies and there are rock slopes from which surface material has been scoured. Deforestation has accelerated this process, particularly in the southern Alps. Considerable areas consist of limestone, notably in the Fore-Alps, and as a result complex underground drainage systems have developed.

A second contribution to the physical landscape is the work of glaciation. In Quaternary times, the High Alps nurtured much more extensive snow-fields and glaciers than exist today (Fig. 22.3). During the maximum Riss stage the glaciers pushed their way well down into the Rhône valley, probably even to the west of Lyons, for erratics have been found within that city. The whole of Bas-Dauphiné was probably covered by a converging piedmont glacier. In the later Würm stages, when the ice-covering was thinner and less extensive, differential erosion was more pronounced.

The glaciers left a marked impress on the relief, notably in the form of overdeepened troughlike valleys in which the present rivers are clearly misfits. The *cluses* separating the individual Fore-Alpine massifs were widened and deepened by glaciers which used the narrow preglacial gorges as exits. They produced all the other familiar features of upland glaciation—cirques, hanging valleys, rock steps and valley benches. The

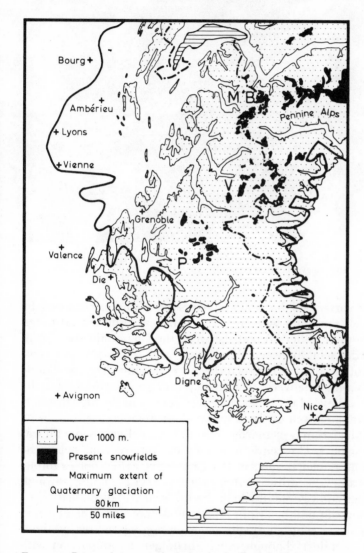

FIG. 22.3. Past and present glaciation in the French Alps
The major snowfields and glaciers at the present time are found in the Mont Blanc region (**MB**), the Vanoise (**V**) and the Pelvoux (**P**).

Based on (*a*) E. de Martonne, *Les Alpes* (1926), p. 42; and (*b*) *Atlas de France* (1939), plate 10.

Plate 62. Mont Blanc and the Vallée de Chamonix, in winter

differing levels of surface of the valley glaciers are also demonstrated by clearcut cols which represent glacial exit channels at different altitudes. Examples include the Col des Montets between the Chamonix and Trient valleys, the Col des Gets between the Dranse and the Giffre (an Arve tributary), the Col de Megève between the Arve and the Arly, the Col de Faverge (or de Tamie) between the Annecy and Isère valleys, and the broad Chambéry valley. Many other cols, particularly in the high frontier-ridges, are the familiar result of 'back to back' cirque recession.

While upland glaciation is primarily erosional in its effects, some till was deposited in the valleys. Crescentic moraines are apparent far below the ends of the present glacier snouts; in the Chamonix valley, for example, well-defined moraines lie athwart the valley near Les Tines, through which the Arve has cut a gorge in which the till is clearly displayed.

In the highest massifs, notably Mont Blanc, the Vanoise and the Pelvoux, snowfields and glaciers (Fig. 22.3) still cover an aggregate area of about 500 sq km (200 sq miles). Though much shrunken in comparison with those of Quaternary times, they afford attractive ingredients in the Alpine landscape.

The varied rocks present different responses to weathering. The massive granite of Mont Blanc, with its prominent vertical joints, weathers into steep buttresses and cleancut pinnacles. The shales and metamorphosed

618

schists form crumbling ridges, flanked by scree slopes, the product of potent frost-shattering. Limestone results in a diverse relief of sharp crests, barren plateaus, vertical cliffs, steepsided gorges and deep chasms. In the south, where the Mediterranean aridity becomes increasingly marked, karstic features are widespread.

The climatic range between the northern and southern ends of the French Alps has resulted in pronounced differences in both landscape and economy. In the north are snowfields and glaciers, dark pine woods, fresh green Alpine meadows and ribbons of agriculture running along the valleys. In the south are semi-arid limestone plateaus and edges, with scrublike vegetation in the higher parts and chestnut woods and olive groves on the lower slopes. As the shores of the Côte d'Azur are approached there is an almost subtropical appearance, with the exotic vegetation of mimosa, oleander, palm and bougainvillaea. A remarkable transition appears southward in the dominant tones of the landscape—a fresh greenness in Savoy, sombre browns in Dauphiny, and harsh greys, dazzling whites and dusty greens in the southern Alps.

Agriculture shows this same contrast. In the north and centre, specialised pastoral industries are based on cattle, utilising both the valley floors and the seasonal alp pastures,² while forest industries are important, especially in the heavily wooded Fore-Alpine massifs. Further south sheep are kept on the patchy upland pastures of the limestone, although not to the same extent as in the past, and an indication of a near-Mediterranean economy is afforded by the cultivation of small plots of hard wheat, maize, almonds and olives.

Nor is agriculture the sole or even the dominant aspect of the economy. The development of hydroelectricity has not only contributed to France's power supplies, but has helped some of the valleys to become important industrial areas, forming a kind of linear industrialisation. Electrochemical and electrometallurgical factories have been established in the upper valleys of the Isère and the Arc, while Grenoble dominates the electrical engineering, textile, glove and other industries of the middle Isère valley.

Finally, the whole region from the shores of Lake Geneva to the Riviera forms a popular and prosperous tourist area, both in summer and winter, capitalising the assets of a most attractive mountain landscape. These two extremities are linked by the 600 km (375 miles) long *Route des Alpes*, one of the finest series of mountain roads in Europe. The high passes are crossed and the lonely valleys are penetrated by motor roads, and hotels are found in the most remote districts.

The various names bestowed on different parts of the French Alps are legion. The two old provincial names, Savoy (*Savoie*) and Dauphiny (*Dauphiné*), are still used to designate the northern and central Alps respectively, and the former is perpetuated in the two *départements* of Savoie and Haute-Savoie. Other regional names have been bestowed upon various groups of the mountain ranges, such as the Graian, Cottian,

Provençal and Maritime Alps. Individual upland blocks, separated by deep valleys, each have their distinctive names, as marked on Fig. 22.1. Several of the glacially-widened troughs, where so much of the life of the Alps is concentrated, form valley *pays*. These include the *Tarentaise*,[1] the *Combe de Savoie* and the *Grésivaudan*, three distinct sections of the upper and middle Isère valley; the *Maurienne*,[3] the long curving valley of the Arc; the *Briançonnais* and the *Embrunais* of the upper Durance; and the *Faucigny* of the Arve valley. Many of these were once administrative units; thus the Maurienne and the Tarentaise were episcopal republics.

It is convenient to describe the French Alps in more detail under their four main structural divisions. These comprise (i) the Fore-Alpine limestone zone to the west (including the small area of Pre-Alps to the south of Lake Geneva); (ii) a longitudinal depression known as the Sub-Alpine Furrow; (iii) a discontinuous series of arcuate crystalline massifs; and (iv) the main sedimentary zone along the Franco-Italian frontier (Fig. 22.1).

## The Fore-Alpine limestone zone

A more or less continuous zone of Jurassic and Cretaceous rocks extends from Lake Geneva to the Mediterranean coast near Monaco. This zone of gentle folds follows for the most part the north–south trend of the High Alps. In the south, however, the trend assumes more of a west–east nature as it becomes involved with the mountain structures of Provence. As a result, this zone, which varies between 20 and 30 km (12 and 20 miles) as far south as the Drôme valley, widens to 100 km (60 miles) or more in the south.

Both the terms 'fore-Alpine' and 'pre-Alpine' zone are bestowed on this unit as a whole. The latter is, however, unfortunate, since the name 'Pre-Alps' is restricted by L. W. Collet and other geomorphologists to the area of nappes extending from Lake Thun in Switzerland to Lake Geneva (the Romande Pre-Alps), and continuing south to the Arve valley as the Chablais Pre-Alps. These Pre-Alps involve a varied stratigraphical sequence with a number of thrustplanes, and their origin is far from clear. Since this term Pre-Alps has received general recognition in its geomorphological connotation, it seems desirable to use the alternative form of Fore-Alps for the uplands other than Chablais.

### The Chablais Pre-Alps

The Chablais massif approaches Lake Geneva so closely between Evian and the Swiss frontier that the roadway has been blasted out along the foot of precipitous limestone cliffs, which drop towards the lake from the summit of the Dent d'Oche. The Chablais consists of a complex series of limestones, sandstones and marls, varying in age from the Upper Triassic to the Oligocene, and much affected by complicated overthrusts. Even a few exposures of granitic rocks appear in the south of this upland, an indication that the Hercynian basement was involved.

The Chablais has been eroded into a maze of limestone ridges and peaks over 2 400 m (8 000 ft), alternating with narrow valleys cut in the marls and more open basins in the sandstones. The Dranse, rising in the southeast of the upland, flows right across the northeast to southwest grain, so producing a most spectacular valley. Below St Jean d'Aulph the stream crosses the heart of the Chablais in a series of magnificent gorges, where steep wooded slopes alternate with sheer limestone cliffs. Then the Dranse suddenly enters the narrow plain bordering Lake Geneva, and the extent of its eroding powers is demonstrated by the lacustrine delta of shingle and sand which it is building out into Lake Geneva. To the west the uplands descend irregularly in a maze of wooded ridges towards the plain which borders the western wing of Lake Geneva.

## The Giffre massif

The southwestern part of the Chablais Pre-Alps is sometimes distinguished (as by Blanchard[4]) as the Massif du Giffre. The two are separated by a zone of Flysch rocks in which the Giffre has worn its valley. This upland area is also complex; part at least was carved out of the Nappe de Morcles-Aravis, one of the most westerly nappes of the High Calcareous Alps, forced over the Aiguilles Rouges granite. The upland, dissected by the rivers Giffre and the Diosaz, culminates in the ridge of the Buet (3 094 m: 10 151 ft), which runs northward, followed by the frontier, into the Dent du Midi group on the western side of the Rhône between Martigny and Lake Geneva.

Although the western part of the Giffre massif, overlooking the Arve valley, is densely wooded, much of the central and eastern uplands consist of rather desolate limestone. The Désert de Platé comprises an area of 10 sq km (4 sq miles) of fissured limestone plateau, almost bare of vegetation.

The impress of past glaciation is shown by the numerous cirques in which usually lie small lakes, morainic mounds and scattered erratics. The Giffre itself rises in the immense Cirque du Fer-à-Cheval to the northeast of Sixt, surrounded by a 300 m (1 000 ft) half-circle of steep crags, down which fall numerous torrents; the floor of this cirque is an infilled lake basin. A few small permanent snowfields and glaciers cover only about 5 sq km (2 sq miles).

## The Fore-Alpine massifs

The zone of the Fore-Alpine massifs has been divided by the river valleys into several well-defined units. The most northerly is the *Genevois*, over-looking the town of Geneva and the Rhône valley below the lake; the higher central part is known specifically as the Plateau des Bornes, while in the east is the Chaîne des Aravis culminating in Mont Charvin. Next to the south is the *Bauges*, to the east of the depression in which lies the Lac du Bourget; this triangular upland is reminiscent of the Jura, though rather higher. The diamond-shaped *Grande Chartreuse* massif is tucked within the angle of the Isère valley to the north of Grenoble, and further to the southwest across that valley lies the *Vercors*, a rugged limestone plateau. The *Dévoluy* massif, crowned by the prominent Obiou 2 790 m (9 164 ft), rises to the south of the Drac, an area of desolate rugged limestone and sandstone. Further south the lower course of the Durance lies across the widest extension of the Fore-Alpine zone, and there is a whole series of these limestone uplands—*Diois*⁵ and *Ventoux* which flank the Rhône valley, *St Christol, Lure* and *Luberon*. Here rocky peaks rise to over 1 800 m (6 000 ft), with rugged ridges, precipitous cliffs, stretches of dreary limestone plateau and deeply cut gorges. The Durance and its tributaries, as well as shorter torrential streams which flow directly to the Rhône, have dissected these uplands into numerous rugged blocks. Beyond the middle Durance basin the Cretaceous limestone country continues eastward to the Mediterranean Sea beyond the Italian frontier, forming a series of upland masses known generally as the *Alpes de Provence*.

The rocks of the Fore-Alps consist mainly of Mesozoic limestones, with surviving patches of Tertiary marls, clays and sands (the *Flysch*). They have been somewhat superficially folded, in much the same manner as the Jura. The degree of complexity decreases southward; the overthrusts of the Bornes and the Bauges are ultimately replaced by a mere gentle flexuring in the Vercors. The steep slopes of the Granier above Chambéry and of the Neyrier above the Lac d'Annecy also reveal a gentle undulation or flexuring of the strata. These folds are clearly autochthonous, that is, they are now more or less in the position in which the sediments which compose them were laid down.

The summits are usually of Lower Cretaceous limestones, sometimes (where denudation is less well advanced) of Upper Jurassic limestone. Occasionally the broken limb of an anticline stands out as a prominent rock peak, or the remains of a syncline forms a saddlelike summit or a flat-topped eminence with precipitous slopes. Thus, for example, in the Chartreuse is the Chamechaude (2 082 m: 6 831 ft), the highest point in the group and a distinct synclinal fragment. One of the most remarkable peaks is Mont Aiguille (2 097 m: 6 880 ft) in the Vercors, overlooking the Drac valley. It has a broad pasture-covered summit, surrounded by steep rocks rising from swathing scree slopes. Though for long known as 'Mont Inaccessible', its challenge is so obvious that it was first climbed as early as 1492 by a party at the behest of Charles VIII of France, using, so it is related, *subtilz engins*. Hundreds of other fantastic peaks can be seen in the

Fore-Alps—obelisks, spires, pyramids, molars, crests, combs and palisades, the product of the folding, faulting, jointing and extreme denudation of the limestone strata. Some ridges are, however, remarkably continuous. One of the most striking is the Haut-du-Seuil, which forms the eastern edge of the Chartreuse overlooking the Grésivaudan; it runs uninterruptedly for 20 km (12 miles) at a uniform height of 1 900 m (6 200 ft), rising but slightly to its highest point, the Dent de Crolles.

Rainfall is heavy in the northern and western Fore-Alps, and river systems are well developed in spite of the extent of the limestone, so most of the plateaus are eroded into a chaos of deeply cut valleys. One of the most impressive gorges is that of the Fier, a stream which flows westwards from the foot of Lac d'Annecy to the Rhône, thus separating the Genevois from the Bauges. The gorge is a water-fretted fissure, nearly 60 m (200 ft) deep, the walls of which are so narrow that they can be touched from either side. In the uplands further south, where the summer aridity is more pronounced (thus emphasising their karstic character), the concentrated runoff of the intense but shortlived autumn and winter rains has produced a fantastic chaos of gullies and gorges.

Although the presence of Cretaceous marls and clays, exposed when a stream has cut through the overlying limestone, ensures plentiful surface water in the more northerly valleys and depressions, complex subterranean drainage systems have developed, and many powerful resurgences appear on the valley sides. The sinkholes and cavern systems form the haunts of French speleologists, sometimes descending for hundreds of metres and extending horizontally for several kilometres. The deepest continuous system yet traced and descended is the Gouffre de Berger. This lies on the Plateau de Sornin in the northeast of the Vercors massif, only 8 km (5 miles) from Grenoble. In recent years its ramifications have been explored to a depth from the surface of 1 130 m (3 707 ft), 'the world depth record' for any underground system.[6] Its passages are traversed by an underground stream, which finally appears in the Isère valley through the fantastic labyrinth of the Cuves de Sassenage at the foot of the limestone cliffs. Another system is in the Chartreuse, the famous Trou de Glaz. Its entry is not far from the summit of the Dent de Crolles, the highest point of the Grande Chartreuse overlooking the Grésivaudan, but the resurgence has been traced to the Grotte de Guiers-Mort in the interior of the Chartreuse massif, 16 km (10 miles) away horizontally and 658 m (2 160 ft) below vertically.[7] These are but two examples of hundreds of cavern systems, many of which have been explored and mapped.

The Fore-Alps are not high enough to carry permanent snowfields and glaciers at the present time, except for some tiny ones on the flanks of the Obiou, but the impress of glaciation is clear. There are some superb cirques; one of the finest is the Combe-Laval in the Vercors, a vast basin with torrent-scored sides, bounded by vertical cliffs of limestone alternating with thickly wooded ledges, with scree slopes below.

## The Sub-Alpine furrow

A distinctly continuous depression can be traced for 180 km (110 miles) between the limestone Fore-Alps on the west and the crystalline massifs on the east. This is given several names by French geographers, such as *la grande dépression intérieure*, or in the phrase of Raoul Blanchard *le Sillon alpin*.[8] Its development has been due to the denudation of sedimentary deposits, mostly of Lower Liassic age, as compared with more resistant crystalline rocks to the east and the Cretaceous limestones of the Fore-Alps to the west. The Lias rocks consist in great part of shales, together with outcrops of other equally soft Jurassic marls. Thus while the main drainage lines were developed in a general direction transversely across the Alpine structures, wherever possible the rivers have taken advantage of this zone of less resistance. The furrow is occupied in succession by portions of the Arve and the Arly, then by the Isère from Albertville to Grenoble, where it is most clearly developed (Fig. 22.1). Further south the floor of the trench, lying at a greater altitude, is occupied by the Drac. It fades out in the neighbourhood of the Col Bayard, the watershed between the Drac and the Durance. The result of this furrow has been to concentrate the outflow of the drainage of the central French Alps towards the river Isère below Grenoble, through the Cluse de l'Isère.

This *cluse* is one of the four 'gateways' between the Rhône valley and the French Alps; the others are the Cluses de Chambéry, d'Annecy and de l'Arve. The second and third are broad open troughs which are in effect offshoots of the main Alpine furrow, since they are floored in part with the same Lias shales, but neither has any through drainage; in the descriptive French term, each forms *une cluse morte*. A low divide occurs near the town of Chambéry in the narrowest part of the *cluse*, between several streams flowing south into the Isère and others flowing north into the Lac du Bourget, 18 km (11 miles) in length, lying in a glacially overdeepened hollow between steep walls. This hollow continues northward into the extensive marshes of the Rhône valley below Seyssel (see p. 603), but the lake is linked to the Rhône only by the artificial Canal de Savières (Fig. 22.4). The charming Lac d'Annecy [9] occupies a curving valley between the Genevois and the Bauges massifs, and likewise drains northwards to the Fier and so to the Rhône.

In the north the Arve, rising in the crystalline Mont Blanc massif, breaks through between the Giffre and the Genevois massifs by means of a prominent gorge, whose character is indicated by the name of the town (Cluses) situated at its mouth. Below Cluses the valley opens out, wide and flat-floored, and the river is braided, with several channels enclosing shingle banks (Plate 60).

### The Pays de Moyenne Durance

Although this area is not strictly part of *le Sillon alpin*, the basin of the middle

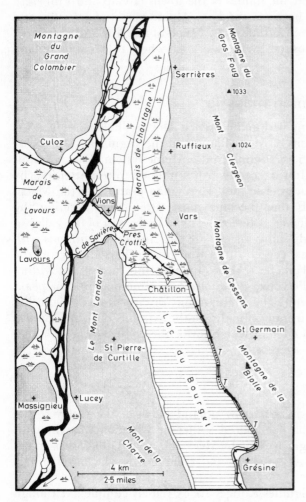

FIG. 22.4. The river Rhône and the Sub-Alpine
depression near the Lac du Bourget
The upland areas are indicated generally by stipple.
**T,** Tunnel.

The Rhône flows southwards through the flat-floored
marshy valley between the Montagne du Grand
Colombier and the Montagne du Gros Foug. It leaves
the Sub-Alpine Depression to the west of the isolated
hill on which stands Vions, and continues southwards
through a parallel syncline towards Lucey and Yenne.
The railway runs on high embankments across the floor
of the depression and then skirts the steep slopes which
bound Lac du Bourget on the east.

Based on *Carte de France au 50 000ᵉ*, sheet XXXIII/31.

Durance,[10] sometimes known as the *Gapençais* in the west and as the *Embrunais* in the east (after the names of the towns of Gap and Embrun), forms a distinct lowland between the Fore-Alpine massif of Dévoluy and the western margins of the Cottian Alps. Much of this lowland is covered with sheets of gravel deposited by the Durance where it leaves its upland course.

## The zone of Hercynian massifs

The crystalline massifs lying within the French Alps are shown on Fig. 22.1. In the north are the massifs of Mont Blanc and the Aiguilles Rouges, the former containing the highest summit in the Alpine system. These crystalline structures are continued southward, although intermittently, by outcrops of Pre-Cambrian gneisses and Hercynian granites in the Massif de Beaufort. The massifs then become more attenuated, forming the arcuate range of the Chaîne de Belledonne, lying to the east of the valley of the Isère. Two smaller adjoining massifs are structurally continuous with the Belledonne: to the east the Grandes Rousses, to the south across the Romanche valley the Taillefer. Then appears the largest individual crystalline mass, that of Pelvoux, culminating in some magnificent peaks and snowfields. Further south the Mercantour (or Argentera) upland lies across the Franco-Italian frontier. Finally, in the extreme south are Maures and Esterel, the southern edge of which forms the coast between Cannes and the Rades d'Hyères (see p. 418).

### The Aiguilles Rouges

The Aiguilles Rouges form a narrow upland between the valley of the Giffre on the west and the flat-floored Vallée de Chamonix on the east. The latter is an erosion groove cut by river action in Upper Lias shales preserved within a narrow syncline, and enlarged by glaciation into a pronounced U-profile.[11]

Morphologically the Aiguilles Rouges are extremely complex. Although the core is composed of granite, most of the higher parts consist of gneiss. Flanking the granites and gneisses are crystalline schists, the remnants of the sedimentary rocks which covered the old Hercynian ranges. Flanking these again are some Carboniferous deposits: conglomerates (especially near Vallorcine), sandstones and schists.

The present form of the Aiguilles Rouges is due to sustained denudation. To the main streams which define the massif (the Arve on the east and south, the Diosaz on the west) flow innumerable torrents, mostly taking their rise in tiny snowfields and glaciers, or in the little lakes. These torrents have furrowed the upland with deep ravines. The culminating ridge of the Aiguilles Rouges is the Brévent, a well-known viewpoint for the Mont Blanc range opposite, falling towards Chamonix in a bold but broken precipice flanked by scree slopes, then by pine forests. This summit ridge, 15 km (10 miles) in length, 2 300 m (7 500 ft) in height, rises at intervals to prominent rocky crests, the highest of which is the Aiguille de Belvédère.

## The Mont Blanc massif

This magnificent mountain mass extends southwestward from the right angle of the Rhône near Martigny for a distance of 40 km (25 miles), with a maximum width of 16 km (10 miles). The northeastern and northern parts of the massif are in Switzerland, the eastern and southeastern in Italy, the western and northwestern in France. The frontier mostly follows the main ridge on the eastern side of the massif, crossing such peaks as the Grandes Jorasses, though the main summit of Mont Blanc is wholly in France (Plate 63).

Much of the Mont Blanc massif consists of homogeneous granite; most of the pinnacled peaks (known as *aiguilles*) are carved from this splendid rock. It is, however, flanked in the Chamonix valley and on the corresponding Italian southeastern slopes by dark-coloured crystalline schists. Moreover, the very highest rocks visible through the snow near the summit of Mont Blanc itself, known as La Tournette, are also of these same dark schists. It is evident, then, that the Mont Blanc massif is of the nature of a batholith, intruded probably in Permian times; in places the Carboniferous rocks have been clearly metamorphosed along the line of contact. The patches of crystalline schists on the higher parts of the range are surviving fragments of the overlying cover of the batholith, now largely removed, thus exposing the granite.[12] The granite was involved in the Alpine folding movements, and was broken into a series of wedge-shaped slices trending northeast to southwest, while hosts of minor faults were produced.

Long-continued denudation, involving glaciation, frost-shattering, and the work of the torrents flowing from the snowfields and glaciers around the margins, has given the massif its present form. There are three distinct elements: the rock pinnacles and ridges, the snowfields, and the glaciers. These elements are shown in generalised form on Fig. 22.5. Viewed from the Aiguilles Rouges on the opposite side of the Chamonix valley, the main line of the rock pinnacles rises above the 'shelf' of the Plan de l'Aiguille, which marks the upper edge of the crystalline schists: Charmoz, Grépon, Blaitière, Plan and dozens more—they project boldly from the rock or ice ridges like a vast serrated comb. If one goes up the Montenvers rack railway behind this frontal wall, many more peaks are revealed, both on the frontier ridge and on the spurs projecting westward between the glaciers. The incredible spire of the Dent du Géant, the fantastic twin-peaked obelisk of the Dru, the dominating pyramid of the Aiguille Verte, are all carved from the massive jointed cleancut granite.

The heart of the massif is occupied by the snowfields. Mont Blanc itself is a snow hump, reaching 4 810 m (15 781 ft), with snow slopes falling away steeply on each side. From the *névés* filling the hollows between the rock ridges the glaciers move downwards and outwards; six major and more than twenty minor ones flow towards the Chamonix valley. The largest is the Mer de Glace, deriving its ice supply from a dozen large cirques in the heart of the massif, and descending to about 1 150 m (3 750 ft) above sea

FIG. 22.5. Peaks and ridges of the Mont Blanc massif
The glaciers and snowfields are shown by light form
lines, the peaks by black triangles, and the major ridges
by heavy lines.
    The Franco-Italian frontier runs southwestward from
Mont Dolent (where the Swiss frontier also converges)
along the ridge through the Grandes Jorasses and the
Dent du Géant to Mont Blanc.
    **Ch,** Aiguille de Charmoz; **D,** Dôme; **Gr,** Aiguille du
Grépon; **GJ,** Grandes Jorasses.

Based on the *Carte Vallot, Tour du Mont-Blanc, Cartes-itinéraires a l'échelle de 1 : 50 000,* by Charles Vallot.

level. Two others, the Glaciers des Bossons and de Bionnassay, descend with remarkable steepness to within a few hundred metres of the Chamonix valley floor; the former falls from 3 600 m to 1 100 m (12 000 ft to 3 600 ft) in only 3 km (2 miles), and so is fantastically crevassed. These glaciers

PLATE 63. The Franco-Italian frontier-ridge. The prominent granite obelisk is the Dent du Géant (4010 m), with the Col du Géant to its right (3345 m). The Glacier du Géant is a headstream of the Mer de Glace.

represent a late stage in the glaciation of the massif, the shrunken remnants of the Quaternary ice sheets, for the whole Vallée de Chamonix must have been filled with ice at one time. The glaciers are still shrinking, as can be seen by examining topographical maps of a century ago; during this present century the recession has been quite marked. Indeed, in 1949 the Glacier du Tour had become so poorly supplied with ice from above that the rockbed was visible through the thin ice above the tongue; this tongue became completely detached and fell as an avalanche in August, unhappily entombing a camp in the valley below. As a result, the glacier in effect 'retreated' 40 m (150 ft) or so, since the mass of débris soon melted. Many of the former lengthy glaciers are now left hanging high up on the slopes, barely protruding from the cirques, and frequent ice avalanches fall from them (Plate 63).

Frost action is very potent at high altitudes among the well-jointed granites, and scree slopes stream away from the buttresses to move down on the glaciers as morainic burden. The milky glacier torrents which emerge from the snouts carry huge quantities of rockflour, the final product of glacial disintegration, down to the Arve and beyond. In 1892 the village of St Gervais-les-Bains was almost destroyed by the torrent issuing from the Glacier de Bionnassay. A vast volume of water had become ponded up behind the glacier tongue, which ultimately collapsed, whereupon the water swept down the valley carrying a huge load of rocks; the results can be seen even now in the rock cone above the village. A tunnel has been hollowed out under the glacier and is carefully maintained so as to allow meltwater to escape freely. Rock avalanches are frequent, sometimes on an enormous scale, especially among the schists on the flanks.

Below the permanent snowline are the *alp* meadows, while the steep sides of the main valleys are thickly wooded with conifers, maintained to provide timber and to act as avalanche breaks. In the valleys are the tourist resorts, the hotels and pensions of Chamonix itself, Argentière, Les Houches and other attractive places.

## Massif de Beaufort

To the southwest of Mont Blanc is the much lower Massif de Beaufort, a triangular upland lying to the north of the Tarentaise valley. Most of the surface consists of Pre-Cambrian rocks, but small exposures of granite appear in the valley of the Doron to the east of the little town of Beaufort. Part of the younger cover survives, forming narrow outcrops of Triassic and even Jurassic rocks parallel to the 'grain' of the structure. The massif is not lofty, the highest peak being Le Roignais (2 999 m: 9 840 ft), with no permanent snowfields and glaciers, but it is dissected into a chaos of ridges by deep valleys radiating to the Isère and its tributary the Doron.

## The Belledonne, Grandes Rousses and Taillefer massifs

To the east of the Grésivaudan rises the elongated massif of the Belledonne, the rocks of which mainly consist of gneisses, with some granite outcrops in the north of the range. The Belledonne is not lofty, and its highest point, the Grand-Pic de Belledonne, rises only to 2 981 m (9 781 ft). No permanent glaciers occur, although occasionally patches of snow survive in north-facing gullies and depressions for several years, and winter snowfall is heavy. It is a wild rugged range, deeply scored by mountain torrents, with many craggy peaks separated by deeply notched cols. The northern part of the range consists of a maze of ridges and rock basins containing seven lakes, and it is given the name of the Massif des Sept-Laux.

To the east of the Belledonne, and separated from it by the valley of the Eau d'Olle (deeply cut into a narrow outcrop of Lias shales), is the small massif of the Grandes Rousses, also composed largely of gneissic rocks with some granite. This massif is nearly 600 m (2 000 ft) higher than the Belledonne; as a result it carries several small permanent snowfields and glaciers.

The Taillefer, south of the Romanche valley, forms a long narrow ridge; it is much dissected by past glaciation and several rocky cirques containing small lakes. Veins of lead and silver ores occur in these crystalline rocks and were worked sporadically in the past.

## The Pelvoux massif

To the east of the southern end of the Belledonne is the extensive Pelvoux massif (Fig. 22.6), almost surrounded by steepsided valleys down which

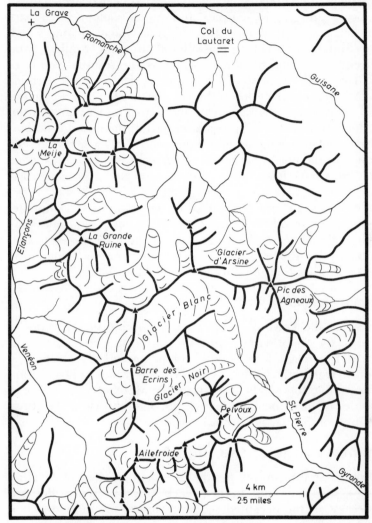

FIG. 22.6. Peaks and ridges of the Pelvoux massif
The glaciers and snowfields are shown by light form lines, the peaks by black triangles, and the major ridges by heavy lines.
   The three main groups of peaks (La Meije, Barre des Ecrins and Pelvoux) are indicated. The complexity of the ridgelines (*crêts*) and summits (*pics, pointes, aiguilles*) indicates the deep dissection of this crystalline massif.
   The Col du Lautaret (one of the celebrated passes for the motorist), is on the watershed between the Romanche (hence to the Isère) and the Durance; the road links Grenoble in the Isère valley with Briançon in the Durance valley.
Based on *Carte de France au 50 000*, sheets XXXIV/35, 36.

631

torrents flow outwards from the heart of the uplands. On the north is the Romanche, on the west and south the Drac, on the east the headstreams of the Durance. Only on the extreme north, at the high Col du Lautaret, are the perimeter valleys interrupted. The massif itself has been dissected into a confusion of peaks and ridges, cirques and radial valleys. There are extensive snowfields, several glaciers (notably the Glacier Blanc, which flows eastwards from the heart of the massif for about 5 km (3 miles)), and some magnificent peaks, the highest of which is the serrated comblike ridge of the Barre des Ecrins with a north face consisting of a superb ice slope. The main summit in the south is the Pelvoux itself, a massive mountain flanked by steep buttresses rising to an undulating upper plateau from which rocky summits protrude. The northern part of the massif is dominated by La Meije, overlooking the climbing-centre of La Grave in the Romanche valley to the north. Its culminating point is the Grand-Pic de la Meije (3983 m: 13068 ft), with its rocky south face and ice-draped northern cliffs.

Ecrins, Meije, Pelvoux—these are the principal summits of Dauphiné, but there are hundreds of other granite *pics* and *aiguilles,* and some snow peaks too, such as the Dôme de Neige and the shapely Pic des Agneaux. The contribution to the Alpine ranges of France, therefore, by the granitic massif of Pelvoux is indeed second only to that of Mont Blanc.

**The Mercantour massif**

To the southeast of the Pelvoux comes an interruption in this series of crystalline massifs for about 65 km (40 miles), until the Mercantour (or Argentera) massif is reached. Much of this upland lies in Italy; the highest point is the Punta Argentera. To the east of the Tinée valley (a headstream of the Var), the frontier follows the crestline of the Mercantour, crossing in succession a series of prominent granite peaks, notably Mont Tenibrés, the highest summit of this massif within France.

## The sedimentary zone of the High Alps

To the east of the crystalline massifs lies the Sedimentary Zone of the High Alps, part of the system of nappes. In the French Alps the Great St Bernard nappe (number IV in the accepted sequence of the six individuals) is dominant; this is the usual name given by Swiss geomorphologists, although some of the French refer to it as the *nappe du Briançonnais.* It can be traced from the Isère valley near the southern end of the Beaufort massif, through the Vanoise into the Briançon district to the east of the Pelvoux, and then southeastward on the Italian side of the Mercantour to the Mediterranean Sea near Savona. The nappe is so well developed in the neighbourhood of Briançon in the valley of the upper Durance that this part of the Sedimentary Alps is sometimes referred to as the Briançonnais zone.

A further minor nappe can be distinguished to the west of the Great St Bernard, known as the *Nappe du Flysch* or *Nappe de l'Embrunais*; it is given the first name because it consists mainly of Tertiary *Flysch* sediments, and the second because it is well developed in the neighbourhood of Embrun. Only a narrow vestige of this nappe exists in the north, extending intermittently from the southern end of the Beaufort range southward to the Pelvoux, but it widens out in the Embrunais and the Ubaye and so makes a substantial contribution to the Sedimentary Zone of the Alps.

The rocks in the western part consist for the most part of sandstones, shales and breccias of Eocene age, known collectively as the *Flysch*. Further east an outcrop of Upper Carboniferous rocks can be traced from the Rhône valley, through the Aosta valley, the Arc valley, and into the Durance valley near Briançon. Some of these Carboniferous strata contain anthracite, worked near La Mure and Avignonnet in the Drac valley, in the Tarentaise and Maurienne valleys, and near Briançon. Mesozoic sediments, especially of Triassic age, include various breccias, dolomitic limestones, and beds of common salt and gypsum. Some narrow outcrops of Jurassic and Cretaceous limestones lie parallel to the 'grain' of the Alpine structures. Finally there are the *Schistes lustrés*, the rocks resulting from sedimentation in the deep parts of the geosyncline, probably of Mesozoic age, but affected by metamorphism since they were so profoundly involved in the folding movements. They overlaid the Great St Bernard nappe, and so have been largely removed by denudation in the west and centre where the nappe was at its highest, but they still survive in the east. They are found in the French Alps on a large scale only in two districts where the frontier makes distinct bends to the east. These districts form part of the Graian Alps, in the neighbourhood of the headstreams of the Arc and the Isère, and part of the Cottian Alps in the district of Queyras.

These sedimentary and metamorphic rocks are of great variety, and denudation has had full scope in producing a diversified landscape. Broad valleys have been worn in the clays and marls. The upper Durance valley has been eroded through the very heart of Briançonnais, from the Col du Lautaret southward past Briançon itself. Similarly, the Isère, which derives its headwaters from a group of small glacier lobes near the Franco-Italian frontier, flows away northwestwards through soft shales and slates in a rather desolate valley, now transformed in appearance by the lake ponded up behind the Tignes barrage (p. 644). A few kilometres to the south the Arc, one of the Isère's main tributaries, flows southwestwards.

These major valleys cut the zone into a number of upland groups—the Vanoise, the Graian Alps, the Cottian Alps and the Maritime Alps.

## The Vanoise

This area of mountains lies between the sharply defined valleys of the Tarentaise and the Maurienne. The upper valleys of the Isère and the Arc are so close together in the east, within 4 or 5 km (2 or 3 miles), that the rivers almost completely surround the massif and give it a distinct unity. The Vanoise is a massive group, with the highest peaks along its southern edge overlooking the Maurienne. Numerous powerful torrents flow northwards to the Isère, thus dissecting the massif into a series of bold ridges, sufficiently high for some considerable snowfields to accumulate. In the northeast is the group of the Grande-Motte and the Grande-Casse (3 852 m: 12 638 ft); the latter, the highest peak of the district, has a remarkable arête-like summit, 20 m (60 ft) long, but less than a metre in width. To the southeast is the group of La Vanoise itself, which has given its name to the whole massif, culminating in the snow peak of the Dôme de Chasseforêt rising from the surrounding snowfields, which cover about 100 sq km (40 sq miles). A few glaciers push their way downwards for a kilometre or two from these snowfields. The third prominent group of mountains within the massif is that of the Péclet-Polset further west, culminating in the Aiguille de Péclet; here also is a small cluster of snowfields.

## The Graian Alps

The mountain groups which form the main ridge line of the Alps between the Petit-St Bernard and the Mont Cenis passes are known collectively as the Graian Alps. The ridge line though sinuous is continuous, and rarely falls below 3 000 m (10 000 ft). The highest peak in the Graians, the Gran Paradiso, is not on the main ridge, but rises to 4 061 m (13 324 ft) from a semidetached mass of uplands well to the east in Italy. The frontier ridge itself culminates in the Grande-Sassière, which looks down upon the desolate stony valley of the upper Isère, the scene of recent great hydro-electric developments (see pp. 644–5). Part of this mountain region has now been designated a national park, continuous with the Gran Paradiso park in Italy.

The ridge line of the Graians is flanked by almost continuous snowfields and glaciers. These occur on a much greater scale on the western side where the precipitation is heavier. One can stand on a rock ridge with extensive snowfields to the west, from which glaciers push down into the lateral valleys towards the Tarentaise and Maurienne, while crumbling rock buttresses and vast slopes of scree fall away to the east.

## The Cottian Alps

The main ridge line of the Alps swings away southeastward from the re-entrant of Italian territory in the Dora Riparia valley towards the Mer-cantour and the Mediterranean. In the neighbourhood of Briançon the headstreams of the Durance have eroded deep valleys in the clays and marls, and tributaries from the east have notched deeply into the uplands. So advanced is this denudation that the frontier ridges are here at their lowest for hundreds of kilometres. Indeed, the much higher summits of the Pelvoux to the west testify to the greater resistance of the granites and gneisses as compared with these sedimentary rocks. To the east of Briançon, the Durance headstream on the French side and the Dora Riparia on the Italian have cut back so deeply into the ridge that it falls to a mere 1 854 m (6 083 ft) in the grassy Col du Mont Genèvre.

The highest point in the Cottians is the graceful pyramid of Monte Viso (3 841 m: 12 602 ft), but it lies wholly in Italy. The parts of the Cottians in France, namely the Queyras massif to the south of the Guil valley and the Parpaillon upland lying between the Durance and its tributary the Ubaye, are much lower. They are, however, dissected by the torrential tributaries of the Durance, and in the south also of the Var. A few peaks in the Parpaillon carry some tiny permanent snowfields. This part of the sedimentary Alps is desolate, with crags, shattered ridges and scree-slopes.

### The Maritime Alps

The term Maritime Alps is applied rather generally to the ranges at the southern end of the High Alps. Structurally they are not wholly part of the Briançonnais zone, but can certainly be regarded as part of the High Sedimentary Alps. They include the ranges of Trois-Evêches and of Mont Pélat, which overlooks the valley of the Var to the east. The former group is interesting in that on the northern slopes is the shrunken Glacier de la Blanche, which has the distinction of being the most southerly glacier in the French Alps.

## Climate

The north–south trend of the French Alps lies transverse both to air-masses moving across France from the Atlantic and to the transition zone that separates the central European climatic region from that of the Mediterranean. Indeed, the distinction between the *Alpes du Nord* and the *Alpes du Sud* rests largely on a climatic basis, indicated by a line drawn westward from Briançon to Valence.

It is difficult to generalise about temperatures, for there is an appreciable latitudinal range between north and south. As a general indication, the mean January and July figures for Chamonix, at about 1 000 m (3 300 ft), are −6°C (22°F) and 17°C (62°F); for Annecy, at 430 m (1 410 ft), in a deep sheltered valley, −1°C (31°F) and 19°C (67°F); and for Gap, much further south, in a tributary valley of the Durance, at 730 m (2 400 ft), 1°C (31°F) and 19°C (66°F) respectively. Aspect, however, is of profound significance. The distinction between south-facing valley slopes (the *adret* or *endroit*) and the shady sides (the *ubac* or the *envers*) is so profound that it dominates the patterns of settlement and land use in those narrow valleys orientated from west to east.

Associated with aspect is the degree of exposure to or shelter from winds from particular directions, and some of these winds are so regularly experienced in the Alps that they possess specific names. The *mistral* affects the Provençal Alps, while to the north of Digne a similar cold, dry, blustery wind is referred to as the *bise*. Winds from a southerly direction are known as the *marin* in the south, as the *vente du midi* in the north. From the southeast the *levant* affects the Maritime Alps, and the *lombarde* the Graian Alps. Most of the southerly winds bring mild damp conditions in winter, with rain or snow at higher altitudes. Stormy conditions with mild temperatures and heavy shortlived precipitation are associated with the *traverse* in the northern part of the Fore-Alps and with the *labech* in the south. The *föhn* is rarely experienced in the French Alps, mainly because of the longitudinal structure and the absence of transverse barriers to a southerly air stream.

Inversion is another common phenomenon; many otherwise sheltered valleys are liable to spells of frost and cold damp fog. It is noticeable that in the Grésivaudan the vines grow on the slopes 30 m (100 ft) or so above the valley floor; the lowest slopes are used for crops less liable to frost damage.

Altitude causes great variation in temperature; during the few years when an observatory on the summit of Mont Blanc was in operation at the end of last century, the lowest temperature recorded was $-43°C$ $(-45°F)$. An average diminution of temperature with height is experienced of $1°C$ per 100 m ($3.3°F$ per 1 000 ft), falling slightly to $2.8°F$ in winter and rising to $3.9°F$ per 1 000 ft in spring, according to Bénévent.[13]

The effects of a well defined division between the outer (western) ranges and the inner (eastern) ranges is shown by the precipitation figures. Though lower, the windward slopes of the upstanding western Fore-Alps receive more than 1 500 mm (60 in) of precipitation. Three stations in the west, centre and east of the Chartreuse (St Laurent-du-Pont, St Pierre-de-Chartreuse and St Pancrasse) have 1 700, 1 700 and 1 500 mm (67, 67 and 59 in) respectively. Thus although the third station is at a height of 1 000 m (3 281 ft), compared with the first at only 410 m (1 345 ft), exposure to the prevailing wind means more than mere altitude. Annecy, slightly in the rainshadow of both the southern Jura and the Fore-Alps, has about 1 270 mm (50 in), and Chamonix, although much higher, is tucked in a deep valley between the Aiguilles Rouges and Mont Blanc and receives about 1 120 mm (44 in).[14] Much of this comes in the form of thunderstorms; the Mont Blanc massif is particularly subject to violent storms in summer which seem to build up from the heated lowlands of Lombardy and the Valle d'Aosta. The deep interior valleys of the Briançonnais, Haute-Maurienne and Haute-Tarentaise have a lower precipitation, about 890 mm (35 in) or less annually; Modane, in the Maurienne, has as little as 610 mm (24 in), and Lanslebourg in the upper Arc valley about 790 mm (31 in).

The distinction between the central and northern Alps as compared with the southern Alps is marked in respect both of seasonal régime and actual totals of precipitation. The northern part is termed by Bénévent the *Zone continentale*; the months with heaviest precipitation (unfortunately from the climber's point of view) are between June and August. There follows the *Zone de transition à tendance continentale*, with a more uniform distribution, though still with an appreciable maximum between June and October. To the south again is the complementary *Zone de transition à tendance méditerranéenne*; at Gap, for example, the two wettest months are October and November, while July and August are drier than the period February to June. Finally comes the *Zone méditerranéenne sublittorale*, with a distinct minimum of almost complete aridity between May and September. Not only then is there a decrease eastward in the total precipitation but also southward, as shown by the figures for Flumet in the Genevois 1 650 mm (65 in) and for Castellane 890 mm (35 in) in the Verdon valley among the southern Fore-Alps.

Much of this precipitation falls in the form of snow, and the French Alpine region is covered in most winters down to the lowest valleys. During the early summer the snowline rapidly recedes, uncovering the *alp* pastures, to the zone of permanent snow. Some indication of the mean duration of the snow cover is given:

*Days with snow cover (altitude in metres)*

|  | 600 | 1 200 | 1 800 | 2 400 |
|---|---|---|---|---|
| High Alps of Savoy | 55 | 125 | 180 | 240 |
| Cottian Alps | 40 | 100 | 150 | 220 |
| Provençal Alps | 5–10 | 80 | 150 | 240 |

Source: E. Bénévent, 'La neige dans les Alpes françaises',
*Recueils de l'Institut de Géographie Alpine*, **5** (1917), pp. 403–98.

It can be seen from this table that at altitudes exceeding 2 400 m (8 000ft) the latitudinal effects are not marked, although at lower altitudes the difference is quite appreciable. It is emphasised that these are mean figures; they vary enormously between the mild winters, the despair of winter sportsmen, and the severe ones when the snow cover is long sustained, and subsequent damage from avalanches and flood meltwater may be considerable. Settlements are carefully sited with respect to known avalanche tracks; a rock spur may be used as protection and the slopes below obvious gullylines are avoided. Above most villages dense plantations of conifers are maintained as avalanche breaks, and critical points on roads and railways are protected by avalanche galleries. The depth of snow varies according to aspect; north-facing hollows will retain it for weeks after southern slopes have been stripped, and above 2 400 m (8 000 ft) drifts may persist throughout the year well below the general snowline. At

Tour (above Chamonix at about 1 430 m (4 700 ft)) an average of 9·5 m (31 ft) of snow is received each year.

A further indication of snowfall is afforded by the information concerning snow-blocking on the Alpine roads (Fig. 22.8). Below about 900 m (3 000 ft) interruption is rare, although some of the roads along deep valley floors may be blocked for a few days. The high passes above 2 000 m (6 500 ft) are usually closed from October to May. Mont Genèvre, between Briançon and Cesanne in Italy, is always kept clear by snow ploughs except for brief periods following heavy storms, as is also the Col du Lautaret between Briançon and La Grave. No effort is made to keep open the highest passes; the Col de l'Iseran is invariably blocked from mid-October to late June or even July.

## Land use

Administratively the French Alps are covered by seven *départements*. Actually the large unit of Isère extends to the Rhône, and Alpes-Maritimes and Var reach the Mediterranean coast, but broadly the land use statistics for these *départements* may be taken as representative of the Alpine regions of France.

*Land use, 1968 (percentage of total area)*

|  | ARABLE | PERMANENT PASTURE | LAND NOT UNDER CULTIVATION | WOODLAND |
|---|---|---|---|---|
| *Northern Alps* | | | | |
| Haute-Savoie | 12 | 26 | 9 | 36 |
| Savoie | 3 | 28 | 40 | 26 |
| Isère | 20 | 23 | 8 | 28 |
| Hautes-Alpes | 7 | 36 | 4 | 27 |
| *Southern Alps* | | | | |
| Alpes-de-Haute-Provence | 11 | 30 | 21 | 32 |
| Alpes-Maritimes | 3 | 29 | 15 | 32 |
| Var | 2 | 7 | 20 | 50 |

Source: Ministère de l'Agriculture, *Annuaire statistique de la France*, 1970–1.

The differences in climatic régime between the northern and southern French Alps are reflected in land use, and it is necessary therefore to consider them separately. It must be remembered that the transition is gradual; while as far north as the Grésivaudan agriculture may reveal southern characteristics (such as the cultivation of maize, vine and even figs), conversely the peaks of the Maritime Alps and Mercantour are sufficiently lofty to carry forests[15] and pasture similar to those of the northern mountains.

## Agriculture in the northern Alps

Within this northern area differences are apparent between the Fore-Alps and the High Alps to the east. The former are more extensively wooded, the result of their copious rainfall and of the presence of clays and marls among the limestone scarps. Fifty-one per cent of the surface of the Chartreuse is wooded, and 47 per cent of the Vercors. There is a definite zoning of tree species, with beech, oak and sweet chestnut to about 900 m (3 000 ft), succeeded by spruce and fir to the treeline, with occasional Arolla pine near the upper limits. Further east in the drier High Alps spruce is the commonest tree. Much is deliberately planted by the state and by the communes for fuel, for the timber industries, to check soil erosion and as avalanche breaks; the first state forest was created in 1860. The forest has been cut into both from below to provide arable fields, orchards and vine-yards on the gentle slopes above the valleys, and from above to extend the *alp* pastures. In the Chablais[16] and the Genevois pasture has largely replaced woodland, except on steep mountainsides.

About a quarter of the active population in Haute-Savoie, Savoie and Hautes-Alpes, and a sixth in Isère, are occupied with agriculture. Many more primarily industrial workers, and others engaged seasonally in the catering for tourists, take part in some agriculture. The proportion is in fact as low as it is because of the development of industry in the Alpine valleys and in such towns as Grenoble.

The traditional Alpine rural economy is dependent on cattle-rearing with ancillary cultivation. In the four northern *départements* there were in 1968 about 527 000 cattle, of which three-fifths were dairy animals. The pattern of the pastoral economy has changed little during the years; more milk is sent off to the towns of the Rhône valley and beyond, there are more milk-using industries, more factory made cheese is produced and less in the farmhouses, but the seasonal rhythm of movement of animals has changed little because it is the best suited to the environment.

This seasonal migration follows a regular pattern. They leave the permanent valley villages and first move up to a valley bench (known as the *montagnette*[17]) above the first steep slopes, each family with its cattle. There they live for the summer in a chalet-cum-barn; in places this building stands isolatedly among its own *alpages*, elsewhere groups form a hamlet ancillary to the permanent village in the valley below. The cattle are grazed there for a while, but as soon as the higher slopes are clear of snow the herds go up for two or three months with a few herdsmen who live in primitive chalets. At the *montagnettes* hay is cut and stored, or carried down to the villages, and the *fromager* carries on with his manufacture of cheese. On most of these *alpages* irrigation channels lead water from torrents and even from glaciers over the slopes to stimulate the growth of rich grass in the long hours of summer sunshine. In autumn the animals return to the *montagnettes*, where they graze on the second growth of the mown pastures, and by October they are back in the valleys, where they feed on the valley pastures until the first snows fall, when they are stall-fed for the winter. Near the rivers irrigated meadows provide perhaps two crops of hay for winter feed. The floor of the Grésivaudan is irrigated by water taken from the endyked Isère through artificial channels, which flow parallel to the river and rejoin it lower down the main valley. Groups of farmers form *syndicats de drainage*, similar to the *wateringues* of Flanders.

There are, of course, many variations in this pattern. In Bornes the tendency is to keep the cattle permanently in the valleys, and the chief labour is to mow, bring down and store sufficient hay from the *alpages* to last the winter. In Chablais many of the valley farmers rent their cattle to the owner of some high pastures, while they, relieved temporarily of the burden, practise arable cultivation and collect hay until the winter, when they recover their animals and resume the making of butter and cheese.

While some dairying is for subsistence (potatoes, bread, cheese and milk are still the staple diet in more remote valleys), most of it is now organised on a commercial basis.[18] Much milk is sent to the industrial towns in the valleys, to Grenoble and to Lyons, and telpherlines, *pipelaits*, lorries and milk tankers provide speedy transport. Cheese is manufactured in the cooperatives, with factories using electric power for the cream separators and churns. *Gruyère*, as in the Jura, is the main cheese made.

A certain amount of arable cultivation is practised for subsistence. In the broad flat-floored valleys in the Sub-Alpine Depression—in the Combe de Savoie, the Grésivaudan and the Chambéry valley in particular—the Lias clays and marls afford good soils. Away from the water-meadows but still on the valley floors flourishes quite an intensive cultivation—wheat and maize, potatoes and other vegetables, growing in strips. In the damper Fore-Alpine valleys, oats becomes the dominant cereal, and in the higher districts rye is still grown. On the lower south-facing slopes are orchards of apples, plums and black cherries and in favoured 'sun traps' apricots, peaches and walnuts. Up the slopes climb the vineyards, particularly in the Arve valley, above Annecy, in the Arly valley, and in the Grésivaudan. No quality wine is made (although such wines as *Crépy* have a more than local repute), but Isère produced in 1968 about 269 000 hectolitres of *vin ordinaire*. Honey is produced mostly for local sale, but some is sent to the large towns. A few hives are placed in or near most orchards, but some bee farms operate on a larger scale.

There is in fact a prosperous cheerful air about Savoy, the valleys seem fresh and fertile, and the houses are attractively built and decorated in the manner of Swiss chalets, with bright gardens.

## Agriculture in the southern Alps

The marked summer aridity and higher temperatures produce striking contrasts between the vegetation of the northern and southern Alps. The proportion of permanent pasture is of course much reduced. The actual area under woodland is oddly enough higher, indeed Var has the highest proportion under wood of any alpine *département*. Actually the figures include large areas of a thin poor scrub-forest, and really indicate that less clearing for pasture and arable land has been effected than in the north. In point of fact man in the past has cleared too much, and as land was abandoned, the result of poor rewards and rural depopulation, the *maquis* and the *garrigue* have spread. So too have the effects of soil erosion, and there is much bare limestone from which the soil has been scoured, with gashed hill slopes no longer protected with trees. On some of the limestone plateaus the *Département des Eaux et Forêts* has established plantations of larch and pine, which are found as high as 2 300 m (7 500 ft). The Aleppo pine and the Atlas cedar both grow on the Ventoux, evergreen oaks and box are common, and the Austrian pine has been established on some of the poorest terrain. Sweet chestnut and cork oak grow on favoured lower slopes. Much of the limestone plateaus of the southern Alps between about 600 and 1 500 m (2 000 and 5 000 ft) has a *maquis*-like aspect. Brushwood and underwood are widespread, consisting of thickets of dwarf evergreen oaks and box, broom, lentiscus, lavender, rosemary, thyme and thorny aromatic shrubs. In other districts are crumbling limestone slopes, gaunt cliffs, fans of gravel choking the valleys of torrents hardly visible in summer, a few prickly tufts of vegetation among the white rock; this is the *garrigue*. Except on the higher summits to the east, where snowmelt nurtures shortlived grasses, pasture is scanty and poor.

The agricultural economy also gradually changes as the Mediterranean coast is approached. Only 36 000 dairy cattle were in Hautes-Alpes in 1968, compared with 254 000 in Isère to the north, while farther south Alpes-de-Haute-Provence and Var had still fewer, about 10 000 each. The higher frontier ranges of Alpes Maritimes were able to support about 6 000 head.

On the limestone pastures sheep become the main feature of the economy; Hautes-Alpes in 1968 had 246 000, Alpes-de-Haute-Provence 249 000 and Var 115 000. The massif of Dévoluy is especially important for sheep-rearing. Large numbers of young lambs are slaughtered to provide skins for the glove industry of Grenoble, and ewes' milk cheese, akin to that of Roquefort in the Causses, is processed. Much seasonal movement of sheep still takes place to the high pastures of Dauphiny and the Maritime Alps in summer, back to the floors of the Durance and its tributaries for the winter, some going even farther down to the pastures of the Rhône delta in the Crau and the Camargue. Flocks of the *mérinos d'Arles*, which live in the Crau, likewise move in summer up to the Maritime Alps, even as far as Dévoluy.

Arable farming in the south is concentrated in the favoured valleys where a thin layer of soil covers the rocks. The northern parts of the Durance valley, although showing a tendency to summer drought, have about

750 mm (30 in) of precipitation. Wheat, maize, tobacco, almonds, apricots and other fruit are patiently and assiduously cultivated, often in un-believably small patches. Not much further down the Durance valley, that symbol of Mediterranean agriculture, the olive, makes its appearance.

The limestone plateaus in southern Alpes-de-Haute-Provence and north-ern Var are of very limited value for agriculture. The former is the most scantily populated *département* in the Alps, with a mere 9 000 agricultural workers; even the *département* of Haute-Savoie, only two-thirds as large and including the high peaks of the Mont Blanc massif, had four times as many. The valley floors of the Durance and its tributaries, and those of the Var and the Tinée, are cultivated intensively with the recent development of irrigation. Thus Digne, in a small embayment floored with Miocene deposits, is the centre of a pleasant fruit-growing area; it is famous for its dried prunes and its delectable *princesses* almonds. Sisteron is the centre of groves of almond trees.

The agricultural economy of these southern Fore-Alps is therefore Mediterranean in character rather than Alpine. Valleys and small depressions among the *maquis* and *garrigue* grow hard wheat and maize; orchards of almonds and walnuts occur in favoured places; olive groves climb up the limestone slopes; there are vineyards and in places gardens of lavender. About 17 000 ha (43 500 acres) in Alpes-de-Haute-Provence and 3 500 ha (8 650 acres) in Var were under wheat in 1968, but the yield per ha was the lowest in France, less than half that of the Paris Basin. A large amount of *vin ordinaire* is produced, in fact Var is the sixth *département* in order of production, but there is no quality wine. Further south still the agricultural economy becomes quite Provençal.

Irrigation has been extensively developed, notably in the lower Durance valley, utilising water ponded behind the Serre-Ponçon dam (p. 645). Water is distributed by canals for the intensive production of fruit and vegetables.

## Power and industry

### Power (Fig. 22.7)

Industrial activity in the Alpine region has expanded considerably as a result of the development of hydroelectricity. The high precipitation, the snowfields and glaciers which form natural reservoirs, the deep valleys penetrating far into the mountains, the narrow *cluses* affording sites for barrages, the rock steps in the main valleys, the moraine dammed lakes, and the torrents emerging from hanging valleys, are all favourable factors. The effects of the long winter freeze and the periods of summer drought are partly remediable by the construction of reservoirs.

The French were pioneers in the production of electricity from water power, for in 1869 the engineer Aristide Bergés used a stream descending 484 m (1 590 ft) into the Grésivaudan to produce electricity, and utilised the power to drive machinery in his wood-pulp and paper mill at Lancey, 16 km (10 miles) from Grenoble. By 1896 ten stations were in operation, which had increased to fifty-seven by 1914, although these were all small-scale by modern standards.

Development continued in the interwar years, and by 1939 a large number of small stations had been constructed in the French Alps. The power produced was for the most part used locally by the electrochemical and electrometallurgical industries, and by the electrified lines of the PLM Company. Most units were in the Maurienne, the Tarentaise and the valleys of the Romanche and Arly, though others were built along the valleys of the Arve, Drac and Durance and one or two small ones high up in the Var valley. A few schemes were on a larger scale. One of the earliest large projects, begun in 1904, is the Sept-Laux or Fond-de-France installation. Four of the seven lakes on the upland to the north of the Belledonne were interconnected and seven barrages built. This has been steadily extended, the latest developments being completed in 1943. Again, between 1931 and 1935 the Bissorte barrage, 60 m (200 ft) high and 550 m (600 yd) in width, was built across the mouth of the hanging valley of the Riveau de Bissorte above La Praz (a few kilometres below Modane in the Maurienne). The surface of the lake lies at 2 082 m (6 830 ft), giving a fall of 1 144 m (3 753 ft)—the longest single chute in the French Alps—to the power station at La Praz, which provides power for the largest electro-metallurgical plant in the Maurienne; this incidentally was destroyed by German forces in 1944 but has been rebuilt. In 1935 the Chambon scheme was begun, completed three years later, in the valley of the Romanche; its storage reservoir is in a hanging valley on the southern side of the Romanche, fed by streams coming from the snowfields at the western edge of the Meije group. Another impressive scheme, completed in 1935, was the construction of the Barrage de Sautet across the upper Drac, ponding up a reservoir along the valleys of the main river and its tributary the Souloise. The Sautet power station did not utilise all the potential head of water thus made available, and in 1946 a second station, the Cordéac, was constructed a few km away. By the end of the 1939–1945 war no less than 118 power stations of over 1 mw capacity were in operation in the French Alps.

By 1969 about 70 per cent of the hydroelectric and 26 per cent of the total power generated in France was produced in the Alps, including the Rhône valley.[19] Schemes are being pushed steadily ahead. The tendency is still to carry out a large number of small projects, though within an integrated plan, rather than a few major schemes, as in the Rhône basin. One project, started as long ago as 1921 but interrupted during the depression of the 'thirties, was completed in 1948, the Castillon barrage built across the gorge of the Verdon near Castillon in the Provençal Alps. This remarkable *Grand-cañon*, as it is known, deeply dissected in the Jurassic limestones, now affords a storage reservoir of 150 million cubic metres and a large power station has been constructed.

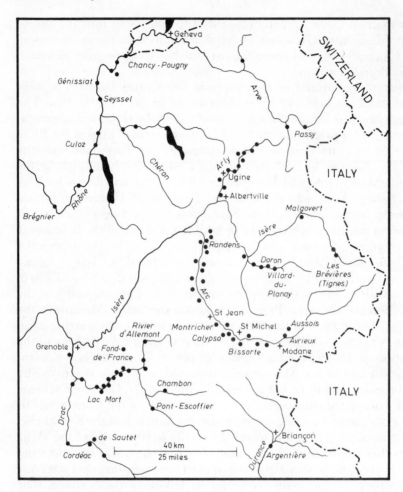

FIG. 22.7. Hydroelectricity stations in the northern French Alps
Only the larger stations are shown; there is a considerable number of
smaller stations along most of the river valleys.

Based on *Atlas de France*, sheet 46, and various official publications.

Chief developments at the present time concern the upper Isère basin,
and three major projects have so far been undertaken. In the upper
Isère valley the first stage of the Tignes scheme was completed in 1954.
Near Tignes the glaciated valley opens out as a broad basin, but narrows
again further down to form a gorge, so providing an ideal site for a reservoir.
A barrage was built 180 m (587 ft) high, creating the largest reservoir in
the French Alps, which unfortunately necessitated the submergence of the
village of Tignes and the compulsory evacuation of its 800 inhabitants to a
new village higher up the valley slopes. The reservoir supplies Les Brévières
power station, with an installed capacity of 32 mW, completed in 1952.

644

Some of the water from the Isère below this reservoir was diverted through an aqueduct down the valley to another marked step in the gradient above Bourg-St Maurice, where a second bigger station, Malgovert (75 mW), was opened in 1954. Another interesting development is the Isère-Drac diversion. At Moutiers the Isère makes a right-angled bend and flows northwestwards through the Tarentaise before it swings south again through the Combe de Savoie. The diversion, accomplished by means of a tunnel 2 000 m (6 500 ft) long beneath the Vanoise massif, was intended to withdraw water from the Isère valley into the much lower Maurienne, so providing a head of 150 m (500 ft) of water. The scheme was largely completed in 1954, when four underground powerhouses, known as the Randens station, of 32 mW each, were opened. The Aussois project utilises streams issuing from snowfields and glaciers on the southern side of the Vanoise, concentrated through aqueducts and tunnels into the Aussois reservoir formed by damming a subsidiary valley of the Arc. The largest hydrostation in the Alps, La Bathie-Roselend (Savoie), was completed in 1961, with an installed capacity of 480 mW.

Other developments have been the Pizançon station on the Isère near where it leaves the Fore-Alps for the Rhône valley, the enlarged Passy station on the upper Arve near St Gervais-les Bains, the Pont-Escoffier station in the upper Romanche, the Ste Tulle station on the Durance just above its junction with the Verdon, and Le Bancairon station on the Tinée before it joins the Var. Another scheme, begun in 1953 and completed in 1959, is an earth barrage across the Durance at Serre-Ponçon[20] below the confluence of the Ubaye. Because of the infilling of alluvium to a depth of at least 90 m (300 ft), affording no foundations, a concrete dam was impracticable. The barrage is made of clay and marl 115 m (377 ft) high and 460 m (1 500 ft) in length; the resulting lake fills the Durance valley for 18 km (11 miles) upstream and that of the Ubaye for 8 km (5 miles). This supplies a head of water for a station at the foot of the dam, with an installed capacity of 352 mW and for a whole series of smaller stations downstream, and also supplies irrigation water in summer for the middle Durance valley; in fact, the Durance waters now rarely reach the Rhône. This dam is the key to the whole multipurpose development of the valley: flood control, irrigation, and hydroelectricity generation.

While the industries of the neighbouring valleys are the prime beneficiary of these enterprises, the Alpine stations are useful contributors to the grid. Since the setting-up of EDF a close degree of integration has been possible, and several high voltage (380 kv) transmission lines have been erected. Thus the Alpine *houille blanche* has indeed become a major contributor to the French industrial economy.

## Industry [21]

For several centuries small-scale industry has been active in the Alpine valleys. Many small blast furnaces and foundries used charcoal for fuel and running water to work the bellows. Iron ore mines were numerous, and other metals mined sporadically were copper, gold and silver; argentiferous galena was worked as early as the twelfth century in the upper Durance valley, and the village of Argentière grew up there, while Argentine in the Maurienne had a similar origin. Small textile factories manufacturing wool, silk, hemp and later cotton were widespread; for example, a string of woollen mills was located along the valley of the Verdon in the south, and the larger towns of Annecy and Chambéry were also important. The glove industry of Grenoble has been highly organised since the sixteenth century. Watch- and clock-making spread to Cluses from the Geneva district in the eighteenth century. Pottery, tiles, bricks and glassware were manufactured in the valleys; glass-making has been important from the mid-eighteenth century at Thorens, Allex and Annecy, using Tertiary sands from the valleys of the Mont Salève, and salt from Trias deposits in the Tarentaise, from the saline springs at Salins near Moûtiers, and from the saline Lac d'Arbonne near Bourg-St Maurice. Paper was made at ten localities before the nineteenth century. Then there was a wide range of village crafts—the making of agricultural implements, domestic utensils, wooden objects, textiles and leather goods. Many of these activities were supplementary to an agricultural livelihood, most of them indeed winter activities. Thus industry, although small-scale, was surprisingly varied.

In the nineteenth century many of these industries declined, largely because the coming of rail communications brought in cheaply made factory products. Correspondingly, the attraction of urban industries drew off an increasing amount of labour. But the railway, an 'agent destructeur de l'industrie ancienne', as G. Veyret-Verner puts it, then became an 'agent de rénovation'. The anthracite of the Mure basin was mined, and the resources of limestone provided the raw material for the first modern industrialisation—the manufacture of cement and the production of agricultural lime, mainly near Grenoble.

The modern development of industry in the Alps is associated with the exploitation of hydroelectric power, and the Alpine valleys, with their focus and 'capital' at Grenoble, now form a distinct industrial region. From adjoining mountains one can look down on a linear industrialisation, a long line of factories and chimneys along the Grésivaudan,[22] Tarentaise, Maurienne and Romanche and on a smaller scale in the upper Arve, the Arly and the middle Durance valleys. Some of the traditional industries such as glove-making, textiles and watch-making have been modernised, but several introductions have resulted from technological developments.

Several large works are engaged in electric steel and alloy production, the most important of which are at Ugine in the Arly valley, at St Michel-de-Maurienne and at Allevarde. Plentiful cheap electricity is essential for the refining of aluminium from its ore, hydrated oxide of aluminium. It was in the French Alps, at Froges in the Grésivaudan a few kilometres from Grenoble, that Héroult first refined aluminium by electrolysis. The main source of bauxite is in the valley of the Argens in the *département* of Var (see p. 409). The ore is reduced to alumina near the area of production, and then sent to the furnaces in the Arc and Isère valleys. It takes about 25 mWh to produce a ton of aluminium, and so the French output of this metal, which totalled 381 000 tons in 1970 (almost all produced in the Alpine valleys but for one or two small refineries in the Pyrenees), consumes a considerable amount of electricity. The largest aluminium factory in France is at St Jean-de-Maurienne, and others are in the same valley at St Michel-de-Maurienne, Prémont and La Praz, a series in the Romanche, in the Tarentaise centred on Moûtiers, though on a smaller scale, and in the valley of the Doron de Bozel.

Many factories specialise in the refining of other metals and in the production of ferro-alloys. The Giffre works in the Arly valley produce ferro-chrome, -tungsten, -molybdenum and -titanium, Chedde produces ferro-vanadium and pure chrome, Ugine a range of ferro-alloys.

Several electrochemical works are situated in the same valleys, for the production of calcium carbide and of its fertiliser derivative calcium cyanamide requires the concentrated and controlled heat of electric furnaces. The largest unit is at Argentière in the upper Durance valley 13 km (8 miles below Briançon. In the Maurienne a series of these electro-chemical factories extends from near Modane as far as Aiguebelle and others are in the Romanche, the Tarentaise and the Arly valley. Other chemicals are made, and an explosives factory is active at Chedde in the Arve valley.

Many small factories, mostly making silk and rayon, are in the Drôme and Aygues valleys under the influence of Lyons, and small isolated ones are at such towns as Gap, Briançon, Faverges, Ugine and Annecy. Silk thread and cloth are made at St Pierre-d'Albigny and La Rochette in the Combe de Savoie. The main textile centre is Grenoble.

The timber-using industries have long been important in the well-wooded northern Fore-Alps. The emphasis is now not so much on small bric-à-brac and manufactured articles generally, as in the Jura, but on sawn timber for joinery, and each small valley in the Fore-Alpine massifs has its saw mills and wood yards. The manufacture of paper, established for centuries, has been developed on modern lines. Factories are in operation in the Grésivaudan (the biggest at Lancey in the lower Drac valley), and a few outlying ones at Annecy, Modane, Sisteron and Malaucène; the tendency is to produce high-quality papers.

The focus of this Alpine industrial region is Grenoble, itself a rapidly expanding manufacturing town. Its main industry was for long the making of gloves, using lamb skins from the Alpine flocks and also brought from the Central Massif and the Pyrenees; this is still largely a domestic industry. Grenoble is the centre of a flourishing textile industry, especially of silk and rayon (a large viscose rayon factory was built in 1926), and also manufactures electro-metallurgical and -chemical products, electrical apparatus (including power station equipment such as turbines and switch gear, ski lifts and cable-cars), paper, plastics and leather. Cement, lime and plaster works are active both to the south of Grenoble in the lower Drac valley and in the Isère valley below the city, using limestone brought down from the Grande Chartreuse by overhead cableways.

In the *département* of Isère almost exactly 50 per cent of the gainfully employed population are engaged in industry. The proportion is less in the other Alpine *départements,* but nevertheless in all about a quarter of a million people are occupied in industry in the French Alps. A large number of these are foreigners, working temporarily in the factories—Italians, Spaniards, Poles and North Africans.

## Population and settlement

The Alpine region stands out clearly as an area of low density, for much consists of uninhabited mountains with rock ridges, snowfields and glaciers, there are considerable areas of merely seasonal occupation by pastoralists, and the forested lands are widespread. Nevertheless, some of the valleys form long narrow strips of surprisingly dense population. At favoured points, particularly where several valleys meet, larger towns have developed; helped by the development of roads and railways (including some international routeways), they have become centres of thriving industry and tourism.

Many small towns and villages are situated along the sides of the valleys, on alluvial fans deposited by streams issuing from tributary valleys or higher up on glacially worn benches, occasionally on the floor of a valley where a transverse resistant rockbar affords a site above floods and facilities for power development. The dominance of the *adret* (sunny side) is always apparent, but more so in the upper narrow valleys orientated from west to east. Population, therefore, though irregularly distributed, is not inconsiderable.[23]

### The northern Alps

The *départements* of Savoie and Haute-Savoie contained in 1968 about 676 000 people, with an average density per sq km of 62 (160 per sq mile). This is surprisingly high when one remembers that the Mont Blanc massif, the Graians and the Vanoise are included. One concentration lies along the southern shore of Lake Geneva and in the valleys of the western Chablais. Thonon- and Evian-les-Bains have long been lakeside spas with mineral springs of international repute, and are excellent tourist centres. A second line of settlements extends along the Arve valley to the market town of Annemasse near the Swiss frontier. The centre for the Mont Blanc area is Chamonix, and with its neighbouring hamlets it provides for tourists both in summer and winter; between 200 000 and 250 000 people visit the district annually. Government finance has been provided to build resorts, hotels and ski lifts, including several new all-season, high-altitude ski complexes, as at Chamrousse and l'Alpe d'Huez. The villages and towns of the Arve valley have hotels, they serve the needs of farmers in the more remote side valleys, and most of them possess industries utilising Arve water power. These include a large electrochemical works, wood industries, the making of butter and cheese, and specifically at Cluses (due to the influence of Geneva) the manufacture of watches and clocks.

The valleys of the Isère and its tributary the Arc, together with the adjacent 'troughs' of Annecy and Chambéry, account for most of the remaining population of the two Savoyan *départements*, the result of the linear industrialisation of the valleys. Many villages and small towns stand away from the river to avoid flooding, usually in an embayment where a tributary enters the main valley or on the gentle slopes of an alluvial fan. The north side is of course much more favoured than the south. Again there are many tourist centres; Bourg-St Maurice, for example, the terminus of the Isère valley railway, lies at the foot of the Petit-St Bernard pass, and the *Route des Alpes* passes southward through the town to the Col de l'Iseran. Other climbing resorts are La Grave in the Romanche and La Bérarde in the Venéon; these are the centres for the Pelvoux massif as Chamonix is for Mont Blanc, but they are less developed and commercialised. Further to the south Modane is the centre for the Maurienne and the southern Vanoise, and has the advantage of being on the main line to Turin via the Mont Cenis tunnel.

Further west in their side valleys are Annecy and Chambéry, the 'capitals' of Haute-Savoie and Savoie respectively. Annecy is exceeded in size in the French Alps only by Grenoble. It is the centre of a prosperous agricultural district, it has become a well-known resort helped by its lake-side position and attractive surrounding hills, and is a notable centre for coach tours. It also has a variety of light engineering, textile and clothing industries. Chambéry, in the flat-floored trough to the south of the Lac du Bourget, is the market centre for a prosperous agricultural district and for the neighbouring Bauges and Chartreuse uplands, it has a variety of manufactures, and the pleasant surrounding country, together with its mild climate, make it a popular resort. Aix-les-Bains on the eastern shores of the Lac du Bourget was for long one of the fashionable European spas, where many thousands have 'taken the cure' from its sulphur and alum warm springs, indeed, the first thermal station (*Aquae Gratianae*) was established as long ago as 125 BC. It has also developed as a centre for winter sports, with the construction of a mountain railway up Mont Revard to the east.

To the southwest of Savoy lies the *département* of Isère, with its population of 768 000 in 1968 and an average density of 97 per sq km (250 per sq mile). This is as high as it is, in spite of the scantily populated uplands, partly because it is crossed by the broad trench of the Grésivaudan, partly because it includes the 'regional capital' of Dauphiny—Grenoble, and partly because it extends to the Rhône and includes the basin of Vienne. The Grésivaudan contains a series of large villages and small towns situated on the lower slopes of the northwestern side of the valley. The valley is so broad that the southeastern side of the valley also has several small towns, since the *ubac* effect is not marked; indeed the railway line (the Grenoble-Mont Cenis-Turin route) follows this side and so links these towns.

Grenoble,[24] at the southern end of the Grésivaudan on the left bank of the Isère, has grown up at a commanding position in the French Alps, since it is the focus of all the Isère valley routes. Not only does the main railway line via the Mont Cenis pass through the town, but it is the centre of a system of electrified light railways serving the neighbouring valleys. Grenoble's importance as a road focus is shown by the fact that from the town a route runs south over the Col de La Croix-Haute to Sisteron and Marseilles, northwest via the Voiron depression to Lyons, northeast up the Isère valley to Chambéry, Annecy and Chamonix, and southeast over the Col du Lautaret to Briançon, thence via the Mont Genèvre pass to Italy. Its title of *La Porte des Alpes* is well deserved, for it receives over 100 000 visitors each year, and at the end of every street one sees a wooded hillside or mountain summit. Moreover it is the administrative, judicial, and servicing centre for Dauphiny, and it has a university with a distinguished school of Alpine Geography. The chief importance of modern Grenoble is as a manufacturing town, as described on p. 647. As a result its population has grown steadily from 24 000 in 1832 to 162 000 in 1968. If the six neighbouring communes which form part of the official agglomeration are included, the total in 1968 was about 332 000. The Grenoble conurbation has grown fourfold since 1945, mainly as a result of its industrial development and its expansion as a tourist metropolis. It has numerous high-rise blocks, new suburbs and the adjacent 'new town' of Echirolles.

## The southern Alps

Great areas of the Fore-Alps are unpopulated, except for some small fertile basins along the Durance and the lower courses of its tributaries. The general density of population is distinctly low; Hautes-Alpes (which lies partly in the northern Alps) had in 1968 a density of 16 per sq km (41 per sq mile), while Alpes-de-Haute-Provence had 15 (39).

Few towns are of any size or importance, for apart from the limited economy even tourism is less developed than in the north; visitors either go north to the High Alps of Savoy and Dauphiny or south to the Mediterranean Riviera coast, and the limestone uplands fall between the two. Gap, the *chef-lieu* of Hautes-Alpes, is the largest town, situated in the Gapençais, where the river Luye flows south in a pleasant vale to join the middle Durance. Further to the northeast in the upper Durance valley is

Briançon, a town of great antiquity, for it was once called *Brigantium,* the capital of a Celtic kingdom. It became a medieval walled town, and was later fortified by Vauban, for it commands the Mont Genèvre pass into Italy. The town consists of steep narrow streets on the slopes below the citadel, with many old forts on the hills around. It is a busy tourist resort, with the Pelvoux massif to the west and the Cottian Alps to the east, while the *Route des Alpes* comes down the Guisane valley. The only other towns, also in the Durance basin, are Sisteron, an attractive old Provençal town with narrow streets climbing the steep sides of a rock eminence near the gorgelike confluence of the Buech and the Durance, and Digne, the chief town of the *département* of Alpes-de-Haute-Provence, and is a pleasant resort for the Provençal Alps. It has been a spa for a long time, with its warm alkaline and sulphurous springs.

## Communications

The pattern of communications in the French Alps, both of roads and railways, is more dense than might be expected, for two main reasons. One is that the Alps lie across lines of movement between central France and northern Italy, facilitated by several transverse valleys, the other is that the whole region has been opened up to cater both for the annual influx of tourists and for the needs of industry. There are several international passes (Fig. 22.8)—the *Petit-St Bernard* between Bourg-St Maurice and Aosta, the *Mont Cenis* between Lanslebourg and Susa, the *Mont Genèvre* between Briançon and Cesana Torinese, and the *Col de Larche* between Barcelonnette and Cuneo.

There are only two main trans-Alpine railways between France and Italy. The more northerly utilises the famous Mont Cenis (or Fréjus) tunnel, 13·7 km (8·5 miles) long, constructed during the years 1857–70, the first of the great trans-Alpine tunnels. It penetrates the Massif de Fréjus at a maximum height of 1 294 m (4 246 ft), while the frontier ridge rises 1 700 m (5 500 ft) above. The section between Culoz and Modane was the first line to be electrified in France, an operation completed in the 1920s. The other trans-Alpine route runs northeastward from Nice into the southern ranges of the Maritime Alps, and then crosses the Col de Tende into Italy before descending to Cuneo, hence to Turin. In addition, a narrow-gauge railway links Chamonix and Martigny in the extreme north by means of a tunnel under the Col des Montets, then following the valley of the Trient into Switzerland.

The French Alps are quite well served by internal railways and roads. A longitudinal line runs from Geneva via Culoz and Chambéry (a section of the Mont Cenis line) to Grenoble, then south to Veynes; this section provides one of the finest railway journeys in the Alps. Beyond Vif the line leaves the Drac valley and crosses the Dévoluy massif by way of the Col de la Croix-Haute; it uses sweeping curves, astonishing loops, long viaducts

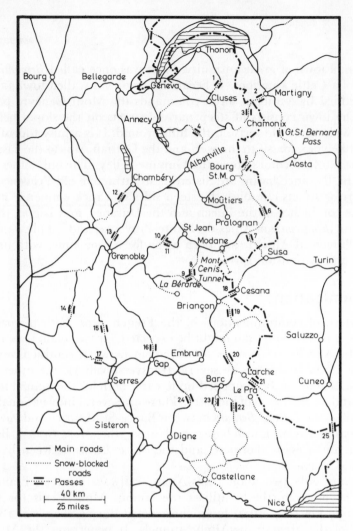

FIG. 22.8. The main roads of the French Alps
The main passes are indicated from north to south by numbers,
with altitudes in metres (feet), as follows: **1.** Col des Gets 1 172
(3 845); **2.** Col du Forclaz 1 528 (5 013); **3.** Col des Montets 1 461
(4 793); **4.** Col des Aravis 1 498 (4 914); **5.** Col du Petit-St
Bernard 2 188 (7 178); **6.** Col de l'Iseran 2 769 (9 085); **7.** Col
du Mont Cenis 2 083 (6 834); **8.** Col du Galibier 2 658 (8 399);
**9.** Col du Lautaret 2 058 (6 752); **10.** Col du Glandon 1 951
(6 401); **11.** Col de la Croix de Fer 2 088 (6 850); **12.** Col du
Granier 1 164 (3 819); **13.** Col de la Porte 1 325 (4 347); **14.** Col
de Rousset 1 411 (4 628); **15.** Col de la Croix-Haute 1 176 (3 858);
**16.** Col Bayard 1 243 (4 077); **17.** Col de Cabre 1 180 (3 871);
**18.** Col du Mont Gènevre 1 854 (6 083); **19.** Col d'Izoard 2 360
(7 743); **20.** Col de Vars 2 111 (6 926); **21.** Col de Larche 1 995
(6 545); **22.** Col de la Cayolle 2 326 (7 631); **23.** Col d'Allos 2 250
(7 382); **24.** Col de Maure 1 347 (4 419); **25.** Col de Tende 1 873
(6 145)

Based on (*a*) the *Michelin* series of road-maps, 1 : 200 000; (*b*) the annual *Guide
Michelin*; and (*c*) *Europe: Strassen Atlas* (*Kümmerly und Frey*, Bern).

and several tunnels. At Veynes, where it is crossed by the line between Livron in the Rhône valley and Briançon, the railway continues south-ward, and from Sisteron it follows the Durance valley into Lower Provence, thence to Marseilles. Other lines run transversely into the French Alps, serving the tourist resorts. Grenoble is the centre of several of these lines converging on the town. The mountain railways and telpherlines (*téléfé-riques*) are obvious concomitants of the mountain resorts. The *téléfériques* are numerous, used not only for tourists but also for bringing down milk, cheese, timber and limestone. The highest of the passenger *téléfériques* goes almost to the summit of the Aiguille du Midi, at a height of 3 607 m (11 834 ft), thence over the snowfields to the Col de Géant on the Italian frontier.

The internal road system is good, and large numbers of cars and an extensive service of autocars penetrate in summer far into the upper valleys and over the cols. The *Route des Alpes* has been developed from Thonon and Evian on Lake Geneva all the way to Nice, crossing from valley to valley by high interconnected roads over the cols. The passes are shown on Fig. 22.8; twenty-five are listed by *Michelin* all over 1 160 m (3 800 ft). The highest is the Col de l'Iseran, open only from early July to mid-October, which links the upper Isère valley with that of the Arc, between Bourg-St Maurice and Lanslebourg. The second highest is the Col du Galibier, which forms a link between St Michel in the Maurienne; the top of the col is pierced by a 370 m (400 yds) long road tunnel, constructed in 1891 to save the last few hundred metres of steep ascent. The successive crossing of these two cols offers a magnificent stretch of Alpine motoring.

In 1965 a road tunnel[25] was opened under Mont Blanc between Chamonix and Courmayeur in Italy. It is 12 km (7·5 miles) long, the longest road tunnel in the world, entering on the French side at 1 200 m (3 950 ft) and leaving on the Italian side at about 1 370 m (4 500 ft).

[1] R. Blanchard, *Les Alpes occidentales* (1944–56), is a monumental work in twelve volumes, dealing in great detail with each part of the French Alps; see also, by the same author, *Les Alpes et leur destin* (1958).

[2] Ph. Arbos, *La Vie pastorale dans les Alpes françaises* (1922) is the classic work on this subject.

[3] H. Onde, *La Maurienne et la Tarentaise: étude de géographie physique* (1938).

[4] R. Blanchard, *Les Alpes occidentales*, vol. i, *Les Préalpes françaises du nord* (1944), pp. 63–102.

[5] J. Masseport, *Le Diois, les Baronnies et leur avant-pays rhodanien: étude morphologique* (1960).

[6] An account of this system and others in the Vercors is given by J. J. Garbier and C. Pommier, 'Explorations au Vercors', *Annales de Spéléologie*, **10** (1955), pp. 5–21; and J. Cadoux *et al.*, *One Thousand Metres Down* (1957), translated by R. L. G. Irving from *Opération-1000* (1955).

[7] See P. Chevalier (translated E. M. Hatt), *Subterranean Climbers* (1951); O. Chevalier, 'Le Dent de Crolles souterrain', *Rev. Géogr. alp.*, **29** (1941), pp. 25–31; and J. Masseport, 'Notes morphologiques sur la Chartreuse Septentrionale', *ibid.*, **41** (1953), pp. 115–33.

[8] J. Miège, *La Vie rurale du sillon alpin: étude géographique* (1961).

9 F. Milon, 'Le Lac d'Annecy', *Annls Géogr.*, **48** (1939), pp. 120–37; this describes its origin and form, variations of level, temperature of waters, and surrounding settlement.

10 P. Veyret, *Les Pays de la moyenne Durance alpestre* (1944), deals in detail with Gap, Embrun, Digne, etc., and their surrounding *pays*.

11 G. Conard, 'Morphologie de la vallée de Chamonix et de ses abords', *Annls Géogr.*, **40** (1931), pp. 396–410; this includes a detailed morphological map (pp. 398–9).

12 Details of this complex structure are summarised, with a full bibliography, by L. W. Collet, *The Structure of the Alps* (1927), pp. 31–45.

13 E. Bénévent, *Le Climat des Alpes françaises (Mémorial de l'Office National Météorologique de France)* (1926).

14 J. Steinberg, 'Le Climat estival de la haute vallée de l'Arve', *Annls Géogr.*, **74** (1965), pp. 129–59.

15 R. Leroy, 'Les forêts des Alpes françaises', *Rev. Géogr. alp.*, **45** (1957), pp. 441–55.

16 A. Reffay, 'Vie pastorale d'une moyenne montagne: le Chablais', *Rev. de Géogr. Alpine*, **55** (1967), pp. 401–68, a very detailed survey with maps and tables.

17 J. Robert, 'Les montagnettes dans les Alpes françaises du Nord', *Mélanges géographiques offerts à E. Bénévent, 1954*, pp. 167–82.

18 M. Allefrosde, 'Les Fabrications fromagères en Haute-Savoie', *Rev. Géogr. alp.*, **40** (1952), pp. 625–41.

19 For a full account, illustrated with maps, see G. Kish, 'Hydro-electric power in France: plans and projects', *Geogrl. Rev.*, **45** (1955), pp. 81–98. See also J. Ritter, 'L'Aménagement hydroélectrique du bassin de l'Isère', *Annls Géogr.*, **68** (1959), pp. 34–53.

20 A. Bertin, 'Le barrage de Serre-Ponçon', *Rev. Géogr. alp.*, **48** (1960), pp. 625–89.

21 A full account of industrial development prior to 1948 is given by G. Veyret-Verner, *L'Industrie des Alpes françaises: étude géographique* (1948), for later years by J. Lefebvre, *L'Evolution des localisations industrielles: l'exemple des Alpes françaises* (1960).

22 D. Bacconnet, 'L'industrialisation d'une grande vallée alpestre et ses répercussions démographiques et rurales: le Grésivaudan', *Rev. Géogr. alp.*, **44** (1956), pp. 99–166.

23 An interesting case study is P. Rambaud, *Economie et sociologie de la montagne* (1962), a study of the commune of Albiez-le-Vieux in the Maurienne.

24 J. E. Brush, 'The function of Grenoble as a central place', *Geogr. Rev.*, **50** (1960), pp. 586–8; and G. Armand and C. Marie, 'Les grandes villes françaises', *La Documentation française*, no. 3288 (1966). See also P. and G. Veyret and F. Germain, *Grenoble capitale alpine* (1967).

25 P. Guichonnet, 'L'achèvement du tunnel du Mont-Blanc', *Rev. Géogr. alp.*, **51** (1963), pp. 145–54.

# 23
# The Pyrenees

The Pyrenees form a mountain barrier more than 400 km (250 miles) in length between the Bay of Biscay and the Mediterranean. In altitude they do not compare with the Alps, for their highest summit, the Pic d'Aneto (or Mont Néthou) in the Maladetta massif (which lies wholly in Spain) attains only 3 404 m (11 169 ft), and the ranges both at the western and eastern ends rarely exceed 1 000 m (3 200 ft). The maximum width of the uplands is only about 80 km (50 miles); in the west it is less than 30 km (20 miles), and in the east the culminating prong of the Mont d'Albères is little more than 8 km (5 miles) across, reaching the coast at Cap Cerbère. The greater part of the Pyrenees, in fact, lies in Spain, forming a complex area of *sierras* and deep valleys drained by the headstreams of the Ebro.

Nevertheless, the Pyrenees are in many ways the most satisfactory of the so-called 'natural frontiers of France'. The effectiveness of the physical barrier is the result partly of the abruptness with which the mountains rise as a long snow-fringed rampart from the foothills bordering the plain of Aquitaine; as M. Sorre[1] expresses it, 'l'impression première est, en somme, d'une crête rigide et continue'. The high-level continuity of this rampart is especially evident in the but slightly serrated central Pyrenees; for a distance of more than 160 km (100 miles) the lowest pass is La Plan de Direts (1 879m: 6 165 ft). While many valleys run southward deep into the mountains, they almost all end in culs-de-sac, and open longitudinal valleys (as in the Alps), which invite penetration by routeways and settlement, are only slightly developed.

For much of its length the main crestline demarcates the Franco-Spanish frontier. The two chief exceptions are in the neighbourhood of the Val d'Aran (Fig. 23.2), where a rightangled bend to the north leaves the whole of the Maladetta massif and the headwaters of the Garonne in Spain, and in the east where the Col de la Perche between the upper valleys of the Têt and the Segre is entirely in France. The Pyrenean frontier, defined by the Treaty of the Pyrenees in 1659, has remained remarkably stable. The effectiveness of the mountains as a physical obstacle must, however, not be exaggerated, for in point of fact sovereign states have straddled the ranges both on the west and the east. Navarre emerged as a unit at the end of the first millennium AD and maintained a high degree of independence until 1516, when Spain annexed the southern side; the northern portion survived until its ruler became Henri IV of France in 1594. In the east Roussillon intermittently formed part of a state of Catalonia, which belonged to France and Spain in turn until the Treaty of the Pyrenees. The barrier quality of the mountain ranges has been due less to the actual physical obstacles (although they are admittedly considerable in the central part) than to the lack of incentive to create trans-Pyrenean routes; the mountains separate no important commercial or industrial regions, as did the Alps lying athwart the routeways between the Mediterranean and central Europe.

## Structure and relief

### Structure

The Pyrenees owe their basic structures to the fold movements of Tertiary times, though of a somewhat earlier date (Eocene and early Oligocene) than the main Alpine systems. The orogeny was one of great complexity, involving masses of granite and of Pre-Cambrian gneissic rocks (fragments of the ancient Hercynian continent), highly metamorphosed Palaeozoic

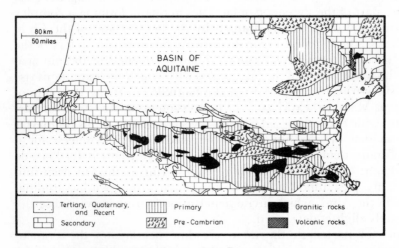

FIG. 23.1. Simplified geological map of the Pyrenees

Based on (*a*) folding map in L. de Launay, *Géologie de la France* (1921); and (*b*) *Carte géologique de la France*, 1 : 1 000 000, published by the Service de la Carte géologique détaillée de la France (1933).

slates, schists and limestones, and flanking Jurassic, Cretaceous and Older Tertiary limestones (Fig. 23.1). The folding was so intense that numerous large-scale recumbent overfolds were formed; in places metamorphosed Palaeozoic rocks overlie Upper Cretaceous limestones. Denudation has however gone on longer and proceeded further than in the Alps, and much of the complicated rock structure overlying the major thrust-planes has been removed.

Faulting was associated both with the main orogenic movements and with late-Tertiary disturbances, involving *en masse* uplift and depression. These resulted in a number of prominent plateaus and lofty basins, especially in the eastern Pyrenees, and were also responsible for the formation of the plain of Roussillon and for the western Mediterranean basin generally, including the Golfe du Lion which separates the Pyrenean ranges from those of Provence.

The net result of these structural processes has been the formation of three more or less longitudinal structural zones in the French Pyrenees, although these are not all everywhere well represented. On the northern flanks occurs what might be called the 'external' or 'frontal' zone (the *Pré-Pyrénées*), where the relatively superficial though closely packed folding involved mainly Upper Cretaceous limestones. Many straight though usually short parallel ridges can be distinguished, now emphasised by erosion which has worn vales in the associated clays and marls. Some French geographers use the name *Petites Pyrénées* for the whole of this zone, although others would restrict this term to the low ridges between the rivers Garonne and Ariège. Another upland within this zone is the Plantaurel. Further west the late-Tertiary fans which spread out over the foothills (Lannemezan, Bigorre, etc., described in Chapter 13) completely mask the structural features of this frontal zone, which reappears in the extreme west.

The second longitudinal zone is that of *Ariège*. Complex folding has here brought diverse rocks into close juxtaposition, so that subsequent differential denudation has emphasised the long narrow exposures of granites and gneissic rocks, Older Palaeozoic schists, and Mesozoic limestones, clays and marls. These varied rocks and structures make equally varied contributions to the landscape. The granitic and other crystalline rocks form *noyaux* elongated from west to east, projecting from the Mesozoic cover: Barousse, Milhas, Castillon, Arize, the curiously named Massif des Trois Seigneurs, St Barthélemy and Agly. The limestones form long *crêtes* separated by longitudinal valleys worn in the marls and clays or such plateaus as those of the Pays de Sault in the east and the Pays de Gave further west. To the east the Ariège zone fades out into the broad trench of Fenouillèdes (the upper Agly valley) to the south of the outlying Corbières massif.[2] The last is structurally not a part of the Pyrenees but of the Central Massif, an upstanding mass of Palaeozoic rocks separated from the Montagne Noire by the Aude valley.

The high central line of the Pyrenees is known as the *zone axiale* or as the *zone des grands massifs*.[3] In the words of D. Faucher, 'l'axe de la chaîne est formé par un affleurement de terrains primaires'. The Palaeozoic rocks were vigorously folded during the Hercynian orogeny, as were those of Corbières and the Montagne Noire, and at the same time batholithic masses of granite were intruded into the cores of the folds. All these were heavily

657

denuded and then involved in the Tertiary orogeny. Long continued erosion has now divided the axial zone into 'un chapelet de massifs' of granite, mica-schists and gneiss: Balaïtous, Vignemale, Néouvielle, Posets, Maladetta, Valira, Campcardos, Carlitte, Puigmal and Canigou; these, elongated more or less from west to east, stand out on Fig. 23.1. Deeply cut valleys, mostly trending transversely northward, but with a few short longitudinal sections (the Tourmalet and part of the upper Garonne, for example), define these upland groups of high plateaus from which rise rugged peaks. A few small intrusions of andesite and kindred rocks have been revealed by denudation; the most notable result is the striking profile of the Pic du Midi de Bigorre, isolated by the removal of the much less resistant surrounding slates of Carboniferous age.

These then are the three main structural zones of the Pyrenees which are represented in France. Further south are two more, the *zones calcaires espagnoles,* a narrow belt of Upper Cretaceous limestones, succeeded by the *zone de l'Aragon* of Eocene and some Oligocene rocks. The latter is wholly in Spain, but the former constitutes the main crestline in a number of places; in succession from west to east are the Pic d'Orhy, the Vizaurin, and the Mont Perdu group. The last forms the frontier to the south of the Cirque de Gavarnie; its back wall rises to a lofty limestone ridge, culminating in Mont Perdu itself (3 351 m: 10 994 ft), the summit of which is in Spain.

## Drainage

For much of its length the main Pyrenean crestline forms a remarkably continuous watershed between streams flowing northwards into France, southwards into Spain, consequent upon the slope of the main axial uplift; the streams originally flowed over a now largely vanished cover of Mesozoic and Tertiary rocks. The two master streams are the Garonne, with its tributary the Ariège draining the central and much of the eastern Pyrenees, and the Adour in the west with its tributaries, each known by its generic name of *gave*, indicating a foaming torrent. Their valleys extend far into the ranges, terminating as steep trough-heads which rise to mere notches forming high-level passes in the ridge-line (Plate 66).

Major longitudinal valleys are notably absent in the central and western French Pyrenees; the only prominent examples are the Val d'Aran on the Spanish side of the frontier and the valley of the Ariège near Ax-les-Thermes. In detail, however, the many streams reveal some degree of adaptation to the structure, and in places they follow narrow outcrops of less resistant rocks in a direction parallel to the main Pyrenean crestline, so that short open west–east valleys alternate with transverse gorgelike sections. In the east the rivers Agly, Têt and Tech occupy prominent west–east valleys of structural origin, as they flow from the uplands of Carlitte and Canigou into the plain of Roussillon (see pp. 438–42).

The Garonne rises in the Val d'Aran in Spain, an open west–east valley developed along a narrow outcrop of slate between crystalline massifs to north and south. It has two headstreams, one rising at the eastern end of the Val, the other emerging as a strong resurgence from a cavern known as the Goueil de Jouéou (Fig. 23.2). It was proved by the French speleologist, Norbert Casteret, that these waters are derived from a sink on the Spanish side of the ridgeline, the Trou de Toro, at a height of nearly 2 000m (6 500 ft), into which pours a torrent from the snowfields and glaciers of the Maladetta massif; a remarkable subterranean drainage system passes under the main watershed.[4] The Garonne leaves the Val d'Aran by the gorge of the Pont du Roi, below which the valley opens out again in the basin of Parignac. Beyond this the river leaves the axial zone of the Pyrenees and crosses the open limestone country of the Ariège zone. Near Montréjeau it receives its large headstream, the Neste; this river flows north through the Val d'Aure, receiving many confluents from the Néouvielle massif, then turns abruptly at rightangles to the east into a trench in the frontal zone to the south of the huge fan of the plateau of Lannemezan (see p. 346). The Garonne continues in this direction through the broad basin of St Gaudens, and after receiving the Salat (which drains the uplands of Couserans) it crosses the Petites Pyrénées and so enters the low Tertiary plateaus of Aquitaine.

The main Pyrenean tributary of the Garonne is the Ariège, which rises on the Pic de Nègre, forming for a short distance the boundary of Andorra. It receives many tributaries from the mountains on the eastern margins of Andorra and from the Carlitte massif. From Ax to Tarascon the river occupies a broad longitudinal trench separating the frontier ridges from the granitic mass of St Barthélemy to the north, and cuts transversely across the crystalline rocks in a narrow steepsided valley. The Ariège then enters the broad basin in which is situated Foix, succeeded below the town by an almost gorgelike valley through the limestone ridges of the Chaîne du Plantaurel. Finally the river flows across the gently undulating Tertiary plateau to join the Garonne.

The dissected Massif de Néouvielle forms a remarkable centre of drainage dispersion, for the Neste drains its eastern flanks, the Adour its northeastern and northern slopes, and the Gave de Pau its western margins. Two streams, the Tourmalet flowing east to the Neste and the Bastan flowing to the west to the Gave de Pau, have cut deep valleys across the massif, separating the Pic du Midi de Bigorre from the Pic d'Aubert–Pic Long group of the Néouvielle massif; their sources are divided only by the Col de Tourmalet, across which passes a fine motor road. The Adour itself flows northwards through its broadening valley; near Bagnères-de-Bigorre the extensive flat-floored well cultivated basin contrasts with the wooded slopes on either side. The river continues through Tarbes (see p. 352) across the gravel fan of Bigorre (Fig. 13.6). The Gave de Pau, the most easterly of the Pyrenean *gaves*, rises in the Cirque de Gavarnie under the frontier ridge, and flows boldly north through its broad detritus-floored vale towards

PLATE 64. The Cirque de Gavarnie in the central Pyrenees

Lourdes, joined by innumerable torrents from the hanging valleys on either side. Near Luz, and again lower down near Pierrefitte-Argelès, the valley broadens into quite extensive basins, but the river crosses the limestone country above Lourdes in a prominent gorge. Below the town the river, whose course is blocked by a vast mass of fluvioglacial material from which streams drain north to the Adour, turns abruptly west and then northwest across the Tertiary fan to Pau.

Two more *gaves*, d'Ossau and d'Aspe, drain the western parts of the High Pyrenees, converging to form the Gave d'Oloron. The Ossau rises among the rugged ridges and basins of the Pic du Midi d'Ossau, the Aspe descends from the frontier ridge in the neighbourhood of the Col du Somport. The latter valley shows well the usual alternation of broad trough and steepsided gorge. Further west the Gave de Saison (or de Mauléon), formed by two small streams which drain the basins in which stand the little towns of Larrau and St Engrâce, flows northwards through a clearly defined valley to join the Oloron. The *pays* name of *Soule* is given to the valley of the Saison; *Haute-Soule* comprises the valleys and ridges of the two headstreams, *Bas-Soule* the broad valley of the middle Saison eroded through Lower Cretaceous marls, with its centre at Tardets. Finally, in the west the Nive rises in the Cretaceous limestone plateau country, and flows through the basin of Cize to join the Adour at Bayonne.

## Underground drainage

The underground section of the course of the upper Garonne already described is one example of a common phenomenon in the Pyrenees, the result of the widespread occurrence of limestones varying in age from Older Palaeozoic to Tertiary. These are found in close juxtaposition with other impermeable rocks, thus causing watersinks, vast ramifications of cavern systems and powerful resurgences. Many hundreds of these cave systems have been explored and named. On the face of the Mont Perdu group, above the Cirque de Gavarnie near the Brèche de Rolande (a huge rectangular rock gash in the frontier ridge), was discovered one of the largest permanently ice-filled caverns in the world (the *Grotte Casteret*), at a

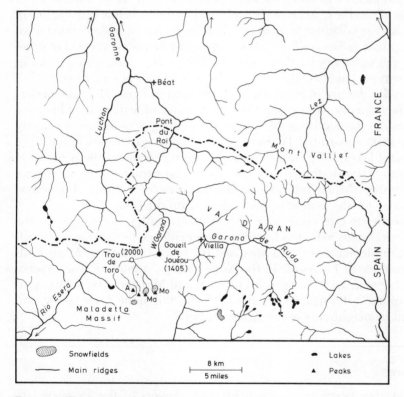

FIG. 23.2. The sources of the Garonne
The possible line of the underground connection between the Trou de Toro and Goueil de Jouéou is indicated by a dotted line.

The high peaks of the Maladetta are indicated as follows: **A,** Pic d'Aneto 3404 m (11 169 ft); **Ma,** Pic Margalide 3258 m (10 689 ft); **Mo,** Pic Moulières 3008 m (9 869 ft).

Based on: (*a*) *Carte de France a 1 : 200 000*, sheet 77; and (*b*) N. Casteret, *Ten Years under the Earth* (1940), pp. 216–17; this is a translation of two of the distinguished speleologist's works, *Dix Ans sous terre* and *Au fond des gouffres*, translated and edited by B. Mussey.

height of 2 700 m (8 800 ft), containing a sort of subterranean glacier which occupies the channel worn by an underground river in bygone periods of milder climate. What was for a time the deepest known abyss in France (the *Gouffre Martel*) was discovered opening into the face of the Pyramid de Serre, the steep upper wall of the Cirque du Lez on the French side of the frontier ridge to the north of the Val d'Aran; it was explored for a vertical depth of 477 m (1 566 ft), with a torrent flowing throughout.[5] Adjacent to the Gouffre Martel, the magnificent stalactite cavern of *La Cigalère* was discovered by Casteret; this had practical results, for the Union Pyrénéenne Electrique drove a tunnel through the mountainside into the cavern and tapped an underground stream through pipes, affording a head of water of over 1 000 m (3 000 ft). There are many more of these cave systems, but the most fantastic is the *Gouffre de Pierre St Martin*, near the Spanish frontier on the side of the Pic d'Arlas in the western Pyrenees; below is the valley of the Licq and the village of St Engrâce. This *gouffre* has been descended to an overall depth of 728 m (2 389 ft). It is entered by an initial vertical shaft no less than 346 m (1 135 ft) deep; beyond lies an inter-connected series of seven enormous caverns, the last of which is large enough to contain a building twice the size of Notre Dame Cathedral in Paris. Here the underground river finally disappears through a mass of sediment. This cave system was the scene during the years 1952 to 1955 of incidents of tragedy and remarkable fortitude.[2] Within all these cavern systems are found large underground lakes, lofty waterfalls and foaming torrents; the watertable fluctuates so violently that many systems can be explored only in August and September. Much information has been derived about this underground water for the benefit of hydroelectric production.

Some of the caverns rival those of the Vezère valley (see p. 338) as the homes of early man, who has left abundant evidence in the shape of wall-paintings, implements and weapons, and the bones of his prey. Many finds have been made at Labastide in the Neste valley ('a salon of Aurignacian and Magdalenian art'), Gargas, Montespan and Marsoulas on the margins of the Garonne valley near St Gaudens, Mas-d'Azil in the Arize valley, and Niaux and its neighbours in the Ariège valley.[7]

## Glaciation[8]

The presentday permanent snowfields and glaciers of the Pyrenees are small in extent, with an aggregate area of only about 34 sq km (13 sq miles). They are confined to the higher mountain groups over 3 000 m (10 000 ft) in the central Pyrenees, where they form small caps to some of the rounded peaks, or lie in north-facing cirques and on high shelves.[9] Most of the present named glaciers are little more than *névés*. The biggest individual glacier in the French Pyrenees is the Glacier d'Aussoue on the eastern flanks of the Pic de Vignemale. Further east a few tiny glaciers exist on the

Montvallier and Montcalm massifs, and some *névés* on Carlitte and Canigou. The largest Pyrenean group is on the Maladetta group within Spain, with five individual glaciers and some snowfields (Fig. 23.2).

In the Pleistocene, snowfields and glaciers were of course very much more widespread, though never comparable with those of the Alps. From the high basins and lofty plateaus glacier tongues pushed northwards along existing river valleys.[10] The glacier which occupied the valley of the Gave de Pau probably had a maximum length of 55 km (34 miles), and a thickness of 900 m (2 900 ft). The glaciers descended in places to 340 m (1 100 ft) above present sea level. At least two definite glacial advances can be distinguished, although some authorities claim to have traced three and perhaps four.

This upland glaciation has left its stamp on the landscape,[11] in the form of cirque basins, lofty arêtes notched by cols, peaks of a distinct pyramidal form, and remarkably over-deepened valleys, with trough heads, rock steps and lateral hanging valleys whose mouths are 400 to 500 m (1 400 to 1 700 ft) above the main valley floors. Large numbers of tiny rock basins now contain lakes (the Néouvielle massif is said to have no less than forty-five); some are very deep, notably the Lac Bleu de Lesponne which is 120 m (394 ft) in depth.[12] The best known cirques are those of Gavarnie and Troumouse at the head of the Gave de Pau on the northwestern flanks of Mont Perdu. Gavarnie is a magnificent amphitheatre nearly 3 km (2 miles) across, backed by cliffs rising in a series of enormous steps for 1 500 m (5 000 ft) to the rocky crestline at twice that altitude (Plate 64). Several cascades descend this cliff wall (the longest fall is over 450 m: 1 500 ft), and huge scree cones rest against the base of the rocks. Troumouse, at the head of the valley of the Héas (a right-bank tributary of the Gave de Pau), is in some ways finer than Gavarnie, with steep walls rising to a crestline of such peaks as the Pic de la Munia.

The upper valleys of the *gaves* are prominently overdeepened, with steep walls and flat floors; several reveal transverse rock bars which cause falls and rapids on the streams and afford sites for hydroelectric stations. Above the walls are the high valley benches. Some hanging tributaries form spectacular falls; in the Carlitte massif a stream leaves the Etang de Naguilhès and falls in a series of rapids for over 900 m (3 000 ft) to join the Oriège, a tributary of the Ariège.

Glacial deposition has contributed a swathing cover to the flat valley floors, and arcs of terminal moraines are present in most of the valleys; these are particularly distinctive near Lourdes in the Gave de Pau and near Arudy in the Gave d'Ossau.[13] Quite large lakes were for a time ponded up behind these moraines, evidence of which can be seen clearly in the valley of the Gave de Pau, but except for the small Lac de Lourdes these lakes have vanished through downcutting of the outflowing stream and some degree of infilling. Other glacial deposition is shown by lateral moraines high on the valley sides, as near Campan in the Adour valley and along the valley of the Neste d'Oo. Beyond the morainic lines are great sheets of fluvio-glacial sands and gravels.

## Weathering and postglacial erosion

The sides of the mountain groups are scored by innumerable gullies, the work of torrents flowing down into the main valleys, fed particularly by the meltwaters from the heavy winter snowfall. Their load of débris is borne away towards the plain of Aquitaine. Weathering, particularly the action of frost, contributes potently to the wastage of the mountains; vast scree slopes flow away from the foot of each crag. The widespread occurrence of limestone enables chemical erosion to produce karstlike features. Large areas are solution-scarred with 'chasms, oubliettes, trap-holes, fissures, tunnels, funnels, knifelike ridges' (Casteret). A vegetation of bracken in the more humid west, of dwarf rhododendron in the centre, and of either *maquis* or *garrigue* in the east only emphasises the rugged character of much of the Pyrenean landscape.

## Regional divisions

On a structural basis three longitudinal zones have been demarcated. It is, however, more convenient in some ways to divide the Pyrenees into three transverse sections: the western, central and eastern Pyrenees. Some French geographers indeed distinguish a fourth, the broad complex mountains on either side of the Ariège basin, hence their name of *Pyrénées de l'Ariège*. This, however, tends to confuse with the longitudinal Ariège structural zone, and it is better to include their western part within the central Pyrenees, their eastern part within the eastern Pyrenees. This division into three sections is further accentuated by marked contrasts in climate, vegetation and agriculture.

The western Pyrenees (*Pyrénées basques* or *atlantiques*) extend from the Bay of Biscay to the Col du Somport; as has been stressed, these uplands are lower and hummocky, and only two peaks, the Pic d'Anie and the Pic d'Orhy, rise much above the general level of about 900 m (3 000 ft). No permanent snow is present. These uplands are crossed by several low passes (although their approaches are indeed steep and strenuous), including the famous Pass of Roncesvalles which is within Spain. While the actual crestline is commonly of Palaeozoic slates and schists, the western Pyrenees consist mainly of Upper Cretaceous limestone plateaus, cut into by the headstreams of the Nive, Saison and Aspe.

The central Pyrenees comprise a series of massifs, eroded into serrated ridges and craggy peaks by the deep valleys of the headstreams of the Adour, Garonne and Ariège. These form the isolated valley *pays*—the Vallée d'Aspe, the Vallée d'Ossau, the Val d'Aure and many more.

The eastern Pyrenees, to the east of the Col de la Perche, partake of a different character, since they consist fundamentally of a series of easterly trending ridges and massifs—Corbières, Canigou and Albères, penetrated by the longitudinal vales of the Agly (*Fenouillèdes*), the Têt (*Conflent*) and the Tech (*Vallespir*), each opening into the Plaine du Roussillon (see p. 438). The frontier here swings south along the eastern margins of the little state of Andorra, leaving the whole Carlitte massif and the upper part of the Segre valley (known as *Cerdagne*) in France. There are also high-level plateaus, notably those of Quérigut, Sault (sometimes known as the *Pays de Sault*)[14] and Capcir,[15] the upper valley of the Aude on the eastern flanks of Carlitte. Much of this lofty area, covered with glacial and fluvioglacial débris brought by the Quaternary glaciers from the adjacent mountains, lies above 1 500 m (5 000 ft).

The Corbières massif is not structurally part of the Pyrenees. Culminating in the Pic de Bugarach, it is a mass of Palaeozoic crystalline rocks similar in character to the Montagne Noire beyond the Aude valley.[16]

# Climate

The Pyrenees reveal the usual diversity of climatic features of mountainous areas, with both temperature and humidity modified locally by altitude and aspect. While the French Alps form a broad system trending from north to south, from continental to Mediterranean régimes, the Pyrenees are orientated from west to east, from Atlantic to Mediterranean régimes. The Pyrenees are neither so lofty nor so extensive, but nevertheless their climates reveal very considerable contrasts.

In the eastern Pyrenees conditions partake of the Mediterranean climatic régime, and the features of the plain of Roussillon (see p. 439) are gradually modified towards the west. The mean annual rainfall varies from about 660 to 840 mm (26 to 33 in); Mont-Louis in the Conflent receives 790 mm (31 in), two-thirds of which falls in intense downpours during the autumn months. There is a marked contrast in the precipitation received by places in the deep valleys and on the intervening uplands. The line of the Conflent and Cerdagne valleys, for example, forms in Faucher's expressive phrase, 'une sorte de couloir de sécheresse'; Puigcerda just inside Spain receives only 580 mm (23 in), while Canigou further east has a precipitation of 1 000 mm (40 in). This same contrast is shown in the valley of the upper Ariège; while Tarascon at 470 m (1 560 ft) receives 790 mm (31 in), Saurat 16 km (10 miles) to the west and at twice the altitude has 1 730 mm (68 in). Temperatures too vary strikingly with position and aspect; the valleys extending into the uplands from Roussillon have the same high temperatures in summer, with means of 21° to 24°C (70° to 75°F) in summer (Amélie-les-Bains in the Tech valley frequently records 29°C: 85°F), while on the surrounding plateaus snow lies for several months and can be expected regularly down to about 600 m (2 000 ft).

The western Pyrenees reveal, on the other hand, obvious indications of an Atlantic régime, with cloudier skies and an annual precipitation varying from 1 000 mm (40 in) to as much as 1 500 mm (60 in) on the west-facing ridges. The distinct autumn-winter maximum is the result of depressions moving eastwards from the Bay of Biscay to the Mediterranean along the northern flanks of the Pyrenees and through the Carcassonne gap. Hendaye, for example, has a mean annual precipitation of 940 mm (37 in); the driest month is July with 60 mm (2·4 in), the wettest is October with 140 mm (5·5 in).[17]

The central Pyrenees naturally form a zone of transition between east and west, though altitude and aspect induce considerable modifications. Thus Arreau at an altitude of 100 m (2 300 ft) receives 960 mm (38 in) of rain, compared with twice as much in the lofty Néouvielle massif to the west. The deep valleys of the western *gaves*, open to moist northwesterly air streams, have an appreciable rainfall; Laruns in the Gave d'Ossau about 1 630 mm (64 in). On the other hand, further up the *gaves* the total diminishes as the result of shelter; while Lourdes in the valley of the Gave de Pau at an altitude of 400 m (1 312 ft) has 1 300 mm (51 in), and Luz at 709 m (2 326 ft) only 890 mm (35 in). However, Gavarnie, higher up still at 1 356 m (4 450 ft) in its basin among high peaks, has 1 220 mm (48 in).

It must again be emphasised that locally the Pyrenean climates show great variations. As in all mountain regions, the importance of aspect is reflected in land use and settlement between the sunny side of a valley (the Alpine *adret*, known in the Pyrenees as the *soulane, sola* or *solana*) and the shady side (the *ubac* or *ubaga*).

## Snowfall

As the greater part of the precipitation is received during the winter half-year, much of it falls in the form of snow. The area of permanent snow is small in the Pyrenees, the result of their southerly latitude, limited altitude and exposure to mild air streams from the Mediterranean; during the long warm summer the snow vanishes from all but the highest summits and north-facing cirques. The permanent snowline therefore lies as high as 2 800 m (9 200 ft) even on the north side of the ranges. The winter snowfall is, however, considerable, much greater in the Pyrenees than in many parts of the Alps. The observatory on the summit of the Pic du Midi de Bigorre usually records a depth of at least 6 m (20 ft) during most winters; all the passes are blocked for varying lengths of time, many of the high villages are virtually isolated, and winter sports have developed in a number of places. The central Pyrenees are in fact covered on an average for a hundred days above 1 200 m (4 000 ft), for about 170 days above 1 800 m (6 000 ft). This duration of the snow cover is much shorter on the eastern flanks. The snowline retreats with amazing rapidity in early summer, and the mountains assume a piebald or striped aspect. Avalanches are widespread and swollen torrents foam down the valleys; many streams are in fact sustained in volume during the summer by snowmelt, especially valuable in the drier eastern valleys, which can use water from the melting snows of Canigou and Carlitte for irrigation.

## Land use and agriculture

Five *départements* whose southern boundaries coincide with the international frontier cover the French Pyrenees and their foothills. Pyrénées-Atlantiques in the west does, however, include the Basque coastlands and part of the Adour lowlands, while Pyrénées-Orientales contains the plain of Roussillon. Hautes-Pyrénées and Ariège consist almost entirely of the main ranges and foothills. Haute-Garonne is least representative of the Pyrenees, for, as its name would imply, it comprises for the most part the valley of the upper Garonne and includes that part of the Basin of Aquitaine around Toulouse; only a narrow 'peninsula' runs up the valley of the Pique to the frontier. The official returns for the other four *départements* do, however, afford some indication of land use in the Pyrenees generally.

*Land use, 1968 (percentage of total area)*

|  | PASTURE | PERMANENT PASTURE | WOODLAND |
|---|---|---|---|
| Pyrénées-Atlantiques | 22 | 22 | 19 |
| Hautes-Pyrénées | 16 | 28 | 26 |
| Ariège | 15 | 34 | 26 |
| Pyrénées-Orientales | 4 | 16 | 25 |

Source: Ministère de l'Agriculture, *Annuaire statistique de la France*, 1970–1.

### Woodlands

The character of the Pyrenean woodlands emphasises the contrasts between the Atlantic and Mediterranean margins. The more humid western uplands were once covered with magnificent forests of ash, which still clothe the steeper slopes, together with considerable areas of chestnut. The largest forest is that of Irati,[18] which runs up to and beyond the frontier to the west of the Pic d'Orhy. In the central Pyrenees the beech is dominant on lower slopes, succeeded by spruce, mountain pine, larch and Scotch fir. On the valley floors, where not cleared for agriculture, are copses and lines of planes, poplars, maple, hazel, lime, birch and alder. In the east the various Mediterranean oaks (especially kerm and cork oaks) gradually become dominant, with pines at higher altitudes.[19]

The story of the gradual past destruction of the forests is much the same as elsewhere in western Europe; the iron forges of the Pyrenean valleys required charcoal, trees were felled for timber, especially for shipbuilding, and the farmers attacked the woodland both from above and below to increase their pasture and arable land. Frequently they resorted to burning to produce the cleared lands. The flocks and herds, especially of goats, prevented regeneration by their close grazing; in the western Pyrenees constant pollarding of the ash trees to provide green shoots for fodder ultimately destroyed many trees. Devastation has been worse in the eastern uplands, where much of the former woodland has degenerated into either a *garrigue* of thyme, lavender, dwarf laurel, oleander, aloe and cistus on the limestones, or a *maquis* of dwarf evergreen oak, broom, box and other shrubs on siliceous rocks. Much land in the east and centre is smothered with a dense low scrub of dwarf rhododendron, which, masking the uneven boulderstrewn surface, forms difficult terrain to cross. In the moister west the bracken fern has spread widely; it can be cut for litter but it spoils much grazing land.

Some afforestation has been effected during this century, and many of the Pyrenean valleys owe much of their charm to their wooded appearance. The forested area has in fact been increased by almost a quarter during the last sixty years. Some of this is planted as avalanche breaks on the hillsides, or to check landslides. Both state owned and communally owned forests have increased appreciably in area.

## Pastoral farming

The table on p. 667 clearly indicates that both *la vie pastorale* and *la vie agricole* contribute to the Pyrenean economy, the former dominating in the high valleys, the latter in the east and on the Aquitaine margins.

In the four *départements* the numbers of sheep (649 000) and of cattle (489 000) are the result of a long steady decline during the last century in the former and a corresponding increase in the latter. Most of the livestock are found in the west and centre, and Pyrénées-Atlantiques had more than a third of each. Several breeds of sheep are represented, some the product of merino crosses; in the high mountains can be seen some attractive long-haired varieties. They are kept for wool, meat and milk; in the central Pyrenees much ewes' milk cheese is made, while from farther east 'raw' cheese is sent to Roquefort for final processing. More lamb and mutton is eaten in the towns and villages along the Pyrenean flanks than in any other part of France.

Cattle are also more common in the west and centre; only 10 000 animals, mostly in the high basins, were recorded for Pyrénées-Orientales in 1968. They are kept both for dairying to supply milk to the Pyrenean towns and for making the various *fromages des Pyrénées*, and also to sell off as stores to the farmers in the plain of Aquitaine and as calves for veal in the markets of Bordeaux and Toulouse. Many are still used as draught animals, especially in the high valleys. Goats totalled only 9 000 in 1968, more than half of them kept in the *garrigue* country of the east; the herds of silky *chèvres noires* are a familiar sight high up on the mountains. The western Pyrenean valleys have long been famous for horse-rearing; these animals are still widely used for draught purposes. About 21 000 were present in 1968. In some valleys herds of brood mares are kept, from which mules are bred (especially in the head valleys of the Ariège) for export to Spain.

A pattern of life has evolved which utilises pastures at different altitudes at various times.[20] The water-meadows on the flat valley floors are crossed by countless runnels fed by the streams descending the steep sides; here the animals graze in spring and autumn, while in summer a crop, sometimes two, of hay is taken. The area devoted to fodder crops has increased appreciably, notably of lucerne grown under irrigation. In winter the cattle are stall-fed and many sheep move down to the gravel-covered plateau of Lannemezan, to the lower lands of Armagnac, to the Adour lowlands, and in the east to the lowlands of Languedoc.

In summer large numbers of animals are taken up to the high pastures, following the receding snowline. Some are open grass slopes on the mountain sides, others on valley benches near the little summer hamlets are carefully surrounded by dry-stone walls and improved by fertilising. The name *estives* is sometimes given to these high pastures, hence the term *estivage* used for the summer pasturing of animals in the Pyrenees and other mountainous districts. The families looking after the animals live in little summer hamlets, or in isolated huts.[21] For centuries the *montagnards* have jealously guarded their rights of movement and pasturage, frequently held in common by a group of communal proprietors; they could, for example, lay down the exact date of opening a particular pasture to the animals and of its closure to grazing. The movement of the animals follows routes delineated by long custom, and safeguarded by 'treaties of covenanted entry'. These rights are especially common and jealously preserved in Canigou and Carlitte, where the sheep come up from the Mediterranean coastlands. Though transhumance and stock-rearing generally has declined during recent decades, as evidenced by the many deserted farms and huts in the hills, this routine of life still persists in many Pyrenean valleys.[22] One reason for the decline in the movement of cattle is that now many remain on the valley floors during the summer, when their milk finds a ready market in the popular resorts. Another development has been of cooperation in the handling and processing of milk, and numerous collecting points are served by fleets of lorries. Butter and cheese factories have been established at many towns in the lower parts of the valleys.[23]

## Arable farming

Within this upland area there is inevitably a scarcity of good soil, and small-scale cultivation is found practised where possible on valley floors away from the water-meadows, on alluvial fans, and on carefully terraced slopes, usually with the lower edges of the fields protected by dry-stone walls. Some of the high basins have flat floors of alluvial soil under a continuous carpet of strip-cultivation. Some land has been improved by fertilising, as evidenced by the replacement of buckwheat and rye in favour of hard wheat or in the west of maize. Much poor or marginal land has been turned into improved pasture or put under fodder crops. Each of the four *départements* has more than half of its arable area devoted to cereals, except for Pyrénées-Orientales where it falls to a third. Pyrénées-Atlantiques and Ariège have a third of their arable areas under fodder crops, the others about a fifth. The overall pattern is thus generally very similar. But in detail contrasts between the western and eastern uplands are again apparent.

In the west maize rivals wheat, with rye in the higher valleys, and large areas of potatoes, haricots, pumpkins and other vegetables are cultivated. There are some vineyards, but the orchards of apples, cherries and plums are far more extensive. Groves of walnuts and hazel-nuts are succeeded on higher slopes by woods of sweet chestnut. In the lower valleys, market gardens now cover a large area, supplying the tourist centres during the summer months. In the central Pyrenees wheat increasingly supersedes maize, and rye and potatoes are grown in the higher valleys. Peaches, apricots and vines appear on sunny south-facing slopes.

In the eastern Pyrenees[2] the agricultural systems are really tongue-like extensions of the Mediterranean patterns of the plain of Roussillon.[24] Among the rock ridges of the Corbières and the Albères, with their stony wastes, has developed a typical Mediterranean terrace cultivation of vines, olives, almonds, peaches, apricots, even oranges and pomegranates in favoured places, nurtured by streams from the melting snows of Canigou. On the high plains of Capcir and Cerdagne are orchards of pear, plum and cherry, growing dessert fruit for the Paris markets; the pears of Osseja and the cherries of Céret[25] (the upper Tech valley) are renowned, the former being the first to arrive on the markets of northern France. Elsewhere fields of hard wheat are cultivated in small basins. In some of the higher valleys and basins, such as the Conflent, much land is devoted to the cultivation of grass for hay and of fodder crops by intensive fertilising and irrigating; this provides winter feed for the cattle coming down from the high pastures. Apples are specially grown in these high valleys.

## Power and industry

### Hydroelectric power

The Pyrenees possess a large potential, as yet only partially realised, of hydroelectric power,[26] for they have the advantages of copious precipitation, long yet accessible steepsided valleys running far into the uplands towards the main crestline, and a multitude of rock basin lakes at a high altitude which require only small barrages to increase their storage capacity appreciably. Many of these lakes are at heights exceeding 1 800 m (6 000 ft), and their outflow into the main valley provides a fine natural head. A few larger barrages have been constructed to create new reservoirs, such as Puyvalador at a height of 1 400 m (4 600 ft) in Capcir. But there has been no construction of major barrages as in the Alps and the Rhône valley.

The emphasis has been on the creation of a large number of small enterprises, rather than of a few major stations. Development started rather later and more slowly in this relatively isolated part of France, to meet local industrial needs and to supply the electrified lines of the former *Midi* railway company. The first high tension transmission lines in France were in fact built from small stations in the Aude valley to Carcassonne and Narbonne as early as 1901. In 1910 the Orlu station in the valley of the upper Ariège had a head of water supplied by a chute of 940 m (3 071 ft), at that time the highest in Europe. After the war of 1914–18 much progress was made, stimulated by electrification of the railways carried out by the Midi company. By 1939 the Paris-Hendaye line had been electrified throughout, together with the transverse line from Bayonne via Toulouse to Béziers and also the two trans-Pyrenean lines. Since the war of 1939–45, Electricité de France and the SNCF have pursued a steady policy of development. Several new generating-stations have been constructed, and the considerable activity of the immediate postwar years culminated in the opening of a number of major stations. Most are small in comparison with those of the Alps and Rhône valley, and only four (Miégebat, Pragnères, Aston and Portillon) have an installed capacity exceeding 50 mW.

The main transformer stations are at Laruns and Pau for the western group of stations, at Lannemezan for the central group, and at Sabart in the east. While the power stations mainly supply local industry and the railways, they also make a contribution to the grid.

At the beginning of 1970 the total installed capacity of the Pyrenean stations was 1 910 mW, responsible for an output in 1969 of about one-tenth of the total French hydroproduction.

**Industry**

The Pyrenean valleys are the scene of two contrasting types of industrial activity, as in the Alps, though developed to a far less degree. On the one hand are the old craft industries, on the other the new factory industries based on hydroelectricity. The former made use of locally produced wool, flax and hemp, of timber from the mountain forests both for fabrication and for charcoal-burning, of small deposits of iron and non-ferrous ores, and of plentiful supplies of fresh water. Many activities grew as the result of isolation and the need for self-sufficiency; these included the spinning and weaving of woollen cloth for clothing. Later the manufacture of cotton and silk developed; these textile industries were widely spread.[27] Wood-using

671

industries included the manufacture of clogs and *sabots* (especially in the Pays Basque), of furniture, rosaries and religious statuary. Iron ore has been mined, smelted with charcoal and used at the forges for many centuries, in Canigou since at least the twelfth century. The forges at Baïgorry and Banca in the west, at Louvie and Arthey in the *gave* valleys, at Foix (one of the chief sources of French wrought iron under the *ancien régime*) and elsewhere made iron objects in great variety, including cannon for the French navy.

Many small-scale attempts have been made to mine and refine various non-ferrous ores, including even gold from the river gravels; the hillsides reveal here and there the scars of ancient workings but little has been won, and as Faucher expresses it, 'quant aux mines, hormis celles de fer, quelle lamentable histoire'.

The iron and steel industry has a considerable presentday importance. The ore, mostly haematite of 50 to 60 per cent metal content, is found in the limestones of the Ariège valley, and in Canigou (Fig. 11.7). While many of the small scattered deposits are now exhausted, the Pyrenean mines still make a fluctuating contribution. In 1913 they produced 370 000 tons, but during the economic crisis between 1932 to 1936 output fell to a mere 22 000 tons. Since the war the deposits have been vigorously worked, and the yield had been increased to 310 000 tons by 1960, though it had fallen to only 50 000 tons by 1968. The modern Pyrenean steel industry dates from the opening of blast furnaces at Tarascon in 1864–67, using coke from Decazeville and Carmaux; later electric furnaces were installed at Pamiers. These two centres still produce about 20 000 tons of steel a year, mostly high-grade alloys or special quality steels. Some special steels are also made in electric furnaces at Rebouc, various alloys at St Antoine and ferro-silicates at Mercus.

The availability of power has facilitated some development of the electro-chemical and electrometallurgical industries.[28] Aluminium is refined at Auzat and Sabart in the Vicdessos valley, at Beyrède in the Aure valley, and at Lannemezan. In the Gave de Pau chemical factories manufacture nitrogenous and phosphoric fertilisers. A factory at Beyrède near Sarrancolin in the Aure valley makes carborundum abrasives, Boussens in the Garonne valley also has a chemical factory, as has Lannemezan, and Marignac near the Garonne-Pique confluence produces explosives. These factories form small oases of industrial activity in the Pyrenean valleys. A rather more extensive area of industrialisation on the Pyrenean flanks is the triangle between Tarbes, Lourdes and Bagnères-de-Bigorre.[29] Here are located a factory which makes insulators, a large electrical and mechanical engineering plant, an arsenal, two electrical and mechanical engineering plants (one making equipment for the SNCF), and an aircraft works at Ossun.

Quarrying is still active, working limestone for cement in the valley of the Oloron, and marble to be processed at Bagnères; part of Napoleon's

PLATE 65. A Pyrenean valley: the thermal spa of Cauterets, situated on the banks of the Gave de Cauterets

tomb in Les Invalides in Paris came from Pyrenean quarries. One large-scale operation is the quarrying of talc (hydrous magnesium silicate), which occurs as large interlaminations within masses of mica-schist, and is worked at the quarry of Trimouns in the St Barthélemy massif. This, with an annual output of 85 000 tons, is the largest individual talc quarry in the world, and France once had a near monopoly of this material, though today only about 10 per cent of the world output is produced.

One further contribution to the economic life of the Pyrenean region is the tourist industry, utilising the attractive scenery of mountain, forest and stream, the heavy winter snowfall which has encouraged winter sports, and numerous mineral springs. More than fifty places have become spas, based on the mineralised springs which issue either from the margins of igneous intrusions or from the Triassic rocks; many towns have in their names the elements *eaux*, *thermes* or *bains*.[2] Le Boulou in the valley of the Tech is sometimes known as 'the Vichy of the Pyrenees'.[30] Towns such as Pau (see p. 358) and Lourdes are indeed 'the gateways to the Pyrenees', and Cauterets is also a winter-sports centre (Plate 65).

## Settlement and communications

It is obvious that the Pyrenees stand out as one of the sparsely populated parts of France; in 1968 the average density per square kilometre in

Hautes-Pyrénées was 50 (130 per sq mile), in Ariège only 28 (73 per sq mile). Further, the population of the higher valleys is steadily declining, a phenomenon common in many of the mountainous parts of Europe.[31] Large areas on the high frontier ridges, on the dissected plateaus between the north-flowing rivers, and on the steep forested slopes, are quite un-populated. Between these empty areas long strips of population extend along the valley floors; at their heads are the temporary summer dwellings of the shepherds and a few permanently inhabited villages such as Gavarnie on the Gave de Pau. Farther down are larger settlements—small market towns, resorts[2] and sometimes centres of small industries. Longitudinal (west–east) communications were for long difficult or impossible, and so the contacts of each valley have tended to be with the margins of the plain of Aquitaine to the north. Small towns therefore grew up at the mouths of the valleys—St Jean-Pied-de-Port and Mauléon in the west; Arudy, Lourdes, Bagnères-de-Bigorre and Montréjeau in the centre; Foix in the east. The development of industries in the triangle between Tarbes, Lourdes and Bagnères-de-Bigorre has led to an area of dense population; there are over 73 000 people in Tarbes and its six adjacent communes in what forms an *agglomération bigourdane*. Towns on the southern edge of the plain of Aquitaine, such as Pau, Tarbes and Pamiers, act as minor regional centres for the uplands to the south, and indeed the spheres of influence of Bayonne, Toulouse and Perpignan extend into the Pyrenees.

In the extreme west lives a group of people, the Basques, whose identity has given rise to the district name of *Pays Basque*.[32] The Basque tongue (an interesting linguistic problem since it seems to be related to no modern European language) is spoken by about 100 000 people in France, and by five times as many in Spain. Though divided by the frontier, the Basques retain much individuality besides their language (though only those living in remote valleys do not speak French as well), including their customs, folk-dancing, costume and their game of *pelote*.

## Communications

The limited pattern of communications reflects the difficulties of the mountain terrain. The south–north valleys contain cul-de-sac roads, linked with one main longitudinal route (N117) which runs from Bayonne via Pau, Tarbes and Foix to Perpignan, parallel to the frontier but 40 to 50 km (25 to 30 miles) away from it. Other links between the Pyrenean valleys are indeed difficult; it is possible to cross from the valley of the Ossau to that of the Pau over the winding Cols de Soulor and d'Aubisque, or from Pau to the Adour valley by the magnificent road over the Col de Tourmalet. These and other roads have been considerably improved in recent years to cope with the tourist traffic. But many of the high valleys are linked, if at all, only by mule-tracks. A continuous *Route des Pyrénées* can be followed only in the east. Most of the roads in the High Pyrenees are snow-blocked from November to May or even later.

Many tracks lead up to the high passes on the frontier ridge, and five cross into Spain—the Roncesvalles in the west, the Somport and the Pourtalet near the Pic du Midi d'Ossau, the Envalira and the Puymorens. The highest, the Envalira, rises to 2 407 m (7 897 ft), linking Ax-les-Thermes via the little state of Andorra to Lerida; it is blocked until late June. Another road into Spain follows the valley of the Garonne from St Béat into the Val d'Aran and on to Viella, from where one can proceed to Lerida either via the Col de Bonaigua or by the road tunnel under the Col de Viella. The easiest routes into Spain are by way of the west flank from Bayonne either to San Sebastian or Pamplona, from the Têt to the Segre valley by the low Col de la Perche, and in the east from Perpignan over the Col du Perthus.

The Pyrenean railway systems are even more limited, although the Hendaye and Cerbère lines around the western and eastern flanks were opened as early as 1864 and 1878 respectively. The Col de la Perche was traversed by a narrow-gauge line to the Spanish frontier at Bourg-Madame in 1911, but a crossing of the main frontier ridge was not effected until 1928, when the line over the Col de Somport was opened; this required sixteen tunnels, including one at the summit (altitude 1 631 m: 5 351 ft) nearly 8 km (5 miles) long. In the following year another line was completed from Ax-les-Thermes up the Ariège valley to the Col de Puymorens, under which the line passes in a tunnel nearly 5·6 km (3·5 miles) long at a height of 1 567 m (5 141 ft), then descending to the frontier station of La Tour-de-Carol. These two lines are but little used, except for tourist traffic within France, for the change of gauge at the Spanish frontier prevents any through traffic.

[1] M. Sorre, *Les Pyrénées* (1922, several editions), is one of the 'classic' French regional monographs. For a further general account, see P. Arque, *Géographie des Pyrénées françaises* (1943). More recent publications are G. Viers, *Les Pyrénées* (1962); and R. Brunet *et al.*, *Les Pyrénées françaises* (1961), Edsco Documents.

[2] P. Brunet, 'Recherches morphologiques sur les Corbières', *Mém. et Documents du Centre* (1958), pp. 59–134.

[3] P. Barrère, 'Le relief des massifs granitiques de Néouvielle, de Cauterets et de Panticosa', *Rev. géogr. Pyr. S.-O.*, **23** (1952), pp. 69–98; this contains maps of the massifs and some fine air-photographs. For a detailed account, see Ch. Jacob, *Zone axiale, versant sud et versant nord des Pyrénées (Livre jubilaire du Centenaire de la Société géologique de France*, 1930).

[4] N. Casteret, *Ten Years under the Earth* (English translation by B. Mussey, 1940), pp. 218–35.

[5] N. Casteret, 'L'abîme le plus profond de France: le Gouffre Martel', *La Montagne*, **62** (1936), pp. 333–6.

[6] Full accounts are given, translated from the French, by H. Tazieff, *Caves of Adventure* (1953), and N. Casteret, *The Descent of Pierre St Martin* (1955).

[7] N. Casteret, *Ten Years under the Earth* (1940), pp. 218–35.

[8] The most convenient summary of Pyrenean glaciation is F. Taillefer, 'Glaciaire pyrénéen: versant nord et versant sud', *Rev. géogr. Pyr. S.-O.*, **28** (1957), pp. 221–44; this

provides a map of the glaciers and moraines, a table of the glacial chronology, and a detailed bibliography.

[9] The extent and names of the present glaciers are shown by P. Barrère, 'Equilibre glaciaire actuel et quaternaire dans l'ouest des Pyrénées Centrales', *Rev. géogr. Pyr. S.-O.*, **24** (1953), pp. 116–34; there is a detailed map on p. 118.

[10] See, for example, D. Faucher, 'Le glacier de l'Ariège dans la basse vallée montagnarde', *Rev. Géogr. alp.*, **20** (1932), pp. 573–89.

[11] For an immensely detailed study of the results of glaciation in the Couserans (the basin of the Salat), see M. Chevalier, 'Le relief glaciaire des Pyrénées du Couserans', *Rev. géogr. Pyr. S.-O.*, **25** (1954), I, 'Les cirques' (pp. 97–124), II, 'Les vallées' (pp. 189–220); this contains detailed maps and some valuable air photographs. See also H. Awad, 'La morphologie de la vallée d'Ossau', *Annls Géogr.*, **48** (1939), pp. 449–58; this deals with the imposition of ice upon the structural and preglacial features, and includes a detailed map of ridges, cirques, moraines, etc. See also G. Viers, 'Le glaciaire du massif du Carlit', *Rev. géogr. Pyr. S.-O.*, **32** (1961), pp. 6–33, with detailed maps.

[12] L. Gaurier, *Les Lacs des Pyrénées françaises* (1934).

[13] These are plotted on a map in Taillefer, *op. cit.*, p. 222.

[14] J.-J. Lagasquie, 'Le relief calcaire du plateau de Sault', *Rev. géogr. Pyr. S.-O.*, **35** (1964), pp. 11–32.

[15] R. Lambert, 'Le Capcir: évolution récente d'un haut bassin des Pyrénées-Orientales', *Rev. Géogr. Pyr. S.-O.*, **36** (1965), pp. 5–22.

[16] J. Malaurie, 'Le relief des Corbières orientales', *Annls Géogr.*, **59** (1950), pp. 259–68, contains a detailed morphological map and sections of the massif.

[17] Features of the climate and vegetation zones of the western Pyrenees are given by H. Boesch, 'Die Natur im Baskenland', *Geographica Helvetica*, **10** (1955), pp. 136–44.

[18] G. Viers, 'La Forêt d'Irati', *Rev. géogr. Pyr. S.-O.*, **26** (1955), pp. 5–27; this deals with past destruction and present measures of maintenance and afforestation.

[19] See (*a*) M. Sorre, *Les Pyrénées méditerranéennes. Etude de géographie biologique* (1913); (*b*) H. Gaussen, *Végétation de la moitié orientale des Pyrénées* (1926); and (*c*) by the same author, *Géographie botanique et agricole des Pyrénées-Orientales* (1934).

[20] Much has been written on this subject. See, for example, H. Cavaillès, *La Vie pastorale et agricole dans les Pyrénées des Gaves, de l'Adour et des Nestes. Etude de géographie humaine* (1931); and M. Chevalier, *La Vie humaine dans les Pyrénées ariégeoises* (1956). The latter is a monumental volume of 1061 pp., with 854 references, many maps and some superb photographs.

[21] These are given numerous local names, including *cayolars, jasses, cujalas, orrys, orhys, bordes* and *pardinas*. The multiplicity of these and other names is due to the fact that in the Pyrenees are spoken Basque, Catalan and the *languedocien, gascon* and *béarnais* dialects.

[22] See, for example, in addition to M. Chevalier (*op. cit.*), (*a*) H. Cavaillès, *La Transhumance pyrénéenne et la circulation des troupeaux dans les plaines de Gascogne* (1931); (*b*) M. Chevalier, 'Les caractères de la vie pastorale dans le bassin supérieur de l'Ariège', *Rev. géogr. Pyr. S.-O.* **20** (1949), pp. 5–84; and (*c*) Th. Lefebvre, 'La transhumance dans les Basses-Pyrénées', *Annls Géogr.*, **38** (1928), pp. 35–60. The last distinguishes five distinct types of movement, and provides two detailed maps (pp. 39 and 53) which show actual routes between the villages and their habitual hill pastures in summer and the lowland pastures of Aquitaine in winter. See also G. Bertrand, 'Vie pastorale et industrie dans le Val d'Ariège', *Rev. géogr. Pyr. S.-O.*, **32** (1961), pp. 63–73.

[23] For example, see M. Bressole and M. Chevalier, 'L'industrie laitière dans les Pyrénées Ariégeoises', *Rev. géogr. Pyr. S.-O.*, **22** (1951), pp. 71–90; this pays special attention to the Ballongue, where the canton of Castillon is known as *le pays des fruitières*.

[24] An attractive study of land use in an east Pyrenean upland valley, based on intensive field-work, is given by R. Peattie, 'The Conflent: a study in mountain geography', *Geogrl. Rev.*, **20** (1930), pp. 245–57.

[25] For a detailed study of orchard cultivation in the high valleys, see P. Fénelon, 'La culture des cerisiers dans la région de Céret', *Rev. géogr. Pyr. S.-O.*, **23** (1952), pp. 5–28.

[26] A summary of the position before the war of 1939–45, with details of installations, is afforded by L. Babonneau, *L'Energie électrique dans la région pyrénéenne* (1941). A more recent study is R. Brunet, 'L'Equipement électrique des Pyrénées', *Rev. géogr. Pyr. S.-O.,* **33** (1962), pp. 123–8.

[27] M. Chevalier, 'L'industrie textile pyrénéenne et le développement de Lavelanet', *Rev. géogr. Pyr. S.-O.,* **21** (1950), pp. 43–60; this includes a map showing the location of former and contemporary factories (p. 44).

[28] Y. Doumergue, 'Electro-chimie et électro-métallurgie dans les Hautes-Pyrénées', *Rev. géog. Pyr. S.-O.,* **36** (1965), pp. 373–402.

[29] P. Duchemin, 'L'industrie moderne à Tarbes et dans sa région', *Rev. géogr. Pyr. S.-O.,* **26** (1955), pp. 176–89.

[30] Details, with a map, are given by R. Balseinte, 'Les stations thermales françaises', *Rev. géogr. Pyr. S.-O.,* **26** (1955), pp. 292–306.

[31] This problem is discussed by G. Lesenne, 'Le dépeuplement des vallées d'Argelès, d'Azun et de Cauterets: ses causes et ses conséquences', *Rev. géogr. Pyr. S.-O.,* **27** (1956), pp. 135–60.

[32] G. Viers, *Pays Basque français et Barretous* (1961).

# Bibliographical note

Footnotes have been used throughout the text to indicate books and articles to which specific reference has been made. The names of journals quoted frequently are abbreviated, as shown in the following list; those to which only rare reference is made are quoted in full.

## Abbreviations

| | |
|---|---|
| *Ann. Ass. Am. Geogr.* | *Annals of the Association of American Geographers* |
| *Annls Géogr.* | *Annales de Géographie* |
| *Bull. Assoc. Géogr. franc.* | *Bulletin de l'Association des Géographes française* |
| *Bull. Soc. belge Etud. geogr.* | *Bulletin de la Société Belge des Etudes Géographiques* |
| *Bull. Soc. roy. belge Géogr.* | *Bulletin de la Société Royal Belge de Géographie* |
| *Bull. Soc. belge Géol.* | *Bulletin de la Société Belge* |
| *Cah. outre-mer* | *Cahiers d'Outre-mer* |
| *Econ. Geogr.* | *Economic Geography* |
| *Geogr. J.* | *Geographical Journal* |
| *Geogr. Rev.* | *Geographical Review* |
| *Rev. Agric.* | *Revue de l'Agriculture (Bruxelles)* |
| *Rev. Géogr. alp.* | *Revue de Géographie Alpine* |
| *Rev. géogr. Pyr. S.-O.* | *Revue géographique des Pyrénées et du Sud-Ouest* |
| *Rev. belge Géog.* | *Revue Belge de Géographie* |
| *Rev. Navig. intér. rhén.* | *Revue de la Navigation Intérieure et Rhénane* |
| *Tijdschr. econ. soc. Geogr.* | *Tijdschrift voor Economische en Sociale Geografie* |
| *Tijdschr. K. ned. aardrijksk. Genoot.* | *Tijdschrift van het Koninklijk Nederlandsch Aardrijkskundig Genootschap* |
| *Tn Plann. Rev.* | *Town Planning Review* |
| *Trans. Inst. Br. Geogr.* | *Transactions of the Institute of British Geographers* |

678

References quoted in the footnotes are not repeated below, except where they are of specific interest. It is necessary to summarise here more general sources, including statistical material.

## Statistical sources

Each of the four countries has an active government statistical department. These are (i) for Belgium the *Institut National de Statistique* (44 Rue de Louvain, Bruxelles); (ii) for France the *Institut Nationale de la Statistique et des Etudes Economiques* (29 Quai Branly, Paris, 7ᵉ); (iii) for Luxembourg the *Office de la Statistique Générale* (19 Avenue de la Porte-Neuve, Luxembourg); and (iv) for the Netherlands the *Centraal Bureau voor Statistiek* ('s-Graven-hage). Each of these organisations publishes a statistical year-book of immense value: the *Annuaire statistique de la Belgique*, the *Annuaire statistique de la France*, the *Annuaire statistique (Grand-Duché de Luxembourg)* (though this is actually published quinquennially) and the *Jaarcijfers voor Nederland* (published biennially). Each of these lists as an appendix the considerable number of other more specialised publications which cover every aspect of national life.

## Belgium

1. *Bibliographie géographique de la Belgique,* compiled by M. E. Dumont and L. de Smet (1954 and 1960); this is a vast compendium of references.
2. *Atlas de Belgique,* in course of publication by the *Comité National de Géographie*; this provides a series of beautifully printed maps on the standard scale of 1:500 000.
3. A. Demangeon, *Belgique–Pays-Bas–Luxembourg* (1927), which is the second volume of the *Géographie universelle*.
4. M. A. Lefèvre, *Notice sur la carte oro-hydrographique de Belgique à* 1:500 000 (1937), which provides an admirable summary of the structure and relief of the country.
5. W. Tuckermann, *Länderkunde der Niederlande und Belgiens* (1931).
6. Y. van Wettere-Verhasselt, 'Les Frontières du nord et de l'est de la Belgique', monograph published in the *Revue belge de Géographie* (1965), no. 89, with 400 pp. and a bibliography of 885 references.

## Benelux

1. F. Dussart, *Le Benelux* (1958).
2. A. Gamblin, *Géographie du Benelux* (1960).
3. F. Gay and P. Wagret, *Le Benelux* (1965).
4. P. George and R. Sevrin, *Belgique, Pays-Bas, Luxembourg* (1967), a recent survey of 282 pp.

## France

1. *Régions géographiques de la France* (1953), produced by a *Commission Centrale* (including E. de Martonne and M. Cholley) for the *Institut National de la Statistique et des Etudes Economiques,* with a most useful folding-map of regions and sub-regions.

2. *Atlas de France,* prepared by the *Comité National de Géographie* founded in 1920, under the sponsorship of the *Académie des Sciences.* Of the eighty-two projected sheets, sixty-nine had been produced before the war. Between 1951 and 1958 a revised edition appeared, with a number of additional sheets.

3. *Atlas aérien,* edited by P. Deffontaines and M.-J. Brunhes-Delamarre, a series of five volumes of magnificent air photographs, with accompanying maps and text. Each major region of France is reviewed.

4. Regional atlases include *Atlas de la France de l'Est* (1960); and *Atlas du Nord* (1961). A vast amount of information is provided by the 46 maps and 200 pp. of accompanying text in *Atlas industriel de la France* (1959).

5. National planning in France is discussed by P. Bauchet, *La Planification française; quinze ans d'expérience* (1962); J. Fourastié and P. Courthéoux, *La Planification économique en France* (1963); and F. Coront-Ducluzeau, *La Formation de l'espace économique nationale* (1964).

6. Ph. Ariès, *Le Peuplement et les migrations intérieures en France métropolitaine* (1961).

7. O. Barré, *L'Architecture du sol de la France* (1903).

8. J. Beaujeu-Garnier, *Le Relief de la France par la carte et le croquis* (1953).

9. J. Beaujeu-Garnier, *La Population française* (1969).

10. L. Bertrand, *Les Grandes Régions géologiques du sol français* (1935).

11. L. Bertrand, *Histoire géologique du sol français* (two volumes, 1944, 1946).

12. P. Vidal de la Blache, *Tableau de la géographie de la France* (1911); this is *Tome I, première partie,* of *Histoire de France illustrée.*

13. J. Brunhes, *Géographie humaine de la France* (two volumes, 1920) (*tome 1^er de l'Histoire de la Nation française,* edited by G. Hanotaux).

14. F. Carrière and Ph. Pinchemel, *Le Fait urbain en France* (1963).

15. G. Chabot, *Géographie régionale de la France* (1966).

16. J. Chardonnet, *Géographie industrielle,* vol. I, 'Les sources d'énergie' (1962).

17. A. Cholley, R. Clazier and J. Dresch, *La France* (n.d.).

18. A. Dauzat, *La Vie rurale en France* (1961).

19. A. Demangeon, *Géographie économique et humaine de la France, 2^e et 3^e vol. du tome vi de la Géographie universelle* (1946, 1948).

20. R. Dion, *Les Frontières de la France* (1947).

21. D. Faucher, with twenty-five contributors, *La France: géographie-tourisme* (1951–2). This magnificent work published by Larousse, in two volumes, describes France on a regional basis, with a wealth of maps and photographs.

22. J. Fèvre and H. Hauser, *Régions et pays de France* (1909).
23. J. Fourastié and H. Montet, *L'Economie française dans le Monde* (1962).
24. L. Gallois, *Régions naturelles et noms de pays* (1911), a classic exposition of French regional geography.
25. L. Gallouédec and F. Maurette, *Géographie de la France* (n.d.).
26. A. Gamblin, *L'Energie en France, étude de géographie* (1961).
27. P. George, *La France* (1967).
28. P. George, *Géographie économique et sociale de la France* (1946).
29. L. Gorny, *Les Economies régionales en France* (1958).
30. E. Jarry, *Provinces et pays de France: essai de géographie historique* (1950).
31. L. de Launay, *Géologie de la France* (1921); this provides a clear account of the regional geology, with a series of folding maps.
32. M. le Lannou, *Les Régions géographiques de la France* (1963).
33. P. Mallet, *La Structure économique de la France* (1958).
34. E. de Martonne, *Les Régions géographiques de la France* (1921).
35. E. de Martonne, *Les Grandes Régions de la France* (1926).
36. E. de Martonne, *Géographie physique de la France* (1947), *1ᵉʳ vol. du tome vi de la Géographie universelle.*
37. E. de Martonne, *France physique* (1942).
38. J. Moniez, *L'Industrie charbonnière française depuis 1946* (1959).
39. H. Ormsby, *France: A Regional and Economic Geography* (1931, second edition 1950).
40. P. Pinchemel, *La Géographie de la France* (1964), two volumes, with a detailed bibliography, perhaps the most comprehensive modern textbook on France, with subsequent editions. English translation, *France: A Geographical Survey*, translated by C. Trollope and A. J. Hunt (1969).
41. C. Précheur, *La Sidérurgie française* (1963).
42. D. I. Scargill, *Economic Geography of France* (1968).
43. J.-M. Sourdillat, *Géographie agricole de la France* (1959).
44. I. B. Thompson, *Modern France* (1970).
45. A. Vigarié, *Les Grands Ports de commerce de la Seine au Rhin* (1964), with an atlas.
46. A most attractive series of texts on the regions of France, entitled *France de Demain*, under the general direction of F.-L. Closon and P. George, has been published since 1959 by *Presses Universitaires de France* (Paris). The country is covered in eight volumes.

## Luxembourg

1. A. Demangeon, *Belgique–Pays-Bas–Luxembourg* (1927), which is the second volume of the *Géographie universelle.*
2. J. Robert, *Geologische Heimatkunde von Luxembourg* (1916).
3. C. Stevens, *Note sur la morphologie du Grand-Duché de Luxembourg interprétée d'après la carte hypsométrique à 1/200,000 de J. Hansen* (1928).

4. *Atlas du Luxembourg,* produced by the Department of Geography of the University of Nottingham, and published by the *Ministère de l'Education Nationale,* Luxembourg.

## Netherlands

1. A. Demangeon, *Belgique–Pays-Bas–Luxembourg* (1927), which is the second volume of the *Géographie universelle.*
2. *Comptes-Rendus du Congrès International de Géographie, Amsterdam, 1938;* this contains numerous accounts of various aspects of the country.
3. C. H. Edelman, *Soils of the Netherlands* (1950); this includes a most detailed folding map on a scale of 1/400 000.
4. F. J. Faber, *Geologie van Nederland* (1933).
5. A. M. Lambert, *The Making of the Dutch Landscape* (1971).
6. G. J. A. Mulder (edited), *Handboek der Geografie van Nederland* (1949–55); this great work deals with the country both subjectively and by regions.
7. M. Schuchart, *The Netherlands* (1972).
8. R. Schuiling, *Nederland, Handboek der Ardrijkskunde* (two volumes, 1934, 1936).
9. A. J. Pannekoek (editor), *Geological History of the Netherlands* (1956); this detailed explanation to the Geological Map of the Netherlands on a scale of 1/200 000, in English, is illustrated with a large number of maps and plates, and includes many bibliographical references.
10. The *Atlas van Nederland,* to comprise 101 maps, with a number of smaller plans and explanatory text (with English translation), is in course of publication.

# Index

*Note.* 1. Strict alphabetical order is maintained, including composite and hyphenated names. The proper name is given first (e.g. Blanc, Mont), except where the generic name has been integrated (e.g. Mont-Louis), and also where Grand-, Petit, Haut- and Bas- are used.

2. References to maps and their captions are indicated by (fig.) after the particular page number; to plates by (pl.).

3. More important page references are given in heavy type.

4. Alternative place-name forms are indexed, and cross-referred to the form actually used in the text.

5. The following abbreviations are used: C. *Canal*; E. *Etang*; F. *Forêt*; I. *Ile* or *Iles*; Pte. *Pointe*; R. *River*.

# A

Aa, R., 78, 79, 82, 85, 154
Aalst, 152
Aarschot, 169
Abbeville, 209
Ache, R., 252
Adour, Pays de l', 318 (fig.), 319, **349–54**; R., 314, 346–54 *passim*, 658, 660
Afgesloten IJ, 60 (fig.), 61
Afsluitdijk, of Zuider Zee, 48–50
Agde, 434, 435; Cap d', 424, 426
Agen, 316, 323
Agenais, **322–3**
Agly, Massif de l', 657; R., 438 (and fig.), 440, 657, 658, 665
Agneaux, Pic des, 631 (fig.), 632
Agout, Massif de l', 658; R.
Ahun, coalfield, 524, 525 (fig.), 572
Aigle, l', power station, 571 (fig.), 572
Aiglemont, Faille d', 484
Aigoual, Mont, 545
Aigues-Mortes, 403 (and pl.)
Aiguilhe, Rocher d', 555 (pl.); 556
Aiguille, Mont, 622
Aiguiller (Mont Dore), 552
Aiguilles Rouges, 614 (fig.), **626–7**
Ain, Côtière d', 381
Ain, R., 381, 603
Aire, C., 83 (fig.), 154
Aire, R., 186, 223 (and fig.), 224

Aisne, R., 186–7
Aisne Lateral C., 188 (fig.)
Aisne-Marne C., 188 (fig.)
Aix-en-Provence, 409
Aix-les-Bains, 649
Alaric, C. d', 351
Albères, Monts, 438 (and fig.), 439, 655, 665, 670
Albert, C., 88, 120, 122 (fig.), 125 (fig.), 128–31 (and figs.), 490, 507
Albi, 316, 345, 346
Albigeois, **343–6**
Albret, Pays d', 357
Alençon, 243
Alès, 531; coalfield, 524 (and fig.), **548**
Alkmaar, 56
Allex, 646
Allier, R., **578–87** *passim*
Almelo, 137
Alpes Maritimes, 614 (fig.), 615 (fig.), 620, 622, 635
Alpilles, Chaîne des, 369, 392, 400 (fig.); C. des, 393, 400 (fig.)
Alprech, Cap d', 206
Alps, 8, **613–54**
Alsace, Ballon d', 372, 378, 521; 515, 513, 520; Grand Canal d', **298–300**, 311; plain of, **292–312**
Alzette, R., 280–3
Ambérieu, 610
Ambès, Bec d', 319; refinery, 328, 330

683

# E

# F

# G

# H

## M

# N

# W